INFORMATION TECHNOLOGY LAW

Third Edition

Cavendish
Publishing
Limited

London • Sydney • Portland, Oregon

INFORMATION TECHNOLOGY LAW

Third Edition

Diane Rowland, BSc, PhD, LLB
Senior Lecturer in Law
University of Wales, Aberystwyth

Elizabeth Macdonald, LLB, LLM
Reader in Law
University of Wales, Aberystwyth

Cavendish
Publishing
Limited

London • Sydney • Portland, Oregon

Third edition first published in Great Britain 2005 by
Cavendish Publishing Limited, The Glass House,
Wharton Street, London WC1X 9PX, United Kingdom
Telephone: + 44 (0)20 7278 8000   Facsimile: + 44 (0)20 7278 8080
Email: info@cavendishpublishing.com
Website: www.cavendishpublishing.com

Published in the United States by Cavendish Publishing
c/o International Specialized Book Services,
5804 NE Hassalo Street, Portland,
Oregon 97213-3644, USA

Published in Australia by Cavendish Publishing (Australia) Pty Ltd
3/303 Barrenjoey Road, Newport, NSW 2106, Australia

© Rowland, D and	
Macdonald, E	2005
First edition	1997
Second edition	2000
Third edition	2005

British Library Cataloguing in Publication Data
Data available

Library of Congress Cataloguing in Publication Data
Data available

ISBN-10: 1-85941-756-6

1 3 5 7 9 10 8 6 4 2

Printed and bound in Great Britain

PREFACE

Our impetus to produce this book arose originally out of our undergraduate and postgraduate teaching in information technology law. One of the difficulties with an emerging subject is that materials are not always readily accessible to students and, in addition, the information technology law student needs to consider a wide range of legal disciplines. Our aim was to include a range of materials sufficient to aid and enhance the student's study of this topic. In such a developing area, we also felt it helpful to include a substantial element of our own text and commentary, where the context required it.

The book is primarily aimed at undergraduate and postgraduate law students. Against that background, we hope that it will provide reassurance that a detailed knowledge of the technology is unnecessary to understand the legal issues. Where some rudimentary understanding is helpful, minimum technical explanations have been included. We think the book may also prove both useful and of interest to computer scientists, who increasingly have to consider the wider implications for their discipline. They, of course, will not require the technological explanations!

We have not changed in our view that information technology has provided and continues to provide exciting challenges and opportunities for the law and lawyers. We hope that we have communicated this to the reader.

We have attempted to state the law as at 1 March 2005 but, where possible, developments since that date have been taken into account.

Diane Rowland
Elizabeth Macdonald
August 2005.

ACKNOWLEDGEMENTS

Grateful acknowledgment is made for permission to reprint copyright material, and in particular to the following to reprint material from the sources indicated.

Playboy v Netscape and Excite (www.bna.com/e-law/cases/planetsc.html) and *Playboy v Calvin* (www.bna.com/e-law/cases/playcalv.html) are reproduced from BNA's Electronic Commerce and Law Reports with the permission of the Bureau of National Affairs (www.bna.com)

Extracts from the All England Law Reports, Stapleton, *Product Liability* (1994) and Howarth, *Textbook on Tort* (1995) are reproduced by permission of the Butterworths Division of Reed Elsevier (UK) Ltd

Cambridge Law Journal and Professor Brian Napier for permission to reproduce extracts from 'The future of information technology law'

Philip Chappatte for the extract from 'Specific problems in the licensing of software'

Columbia Journal of Transnational Law for an extract from Nehf, 'Borderless trade and the consumer interest: protecting the consumer in the age of e-commerce'

Columbia Law Review for permission to reprint extracts from Velasco, 'The copyrightability of non-literal elements of computer programs'

Council of Europe for extracts from the Convention for the Protection of Individuals with regard to Automatic Processing of Personal Data

Elsevier Applied Science Ltd for an extract from Lloyd, 'Liability for defective software'

European Patent Office for extracts of decision T 1173/97, taken from www.european-patent-office.org/dg3/biblio/1971173ex1.htm

Federal Trades Commission for permission to reproduce extracts from *Privacy Online*, 1998 and 2000

Hart Publishing, Hector MacQueen and Charlotte Waelde for extracts from MacQueen, 'Copyright and the Internet' and Waelde, 'Domain names and trade marks: what's in a name?'

Harvard International Law Journal for the extract from Delacourt, 'The international impact of Internet regulation'

Harvard Law Review and Professor AR Miller for permission to reproduce extracts from 'Copyright protection for computer programs, databases and computer-generated works' © 1993 Harvard Law Review Association

Harvard Law Review for permission to reproduce extracts from the case note on *Computer Associates v Altai* © 1992 Harvard Law Review Association

HMSO for extracts from Command Papers, Law Commission Reports and Working Papers, and reports of patents, design and trademark cases. Crown copyright is reproduced with the permission of the Controller of Her Majesty's Stationery Office

Incorporated Council for Law Reporting for England and Wales for extracts from the Law Reports and the Weekly Law Reports

Indiana Journal of Global Legal Studies for an extract from the article which appeared as Reed, 'Controlling world wide web links: property rights, access rights and unfair competition'

Institution of Electrical Engineers for extracts from *Safety-Related Systems: A Professional Brief for the Engineer*

Extracts from Poullet, 'Data protection between property and liberties', and Bently and Burrell, 'Copyright and the Information Society in Europe: a matter of timing as well as content', are reproduced with the kind permission of Kluwer Law International

Lawrence Erlbaum Associates Inc for permission to reprint Sableman, 'Link law : the emerging law of Internet hypertext links'

Lloyd's Law Reports, published by LLP Professional Publishing, 69–77 Paul Street, London EC2A 4LQ, for an extract from *Kent v London Ambulance Service* (1999)

Michigan Law Review for extracts from Englund, 'Idea, process or protected expression?'

MIT Press for the extract from Mayer-Schönberger, 'Generational development of data protection in Europe'

Guidelines on the Protection of Privacy and Transborder Flows of Personal Data 1980 are reproduced by kind permission of the Organisation for Economic Co-operation and Development

Oxford University Press for extracts of works by Blume, Glatt, Ogus, Carson and Stapleton

ES Singleton for the extract from 'Computer software agreements and the implementation of the EC Directive'

Stanford Law Review and Fred B Rothman and Co for extracts from Menell, 'An analysis of the scope of copyright protection', and Dunn, 'Defining the scope of copyright protection for computer software'

Sweet & Maxwell Ltd for extracts from Fleming, *The Law of Torts* (1992), *Winfield and Jolowicz on Tort* (1994) and various journals and reports

Sydney Law Review for an extract from Kohl, 'Defamation on the Internet – a duty free zone after all?'

Taylor and Francis (www.tandf.co.uk/journals) for extracts from Information and Communications Technology Law

UN Publications for various extracts related to UNCITRAL

West Publishing Co for extracts from *The Federal Reporter*

World Intellectual Property Organization for permission to reproduce parts of the Introduction to the WIPO Model Provisions on the Protection of Computer Software 1978 and extracts from the Administrative Panel decision in Case No D 2000-0235, *Jeanette Winterson v Mark Hogarth*

The publishers have made every effort to contact the owners of copyright for material reprinted in 'Information Technology Law', however, this has not been possible in every case. We would welcome information from any rights holders that have not been acknowledged here and will endeavour to make any corrections in subsequent editions.

CONTENTS

PART I

THE CHALLENGES OF COMPUTER SOFTWARE

PART II

THE CHALLENGES OF COMPUTER NETWORKS

TABLE OF CASES

TABLE OF EUROPEAN LEGISLATION

DIRECTIVES

DECISIONS

REGULATIONS

TREATIES AND CONVENTIONS

TABLE OF STATUTES

AUSTRALIA

GERMANY

MALAYSIA

TABLE OF STATUTORY INSTRUMENTS

TABLE OF ABBREVIATIONS

ASEAN	Association of South East Asian Nations
BBO	Bulletin board operator
C & L	Computers and Law
CCRO	Community Charge Registration Officer
CDA	Communications Decency Act 1996 (US)
CDPA	Copyright, Designs and Patents Act 1988
CL	Computer Law
CL & P	Computer Law and Practice
CLR	Commonwealth Law Reports
Comm L	Communications Law
COPA	Child On-line Protection Act 1998 (US)
CPA	Consumer Protection Act 1987
ECR	European Court Reports
EDI	Electronic data interchange
EFTA	European Free Trade Area
EIPR	European Intellectual Property Review
EPC	European Patent Convention
EPIC	Electronic Privacy Information Center
EPO	European Patent Office
FSR	Fleet Street Reports
FTC	Federal Trade Commission
GATT	General Agreement on Tariffs and Trade
HTML	Hypertext mark-up language
ICANN	Internet Corporation for Assigned Names and Numbers
ICP	Internet content provider
Int JLIT	International Journal of Information Technology
ISP	Internet service provider
JANET	Joint Academic Network

JBL   Journal of Business Law

NAFTA   North Atlantic Free Trade Area

OECD   Organisation for Economic Co-operation and Development
OPEC   Organisation of Petroleum Exporting Countries

ROM   Read only memory
RPC   Report of Patent Design and Trademark Cases
RSC   Rules of the Supreme Court
RTR   Road Traffic Reports

SGA   Sale of Goods Act 1979/1893
SGSA   Supply of Goods and Services Act 1982
SRA   Self-regulatory agency
SSGA   Sale and Supply of Goods Act 1994
SSO   Structure, sequence and organisation

TLD   Top level domain
UCTA   Unfair Contract Terms Act 1977
UNCITRAL   United Nations Commission on International Trade Law

Web JCLI   Web Journal of Current Legal Issues
WIPO   World Intellectual Property Organisation
WTO   World Trade Organisation

CHAPTER 1

INTRODUCTION

The rapid development of information technology presents challenges for the law; challenges which are not just confined to any single one of the traditional legal categories but which arise in, for example, criminal law, intellectual property law, contract and tort. Even land law may not be untouched![1] Initially, these challenges manifested themselves at the micro, rather than the macro, level, with questions such as the applicability of copyright protection for computer programs. More recently, with the accelerating growth of the internet and the world wide web, some of these problems, such as privacy, have been exacerbated, and others, including the regulation of offensive material, have come to the fore. In effect, the questions posed for the law by the advancing technology are many and various but some idea of their scope can be gained by brief illustration:

- How does the law deal with computer hackers or those who introduce viruses?[2]
- Should a contract for the acquisition of software be categorised as one dealing with goods?[3]
- The exponential growth of e-commerce generates many issues, for example, how does the law deal with the new phenomenon of mass consumer purchases from other jurisdictions?[4]
- Can copyright subsist in a computer program? Would patent protection be more appropriate?[5]
- Does the widespread dissemination of text on networks herald the death of copyright?[6]
- Should the law regulate 'cybersquatting' and trafficking in domain names?[7]
- Should the content of material on the internet be regulated and, if so, by whom?[8] What about freedom of information and expression?[9]
- How is the privacy of the individual to be protected amid the increasing capacity for storing, gathering and collating information?[10]

---

1 Through, eg, computerisation of the Land Registry, raising the question of who could be liable if a defect in the software resulted in an inaccurate certificate. See *Minister of Housing and Local Government v Sharp* [1970] 2 QB 223 (below, p 227) for consideration of a slightly different question.
2 See below, Chapter 8.
3 See below, Chapter 4.
4 See below, Chapter 6.
5 See below, Chapter 2.
6 See below, Chapter 9.
7 See below, Chapter 9.
8 See below, Chapter 8.
9 See below, Chapter 7.
10 See below, Chapter 7.

The point has already been made that the developments in information technology present challenges for many of the established categories of law. This leads to the question of whether information technology law should be regarded as a subject in its own right. Obviously, the initial reaction in attempting to deal with novel problems is to try to accommodate them within existing legal frameworks. This results in a fragmentary approach, which may or may not be appropriate in the particular case. One of the important benefits of looking at the subject of information technology law as a whole is the opportunity to consider how apposite and coherent are piecemeal solutions which borrow from the different established legal areas. It may even lead to the recognition that there is a need for new legal concepts, transcending the traditional boundaries. The acknowledgment of information technology law as a subject worthy of study in its own right also produces a focus upon the issues which might not otherwise occur, with the risk that the particular problems generated by the scientific advances are otherwise merely regarded as footnotes to the established categories. Nonetheless, we have found it convenient to divide the discussion which follows in a way which largely reflects different established legal subjects, and this also reflects the current state of the law. We have also found it useful to divide the book into two parts – the first of these concentrates on problems generated by the nature of computer software, whereas the second considers the impact of computer networks. However, the reader is invited to consider the aptness of the solutions arrived at and the desirability of a more integrated approach.

PART I

THE CHALLENGES OF COMPUTER SOFTWARE

CHAPTER 2

PROTECTING AND EXPLOITING RIGHTS IN SOFTWARE – INTELLECTUAL PROPERTY RIGHTS

INTRODUCTION

Although it may be rather hackneyed to repeat the practical test of Petersen J in *University of London Press Ltd v University Tutorial Press Ltd*,[1] namely, that what is worth copying is *prima facie* worth protecting, the truth underlying this statement is demonstrated nowhere so strikingly as in the commercial exploitation of computer software. As the industry has developed, there has been a trend towards general applications programs, rather than specific bespoke software, and a massive amount of research and development time and money is devoted to the creation of such new computer software. A further feature is the vulnerability of the medium to reproduction by individuals and the consequent threat of widespread copying and piracy. The commercial factors alone would suggest powerful reasons for protecting the intellectual property rights in such software, but, when coupled with the ease of copying, they make protection imperative.

Despite these reasons, and the fact that computers have now been in existence for over half a century, protection of the intellectual property rights in computer programs has only really become an issue since the advent of microcomputers, a much more recent development. In the early stages of development of the industry, the problem was not particularly acute, since computer systems were large, custom built affairs. They were only used by large institutions, whether commercial, industrial or educational, and the public had no general access to them. In those cases where intellectual property rights might have been an issue, the software and programs written for them could be adequately protected by contract, supplemented by actions for breach of confidence. These methods may still provide a useful remedy in certain cases.[2] This situation changed dramatically as microprocessors and personal computers became commonplace; their use became widespread and was no longer confined to large institutions. At this point, it was not possible to rely purely on contract and confidence to protect intellectual property rights in computer programs. As early as the beginning of the 1970s, the World Intellectual Property Organisation (WIPO) had begun to turn its attention to the issue and, in 1978, produced Model Provisions for the Protection of Intellectual Property Rights in Computer Software. These concluded that, even at that time, legal protection of computer software was desirable for a number of reasons. First, time and investment were expended on the creation and maintenance of software systems; second that, as the technology progressed, the total expenditure on software was likely to continue to increase; third as an incentive to disclosure so that there was no need to rely on the vagaries of secrecy; fourth as a basis for trade to ensure the dissemination of new software and

---

1   [1916] 2 Ch 601, p 610, *per* Petersen J.
2   The case of *Ibcos Computers Ltd v Barclays Mercantile Highland Finance Ltd* (1994) (discussed below, p 40) concerned an action for breach of confidence, as well as an action for copyright infringement.

fifth to cater for the vulnerability of software to copying. Although the WIPO document was prepared approximately 30 years ago and, therefore, has the status of a historical document as far as the computer industry is concerned, it shows that major problems were evident even at this early stage. The technology still had a long way to progress before it would be recognisable by present standards, but the trend towards standard application packages was noted, together with the ease of copying and the global nature of the technology.

The purpose of the Model Provisions was to provide a framework which countries that were signatories to the agreement could use. Accepting that the legal protection of computer programs was desirable, the question that then had to be addressed was what was to be the most appropriate and effective method of protecting the intellectual property rights in computer software and programs. The document reviewed the potential use of both patent and copyright protection and also considered other areas of law including the use of contractual provisions and the law on trade secrets. It identified with accuracy a number of issues which were to trouble the courts. In particular, it noted the legal difficulties in patenting software which, as discussed later, remain substantially the same and estimated that perhaps only 1% of computer programs would exhibit the necessary inventiveness to qualify for patent protection. In contrast, copyright protection was considered far more appropriate taking into account the fact that a computer program could be regarded as a form of expression of the ideas behind it. The problems which some jurisdictions would encounter with according copyright protection to such a utilitarian work were noted but, overall, copyright was found to have more advantages than disadvantages.

The approach taken by the Model Provisions was essentially one of copyright drafted to protect the form of an original program, rather than the concepts on which it is based. This approach, which rewards the results of the creator's own intellectual efforts, has proved to be very influential. In view of the huge commercial significance of software development, it might be necessary to amalgamate the reasons and rationale underlying the continental and common law notions of copyright and take into account the encouragement of commercial innovation, the rights of the author as creator and also the public interest.

The resolution to use copyright and protect the intellectual property rights in software as if it was a literary work was, in many ways, a pragmatic response to an immediate problem. In formulating the Model Provisions, WIPO was not envisaging that they should be implemented as *sui generis* legislation but that the principles would be absorbed into the existing framework of protection. It was also hoped that the choice of copyright principles would lead to international protection based on the Berne Convention, although this would clearly depend on whether a particular jurisdiction regarded computer programs as appropriate subject matter for such protection.[3] But computer programs are sufficiently dissimilar to other literary works that this decision was not adopted without dissent, and neither has this dissent been completely silenced by the application of current copyright law to computer programs. The following extract explains in more detail the reasons for the choice of copyright.

---

3   See, also, Cornish, 1993, and below, p 51 *et seq* in relation to the EC Software Directive.

Copyright protection of computer software in the United States and Japan, Part I
Dennis S Karjala
[1991] 6 EIPR 195, pp 195–96

The decision to protect computer programs under copyright was in fact a radical departure from traditional intellectual property principles. The reason is that computer software is functional – the technological means for using general purpose computing devices. Software is not art, music, or even literature. Software is developed with an end use in mind – an end use usually involving the performance of a task other than to please or inform human beings. Like all other technologies, software technology grows by incremental additions to the existing technological base. Programmers learn by studying existing programs, both at school and at their workplaces, and they adapt what they have learned to the new tasks that are placed before them.

... The famous case of *Baker v Selden* [101 US 99 (1879)] says that the functional aspects of works are properly the subject matter of patent law. Thus, under traditional intellectual property law, protected works of technology must show a considerable degree of inventiveness that is passed upon by an administrative review. Technological works that are insufficiently inventive to qualify for a patent are protected only for such time as they remain secret or invulnerable to reverse engineering.

Technology enjoys such limited protection, not because it is believed that technological creativity should go unrewarded. Rather, the law's contribution is limited because too much protection would impede technological progress rather than advance it, by restricting subsequent creators in what they could draw from the existing technological base. While not perfect, the traditional scheme for protecting technology under intellectual property law has worked tolerably well in balancing the tension between incentives (rewarding creators through legal protection) and technological advance that builds on past creations (limitation or denial of legal protection).

Notwithstanding this long and nearly uniform history of denying copyright protection to functional works, a conscious choice has been made to protect computer programs under copyright. The reasons were perfectly sound, but it is worth spelling them out explicitly because they have implications for interpreting the appropriate scope of copyright protection in a program. First, programs are easy to pirate, notwithstanding that their creation can require a large investment of time, money and energy. Yet, traditional patent law could cover at most a small percentage of programs, because most programs are simply an application of well known techniques to a well defined problem. If an incentive is to be supplied for the production of useful but complex programs, patent law will often not be up to the task. Moreover, in the absence of contractual restrictions, trade secret law does not protect against taking a program from a disk or tape that was lawfully acquired. It, too, therefore fails to protect programs that are widely distributed.

Traditional copyright protection, on the other hand, arises immediately on creation and in most countries requires little or no showing of 'inventiveness'. Moreover, copyright clearly protects against the one form of piracy that everyone agrees should be unlawful, namely, disk-to-disk, ROM-to-ROM, and similar mechanical copying and translating from object code as well as line-by-line copying of source code. Copyright has the further advantage over a *sui generis* copyright-like statute in that protection against this kind of piracy is immediately international, without the need for formal action of any kind. When the problem to be solved is viewed as 'piracy' of this type, copyright law appears as a nearly obvious solution. It is hardly surprising, therefore, that so many countries have adopted it.

This seems to suggest that one of the most powerful arguments for copyright protection is a negative one:[4] that, if such protection were to be denied, the patent system would not be of use either, since most programs are an application of well known techniques, often to well known problems.[5] Another argument for the choice of copyright centres on the ease of copying:

> Because of the tremendous ease with which the creativity embodied in a program can be copied, copyright's originality standard, rather than patent's non-obviousness standard, better defines the level of creativity the law should require before it protects the typical computer program from copying.[6]

This, coupled with the ease of piracy, would make innovations very vulnerable to having intellectual endeavour and investment in time and money abused. As we shall see, notwithstanding the objectives, both philosophical and pragmatic, for the choice of copyright for the protection of computer software, this choice can, at times, seem to raise as many problems as it solves. In addition, the courts have not always approached the issue with a unanimity of purpose. For these reasons, there are still a number of academics and practitioners who advocate a *sui generis* protection for computer software.[7]

Samuelson *et al*, for instance, suggests that programs cannot be regarded merely as texts because 'a crucially important characteristic of programs is that they behave; programs exist to make computers perform tasks'. Since this attribute is central to the essential nature of programs, it gives them a 'dual character': they can be regarded simultaneously as both 'writings and machines'. This means that, in their view, neither copyright nor patent law are suitable for protecting software innovation.[8] On the other hand, this view has been criticised as being overly pessimistic about the capabilities of existing legal regimes to accommodate new technological advances,[9] although the very evolution of existing law to take into account new developments has been likened to a form of *sui generis* protection.[10]

---

4   This argument can be compared with Scott Baker J's more recent comment in relation to software as goods in *St Albans City and DC v ICL* [1995] FSR 686 (see, also, below, Chapter 4) that, 'if the supply of software is not the supply of goods, it is difficult to see what it can be other than something to which no statutory rules apply, thus leaving the recipient unprotected in the absence of express agreement'. For a more recent assessment of the pros and cons of applying patent law and copyright law to computer programs see Koo, 2002.

5   See below, p 60.

6   Lunney, 1996, p 243.

7   It should also be noted that there is a limited precedent for the use of *sui generis* protection for new technologies in respect of the protection available to the topography of semiconductor chips. However, this is in the context of a market with a completely different structure, heavily dominated by the US, which, therefore, found itself in a position to enforce its standards on the rest of the world. Basically, the US Semiconductor Chip Protection Act 1984 did not protect the design of non-US chips unless reciprocal protection was available in that State. In view of US dominance, a number of States legislated accordingly, including the EC – in Council Directive 87/54/EEC (Legal Protection of Topographies of Semiconductor Products). The UK provisions are now contained in the Design Right (Semiconductor Topographies) Regulations 1989 (SI 1989/1100). It is unlikely that consensus over the form of a *sui generis* protection for computer software would be achieved so easily.

8   Samuelson *et al*, 1994, on sui generis protection, see also, Gordon, 1998. Compare the discussion below, p 82 on intellectual property rights in databases.

9   Ginsburg, 1994.

10 Davidson, 1986.

The two views expressed below perhaps summarise the opposite poles of the argument.

Is the centre beginning to hold in US copyright law?
Richard H Stern[11]
[1993] 2 EIPR 39, p 40

That courts are beginning to learn how to be more rational in applying copyright principles to computer software does not mean that copyright is a legal scalpel, after all, rather than a blunt instrument. When both the Second Circuit in *Altai*[12] and the Ninth Circuit in *Accolade* warned against 'forcing a square peg into a round hole', they meant that when one tries to apply ordinary principle of copyright law to computer software one gets very peculiar results – sometimes quite startling and unsatisfactory ones. Unless and until we devise a round peg for a round hole, we shall continue to lurch from one to another software law crisis ...

We need a properly thought out utility model or petty patent type of law for computer software, treating it as the industrial property that it is, not as a species of poem or some other *belle lettre* or *beau art*. Copyright does not belong to the right one of Snow's cultures to do the job properly. Bridging the two cultures may be a noble idea, but there would be much less wear and tear on the industry if the experiment were carried out at some other experimental subject's expense ... We need a system that borrows appropriately from copyright law, patent law, and utility model law – perhaps slavish imitation law as well – and combines selected features of each, and new features where the nature of software dictates it, to provide a form of legal protection congruent to the subject matter, the commercial needs of industry, software professionals, and software users, and the interests of the public. The task of crafting such a system is not easy, but the alternative is perennial ineptitude and recurrent crisis.

In contrast, Miller warns against the 'false icon of *sui generis* protection':

... seeking genre-specific limitations on particular program aspects or excluding them from copyright protection in favour of some – as yet undefined – form of *sui generis* protection is unnecessary and potentially mischievous. The effect would be to discard the growing experience under the present copyright law and the increasing certainty that it provides, in favour of something unknown, uncabined and unpredictable. This is especially dangerous given the dynamism of the software industry and the likelihood that today's restrictions will be ill-suited to tomorrow's innovations. Today's attempt to draw a bright defensive perimeter may produce tomorrow's Maginot line. Judgments as to the precise scope of copyright in the computer context are best left to judicial decision-making under a loosely textured and familiar statutory formula that can mature over time ...

... Courts always have had to struggle with the delicate questions of where the commonplace becomes originality and where legitimate imitation shades into infringement, especially in the environment of a new mode of expression. This process admittedly is even more difficult when it involves computer programs of the size, complexity, and sophistication of modern operating systems. But this difficulty is an inevitable aspect of fact-based determinations, which would not be easier under any genre-specific provisions that might be inserted in the copyright law or under some other – most assuredly less predictable – *sui generis* regime invented out of the whole cloth.

---

11   Maintaining an earlier view expressed in Stern, 1986.
12   See below, p 28.

It is a mistake to believe that creating highly refined legislative prescriptions or inventing an entirely new legal structure for software at this time will produce better results than carefully applying existing copyright principles to individual situations. As the case law involving the idea/expression dichotomy attests,[13] the court decisions in this area are, by degree, crystallising into an understandable and sensible doctrinal matrix, obviating any need for a *sui generis* approach.[14]

Doubtless, readers will formulate their own arguments about the most appropriate form of protection for the intellectual property rights in computer software, but whatever protection is developed needs to take into account the 'distinctive character of software programs'.[15]

Copyright has been chosen (even if by default) as the basis for protection, but what is it about computer programs and computer technology that might cause problems for traditional copyright law? In simple terms, there are two broad areas which need to be considered. The first, and simplest in conceptual terms, if not in solution, is the mode of operation of computers and the ease of copying. Computer programs were made to be copied. It is impossible to run a computer program and avail oneself of its useful effects without copies being made, however transient, within the depths of the computer. Also, because programs may be corrupted or inadvertently erased, it is good computing practice to take and keep a back-up copy of each computer program. Whilst even this level of copying could constitute a technical breach of copyright unless express provision is made,[16] it is clear that such copying cannot be construed as a threat to the commercial exploitation of that program. However, it is precisely the fact that the success of computer technology relies heavily on the ease with which programs can be copied that also makes it a trivial matter to produce multiple illicit copies, whether for private use, use within a commercial organisation or for selling on the open market. This is not an issue as far as the application of copyright law is concerned but causes significant problems for the enforcement of such law in relation to straight disk to disk copying and piracy of computer programs.[17] No special equipment is needed to make copies and multiple copies can be made quickly and for minimal capital outlay. These can then be marketed at much lower prices than the authentic version. The widespread copying of software within an organisation can also have a severely prejudicial effect on the rights of the copyright owner. This problem of enforcement in relation to straight copying has been further exacerbated by the growth of the internet and the consequent ease with which software can be downloaded from remote sites.

It has proved much more difficult for traditional copyright rules to be applied to the actual process of copying at the stage at which the computer program is written by

---

13 See below, p 23.
14 Miller, 1993.
15 Raskind, 1986.
16 See below, p 52.
17 In an early note, now of only historical significance, it was nevertheless recognised that widespread piracy was likely to be a problem in the industry, even in an age when *only those large enough to own computers are well established businesses* – see 1964.

the programmer. Why should this be? Copyright was developed to protect the authors of literary, artistic and other works from those who might copy the way in which their ideas had been expressed, especially where this was done for commercial gain. On the face of it, therefore, it would seem to be an appropriate method for protecting the intellectual property rights in computer programs and, as we shall see, the way in which the law has developed in most jurisdictions, has been to protect programs as literary works. However, computer programs differ from conventional literary works in a number of important and fundamental ways, bringing into question the suitability of copyright for this purpose.

One important difference is that, in a computer program, the literary is combined with the technical,[18] causing technology to operate to produce a defined result, either within the computer system itself or in the real world. Neither can programs, in their 'literary form', be readily understood other than by a person skilled in the particular programming language employed. Indeed, end users of the program will often have no knowledge of the underlying program which is causing their computer to perform a particular task, nor will they have any need for such knowledge. Such characteristics are not shared by other literary works, even those of a utilitarian nature.

NavitaireInc v EasyJet Airline Company
[2003] EWHC 3487
High Court

12. To protect a computer programme as a literary work encumbers this field of copyright with many accretions which the protection of literary works has attracted down the years, such as the protection of plots which have no direct relevance to computer software as such at all, but which may provide a valuable jumping off point for the formulation of a modern system of protection for computer programmes by a process of reasoning by analogy or by similarity.

13. Computer programmes are curious literary works in that they are the prescriptive expression of the manner in which a completely deterministic machine is required to operate. Something more different from an imaginative work of fiction which attracts exactly the same protection it is difficult to imagine.

The situation is further complicated by the fact that computer programs can be encapsulated in so many different media, ranging from hard-wired circuitry to transient impulses sent down telephone lines, neither of which, *prima facie*, has much in common with a literary work. In between these two extremes, programs may be held on disks or tape that, perhaps, seem to have more in common with sound recordings, for instance. To appreciate the problems that computer programs have caused for intellectual property law, it will be instructive to examine both the nature of the beast and the problems encountered in applying some of the concepts of copyright law to computer programs.

The first issue to be dealt with is the manner in which computer programs are written and constructed; it is common for cases concerning these issues to contain some brief explanation of these mysteries.

---

18 Cf Samuelson *et al's* 1998, discussion of the 'behavior' of software.

John Richardson Computers Ltd v Flanders
[1993] FSR 497, p 503
High Court

Ferris J   In order for a computer to be given the appropriate instructions it is necessary to communicate with it in some way. The only instructions which a computer can understand are those which consist of a series of 0s and 1s. Instructions set out in this way are said to be written in 'machine language' or machine code. (This may represent something of an oversimplification. I gather that at least in some cases the machine code which is fed into the computer will be translated by the machine into a more elaborate series of 0s and 1s. However this description will suffice for present purposes.) The machine code for one type of computer will usually be different from that for another type, although there may, of course, be compatibility between different manufacturers' products.

A suitably trained or skilled programmer will be able to write a program in machine code for a particular model of computer. But the process is slow and tedious and the program, although intelligible to the computer, will be virtually unintelligible to anyone except an equally skilled programmer. From the comparatively early days of computers, therefore, an alternative language for writing programs was devised. This was known as 'assembler language'. It used a variety of abbreviations more akin to ordinary language than machine code. A computer could not itself understand such a language directly but a program could be, and was, devised which enabled a computer to convert assembler language into the machine code which could be understood by the computer. The translation process is usually possible only in one direction. Assembler language can be translated into machine code, but not vice versa.

While assembler language has advantages over machine code it still requires many instructions to be written in order to achieve the simplest tasks. A variety of so-called high level languages has been devised in order to simplify the task of the programmer. These high level languages have been given names. They include such languages as Basic and derivatives of it, Fortran, Cobol and Pascal. The use of these languages enables the programmer to write a program in terms which more nearly resemble ordinary English than those used in lower level languages. They also permit what is, for the computer, quite a complex operation to be directed by a relatively compact command. Like assembler language, high level languages have to be translated into machine code before they can be understood and acted upon by a computer. The programs which have been devised to achieve this are called compilers. As with assembler language, the translation process is usually possible in one direction only. It is not generally possible to recreate a program in its higher language form from its translation into machine code.

In computer parlance the program as written in whatever language used by the programmer (whether machine code, assembler language or a high level language) is known as the source code. When this is converted by an assembler or a compiler into machine code it is known as the object code. In cases where the program is written in machine code, the source code and the object code are the same. When computer programs are exploited commercially it is usual for the end user to be supplied only with the object code, this being all that the customer needs to load into his computer. The customer does not generally have access to the source code and, because of the difficulties concerning re-translation, cannot generally reconstruct the source code from the object code.

This suggests that the computer programs themselves are rarely seen by the user – merely their effects are seen – but in written form can be expressed as *source code* and *object code*. The source code is the program as written by the programmer and can be in any one of a whole host of different languages. Many of these are the so called high level programming languages, that bear a certain resemblance to literary language and have their own rules of syntax and grammar. An example of part of a program written in the language C is shown below:

```
int bubblesort(int num_list[],int length)
{
int i,j,temp;
for (i=length-1;i>0;i—)
{
for (j=length-1;j>0;j—)
    if (num_list[j]<num_list[j-1])
    {
    temp = num_list[j];
    num_list[j] = num_list[j-1];
    num_list[j-1] = temp;
    };
};
return 0;
}
```

That there are similarities with literary language is clear. However, it is also evident that, without further specialist knowledge, the lay reader may get little further information. In fact, the purpose and function of this part of the program is to sort, in ascending order, an array of numbers. Readers with some knowledge of programming might have deduced this from the title 'bubblesort' and the fact that the variables have been given meaningful names: 'num_list' for number list, for instance. This represents a very simple routine which would be likely to be part of a more complex program. Due to its simplicity, it is unlikely that a programmer would annotate these lines of code any further. However, for longer and more elaborate programs, to assist understanding, comments are frequently added in literary language as markers to particular stages of the program. Thus, the program above could, if required, be annotated as follows:

```
/* function bubblesort; takes an integer array and its length and reorders its elements into
ascending order. */
int bubblesort(int num_list[],int length)
{
int i,j,temp;
for (i=length-1;i>0;i—) /* iterate over whole array */
{
for (j=length-1;j>0;j—)
    if (num_list[j]<num_list[j-1]) /* compare adjacent elements */
    {
    temp = num_list[j];
    num_list[j] = num_list[j-1]; /* ...and swap if required */
    num_list[j-1] = temp;
    };
```

```
};
    return 0;
}
```

Although this program is beginning to appear more intelligible to the layperson, and certainly more understandable to a programmer, this version cannot be put into effect by the computer in its present form. In order that the function intended be performed, the source code has to be translated, or *compiled,* into the object code – a list of binary instructions which are represented on paper by a series of noughts and ones. It would be highly improbable for programmers to write directly in binary; most would select a suitable high level language,[19] which would then be compiled as described, by means of another program, the compiler. Some of the simpler programming languages such as machine and assembly code do approach simple binary form; these are much more difficult for even skilled programmers to follow but, nevertheless, are favoured by some programmers, as indeed was the case with Flanders in the previous extract.

In some respects, the explanation of Ferris J, above, oversimplifies the task of creating a workable computer program.[20] When the source code is first compiled, the compiler translates the high level language into binary code, the so called *relocatable object code,* which is not quite the version which will produce the desired effect. Then, as the compilation proceeds, this relocatable object code will be linked to standard libraries of code which perform certain common functions and which would otherwise have to be written into the program from scratch – the PRINT command, for instance. The end result is the *executable object code,* which will cause the computer to perform the desired function.

Thus, a program is not created in a linear fashion, but has a particular structure at the level at which the computer operates. In addition to this, it will also have a certain structure at the higher level.

Ideas, process or protected experience?
Steven R Englund
(1990) 88 Mich L Rev 866, pp 867–72 (footnotes omitted)

A 'computer program' is defined in the 1976 Act as 'a set of statements or instructions to be used directly or indirectly in a computer in order to bring about a certain result'. Although computers are only capable of *directly* executing 'computer instructions', which may be expressed as combinations of the binary digits zero and one, most programs are written in some sort of programming language that is more convenient to use. Such programs may only be *indirectly* executed by computer.

To understand how a computer program comes to have structure and why it is important that the processes implemented by programs and the ideas embodied may not be protected by copyright law, it is necessary to have some appreciation of computer programming. 'Computer programming' refers to the 'designing, writing and testing' of

---

19 Many are developed for specific applications, eg, ADA is often used for safety related programming.

20 For a more detailed consideration see the Appendices to the judgment in *Cantor Fitzgerald v Tradition* [2000] RPC 95, 145 which begin by explaining matters concerning the use of programming languages and software development and continue with a specific explanation of the software systems at issue in the case.

programs. Almost all programs are written with some concern for the efficient use of resources such as memory space and computer, programmer and user time. Since it will seldom, if ever, be possible to write a program minimising the use of all of these resources, programmers must choose some balance of these criteria appropriate to the nature of the particular program. There are as many ways to approach the task of writing a program to achieve certain efficiency objectives as there are programmers. It is, however, possible to make some generalisations about the techniques that most programmers use.

A programmer begins the process of writing a program by precisely defining the program's 'function'. A program's function is what the program actually does, in contrast to its 'implementation', which is the method, including the instructions, that allow a program to accomplish that function. After the function of a program has been precisely defined, a programmer decomposes that function into simpler constituent problems or 'subtasks'. Subtasks themselves may be decomposed similarly. This process of decomposition requires skill and judgment on the part of the programmer; decisions made at this stage of the programming process can profoundly affect the quality of the resulting program by determining whether a program will be more or less efficient in its use of computer and human resources. The resulting decomposition is determined both by the nature of the problem and by the approach of the programmer. Different programmers faced with the same problem would ordinarily be expected to produce somewhat different decompositions.

Once the function of a program has been decomposed into subtasks, a programmer can determine how best to implement the functions of the subtasks and then write instructions in some programming language to do so. This Note refers to the portion of a program implementing a subtask as a 'module'. A module is thus nothing more than a relatively short sequence of instructions in some programming language that, when executed, performs some well defined function that is one of the subtasks defined in the course of decomposing the ultimate function of the program. The functions of the modules in a program together with each module's relationship to other modules constitute the 'structure' of the program.

The logic and instructions for implementing a subtask may often come from the work of others. The computer industry has long been characterised by the free sharing of programs and program parts among programmers. Not only does the borrowing of the implementation details eliminate the need to 'reinvent the wheel' with each new program, but borrowing and improving upon more general ideas is an important way in which the computer art progresses. This is important because, in order to ensure [that] its decisions in copyright cases involving computer programs promote progress in the computer art, a court should have some understanding of the role of copyright law in promoting progress in that art.

Thus, many aspects of a computer program may be copied, from straight line to line copying of both source and object code – so called *literal copying*, to copying of the structure of the program, often referred to as *non-literal copying*. Should all these aspects of copying be subject to the law of copyright, or only those which correspond to literal copying of the work, by analogy with a literary work? How far can computer programmers use the work done by others in their own creation of new programs without infringing the original developer's rights? At what point does the code for a commonly used routine enter the public domain? These, and other issues, have resulted in discussion in many jurisdictions as to the extent of the scope of copyright protection for computer programs and the literature on the subject is now voluminous. As a number of these arguments continue to surface in discussions, both in academic literature and in judicial deliberations, it is worth considering, in brief, the manner in which the arguments have developed thus far.

The first issue to be resolved was whether copyright could subsist in both source and object code. It has been accepted for a long time that copyright can subsist in code,[21] that is, that a code could be construed as an original literary work. Did this, by analogy, mean that copyright could subsist in both source code and object code? This question caused a debate that will be examined in some detail, as it is highly illustrative of the way in which intellectual property law has been used to argue both for and against copyright protection for computer programs. US copyright law required the subject of copyright protection to be a 'writing' and also denied copyright protection to works of a utilitarian nature. This led to the suggestion that, although there might be copyright in the source code, this could not be true of the object code, which could not be construed as a 'writing'. Further credence was given to this view by the argument that object code was created not by a person but by a machine, referring to the process of compilation described above. On the other hand, computer programs are contained within the definition of 'literary work' in the US Copyright Act 1976, and amendments introduced in 1980 included the definition 'a set of statements or instructions to be used directly or indirectly in a computer in order to bring about a certain result', suggesting that the use of the word 'indirectly' must be taken to include object code. In addition, the US courts were beginning to recognise that object code was subject to copyright protection in cases such as *Apple Computer Inc v Franklin Computer Corp*.[22] These developments were mirrored in other jurisdictions, as, for example, in *SEGA Enterprises v Richards*.[23] Whilst the court was happy to accept in principle that computer programs could be the subject of copyright, there was some discussion as to whether copyright could subsist in both the source code and the object code.

The above argument both depends upon and presupposes that copyright protection will be extended to software because of the writing requirement or, in many jurisdictions, that a computer program is a form of 'literary work', as opposed to any other type of creation attracting copyright protection. Even this view was challenged by the Australian case of *Apple Computer v Computer Edge Pty Ltd*,[24] in which it was said that the purpose of literary works was for enjoyment,[25] and so the court declined to think that computer programs could be protected in this way. This decision was subsequently reversed, the Full Court of the Federal Court holding that the source programs were protected by copyright as new and original literary works and that the object programs were protected in consequence as adaptations of the source programs.[26] The issue was again considered on a further appeal to the High Court of Australia, which concluded, although not without difficulty, that the *source* programs were protected as literary works. The court was divided, however, over whether protection could be afforded to the object code on any basis. Gibbs J, for instance,

---

21   *DP Anderson & Co v Lieber Code Co* [1917] 2 KB 469.
22   714 F 2d 1240 (3rd Cir 1983).
23   [1983] FSR 73.
24   (1983) 50 ALR 581; [1984] FSR 246.
25   A view which echoes the *dictum* of Davey LJ in *Hollinrake v Truswell* [1894] 3 Ch 420, p 428.
26   (1984) 53 ALR 225.

found that nothing had persuaded him that 'a sequence of electrical impulses in a silicon chip, not capable itself of communicating anything directly to a human recipient, and designed only to operate a computer, is itself a literary work, or is the translation of a literary work'. This was reflected in the view of the majority that, as the only manifestation of the object code at issue was as electrical impulses in a silicon chip which could neither be detected by nor had any meaning for humans, it could not be construed as a literary work.

Computer Edge Pty Ltd v Apple Computer Inc
(1986) 161 CLR 171, p 201

Brennan J   A literary work need not have literary merit ... The words 'literary work', as Peterson J pointed out in *University of London Press Ltd v University Tutorial Press Ltd*, 'cover work which is expressed in print or writing, irrespective of the question whether the quality or style is high'. A 'literary work', according to Davey LJ in *Hollinrake v Truswell*, is a work 'intended to afford either information and instruction, or pleasure, in the form of literary enjoyment' ... The observation is not unduly restrictive. If the print or writing in which the work is expressed conveys information or instruction, albeit to a limited group with special knowledge, it is immaterial that the information or instruction is not expressed in the form of words, phrases or sentences. Thus a telegraphic code has been held to be a literary work though the words of the code were meaningless in themselves ... The source programs were the product of substantial originality and skill, they were prepared as instructions for the manufacture of Apple II ROMs, they were in writing and they conveyed meaning at least to computer scientists and technicians. That is sufficient to bring them within the scope of literary copyright. The argument that a source program is not a literary work proposes a dichotomy between literary works and what are 'merely adjuncts to the operation of a mechanical device'. The dichotomy is false, for it cannot be said that every book of instructions for the operation of a machine is outside the scope of copyright protection. Copyright might not protect every minor direction for use of a machine or device, but that is not the present case. Here, the source programs are a set of complex and precise instructions for the manufacture of Apple II ROMs. The source programs are substantial original compilations. It would be an infringement of Apple's copyright in a source program to do in relation to that program in Australia without Apple's licence any of the acts prescribed in s 31(1)(a) of the Act.

The corresponding object programs, on the other hand, are not in writing. The electrical charges which constitute them may be represented in writing, using the conventional binary or hexadecimal notations. However, the written representation must not be confused with what is represented but not written. Copyright protection under Pt III of the Act is given only to works; under Pt IV of the Act it is given to subject matter other than works. The object programs do not come within Pt IV. To be a 'work' within Pt III, an object program must be one of the four classes of works as defined by s 101(1) – literary, musical, dramatic or artistic. To come within the scope of 'literary work' as that term was defined in the Act prior to the 1984 amendment, a literary work had to be in print or writing. Peterson J in *University of London Press* said:

> Copyright Acts are not concerned with the originality of ideas, but with the expression of thought, and in the case of 'literary work', with the expression of thought in print or writing.

And in *Ladbroke (Football) Ltd v William Hill (Football) Ltd* Lord Hodson regarded it as the undoubted truth that 'copyright is not concerned with the originality of ideas, but with the expression of thought, in the case of literary work with the expression of thought in print or writing'.

... Section 22 implies that the form in which a literary work is expressed is writing or some other material form. A material form is a form which can be perceived by the senses. That is not to say that copyright subsists in a document on which the writing of an original literary work appears ... Copyright in a work is a right in respect of the form to which the work has been reduced, not a right of property in the object in or from which the form is perceptible. But a form from which the words, letters or figures of a literary work cannot be perceived by sight or touch (or, possibly, hearing) is not a material form to which the work has been reduced. The electrical charges which constitute the object programs cannot be seen or touched or heard or, if they can, they do not communicate the letters of the original literary work, the source programs. Nor, for that matter, do the electrical charges communicate the letters or figures by which an object program may be represented. The object programs are not literary works.

Neither, in the view of the majority, were they protected as adaptations of the source program.

Computer Edge Pty Ltd v Apple Computer Inc
(1986) 161 CLR 171, p 204

Brennan J   The action or process of turning the source program in '6502 Assembly Language' into the object program in what is called 'machine readable language' is said to be a translation. It strains the meaning of 'language' to include within its denotation the alphabetic symbols in which the source programs were written. Although the alphabetic symbols of the source programs may be classified as literary in form for the purposes of the Act, I would not describe those symbols as a language, the primary meaning of which is 'the whole body of words and of methods of combining them used by a nation, people or race' (*Shorter Oxford Dictionary*). It is difficult to divorce 'language' from human speech, and a means of communicating ideas which does not consist of words is not properly to be described as a language. A chemical formula or a mathematical equation are apt to communicate ideas, but I should not classify either as a language. '6502 Assembly Language' is not a language; it is a code. Even if the code were thought to be susceptible of 'translation' into another language, it was not so translated: the electrical charges which constitute the object programs are clearly not a language. To describe such electrical charges – no doubt helpfully enough for the purposes of computer science – as 'machine readable language' is to make metaphor serve as reality. The machine has no comprehension of thought which it is the essential purpose of language to convey, and the fact that a microprocessor is activated by a sequence of electrical charges in a predictable way does not mean that it has understood and executed some command.

The secondary meaning of translation comes closer to describing the connection between the sequences of electrical charges constituting the source programs and corresponding object programs. Like the messages sent by a morse telegraphist, the object programs might be regarded as an expression of the original text in a different medium: a translation of a written text into a sequence of electrical charges. The fact that an object program will so operate upon a suitably programmed computer as to cause it to print out either the original written text (the source program) or a binary or hexadecimal notation of the electrical charges (the object program) makes it arguable (I need put it no higher) that an object program is an expression of a source program in another medium and is a 'translation'. This approach, freed from the confusion arising from the metaphorical use of 'language', might command acceptance if it were not for the necessity of the 'adaptation' being itself a 'work'. In the Full Federal Court, the majority did not think it necessary to decide whether an 'adaptation' (that is, a 'translation') was a 'work' but I respectfully disagree. The language of s 31(l)(a)(vii) is clear, 'a work that is an adaptation'. We have seen that a sequence of electrical charges constituting an object program is neither a literary work nor any other kind of 'work'. An object program is therefore not 'a work that is an adaptation' of the source program in which copyright subsists.

As we shall see, this view has not survived although it is prudent not to dismiss these arguments in their entirety as they are illustrative of some of the difficulties of accommodating the protection afforded to computer programs within that for literary works. Nevertheless it does not represent the protection offered to computer programs in any jurisdiction. With the benefit of hindsight, it may be that the dissenting judgments of Mason and Wilson JJ have turned out to be more influential, or, at least, to be a more accurate assessment of the current protection afforded to computer programs.

Computer Edge Pty Ltd v Apple Computer Inc
(1986) 161 CLR 171, p 193

Mason and Wilson JJ   We have no hesitation in coming to the conclusion that each of the source programs was an original literary work ... Whether or not a literary work must be in writing, these programs were written. Although the substance of the program in each case was expressed in 6502 Assembly Code, this is a language which was readily intelligible to anyone versed in computer science. Each program was the product of skill, time and effort. It was a particular kind of vehicle for the communication of useful information to persons who may desire it. The fact that its creation was a step towards the goal of facilitating the operation of a computer does not warrant its dismissal by the appellants as no more than a mere adjunct to the operation of a mechanical device ... On any view, in the form in which it was created and before it was transformed into another medium, each source program had an existence which was entirely independent of the machine. It was capable of conveying meaning as to the arrangement and ordering of instructions for the storage and reproduction of knowledge. In that form it was entitled to copyright protection.

The second submission of the appellants is that even if the source programs are the subject of copyright, the object programs are not. It is said that the members of the Full Court who formed the majority erred in holding each object program to be a 'translation' of the relevant source program and therefore an adaptation of a literary work within the meaning of that term as defined in s 10(1). The arguments advanced in support of the submission may be summarised as follows: (a) the object programs are merely sequences of electrical impulses within the computer; (b) a translation, in order to constitute an adaptation, must be a translation from one human language to another; (c) a translation of a literary work must itself be a literary work; (d) a translation of a literary work must convey a clear idea of the literary work to human beings. It is not correct to describe an object program as *merely* a sequence of electrical impulses within the computer. Electrical impulses there are, but those impulses serve to identify a set of instructions in machine readable language designed to guide the machine in its basic operations. They do not form part of the computer itself, notwithstanding that they may be embodied in a ROM or ROMs located permanently in silicon chips in a machine. They might equally well be contained in a magnetic disc or tape which can be inserted into or removed from the machine at will. The language may be recorded in visible form in binary or hexadecimal notation. The same result as is achieved by the use of an object program could be achieved by the manual operation of a computer in accordance with instructions written out in ordinary English and contained in a manual. The only problem would be that such a process would be impossibly tedious and therefore wholly impracticable.

The next question is whether the object program is a translation of the source program. The word 'translation' is not defined in the Act. One of the meanings given in the *Shorter Oxford Dictionary* is 'the expression or rendering of something in another medium or form'. In the Federal Court, Sheppard J was of the opinion that a translation did not encompass something which could neither be seen nor heard. With all respect to his Honour, we are unable to share that view. True it is that the object program can be neither seen nor heard, but there can be no doubt that it exists and one knows where it can be found and how it can be activated. It seems to us that the conversion of a source code into an object code, albeit by the mechanical operation of a computer, is a process which effects a 'translation' of the source code from one language into another language. It is immaterial that the last-mentioned language takes a form which can only be read and understood in that form by a machine. It is an adaptation of a literary work. This conclusion finds support in the statement from the 1979 report of the United States National Commission on New Technological Uses of Copyright Works, p 21, n 109, which was cited by Fox J in his Honour's judgment in the Federal Court:

> A source code is a computer program written in any of several programming languages employed by computer programmers.

> An object code is the version of a program in which the source code language is converted or translated into the machine language of the computer with which it is to be used.

We therefore reject the argument of the appellants that the only relevant translation is that which translates one human language into another human language. We also find no warrant for the argument that a translation must convey a clear idea of the literary work to human beings although, if it matters, there is no reason why an object program may not be reduced to writing and understood by those skilled in the art.

The question whether an adaptation of a literary work must itself be a literary work is more difficult of resolution ... Section 31(1)(a)(vii) provides that copyright, in relation to a literary work, is the exclusive right, *inter alia*, to reproduce in a material form a work that is an adaptation of that literary work. 'Work' is defined in s 10(1), unless the contrary intention appears, to mean *inter alia* a literary work. *Prima facie*, therefore, an adaptation of a literary work must itself satisfy the description of a literary work. Of course, one would expect that an adaptation, in this case a translation of the original literary work constituted by the source codes, would continue to display, in its new form, the characteristics which enabled the original work to satisfy that description. But it is argued for the appellants that that is not so in the present case because a literary work must be in writing. Ordinarily and traditionally it is no doubt true that a literary work would take a written form. But the Act does not require it to be so. Indeed, s 22(1) of the Act identifies the time when a work is made as the time when 'the work was first reduced to writing *or to some other material form*' (our emphasis): see also s 21 of the Act. There seems to be no reason to doubt that a literary work is made and entitled to copyright protection from the time it is first recorded on tape, if that be the first material form that the work takes: In our opinion, an object code, although brought into existence by mechanical means, takes on the same literary character as is possessed from the source code from which it is derived. This conclusion seems necessarily to follow, if the protection secured by the Act to the source programs as original literary works is to be effective. If there is no copyright in the object programs which are a natural and necessary derivative of the source programs then there is no point in protecting the source programs.

Notwithstanding this dissenting view, the majority decision led to some consternation in the common law world as to the correct mode of application of copyright principles to computer programs. Some of this was based on theoretical argument, but some related to the practical issue of whether or not intellectual property rights in object code could be protected at all, if copyright was not deemed to be an appropriate medium for that protection. This confusion led directly to statutory action being taken in the UK: the Copyright (Computer Software) Amendment Act was passed in 1985 and its provisions have now been re-enacted in the Copyright, Designs and Patents Act (CDPA) 1988. Further amendments to this statute have now been incorporated by virtue of the Copyright (Computer Programs) Regulations 1992 and these will be discussed later.[27]

CDPA 1988 (as amended)

3(1) 'literary work' means any work which is written, spoken or sung and accordingly includes –

(a) a table or compilation;

(b) a computer program;

(c) preparatory design material for a computer program.

...

17 (1)   The copying of the work is an act restricted by the copyright in every description of copyright work ...

(2)   Copying in relation to a literary, dramatic, musical or artistic work means reproducing the work in any material form. This includes storing the work in any medium by electronic means.

Thus, *prima facie*, copyright law applies to both source code and object code and the owners of the copyright in the computer programs represented by this code have a legal remedy available in the case of unauthorised copying of those programs.

THE SCOPE OF PROTECTION

How much needs to be copied before an infringement occurs is defined differently in different jurisdictions. In the UK, the concept is one of taking a substantial part (s 16(3) of the CDPA 1988), whilst the US considers unauthorised copying in terms of substantial similarity. While the detail of these may differ, they both require some assessment of what and how much has been copied in comparison with the whole. A consideration of the manner of constructing computer programs, to which reference has already been made, will reveal that many aspects of a program can be copied, from straight, line by line copying of the source or object code (literal copying) to copying of the structure, sequence and organisation (SSO) of the program (non-literal copying). It has been established, in relation to other areas of copyright law, that the test of substantial taking may be either quantitative or qualitative.[28] Thus, if part of a work is copied which is small in quantity but highly significant in terms of its overall contribution to the work, then an action will lie. It is common practice for programmers to include spurious lines of code which are not essential to the execution of the program but make the detection of copying easier. Other evidence may also

---

27   See below, p 54.

28   See, eg, *Hawkes & Son (London) Ltd v Paramount Film Services Ltd* [1934] Ch 593; *Ladbroke (Football) Ltd v William Hill (Football) Ltd* [1964] 1 WLR 273, in which Lord Pearce said: 'Whether a part is substantial must be decided by its quality rather than its quantity.' This latter case was relied upon by Ferris J in *John Richardson Computers v Flanders* [1993] FSR 497: see below, p 36.

raise a strong presumption of literal copying. Thus, in MS Associates v Power,[29] it was noted that there were a number of similarities in the names of the variables in the defendants' and plaintiffs' programs – names which would be expected to be decided quite arbitrarily. It was also noted that the function 'vtprs' appeared in both the defendants' and the plaintiffs' list of variables, although the facts showed that the function was not used in the defendants' program.

Where there are similar errors in two programs, a strong presumption of copying may be raised. However, this may be capable of rebuttal because of another difference between computer programs and other forms of literary work. Whereas it is statistically improbable that, if two authors independently have the same idea for a novel, they will write it in the same words and sentence construction, this is not such a remote possibility in the case of a computer program. If two programmers independently write a program to perform the same task, especially if this is a relatively simple task or sub-routine, it may be very likely that they will write the same or similar program. It is also equally possible that they may make the same errors. If such programs contain the same errors, then, although this may provide persuasive evidence, copying will not be a foregone conclusion, as some errors are more frequent and obvious than others. Illustrations of these issues are again to be found in MS Associates v Power, in which the same errors were noted in one part of the program but, in relation to another part, it was perhaps possible to explain the observed similarities.

MS Associates v Power
[1987] FSR 242, p 248

In the plaintiffs' program the 'oct' function is arbitrarily grouped with the 'hex' function following it. In the defendant's B-tran, the 'oct' function similarly is grouped with the 'hex' function in the source file called 'hex c'. It is Mr Maskell's evidence that there is no obvious reason why it should be grouped with the 'hex' function, other than that the plaintiffs had so grouped them together, and indeed that it would have been better not to put it there but to allocate it to a separate source file of its own. However, on commenting on this point, the first defendants' evidence is that the 'hex' and 'oct' functions are commonly grouped together and are so in Microsoft BASIC.

Problems of this type create some fundamental difficulties in applying the law of copyright to computer programs. Copyright was developed to protect the form in which authors or artists create their work; to protect the expression of their idea rather than the idea itself. If, in the previous example, there is indeed only one way in which the program or part of the program can be written, can this reasonably be treated as the expression of an idea, or has the expression merged with the idea, so that the whole cannot be protected by copyright? This issue, referred to as the idea/expression dichotomy, has now become central to some discussions on the scope of copyright protection for computer programs. Although the concept enjoyed a renaissance in connection with computer software, this is not a new idea for copyright law to accommodate and the boundaries of what is and is not copyrightable have been discussed elsewhere, particularly in the US, where the distinction has been given a

---

29 [1987] FSR 242.

statutory basis.[30] This has resulted in extensive discussion in the case law on the subject in the US, concerning the formulation of rules and tests to distinguish idea from expression. In particular, Learned Hand J, in *Nichols v Universal Pictures Corp*,[31] devised the 'levels of abstraction' test:

> Upon any work, and especially upon a play, a great number of patterns of increasing generality will fit equally well, as more and more of the incident is left out. The last may perhaps be no more than the most general statement of what the play is all about, and at times might consist only of its title; but there is a point in this series of abstractions where they are no longer protected, since otherwise the playwright could prevent the use of his 'ideas' to which, apart from their expression, his property is never extended.

But he went on to say, referring to the line between idea and expression, that nobody 'has ever been able to fix that boundary and nobody ever can'.

The problems caused by the idea/expression dichotomy have been further exacerbated by the dispute surrounding the extent to which the non-literal elements of a program, the SSO, can be protected by copyright, coupled with the extent to which elements of the structure form part of the expression of that program.

These non-literal elements are often referred to as the 'look and feel'[32] of a program and are often precisely those factors that are likely to give a particular program a competitive edge over its rivals, and, therefore, precisely those elements which the originators of the program will most want to protect. Thus, the 'look' of a program may include elements of the user interface, such as the screen display, and determine the way in which the computer program appears to the user. The 'feel', on the other hand, includes those elements which determine the experience of using the program, such as the keystroke sequences or other means of operating the program. The generic term 'look and feel' recognises that these concepts may frequently overlap or be interdependent.

The situation in the US

The extent to which this SSO of a program can be regarded as the idea of the program or, alternatively, be protected by copyright law as part of the expression of that idea has, as already mentioned, been debated extensively by the courts in the US. Some of the arguments raised in these cases have been highly influential in stimulating the debate on the correct application of copyright principles to computer programs. The first such case was *Whelan Associates v Jaslow Dental Laboratory Inc*.[33] A computer program had been devised by an employee to keep records in a dental laboratory. The

---

30 US Copyright Act 1976, 17 USCS s 102(b), which provides that copyright protection does not extend to any 'idea, procedure, process, system, method of operation, concept, principle or discovery'.

31 45 F 2d 119, p 121 (2nd Cir 1930), discussed in, eg, Englund, 1990; Daniels, 1994; Wilkins, 1994.

32 A concept which originated in relation to greetings cards and children's books and entered the analysis of copyright infringement of computer programs in cases involving video games. See, eg, Ogilvie, 1992, Velasco, 1994.

33 [1987] FSR 1.

employee concerned subsequently left that employment and later created another software package to perform the same function. It was accepted that both packages provided the same service, that is, the end product was the same, but that the coding was different; thus, literal similarities were absent. It was argued, for the defendants, that the structure of a computer program must be the idea, rather than the expression of that idea, and would therefore be beyond the scope of copyright protection. The US Court of Appeals for the Third Circuit responded by trying to devise a rule for distinguishing idea from expression which they could then apply to the facts of the case.

Whelan Associates v Jaslow Dental Laboratory Inc
797 F 2d 1222, 1234
US Court of Appeals, Third Circuit (1987)

1 A rule for distinguishing idea from expression in computer programs

It is frequently difficult to distinguish the idea from the expression thereof. No less an authority than Learned Hand J, after a career that included writing some of the leading copyright opinions, concluded that the distinction will 'inevitably be *ad hoc*' ... Although we acknowledge the wisdom of Judge Hand's remark, we feel that a review of relevant copyright precedent will enable us to formulate a rule applicable in this case. In addition, precisely because the line between idea and expression is elusive, we must pay particular attention to the pragmatic considerations that underlie the distinction and copyright law generally. In this regard, we must remember that the purpose of the copyright law is to create the most efficient and productive balance between protection (incentive) and dissemination of information, to promote learning, culture and development ... We begin our analysis with the case of *Baker v Selden*, which, in addition to being a seminal case in the law of copyright generally, is particularly relevant here because, like the instant case, it involved a utilitarian work, rather than an artistic or fictional one. In *Baker v Selden*, the plaintiff Selden obtained a copyright on his book, *Selden's Condensed Ledger, or Bookkeeping Simplified*, which described a simplified system of accounting. Included in the book were certain 'blank forms', pages with ruled lines and headings, for use in Selden's accounting system ... The dispute centred on whether Selden's blank forms were part of the method (idea) of Selden's book, and hence non-copyrightable, or part of the copyrightable text (expression). In deciding this point, the court distinguished what was protectable from what was not protectable as follows:

> ... where the art [that is, the method of accounting] it teaches cannot be used without employing the methods and diagrams used to illustrate the book, or such as are similar to them, such methods and diagrams are to be considered as necessary incidents to the art, and given to the public.

Applying this test, the court held that the blank forms were necessary incidents to Selden's method of accounting, and hence were not entitled to any copyright protection. The court's test in *Baker v Selden* suggests a way to distinguish idea from expression. Just as *Baker v Selden* focused on the end sought to be achieved by Selden's book, the line between idea and expression may be drawn with reference to the end sought to be achieved by the work in question. In other words, *the purpose or function of a utilitarian work would be the work's idea, and everything that is not necessary to that purpose or function would be part of the expression of the idea* ... Where there are various means of achieving the desired purpose, then the particular means chosen is not necessary to the purpose; hence, there is expression, not idea. Consideration of copyright doctrines related to *scènes à faire* and fact-intensive works supports our formulation, for they reflect the same underlying principle. *Scènes à faire* are 'incidents, characters or settings which are as a practical matter indispensable ... in the treatment of a given topic' ... It is well settled doctrine that *scènes à faire* are afforded no copyright protection. *Scènes à faire* are afforded no protection because the subject matter represented can be expressed in no other way than through the particular *scène à faire*. Therefore, granting a copyright 'would give the first author a monopoly on the commonplace ideas behind the *scènes à faire*' ... This is merely a restatement of the hypothesis advanced above, that the purpose or function of a work or literary device is part of that device's 'idea' (unprotectable portion). It follows that anything necessary to effecting that function is also, necessarily, part of the idea, too. Fact intensive works are given similarly limited copyright coverage ... Once again, the reason appears to be that there are only a limited number of ways to express factual material, and therefore the purpose of the literary work – telling a truthful story – can be accomplished only by employing one of a limited number of devices. Those devices therefore belong to the idea, not the expression, of the historical or factual work. Although the economic implications of this rule are necessarily somewhat speculative, we nevertheless believe that the rule would advance the basic purpose underlying the idea/expression distinction, 'the preservation of the balance between competition and protection reflected in the patent and copyright laws' ...

As we stated above, among the more significant costs in computer programming are those attributable to developing the structure and logic of the program. The rule proposed here, which allows copyright protection beyond the literal computer code, would provide the proper incentive for programmers by protecting their most valuable efforts, while not giving them a stranglehold over the development of new computer devices that accomplish the same end. The principal economic argument used against this position – used, that is, in support of the position that programs' literal elements are the only parts of the programs protected by the copyright law – is that computer programs are so intricate, each step so dependent on all of the other steps, that they are almost impossible to copy except literally, and that anyone who attempts to copy the structure of a program without copying its literal elements must expend a tremendous amount of effort and creativity. .... A further argument against our position is not economic but jurisprudential; another commentator argues that the concept of structure in computer programs is too vague to be useful in copyright cases ... He too would therefore appear to advocate limiting copyright protection to programs' literal codes.

Neither of the two arguments just described is persuasive. The first argument fails for two reasons. In the first place, it is simply not true that 'approximation' of a program short of perfect reproduction is valueless. To the contrary, one can approximate a program and thereby gain a significant advantage over competitors even though additional work is needed to complete the program. Second, the fact that it will take a great deal of effort to copy a copyrighted work does not mean that the copier is not a copyright infringer. The issue in a copyrighted case is simply whether the copyright holder's expression has been copied, not how difficult it was to do the copying. Whether an alleged infringer spent significant time and effort to copy an original work is therefore irrelevant to whether he has pirated the expression of an original work.

As to the second argument, it is surely true that limiting copyright protection to computers' literal codes would be simpler and would yield more definite answers than does our answer here. Ease of application is not, however, a sufficient counterweight to the considerations we have adduced on behalf of our position.

Finally, one commentator argues that the process of development and progress in the field of computer programming is significantly different from that in other fields, and therefore requires a particularly restricted application of the copyright law. According to this argument, progress in the area of computer technology is achieved by means of 'stepping stones', a process that 'requires plagiarising in some manner the underlying copyrighted work' (Note, 68 Minn L Rev at 1292). As a consequence, this commentator argues, giving computer programs too much copyright protection will retard progress in the field.

We are not convinced that progress in computer technology or technique is qualitatively different from progress in other areas of science or the arts. In balancing protection and dissemination, the copyright law has always recognised and tried to accommodate the fact that all intellectual pioneers build on the work of their predecessors. Thus, copyright principles derived from other areas are applicable in the field of computer programs.

2 Application of the general rule to this case

The rule proposed here is certainly not problem-free. The rule has its greatest force in the analysis of utilitarian or 'functional' works, for the purpose of such works is easily stated and identified. By contrast, in cases involving works of literature or 'non-functional' visual representations, defining the purpose of the work may be difficult. Since it may be impossible to discuss the purpose or function of a novel, poem, sculpture or painting, the rule may have little or no application to cases involving such works. The present case presents no such difficulties, for it is clear that the purpose of the utilitarian Dentalab program was to aid in the business operations of a dental laboratory. It is equally clear that the structure of the program was not essential to that task: there are other programs on the market, competitors of Dentalab and Dentcom, that perform the same functions but have different structures and designs.

This fact seems to have been dispositive for the district court.

The mere idea or concept of a computerised program for operating a dental laboratory would not in and of itself be subject to copyright. Copyright law protects the manner in which the author expresses an idea or concept, but not the idea itself ... There are many ways that the same data may be organised, assembled, held, retrieved and utilised by a computer. Different computer systems may functionally serve similar purposes without being copies of each other. There is evidence in the record that there are other software programs for the business management of dental laboratories in competition with plaintiff's program. There is no contention that any of them infringe although they may incorporate many of the same ideas and functions. The 'expression of the idea' in a software computer program is the manner in which the program operates, controls and regulates the computer in receiving, assembling, calculating, retaining, correlating, and producing useful information either on a screen, print-out or by audio communication.

... The conclusion is thus inescapable that the detailed structure of the Dentalab program is part of the expression, not the idea, of that program.

... The Copyright Act of 1976 provides further support, for it indicates that Congress intended that the structure and organisation of a literary work could be part of its expression protectable by copyright. Title 17 USC § 103 (1982) specifically extends copyright protection to compilations and derivative works. Title 17 USC § 101 defines 'compilation' as 'a work formed by the collection and assembling of pre-existing materials or of data that are selected, co-ordinated, or arranged in such a way that the resulting work as a whole constitutes an original work of authorship', and it defines 'derivative work' as one 'based upon one or more pre-existing works, such as ... abridgement, condensation, or any other form in which a work may be recast, transformed, or adapted'. Although the Code does not use the terms 'sequence', 'order' or 'structure', it is clear from the definition of compilations and derivative works, and the protection afforded them, that Congress was aware of the fact that the sequencing and ordering of materials could be copyrighted, that is, that the sequence and order could be parts of the expression, not the idea, of a work.

Despite the reference to Learned Hand, this judgment does not build on his famous abstractions test but, instead, relies on another line of case law and also on statute to show that the SSO of the program, the non-literal elements, should be afforded copyright protection. In brief, the court found that the purpose of the program at issue was the organisation of the dental laboratory records and that the structure of the program was not necessary to that purpose, following from the analogy with the reasoning in *Baker v Selden* (1879). In consequence, the structure of Whelan's program was entitled to copyright protection.

One possible virtue of this approach is its simplicity, but, as Englund identifies below,[34] this may generate its own problems:

> Perhaps the single virtue of the *Whelan* rule is that it is easy to apply. The widespread application of the rule is likely to have undesirable consequences. Given the court's broad conception of the purpose of a program as what a user might do with it rather than what the program actually does, almost any particular structure could be seen as not necessary to that purpose. The court failed adequately to consider the possibility that broad protection might allow *Whelan* to make it impossible for others to program a computer efficiently to perform the same function and employ the same process. Although the court purported to consider the need to 'create the most efficient and productive balance between protection (incentive) and dissemination of information to promote learning, culture and development', the court's rule may thus actually impair progress in the computer art.

Velasco[35] makes the point that the ideal test would be one which is both simple and accurate. In such a technically complex area as computer software, it has proved difficult to pursue either of these aims without compromising the other and it is unsurprising, therefore, that certain inadequacies have been identified in the straightforward test enunciated in *Whelan*. It can thus be criticised as being over-simplistic in its suggestion that it may be possible to both define and isolate a single purpose for a particular program. An obvious consequence of this is that, if programmers are to be able to devise other programs that perform the same function but do not infringe copyright, then there has to be a number of other possible structures for the program which could, reasonably and efficiently, fulfil that same purpose. If not, the *Whelan* formulation is capable of conferring an almost patent-like protection on the first programmer to develop a suitable structure. In reality, most commercially important programs consist of a number of sub-routines and modules, each of which could, validly, be considered as an idea, a fact which was later recognised in *Computer Associates v Altai*, discussed below. These problems were summarised accurately by Menell:

> ... it is apparent that the emerging interpretation of copyright protection for application program code is quite far off the mark. Under the *Whelan* test, copyright extends to the structure, sequence and organisation of application code as long as the overall purpose of the entire program, broadly defined, can be implemented in another manner. Since many aspects of application code are dictated by basic principles of software engineering, the *Whelan* rule makes it difficult for others wishing to market programs performing the same task as the first comer to perform it as effectively. In effect, the *Whelan* test enables first comers to 'lock up' basic programming techniques as implemented in programs to perform particular tasks. This gives the first comer significant market power. In addition, since the programmer did not have to contribute novel and non-obvious programming techniques to our state of knowledge in order to get this legal protection, the monopoly power bestowed will not, in most cases, be justified on the basis of sound public policy analysis.

---

34   Englund, 1990, p 881.
35   Velasco, 1994.

Furthermore, in the light of the importance of sequential research in the application program industry, the *Whelan* test is likely to affect detrimentally the direction and cost of research and development. This can be seen clearly by analysing the set of options open to an application programmer who wishes to improve on an existing program that employs nothing more than good programming practice. In a world protecting only useful, novel and non-obvious programming elements, the programmer would be free to build upon the functional aspects of the first program. The *Whelan* test, however, prohibits the programmer from innovating in this way. The programmer would either have to: (1) secure a licence for the original program (or its desired aspects) from the copyright owner; (2) circumvent the copyrighted material by expressing the desired functional aspects of the original program in a way that does not infringe its overall structure, sequence and organisation; or (3) independently develop the functional programming techniques. Plainly, all three of these options substantially raise the costs of innovative activity. [36]

Karjala goes further and suggests that the reasoning based on the use of *scènes à faire* is inappropriate:[37] '... computer programs are literary works only in form ... In operation, they are pure works of function, that is, of technology. The analogy with novels and plays ... is totally inapt for works of technology.' Although expressed as a criticism of the reasoning in *Whelan*, this could be regarded, more correctly, as a comment on the classification of computer programs as literary works for copyright purposes.

The US Court of Appeals Second Circuit recognised some of these problems in the later case of *Computer Associates v Altai*,[38] noting that the decision in *Whelan* had received a 'mixed reception' in the courts and that '*Whelan* has fared ... poorly in the academic community where its standard ... has been widely criticised for being overbroad',[39] and went on to use rather different reasoning. The case concerned the development of an 'operating system compatibility component' by Computer Associates which enabled a program to work with a number of different operating systems. One of the members of the team that developed this feature was later employed by Altai to develop a version of one of its own programs which could be used on various operating systems. Without the knowledge of Altai, the programmer based the program on the Computer Associates program, including the literal copying of some 30% of the code. When Altai were made aware of this (by Computer Associates suing for copyright infringement!), they used different programmers to create a new version. Nonetheless, Computer Associates went on to sue for infringement of both programs, alleging that even the second program made use of the non-literal elements of their original program.

Not surprisingly, at first instance, the court found that there had been infringement in relation to the first program. However, this court absolved Altai of liability in relation to the second program and Computer Associates appealed, leading to the Second Circuit formulating what has become known as the 'abstraction-filtration-comparison' test as they struggled to formulate a suitable method for determining the copyrightability of the non-literal elements of a computer program. It was accepted in

36   Menell, 1989, p 1082.
37   Karjala,1991, p 198.
38   982 F 2d 693 (2nd Cir 1992).
39   *Ibid*, p 705.

the case that copyright protection of computer programs extends beyond literal similarities in code and also includes similarities in structure. In contrast to the decision in *Whelan*, the judgment of the Second Circuit utilised Learned Hand's famous abstractions approach, at least for the first part of the test, and the *Whelan* formulation, that the overall purpose of the program can be equated with its idea, was roundly criticised on the basis that the majority of programs do not consist of a single 'idea' but are more accurately described as composites. Circuit Judge Walker therefore introduced a different test and, in presenting this test, the Second Circuit suggested that, when faced with this problem, courts:[40]

> ... would be well advised to undertake a three step procedure based on the abstractions test utilised by the district court, in order to determine whether the non-literal elements of two or more computer programs are substantially similar. This approach breaks no new ground; rather it draws on such familiar copyright doctrines as merger, *scènes à faire* and public domain. In taking this approach, however, we are cognisant that computer technology is a dynamic field which can quickly outpace judicial decision making. Thus, in cases where the technology in question does not allow for a literal application of the procedure we outline below, our opinion should not be read to foreclose the district courts of our circuit from utilising a modified version.
>
> In ascertaining substantial similarity under this approach, a court would first break down the allegedly infringed program into its constituent structural parts. Then, by examining each of these parts for such things as incorporated ideas, expression that is necessarily incidental to those ideas, and elements that are taken from the public domain, a court would then be able to sift out all non-protectable material. Left with a kernel, or possibly kernels, of creative expression after following this process of elimination, the court's last step would be to compare this material with the structure of an allegedly infringing program. The result of this comparison will determine whether the protectable elements of the programs at issue are substantially similar so as to warrant a finding of infringement.

This was the source of what has become known as the abstraction-filtration-comparison test, which was subsequently enlarged upon by the court.[41]

Step 1: Abstraction

> ... As applied to computer programs, the abstractions test will comprise the first step in the examination for substantial similarity. Initially, in a manner that resembles reverse engineering on a theoretical plane, a court should dissect the allegedly copied program's structure and isolate each level of abstraction contained within it. This process begins with the code and ends with an articulation of the program's ultimate function. Along the way, it is necessary essentially to retrace and map each of the designer's steps – in the opposite order in which they were taken during the program's creation ...
>
> At the lowest level of abstraction, a computer program may be thought of in its entirety as a set of individual instructions organised into a hierarchy of modules. At a higher level of abstraction, the instructions in the lowest level modules may be replaced conceptually by the functions of those modules. At progressively higher levels of abstraction, the functions of higher level modules conceptually replace the implementations of those

---

40   *Ibid*, p 706.
41   *Ibid* p. 707.

modules in terms of lower level modules and instructions, until finally, one is left with nothing but the ultimate function of the program. A program has structure at every level of abstraction at which it is viewed. At low levels of abstraction, a program's structure may be quite complex; at the highest level it is trivial ...

Step 2: Filtration

... This process entails examining the structural components at each level of abstraction to determine whether their particular inclusion at that level was 'idea' or was dictated by considerations of efficiency, so as to be necessarily incidental to that idea; required by factors external to the program itself; or taken from the public domain and hence is non-protectable expression ...

(a) Elements dictated by efficiency

... Copyrighted language may be copied without infringing when there is but a limited number of ways to express a given idea ... In the computer context, this means that when specific instructions, even though previously copyrighted, are the only and essential means of accomplishing a given task, their later use by another will not amount to infringement.

... In the context of computer program design, the concept of efficiency is akin to deriving the most concise logical proof or formulating the most succinct mathematical computation. Thus, the more efficient a set of modules are, the more closely they approximate the idea or process embodied in that particular aspect of the program's structure.

... Efficiency is an industry-wide goal. Since, as we have already noted, there may be only a limited number of efficient implementations for any given program task, it is quite possible that multiple programmers, working independently, will design the identical method employed in the allegedly infringed work. Of course, if this is the case, there is no copyright infringement.

... Thus, since evidence of similarly efficient structure is not particularly probative of copying, it should be disregarded in the overall substantial similarity analysis ...

(b) Elements dictated by external factors

... Professor Nimmer points out that 'in many instances it is virtually impossible to write a program to perform particular functions in a specific computing environment without employing standard techniques' ... This is a result of the fact that a programmer's freedom of design choice is often circumscribed by extrinsic considerations such as (1) the mechanical specifications of the computer on which a particular program is intended to run; (2) compatibility requirements of other programs with which a program is designed to operate in conjunction; (3) computer manufacturers' design standards; (4) demands of the industry being serviced; and (5) widely accepted programming practices within the computer industry ...

(c) Elements taken from the public domain

... Such material is free for the taking and cannot be appropriated by a single author even though it is included in a copyrighted work ... We see no reason to make an exception to this rule for elements of a computer program that have entered the public domain by virtue of freely accessible program exchanges and the like.

Step 3: Comparison

The third and final step of the test for substantial similarity that we believe appropriate for non-literal program components entails a comparison. Once a court has sifted out all elements of the allegedly infringed program which are 'ideas' or are dictated by efficiency or external factors, or taken from the public domain, there may remain a core of protectable expression. In terms of a work's copyright value, this is the golden nugget ...

The court then went on to discuss what it believed to be the relevant policy issues in drawing the line between idea and expression. In doing this, they recognised that assessing non-literal similarity in this way is far more favourable to the defendant than the method of assessing non-literal copying used in *Whelan* which the court in *Computer Associates* explicitly rejected. Nonetheless, they felt that a correct application of copyright principles was of overriding importance and were of the view that this would not have disastrous consequences for the industry:[42]

> ... we are unpersuaded that the test we approve today will lead to the dire consequences for the computer program industry that the plaintiff and some *amici* predict. To the contrary, serious students of the industry have been highly critical of the sweeping scope of copyright protection engendered by the *Whelan* rule, in that it enables first comers to 'lock up' basic programming techniques as implemented in programs to perform particular tasks.
>
> While incentive based arguments in favour of broad copyright protection are perhaps attractive from a pure policy perspective, ultimately they have a corrosive effect on certain fundamental tenets of copyright doctrine. If the test we have outlined results in narrowing the scope of protection, as we expect it will, that result flows from applying, in accordance with Congressional intent, long standing principles of copyright law to computer programs. Of course, our decision is also informed by our concern that these fundamental principles remain undistorted.

This judgment was generally well received as demonstrating a good understanding of the way in which computer programs are designed and written. It was acknowledged by some writers that the decision was also able to deal with constraints of interoperability and compatibility:[43] '... together, *Altai* and *Sega* provide a method by which the courts can permit copying of internal interface elements necessary for compatibility while protecting elements not needed for compatibility.'[44] On the other hand, some reservations were expressed.

Case note on Computer Associates v Altai
(1992) 106 Harv L Rev 510

> Although the *Altai* court attempted to balance the interests involved in the protection of these basic elements, the court was unduly constrained by a uniquely literary view of the creative process and thus failed to recognise its own ability to 'keep pace' with technological change within the traditional copyright framework. Because the court protected more than the 'only and essential means' of accomplishing a programming task, its test will discourage innovative programming techniques and leave non-literal elements of computer programs under-protected.

Notwithstanding this criticism, the writer still found some positive features in the judgment which might form the basis of a workable test, as long as certain provisos were taken into account:

> In certain cases, it may be necessary to limit the copyrightability of an 'essential means' of accomplishing a particular programming objective in order to allow continuing innovation but this will rarely preclude copyrightability. Even assuming, as the *Altai*

---

42   *Ibid*, p 712.
43   See, also, below, p 47.
44   Teter, 1993, p 1084.

court did, that 'efficiency' takes a lot of the creativity out of programming, the court did not assert that *no* creativity is involved. Rarely is there only one way to accomplish a given programming task.

The 'abstraction-filtration-comparison' method of determining the copyrightability of a computer program's non-literal elements may be imperfect, but is arguably a 'practical necessity' in the computer program context. Abstracting and then filtering out unprotected elements 'eases the court's task of discerning the boundaries of protectable expression' by 'separating the program into manageable components'. However, the only elements – whether literal or non-literal – that should be filtered out are those that constitute the 'only and essential means' of accomplishing a given task. Although there is 'no statutory basis for treating computer programs differently from other literary work', courts should attempt to develop an approach to copyrightability that acknowledges the unique creative challenges posed by computer programming.

The decision in *Altai*, although taking more accurate recognition of the way in which computer programs are developed and written, cannot deal satisfactorily with the situations such as that which occurred in *Apple Computer Inc v Microsoft Corp*.[45] In this case, applying the abstraction-filtration-comparison test would result in there being little to compare, because the program had been constructed from existing sub-routines already in the public domain or dictated by efficiency requirements, with a consequent denial of copyright protection.

Apple v Microsoft: has the pendulum swung too far?
Steve S Moutsatsos and John CR Cummings
(1993) 9 CL & P 162

It could be strongly argued that the decision in *Apple v Microsoft* simply turned on its facts and that the 'analytical approach' remains a sound legal process through which to examine software copyright issues. On the other hand, it is also possible to assert that the 'analytical approach' as it is applied to computer software, by its nature, may inevitably lead to the conclusion that the constituent elements of a computer program are not protectable under copyright law. The analytical dissection of a computer program, which is essentially a utilitarian work, is more likely to produce constituent parts that are found to be functional, as opposed to a movie or a novel ...

In such cases, whether or not there is any copyright protection will depend on an assessment of the way in which they have been assembled and interlinked. It will be at this stage that the case law on the copyright of compilations may become very relevant.[46]

The discussion on the previous pages has focused exclusively on the cases of *Whelan and Altai*, largely because they have subsequently been the ones referred to in the UK cases, but also because they have generally proved to be influential and have both generated much debate. Also, in some ways, they can be viewed as two ends of the spectrum of copyright protection for computer programs. As noted by Moutsatsos and Cumming,[47] 'Both approaches are rooted in and use the language and legal

---

45   35 F 3d 1435 (9th Cir 1994).
46   In the US, see *Feist Publications Inc v Rural Telephone Service Co* 113 L Ed 2d 358 (1991), cited in *Altai* and discussed in the context of databases below p 82. In the UK see the discussion of *Richardson v Flanders*, below, p 35.
47   Moutsatsos and Cummings 1993.

precedent of copyright law but with vastly differing results'. *Whelan*, with its almost patent-like protection, operates in favour of the original developer of the program, whereas application of the test in *Altai* reduces considerably this protection. The opposing effects of these two judgments may be of significance for certain sectors of the industry. Thus, in the appeal in *Altai*, the Software Publishers Association supported Computer Associates in opposing the lower court's decision and in support of the *Whelan* approach, whereas the American Committee for Interoperable Systems favoured rejection of the *Whelan* rationale.[48] Different commentators have both supported and opposed the decision in *Altai*, but Miller believes that *Altai* can be viewed as a further refinement of the approach begun in *Whelan* and suggests that the difference between the two has been overstated:[49] '... it seems more accurate to view *Altai* as adopting a series of modifications of *Whelan's* generalised statements and as using different terminology without deviating markedly from the *Whelan* court's fundamental reliance on the idea/expression dichotomy.'

Whatever view is taken of the relationship between the decisions in these two cases, the situation in the US courts has been more complex than the analysis above might suggest. As we have seen, both *Whelan and Altai* were decided in different circuits of the US Court of Appeals and, despite the criticisms of *Whelan* contained in the court's judgment in *Altai*, it was certainly not the case that the test in *Altai* immediately eclipsed that in *Whelan*. In addition, other circuits devised other tests which might be based in part on either of these tests. This resulted, at times, in certain contradictions and confusions and, in the words of the court in *Altai*,[50] 'many of the decisions in this area reflect the courts' attempt to fit the proverbial square peg in a round hole'. The Ninth Circuit, for instance, developed its own test (the intrinsic/extrinsic test) for copyrightability of computer programs in *Brown Bag Software v Symanthec Corp*.[51] The proliferation of such tests and their subsequent modification led one commentator to state that 'The "look and feel" cases ... can fairly be characterised as a mess'.[52] Thus, the situation with regard to copyrightability of computer software in the US courts has been more confused than is sometimes presented,[53] although the *Altai* test now appears to be accepted in many US courts.[54]

Velasco has compared the various tests and has concluded that the test devised in *Computer Associates v Altai* is the best on offer from the courts.

---

48 Zadra-Symes, 1992.
49 Miller, 1993, p 1002.
50 982 F 2d 693 (2nd Cir 1992), p 712.
51 960 F 2d 1465 (9th Cir 1992).
52 Hayes, 1993.
53 A more detailed analysis is beyond the scope of this publication; see, eg, Hayes, 1993; Miller, 1993; Velasco, 1994; Karjala, 1994; Drexl, 1994.
54 Lai, 2000, Chapter 2.

The copyrightability of non-literal
elements of computer programs
Julian Velasco
(1994) 94 Colum L Rev 242, p 284

... only the *Altai* test *explicitly* incorporates in a *systematic* way the abstractions test, the concept of merger, a very sophisticated understanding of the concept of *scènes à faire*, and the concept of public domain materials. In short, from the perspective of copyright doctrine, the *Altai* test is superior to the others.

Despite this tribute, he nevertheless goes on to point out a failing and suggest an improvement:

An inescapable failing of the *Altai* test is that its thoroughness in filtering out unprotectable elements of expression leads to underprotection ... Application of the compilations doctrine rectifies this failing ... works consisting entirely of uncopyrightable elements are often protected by the copyright law under the rubric of 'compilations'. Based on an analogy to compilations, copyright protection should subsist in computer programs even if they consist entirely of uncopyrightable elements if those elements were selected or arranged in an original manner. Therefore, an additional step should be added to *Altai*'s 'abstraction-filtration-comparison' test. After the court has completed the successive filtering of the second step of the *Altai* test, it should re-evaluate the elements that have been excluded as uncopyrightable to determine whether there are elements, or groupings of elements, that, in their selection, co-ordination or arrangement, are sufficiently original to merit copyright protection as a group in a manner analogous to compilations. This would be a 're-incorporating' stage since elements previously excluded from copyright protection are now reincorporated in the analysis, albeit as compilations ... The addition of the compilations doctrine expands the scope of the *Altai* test ... while simultaneously avoiding the overbreadth of 'total concept and feel'. It strikes the appropriate balance between the two, providing the substance needed for analysis while ensuring that only expression is protected.

One final point should be made with regard to the proposed re-incorporating stage. In applying it, the court should recognise the fact that a work may be held to consist of *more than one* compilation, just as a work 'may consist of a mixture of numerous ideas and expressions' ...

With the elimination of the unnecessary limitations imposed by the court and the addition of this re-incorporating stage, the *Altai* test becomes complete. In theory, at least, it should provide protection to *all* the elements and *only* to the elements of a computer program that deserve protection. Although decisions will still be '*ad hoc*' to a certain extent, this modified *Altai* test provides the decision maker with a framework for determining copyrightability that is solidly grounded in well established copyright principles.

Despite dissent in some quarters and the evolution of different tests (as mentioned earlier, the Court of Appeals in *Altai* itself thought that modifications would be appropriate in some circumstances), the test was generally greeted with favour and the prevailing opinion seemed to be that this was likely to become the preferred approach:[55]

---

55 Rinck, 1992, p 356.

Given the prestige of the Second Circuit and the considerable persuasiveness of the opinions, it is fair to conclude that *Computer Associates* has now become the analytical starting point for further analysis in the United States of the appropriate scope of copyright protection for computer programs ... The effects intended by the court in *Computer Associates*, of course, are greater competition, increased incremental innovation and a more public exchange or market in 'ideas'. Wherever United States' case law or legislation next turns, these should continue to be important objectives.

The situation in the UK

During the period in which the US courts were debating these issues, those involved in the UK waited impatiently for the first case to go to full trial. There was academic debate about how the approach of the UK courts might be influenced by the difficulties experienced by the US courts. There was also evidence provided by interlocutory hearings such as that of *Computer Aided Design v Bolwell*,[56] in which Hoffman J made reference to the decision in *Whelan v Jaslow*, that, at the least, the judiciary were taking cognisance of the US decisions. Computer Aided Design (CAD) were suppliers of both software and hardware. In particular, they marketed a software package called BUSNIX-FLEET. In a common scenario in this type of case, three employees, including Bolwell, left CAD to set up a rival business, with the promise of both orders and financial assistance from a former customer of CAD who was dissatisfied with BUSNIX-FLEET. The defendants wrote a program using the fourth generation language, PROGRESS, and called the package the Towquest system. CAD then alleged that this had incurred both a breach of copyright and a breach of confidence. The respective programs used different codes and there was no allegation that the code itself was copied, rather that the overall design and structure, that is, the *'look and feel'*, of BUSNIX-FLEET had been substantially copied.

Although CAD failed to obtain an injunction because they were unable to satisfy the court that Towquest was arguably a substantial copy of BUSNIX-FLEET, Hoffman J said that the overall structure of a computer program was a form of literary expression in which copyright could exist and, in his express reference to the reasoning in *Whelan v Jaslow*, seemed to be condoning the approach in that case.

It was not until the end of 1992 that the High Court began to hear the case of *John Richardson Computers Ltd v Flanders*.[57] The facts of the case are complex but, in brief, both parties developed and marketed programs to print labels for prescriptions at pharmacists and keep details of the stock of drugs. Flanders, a self-taught programmer with a penchant for writing programs in machine code, had worked for Richardson in the past, first as an employee and then as a self-employed consultant. After all ties with Richardson ceased, Flanders wrote a program in QuickBASIC for an IBM personal computer which he marketed through a company that he had established, called Chemtec. Richardson alleged that this program infringed his copyright in an earlier program written, with the help of Flanders, in assembler language for a BBC computer.

---

56   (1989) unreported, 23 August.
57   [1993] FSR 497.

Ferris J identified a number of issues, of which the most important and interesting for our purposes was: 'What ought to be the approach of the court to the appraisal of an allegation of breach of copyright in a computer program where it is not claimed that the source code has itself been copied?'

John Richardson Computers Ltd v Flanders
[1993] FSR 497, p 519
High Court

6 Approach to be adopted by the court in this type of case

... it is apparent now that this is not a case where it can be said that any substantial parts of the source code of the BBC program have been copied in the Chemtec program. The two programs are, of course, written in different computer languages. This by itself would not avoid infringement if the Chemtec program could be said to be a translation of the BBC program, or a substantial part of it, into a different language (see section 1(2) of the 1985 Act, now section 21(4) of the 1988 Act). But this is not what is said to have happened. What is said is that the defendants have taken the general scheme of the BBC program, including the detail of certain routines of an idiosyncratic nature. The case was likened ... to one in which the plot of a book or other literary work has been taken ...

In making the analogy with novels and plays, this recalls the reasoning adopted in *Whelan v Jaslow*, and the argument continued to include both UK and US authorities. Ferris J then went on to discuss the proposition that the program could be protected as a compilation:

Mr Wilson, on behalf of JRC, also relied upon *Ladbroke (Football) Ltd v William Hill (Football) Ltd*. In that case Ladbrokes admitted having copied some parts of Hills' fixed odds football betting coupons, but denied that Hills were entitled to copyright in those parts. They admitted that certain other parts of Hills coupons were protected by copyright, but they had not copied those parts. It was held by the House of Lords that the coupon had to be looked at as a single literary work and that, having regard to the skill and effort involved in working out certain parts of Hills coupon, the coupon as a whole was an original compilation which was protected by copyright. I quote from the speech of Lord Pearce at page 291:

In deciding therefore whether a work in the nature of a compilation is original, it is wrong to start by considering individual parts of it apart from the whole, as the appellants in their argument sought to do. For many compilations have nothing original in their parts, yet the sum total of the compilation may be original ...

In such cases the courts have looked to see whether the compilation of the unoriginal material called for work or skill or expense. If it did, it is entitled to be considered original and to be protected against those who wish to steal the fruits of the work or skill or expense by copying it without taking the trouble to compile it themselves.

This approach, of course, gives rise to a further question where it is contended that what the defendant has copied is one or more of the unoriginal parts, not the compilation as a whole. As to this question, Lord Pearce said (at p 293):

Whether a part is substantial must be decided by its quality rather than its quantity. The reproduction of a part which by itself has no originality will not normally be a substantial part of the copyright and therefore will not be protected. For that which would not attract copyright except by reason of its collocation will, when robbed of that collocation, not be a substantial part of the copyright and therefore the courts will not hold its reproduction to be an infringement. It is this, I think, which is meant by one or two judicial observations that 'there is no copyright' in some unoriginal part of a whole that is copyright. They afford no justification, in my view, for holding that one starts the inquiry as to whether copyright exists by dissecting the compilation into component parts instead of starting it by regarding the compilation as a whole and seeing whether the whole has copyright. It is when one is debating whether the part reproduced is substantial that one considers the pirated portion on its own.

In using the *William Hill* case by way of analogy, Ferris J found an English authority on which to base argument concerning the structure of the program, a process which begins to bear a resemblance to the assessment of substantial similarity required by US law. Having made reference to the non-literal elements in the fact that the compilation is itself an appropriate subject for copyright protection, Ferris J went on to apply the test from *Computer Associates v Altai*.

John Richardson Computers Ltd v Flanders
[1993] FSR 497, p 526
High Court

Ferris J In the test propounded in *Computer Associates* the discovery of a program's abstraction levels is the first step. The second step is to filter these abstractions in order to discover a 'core of protectable material'. In the process of filtration there are to be excluded from consideration (a) elements dictated by efficiency; (b) elements dictated by external factors; and (c) elements taken from the public domain. Each of these categories is explained at some length. The essence of the 'elements dictated by efficiency' is that if there is only one way to express an idea the idea and its expression are inseparable and copyright does not prevent the copying of the expression. The exclusion of 'elements dictated by external factors' arises from the fact that if two persons set about the description of the same event there may be a number of particular facts which can only be described in a particular way. The Court of Appeals cited with evident approval the observation of Professor Nimmer (a well known academic commentator on United States copyright law) that:

> ... in many instances it is impossible to write a program to perform particular functions in a specific computing environment without employing standard techniques.

As to 'elements in the public domain':

> ... plaintiffs may not claim copyright of an ... expression that is, if not standard, then commonplace in the computer software industry.

The third step in the process suggested in the *Computer Associates* case is to compare what is left of the 'abstractions' made from the plaintiff's case after filtering out these elements with the program which is said to be an infringement of that program.

I have thought it right to deal at some length with the *Computer Associates* case because it explores the difficulties which arise in applying copyright law to computer programs to a greater extent than an English authority does. In the even more recent case of *Sega Enterprises Ltd v Accolade Inc*, the United States Court of Appeals for the Ninth Circuit approved the approach adopted by the Court of Appeals for the Second Circuit in *Computer Associates*. Not surprisingly, neither of these decisions have yet been considered in an English case. There are references to *Whelan* in the judgments of Hoffman J in *Computer Aided Systems v Bolwell*, and of Judge Paul Baker, QC in *Total Information Processing Systems Ltd v Daman Ltd*, but both these references are very general and neither of them can be said to indicate a preference for the *Whelan* approach over the approach which has since been adopted on two federal circuits in the United States.

There is thus nothing in any English decision which conflicts with the general approach adopted in the *Computer Associates* case. I think that in preference to seeking the 'core of protectable expression' in the plaintiff's program an English court will first decide whether the plaintiff's program as a whole is entitled to copyright and then decide whether any similarity attributable to copying which is to be found in the defendant's program amounts to the copying of a substantial part of the plaintiff's program. This was the approach which was held to be appropriate in the *William Hill* case. But at the stage at which the substantiality of any copying falls to be assessed in an English case the question which has to be answered, in relation to the originality of the plaintiff's program and the separation of an idea from its expression, is essentially the same question as the United States court was addressing in *Computer Associates*. In my judgment it would be right to adopt a similar approach in England. This means that consideration is not restricted to the text of the code, as Mr McEwen submitted that it was when putting the defendant's case at its highest level. Moreover the argument that consideration should be limited to the 'structure and organisation' of the program imports an unacceptable degree of uncertainty, because it is unclear at what level of abstraction (to use that term in the sense in which it was used in *Computer Associates*) the structure and organisation is to be discerned.

Despite the above analysis, when it came to applying the test to the facts of the case, there was no actual comparison of the BBC program code with the code of the Chemtec program, as might have been expected if the *Computer Associates* test had been used without modification. The expert witness had compared both codes in the report he compiled for the court. One factor that seems to have had a bearing on the lack of such comparison in arriving at the final decision appears to be that Ferris J had trouble in understanding this part of the report, and also that the situation was not made any clearer during cross-examination.

The test which was evolved in the case can perhaps be summarised by the following steps:

* is the claimant's program as a whole entitled to copyright protection?;
* are there similarities to the claimant's program in the defendant's program?;
* is any similarity attributable to copying?;
* do any such similarities amount to the copying of a substantial part of the claimant's program assessed by application of the abstraction-filtration-comparison test of *Computer Associates v Altai*?

The outcome of the case was that some infringement of Richardson's copyright was found, but this was fairly minor and in only a few limited respects. In writing the new program, it appeared that Flanders had not copied or translated all or a substantial part of the source code of the BBC program; instead, he had created another program to fulfil a similar purpose and thus compete on the same market.

How are we to assess the first complete decision relating to copyright infringement of computer software in a UK court? In view of the length of time that such a case had been awaited, the judgment of Ferris J was perhaps subjected to more detailed scrutiny and analysis than is customarily awarded to decisions of the High Court. One aspect on which all seem to agree is that, in English law, as has been determined in the US, copyright infringement does not only occur in cases of literal copying but may be found when copying of non-literal elements of the program can be established. The question is, what is an appropriate test in such cases? It appears that, in starting from the judgment in *William Hill*, Ferris J does not believe that the abstraction-filtration-comparison test should be applied directly in an English case.

Although the abstraction process advocated in *Altai*, based as it is on earlier US authorities, in particular the judgments of Learned Hand J, may not be compatible with the way in which copyright law has developed in the UK, neither does it mean that the attempt of Ferris J in formulating a suitable test is any more successful. In particular, an important consideration is the appropriateness of the analogy between a compilation and a computer program, on which the application of the *William Hill* authority depends. Such an analogy might be appropriate in the case where a program is assembled from existing sub-routines, but it is questionable as to whether it is capable of more general application. A similar point was noted by Baker J in *Total Information Processing Systems Ltd v Daman Ltd*,[58] who said that 'The mere linking of programs is not in my judgment itself an original, literary or artistic work in the way that the collective presentation of literary works by divers authorities is'. Nor could the compilation be regarded as a computer program separate from and in addition to the individual programs. However, this statement was later to be criticised by Jacob J in *Ibcos Computers v Barclays Finance Ltd*,[59] as not being capable of general application, although relevant to the facts in *Total Information*.

A second point is how far it is sensible to apply the three stage test, based as it is on the more rigidly imposed distinction between idea and expression embodied in US law. Whether or not it is articulated as such, the distinction does exist in the UK, albeit expressed in rather a different way. Thus, in *Donoghue v Allied Newspapers Ltd*,[60] Farwell J said: '... there is no copyright in an idea or ideas ... If the idea, however original, is nothing more than an idea, and is not put into any form of words, or any form of expression ... then there is no such thing as copyright at all.' This notion was also taken up by Baker J in *Total Information*:[61] '... stemming from the principle that copyright does not exist in ideas but in the expression of them, is the line of authorities commencing with *Kenrick and Company v Lawrence and Company*,[62] that if there is only one way of expressing an idea that way is not the subject of copyright.'

The US basis for copyright infringement of substantial similarity requires much more wrestling with the idea/expression dichotomy than the UK test of establishing whether there has been copying of a substantial part, and the attempt by Ferris J to marry the US and UK approaches has received a mixed reception. The above criticisms have been discussed by Arnold.

Infringement of copyright in computer software by non-textual copying: first decision at trial by an English court
Richard Arnold
[1993] EIPR 250, p 253

So far as the analysis of the law is concerned, it is submitted that much of what Ferris J says is sound. In particular, he was plainly right to reject the submissions that a substantial part can only be reproduced if there is textual copying. Furthermore, there is force in the criticism of the *Whelan* approach, although the criticisms underplay the detail in which the court in that case did in fact compare the code structure. Equally, the judge was correct that the *Computer Associates* approach of extracting a 'core of protectable

---

58   [1992] FSR 171.
59   [1994] FSR 275.
60   [1938] Ch 106, pp 109, 110.
61   [1992] FSR 171, p 181.
62   (1890) 25 QBD 99.

expression' is incompatible with English authority, and in particular the speeches of the House of Lords in *William Hill.*

Where the analysis may be questioned, however, is when Ferris J states that in considering substantiality it is right to adopt a similar approach to the approach set out in *Computer Associates.* Although Ferris J is not explicit about this, it appears that he has in mind the point made by Lord Pearce in the passage quoted above. It is submitted that what Lord Pearce envisaged was a different procedure however. This involves the following steps. (1) Decide whether copyright subsists in the plaintiff's work. (2) If so, decide whether there is a derivation. (3) If so, decide whether a substantial part has been reproduced; if the only part which has been reproduced is a part which by itself has no originality, then that part is not substantial. This is not the same thing as the filtering process described by the Court of Appeals in *Computer Associates.* It should be borne in mind that Lord Pearce was dealing with what was essentially a compilation case. At various places in the judgment Ferris J refers to a computer program as a compilation, but this does not seem to be correct except in the particular case where a program has been compiled from pre-existing sub-routines.

Although *dicta* may be found in English cases to the effect that there is 'no copyright in ideas', the general trend of English authority is rather against attempts rigidly to distinguish between 'idea' and 'expression'. As Ferris J acknowledged, the position is different in the United States because the distinction has a statutory basis. Furthermore, as the judge has also acknowledged, reliance on the distinction can be dangerous. Despite this, Ferris J appears to have accepted that an English court should attempt to draw this distinction and moreover should engage in the *Computer Associates* filtering process in doing so. It is open to question whether this is the right approach under English law.

Even if the test is an appropriate one, it is difficult to apply – a fact which was recognised in the judgment itself – and the result of the case was, in fact, more dependent on practical and pragmatic considerations relating to the comparison of the mode of operation of the two programs and an assessment of the opportunity for copying.

Richardson v Flanders was soon followed by another case, that of *Ibcos Computers Ltd v Barclays Finance Ltd.*[63] Again, the facts are rather complex, but the main features are as follows. In the 1970s, a programmer, Poole, wrote software for agricultural applications for a dealer, Clayton. Eventually, a company was set up in which both Poole and Clayton owned shares. Poole was the only employee of this company and continued to develop the software, now known as ADS. A deal between the company and a subsidiary of Barclays fell through but Poole, himself, was offered a two year consultancy and parted company with Clayton. As a result, Poole and Clayton signed an agreement by which Poole was to return all company property and agreed not to modify or provide customer support for the ADS package. Poole acknowledged that the software and manuals were the sole property of the company, whose assets were later transferred to Ibcos. Poole also agreed not to develop any agricultural software for two years.

In 1986, Poole rewrote the ADS package but it was not marketed until the two years had expired, in order to comply with the restrictive covenant. Poole received 10% of the licence fees.

---

63   [1994] FSR 275.

The court agreed that there had been no breach of the restrictive covenant, but also had to decide whether Poole's new version constituted a breach of copyright. Copyright infringement was claimed in the individual programs and sub-routines, the general structure and certain general features of the system which were identified in the expert witnesses' report.

Jacob J first set out the basic steps to ascertain whether there had been copying namely; what are the work or works in which the plaintiff claims copyright? Is each such work 'original'? Was there copying from that work? If there was copying, has a substantial part of that work been reproduced? He then directed attention to the idea/expression issue.

Ibcos Computers v Barclays Finance Ltd
[1994] FSR 275, p 290
High Court

Jacob J   It was sometimes suggested in a general sort of way that because a particular program had a function, and especially if that function could only be achieved in one or a limited number of ways, there could be no copyright on it. The extreme form of this idea is expressed by Judge Baker in the *Total* case. He said:

> Secondly, stemming from the principle that copyright does not exist in ideas but in the expression of them is the line of authorities commencing with *Kenrick v Lawrence* that if there is only one way of expressing an idea that way is not the subject of copyright.

That statement is in error in two ways. First, *Kenrick* (the case of the drawing of a hand showing voters which way to vote on a voting slip) did not decide that if there is only one way of expressing an idea then no copyright can subsist in it. What was held was that there was no copyright infringement in taking the idea of using a picture of a hand showing how to vote. Accordingly, a different picture embodying the same idea was not taking a substantial part of the copyright work. In that sense, only the principle that there is no copyright in an idea applied.

Secondly, there is, I think, danger in the proposition that 'If there is only one way of expressing an idea that way is not the subject of copyright'. As Lord Hailsham observed in *LB Plastics v Swish*:

> But of course as the late Professor Joad used to observe it all depends on what you mean by 'ideas'. What the respondents in fact copied from the appellants was a mere general idea.

It is of course true that copyright cannot protect any sort of general principle, such as the principle of drawing a hand to show how to vote, but it can protect a detailed literary or artistic expression ... The true position is that where an 'idea' is sufficiently general, then even if an original work embodies it, the mere taking of that idea will not infringe. But if the 'idea' is detailed, then there may be infringement. It is a question of degree.

Jacob's notion of a *detailed* idea that might be protected by copyright is, presumably, in the context of computer programs, that found when a number of sub-routines are put together to form one program. This would be the result of the intellectual effort, skill and judgment of the software writer, as opposed to a *general* idea, which would not be protected by copyright, and presumably might equate with the 'function' in the *Whelan* sense. Thus, he did not give credence to the idea/expression dichotomy which has been much discussed in US law and, indeed, went on to discuss the use of US copyright principles in English cases. He pointed out that US copyright law is different from that in the UK, particularly in the fact that the idea/expression distinction has a statutory basis which has, necessarily, resulted in a different interpretation of that issue in the courts. On the question of judging substantial part, he found it unnecessary to consider US authorities as he felt that it unnecessarily complicated the issue, which could be resolved by applying the standard principles of UK copyright law.

Ibcos Computers v Barclays Finance Ltd
[1994] FSR 275, p 302
High Court

Jacob J For myself I do not find the route of going via United States case law particularly helpful. As I have said, United Kingdom copyright cannot prevent the copying of a mere general idea but can protect the copying of a detailed 'idea'. It is a question of degree where a good guide is the notion of the overborrowing of the skill, labour and judgment which went into the copyright work. Going via the complication of the concept of a 'core of protectable expression' merely complicates the matter as far as our law is concerned. It is likely to lead to overcitation of United States authority based on a statute different from ours. In the end the matter must be left to the value judgment of the court. Having expressed this reservation, however, I thoroughly agree with what Ferris J went on to say: 'Consideration is not restricted to the text of the code ...' That must be right: most literary copyright works involve both literal matter (the exact words of a novel or computer program) and varying levels of abstraction (plot, more or less detailed of a novel, general structure of a computer program).

I therefore think it right to have regard in this case not only to ... 'literal similarities' but also to ... ' program structure' and 'design features'.

Thus, whether or not there is agreement on the reasoning, it appears that there is agreement that non-literal elements can be protected by copyright in the UK, as well as in the US. Despite Jacob J's criticisms of the judgment in *Richardson v Flanders*, the *Ibcos* case was one in which there had been literal copying and so the assessment of a substantial part of the non-literal elements was not crucial to the case. What was a 'substantial part' was one of the crucial issues in *Cantor Fitzgerald v Tradition*. Pumfrey J, agreeing with the general approach of Jacob J in *Ibcos*, went on to 'deal with an aspect of this case which is of considerable importance, and that is the interrelationship of the originality of the work (the prerequisite for the subsistence of copyright) and substantiality of the part of the work copied (the prerequisite for infringement)'.[64] In so doing he made a number of pertinent observations on the problems of applying law developed for literary works to computer programs.

Cantor Fitzgerald v Tradition
[2000] RPC 95
High Court

74. ... I think that there is a real risk of making an error if one adapts well-known principles which have been developed in the context of literary works addressed to humans and applies them uncritically to literary works whose only purpose is to make a machine operate in such and such a manner. A program expressed in a computer language must not contain any errors of syntax (or it will not compile) and it must contain no semantic errors. Computers do not have the capacity to deduce what the author meant

when they encounter errors in the kind of software with which this action is concerned. If the software contains semantic errors it will produce the wrong answer or no answer at all: it may merely fail to run. The only opportunity that the programmer gets to express himself in a more relaxed way is provided by the comments in the code, which are for the benefit of the human reader only and are ignored when the code comes to be compiled. These considerations might suggest that every part of a computer program is essential to its performance, and so every part, however small, is a "substantial part" of the program.

Pumfrey J then considered the Australian case of *Autodesk v Dyason*,[65] as a precedent that this was the correct view, but dismissed the reasoning in that case as 'simplistic' as it would 'result in any part of any computer program being substantial since without any part the program would not work, or at best not work as desired.' The programs in question consisted of a number of modules and the contents of the source file were divided between these modules. He went on to explain how this affected his interpretation of substantial on these particular facts.

76. In my judgment, so far as English law is concerned the correct approach to substantiality is straightforward. It is the function of copyright to protect the relevant skill and labour expended by the author on the work. I say relevant skill and labour because (for example) a purely literary contribution is not relevant skill and labour so far as an artistic copyright is concerned, the latter being concerned purely with visual impression … It follows that a copyist infringes if he appropriates a part of the work upon which a substantial part of the author's skill and labour were expended. …

77. … If it is said that a substantial part of it has been reproduced, whether that part can properly be described as substantial may depend upon how important that part is to the recognition and appreciation of the "artistic work". If an "artistic work" is designed to convey information, the importance of some part of it may fall to be judged by how far it contributes to conveying that information, but not, in my opinion, by how important the information may be which it conveys or helps to convey. What is protected is the skill and labour devoted to making the "artistic work" itself, not the skill and labour devoted to developing some idea or invention communicated or depicted by the "artistic work". The protection afforded by copyright is not, in my judgment, any broader, as counsel submitted, where the "artistic work " embodies a novel or inventive idea than it is where it represents a commonplace object or theme."

This statement of principle cannot be applied directly to infringement of literary copyrights in general or literary copyrights subsisting in computer programs in particular but it reflects nonetheless the approach which I consider is appropriate. So in the general case, it is well established that a substantial part of the author's skill and labour may reside in the plot of a novel or a play: and to take that plot without taking any part of the particular manner of its expression may be sufficient to amount to copyright infringement …

The closest analogy to a plot in a computer program lies perhaps in the algorithms or sequences of operations decided on by the programmer to achieve his object. But it goes wider. It seems to be generally accepted that the "architecture" of a computer program is capable of protection if a substantial part of the programmer's skill, labour and judgment went into it. In this context, "architecture" is a vague and ambiguous term. It may be used to refer to the overall structure of the system at a very high level of abstraction. …

---

65   [1992] RPC 575.

78. ... It seems to me on the evidence that the choice of module content, if not arbitrary, is based on an assessment of considerations which have nothing to do with the computer program as a functional unit but relate to extraneous matters such as availability and skill of programmers, convenience of debugging and maintenance and so on. It is not possible to say that the skill and labour involved in making such a choice could never amount to a substantial part of the copyright subsisting in the various modules, but it seems to me to be unlikely. So in my judgment the substantiality of what is taken has to be judged against the collection of modules viewed as a whole. Substantiality is to be judged in the light of the skill and labour in design and coding which went into the piece of code which is alleged to be copied. It is not determined by whether the system would work without the code; or by the amount of use the system makes of the code.

The problem of non-literal copying was considered further in *Navitaire v EasyJet*.[66] The case concerned the creation of an airline reservation system for EasyJet which had the same functionality as that of Navitaire. Easyjet had originally been a licensee of the Navitaire software but wished to create a similar system for its own requirements while maintaining the same functionality. EasyJet had had no access to the original source code and the new system had been created purely by observation of the first system. Pumfrey J took a pragmatic approach to non-literal copying.

NavitaireInc v EasyJet Airline Company
[2004] EWHC 1725
High Court

118 ... Since copyright in computer programs is a literary copyright, the natural approach for Navitaire is to base its contentions on the analogy between the function of a computer program and the plot of a literary work. Mr Carr QC employs the law in this area as a cornerstone of his submissions, and it is necessary to consider the cases.

119. In *Designer's Guild v Russell Williams Textiles Ltd* [2000] 1 WLR 2416, Lord Hoffman says at 2422:

It is often said, as Morritt L.J. said in this case, that copyright subsists not in ideas but in the form in which the ideas are expressed. The distinction between expression and ideas finds a place in the Agreement on Trade-Related Aspects of Intellectual Property Rights (TRIPS) ..., to which the United Kingdom is a party (see Article 9.2: "Copyright protection shall extend to expressions and not to ideas ..."). Nevertheless, it needs to be handled with care. What does it mean? As Lord Hailsham of St. Marylebone said in *L.B. (Plastics) Ltd v Swish Products Ltd.* [1979] RPC 551, 629, 'it all depends on what you mean by "ideas."'

Plainly there can be no copyright in an idea which is merely in the head, which has not been expressed in copyrightable form, as a literary, dramatic, musical or artistic work. But the distinction between ideas and expression cannot mean anything so trivial as that. On the other hand, every element in the expression of an artistic work (unless it got there by accident or compulsion) is the expression of an idea on the part of the author. It represents her choice to paint stripes rather than polka dots, flowers rather than tadpoles, use one colour and brush technique rather than another, and so on. The expression of these ideas is protected, both as a cumulative whole and also to the extent to which they form a 'substantial part' of the work. Although the term 'substantial part' might suggest a quantitative test, or at least the ability to identify some discrete part which, on quantitative or qualitative grounds, can be regarded as

---

66   [2004] EWHC 1725.

substantial, it is clear upon the authorities that neither is the correct test. ... Or to take another example, the original elements in the plot of a play or novel may be a substantial part, so that copyright may be infringed by a work that does not reproduce a single sentence of the original. If one asks what is being protected in such a case, it is difficult to give any answer except that it is an idea expressed in the copyright work.

120. This passage encapsulates the state of the law. ...

Pumfrey J then went on to review a number of judgments, including those in *Flanders* and *Ibcos* discussed above, but found them to be of little help in the instant case.

125. This does not answer the question with which I am confronted, which is peculiar, I believe, to computer programs. The reason it is a new problem is that two completely different computer programs can produce an identical result: not a result identical at some level of abstraction but identical at any level of abstraction. This is so even if the author of one has no access at all to the other but only to its results. The analogy with a plot is for this reason a poor one. It is a poor one for other reasons as well. To say these programs possess a plot is precisely like saying that the book of instructions for a booking clerk acting manually has a plot: but a book of instructions has no theme, no events, and does not have a narrative flow. Nor does a computer program, particularly one whose behaviour depends upon the history of its inputs in any given transaction. It does not have a plot, merely a series of pre-defined operations intended to achieve the desired result in response to the requests of the customer.

...

128. I think that the answer to the problem is to be gathered from the passage in Lord Hoffmann's speech immediately following that quoted above (paragraph 119) from the *Designers' Guild* case:

My Lords, if one examines the cases in which the distinction between ideas and the expression of ideas has been given effect, I think it will be found that they support two quite distinct propositions. The first is that a copyright work may express certain ideas which are not protected because they have no connection with the literary, dramatic, musical or artistic nature of the work. It is on this ground that, for example, a literary work which describes a system or invention does not entitle the author to claim protection for his system or invention as such. The same is true of an inventive concept expressed in an artistic work. However striking or original it may be, others are (in the absence of patent protection) free to express it in works of their own: see *Kleeneze Ltd. v DRG. (UK) Ltd* [1984] FSR 399. The other proposition is that certain ideas expressed by a copyright work may not be protected because, although they are ideas of a literary, dramatic or artistic nature, they are not original, or so commonplace as not to form a substantial part of the work. *Kenrick & Co v Lawrence & Co* (1890) 25 QBD. 99 is a well known example. It is on this ground that the mere notion of combining stripes and flowers would not have amounted to a substantial part of the plaintiff's work. At that level of abstraction, the idea, though expressed in the design, would not have represented sufficient of the author's skill and labour as to attract copyright protection. Generally speaking, in cases of artistic copyright, the more abstract and simple the copied idea, the less likely it is to constitute a substantial part. Originality, in the sense of the contribution of the author's skill and labour, tends to lie in the detail with which the basic idea is presented. ...

129. The questions in the present case are both a lack of substantiality and the nature of the skill and labour to be protected. Navitaire's computer program invites input in a manner excluded from copyright protection, outputs its results in a form excluded from copyright protection and creates a record of a reservation in the name of a particular passenger on a particular flight. What is left when the interface aspects of the case are

disregarded is the business function of carrying out the transaction and creating the record, because none of the code was read or copied by the defendants. It is right that those responsible for devising OpenRes [the Navitaire system] envisaged this as the end result for their program: but that is not relevant skill and labour. In my judgment, this claim for non-textual copying should fail.

Thus copyright protection could not be relied on to prevent the creation of a competing product. However, this is not necessarily an unusual position and, although the American authorities were not relied upon, it seem likely that, on these facts, a similar result would be obtained by applying the *Altai* test. [67]

At an international level, both the TRIPS Agreement (as noted by Pumfrey J in the previous extract) and the European Community (EC) Software Directive[68] preserve the idea/expression dichotomy,[69] but without creating guidance on the practical impact on copyright protection. It has been pointed out that, although there are a number of international agreements on copyright, there remains uncertainty over the scope of copyright protection for the non-literal elements of computer programs. In a global market, this can lead to software writers lacking confidence in the protection available in jurisdictions which are signatories to those agreements.[70] Having reviewed the situation in the US, UK and Canada, Zimmerman calls for international guidance in the form of 'a set of limiting doctrines that signatory nations and their courts can follow in delineating the scope of software copyright'.[71] There has been no corresponding activity in this direction, but it may be that the *Altai* approach has become the *de facto* standard, both within[72] and outside the US.

Pun notes that, since China introduced new software copyright law in 1990, the ongoing legal trend in China has been in step with most Western jurisdictions.[73] In the Australian case of *Data Access Corporation v Powerflex Services Pty Ltd*, Jenkinson J, at first instance,[74] referred extensively to US case law and seemed to suggest that the Australian courts were likely to follow the *Altai* test. The central issue in the case was whether user interface commands represented computer programs and were thus subject to copyright protection; if they were, the court would then need to consider whether a substantial part had been reproduced.[75] The court took into account the *dictum* of Lord Pearce in *Ladbroke (Football) Ltd v William Hill (Football) Ltd* that substantial copying was an issue of quality rather than quantity.[76]

---

67   See also discussion in Marchini, 2005.
68   See below, p 51.
69   See further discussion above p 23.
70   Zimmerman, 1996.
71   *Ibid*, p 521.
72   See Lai, 1994.
73   Pun, 1997.
74   (1996) 33 IPR 194; text available at www.austlii.edu.au/au/cases/cth/FCAFC/2002/112.html. For a discussion of the use of the *Altai* test in Canada see Handa and Buchan, 1995.
75   See, also, discussion and commentary in Fong, 1997; Hunter, 1998.
76   [1964] 1 All ER 465, p 481.

Data Access Corp v Powerflex Services Pty Ltd
[1999] HCA 49
High Court of Australia

84   ... in determining whether something is a reproduction of a substantial part of a computer program, the 'essential or material features of [the computer program] should be ascertained by considering the originality of the part allegedly taken'.

85   In order for an item in a particular language to be a computer program, it must intend to express, either directly or indirectly, an algorithmic or logical relationship between the function desired to be performed and the physical capabilities of the 'device having digital information processing capabilities'. It follows that the originality of what was allegedly taken from a computer program must be assessed with respect to the originality with which it expresses that algorithmic or logical relationship or part thereof. The structure of what was allegedly taken, its choice of commands, and its combination and sequencing of commands, when compared, at the same level of abstraction, with the original, would all be relevant to this inquiry.

86   That being so, a person who does no more than reproduce those parts of a program which are 'data' or 'related information' and which are irrelevant to its structure, choice of commands and combination and sequencing of commands will be unlikely to have reproduced a substantial part of the computer program. We say 'unlikely' and not 'impossible' because it is conceivable that the data, considered alone, could be sufficiently original to be a substantial part of the computer program.

88   ... the Reserved Words are irrelevant to the structure, choice of commands and combination and sequencing of the commands in source code. They are merely literal strings which, from the computer's perspective, could be replaced by any other literal string. Accordingly, they are not a substantial part of the Dataflex program as it appears in source code unless they have their own inherent originality.

REVERSE ENGINEERING AND DECOMPILATION

One feature which may be desirable in a computer program but which has no clear parallel in relation to more conventional literary works is the need for interoperability, that is, the capacity of the computer program to be compatible with other computer programs or hardware elements in a system, such as a printer. It will be remembered that the computer program at issue in *Computer Associates v Altai* had this property. If a computer program is to be interoperable with another, it may need to contain some of the same features, at least at the interface between the two. One way of producing a computer program which is interoperable with other programs is by decompiling (that is, compiling in reverse), or reverse engineering, the object code of the program with which interoperability is desired, to obtain the source code in a high level language. This can then be used in the creation of the interface between the existing and the new or proposed program. Where the creator of the new program does not have the copyright in the other program, this can lead to allegations of copyright infringement as a result of the decompilation and subsequent development of the new program. Those sections of the industry that create software primarily for running on operating systems created by others clearly have a vested interest in allowing decompilation to the maximum extent without fear of infringement, whereas other sectors of the industry, such as those which produce complete systems, are less likely to wish to permit decompilation or any other form of reverse engineering or analysis.

To what extent can copyright holders prevent decompilation for this purpose? Until the advent of the EC Software Directive and implementing legislation, such activity was likely to breach copyright unless it could be brought within the fair dealing exceptions contained in the CDPA 1988. Similar principles pertained in the US under the fair use doctrine, which attempts to balance the author's right to exploit his or her work against the public interest in the widest possible dissemination of information. The relevant provisions are contained in s 107 of the US Copyright Act 1976 and allow what would otherwise be infringements for such purposes as criticism, comment, news reporting, teaching, scholarship or research, always provided that the use is non-commercial, does not affect the potential market or value of the work, etc.[77]

There was much discussion surrounding the application of these provisions to reverse engineering and decompilation, but with no unanimity of opinion. The opposing points of view are well explained in the following two extracts.

Defining the scope of copyright protection for computer software
Susan A Dunn
(1986) 38 Stan L Rev 497, p 518

Copyright law should not prohibit disassembly of computer programs. If disassembly leads to the creation of a final product that is not substantially similar to the original program, consumers will be enriched by a wider choice of programs. Their options are enhanced at the expense of the owner of the original copyright, who will find the scope of his monopoly is narrowed. But copyright law inevitably balances the proprietor's interest in protection against the public's interest in disclosure. For example, copyright law protects only expression and not ideas so that the public can profit by using the ideas in copyrighted works. If examining a copyrighted computer program through disassembly were illegal, the public could not take advantage of many of the ideas it contains. Replacing the substantial similarity test with evidence of the course of development would sharply alter the balance of competing rights in favour of copyright proprietors.

Copyright protection for computer programs, databases, and computer-generated works: is anything new since CONTU?
Arthur R Miller
(1993) 106 Harv L Rev 977, p 1026

The simple truth is that permitting decompilation allows a second comer to create a market substitute and reap the benefits of a successful program after others have incurred the risk and expense of its development – an especially inappropriate result given the extraordinary discrepancy between the cost of creating the software and the cost of duplicating it. If an exemption from copyright is permitted, the decompiler will be able to reproduce the entire program of competitor – appropriating in one relatively simple procedure what may represent years of creative effort and investment – and then electronically massage the copy until every trace of that illicit reproduction is obscured. Yet the resulting program may be no less a derivative work founded on the first program

---

77 See, eg, Asarch 1996 for comment on *AMI System Corp v Peak Computers Inc* 991 F 2d 511 (9th Cir 1993) and problems encountered when an independent service organisation could not satisfactorily carry out computer maintenance without loading software into RAM, ie, making a copy, which was held to be a breach of copyright.

than is a motion picture based on the cleverest plot details and juiciest dialogue of a novel. Both works encroach on the copyright proprietor's statutory rights. Freedom to decompile also eliminates any incentive to produce an innovative or creative expression of one's own, thereby debilitating one of the basic objectives of the copyright regime.

The court in *Atari Games Corp v Nintendo of America Inc* concluded that reverse engineering object codes to discern the unprotectable ideas in a computer program is 'fair use'.[78] In *SEGA Enterprises v Accolade*,[79] the Court of Appeals for the Ninth Circuit, reversing the decision of the district court, seemed to suggest that decompilation may be permissible in certain circumstances and found its reasoning to be compatible with that of *Atari v Nintendo*. In particular, there was likely to be fair use where the end product did not contain copyright material and the copying was necessary to obtain access to the functional elements of the program. More recently the Ninth Circuit again considered the application of the four fair use factors to acts of decompilation. The Sony 'PlayStation' is a well-known computer games console. Connectix intended to create 'emulator software' which would allow Sony games to be used, not only on the proprietary console, but also on a standard PC. Although, as in the *SEGA* case, Connectix's final product contained none of Sony's code, in order to produce its version it had to decompile Sony's software to ensure compatibility. During the development process, Connectix contacted Sony for 'technical assistance' but, although there was a meeting of representatives from the two companies, the request was declined. Sony subsequently filed a complaint for copyright infringement.[80] The Ninth Circuit found that the decompilation was protected by the fair use provisions, Decompilation was necessary to provide access to the unprotected functional elements; although the whole of Sony's software had been copied, there was no infringing material in the final product and so this factor could be accorded little weight; Connectix's use was 'modestly transformative'; and the new product was a 'legitimate competitor'. In finding a transformative use, the court noted that the 'innovation affords opportunities for game play in new environments' and that, notwithstanding the similarity of uses, the Virtual Game Station was a wholly new product and one which would be compatible with games designed for the Sony PlayStation.

Further developments in the US have centred around the extent to which decompilation and reverse engineering of software can be controlled or precluded by contractual provisions. The Digital Millennium Copyright Act of 2000,[81] introduced a new §1201 into the US Copyright Act which generally prohibits the circumvention of copyright protection systems. Nevertheless, §1201(f) appears to allow reverse engineering along similar lines to that developed by the judiciary. As discussed below, the Software Directive specifically prohibits contractual provisions which attempt to exclude the decompilation right, but the extent to which decompilation or reverse

---

78 975 F2d 832, p 843 (Fed Cir 1992).
79 *Sega Enterprises Ltd v Accolade Inc* 977 F 2d 1510 (9th Cir 1992). Compare the views of, eg, Miller,1994, p 1014 *et seq*; Stern, 1992 discussing the district court's decision; Stern, 1993 following the judgment of the Court of Appeals. Hunter, 1993, notes that the Australian courts would not arrive at the same conclusion: 'Reverse engineering computer software – Australia parts company with the world'.See, also, Waters and Leonard, 1991.
80 *Sony v Connectix* 203 F3d 596 (9th Cir 2000), see also discussion in Prestin, 2002.
81 See further discussion in Chapter 9.

engineering could be prohibited by contractual terms in the US remains unclear. Neither has the situation been clarified by the Uniform Computer Information Transactions Act (UCITA) although the official comment to §105 notes that there is recognition of 'a policy not to prohibit some reverse engineering where it is needed to obtain interoperability'.[82]

Although the issue of decompilation has not been discussed in the UK courts, making it difficult to ascertain whether or not the fair dealing provisions in s 29 of the CDPA 1988 apply to reverse engineering,[83] similar arguments have been aired before the High Court of Singapore concerning the fair dealing provisions in the Singapore Copyright Act. *Aztech Systems Pty Ltd v Creative Technology Ltd*,[84] concerned the development of computer sound cards which would be interoperable with the 'Sound Blaster' card – the market leader. Although it was alleged that this had been achieved by disassembly, the court found that there had been no actual decompilation but that the operation of the program had been studied using a logic analyser, a non-invasive operation, together with the use of program DEBUG, designed for fault-finding during program development and which could therefore be used to observe the operation of a program. Then, by a 'process of trial, error and inference, they worked out what features a sound card must have to be compatible with "Sound Blaster" and designed their card accordingly'. Did this come within the provisions contained in s 35 of the Singapore Copyright Act of 1988, which allow for fair dealing for research and private study?

Research for industrial purposes or by companies was expressly excluded in the relevant legislation, and so reliance was placed on fair dealing for private study. The court found that 'study' meant 'the devotion of time and attention to acquiring information and knowledge' and the operations which had been carried out fell within this definition. As to the commercial aspect, it was held that the purpose had to be considered along with other relevant factors and that, in this case, there were public interest benefits in allowing this type of activity in terms of advantages to the consumer. However, notwithstanding this reasoning, the case was subsequently reversed by the Singapore Court of Appeal in November 1996,[85] which held that the meaning of 'private study' should not be extended to include any study, the results of which were used for commercial purposes, otherwise this would 'render otiose the specific exclusion of commercial research under s 35(5)'.[86] On this reasoning, Aztech did not even qualify for the defence of 'fair dealing', and so there was no need to consider further the question of substantive fairness.

The issue of reverse engineering of software also arose in *Data Access v Powerflex*,[87] and, insofar as the High Court of Australia found this to be a breach of copyright in

---

82 Further discussion of this point is beyond the scope of this chapter but for a more complete consideration see e.g. Douma, 2001; *Bowers v Baystate Technologies* 320 F 3d 1317 (Fed Cir 2003) together with Kwong, 2003; Andrews, 2004; Son, 2004.

83 For a discussion of the application of the UK fair dealing provisions to copyright of computer programs see Reed, 1991.

84 [1996] FSR 54.

85 [1997] FSR 491.

86 *Ibid*, p 505.

87 Above, p 46.

relation to the disassembly of a particular table, the court noted that this finding might 'have wider ramifications for anyone who seeks to produce a computer program that is compatible with a program produced by others'. However, the Court considered that this consequence of its judgment was something which could be resolved only by the legislature reconsidering the appropriate legal framework for copyright in computer software. In Europe, this was effectively what had happened with the adoption of the 'Software Directive'.

THE 'SOFTWARE DIRECTIVE'

In parallel with the courts' development of the interpretation of the existing copyright law to copying of computer programs, changes in the legislation itself, to take into account the nature of computer programs, were imminent, precipitated by the need to implement the EC Directive on Legal Protection of Computer Programs – the so called 'Software Directive'.[88] This Directive was a recognition of the issues that had caused debate in relation to the protection of intellectual property rights in computer programs, and also of the fact that, without harmonisation of these provisions, the completion and operation of the Single European Market in goods and services might be compromised. This was particularly necessary in view of the fact that different States had adopted quite different attitudes to the legal protection of computer programs. Thus, notwithstanding that many other jurisdictions, both inside and outside Europe, were basing their protection on copyright principles, this was not possible in Germany, for instance, where computer programs were viewed as technical and scientific products, rather than literary works.[89] The fact that such States might be signatories to the Berne Convention was of little relevance, as the issue was one of the categorisation of computer programs as copyright material. The Directive had a protracted gestation, not least because of a vociferous lobby from both sides of the industry relating to the scope of permissible decompilation contained in Art 6.[90] *Prima facie*, the agreed Directive extends copyright protection to computer programs as literary works and makes it clear that this protection is afforded to expression rather than idea.[91]

Article 1
Object of protection

1   In accordance with the provisions of this Directive, Member States shall protect computer programs, by copyright, as literary works within the meaning of the Berne

---

88   Council Directive 91/250/EEC, 14 May 1991 (Legal Protection of Computer Programs). There has been a recent Report on the implementation of this Directive: See Report from the Commission to the Council, the European Parliament and the Economic and Social Committee on the Implementation and Effects of Directive 91/250/EEC on the Legal Protection of Computer Programs COM (2000) 199 final.

89   See, eg, Wiebe, 1993.

90   A detailed account of the extended discussions preceding the adoption of the Directive is beyond the scope of this work, but see Czarnota and Hart, 1991.

91   For implementation in different Member States see Lehmann and Tapper, fn 3. and see also Report from the Commission to the Council, the European Parliament and the Economic and Social Committee, COM(2000) 1999 final. For the UK position see below, p 63.

Convention for the Protection of Literary and Artistic Works. For the purposes of this Directive, the term 'computer programs' shall include their preparatory design material.

2   Protection in accordance with this Directive shall apply to the expression in any form of a computer program. Ideas and principles which underlie any element of a computer program, including those which underlie its interfaces, are not protected by copyright under this Directive.

3   A computer program shall be protected if it is original in the sense that it is the author's own original intellectual creation. No other criteria shall be applied to determine its eligibility for protection.

The rights permitted to copyright holders are defined by Arts 4–6.

Article 4
Restricted acts

Subject to the provisions of Articles 5 and 6, the exclusive rights of the rightholder within the meaning of Article 2, shall include the right to do or authorise:

(a) the permanent or temporary reproduction of a computer program by any means and in any form, in part or in whole. Insofar as loading, displaying, running, transmission or storage of the computer program necessitates such reproduction, such acts shall be subject to authorisation by the rightholder;

(b) the translation, adaptation, arrangement and any other alteration of a computer program and the reproduction of the results thereof, without prejudice to the rights of the person whom alters the program;

(c) any form of distribution to the public, including the rental, of the original computer program or of copies thereof. The first sale in the Community of a copy of the program by the rightholder or with his consent shall exhaust the distribution right within the Community of that copy, with the exception of the right to control further rental of the program or a copy thereof.

Article 5
Exceptions to the restricted acts

1   In the absence of specific contractual provisions, the acts referred to in Article 4(a) and (b) shall not require authorisation by the rightholder where they are necessary for the use of the computer program by the lawful acquirer in accordance with its intended purpose, including for error correction.

2   The making of a back-up copy by a person having a right to use the computer program may not be prevented by contract insofar as it is necessary for that use.

3   The person having a right to use a copy of a computer program shall be entitled, without the authorisation of the rightholder, to observe, study or test the functioning of the program in order to determine the ideas and principles which underlie any element of the program if he does so while performing any of the acts of loading, displaying, running, transmitting or storing the program which he is entitled to do.

Article 6
Decompilation

1   The authorisation of the rightholder shall not be required where reproduction of the code and translation of its form within the meaning of Article 4(a) and (b) are indispensable to obtain the information necessary to achieve the interoperability of an independently created computer program with other programs, provided that the following conditions are met:

(a) these acts are performed by the licencee or by another person having a right to use a copy of the program, or on their behalf by a person authorised to do so;

(b) the information necessary to achieve interoperability has not previously been readily available to the persons referred to in subparagraph (a); and

(c) these acts are confined to the parts of the original program which are necessary to achieve interoperability.

2 The provisions of paragraph 1 shall not permit the information obtained through its application:

(a) to be used for goals other than to achieve the interoperability of the independently created computer program;

(b) to be given to others, except when necessary for the interoperability of the independently created computer program; or

(c) to be used for the development, production or marketing of a computer program substantially similar in its expression, or for any other act which infringes copyright.

3 In accordance with the provisions of the Berne Convention ... the provisions of this Article may not be interpreted in such a way as to allow its application to be used in a manner which unreasonably prejudices the rightholder's legitimate interests or conflicts with a normal exploitation of the computer program.

Notwithstanding the explicit reference to contract in Art 5(2), Art 9(1) further provides that 'Any contractual provisions contrary to Article 6 or to the exceptions provided for in Art 5(2) and (3) shall be null and void'. The provision regarding back-up copies was non-contentious. Taking a back-up copy of a program is good computing practice but, without such a right being included explicitly in the licence to use the software (as is the usual practice), such a practice would be a technical infringement. In the US, amendments introduced in 1980 to the Copyright Act 1976 had served a similar purpose. However the rights, contained in a limited way in Art 5(3) and in more extensive form in Art 6, to undertake reverse analysis or decompilation under certain circumstances were to provoke much spirited debate both during the gestation of the Directive,[92] and after its adoption,[93] in academic circles and also between representatives of different parts of the industry, in which the main protagonists took up positions similar to those evident in the extracts from Dunn and Miller, above.

One problem in framing the terms of Art 6 was the need to reconcile the common law approach, in which reverse analysis might be permitted, in certain circumstances, under fair dealing or fair use exceptions, with a civil law tradition which looks for legal certainty in the legislation. The situation was made more complex by the view of different sectors of the industry, discussed further below, of the extent to which any type of reverse analysis should be permitted. The resulting provision covers the circumstances in which decompilation, in particular, is allowed to take place, and also the purposes for which the information gained as a consequence can be used. The compromise arrived at in the Directive appears to be aimed at allowing products to be

92 See, eg, the debate between Cornish 1989, 1990, Lake *et al*, 1989, and Colombe and Meyer 1990a, 1990b.

93 See, eg, Huet, and Ginsburg, 1992; Haaf, 1992; Hidalgo, 1993; *op cit*, Waters and Leonard, *op cit* fn 79; Bainbridge, 1993.

developed which are compatible with the original, rather than those which might be viewed as being in competition with the original.[94] This is a fine line to draw.

The EC has thus tried to use legislation to deal with issues which have previously been dealt with by the courts in a number of jurisdictions. Although the Directive has attempted to grapple with particular aspects of computer programs, its provisions do not necessarily assist in the problem of defining the scope of protection itself, which may still fall to be determined by the courts.

**Scope of protection in the European Community, in
recent United States and international
developments in software protection, Part 2
Dennis S Karjala
[1994] EIPR 58, p 63**

The EC Software Directive, of course, fails almost completely to address either the scope-of-protection problem or the degree of copyright protection in user interfaces. Notwithstanding the Directive's purported goal of uniformity, therefore, one can expect courts in the various Member States to grope their way towards appropriate solutions much as do courts in the US federal system. In the long run, this is likely to lead to a better and more stable balance of the social policy tensions involved in software protection than detailed statutory coverage adopted in a highly charged political atmosphere. Perhaps the courts in Europe will benefit from the opportunity to observe the successes and failures of the American courts. Even so, one should expect a good deal of lurching, backtracking and zigzagging before a general consensus is reached.

The directive had to be implemented by 1 January 1993. A subsequent report from the European Commission on its implementation[95] found that overall implementation by Member States was satisfactory and that the effects of the implementation were beneficial. It therefore concluded that 'experience to date does not lead to the view that the substantive copyright provisions of the Directive should be revisited at this time'. This view was effectively endorsed by the fact that no amendments to this directive were included in the later Copyright Directive,[96] Recital 20 of which notes that it is 'based on principles and rules already laid down in the directives currently in force in this area, in particular directive 91/250/EEC ... '. Further the substantive provisions of the Directive on Technical Circumvention do not modify or amend the provisions in Arts 5 and 6 of the software directive which 'exclusively determine exceptions to the exclusive rights applicable to computer programs.'[97]

UK implementation of the Software Directive

The UK implemented the Software Directive by means of the Copyright (Computer Programs) Regulations 1992,[98] which amended the 1988 Act, particularly in relation to

---

94 See, Huet and Ginsburg. The balance of rights created by the Directive, specifically in relation to decompilation, is discussed in Krocker, 1997.
95 See also Report from the Commission to the Council, the European Parliament and the Economic and Social Committee, COM(2000) 1999 final.
96 Directive 2001/29/EC – see further discussion in Chapter 9.
97 *Ibid* Recital 50.
98 SI 1992/3233.

the new permitted acts, the creation of back-up copies, error correction and decompilation. The first two of these were covered by the introduction of new ss 50A and 50C.

CDPA 1988 (as amended)

50A (1) It is not an infringement of copyright for a lawful user of a copy of a computer program to make any back up copy of it which is necessary for him to have for the purposes of his lawful use.

   (2) For the purposes of this section and sections 50B and 50C a person is a lawful user of a computer program if (whether under a licence to do any acts restricted by the copyright in the program or otherwise), he has a right to use the program ...

50C (1) It is not an infringement of copyright for a lawful user of a copy of a computer program to copy or adapt it, providing that the copying or adapting –

   (a) is necessary for his lawful use; and

   (b) is not prohibited under any term or condition of an agreement regulating the circumstances in which his use is lawful.

   (2) It may, in particular, be necessary for the lawful use of a computer program to copy it or adapt it for the purpose of correcting errors in it ...

This right to adapt, insofar as it is necessary for lawful use, extending even to the correction of errors, should be read in conjunction with the definition of 'adaptation' introduced by a new s 21(3)(ab), namely, 'an arrangement or altered version of the program or translation of it'.

The manner of incorporating the decompilation right was to remove decompilation from the ambit of the fair dealing provisions relating to research and private study contained in s 29 and then to introduce it as a new permitted act in s 50B. The provisions of s 29 will still apply to computer programs in relation to activities other than decompilation.

CDPA 1988 (as amended)

29(4) It is not fair dealing –

   (a) to convert a computer program expressed in a low-level language into a version expressed in a higher level language; or

   (b) incidentally in the course of so converting the program, to copy it ...

50B (1) It is not an infringement of copyright for a lawful user of a copy of a computer program expressed in a low-level language –

   (a) to convert it into a higher level language; or

   (b) incidentally in the course of so converting the program, to copy it (that is to 'decompile it'), provided that the conditions in subsection (2) are met.

   (2) The conditions are that –

   (a) it is necessary to decompile the program to obtain the information necessary to create an independent program which can be operated with the program decompiled or with another program ('the permitted objective'); and

   (b) the information so obtained is not used for any purpose other than the permitted objective.

   (3) In particular, the conditions in subsection (2) are not met if the lawful user –

(a) has readily available to him the information necessary to achieve the permitted objective;

(b) does not confine the decompiling to such acts as are necessary to achieve the permitted objective;

(c) supplies the information obtained by the decompiling to any person to whom it is not necessary to supply it in order to achieve the permitted objective; or

(d) uses the information to create a program which is substantially similar in its expression to the program decompiled or to do any act restricted by copyright.

(4) Where an act is permitted under this section, it is irrelevant whether or not there exists any term or condition in an agreement which purports to prohibit or restrict the act ...

It is by no means clear that the definitions of decompilation contained in the Directive and the implementing regulations coincide.[99] The regulations seem to confine decompilation exclusively to the situation in which the decompiler is working upwards from the low to the high level language. The Directive, on the other hand, refers to 'reproduction of the code and translation of its form' which appears to represent a much wider view of the scope of decompilation. The meaning of 'translation' of a computer program contained in s 21(4) of the 1988 Act includes 'a version of the program in which it is converted into or out of a computer language or code or into a different computer language or code'. This corresponds more accurately with the terminology in the Directive but would not be included in the new definition of decompilation introduced by the Regulations.

The new s 50B(2) provides that decompilation will be allowed where it is 'necessary to create an independent program which can be operated with the program decompiled or another program'. This, taken together with s 50B(3), suggests that it may be lawful to create a competing program, provided that it is not substantially similar to the original program, but that it would be impermissible to devise modifications to an existing program to make it interoperable with another. This latter act would, apparently, be permitted under the terms of the Directive, which allows decompilation where it is 'indispensable to obtain the information necessary to achieve the interoperability of an independently created computer program with other programs'.

The Directive, in Art 5(3), refers expressly to the right to 'observe, study or test the functioning of the program', this being done 'in order to determine the ideas and principles underlying any element of the program'. It might appear that this aspect has not been incorporated, since the only reference to 'observation' is to be found in the new s 296A(1), making any contractual terms purporting to place limits on this process void. On the other hand, fair dealing for the purposes of research and private study is still permissible under s 29(1) and it may be that observation can legitimately be construed as such research or private study.

In implementing the Directive, no express enactment relating to the idea/expression distinction referred to in Art 1 was included, so, insofar as this

---

99 See also criticism in COM(2000) 199 final pp 13–14.

doctrine is a part of UK law, it remains on a case law basis, rather than having a statutory basis, as found in the US. The Commission Report noted that the provision in Art 1(2) on the idea/expression distinction had not been implemented by a number of Member States, including the UK, but that it would appear that 'it is standing practice of such Member States to apply the idea/expression dichotomy as a general principle of copyright law'.[100] Thus far, as intimated in *Navitaire v EasyJet*,[101] no case in the UK has relied on provisions which originate from the directive, however there was some consideration of the idea/expression distinction at the full trial. One of the issues in the case was the extent to which the interface commands, which could virtually be construed as a separate language, could be protected by copyright.

Navitaire Inc v EasyJet Airline Company
[2004] EWHC 1725
High Court

87. I think the problem should be approached in the following way. To define a series of commands and their syntax to be recognised by the computer is to define a computer language. It is exactly the same as defining a language such as BASIC or a simple language to control a calculator program. A program consists of a statement or series of statements in that 'language'. ... Recitals 13, 14 and 15 of the Software Directive are as follows:

[13] Whereas, for the avoidance of doubt, it has to be made clear that only the expression of a computer program is protected and that ideas and principles which underlie any element of a program, including those which underlie its interfaces, are not protected by copyright under this Directive;

[14] Whereas, in accordance with this principle of copyright, to the extent that logic, algorithms and programming languages comprise ideas and principles those ideas and principles are not protected under this Directive;

[15] Whereas, in accordance with the legislation and jurisprudence of the Member States and the international copyright conventions, the expression of those ideas and principles is to be protected by copyright.

88. The Software Directive is a harmonising measure. I must construe any implementing provision in accordance with it: if the implementing provision means what it should, the Directive alone need be consulted: if it departs from the Directive, then the latter has been incorrectly transposed into UK law. The recitals quoted are said by Laddie *et al.*, *Modern Law of Copyright and Designs*, (3rd Edn) paragraph 34.19 to make it clear that 'computer languages are not included in the protection afforded to computer programs'. With this conclusion I agree, although the point cannot be said to be entirely clear and will require to be referred to the Court of Justice. In my view, the principle extends to *ad hoc* languages of the kind with which I am here concerned, that is, a defined user command interface. It does not matter how the 'language' of the interface is defined. It may be defined formally or it may be defined only by the code that recognises it. Either way, copyright does not subsist in it. This is of course not to suggest that the expression of a program in a particular language is not entitled to copyright. Quite the reverse. What this recital, and the associated dispositive provision of Art 1(2), appear to be intended to do, is to keep the language free for use, but not the ideas expressed in it: Art 1(2): Protection

100 COM(2000) 199 final p 9.
101 [2003] EWHC 3487 para 13.

in accordance with this Directive shall apply to the expression in any form of a computer program. Ideas and principles which underlie any element of a computer program, including those which underlie its interfaces, are not protected by copyright under this Directive.

89. There is here more than an echo of a conceptual distinction between idea and expression, but it is unprofitable to pursue this approach in the light of the express reference to computer languages and interfaces in the recital and to the interfaces in Art 1(2).

...

94. Copyright protection for computer software is a given, but I do not feel that the courts should be astute to extend that protection into a region where only the functional effects of a program are in issue. There is a respectable case for saying that copyright is not, in general, concerned with functional effects, and there is some advantage in a bright line rule protecting only the claimant's embodiment of the function in software and not some superset of that software. The case is not truly analogous with the plot of a novel, because the plot is part of the work itself. The user interface is not part of the work itself. One could permute all the letters and other codes in the command names, and it would still work in the same way, and all that would be lost is a modest mnemonic advantage. To approach the problem in this way may at least be consistent with the distinction between idea and expression that finds its way into the Software Directive, but, of course, it draws the line between idea and expression in a particular place which some would say lies too far on the side of expression. I think, however, that such is the independence of the particular form of the actual codes used from the overall functioning of the software that it is legitimate to separate them in this way, and not to afford them separate protection when the underlying software is not even arguably copied.

Sui generis rights revisited

At the beginning of this chapter, the reasons for the choice of a copyright scheme rather than a *sui generis* right for the protection of the intellectual property rights in computer programs was discussed. As we have seen, the law in a number of jurisdictions has struggled with, and has sometimes needed to modify, traditional copyright principles in order to apply them satisfactorily to computer programs. In the European Commission Green Paper, *Copyright and The Challenges of Technology – Copyright Issues Requiring Immediate Action*,[102] a *sui generis* right for computer programs was rejected under the influence of the observed case law trend towards copyright already formulated by the courts in a number of jurisdictions. Nonetheless, it could be argued that some of the modifications that were negotiated for inclusion in the Software Directive, and that have led to the new derogations with respect to decompilation rights, modify traditional copyright principles to such an extent that the resulting protection is, more accurately, described as a *sui generis* right.[103] Goldstein,[104] observes that *sui generis* protection for the intellectual property rights in computer programs is now less frequently advocated, and relates this to the protection which has evolved from the conventional copyright framework, both in the US and in Europe:

102 COM (1988) 172 final.
103 See, eg, the views expressed by Wiebe, *op cit,* fn 89.
104 Goldstein, 1993.

The principle reason in the decline in calls for *sui generis* legislation is that, in a very real sense, *sui generis* protection for computer programs is already being implemented throughout the world – albeit under the nominal auspices of copyright. Section 117 of the United States Copyright Act is specifically tailored to the special features of computer programs; sections 102(b) and 107 of the Act have also been interpreted with particular attention to the particular nature of software. The EC Directive represents, to date, the most systematic tailoring of copyright to meet the special needs of computer programs. Indeed, apart from its relatively long term of protection, the Directive more closely resembles a *sui generis* law than it does copyright. Most important, the deliberations on the Software Directive have shown that the Berne Convention's rigorous standards, once thought to pose the most serious impediment to a copyright accommodation for computer programs, are sufficiently flexible to admit needed derogations from the reproduction and adaptation rights.

Widdison, on the other hand, having reviewed some of the problems of both copyright and patent law concludes that a *sui generis* system may be the only sensible way forward.

Robin Widdison
Software Patents Pending?
[2000] 3 JILT[105]

… we could renew our search for a third way – a sui generis regime. Such a regime might be broadly similar to that adopted by the European Union for the protection of databases albeit with a few key differences. What might such a regime involve? To open the debate, I propose the following scheme, which I argue strikes a fair balance between the interests of existing owners, would-be creators and the public at large:

> Existing owners of computer programs who could demonstrate that their software was substantially their own intellectual creation would be entitled to protection. No further account would be taken of such issues as novelty, inventiveness or industrial application.

> Protection would extend to every aspect of programs - from initial design algorithms, to code listings, and beyond to all functional characteristics.

> The duration of legal protection would be appropriate to the useful life of a computer program - say a maximum of five years, renewable annually. A new version of a program that involved a substantial change might quality for a new term of protection.

> During the period of protection, other would-be creators could decompile a program for the limited purpose of studying and understanding the concepts, processes and techniques used.

> During the period of protection, would-be creators could demand a licence of right in respect of part or all of a protected program. The fee for such a licence would then be agreed by the parties or, in default, by a suitable independent body.

At present, it may seem that TRIPS is the very last word on global software protection. However, I believe that we will eventually see it as no more than the first word. It is true that *sui generis* protection of computer programs is an unfashionable topic, particularly since the advent of TRIPS. In time, though, growing distortions and disruptions in the global software market will force TRIPS signatory states to come together again in order to search for a software protection regime that is not only applicable world-wide, but also seen to be both even-handed and workable on that same global scale.

PATENTS AND COMPUTER PROGRAMS

Whereas it appears that, in the majority of cases, copyright will be the appropriate method of protecting the intellectual property in computer software, the question has also arisen as to whether patent protection might also, or alternatively, be available for computer programs.[106] Koo sets out the advantages and disadvantages of software patents in the following extract.[107]

Daehwan Koo
Patent and Copyright Protection of Computer Programs
[2002] IPQ 172, 199 et seq.

[1] Pros for Software Patents

The most significant feature of patent protection for software is that a patent can protect the idea or concept underlying the invention. The ideas or concepts embodied in computer programs may have great value. As the importance of business on the Internet grows, protection for the business concept underlying the software, which has been developed for its specific purpose, becomes increasingly necessary. The growing necessity to protect software by patenting rather than copyright is extending the scope of software patentability.

Software patenting protects against independent inventors, not just against copiers. This means that patents protect against independently developed programs that are based on the same concept. In addition, patent documents stimulate development, because the public can build on published software patents. Patents provide software developers with a potential source of income.

Advocates of extended software patentability assert that expanded protection provides stronger incentives for the generation and diffusion of new technologies, and that the inadequacies in intellectual property protection create loss of export sales and trade distortions in international trade. Software patentability makes it worthwhile for investors to sink large resources into new and existing companies, and for new entrants to devote resources to R&D. A patent portfolio can also be used to bargain with companies for use of their patents. A major advantage of a patent over copyright is that it can protect against competitors creating equivalent solutions.

[2] Cons for Software Patents

Patents have limited application in the protection of behaviour, because patents typically issue for particular methods of achieving results, rather than for results themselves. A patent on a method of generating certain results cannot prevent the use of another method, even though those results are the principal source of value of the software. Hence, patents on methods would not protect behaviour, which is one of the primary entities of value in software. On the other hand, a patent with claims for any means of achieving particular results would inhibit competition in the development of useful program behaviours out of proportion to the innovation actually contributed by the applicant.

Disadvantages can also be exhibited by the characteristics of software innovation. Cumulative, sequential innovation and re-use prevail in the software industry. Software innovation typically proceeds via a mix of new coding, modifications to some existing

---

106 See also Karjala, 2003 noting that 'Functionality is the basic determinant of the patent/ copyright boundary.'
107 See also Attridge, 2001.

modules or subroutines, and re-use of others. Moreover, patterns of improvement and re-use are constrained to a substantial degree by the need to preserve interoperability between program, system and network components. Interoperability constrains the range of options available to the second-comer. Patenting incremental innovations, which are not inventive, would not be appropriate for the economic goals of patent system, since a patent is given for a substantial contribution to the art. ...

According to the concept of 'sequential innovation' systems, which was generalised by Bessen and Maskin, software patents are not economically useful as far as the ideal form of organisation for the software industry is not a monopoly. A regime without patents induces more efficient investment than one with patents. They argue that when innovation is sequential and complementary, contrary to standard reasoning about patents and imitation, imitation becomes a spur to innovation and strong patents become an impediment. ...

Based on the characteristics of sequential innovations, opponents of software patenting argue that almost all authors of software will involuntarily infringe a software patent when they publish their software, because typical software comprises several thousands different processes (and major software, several tens of thousands) and depends on earlier programmers' solution to a problem. It is impossible to check to ensure that none of these processes infringes one of the software patents already granted.

Since software development requires relatively less investment of time and money and the barrier to innovation is so small in the software sector, the absence of patents does not discourage innovation. In addition, the economic life of a software innovation is normally quite short. It is much shorter than the 20-year term conferred by the patent law. A software patent expanded to cover later improvements will exert control over many more generations of improvements than a conventional patent with a longer effective term. This means that the market-distorting effect of a software patent will be substantially greater than that of other types of patents. Software patents would also reserve for first-comers the rights to rule the market. To a greater degree than in other areas, second-comers would need permission to develop and market their innovations.

To be patented an invention must fulfil certain criteria: novelty, inventiveness and capability of industrial application. Computer programs are generally complex. Application documents for software patents are highly complicated. Due to these requirements and complexities, the cost of using the patent system, that is, filing, maintaining and defending a patent, is high, particularly for SMEs.

The introduction of software patenting may also increase secrecy of practical technical knowledge and hinder the sharing of knowledge. It is because the publication of the source code facilitates a competitor's search for patent infringements (whereas the publication of the binary code prevents a competitor's search for patent infringements due to the prohibition on decompiling), that publishers keep source codes secret to reduce patent infringement lawsuits. ...

Software patenting also has inappropriate aspects in that relevant prior art is not disclosed sufficiently, because patent protection for software has been limited and software developers have kept secret the software source codes that they have developed. Also, because the vast majority of software innovation takes place outside traditional research institutions, many software improvements are not recorded in the formal system of technical documentation. Software innovations exist in the source code of commercial products and services that are available to customers. This source code is difficult to catalog or search for ideas. This trend results in insufficient published prior art, which makes it difficult to search for prior art and to examine patent applications properly. ...
Software patents tended to be classified according to the field in which the software will eventually be used (for example, game machine, ovens, washing machine, etc), rather than according to the nature of the software invention. This makes it much harder for

examiners to find relevant prior art. As a result, software patents are more likely to receive a broader scope than they deserve.

This list reveals many more general disadvantages than advantages to the granting of software patents. Nevertheless for the applicant, if a patent can be obtained, it can be very valuable in providing the opportunity to those developing the programs to recoup their research and development costs. In recent years, therefore, a steady increase in the number of patent applications relating to computers and processing systems has been noted,[108] many of which have been for specific apparatus containing software which is, itself, novel or is used in a novel application, or for processes where the claimed invention is neither a pure mathematical algorithm nor a mental step. Clearly, these will be highly specialised situations and, to determine the conditions under which a patent might be available for such an invention, it is necessary to consider the relevant legal provisions in more detail.

In the UK, the Patents Act 1977 gave effect to the European Patent Convention (EPC) of 1973, the relevant provisions being Art 52 of the Convention and s 1 of the Act.

EPC 1973
Article 52 Patentable inventions

(1) European patents shall be granted for any inventions which are susceptible of industrial application, which are new and which involve an inventive step.

(2) The following in particular shall not be regarded as inventions within the meaning of paragraph 1:

  (a) discoveries, scientific theories and mathematical methods; ...

  (c) schemes, rules and methods for performing mental acts, playing games or doing business, and programs for computers;

  (d) presentations of information.

(3) The provisions of paragraph 2 shall exclude patentability of the subject matter or activities referred to in that provision only to the extent to which a European patent application or European patent relates to such subject matter or activities as such.

Patents Act 1977
1 Patentable inventions

(1) A patent may be granted only for an invention in respect of which the following conditions are satisfied, that is to say –

  (a) the invention is new;

  (b) it involves an inventive step;

  (c) it is capable of industrial application;

  (d) the grant of a patent for it is not excluded by subsection(s) (2) ...

---

108 See, eg, Sterne et al, 1994, p 30; Lenno, 1994. Notwithstanding the legal obstacles to patentability discussed in this chapter, a large number of computer-related inventions have been granted patents by the EPO. For a list of applications that have been successful see www.swpat.ffii.org/patents/txt/ep/2003.en.html. Some which have not succeeded are listed at www.patent.gov.uk/about/ippd/issues/cii-examples.htm.

(2) It is hereby declared that the following ... are not inventions for the purposes of this Act, that is to say, anything which consists of –

    (a) a discovery, scientific theory or mathematical method; ...

    (c) a scheme, rule or method for performing a mental act, playing a game or doing business, or a program for a computer;

    (d) the presentation of information,

but the foregoing provision shall prevent anything from being treated as an invention for the purposes of this Act only to the extent that a patent or application for a patent relates to that thing as such.

The Patents Act 1977, in recognition of its origins, directs that other legal rules will be of relevance:

91 Evidence of conventions ...

(1) Judicial notice shall be taken of the following, that is to say –

    (a) the European Patent Convention, the Community Patent Convention and the Patent Co-operation Treaty ...;

    (b) any bulletin, journal or gazette published under the relevant convention ...;

    (c) any decision of, or expression of opinion by, the relevant convention court on any question arising under or in connection with the relevant convention.

Clearly, the interpretation of *'as such'* in Art 52 of the EPC and s 1 of the Patents Act 1977 is a key issue in determining the patentability or otherwise of inventions in which the inventive step falls within a computer program. The crucial question would seem to be, is the claim for a patent for an invention involving a computer program an application for a patent for a program *'as such'* or, rather, is the effect to create an entirely new product or process within which the computer program can merely be regarded in the same light as any other component might be? In the US, where there was a similar statutory exclusion under 35 USC § 101, views on this matter have, arguably, polarised more distinctly. Many expressed the view that claims for patents involving computer software should be treated in the same way as those concerning computer hardware. On the other hand, others advocate the opposite view[109] on the basis that software technology is significantly different from that which applies to hardware.[110]

Some of the perceived difficulties appear to have arisen from definitional difficulties. Since the statutory exclusion is for a computer program *as such*, a uniform interpretation of the exclusion is very dependent on an accepted and acceptable definition. What is a computer program? The origin of the exclusion appears to derive from the same source as the exclusion for mathematical methods, since computer programs can be expressed in the form of algorithms. For some time, there have been arguments that such an exclusion was unnecessary and that any bar to patentability should rest merely on the standards of novelty and non-obviousness. Chisum poses the question, 'Why are new and useful developments in *mathematics* with direct

---

109 See, eg, Sterne *et al*, 1994.

110 For a more philosophical discussion of the nature of technology and the purpose and application of both patents and exclusion from patentability see, eg, Von Helfeld, 1986.

industrial applications *per se* excluded from the patent system when developments in all other areas of applied technological knowledge are included?'.[111] In his view, the confusion over patentability was entirely due to the decision of the Supreme Court in *Gottschalk v Benson*, which had held that a mathematical algorithm could not be patented, no matter how new and useful, and that 'policy considerations' indicated that patent protection was as appropriate for mathematical algorithms that are useful in computer programming as for other technical innovations.[112]

More recently, Harrington[113] has suggested that the crux of the problem is the difference in the definition of 'computer program' as between lawyers and electronic or electrical engineers. Whereas lawyers tend to define a computer program in terms of instructions, creating a *prima facie* impression of non-patentability, electrical engineers are more likely to think in terms of 'a process for performing a specific function or a means for creating circuitry in a block of silicon', that is, a process for creating a new device; such an activity sounds much more like the substance of a patent claim. He cites with approval *In re Allapat*,[114] in which Judge Rich said that it was 'inaccurate and confusing to speak in terms of a mathematical algorithm as excluded subject matter when assessing the patentability of a computer related invention' and used an approach which was much more in accordance with engineering definitions of 'computer program'. In Harrington's view, this approach 'recognises the reality of what actually occurs when a program is run on a computer and the utility of the mathematical sciences as a powerful vehicle for applied technology'.

Some of the propensity for confusion can be observed in *Data Access v Powerflex*,[115] where, albeit for the purposes of copyright law rather than the granting of a patent, it was vital to ascertain whether the user interface commands (the 'Reserved Words') could be computer programs based on a legal definition of a computer program as a set of instructions. The High Court of Australia noted that 'the definition of a computer program seems to have more in common with the subject matter of a patent than a copyright' but the lower courts nevertheless had conflicting views on whether the particular features at issue could be construed as a computer program.

Data Access Corporation v Powerflex Services Pty Ltd
[1999] HCA 49
High Court of Australia

30 The trial judge held that each Reserved Word was itself a computer program. Jenkinson J said:

Each of the words of the DataFlex language found also in the PFXplus language is in my opinion an expression of a set of instructions intended to cause a device having digital information processing capabilities to perform a particular function. The circumstance that the expression of those instructions in source code is different is in

---

111 Chisum, 1986, p 1007, following *In re Pardo* 684 F 2d 912 (1982).
112 409 US 63 (1972). But note the comment on the nature of algorithms in response to Chisum's article in Newell, 1986.
113 Harrington, 1996.
114 33 F 3d 1526 (Fed Cir 1994), see below p 81. See, also, Lowrie, 1997.
115 www.austlii.edu.au/au/cases/cth/FCAFC/2002/112.html.

my opinion immaterial. At the level of abstraction under consideration the objective similarity is complete: the set of instructions intended to cause the performance of the particular function is expressed, at that level where the 'language, code or notation' is based upon concatenations of letters of the alphabet, by the same concatenation of letters in each language. If at that level some of the concatenations constitute or resemble words of the English language descriptive or suggestive of the functions to be performed, that may facilitate the use of the computer program by those who understand English. But each concatenation of letters is nonetheless an expression of a set of instructions intended to cause the device to perform a particular function, in my opinion, and therefore a 'computer program' within the meaning of that expression in the Copyright Act.

31   The Full Court came to the opposite conclusion. It said:

> Each of the words in the so called Dataflex language is but a cipher. The underlying program is the set of instructions which directs the computer what to do when that cipher is in fact used, for example by being typed on to the screen. It is not to the point that the cipher bears some resemblance to an ordinary English word. The cipher or command is not an expression of the set of instructions, although it appears in that set of instructions. It is the trigger for the set of instructions to be given effect to by the computer.

> It may not be inaccurate to describe each of the commands as itself an instruction. It is likewise not necessarily inaccurate to talk of each of those words as representing the set of instructions in the sense that the use of one of them triggers the instructions contained in the computer program to be acted upon. But it is in our view not accurate to refer to each of the words as being an expression of the set of instructions. The set of instructions is expressed in the source code which is the computer program and, at least at a higher level, includes the particular word which is a command. The computer program will also in other forms exist in lower level language, ultimately through to an object code in non-visible form. Each of these representations will fall within the definition of 'computer program'. In each of them, in some language, code or notation, the word said to be part of the computer language will be able to be found.

In whichever jurisdiction they arise, relevant patent applications will, typically, fall into one of two basic categories:

(a) where the program embodies a procedure for performing a useful operation or a physical phenomenon forming part of the real world outside the computer;

(b) the program solves a technical problem in the operation of the system of which the computer on which it is running forms a part.

Notwithstanding the ongoing debate over the interpretation of the exclusions, it is still the case that no patent will be granted where the application relates merely to the operation of the computer under the control of the program. This was emphasised as early as 1979, in Guidelines from the European Patent Office (EPO):[116]

> A computer program may take various forms, for example, an algorithm, a flow-chart or a series of coded instructions which can be recorded on a tape or other machine-readable record-medium, and can be regarded as a particular case of either a mathematical method or a presentation of information. If the contribution to the known art resides solely in a

116 Quoted in Gall, 1985.

computer program the subject matter is not patentable in whatever manner it may be presented in the claims. For example, a claim to a computer characterised by having a particular program stored in its memory or to a process for operating a computer under control of the program would be as objectionable as a claim to the program *per se* or the program when recorded on magnetic tape.

However, because the statutory exclusions are well known, it is unusual for a patent application to relate to a computer program without more, and there will always be an attempt to associate the application with some technical effect made possible by the novelty of the invention as a whole. The whole must therefore be examined for novelty and inventive step, taking into account the exclusions.

European Patent Office Guidelines 1985 on the
Protection of Inventions relating to Computer Programs
G Gall
(1985) 2 CL & P 1985

Inventions which relate to computer programs or in which such programs constitute an essential element are subject to the general rules of patent law. Thus, in the case of inventions relating to programs for computers the relevant question is whether the invention is of a *technical* nature ... Guidelines make it clear that the basic test of whether there is an invention within the meaning of Art 52(1) EPC is 'separate and distinct from the question whether the subject matter is susceptible of industrial application, is new and involves an inventive step'. If the subject matter claimed is not excluded from patentability as 'non-technical subject matter' the invention must still pass *inter alia* the test whether the invention involved an inventive step (Art 56 EPC). Patent protection is reserved for such inventions which go beyond the capacities of the so called 'ordinary men skilled in the art'.

Faced with making such decisions, therefore, both the Technical Board of Appeals of the EPO and the courts in the UK need to assess whether there is a *technical* contribution to known art. If this is found, then the fact that the best method of doing it is by computer is no bar to patentability. However, the precise meaning of technical contribution in this sense has proved elusive; Tapper,[117] suggests that the 'concept of "technical effect" is not self-evident' and Lloyd[118] has remarked that the 'question what constitutes a technical advance is not always susceptible of ready or precise answer'.

Commentators are divided over the EPO's approach to the interpretation of the computer program exclusion and the definition of 'technical'. Watkins and Rau[119] comment favourably on 'the establishment by the EPO of a consistent policy towards computer related inventions' and say that, in relation to the computer program exclusion, 'the EPO now holds consistently that an innovation based on a new computer program can be patentable if it falls within one of two categories: (a) if it solves a technical problem associated with a computer apparatus; or (b) if it makes a contribution to another technical field'. Although 'technical' is not defined by either

---

117 Tapper, 1993.
118 Lloyd, 1995.
119 Watkins and Rau, 1996.

the EPC or the EPO Guidelines, they believe that, nevertheless, the EPO has been fairly 'generous to the patentability in principle of computer related inventions'.

In marked contrast, Newman[120] is of the view that the 'description of computer programs as non-technical sits uncomfortably with the reality that many programs are of technical 'real world' significance' and states baldly that, '[b]y any standards, the EPO has failed clearly to set out the criteria for determining which of the products of the computer industry are patentable'. Meanwhile, Davies[121] points out that, during the 1990s, the European practice on software inventions had diverged from that of its two major trading partners, the US and Japan,[122] both of which had become more flexible over the issue of patents for computer program claims. Neither need a parallel development in Europe be hindered by the requirements of the EPC:

> ... the EPO rejection of explicit computer program claims for inventions which are acknowledged as patentable represent an unjustified obsession with form over substance ... there is a reasonable self-consistent interpretation of Art 52(2) EPC which recognises that an arbitrary computer program is not, of itself, an invention, but that this does not prevent acceptance of claims directed to computer program embodiments of technical inventions.

The apparently imprecise scope of the concept of 'technical' is summed up by Cohen:[123]

> What has always been patentable is software which produces a technical effect. What is meant by a technical effect has moved since the first questions were raised in the early 1980s, somewhat more in favour of allowing patents to be granted

The issue has been further complicated by the fact that different approaches to the interpretation of the exclusion are possible. Gall[124] further points out that the EPC is a multilateral international treaty, so it should be construed in the light of the corresponding international law, in particular Art 31(1) of the Vienna Convention, which requires the provisions of a treaty to be interpreted in good faith, taking into account the meaning of the words in context and having regard to the object and purpose of the provisions in question. Evidence of such a purposive construction can perhaps be identified in some of the decisions made under the EPC. In contrast, the UK courts lean towards a more literal, or technical, interpretation of 'as such'.[125] However, since decisions under the EPC have been both referred to and taken into account in judgments under the Patents Act 1977 (as would be expected, taking into account s 91(1) of that Act), the situation is by no means clear cut. Other jurisdictions have struggled with the same issues as shown by the following extract concerning the relationship between the EPC and the German law on patents (PatG).

---

120 Newman, 1997.
121 Davies, 1998.
122 For details of the situation in the US see, eg, Fellis, 1999; For Japan see Mashima, 1999.
123 Cohen, 1999.
124 COM(2000) 199 final p 9.
125 On the relationship between the European Patent Convention and the Patents Act, Aldous LJ remarked in *Fujitsu Ltd's Application* [1997] RPC 608, p 611 that 'the intention of Parliament was that there should be uniformity in this regard. What is more, any substantial divergence would be disastrous'. For a consideration of the divergence of the case law of the EPO and the UK courts see Newton, 1996.

R v Re IBM's Patent Application
('search for incorrect strings')
[2003] ENPR 2
Bundesgerichthof (Federal Court of Justice)

17 This distinction between programs for computers, for which as such protection is
sought, and computer-related subject-matter not covered by Art 1(2), point 3, PatG
means that claims which propose ways in which a computer can work its way
through certain procedural steps in order to solve a problem in the conventional
technical fields, i.e. engineering, physics, chemistry or biology, are in principle
patentable. ...

18 ... a program can be patented if it is incorporated into technical processes, for
example in such a way that it processes measured values, monitors the operation of
technical devices or performs any other external controlling or regulating function
.... A method whereby a computer is used to examine and compare data in order to
perform an intermediate step in the manufacture of technical articles is also
comparable to inventions which can generally be granted patent protection, if this
solution is characterised by a finding based on technical considerations and the
implementation of that finding. The same is true if the invention concerns the
operability of the computer as such and thereby permits the direct interaction of its
elements ... Nor are instructions for the particular construction of a computer or for
its use in a special way ... necessarily covered by the exclusion from patent
protection.

19 ... The scientific theories and mathematical methods ... as well as the schemes, rules
and methods for performing mental acts ... are excluded from patent protection only
in so far as they are claimed in isolation from a specific function. But when used to
solve a specific technical problem they are–in that context–in principle patentable ...

20 ... When the EPC was being drafted, there were no clear ideas about what definition
should be adopted for the patenting of computer-related inventions. During the
diplomatic conference to conclude the Convention, it was expressly pointed out that
attempts had been made in vain to give the abstract concepts more solid form and
that their interpretation would have to be left to everyday legal practice ...

21 Nevertheless, the choice of words adopted in the EPC and the PatG reflects the desire
to refrain from hampering the development of the then still relatively new field of
computer technology by not setting bounds to the scope of patent protection. Clearly,
inventions in fields not traditionally regarded as technical should not be considered
patentable simply because they are intended to be used with the aid of a computer.
On the other hand, it would go beyond the stated aim to deny patent protection to
an invention characterised by technical processes or considerations on the grounds
that it is meant for use on a computer and/or a number of computer specialists
regard it as a program for a computer in the narrower sense.

Without doubt, therefore, the test for patentability of inventions relating to computer
technology has proved difficult both to apply and to explain, and the most appropriate
way of examining it is to consider some of the applications made and whether or not it
proved possible to establish a case for patentability.

Decisions of the Board of Appeals of the EPO[126]

One of the leading cases in this area remains the decision of the Technical Board of Appeal in *Vicom*.[127] The application concerned a claim for a method of digitally processing images in the form of a two-dimensional array which could be used to enhance or restore the technical quality of such images. It was the computer program that embodied the inventive idea which both controlled the process and gave it its value, but it was held that the application was not for the program *as such*, but for the invention it was used to perform. A decisive point was that the application was susceptible of industrial application, since it could be used for investigating the properties of a real or simulated object or for designing an industrial article. The requisite technical effect could therefore be ascertained.

Vicom/Computer-related invention
T208/84 [1987] EPOR 74
Technical Board of Appeal

12 The Board of Appeal is of the opinion that a claim directed to a technical process which process is carried out under the control of a program (be this implemented in hardware or software) cannot be regarded as relating to a program *as such* within the meaning of Article 52(3) EPC, as it is the application of the program for determining the sequence of steps in the process for which in effect protection is sought. Consequently, such a claim is allowable under Article 52(2) and (3) EPC ...

15 ... Generally, claims which can be considered as being directed to a computer set-up to operate in accordance with a specific program (whether by means of hardware or software) for controlling or carrying out a technical process cannot be regarded as relating to a computer program *as such* and thus are not objectionable under Article 52(2) and (3) EPC ...

16 ... Generally speaking, an invention which would be patentable in accordance with conventional patentability criteria should not be excluded from protection by the mere fact that, for its implementation, modern technical means in the form of a computer program are used. Decisive is what technical contribution the invention as defined in the claim when considered as a whole makes to the known art ... it would seem illogical to grant protection for a technical process controlled by a suitable programmed computer but not for the computer itself when set up to execute control.

In contrast, the *IBM/Semantically related expressions* application[128] was found not to be patentable. The claim was for a method of generating a list of expressions semantically related to an input linguistic expression using a programmable data processing system. The semantic relationship was of abstract linguistic information content and did not relate to any physical entity.

It may be argued that the test is easier to apply to claims such as those of *Vicom* and *IBM/Semantically related expressions*, which could be said to represent opposite ends of

---

126 The text of these decisions is available by searching the database of EPO decisions via www.legal.european-patent-office.org/dg3/search_dg3.htm.

127 [1987] EPOR 74.

128 T52/85 [1989] EPOR 454.

the spectrum.[129] However, the application *IBM/Data processor network*[130] is, perhaps, more equivocal. It referred to a data processing system consisting of a plurality of data processors interconnected as nodes in a telecommunications network. Novel procedures enabled this network of computers to maintain concurrent connections between a terminal and more than one applications program and to provide simultaneous online processing, using several data files located at remote processors. Notwithstanding that the end result, an enhancement of the range of practical steps which could be performed by linked computers, was achieved using software, it was said to solve a problem which was essentially technical, even though that technical effect was manifested within the computer itself.

As has been indicated, one of the criticisms of the EPO's interpretation of the computer program exclusion was that it was out of line with what was happening in some other jurisdictions. This argument was fuelled by the TRIPS Agreement, Art 27(1) of which states that 'patents shall be available for any inventions, whether products or processes, in all fields of technology, provided they are new, involve an inventive step and are capable of industrial application'. Although no definition of 'all fields of technology' is provided, there seems to be no reason, *per se*, why computer technology should be excluded. Two recent decisions of the Board of Appeals[131] in which the applicant referred to both the TRIPS Agreement and the developments in the US and Japan have provided the EPO with the opportunity to review its interpretation of the computer program exclusion.

T1173/97 was a claim for an asynchronous resynchronisation of a commit procedure, a novel mechanism for resource management in distributed systems[132] and the examining division, following previous decisions such as that in *Vicom,* concluded that the device was not patentable:

> ... since the data medium and the program recorded thereon were not technically related, except for features which were already known from the prior art, the technical character of the computer program could not be derived from the physical character of the storage medium on which it was recorded. The technical character could also not be derived from the method or system in which the computer program was used.

On appeal, in response to the points raised about TRIPS, the Board of Appeals, in its summary of its preliminary view, was swift to point out that this was not of immediate relevance to decisions of the EPO and that, although it should take cognisance of such developments, its duty was to interpret the EPC.

---

129 Compare, also, *IBM/Computer-related invention* T115/85 [1990] EPOR 107 and *IBM/Text processing* T65/86 [1990] EPOR 181.

130 T06/83 [1990] EPOR 91.

131 T935/97 (4 February 1999), T1173/97 (1 July 1998), [1999] RPC 861; a summary can be found at (2000) 31 IIC 189.

132 A distributed system is a cluster of interconnected computers.

In re IBM Corp
T1173/97
EPO Board of Appeals

Regarding the TRIPS Agreement, it was not clear whether this international treaty applied to the EPC at all ...

In addition, there was no indication that the member states of the TRIPS Agreement intended to include computer programs within the scope of patentable subject matter ...

When it came to the written reasons for the decision, after having agreed that it shared the appellant's opinions about the significance of TRIPS in this context, it nevertheless appeared to be taking the same line:

However, for the time being it is not convinced that TRIPS may be applied directly to the EPC. Apart from any other considerations TRIPS is binding only on its Member States. The European Patent Organisation itself is not a member of the WTO and did not sign the TRIPS Agreement.

Having made this fundamental position clear, the Board then went on to say:

2.3 But although TRIPS may not be applied directly to the EPC, the Board thinks it appropriate to take it into consideration, since it is aimed at setting common standards and principles concerning the availability, scope and use of trade-related intellectual property rights, and therefore of patent rights. Thus TRIPS gives a clear indication of current trends.

Article 27(1) of TRIPS states that 'patents shall be available for any inventions, whether products or processes, in all fields of technology, provided they are new, involve an inventive step and are capable of industrial application'. This general principle, when considered together with the provisions pursuant to paras 2 and 3 of Art 27 concerning exclusion from patentability (which, however, do not comprise any of the subject matter mentioned in Art 52(2) of the EPC), can be correctly interpreted, in the Board's opinion, as meaning that it is the clear intention of TRIPS not to exclude from patentability any inventions, whatever field of technology they belong to, and therefore, in particular, not to exclude programs for computers as mentioned in and excluded under Art 52(2)(c) of the EPC. Similarly, with respect to developments in the US and Japan, the Board said:

2.5 The appellant also referred to current practice in the US and Japanese Patent Offices and pointed out that, according to the recently revised guidelines for examination in both offices, claims for computer program products are now allowed ...

The Board has taken due notice of these developments, but wishes to emphasise that the situation under these two legal systems ... differs greatly from that under the EPC in that it is only the EPC which contains an exclusion such as the one in Art 52(2) and (3).

2.6 Nevertheless, as pointed out by the appellant, these developments represent a useful indication of modern trends. In the Board's opinion they may contribute to the further highly desirable (worldwide) harmonisation of patent law.

Having pointed out that the only applicable law which the Board could be bound to consider was the EPC, it continued in its review of the interpretation of the exclusions in the light of the developments described:

3   ... The Board will therefore now investigate what in its view would be the proper interpretation of the exclusion from patentability of programs for computers under Art 52(2) and (3) EPC ...

5.5   The main problem for the interpretation of said exclusion is therefore to define the meaning of the feature 'technical character', in the present case with specific reference to programs for computers ...

6.5   ... a patent may be granted not only in the case of an invention where a piece of software manages, by means of a computer, an industrial process or the working of a piece of machinery, but in every case where a program for a computer is the only means, or one of the necessary means, of obtaining a technical effect within the meaning specified above, where, for instance, a technical effect of that kind is achieved by the internal functioning of a computer itself under the influence of said program.

In other words, on condition that they are able to produce a technical effect in the above sense, all computer programs must be considered as inventions within the meaning of Art 52(1) EPC, and may be the subject matter of a patent if the other requirements provided for by the EPC are satisfied ...

9.4   ... Once it has been clearly established that a specific computer program product, when run on a computer, brings about a technical effect in the above sense, the Board sees no good reason for distinguishing between a direct technical effect on the one hand and the potential to produce a technical effect, which may be considered as an indirect technical effect, on the other hand.

A computer program product may therefore possess a technical character because it has the potential to cause a predetermined further technical effect in the above sense ...

9.5   In contrast to the reasons given in the decision under appeal, the Board has derived the technical character of the computer program product from the potential technical effect the program possesses, which effect is set free and may reveal itself when the program is made to run on a computer ...

9.6   A computer program product which (implicitly) comprises all the features of a patentable method (for operating a computer, for instance) is therefore in principle considered as not being excluded from patentability under Art 52(2) and (3) EPC ...

10.1 The Board has analysed some aspects of the meaning of the expression 'computer programs as such', with the emphasis on the 'as such', and has arrived at the conclusion that a computer program product is not excluded from patentability if it possesses the potential to bring about a 'further' technical effect.

10.2 ... the Board has arrived at its interpretation in the light of developments in information technology. This technology tends to penetrate most branches of society and leads to very valuable inventions. In its interpretation the Board has in its view not gone beyond the ordinary meaning given to the terms of the EPC ...

11.5 The present Board concludes from all this that, although the present decision may be based on a slightly different approach in thinking and reasoning than the case law of the boards of appeal of the EPO, it does not go directly against the existing case law when that case law is considered in the light of what was decided in the decisions concerned ...

... a computer program claimed by itself is not excluded from patentability if the program, when running on a computer or loaded into a computer, brings about, or is capable of bringing about, a technical effect which goes beyond the 'normal' physical interactions between the program (software) and the computer (hardware) on which it is run.

The result of this difference in approach was that the decision of the examining division was set aside and the matter was remitted back for reconsideration in the light of the decision of the Board of Appeal. An essentially similar judgment and resultant outcome occurred in T935/97. Following these decisions, the nature of technicality was subsequently revisited by the Technical Board of Appeal in T931/95 *Pension Benefit*

Systems Partnership. One of the other exclusions from patentability 'as such' is a claim for a 'business method'. Because most business methods are nowadays effected by computer these two issues are often discussed together, and even where they are not, similar concepts are involved, notably the need for a technical contribution. T 931/95 contained a claim for a process for managing and controlling pension benefits program and also for an apparatus for performing this process. The former was rejected as being a claim for a business method, as such, which was therefore unpatentable. In relation to the latter, the Board decided that 'a computer system suitably programmed for use in a particular field, even if that is the field of business and economy, has the character of a concrete apparatus in the sense of a physical entity, manmade for a utilitarian purpose and is thus an invention within the meaning of Article 52(1) EPC.' The Board was critical of the 'contribution approach' to technicality which had been used in a number of previous cases, namely that it was necessary to identify the real contribution which the subject matter claimed, considered as a whole, added to the known art. If this contribution was not of a technical character then, on the previous reasoning, there would be no invention. The Board held that this approach confused the requirement of 'invention' with the requirements of 'novelty' and 'inventive step'. The Board referred to both T1193/97 and T935/97 and concluded that possession of technical character was an implicit requirement of an invention and there was no basis for distinguishing between 'new features' of an invention and features of that invention which are known from the prior art. Likhovski has remarked that this decision 'in marked contrast to previous pronouncements on the importance of substance over form ... elevates the form of the claim over its substance. In essence, it sanctions what seem to be almost automatic findings of technicality for apparatus claims'.[133] Laakkonen and Whaite suggest that the ruling was intended to 'end the discussion on the patentability of programs for computers and that it 'appears to remove practically all restrictions derived from patentability of programs as such'.[134]

The reasoning in T931/95 was developed and applied in the more recent case T258/03 involving Hitachi's claim for an automatic auction method. Noting that the term 'invention' is to be construed as 'subject-matter having technical character' the Board appeared then to resolve some of the criticism that T258/03 exalted form over substance.

Hitachi's Application
('Automatic auction method')
EPO Technical Board of Appeal (2004)

3.5 Therefore, taking into account both that a mix of technical and non-technical features may be regarded as an invention within the meaning of Article 52(1) EPC and that prior art should not be considered when deciding whether claimed subject-matter is such an invention, a compelling reason for not refusing under Article 52(2) EPC subject-matter consisting of technical and non-technical features is simply that the technical features may in themselves turn out to fulfil all requirements of Article 52(1) EPC.

---

133 Likhovski, 2000 and see comments in *R v Hutchins' Application* [2002] RPC 8 at paras 33 and 34 extracted below at pp 79–80.
134 Laakkonen, and Whaite, 2001.

As pointed out later in the decision, 'this reasoning is independent of the category of claim'. However the Board then went on to apply the reasoning on technicality in T931/95 to the substance of the claim.

4.3 However, in order to be consistent with the finding that the so-called 'contribution approach', which involves assessing different patentability requirements such as novelty or inventive step, is inappropriate for judging whether claimed subject-matter is an invention within the meaning of Article 52(1) EPC, there should be no need to further qualify the relevance of technical aspects of a method claim in order to determine the technical character of the method. In fact, it appears to the Board that an assessment of the technical character of a method based on the degree of banality of the technical features of the claim would involve remnants of the contribution approach by implying an evaluation in the light of the available prior art or common general knowledge.

4.4 From a practical point of view, this inconsistency becomes fully apparent when considering the question of whether technical character is conferred to a method using technical means for a purely non-technical purpose. In this case, following the approach taken in T 931/95, the mere presence of such means would not necessarily be sufficient to lend the method technical character. In the Board's opinion, any practical answer to this question would have to rely on some weighting of the importance of the features to determine the 'core' of the invention, necessarily including considerations on their technical relevance, in particular possible novel or inventive contributions, with respect to the prior art. The Board would like to add that such weighting has already been rejected in early case law of the boards of appeal (see Decision T 26/86, OJ EPO 1988,19; headnote II).

4.5 Finally, the Board in its present composition is not convinced that the wording of Article 52(2)(c) EPC, according to which 'schemes, rules and methods for performing mental acts, playing games or doing business' shall not be regarded as inventions within the meaning of Article 52(1) EPC, imposes a different treatment of claims directed to activities and claims directed to entities for carrying out these activities. What matters having regard to the concept of 'invention' within the meaning of Article 52(1) EPC is the presence of technical character which may be implied by the physical features of an entity or the nature of an activity, or may be conferred to a non-technical activity by the use of technical means. In particular, the Board holds that the latter cannot be considered to be a non-invention 'as such' within the meaning of Article 52(2) and (3) EPC. Hence, in the Board's view, activities falling within the notion of a non-invention 'as such' would typically represent purely abstract concepts devoid of any technical implications.

4.6 The Board is aware that its comparatively broad interpretation of the term 'invention' in Article 52(1) EPC will include activities which are so familiar that their technical character tends to be overlooked, such as the act of writing using pen and paper. Needless to say, however, this does not imply that all methods involving the use of technical means are patentable. They still have to be new, represent a non-obvious technical solution to a technical problem, and be susceptible of industrial application.

4.7 It is therefore concluded that, in general, a method involving technical means is an invention within the meaning of Article 52(1) EPC.

Case law in the UK

In the UK, both *Hitachi's Application*,[135] and *Wang Laboratories Inc's Application*,[136] failed to gain patent protection for their products. In the *Hitachi* case, the application was for a particular type of compiler program which was able to increase the speed of operation significantly. Hitachi tried to rely on the *Vicom* decision, saying that as the compiler was acting on a physical entity (the source program) this, therefore, could be regarded as constituting a technical process. The examiner found that just because a mathematical method operated on a physical entity it did not automatically follow that it was used in a technical process. The invention claimed amounted to a claim for the compiler program itself and therefore must be excluded.

Wang Laboratories Inc's Application was an attempt to patent a computer system shell and expert system. Expert systems are computer programs that have been constructed, using the knowledge from a human expert, in such a way that they are capable of functioning at the same standard (at least) of human experts in a given field. They are used as high level intellectual aids to their users. Most expert systems contain of a set of facts describing a particular problem domain and a set of assertions or inference rules defining relationships between the facts and specifying how new facts can be deduced from existing facts by means of the assertions. These attributes are known as the 'knowledge base'.

In this case, the examining officer said that this was merely a claim for a computer program, *as such*, and should be excluded. The applicant's argument was that this was use of a computer program in a novel way, and was not a claim for a program, *as such*. In addition, it was submitted that the words 'a scheme, rule or method for performing a mental act' in s 1(2)(c) were intended only to exclude those schemes which were intended to be, and could be, performed by a human mind. The Patents Court disagreed: this was not the correct interpretation of the phrase. A 'scheme, rule or method' for performing a mental act was excluded, whatever steps or processes were involved, and such a scheme was still excluded if the method was performed by computer, whether or not the computer program adopted steps that would not ordinarily be used by a human mind. Accordingly, the claim relating to the expert system was a claim to a scheme or method for performing a mental act using a computer program and was not allowable. The claim relating to the computer system shell was a claim for a computer program and nothing more. The computer remained separate even when programmed and did not combine with the program to form a new machine. It is this last fact which seems to be the salient feature on which patentability of computer software depends.

The difficulty of applying the test can be seen in *Re Gale's Application*, which was a claim for a new method of calculating square roots, encapsulated in ROM (read only memory). This was first of all refused by the patents examiner on the ground that it was merely an application for a computer program. This decision was reversed by the Patents Court, in which Aldous J argued that a distinction could be made between a

135 [1991] RPC 415.
136 [1991] RPC 463.

disk containing a software program, which would not be patentable, and the hard-wired ROM. This distinction could be made, in his view, because the ROM was used as a dedicated piece of apparatus to perform a particular task. This reasoning was not accepted by the Court of Appeal, in which Nicholls LJ acknowledged the importance of decisions made under the EPC in deciding such cases, and, referring to the *Vicom* claim, restored the original decision.

Re Gale's Application
[1991] RPC 305, p 327
Court of Appeal

Nicholls LJ   In the present case Mr Gale claims to have discovered an algorithm. Clearly that, *as such*, is not patentable. It is an intellectual discovery which, for good measure, falls squarely within one of the items, mathematical method, listed in section 1(2). But the nature of this discovery is such that it has a practical application, in that it enables instructions to be written for conventional computers in a way which will, so it is claimed, expedite one of the calculations frequently made with the aid of a computer. In my view the application of Mr Gale's formulae for the purpose of writing computer instructions is sufficient to dispose of the contention that he is claiming a mathematical method *as such*.

That still leaves the difficulty that those instructions when written, and without more, are not patentable, because they constitute a computer program. Is there something more? In the end I have come to the conclusion that there is not. The attraction of Mr Gale's case lies in the simple approach that, as claimed, he has found an improved means of carrying out an everyday function of computers. To that extent, and in that respect, his program makes a more efficient use of the computer's resources. A computer, including a pocket calculator with a square root function, will be a better computer when programmed with Mr Gale's instructions. So it may. But the instructions do not embody a technical process which exists outside the computer. Nor, as I understand the case as presented to us, do the instructions solve a 'technical' problem lying within the computer ... I confess to having difficulty in identifying clearly the boundary line between what is and what is not a technical problem for this purpose ... in the present case Mr Gale has devised an improvement in programming. What his instructions do, but it is all they do, is to prescribe for the CPU [central processing unit] in a conventional computer a different set of calculations from those normally prescribed when the user wants a square root. I do not think that makes a claim to those instructions other than a claim to the instructions as such. The instructions do not define a new way of operating the computer in a technical sense ...

Although there have been suggestions from time to time that the basic test of the 'technical contribution to the known art' might be subject to modification from time to time,[137] the centrality of the basic test was affirmed in *Fujitsu Ltd's Application,* a case which was welcomed by Newton as an 'attempt to resolve these conflicting positions with a view to clarifying precise circumstances in which a patent may be obtained for a software related invention'.[138] The application was for a method and apparatus for modelling a synthetic crystal structure for designing inorganic materials. The applicant argued that, where there had been a technical contribution to known art, a patent

137 See, eg, Press, T, '1996.
138 Newton, 1994, p 204.

should not be refused and, once a mental act had been tied to a technical application, it ceased to be merely a mental act and could, therefore, become the subject matter of a patent. The examiner distinguished a manipulation of the technical quality of the data (as in *Vicom*) and the manipulation of the content of the information in this application. The question then was whether the fact that the image represented, that is, the crystal structure, was a 'technical artefact', gave the whole application a technical character. The examiner found that, on the evidence, the application was not only for a computer program, but was, in substance, a scheme or method for performing a mental act and was therefore unpatentable. This decision was upheld on appeal, in which Laddie J summarised the requirements for patentability of computer programs.

Fujitsu Ltd's Application
[1996] RPC 511, p 530
Patents Court

Laddie J   It seems to me that the relevant provisions of the Act and the EPC ... produce the following principles:

1   The types of subject matter referred to in section 1(2) are excluded from patentability as a matter of policy. This is so whether the matter is technical or not.

2   The exclusion from patentability is a matter of substance not form. Therefore the exclusion under section 1(2) extends to any form of passive carrier or recording of excluded subject matter. Thus, merely because a piece of paper is in principle patentable (save to the extent that it lacks novelty), it is not permissible, for example, to record a literary work (section 1(2)(b)) or a computer programs (section 1(2)(c)) on a piece of paper and then seek patent monopoly for the paper bearing the recorded work. Similarly, it is not permissible, without more, to seek protection for a computer program when it is stored on a magnetic medium or *merely* loaded into a computer.

3   *Prima facie* a computer running under the control of one program is a different piece of apparatus from the same computer when running under the control of another program. It follows that a claim to a computer when controlled by a program or to a method of controlling a computer by a program or to a method of carrying out a process by use of a computer so controlled *can* be the subject of patent protection. However, because the court is concerned with substance not form, it is not enough for the designer of a new program to seek protection for his creation merely by framing it in one of these terms. The court or patent office must direct its attention not to the fact that the program is controlling the computer but to what the computer, so controlled, is doing.

4   Therefore a data processing system operating to produce a novel result would not be deprived of protection on the ground that it was a program as such. On the other hand, even if the effect of the program is to make the computer perform in a novel way, it is still necessary to look at precisely what the computer is doing, that is, at the nature of the process being carried out. If all that is being done, as a matter of substance, is the performance of one of the activities defined under section 1(2) as unprotectable, then it is still unprotectable.

In accordance with these principles, just as it would be possible to obtain a patent, considerations of novelty aside, for a faster chip or a more effective storage medium, there is no reason in principle or logic why modification of the computer to achieve the same speed or storage increase by means of software should be excluded from protection. The fact that the advance is achieved in software rather than hardware should not affect patentability. To use in a slightly different context Nicholls LJ's words from *Gale's Application*, that would be to exalt form over substance. Similarly, if a new process achieved by mechanical means would be patentable, there is no reason why the same process achieved by computer means should be any less patentable. If that is so, it does not matter whether the patent claims are drafted in terms of a process controlled by a computer, a computer when programmed in particular way or a method of controlling a computer. In each case the substance of the invention is the same.

... Is it enough for [counsel for the applicant] to demonstrate that his client's advance is of a technical character and relates to a technical field? The answer depends on what is meant by the word 'technical'. [He] appeared to me to use it as if it covered all areas of practical development which were not associated with the liberal arts. That is not what I understand to have been the way in which it was used in the decided cases. In particular in *VICOM* and *IBM* it is only processes or methods which do not fall foul of the express exclusions from patentability under section 1(2) which are treated as suitably 'technical'. Therefore use of the word 'technical', the meaning of which takes its colour from its context, is apt to confuse. What counts in this area is whether the method or process controlled by the program or the computer running it is one which itself is excluded from patentability.

The Court of Appeal dismissed a further appeal,[139] finding that the only question was whether there was a technical contribution in order that it could not be said that the invention consisted merely of a computer program *per se*. However, the Court produced little clarification of the meaning of 'technical contribution', Aldous LJ finding little help from *Vicom* – 'The reasoning in *Vicom* as to what was the technical contribution is not easy to ascertain' – and holding that, overall, 'what was and was not a technical contribution was not a clear one', so that each case had to be decided on its own facts.

The cases above were, of course, decided before the significant EPO decisions in T1193/97 and T935/97 and, as a result of these two decisions, the UK Patent Office issued a Practice Direction explaining their impact. The Practice Direction reviewed the decisions and previous case law within the UK and then went on to outline its existing practice which would be changing to conform to the new direction given by the EPO.

Patent Office Practice Direction
[1999] RPC 563

13. ... The Patent Office has taken the view that the authorities decide that it is the absence of a substantive technical contribution in the subject matter which would render an invention unpatentable and that it is not possible to rescue inherently unpatentable subject matter from its fate merely by changing the semantic form of the claims, e.g. by dressing a program for a computer up as a carrier or a conventional computer containing the program. However, the courts were not able to identify any substantive technical contribution in any of these authorities and as a result they rejected the applications for that reason. Consequently, they did not elaborate on the position in the event there is such a contribution.

14. From this, the erstwhile practice of the Patent Office developed alongside that in the European Patent Office such that if there is a substantive technical contribution, claims to a conventional computer programmed to perform that technical contribution, or to equivalent methods or processes, are accepted. However, the practice of the Patent Office has been not to accept claims to the programs, whether in the form of a carrier bearing the program or otherwise, essentially because such a claim of itself does not actually deliver the technical contribution which underpins

---

139 [1997] RPC 608.

the invention; only when the program is run on a computer does that happen. That practice will now change to remain in step with that of the European Patent Office.

Notwithstanding this Practice Direction and the subsequent application of the reasoning in T1193/97 and T935/97 in the *Pensions Benefit System* case, the approach in the latter was subject to criticism in *Hutchins' Application*. This was a claim for a computer system providing guidance to rescue personnel providing cardio-pulmonary resuscitation to a patient. Users were able to input data regarding the condition of the patient and, in response, the system provided both visual and synthesised speech advice. It was held that, even though this was a claim for an apparatus, it did not thereby avoid the exclusions in the Patents Act 1977. It was clear that the substance of the claim was for a computer program 'as such' and therefore could not be afforded patent protection. The claimant had sought to rely on similar reasoning to that in *Pensions Benefit System* that the claim had 'the character of a concrete apparatus in the sense of a physical entity, man-made for a utilitarian purpose and is thus not an excluded item within the meaning of section 1(2) of the Act' – but to no avail.

Hutchins' Application
[2002] RPC 8

32 The apparent conflict between the EPO Board of Appeal's decision in Pension Benefit Systems and established law in the United Kingdom was considered recently by the Comptroller's hearing officer in Pintos Global Services Ltd's Application. The following passage at paragraphs 25 to 28 of the hearing officer's decision in that case sets out the position very clearly:

'25. There is therefore a conflict between the recent decision of the EPO Technical Board of Appeal in Pension Benefit Systems, which specifically disapproved of the so-called "contributions" approach, and the long established practice of the United Kingdom courts, originating from the Merrill Lynch judgment, from which it is clear that the decision as to what is patentable depends upon substance not form.

26. Furthermore, the approach suggested by the Board in Pension Benefit Systems conflicts with the practice of the courts in this country in one other, very important respect. At paragraph 8 of its reasons, and following on from its decision that a claim in the form of apparatus was not excluded by Article 52(1), the Board went on to consider whether the invention as claimed satisfied the requirements for novelty and inventive step. They said:

Indeed, the improvement envisaged by the invention according to the application is an essentially economic one, that is, lies in the field of economy, which, therefore, cannot contribute to inventive step. (Emphasis provided)

27. The Board's approach in this respect is summarised at the beginning of its decision in the following words:

... the subject-matter as claimed, considered as a whole, did not provide any contribution to the art in a field not excluded from patentability under Article 52(2)EPC ...

28. Interestingly, the Board is here adopting an approach that was accepted by the Court of Appeal to be "erroneous" as long ago as 1989 in the *Merrill Lynch* case, and that is that on the determination of the question whether or not an application relates to an excluded matter it is necessary to take into account whether the non-excluded features are already known and obvious. In the event, I am in no doubt but that I am bound to follow the practice laid down by the courts in the United Kingdom.'

33 I too believe that I am bound to follow the practice laid down by the UK courts, and therefore I do not place much (if any) importance on the actual form of the claim, in deciding whether or not the invention defined in the claim is excluded from patentability by section 1(2). Instead I have looked to the substance of the invention, and taking the best view I can of the matter, it is clear to me that the invention as described and as claimed in this application is a program for a computer as such. As stated above, I do not consider that the program produces, or has the potential to produce, the necessary technical effect that would have demonstrated that the invention is more than a computer program as such. Consequently, the invention as claimed in this application is excluded by section 1(2)(c).

34 I note in passing that, had the issue been entirely free from authority, I would in any event have preferred the approach adopted by the UK courts. The reasoning of the EPO Board of Appeal in Pension Benefit Systems appears to me to exalt form over substance, and (in relation to Article 52 at least) to determine the patentability of an invention in accordance with the manner in which it is claimed. At least in so far as the Patents Act 1977 is concerned, there does not appear to be any basis for determining the patentability of an invention by considering the form in which it is claimed

A comparison with the US system

The problems surrounding the application of the test for patentability of computer programs are unlikely to deter the large producers of computer systems from seeking patents for their products where they feel that this is appropriate, especially in the light of a certain apparent relaxation of the rules in the Patent Offices of the US and Japan and the recent decisions of the EPO Board of Appeals. This may, perhaps, be given additional impetus in the light of some of the uncertainty surrounding the application of copyright principles to computer programs. If a computer program can be granted a patent, then the producer will enjoy the monopoly that goes with it and will cease to be concerned about issues of decompilation, adaptation, and so on. Given the commercial importance of many software products and products containing software, it is not surprising that patent applications are filed in instances where designers/developers perceive novelty and inventiveness. The US law on patents is contained in the Patents Act of 1952 and it is, therefore, unsurprising that it contains no reference to computer programs as potential subject matter for patent claims. This fact, together with the absence of general exclusions, has meant that the law on software patents has developed along a rather different trajectory than that in the EU. By virtue of 15 USC §101, patents are available for 'any new and useful process, machine manufacture, or composition of matter or any new and useful improvement thereof'. Historically this has not meant, however, that patents were available for all things and the exclusion of algorithms from patentability in *Gottschalk v Benson*, referred to earlier in the chapter, had a lasting effect on preventing the success of computer program claims. Subsequent cases began to develop tests for the patentability of software based on the overall functioning of the system in cases where the whole system could be considered the subject matter of the claim.[140] This reasoning was relaxed further in *Re*

---

140 See eg, *Re Abele* 648 F2d 902 (US Court Customs and Patents Appeals 1982).

Alappat,[141] in which the approach taken was to consider the computer as a machine so that a program could be construed as a 'new and useful improvement thereof' within the meaning of §101. More recently, in the cases of *State Street Bank v Signature*[142] and *AT & T Corp. v Excel Communications,*[143] the courts have enunciated a test which is based on the identification of a 'useful concrete and tangible result'. This represents a considerable departure from the early approaches and has resulted in a consequent liberalisation of the criteria for patentability of computer software in the US[144] as compared with the EU as summarised in the following extract.

Tim Press
Patent Protection for Computer-related inventions
Ch. 4 in Chris Reed and John Angel (eds)
Computer Law 5th ed
Oxford: OUP (2003) p. 166

> ... why is the position in Europe commonly viewed as being more restrictive? First there is the gap between perception and reality – the existence of a specific exclusion in the EPC leads to considerable misconception as to the true position. But there is also a real difference between Europe and the US, certainly in relation to the recent explosion of activity in the field of patents for computerised business methods. ... in the US (as now in Europe), such claims will be most unlikely to be refused because the subject-matter is non-patentable or excluded. In both jurisdictions also, the claim will have to proceed to examination for novelty and non-obviousness/inventive step. But in the US, in contrast to Europe, there is no specific requirement that the inventive step be of a technical nature. This difference in approach will result in a wider scope of matter being held unpatentable in Europe than is the case in the US.

Current proposals

The issue of patentability of computer programs has also being pursued by the European Commission as a consequence of the follow-up to the Green Papers on *Innovation* and the *Community Patent.*[145] Ostensibly, both the Commission and the European Parliament support the patentability of computer programs,[146] both for internal market reasons and also in order to be on a par with the US and Japan as important trading partners. For these reasons, in 2002, the Commission introduced a proposal for a Directive, aimed at harmonising Member States' legislation on the patentability of computer programs.[147] The intention is that this Directive should ensure uniform application and interpretation of the new rules on the patentability of computer programs throughout the Community. However despite apparent agreement about the overall objectives of such a directive, the proposal itself has had a

---

141 33 F3d 1526 (Fed Cir 1994).

142 149 F 3d 1368 (Fed Cir 1998).

143 172 F3d 1352 (Fed Cir (1999).

144 For further discussion see eg, Fellas, 1999; Attridge 2001; Koo, 2002.

145 COM (1999) 42 final.

146 See *op cit,* Report from the Commission, fn 88.

147 Proposal for a Directive of the European Parliament and of the Council on the patentability of computer-implemented inventions, COM (2002) 92 final, for commentary on the proposal see eg, Booton and Mole, 2002; Pangiotidou, 2003; Williams, 2004.

stormy ride through the various stages of the co-decision procedure.[148] The text finally adopted by the Council of Ministers by qualified majority on 7 March 2005 shows marked changes from the original proposal and ignored most of the Parliament's amendments. At the plenary debate in the European Parliament on 8 March 2005, the Commission came under criticism for refusing to go back to the drawing board and submit a new proposal[149] and so, a the time of writing, the future of the draft directive remains uncertain.

INTELLECTUAL PROPERTY
RIGHTS IN DATABASES

Computer technology has revolutionised information storage and retrieval and this has facilitated the creation and commercial exploitation of databases, providing ready access to information on a wide range of subject matter. Collections and compilations are not new, but the ease of search and correlation made possible by computerisation of such products has had a dramatic effect on both the ease of use and the ultimate usefulness. It is frequently the case that the value of the database lies not in the individual entries *per se,* since, depending on the nature of the database, these may be obtained from public domain material or be brief facts which are not individually subject to copyright protection. Instead, the value lies in the way in which this material is available for retrieval, the sheer volume and comprehensive nature of the material which may be accessed and the manner in which it is presented to the user. Cerina,[150] points out that databases are invaluable tools of vital importance for users in many segments of the economy, but can be copied in a minute with almost no effort, despite the considerable effort and expenditure necessary to their development. This fact, coupled with the truth of Peterson J's *dictum* quoted at the beginning of this chapter, suggests that some consideration of the way in which intellectual property rights in databases can be protected is essential.

Neeta Thakur
[2001] IPQ 100
Database protection in the European Union and the United States:
The European Database Directive as an optimum global model

Electronic databases and other compilations of factual material are indispensable to the global economy. These informational products are an essential tool for improving productivity, advancing education and promoting science. They are the lifeblood of a dynamic commercial information industry. Databases are rapidly becoming the forums for electronic intellectual creativity, and the extent to which intellectual property rights protect, or indeed hamper, the use of databases has long been a topic of scholastic debate. Copyright is a particularly vital area for businesses. It is very desirable for multimedia product creators to have a right over their product, and underlying processes, as a whole, as in principle it is easier and therefore, cheaper to enforce a single right over the database

---

148 For the various stages see europa.eu.int/comm/internal_market/en/indprop/comp/ index.html and for an analysis of some of the contentious issues between the European Parliament and the Council see Egitto, 2004.
149 See European Parliament Press release 9/03/05 at www.europarl.eu.int/press/index_en.htm.
150 Cerina, (1993).

rather than attempting to enforce a range of (perhaps non-exclusive) rights over its contents. The computer and information industry's increasing importance in the global economy has prompted governments world-wide to reassess their treatment of the law in an attempt to strengthen protection for on-line and real time databases.

Even prior to the burgeoning of the market in databases, many jurisdictions had found difficulty in extending copyright protection to collections, compilations and directories.[151] There was a marked division also between the common law and civil law approaches to copyright based on a different view of originality and its role in imparting copyrightability.[152] The acceptable standard of originality in the civil law 'droit d'auteur' reflects the fact that the material should exhibit something of the author's personality and creativity or demonstrate original, in the sense of novel, intellectual activity. Such a standard will, inevitably, exclude many databases from being protectable by copyright.[153]

The common law approach, on the other hand, is based on a literal 'copyright' – a legal method of safeguarding work against commercial exploitation arising as a result of copying by a third party. This requires only a low threshold of originality. It may be sufficient merely that the work is the author's independent creation, and not copied from elsewhere, rather than the necessity of a finding of particular novelty. Instead of novelty, the common law courts have tended to look for a 'sweat of the brow' test for the subsistence of copyright. Lord Atkinson said that 'it is necessary that labour, skill and capital should be expended sufficiently to impart to the product some quality or character which the raw material does not possess and which differentiates the product from the raw material'.[154] Lord Pearce agreed with this reasoning, commenting that 'the courts have looked to see whether the compilation of the unoriginal work called for work or skill or expense. If it did, it is entitled to be considered original and to be protected against those who wish to steal the fruits of the work or skill or expense by copying it'.[155]

However, the 'sweat of the brow' test has become controversial, even in the common law world, as can be seen from the US case of *Feist Publications Inc v Rural Telephone Service Company Inc*, in which the Supreme Court did not extend copyright protection to a telephone directory. Despite earlier decisions which had found copyrightability in a 'sweat of the brow' or 'industrious collection test', the court held that originality was the only standard for deciding whether or not a factual compilation is protectable by copyright. It is clear from *Feist*, however, that this standard of originality is somewhat lower than the civil law standard and is related purely to independent creativity.

---

151 For a review of the situation in a number of jurisdictions at the beginning of the 1990s see Dommering, and Hugenholtz, 1991.

152 See, also, Rowland, 1997. For a review of the treatment of originality in relation to fact-based compilations in a number of jurisdictions see e.g. Devici, 2004.

153 See, also Cerina, 1993, *op cit* fn 150. For a review of the treatment of originality in relation to fact-based compilations in a number of jurisdictions see e.g. Deveci, 2004.

154 *Macmillan & Co Ltd v Cooper* (1924) 40 TLR 186, p 188.

155 *Ladbroke (Football) Ltd v William Hill (Football) Ltd* [1964] 1 WLR 273, p 291. For a comprehensive review of the relevant cases see *Desktop Marketing Systems Pty ltd v Telstra Service Company Inc.* [2002] FCAFC 112 paras 20–160, available at www.austlii.edu.au/au/cases/cth/FCAFC/2002/112.html.

Feist Publications Inc v Rural Telephone Service Co Inc
113 L Ed 2d 358 (1991)
US Supreme Court

... Originality does not signify novelty; a work may be original even though it closely resembles other works so long as the similarity is fortuitous, not the result of copying [p 369] ...

... originality is not a stringent standard; it does not require that facts be presented in an innovative or surpassing way. It is equally true, however, that the selection and arrangement of facts cannot be so mechanical or routine as to require no creativity whatsoever. The standard of originality is low, but it does exist [p 379] ...

Nevertheless, the court was at pains to point out that the decision would not deprive all compilations of copyright protection.

... Factual compilations ... may possess the requisite originality. The compilation author typically chooses which facts to include, in what order to place them, and how to arrange the collected data so that they may be used effectively by readers. These choices as to selection and arrangement, so long as they are made independently by the compiler and entail a minimal degree of creativity, are sufficiently original that Congress may protect such compilations through the copyright laws ... Thus even a directory that contains absolutely no protectable written expression, only facts, meets the constitutional minimum for copyright protection of it features an original selection or arrangement [p 370] ...

Thakur has commented that 'Feist caused ripples of alarm in Europe'[156] and it was against this general background of inconsistency and doubt over both the existence and scope of copyright protection for databases and factual and other compilations that the EC Database Directive was drafted and adopted. The main impetus was a desire to harmonise the legal protection provided for databases and, as an adjunct, to ensure there was no impediment to the free market in both information products and information services. Even before the judgment in *Feist*, some commentators[157] had expressed concern that insistence on a high threshold of originality for copyright protection would cause problems for modern informational works and that copyright, at least in its common law manifestation, had always needed to balance creative aspects of the work with commercial demands. Ginsburg's suggested solution was to recognise a differential between works of 'high' and 'low' authorship and to provide corresponding protection. In essence, this could be said to be what the Database Directive does by extending conventional copyright protection to those works which satisfy the requisite originality requirement and providing a *sui generis* right for those databases which do not satisfy this test but are, nevertheless, the result of considerable investment.

THE DATABASE DIRECTIVE[158]

The Directive applies to both electronic and non-electronic databases, but not to the underlying computer programs:

---

156 Thakur, 2001, p 110.
157 See, eg, Ginsburg, 1990.
158 Directive 96/9/EC, 11 March 1996 (Legal Protection of Databases).

1 Scope

2   ... 'database' shall mean a collection of independent works, data or other materials arranged in a systematic or methodical way and individually accessible by electronic or other means.

3   Protection under this directive shall not apply to computer programs used in the making or operation of databases accessible by electronic means.

The copyright protection which is appropriate for databases is detailed in Art 3:

3 Object of protection

1   In accordance with this Directive, databases which, by reason of the selection or arrangement of their content, constitute the author's own intellectual creation shall be protected as such by copyright. No other criteria shall be applied to determine their eligibility for that protection.

2   The copyright protection of databases provided for by the Directive shall not extend to their contents and shall be without prejudice to any rights subsisting in those contents themselves.

Since 'selection' or 'arrangement' is essential criteria, large comprehensive databases may be excluded unless 'the particular arrangement of material is capable, by dint of personal creativity, of satisfying the "own intellectual creation" test'.[159]

The EC Database Directive: an original
solution to an unoriginal problem?
Diane Rowland
[1997] 5 Web JCLI

The standard required for copyright protection is higher than the 'sweat of the brow' test and in some cases there will be room for debate as to whether a database qualifies for protection. In such cases it will be a matter for national tribunals, in the first instance at least, to determine the boundaries of 'originality'. One of the most significant legal reasons why copyright protection for databases in different Member States was so much at variance was the divergence over the most appropriate definition of originality and, notwithstanding the warning of the Economic and Social Committee to the Council to 'resist being sidetracked into a debate on the legal philosophies which underlie the Directive, particularly on the subject of "originality"', it is difficult at one level to see how this can be avoided. Any assessment of the likely effect of the directive as it stands will need to consider the test for copyrightability and Member States will need to consider the issue in ascertaining how it can be implemented into their domestic legislation.

This protection is then qualified by the restricted acts and their exceptions in Arts 5 and 6, which are similar in nature to those from conventional copyright regimes. In common with other copyrights in the EU, the term of protection is 70 years. The duration of the *sui generis* database right, on the other hand, is 15 years (Art 10). Articles 7–9 delineate its scope, the rights and obligations of lawful users and exceptions to the right.

---

159 Rowland, 1997. The standard of copyright protection for databases in Art 3 also accords with that suggested under TRIPS, Art 10.2 and the 1996 WIPO Copyright Treaty, both of which provide no protection for databases that do not attain this standard.

Sui generis right

7 Object of protection

1   Member States shall provide for a right for the maker of a database which shows that
there has been qualitatively and/or quantitatively a substantial investment in either
the obtaining, verification or presentation of the contents to prevent extraction
and/or re-utilisation of the whole or of a substantial part, evaluated qualitatively
and/or quantitatively, of the contents of that database.

2   ...

(a) 'extraction' shall mean the permanent or temporary transfer of all or a
substantial part of the contents of a database to another medium by any means
or in any form;

(b) 're-utilisation' shall mean any form of making available to the public all or a
substantial part of the contents of a database by the distribution of copies, by
renting, by on-line or other forms of transmission ...

4   The right ... shall apply irrespective of the eligibility of that database for protection by
copyright or by other rights. Moreover, it shall apply irrespective of the eligibility of
the contents of that database for protection by copyright or other rights ...

5   The repeated and systematic extraction and/or re-utilisation of insubstantial parts of
the contents of the database implying acts which conflict with a normal exploitation
of that database or which unreasonably prejudice the legitimate interests of the
maker of the database shall not be permitted.

In many European jurisdictions, databases which satisfy the requirements of Art 3(1)
would be likely to qualify for copyright protection, even in the absence of the
Directive. However, in the UK in particular, there are likely to be many databases
which would have qualified for protection under the old 'sweat of the brow' test
which will now be denied copyright protection. As long as these fulfil the requirement
of 'substantial investment', which is not defined in the Directive, they will still qualify
for the *sui generis* database right in Art 7.

This approach has been criticised on the basis that a 'two tier' system has implicit
connotations of a higher and lower mode of protection, There have also been
expressions of doubt as to whether the compromise solution of the combination of a
traditional copyright with a new form of right is the correct model.[160]

The EC Database Directive: an original
solution to an unoriginal problem?
Diane Rowland
[1997] 5 Web JCLI

During the consultation process, the Economic and Social Committee commented on the
inadequacy of compromise solutions, expressing the view that once protection is deemed
to be necessary, only a high standard of protection will suffice. It may be misguided
though, to view the protection afforded by the *sui generis* right as second rate. A major
threat to large databases is that of piracy and a fifteen year term of protection against

---

160 There have also been criticisms based on the fact that a 'neighbouring rights' regime would
have provided a suitable solution without necessitating the creation of a specific *sui generis*
right. See, eg, Garrigues, 1997. Cornish, 1999, on the other hand, suggests that the *sui generis*
right is to take account of the fact that there is no harmonised law of fair competition in the
EU.

copying is, in most cases, likely to be sufficiently extensive to accommodate the shelf-life of even the most enduring database. This should not be divorced from the fact that any further substantial investment, such as might be required by necessary revision and updating, will generate a further term of protection. It can thus be said that the two tier system, rather than providing a superior and an inferior protection, instead maintains the necessary balance between creativity and investment.

That is not to say, however, that the line between creative and non-creative databases will be an easy one to draw. Smith-Ekstrand's consideration of the similar problem confronting the US courts post-*Feist* revealed judicial analysis which 'bordered on hair-splitting, infinitesimal detail, as courts attempted to peel back each layer of the work, attempting to find its creativity or lack thereof'. She concludes that a flexible test is needed to determine when a compilation is sufficiently creative on because 'a creative database may be comprised of creative parts but uncreative selection, arrangement or co-ordination; or it may be comprised of creative selection, co-ordination and arrangement with uncreative parts. Databases may lie anywhere along the continuum.'[161]

The Database Directive was implemented in the UK[162] by the Copyright and Rights in Databases Regulations 1997.[163] These amend the CDPA 1988 in relation to copyright, by inserting definitions of 'database' and 'originality in databases' (new s 3A); making relevant amendments to s 29 (fair dealing) and s 50 (permitted acts). They also insert a new s 296B, which provides that acts permitted by virtue of the amended s 50 cannot be excluded by contract.

The new database right contained in Pt III of the Regulations, not being a copyright as such, has not been subsumed within the text of the 1988 Act, although certain of the available rights and remedies are, nevertheless, those contained in that statute (see reg 23). The basic database right is contained in reg 13:

13 (1) A property right ('database right') subsists ... in a database if there has been substantial investment in obtaining, verifying or presenting the contents of the database.

    (2) For the purposes of paragraph (1) it is immaterial whether or not the database or any of its contents is a copyright work within the meaning of Part I of the 1988 Act.

It will be recalled that the Directive only provides a definition of 'extraction and re-utilisation', but the Regulations provide explicit definitions of both 'substantial' (whose meaning is implicit within the Directive with regard to extraction and re-utilisation) and 'investment':

12 Interpretation

(1) ... 'investment' includes any investment, whether of financial, human or technical resources; ...

'substantial', in relation to any investment, extraction or re-utilisation, means substantial in terms of quantity, quality or a combination of both.

---

161 Smith-Ekstrand, (2002) p 334.
162 See, eg, Rowland, 1997; Lai, 1998; Chalton, 2000.
163 SI 1997/3032.

Subsequent regulations deal with other aspects of the database right, including infringement.

16 Acts infringing database right

(1) ... a person infringes database right in a database if, without the consent of the owner of the right, he extracts or re-utilises all or a substantial part of the contents of the database.

(2) ... the repeated and systematic extraction or re-utilisation of insubstantial parts of the contents of databases may amount to the extraction or re-utilisation of a substantial part of those contents.

The first UK case to take note of the new provisions concerned none of the more fundamental issues that were to be the subject of later litigation. For the purposes of the relevant discussion in *Mars UK Ltd v Teknowledge Ltd*,[164] the pertinent question was whether there was any right of repair which could be read into the Database Regulations. Having decided that, notwithstanding the rights of error correction, etc, the permitted acts in relation to computer programs themselves revealed no such defence, Jacob J went on to consider the Database Regulations. He pointed out that the situation with respect to databases could be distinguished from that for software because the Database Directive itself allowed, in Art 6(2)(d), a defence 'where other exceptions to copyright which are traditionally authorised under national law are involved'. This, in Jacob J's view, gave Parliament a right to impose limitations on the scope of rights but, in the absence of such legislative activity, gave no discretion to the courts *in lieu*.

Since that time there has been a steadily increasing number of cases for alleged infringement of the database right in many of the Member States of the European Union, all of which have, by now, implemented the Database Directive.[165] A comprehensive review of this litigation is beyond the scope of this chapter, but it is instructive to consider a representative selection of the cases highlighting the approach to some of the essential elements of the *sui generis* right. Hugenholtz has noted that 'the Directive does not offer much guidance in interpreting the notion of 'substantial investment. It does not clarify how much 'blood, sweat and tears' the database producer must have spent to qualify for protection.'[166] Predictably the interpretation of 'substantial investment' has been a key issue in much of the litigation, especially in relation to so-called 'spin-off' databases – those in which compilations of data arise incidentally to the main activities of the database owner. Typical examples include travel timetables, TV programme listings, details of sports fixtures etc. In such cases the primary investment is in the activities, rather than the database which catalogues those activities, or their results or outcomes. There is a school of thought, sometimes referred to as the 'spin-off' theory which suggests that the database right should not protect such databases. Hugenholtz[167] suggests that, in reality, the 'spin-off' argument is a 'mix of independent arguments'. These arguments include the fact that the database right is based on utilitarian reasoning in order to promote investment in

---

164 [2000] FSR 138.
165 For details of these cases and implementation of the directive in the Member States, see www.ivir.nl/files/database/index.html.
166 Hugenholtz, 2003.
167 *Ibid*

databases. On this basis there would be no need to extend protection to databases which were the (inevitable) by-product of other activities. This also makes it difficult to establish a direct link between the investment and the database at issue. An alternative argument is that investment costs should be recouped from primary, rather than incidental activities, that is, from the TV programmes, sports fixtures etc. themselves. He notes further that Laddie J, in the first instance decision in *British Horseracing Board v William Hill*,[168] distinguishes 'creating' and obtaining', the latter implying an object with a prior existence.

P. Bernt Hugenholtz
Program Schedules, Event data and Telephone subscriber listings under the Database Directive
Eleventh Annual Conference on International IP Law and Policy
Fordham University School of Law, New York, 2003

... a lot is to be said in favour of the 'spin-off doctrine'. In view of the principal rationale of the database right, ie, promoting investment in databases, it would be irrational to protect databases that are generated automatically as by-products of other activities. By the same token, any cost and labour spent must be attributable to the database for it to qualify as relevant investment. ... A different, but equally compelling argument is that investments in generating (creating) data are not protected by the database right as a matter of principle. ... The database right was introduced to protect investment in gathering, processing and publishing pre-existing data. Granting exclusive intellectual property rights in novel (newly created or discovered) data, which can not be obtained from alternative sources almost by definition, would lead to unwanted monopolies, and unduly restrict the freedom of expression and information.

The spin-off doctrine is unlikely to be popular with database producers as it severely restricts the scope of protection, but the obverse of this argument is that it fosters a 'broader public domain'.[169] Given that the doctrine apparently originated in the Netherlands,[170] it was entirely foreseeable that it should be referred to in decisions in that jurisdiction.

NV Holdingmaatschappij de Telegraaf v Nederlandse Omroep Stichting
[2002] ECDR 8
Court of Appeal of the Hague

16. ... it must be assumed in the absence of any evidence supporting a reasonable assumption to the contrary, that the mere compilation of programmes does not entail any (separate) substantial investment in the form of time, money or anything else.

17 The court also finds support for this view in the position adopted by the Minister of Justice, from which one may conclude that there need be no substantial investment where information about television programmes represents nothing more than a broadcaster's programming spin-off (parliamentary records on the Databankenwet memorandum in response to the report–Lower House). This state of affairs means that insufficient evidence has been presented to substantiate a reasonable assumption that an investment has been made under the terms of section 1(1)(a) of the Databankenwet. ...

---

168 [2001] 2 CMLR 12.
169 Derclaye, 2004.
170 See eg, Hugenholtz 2003 and Derclaye, *ibid*.

Similar reasons have been used in other courts in the Netherlands. In *Algemeen Dagblad v Eureka Internetdiensten* (the 'kranten.com' case), for instance, the District Court of Rotterdam declined to offer the protection of the database right to a list of headlines from newspapers,[171] but other Member States have not embraced the theory so readily. In *Danske Dagblades Forening (DDF) v Newsbooster*, the Copenhagen City Court, on similar facts to those in the kranten.com case, did extend protection to a collection of headlines and articles.[172] A number of cases in which the spin-off theory could be deemed to be relevant involved Fixtures Marketing Ltd and concerned a database created by the English and Scottish Football leagues and containing lists of football fixtures. The information on football fixtures in this database was used, *inter alia*, by companies in Sweden, Finland and Greece which organised pools games or other gambling activities based on forecasting the results of these matches. Applying the spin-off theory, it could be concluded that the lists were a mere by-product of the Football Leagues' main activity – was this how the courts in the three jurisdictions decided? All three disputes led to questions being referred to the European Court of Justice (ECJ) and judgment was given in all three on 9 November 2004.[173] In particular, the Högsta Domstolen of Sweden referred, *inter alia*, the following questions.

**Case C-338/02 *Fixtures Marketing v Svenska Spel*
European Court of Justice
9 November 2004**

1. In assessing whether a database is the result of a substantial investment within the meaning of Article 7(1) of the directive can the maker of a database be credited with an investment primarily intended to create something which is independent of the database and which thus does not merely concern the obtaining, verification or presentation of the contents of the database? If so, does it make any difference if the investment or part of it nevertheless constitutes a prerequisite for the database?

2. Does a database enjoy protection under the database directive only in respect of activities covered by the objective of the database maker in creating the database?

The ECJ's decision was as follows:

28. Investment in the creation of a database may consist in the deployment of human, financial or technical resources but it must be substantial in quantitative or qualitative terms. The quantitative assessment refers to quantifiable resources and the qualitative assessment to efforts which cannot be quantified, such as intellectual effort or energy, according to the 7th, 39th and 40th recitals of the preamble to the directive.

29. In that light, the fact that the creation of a database is linked to the exercise of a principal activity in which the person creating the database is also the creator of the materials contained in the database does not, as such, preclude that person from claiming the protection of the sui generis right, provided that he establishes that the obtaining of those materials, their verification or their presentation, in the sense described in paragraphs 24 to 27 of this judgment, required substantial investment in quantitative or qualitative terms, which was independent of the resources used to create those materials.

---

171 [2002] ECDR 1.

172 [2003] ECDR 5. Both of these cases also involved the legality of hypertext links to the websites containing the lists of headlines and articles – see also discussion in Chapter 9.

173 Cases C-338/02 *Fixtures Marketing v Svenska Spel*, C-46/02 *Fixtures Marketing Ltd v Oy Veikkaus Ab.* and C-444/02 *Fixtures Marketing Ltd v Organismos prognostikon agonon podosfairou AE.*

30. In those circumstances, although the search for data and the verification of their accuracy at the time a database is created do not require the maker of that database to use particular resources because the data are those he created and are available to him, the fact remains that the collection of those data, their systematic or methodical arrangement in the database, the organisation of their individual accessibility and the verification of their accuracy throughout the operation of the database may require substantial investment in quantitative and/or qualitative terms within the meaning of Article 7(1) of the directive.

31. In the case in the main proceedings, the resources deployed for the purpose of determining, in the course of arranging the football league fixtures, the dates and times of and home and away teams playing in the various matches represent, as Svenska Spel and the Belgian, German and Portuguese Governments submit, an investment in the creation of the fixture list. Such an investment, which relates to the organisation as such of the leagues is linked to the creation of the data contained in the database at issue, in other words those relating to each match in the various leagues. It cannot, therefore, be taken into account under Article 7(1) of the directive.

32. Accordingly, it must be ascertained, leaving aside the investment referred to in the previous paragraph, whether the obtaining, verification or presentation of the contents of a list of football fixtures constitutes a substantial investment in qualitative or quantitative terms.

33. Finding and collecting the data which make up a football fixture list do not require any particular effort on the part of the professional leagues. As Fixtures itself points out in its observations, those activities are indivisibly linked to the creation of those data, in which the leagues participate directly as those responsible for the organisation of football league fixtures. Obtaining the contents of a football fixture list thus does not require any investment independent of that required for the creation of the data contained in that list.

34. The professional football leagues do not need to put any particular effort into monitoring the accuracy of the data on league matches when the list is made up because those leagues are directly involved in the creation of those data. The verification of the accuracy of the contents of fixture lists during the season simply involves, according to the observations made by Fixtures, adapting certain data in those lists to take account of any postponement of a match or fixture date decided on by or in collaboration with the leagues. Such verification cannot, therefore, be regarded as requiring substantial investment.

35. The presentation of a football fixture list, too, is closely linked to the creation as such of the data which make up the list, as is confirmed by the absence of any mention in the order for reference of work or resources specifically invested in such presentation. It cannot therefore be considered to require investment independent of the investment in the creation of its constituent data.

36. It follows that neither the obtaining, nor the verification nor yet the presentation of the contents of a football fixture list attests to substantial investment which could justify protection by the *sui generis* right provided for by Article 7 of the directive.

37. In the light of the foregoing, the answer to the first question referred should be that the expression investment in … the obtaining … of the contents' of a database as defined in Article 7(1) of the directive must be understood to refer to the resources used to seek out existing independent materials and collect them in the database. It does not cover the resources used for the creation of materials which make up the contents of a database. In the context of drawing up a fixture list for the purpose of organising football league fixtures, therefore, it does not cover the resources used to establish the dates, times and the team pairings for the various matches in the league.

Whilst paying lip service to the fact that such databases *could* involve substantial investment (paras 29 and 30), that is, it is not automatic that a spin-off database is not protected by the database right, in these particular cases the outcome is the same as if the spin-off doctrine had been applied, both in the distinction made between creating and obtaining in para 33 and the overall outcome. Advocate Generakl Stix-Hackl had considered the spin-off theory in her opinion in C-444/02 *Fixtures Marketing Ltd v Organismos prognostikon agonon podosfairou AE* although, after a consideration of the factors surrounding 'obtaining', had concluded that it did not apply.

C-444/02 *Fixtures Marketing Ltd v Organismos prognostikon agonon podosfairou AE*
[2005] 1 CMLR 16
European Court of Justice

AG56 Many of the parties submitting observations based their observations on the so-called 'spin-off theory' according to which by-products are not covered by the right. It is only permissible to protect profits which serve to repay the investment. Those parties pointed out that the database at issue in the proceedings was necessary for the organisation of sporting bets, that is to say, it was made for that purpose. The investment was for the purpose of organising bets and not, or not exclusively, for that of creating the database. The investment would have been made in any event, as there is an obligation to undertake such organisation. The database is thus merely a by-product on another market.

AG57 In the present proceedings it must thus be clarified whether and in what way the so-called 'spin-off theory' can be of relevance to the interpretation of the Directive and in particular of the *sui generis* right. In the light of the reservations expressed in these proceedings regarding the protection of databases which are mere by-products, a demystification of the 'spin-off theory' seems called for. This theory, leaving aside its origins at national level, can be traced back, first, to the purpose implied by the Tenth to Twelfth Recitals of the Directive, which is to provide incentives for investment by improving the protection of investment. However, it is also based on the idea that investments should be repaid by profits from the principal activity. The 'spin-off theory' is also bound up with the idea that the Directive only protects those investments which were necessary to obtain the contents of a database. All these arguments have their value and must be taken into account in the interpretation of the Directive. However that must not result in the exclusion of every spin-off effect solely in reliance on a theory. The provisions of the Directive are and remain the decisive factor in its interpretation. ...

AG73 ... it should be pointed out that the so-called 'spin-off theory' cannot apply. Nor can the objective pursued in obtaining the contents of the database be of any relevance. That means that protection is also possible where the obtaining was initially for the purpose of an activity other than the creation of a database. For the Directive also protects the obtaining of data where the data was not obtained for the purposes of a database. That implies that an external database, which is derived from an internal database, should also be covered by protection.

Although in databases such as the ones at issue in these cases, it is a simple matter to distinguish between creating and obtaining, this may not always be the case.

Mark J Davison and P Bernt Hugenholtz
Football fixtures, horseraces and spinoffs: the ECJ domesticates the database right
[2005] EIPR 113, 115

While the ECJ appears to be confident it can distinguish between 'creating' and 'obtaining' data, the distinction is not always so easy to make. For instance, is the derivation of data from naturally occurring phenomena an act of creation or obtaining?

One example may be the recording of meteorological data such as the daily maximum temperature in a particular location. Are those data created or obtained? Similarly, do scientists obtain the genetic sequences of living organisms or do they create them? The strict approach taken by the ECJ in these four cases would suggest that the answer is that such data are created. Meteorological data and genetic sequences are records and representations of natural phenomena, not the phenomena themselves, and it would be difficult for scientists to argue that they have simply collected the data as opposed to creating them. On the other hand, when a large mass of such data has been created, there are also significant costs associated with presentation and verification which may meet the requirements in Art 7(1) of the Directive. In any event, these metaphysical distinctions will undoubtedly continue to concern courts and commentators for some time to come.

At the same time as the *Fixtures Ltd* cases, the ECJ also gave judgment in a similar, albeit rather more complex, case, C-203/02 *British Horseracing Board v William Hill*. BHB operated a database of various facts related to horse racing. The size of this database was significant and the estimated cost of keeping the 20 million records up to date was £4m p.a. The information was made available to other interested organisations and was licenced to a number of bookmakers, including William Hill. William Hill also provided on-line betting services and BHB alleged that this process used information derived from the BHB database without the requisite licence. Laddie J, at first instance, gave a wide interpretation to the directive, leading to questions being referred by the Court of Appeal to the ECJ.[174] The ECJ reiterated its view in the *Fixtures* cases that in this case there was no substantial investment in the obtaining or verifying the contents of a database (see paras 29–41). None of these cases, however, provide any real guidance on the quantum which would be considered 'substantial' in terms of investment because in all of the cases the investment was judged to be minimal.

A number of questions had also been referred to the ECJ in this case about the meaning of 'substantial part' of a database.

Case C-203/02 *British Horseracing Board v William Hill*
European Court of Justice
9 November 2004

68. By its fourth, fifth and sixth questions, the referring court raises the question of the meaning of the terms 'substantial part' and 'insubstantial part' of the contents of a database as used in Article 7 of the Directive. By its first question it also seeks to know whether materials derived from a database do not constitute a part, substantial or otherwise, of that database, where their systematic or methodical arrangement and the conditions of their individual accessibility have been altered by the person carrying out the extraction and/or re-utilisation.

69. In that connection, it must be borne in mind that protection by the *sui generis* right covers databases whose creation required a substantial investment. Against that background, Article 7(1) of the Directive prohibits extraction and/or re-utilisation not only of the whole of a database protected by the *sui generis* right but also of a substantial part, evaluated qualitatively or quantitatively, of its contents. According to the 42nd Recital of the preamble to the directive, that provision is intended to prevent a situation in which a user 'through his acts, causes significant detriment, evaluated qualitatively or quantitatively, to the investment'. It appears from that recital that the assessment, in

---

174 [2001] 2 C.M.L.R. 12 (High Ct), [2002] ECC 24 (CA).

qualitative terms, of whether the part at issue is substantial, must, like the assessment in quantitative terms, refer to the investment in the creation of the database and the prejudice caused to that investment by the act of extracting or re-utilising that part.

70. The expression 'substantial part, evaluated quantitatively', of the contents of a database within the meaning of Article 7(1) of the directive refers to the volume of data extracted from the database and/or re-utilised, and must be assessed in relation to the volume of the contents of the whole of that database. If a user extracts and/or re-utilises a quantitatively significant part of the contents of a database whose creation required the deployment of substantial resources, the investment in the extracted or re-utilised part is, proportionately, equally substantial.

71. The expression 'substantial part, evaluated qualitatively', of the contents of a database refers to the scale of the investment in the obtaining, verification or presentation of the contents of the subject of the act of extraction and/or re-utilisation, regardless of whether that subject represents a quantitatively substantial part of the general contents of the protected database. A quantitatively negligible part of the contents of a database may in fact represent, in terms of obtaining, verification or presentation, significant human, technical or financial investment.

72. It must be added that, as the existence of the *sui generis* right does not, according to the 46th Recital of the preamble to the Directive, give rise to the creation of a new right in the works, data or materials themselves, the intrinsic value of the materials affected by the act of extraction and/or re-utilisation does not constitute a relevant criterion for the assessment of whether the part at issue is substantial.

73. It must be held that any part which does not fulfil the definition of a substantial part, evaluated both quantitatively and qualitatively, falls within the definition of an insubstantial part of the contents of a database.

74. In that regard, it appears from the order for reference that the materials displayed on William Hill's internet sites, which derive from the BHB database, represent only a very small proportion of the whole of that database, as stated in paragraph 19 of this judgment. It must therefore be held that those materials do not constitute a substantial part, evaluated quantitatively, of the contents of that database.

75. According to the order for reference, the information published by William Hill concerns only the following aspects of the BHB database: the names of all the horses running in the race concerned, the date, the time and/or the name of the race and the name of the racecourse, as also stated in paragraph 19 of this judgment.

76. In order to assess whether those materials represent a substantial part, evaluated qualitatively, of the contents of the BHB database, it must be considered whether the human, technical and financial efforts put in by the maker of the database in obtaining, verifying and presenting those data constitute a substantial investment.

77. BHB and Others submit, in that connection, that the data extracted and re-utilised by William Hill are of crucial importance because, without lists of runners, the horse races could not take place. They add that those data represent a significant investment, as demonstrated by the role played by a call centre employing more than 30 operators.

78. However, it must be observed, first, that the intrinsic value of the data affected by the act of extraction and/or re-utilisation does not constitute a relevant criterion for assessing whether the part in question is substantial, evaluated qualitatively. The fact that the data extracted and re-utilised by William Hill are vital to the organisation of the horse races which BHB and Others are responsible for organising is thus irrelevant to the assessment whether the acts of William Hill concern a substantial part of the contents of the BHB database.

79. Next, it must be observed that the resources used for the creation as such of the materials included in a database cannot be taken into account in assessing whether the

investment in the creation of that database was substantial, as stated in paragraphs 31 to 33 of this judgment.

80. The resources deployed by BHB to establish, for the purposes of organising horse races, the date, the time, the place and/or name of the race, and the horses running in it, represent an investment in the creation of materials contained in the BHB database. Consequently, and if, as the order for reference appears to indicate, the materials extracted and re-utilised by William Hill did not require BHB and Others to put in investment independent of the resources required for their creation, it must be held that those materials do not represent a substantial part, in qualitative terms, of the BHB database.

A particularly significant point is that in para 78 above, in which the ECJ rejects the notion that 'substantial part' bears any relation to the intrinsic value of the data. This is important since holding otherwise would be to afford a very wide protection to database owners who could presumably usually argue that the data was valuable to them. The judgment then goes on to discuss the interpretation of 'repeated and systematic extractions of insubstantial parts' and concludes that these will only infringe if they are sufficient to allow the alleged infringer to reconstitute the whole, or a substantial part of the database (paras 86 and 87). In this case, given the size of the BHB database, there was 'no possibility, that through the cumulative effect of its acts, William Hill might reconstitute and make available to the public the whole or a substantial part of the contents of the BHB database' (para 91).

A final point, which had been referred as a question by the Court of Appeal, but remains unresolved by the ECJ decision, is the extent of the term of protection in relation to dynamic databases. Very few databases remain static but are regularly updated in an incremental fashion. What effect does this have on the term of protection? Does each amendment effectively create a new database so that a new term of protection is initiated? If so, that can have the effect of extending the protection for dynamic databases in perpetuity – an ironic result given that the original philosophy behind the database right is to provide a weaker protection for those databases that do not qualify for full copyright protection. Given that the ECJ's decision had the effect of depriving BHB of the benefit of the database right, it did not feel it necessary to answer the Court of Appeal's question on this topic but the matter was discussed by the Advocate General.

British Horseracing Board v William Hill
Opinion of the Advocate General
8 June 2004

146. It is obvious that the new term of protection laid down by Article 10(3) can only relate to a specific object. It is clear from the background to the drafting of this provision that the result of the further investment was meant to enjoy protection. Limiting the object of protection to the resulting database is consistent with the objective of providing for a new term of protection.

147. It should be recalled, here, that the database at issue in these proceedings is what is known as a dynamic database, that is to say, a database which is constantly updated. It must be borne in mind that not only deletions and additions but also, as is clear from the 55th recital, verifications are to be considered changes within the meaning of Article 10(3) of the Directive.

148. It is characteristic of dynamic databases that there is only ever one database, namely the most recent. Previous versions 'disappear'. That raises the question of what the new

term of protection covers, in other words, what the object of protection, that is to say, the new one, is.

149. The point of departure must be the objective of the changes, which is to bring the database up to date. That means that the whole database is the object of the new investment. Thus, the most recent version, that is to say, the whole database, is always the object of protection.

150. The background to the drafting of the Directive also supports that interpretation. Although Article 9 of the original proposal still made provision for extension of the term of protection of a database, in its explanatory statement to the proposal the Commission expressly referred to a new 'edition' of the database. A clarification as regards constantly updated databases was then included in an amended proposal. In the legal definition in Article 12(2)(b) the successive accumulation of small changes typical of dynamic databases is expressly mentioned.

151. Viewed in that light Article 10(3) of the Directive provides for a 'rolling' *sui generis* right.

152. Ultimately, the solution proposed here for dynamic databases reflects the principle that it is always the result, that is to say, the new and not the old database, which is protected. Dynamic databases differ from static databases simply in that, in the case of dynamic databases, the old database ceases to exist because it is constantly transformed into a new one.

153. Further, the fact that in the case of dynamic databases the whole database and not only the changes as such enjoy a new term of protection can, regardless of the objective and subject-matter of the new investment, be justified by the fact that only an assessment of the whole of the database as such is practicable.

154. The objective of protecting investments and of providing an incentive for investment lends further support to the argument for assessment as a whole. In the case of dynamic databases these objectives can only be attained if updates are also covered. Otherwise investment in dynamic databases would be disadvantaged.

Although the logic behind this argument cannot be denied, how easily it sits with the ECJ's generally restrictive interpretation to other provisions of the directive is difficult to assess. Overall the four cases decided at the end of 2004 have curbed what had been seen as the wider excesses of the directive which had the potential to harm the public domain of information and ideas.[175] Although they will certainly not be welcomed by certain database owners they probably represent a more realistic approach to the position of the database right in the general hierarchy of intellectual property rights.

At present, the creation and harmonisation of database rights in the European Union is specific to that jurisdiction and, despite attempts in the US Congress, similar modifications have not yet been adopted elsewhere. Following *Feist* (1991), Lavenue noted the paradoxical impact of the effect of this judgment:

... the US stands at the forefront in the development of computer technology, representing the world leader in the database market. Nevertheless, the US currently recognises no intellectual property protection for the content of databases such as a database right.[176]

175 Lipton, 2003.
176 Lavenue, 1997, p 46.

Nevertheless, recent cases in the US continue to support the *Feist* reasoning.[177] In addition, there have been a number of attempts to legislate in the US including, for instance, attempts to pass the Collections of Information Antipiracy Act and the Consumer and Investor Access to Information Act at the end of the 1990s and, most recently, the Database and Collections of Information Misappropriation Act in 2003,[178] but as yet no legislation has been enacted. There are powerful lobby groups on both sides of the debate and academic opinion over the need for and suggested form of a database right is divided. Thakur concludes that 'a robust global model with an international *sui generis* regime is, undoubtedly, a necessity so as to bring the United States' database industry also under the protective umbrella for an effective stimulation of databases in the global community',[179] whereas Greenbaum warns that 'the United States should not be pressured by the European Union to follow in its unproven protectionist policies'.[180]

A completely different approach has been taken in Australia where, notwithstanding the apparent impact of *Feist* in the common law world, the sweat of the brow test has certainly not been rejected. In *Desktop Marketing Systems Pty Ltd v Telstra Corporation Ltd*,[181] the Federal Court of Australia allowed copyright protection to a database on the basis of 'industrious collection'. The database in question was a purely factual compilation being, as in *Feist*, a public telephone directory produced by Telstra. After an extensive review of relevant case law and a consideration of a number of issues related to originality, the decision was that the overriding concern was whether the work *originated* with the creator rather than being copied.

Desktop Marketing Systems Pty Ltd v Telstra Corporation Ltd
[2002] FCAFC 112
Federal Court of Australia

160 While it is possible to distinguish particular cases on their facts, in my opinion the course of authority in England and Australia examined above supports the following propositions of relevance to the subsistence of copyright in compilations of factual information:

1. The concept of originality is correlative with that of authorship …

2. Authorship (likewise originality) does not require novelty, inventiveness or creativity, whether of thought or expression, or any form of literary merit …

3. Not all works, even literary works, are of the same kind and one must identify and keep in mind the particular kind of work within the Act in which copyright is claimed to exist – in the present case, a particular form of literary work, namely, a 'compilation' …

4. It appears to be a necessary feature of a factual compilation that it supply 'intelligible information' … Accordingly, a totally random collection and listing of unrelated pieces of factual information would not be a compilation within the Act. (Apparently the position would be different if the compilation included a statement that it was a

---

177 See e.g. *Assessment Technologies of WI, LLC v Wiredata Inc* 350 F 3d 640 (7th Cir 2003) and case note by Blanke, 2004.

178 See e.g. Gibson, 2004 and Loy, 2003.

179 Thakur, 2001, p. 130.

180 Greenbaum, 2003, p 501 and see also Edwards 2004.

181 Above fn.155 and see also Strasser, 2002.

random selection, since that very statement would give the whole a significance it would otherwise lack). A telephone directory satisfies the apparent requirement that a compilation convey a significance of its own which is independent of that of its component items considered individually and in isolation from one another. A telephone directory purports to be an alphabetical listing of particulars of all listable telephone subscribers within a given geographical area, and therefore to perform the function of providing access to the telephone number of every subscriber. It impliedly proclaims: 'These are the names, addresses and telephone numbers of all listable subscribers within the stated geographical region, and if a name does not appear in its alphabetical position, there is no listable subscriber by that name'.

5. One must apply the test of originality to the literary work, including a compilation, in which copyright is claimed to exist, as a whole, rather than dissecting it and applying the test to the individual parts …

6. The test of originality is whether the work was not copied, but originated from the putative author …

7. This test is not an 'all or nothing' one but raises a question of fact and degree as to the extent of the putative author's contribution to the making of the particular literary work in question, in the present case, a compilation …

8. For this purpose, no particular kind of antecedent work contributed by the putative author is, a priori, to be left out of account, except, perhaps, antecedent work which was undertaken for a purpose or purposes which did not include the making of the literary work at all …

9. It is not the law that where there is only one way of expressing and arranging a whole-of-universe factual compilation, the compilation cannot attract copyright protection …

10. Decisively for the present case, there is no principle that the labour and expense of collecting, verifying, recording and assembling (albeit routinely) data to be compiled are irrelevant to, or are incapable of themselves establishing, origination, and therefore originality; on the contrary, the authorities strongly suggest that labour of that kind may do so …

161 To recognise copyright in compilations of factual data which do not involve selection or scope for variance in expression or arrangement may be seen, as a practical matter, to be an acceptance of the proposition that copyright can subsist in facts. No doubt policy reasons can be suggested for withholding, as for according, copyright protection in such cases. There are those who point to the advantages of permitting others to build on the first compiler's work, without first having to repeat that work independently. Others point out that to deny the first compiler copyright protection is to discourage research by would-be first compilers. The Act does not provide for the compulsory licensing of copyright for reasonable remuneration in aid of the commercial objectives of a would-be licencee. Accordingly, the situation in cases such as the present under Australian law is an 'all or nothing' one.

162 Consideration has been given to some of the policy issues involved in Europe. In the United Kingdom the Copyright and Rights in Databases Regulations 1997 (SI 1997 No 3032) ('the Regulations'), made pursuant to Directive 96/9/EC of the European Parliament and Council of 11 March 1996 on the Legal Protection of Databases ('the Directive'), has amended the definition of 'literary work' in subs 3(1) of the 1988 UK Act by adding after the word 'compilation', the words 'other than a database', and including and dealing with databases as a special kind of literary work in their own right. … Unlike its United Kingdom counterpart, the Commonwealth Parliament has not amended the legislation to give effect to a policy in respect of the issues raised by the present case.

163 The task of carefully identifying and listing all the units constituting a defined

universe is usefully and commonly, undertaken. Moreover, alphabetical order is a common form of arrangement according to which such lists are made up. There are two special benefits offered by the compiler in such cases. The first is the assurance that the universe has been thoroughly explored, and that all members of it have been captured. 'Whole-of-universe certification' gives value to the list. A compilation which can only profess to have captured 'nearly all' the members of a defined universe is not as valuable as one that can claim to have captured all of them. But whole-of-universe certification is a benefit only if the second special benefit to which I referred is also present: an intelligible arrangement of the data compiled. Who would want a telephone directory containing particulars of all subscribers listed randomly and therefore inaccessibly?

164 The making of accessible whole-of-universe compilations is arguably to be encouraged by the giving of copyright protection on account of the industrious collection, verification, recording and assembly necessarily undertaken for the purpose. But ultimately the weighing of the competing policy considerations is a matter for the legislature.

The above discussion shows that there is a considerable divergence of approaches to the appropriate form of intellectual property protection for factual databases, if indeed such protection is considered desirable at all. The overall situation is summed up in the following extract.

Georger Wei
Telephone Directories and Databases:
The policy at the helm of copyright law and a tale of two cities
[2004] IPQ 316, 362

The debate over the appropriate scope of protection for databases in Europe, the United States and elsewhere reveals many points of difficulty and controversy. First, in respect of copyright, whilst the US Supreme Court has rejected the 'sweat of the brow' approach to originality and databases, a different view has been taken by the Federal Court of Australia. Secondly, in respect of any new database right that might be introduced, there is the ongoing dispute as to the nature of the right that is to be conferred. Proponents of the European model will argue in favour of a strong *sui generis* property right characterised by: ownership, transferability, definite terms of protection, broad exclusive rights and limited defences and exceptions. On the hand, whilst the United States has yet to enact any new database legislation, the experience with the various versions of the Collections of Information Antipiracy Bills demonstrate a preference for a more nebulous right in the nature of an unfair competition remedy. Underlying the debate over a true property right and a lesser right to prevent unfair competition are a broad range of issues such as the nature of the harm (actual or potential) which has to be proven in order to succeed in an infringement action, the range of defendants who might be liable and the scope of defences and exceptions. Whether the international community can come to any consensus as to the approach to be taken and the balance to be achieved within the chosen approach, remains to be seen. What is clear is that a careful consideration of the needs of the database industry and the public at large is essential before any new intellectual property right is introduced. ...

The telephone directories cases lie at the heart of debate over the extent to which databases and other factual compilations are and should be protected by intellectual property rights. Given that the primary vehicle in many common law countries including the United States, Canada and Australia for protecting the effort, labour and expense invested by the compiler in such works is copyright, it is not surprising to find that cases on white and yellow page directories have come to occupy such a prominent position in the debate. Telephone directories, especially white page listings, are amongst the most factual of factual compilations with only, at best, a thin veneer of authorial expression over and above the underlying raw data. Decisions on the copyright status of white and yellow page directories not only reflect the copyright culture of the country, they are searchlights that indicate the extent to which databases and other factual compilations might be protected by copyright law. At the same time, the development of information technology and the information society has greatly magnified the importance of factual works and databases stored in electronic form suitable for use in computer systems. Any country that embraces the information age will recognise the importance of encouraging the development of 'whole-of-universe' primary databases. Around the periphery of such databases the law offers a variety of ways whereby indirect protection is offered to the compiler. Thus, in some cases, contract law, confidential information and trade secrets law and computer program rights may play a role in safeguarding databases. Important though these rights are, primary data compilers are seeking not just peripheral protection but direct protection for the effort, labour and expense invested in the collection, verification and storage of the facts in a user friendly format. Using copyright to achieve this goal inevitably causes problems with the originality requirement and the principle that copyright does not protect underlying basic facts and ideas. A country's response to the question of what is the policy of copyright law strongly informs the approach to be taken on originality. Those countries that are prepared to take a robust approach and to protect industrious collection will find that copyright law confers extensive protection even on the most factual of factual compilations. Those that have rejected industrious collection in favour of a creativity approach will find that copyright protection for whole-of-universe primary databases is rather thin. If copyright does not give adequate protection for industrious collection of facts in a database, the question that then arises is whether *sui generis* database rights should be introduced. If an affirmative answer is forthcoming, the beauty of this approach is that the law-makers will then have an opportunity to craft a fresh balance between rights in the database and exceptions and limitations unfettered by pre-existing principles or provisions in the copyright legislation. Ultimately, what the international community may need is an agreement on the extent to which databases should be protected. Otherwise, there is danger that there may be a proliferation of approaches to database protection: from 'plump' copyright protection under industrious collection, to different forms of *sui generis* database protection all the way through to approaches that offer only 'thin' copyright protection and nothing much else. An information age that embraces the world needs an international solution and perhaps the recent Australian *Telstra* phone directory litigation indicates that the time has come for the WIPO to reinvigorate its attempts to achieve a Treaty on Intellectual Property in Respect of Databases.

CONCLUDING REMARKS

The discussion in this chapter has demonstrated that the unique nature of computer software and the particular products and inventions which it makes possible have created a considerable challenge for intellectual property law. Despite the individual protagonists who champion copyright, patents or *sui generis* rights, it is apparent that, in appropriate situations, all these mechanisms have been, and are being, used to foster and protect exploitation of computer software and products relying on it. Globalisation is a significant feature of the software market and this has forced different jurisdictions, even in the absence of suitable international treaties, to take account of the legal and regulatory activity in other jurisdictions to an unprecedented degree. It should perhaps be no surprise that the needs and requirements of a worldwide market may operate as a more potent force for international harmonisation than intergovernmental co-operation.

CHAPTER 3

PROTECTING AND EXPLOITING RIGHTS
IN SOFTWARE – CONTRACT

INTRODUCTION

Types of contract

There are numerous different types of contract which can relate to computer hardware and software: contracts for the sale or lease of hardware, or of a hardware and software package; contracts licensing software; contracts for the maintenance of hardware or software (which may be called support contracts); distribution agreements between manufacturers and distributors of software or hardware; bureau services contracts, under which one party which has computer hardware and software supplies computer services or facilities to a party which does not have its own hardware or software. These are just some examples of the different types of contract dealing with computer hardware and software. It is not intended here and in Chapter 4 to set out in detail the terms that might occur in each type of contract; rather, these chapters will deal with some of the issues that may arise in relation to contracts concerned with computer software. The focus is on the supply of software or of systems involving both hardware and software. Hardware clearly constitutes goods, and contracts dealing with goods are familiar from other contexts. It is software which poses the significantly different questions. Although the term 'software' can be used to mean anything that is not hardware, it will be used here to mean computer programs unless otherwise indicated. This is the type of software which raises significant issues for information technology law.

Bespoke and standard software

Discussion of contracts dealing with software requires a distinction to be made between different basic types of software. At one end of the spectrum is 'bespoke' software. That is software written for a particular user. At the other end is mass produced software, which is simply bought 'off the shelf' by many users. Somewhere in between will be modified standard software, for which the basic program will be the same in each case, but it will then be modified to some extent to meet the needs of the individual user. This division may be relevant, for example, in considering whether a contract for the supply of software should be regarded as a contract for the sale of goods or the supply of services (or something else).

The software licence[1]

When computers first began to be sold, the software was merely something that came with them. It simply was not seen as something to be separately exploited. The focus

---

1   Freed, 1982; 1986; 1990–91, p 155; (1992).

was on the hardware. It was in the early 1970s that serious consideration began to be given to software as a resource to be protected and exploited, and the practice grew up of using licences to do so. The licence would set out what the acquirer could, and could not, do with the software. Despite initial uncertainly, it became clear that licensing does, indeed, provide an appropriate approach to the exploitation of software. With the recognition that copyright can exist in software,[2] the licence has become the vehicle by which the acquirer is given rights to use the software. In so doing, it provides the means by which those who develop software can recoup the large costs of that development, make a profit, and encourage further development.

There are difficulties in licensing software when the developer does not deal directly with the end user and, with the trend away from bespoke to 'off the shelf' software, this has become a common situation. If the end user does not deal with the developer, how is his or her use to be licensed? There may be a chain of contracts. The end user may be a sub-licensee of a distributor who obtained a licence from the developer – the distributor's licence, including the right to create sub-licenses. However, the mass production of standard software has posed its own legal difficulties. How are licenses to be 'mass produced' when someone can acquire software simply by walking into a shop, selecting software from a display and paying for it at a till? The attempt to create licenses in this type of case by means of what has been called the 'shrink wrap' licence will be returned to below (see p 113).

Goods or services or something else?

One problem which is of particular conceptual and practical significance is the legal nature of software. Obviously, a program is, basically information and is protected by intellectual property rights in the form of copyright. However, could software also be regarded as 'goods'? Should the supply of software be regarded as a service? On a practical level, these questions arise in the context of the applicability of legislation such as the Sale of Goods Act (SGA) 1979, the Supply of Goods and Services Act 1982 and the Commercial Agents (Council Directive) Regulations 1993. The issue of classification will be returned to in Chapter 4, which addresses the question of liability for defective software.

Scope of the chapter

Two chapters in a book on information technology law cannot deal in depth with all aspects of contract law. Instead, the discussion here will focus on some aspects of contract law that are particularly relevant in the context of software transactions. As the title implies, this chapter deals with the licensing of software and related issues. Chapter 4 deals with the issues around the suitability/quality of the software.

---

2   See, now, CDPA 1988, ss 1, 3.

TERMS

When software is in question, some of the most significant terms will be those licensing its use. (Licence terms will be considered below.) First, we should briefly consider sources of contractual terms, although pre-contractual statements becoming terms will be looked at below in relation to the quality/functionality of the software.

If the relevant party signed a contractual document, its contents will provide contractual terms, whether he or she has any knowledge of them or not.[3] If such a document is not signed, then, in the absence of actual knowledge of its contents, its effectiveness to import terms into the contract will depend upon whether there has been reasonably sufficient notice of it.[4] That is an objective test, requiring sufficient notice for the reasonable person, rather than the particular individual concerned.[5] Even if clauses have not been appropriately introduced into a particular transaction, they may be imported if there has previously been a consistent course of dealings between the parties, involving those terms.[6] There is a considerable degree of artificiality in the way in which clauses can become terms of a contract. It means that written contractual terms, particularly standard terms, may be seen as having very little to do with the agreement of the parties in any subjective sense.

Contract terms may be implied[7] as well as express. They may be implied by statute, as, for example, with the terms implied by ss 13–15 of the SGA 1979, which are considered in Chapter 4. Otherwise, at common law, they may be implied in fact, in law or by custom. Terms are implied in fact on the basis of the parties' intention, but within very narrow confines. The tests applied are whether it is necessary to imply the term to give the contract 'business efficacy'[8] and also the 'officious bystander' test, that is, whether the term was so obvious that, had an officious bystander approached the contracting parties and suggested it, they would have said that of course the term in question was included.[9] The implication of terms in law is not based on the intention of the parties, but upon necessity and the type of contract;[10] that is, the term must be one which it is 'necessary' to imply into the type of contract in question. Intention is relevant only to the extent that a term will not be implied in the face of a contrary term.[11]

---

3   *L'Estrange v F Graucob Ltd* [1934] 2 KB 394. There are limited exceptions. If the content of the terms has been misrepresented, then the part misrepresented will not be enforced (*Curtis v Chemical Cleaning and Dyeing Co* [1951] 1 KB 805). Signed terms are also subject to a claim of *non est factum*.

4   *Parker v South Eastern Rly Co Ltd* (1877) 2 CPD 416. See, generally, Koffman and Macdonald, 2004, pp 141–48. See further, below, p 114.

5   *Thompson v LM & S Rly* [1930] 1 KB 41.

6   See, eg, *Kendall v Lillico & Sons* [1969] 2 AC 31; *Circle Freight International v Medeast Gulf Exports* [1988] 2 Lloyd's Rep 427. See, generally, Macdonald, 1988; Koffman and Macdonald, 2004, paras 9.25–9.38.

7   See, generally, Koffman and Macdonald 2004, paras 7.26–7.50.

8   *The Moorcock* (1889) 14 PD 64.

9   *Shirlaw v Southern Foundries Ltd* [1939] 2 KB 206, p 227, *per* Mackinnon LJ.

10   *Liverpool CC v Irwin* [1976] 2 All ER 39.

11   *Johnstone v Bloomsbury HA* [1991] 2 All ER 293 – the Court of Appeal indicated that an express contrary term might be treated as an exclusion clause falling within UCTA 1977 in appropriate circumstances (see Macdonald, 1992).

The final issue to be addressed here is the question of the interpretation, or construction, of the contract. Obviously, once the terms have been established, the interpretation of the contract has to be ascertained. The objective when construing or interpreting a contract is that of determining the parties' intention, objectively ascertained. Traditionally, there has been an overwhelming emphasis upon the written words used and a restrictive approach to what further evidence of the parties' intention could be considered. However, in *Investors Compensation Scheme Ltd v West Bromwich Building Society*,[12] the House of Lords took the view that a 'fundamental change ... has overtaken this branch of the law' and that the result has largely been:[13]

> to assimilate the way in which such documents are interpreted by judges to the common sense principles by which any serious utterance would be interpreted in ordinary life. Almost all the old intellectual baggage of interpretation has been discarded.

Lord Hoffmann provided a summary of principles, which is now frequently referred to by the courts. He said:[14]

> (1) Interpretation is the ascertainment of the meaning which the document would convey to a reasonable person having all the background knowledge which would reasonably have been available to the parties in the situation in which they were at the time of the contract.

> (2) The background was famously referred to by Lord Wilberforce as the 'matrix of fact', but this phrase is if anything an understated description of what the background may include. Subject to the requirement that it should have been reasonably available to the parties and to the exception mentioned next, it includes absolutely anything which would have affected the way in which the language of the document would have been understood by a reasonable man.

> (3) The law excludes from the admissible background the previous negotiations of the parties and their declarations of subjective intent. They are admissible only in an action for rectification. The law makes this distinction for reasons of practical policy and, in this respect only, legal interpretation differs from the way we would interpret utterances in ordinary life ...

> (4) The meaning which a document (or any other utterance) would convey to a reasonable man is not the same thing as the meaning of its words. The meaning of words is a matter of dictionaries and grammars; the meaning of the document is what the parties using those words against the relevant background would reasonably have been understood to mean. The background may not merely enable the reasonable man to choose between the possible meanings of words which are ambiguous but even (as occasionally happens in ordinary life) to conclude that the parties must, for whatever reason, have used the wrong words or syntax (see *Mannai Investments Co Ltd v Eagle Star Life Ass Co Ltd* [1997] 3 All ER 352) ...

> (5) The 'rule' that words should be given their 'natural and ordinary meaning' reflects the commonsense proposition that we do not easily accept that people

12 [1998] 1 All ER 98
13 *Ibid* at p 114.
14 *Ibid*.

have made linguistic mistakes, particularly in formal documents. On the other hand, if one would nevertheless conclude from the background that something must have gone wrong with the language, the law does not require judges to attribute to the parties an intention which they plainly could not have had.

COPYRIGHT OWNERSHIP

When software is acquired, the copyright interest in it is not usually acquired as well, merely a right to use it under the terms of a licence. However, there will be some cases in which the acquirer also acquires the copyright . This might happen in relation to software which the acquirer commissioned the developer to devise for him or her. The desirability of copyright ownership for both such parties is put in context by Chappatte.

Specific problems in the licensing of software
Philip Chappatte
(1995) 11 CL& P 16

The ownership of software is not normally an issue in commercial transactions except where one person (the software house) has agreed to develop application software for another (the user) involving either the developing of a complete software system or developing additions and improvements or adaptations to an existing system.

Let us take an example. If a manufacturer of heavy machinery asks a software house to develop application software to suit its specific needs and business environment, the software house may be able to suggest a standard software package which is 30 or 40 per cent fit for the user's requirements. The rest of the software system will have to be specifically developed by the software house for the user.

Benefits of ownership for user

The user may acquire substantial benefits by obtaining ownership. I will mention three benefits:

(i)   the user will be able to avoid all restrictions on use and transferability and the problems associated with a revocable licence if he acquires ownership;

(ii) if the software house uses the whole or part of the software developed for the user for the benefit of other persons, the user may be able to extract royalties from the software house for subsequent use and sub-licenses;

(iii) ownership of the software means control over software. What can often be the most important benefit for the user is that ownership will enable the user to ensure that none of his competitors will be able to obtain the right to use the software developed for him.

Disadvantages for the software house

If the user acquires proprietary rights, the software house will obviously lose the corresponding benefits acquired by the user. For example, the software house will not freely be able to use certain software routines developed for the user in our example for the benefit of another person or to incorporate those routines in one of its standard software packages. But the software house may also face real practical difficulties if a user does acquire proprietary rights.

It may be administratively burdensome for the software house to develop an internal register dividing software it has developed in which it has a proprietary right and other software it has developed owned by its customers. It may be difficult for the software house to prevent its programmers and designers from drawing on their previous experience which may unwittingly involve the copying of customised software developed for and owned by a particular user.

THE LICENCE

Licence terms

The software licence will deal with such matters as:

- to whom the licence is granted;
- the equipment on which, and location at which, it may be used;
- the use to which the software can be put[15] (for example, sub-licensing is usually forbidden);
- whether the source code or object code is supplied (normally, the acquirer only receives the object code);
- whether the licence is exclusive or non-exclusive (normally, it will be non-exclusive, unless it is being granted to a distributor who is to exploit the software through sub-licensing it);
- whether the licensee can transfer the licence;[16]
- the duration of the licence, which may be for a fixed or indefinite period. It will normally state that it is to terminate on the occurrence of certain breaches by the licensee or on the licensee's insolvency;[17]
- confidentiality – the licence may state that the 'software' is confidential information which should not be disclosed, if the licensor is attempting to gain the protection afforded to such information;
- exemption clauses – the licensor will insert an exemption clause in an attempt to exclude or restrict any liability he or she might incur to the licensee.

The effectiveness of exemption clauses must be considered in the light of the Unfair Contract Terms Act (UCTA) 1977, which is considered below (see p 187). In addition, the Unfair Terms in Consumer Contracts Regulations 1999 will subject to a test of 'fairness' many non-individually negotiated terms in contracts between sellers or suppliers and consumers. The Regulations are also considered below.[18] Here some

---

15 Defining the use rendered 'lawful' by the licence may be particularly important in the light of the CDPA 1988, s 50C, which bases its limited 'right' to, eg, copy, adapt or correct errors in software on what is necessary for the software's 'lawful' use.

16 The copyright holder may wish to prevent a licence from being transferred to a rival.

17 Such termination has serious potential consequences for a licensee whose business is organised around the use of the software. The purchaser of such a business may require a check to see that the relevant software licenses have not been infringed.

18 SI 1999/2083; see p 203.

further consideration should be given to the importance of the source code and the recognition of its significance by the courts.

SOURCE CODE

As has been indicated, the licence will normally include a term dealing with whether the acquirer is entitled to the object code or the source code and usually it will merely be the object code. Some further consideration should be given to the difference between them, the significance of which is available to the acquirer, and the courts' recognition of the importance of the source code under certain circumstances.

First, the basic distinction between source code and object code should be made. They have been defined as:[19]

> 'Source code' may be defined as a version of the program using alphanumeric symbols, which cannot be processed directly by a computer without first being 'translated' (or 'compiled') into a machine-readable form. 'Object code' is the machine readable form of that program which essentially comprises a long series of ones and zeroes, corresponding to the complex 'on-off' instructions used to process data.

As it stands, the object code is not really intelligible to human beings. The source code is used to write the program and, essentially, it is needed if any bugs are to be corrected or improvements made. Obviously, the acquirer of the program would prefer to have a licence which extends not only to the object code but to the source code, but the supplier will want to maintain control of the source code to prevent the program information from becoming known. The most likely form of arrangement which the acquirer might achieve to provide access to the source code in limited circumstances is an escrow arrangement:

> whereby the supplier agrees to deposit a copy of the source code with an independent third party (the escrow agent) and then the supplier, customer and escrow agent enter into a tripartite arrangement to govern its release. The escrow arrangement will provide for the initial deposit of the of the source code, and for its updating with error correction and new releases. On the happening of certain specified events (for example, such as the supplier going into liquidation, or failing to provide maintenance services as contracted for), the escrow agent will release the source code to the customer for the purposes of maintaining the software.[20]

The courts have recognised the significance of the source code. They have shown some willingness to interpret the contract, or imply terms to allow the acquirer to use the source code in circumstances where it is necessary to make the contract commercially viable.[21]

In *Saphena Computing Ltd v Allied Collection Agencies*,[22] the availability and use of source codes for error correction was considered. The case was concerned with an

---

19 Reed and Angel, 2003, para 1.4.2.2.

20 *Ibid.*

21 But see *Mars Uk v Teknowledge Ltd* [2000] FSR 138.

22 [1995] FSR 636.

attempt to provide an 'online' computer system for a debt collecting agency. The plaintiff suppliers experienced difficulties in trying to make the software function as required. The time they spent in attempting to deal with the problems eventually led the defendant acquirers to agree to a termination of the contract. They then called in a third party to deal with the problems. The particular point which needs to be considered here is the question of whether the defendants were entitled to possession of the source code, and in order to remedy the defects in the software. Havery QC (Official Receiver) considered the question in general terms under the original supply agreement and in the more specific situation of the agreement to terminate an incomplete supply contract. In general, he thought there was no right to the source code but he was prepared to imply a term to give business efficacy to the termination agreement (on applied terms see above p 103).

Saphena Computing Ltd v Allied Collection Agencies
[1995] FSR 636

[The] fact that source programs remain the property of the plaintiffs must entail two propositions: first, that once the plaintiffs have completed the supply of the software that has been agreed to be supplied, that is, the object programs, they are entitled to remove the source program from the defendants computer. The only way of doing that is by deleting them. Secondly, it entails that the defendants are not entitled to copy the source programs if they do remain in their possession, since the source programs remain the property of the plaintiffs ... and no licence is granted for their reproduction or adaptation.

In my judgment, this conclusion is not affected by the decision in *British Leyland Motor Corp Ltd v Armstrong Patents Co Ltd* [1986] AC 577. The factual basis of that case was that during its expected lifetime a car supplied by the plaintiffs and originally fit for its purpose would require, in order to continue to be fit for its purpose, to have its exhaust pipe replaced by a new one, the manufacture of which would involve the reproduction of the plaintiff's copyright drawings. The ultimate purchaser would have no remedy against the person who supplied the car to him or against anyone else (subject, no doubt, to competition law) if he, the purchaser, could obtain no replacement exhaust pipe.

In the present case, on the other hand, once the software is fit for its purpose, it stays fit for its purpose. If by any chance a flaw is discovered showing that it is unfit for its purpose (which is hardly likely after prolonged use) there is a remedy in damages against the supplier, if solvent, until the expiry of the period of limitation. It may well nevertheless be that the effect of *British Leyland* is that if the software supplied by the plaintiffs to the defendants in the present case turns out to be unfit for its purpose, and the defendants at the time have access to the source code, the plaintiffs cannot restrain reproduction of the source code for the purpose of rendering the software fit for its purpose. But that does not mean either that the defendants can retain the source code against that eventuality, or that they are entitled to require the plaintiffs to supply it to them in that event.

... In the present case, I am satisfied from the evidence ... that at any rate in the case of ready written programs, unlike the case of motor cars, the purchaser is not normally in a position, and therefore cannot reasonably expect, either to repair them or improve them. The factual basis for restricting what would otherwise be the plaintiff's rights in their source code does not therefore exist.

But the position so far as completion of the software originally agreed to be supplied ... is different. At the time that the relationship came to an end, the plaintiff was in the course of ... removing bugs from it in order to make it fit for the purposes communicated to the plaintiff ... It was not entirely fit for those purposes on [the termination date]. In my judgment, it cannot reasonably be held to have been the intention of [the defendants] and [the plaintiffs] when they determined their business relationship, that the software should remain with its bugs and though usable, not entirely fit for the purposes I have mentioned. Although [the plaintiff] was no longer to be involved, it must, in my judgment, have been implicit that he would let the defendants have the use of the source programs which were necessary to put the software into a state where it was fit for those purposes. It was indeed accepted by counsel for the plaintiffs that the defendants were entitled to reproduce source programs for that purpose ...

... the defendants would be entitled to copy the source programs to the extent necessary to complete the software ... to make it reasonably fit for the purposes specified ... In my judgment implied terms to that effect are necessary to give business efficacy to the agreement to bring the relationship between the parties to an end.

(If the source program is available to the acquirer, s 50C(2) of the Copyright, Designs and Patents Act 1988 will now be relevant to the question of whether it can be copied in order to correct errors. See further below.)

There are indications of willingness to go somewhat further to make the contract workable in *Psychometric Services v Merant*,[23] in that what was in question there was ordering the supply of the source code to the acquirer. The case was again concerned with a problem caused by uncompleted software. The acquirer was arguing that the supplier was in breach and that it wanted to have the software completed by someone else. Laddie J only had to consider whether as a matter of interim relief, to order the supply of the source code to the acquirer. (The dire financial situation of the acquirer if the program was not swiftly made to function pointed to such relief.) However, what is of interest are the indications of his willingness to interpret the contract so as to find an entitlement to the source code by the acquirer. He found an express term which 'strongly supports PSL's claim to the source code',[24] and he had already pointed out that, in any event, had everything happened as it should have done under the contract, the 'loyalty period' of maintenance by the supplier needed only to last for two years (and might even have been shorter in some circumstances). At the end of that period, if the acquirer was not entitled to the source code 'none of the inevitable bugs [would] be able to be fixed. No development [would] be possible'.[25] Laddie J made the point that the suppliers did not 'dissent strongly' from the proposition that, if that was correct, 'the agreement made no commercial sense at all'.[26] (There is an impetus to interpret contract terms in a way that makes good commercial sense[27] and against a construction which achieves an unreasonable result. The 'more unreasonable the result the more unlikely it is that the parties can have intended it, and if they do intend it the more necessary it is that they [should] make that intention abundantly clear'.[28])

23   [2002] FSR 8.
24   At [37].
25   At [36].
26   At [36].
27   *Antaios Cia Naviera SA* v *Salen Rederierna AB* [1985] AC 191, 221.
28   *Schuler v Wickman Machine Tools* [1974] AC 235, 251.

EC DIRECTIVE

Basic use of software

It is generally said that using software will be in breach of copyright unless the user has a licence. This is because its use almost inevitably requires it to be copied onto hardware and, in the absence of a licence, such copying has generally been said to entail a breach of copyright.[29] However, what must be considered is the effect on this of Art 5(1) of the EC Directive on the Protection of Computer Programs. This might be seen as providing the acquirer with a right to make the copy required for the basic use of software.

Article 5(1) states:

> In the absence of specific contractual provisions, the acts referred to in Article 4(a) and (b) shall not require authorisation by the rightholder where they are necessary for the use of the computer program by the lawful acquirer in accordance with its intended purpose, including for error correction.

The 'acts' referred to in Art 4(a) and (b) are, *inter alia*, the 'permanent or temporary reproduction of computer programs' and 'the translation, adaptation, arrangement and any other alteration of a computer program and the reproduction thereof'. This means that the Directive might be seen as providing the right to make the copy of software which its basic use requires. However, any such right would be limited and it would seem that the copyright owner could prevent any such right from being acquired by including an express contrary term.

Article 5(1) is reflected in what is now s 50C of the Copyright, Designs and Patents Act (CDPA) 1988, which states:

(1) It is not an infringement of copyright for the lawful user of a copy of a computer program to copy or adapt it, provided that the copying or adapting–

    (a) is necessary for his lawful use; and

    (b) is not prohibited under any term or condition of an agreement under which his use is lawful.

(2) It may, in particular, be necessary for the lawful use of a computer program to copy or adapt it for the purpose of correcting errors in it ... [30]

It should be noted that the section seems generally restrictive of any notion of a right to make basic use of software. There is an important difference to be noted between the Directive's references to 'lawful acquirer' and use of the software in accordance with its 'intended purpose', and the statutory references to 'lawful user' and 'lawful use'. It would seem that someone might well be argued to be a 'lawful acquirer' although they lacked the rights to make them a 'lawful user' (the same point can be made in relation to 'lawful use' and 'intended purpose' ('lawful user' is defined in s 50A(2)). *Prima facie*, the person who purchases software in a shop should be regarded as a

---

29   See CDPA 1988, s 17(1), (2), (6).

30   It should be noted that s 50C would require a contrary contract term. If the Directive is construed so that there is no right under Art 5(1) where there is a contrary agreement, it does not seem to require any such agreement to be contractual.

'lawful acquirer' but, on any natural meaning of the words, it seems doubtful that they can be registered as a 'lawful user' unless they have an effective licence. However, whatever the natural meaning of the words, the Act is an implementation of an EC measure and should be construed so as to achieve that implementation – 'lawful user' may here be understood as 'lawful acquirer'.

Back-up copies

Making back-up copies of software is commonly regarded as sound practice. A disk can be affected, and the program corrupted by a number of factors, such as a faulty disk drive, heat or an electro-magnetic field. Some copyright holders even put instructions in the manual that, before the software is put to any other use, it should be copied and a copy put in a safe place, to be used in the event of the other becoming corrupted. However, some copyright holders do not want any copies of this type made, perhaps for security reasons. Consideration should now be given to s 50A of the 1988 Act, which states that it is not an infringement of copyright for a 'lawful user' of a copy of a computer program to make any back-up copy of it 'which it is necessary for him to have for the purposes of his lawful use' (s 50A(1)). This 'right' to make a necessary back-up copy cannot be removed by any contrary agreement. Section 50A(3) states that, where an act is permitted by the section, 'it is irrelevant whether or not there exists any term or condition in an agreement which purports to prohibit or restrict the act'. Any such term is void under s 296A.

Section 50A is based on Art 5(2). Both are of limited scope. The right to make a back-up copy, irrespective of contrary agreement, is limited to cases where it is 'necessary' to make such a copy. If 'necessary' is strictly construed, this would be of very limited application. In most cases, a back-up copy will be highly desirable, but not strictly necessary , in the sense of 'essential to', the actual use of the program. However, 'necessary' may be understood in its context. In a commercial context, it might be taken to mean 'necessary' for the commercial use of the software. It might then be found that having a readily accessible back-up copy would often be necessary for its commercial use, the business user effectively being unable to use it if it could become unavailable to him, or her, for a time, through corruption of the disk, for example. The latter type of approach to necessity was obviously envisaged by Susan Singleton in her consideration of how a copyright holder who wished to avoid back-up copies being made might redraft his or her licenses appropriately.

Computer software agreements and the
implementation of the EC Directive
Susan Singleton
(1993) 9 CL & P 50

Although many licenses do permit the making of back-up copies, in which case there is no need to amend licence provisions, some companies do not want a back-up copy [to be made] for security or other reasons. Indeed, they may make devices on the software which prevent the making of a back-up copy. How are they affected by the new law? If it is necessary for the user to make a back-up copy for his lawful use then he is allowed to do so and any condition prohibiting it is void. There are no restrictions on placing copyright protection devices on software. Those wanting to restrict copying can continue to use such devices ...

The question will be 'what is necessary?'. Licensors should consider adding words such as the following, provided they reflect the true facts:

> The licensor has available a 24 hour service for the provision of duplicate software to that licensed under this agreement in the event that the licensee requires a back-up copy, whether through total destruction of the software licensed, or its corruption. Given such availability there is no necessity for the licensee to have a right to make such copies of the software for any purpose, including without prejudice to the foregoing generality, for back-up purposes and therefore such right is prohibited in accordance with the provisions of section 50A of the Copyright, Design and Patents Act 1988.

If 24-hour facilities cannot be provided then a copy could be made available to a bank or other organisation under terms providing for release of the program when designated disaster circumstances arise.

Error correction

Error correction will normally require the use of the source code, rather than merely the object code. It will not normally be undertaken by the acquirer of software. In particular, a maintenance agreement will often be made in relation to software, coming into effect once acceptance has occurred and encompassing error correction.[31] The question may arise as to whether the error in question amounts to a breach of the supply contract and that will depend upon the express and implied terms of that contract (see Chapter 4).

However, the point which should be focused on here is whether the acquirer can correct errors in the software. This question is affected by the EC Directive and what is now s 50C of the CDPA 1988. Article 5 of the Directive includes 'error correction' within the acts which are not in breach of copyright when they are necessary for the intended purpose of a program.[32] Similarly, s 50C states that, subject to contrary agreement, the copying or adapting which is necessary for the lawful use of a program is not a breach of copyright. Section 50C(2) makes it clear that 'it may, in particular, be necessary for the lawful use of a computer program to copy or adapt it for the purpose of correcting errors in it'. Some of the difficulties in interpreting these provisions were outlined above. It should be noted that, whatever the extent of the 'right' conferred by the Directive, it is not the acquirer's 'right' to have errors corrected; he or she can merely correct them without being in breach of copyright. In addition, it would seem that there is no obligation, in these provisions, on the seller to supply the source code, which is generally needed for error correction. The contractual obligation is normally

---

31 There will be difficulties for the acquirer of software if access to the source code for necessary error correction is denied because the copyright holder becomes insolvent or otherwise ceases to function. To deal with these situations, 'source code escrow' is sometimes used; ie, the source code is held by a third party, to be released to the acquirer on the happening of certain specified events, such as the copyright holder's insolvency. There may, however, be difficulties with this under insolvency law.

32 It has been argued to the contrary that, on its wording, Art 5(1) does not only encompass error correction which is necessary for the intended purpose of the program, but rather treats error correction as an intended purpose: see Sherwood-Edwards, 1993.

only to supply the object code, but it may provide for the supply of the source code. The Directive and the legislation would not seem to make the source code, as such, available to any greater extent to the acquirer.

THE 'SHRINK WRAP' LICENCE[33]

Software may be acquired via the web, directly from the copyright holder. In such a situation, there is obviously no difficulty in creating a contractual licence for the acquirer of the software – all that is required is that the licence terms appear appropriately on the website for them to be incorporated (see p 103). However, the more common situation is for the end user to acquire the software from a supplier who is not the copyright holder. This raises the issue of the creation of the licence, which has been termed the 'shrink wrap' licence problem.

The problem of the effectiveness of the shrink wrap licence can be epitomised by the purchase of software 'off the shelf' from a shop. The purchaser will take his or her newly-acquired software home, open the box and discover that it is contained in an envelope, on which it is stated that opening the envelope constitutes acceptance of the copyright holder's licence terms. (These are also included in the box.) Alternatively, on starting to use the software, the acquirer may discover an on screen message stating that the software cannot be used unless there is an agreement to licence terms by 'clicking' on a button (if the acquirer is online, that may generate a message to the copyright holder). This is referred to as 'click wrap'. Whatever form it takes, the statement on screen or on the box may also state that, if the purchaser does not want to accept the licence terms, the software may be returned to the shop from which it was purchased for a full refund.[34]

There are numerous variations on the fact situation indicated above. The packaging arrangements may vary, but all raise the same type of issues. It may also be that the software is not acquired from a shop but by mail or telephone order. The software may also be downloaded from the web, from a supplier's website, and a form of 'click wrap' will then be in question. Again, many of the same issues arise as under the above fact situation. Primary consideration will be given to the purchase in a shop, with comments on other situations where that is required. The basic question in each situation is whether the shrink wrap licence is effective, and there are two basic possibilities to consider.[35] It might be argued that it is part of the contract made between the supplier, S, and the acquirer, A, for the acquisition of the software (that is, the supply in the shop), or part of a contract formed, between A and the copyright holder, C, when the envelope is opened.

33 See, generally, Lemley, 1995; Millard, 1988; Smith, 1986.
34 There may be difficulties in finding that the supplier is under an obligation to the acquirer to take back the software and return the price paid – see below, p 117.
35 A third possibility, combining elements of the two considered, was arrived at in the Scottish court in *Beta Computers (Europe) Ltd v Adobe Systems (Europe) Ltd* [1996] FSR 371.

Acquisition contract

In considering the acquisition of software from a shop, the first point to consider is whom the acquirer, A, contracts with. *Prima facie*, at that stage, there is simply a contract between the shop, S, and A. The transaction certainly looks like a simple sale of the software by S to A. On this basis, two issues need to be addressed: first, the timing of the introduction of the licence terms; and, secondly, the fact that the copyright holder, C, is a third party to the acquisition contract.

The first point to be made is simply that new terms cannot be introduced into a contract, once it has been made.[36] If the licence terms are not introduced into the transaction until after the contract in the shop has been made, they cannot be part of the contract between A and S.

Contract formation is normally analysed in terms of offer and acceptance. An offer expresses a willingness to be contractually bound by certain terms,[37] if the other party accepts them. An acceptance occurs when the other party agrees to the same terms.[38] In a shop, the offer is normally made by the customer when the goods are taken to the till, and it is accepted by the assistant.[39] If the existence of licence terms does not become apparent until after the box has been opened, and that does not take place before offer and acceptance have occurred, obviously, they have been introduced after the contract was made, and cannot be part of it. This was recognised in the Scottish case of *Beta Computers (Europe) Ltd v Adobe Systems (Europe) Ltd*.[40] The same point can also be made in relation to the mail order, or telephone order, of software. In those cases, the contract will normally be made when the acquirer's order (the offer) is accepted by dispatch of the goods (in the case of mail order) or by express acceptance on the telephone, in the case of a telephone order. If not even the existence of the licence was indicated prior to A's opening of the box, it cannot form part of the contract terms and a similar point can be made in relation to web-based order and delivery.

The situation also has to be considered in which the licence terms are referred to on the outside of the box[41] (or on the website, when that is where the software is acquired). Clauses may be incorporated into contracts from unsigned documents on the basis of reasonably sufficient notice.[42] It should also be noted that incorporation by

---

36 *Olley v Marlborough Court Hotel* [1949] 1 KB 532; *Thornton v Shoe Lane Parking* [1971] 2 QB 163.
37 See, eg, *Gibson v Manchester CC* [1979] 1 WLR 294.
38 *Jones v Daniel* [1894] 2 Ch 332.
39 *Pharmaceutical Society of Great Britain v Boots Cash Chemists* [1953] 1 QB 401.
40 [1996] FSR 371; see below, p 117.
41 This fact seems to have been emphasised by the US court in *ProCD v Zeidenberg* No 96-1139 (US Ct App 7th Cir) 20 June 1996. See below, p 118.
42 *Parker v South Eastern Rly Co* (1877) 2 CPD 416. The 'red hand rule' has been added to this, so that the more unreasonable or unusual a clause, the greater the degree of notice required to provide reasonably sufficient notice – *Thornton v Shoe Lane Parking* [1971] 1 QB 163; *Interfoto Picture Library v Stiletto Visual Programmes* [1988] 1 All ER 348. (The name of the rule stems from a famous *dictum* of Denning LJ, as he then was, in *Spurling v Bradshaw* [1956] 1 WLR 461. He said (p 461): 'The more unreasonable a clause is, the greater the notice which must be given of it. Some clauses which I have seen would need to be printed in red ink on the face of the document with a red hand pointing to [them] before the notice could be held to be sufficient.') On incorporation by notice generally, see Koffman and Macdonald, 2004, pp 141–48.

reference is possible, that is, the document providing notice does not have to contain the terms but can merely refer to where they can be found.[43] The test is objective[44] and whether incorporation by notice occurs is basically[45] a question of fact in each case,[46] dependent upon such matters as the legibility and prominence of the relevant writing. One factor which has been seen as relevant to the test generally is whether the place where the notice is to be found is the type of place in which the reasonable person would expect to find a contractual term. One reason why the clause on the deck chair ticket in *Chapelton v Barry UDC*[47] did not provide reasonably sufficient notice of an exemption clause was that the ticket was seen as something which the reasonable person would view merely as a method of proving that the deck chair hire charge had been paid, rather than as a document containing contract terms. One question is whether people normally expect to find contract terms referred to on the back of a box containing software. The size and position of any such notice on the box would also be relevant and it would, for example, be ineffective if the shop had stuck a price tag, or some other label, over it.[48] It should be easier for such incorporation to take place as acquirers, in general, begin to assume that the acquisition of software will involve licence terms.[49]

However, if the licence is incorporated into the contract between S and A, the fact that C is a third party to that agreement must now be considered. Traditionally, the response in English law would have been that incorporation of the licence into the contract between A and S could not assist C. Traditionally, the doctrine of privity of contract would not have allowed a third party, C, to enforce contract terms, even if they were for the third party's benefit. However, privity has now been considerably modified by the Contracts (Rights of Third Parties) Act 1999. Basically, a third party may now enforce a term of the contract if either (a) 'the contract expressly provides that he may', or (b) 'the term purports to confer a benefit on him' and it does not appear that the parties did not intend the term to be enforceable by the third party.[50] The overall effect of this would seem to be that if the licence terms are appropriately drafted (and they are drafted by C), then A will indirectly acquire a licence to use the software (through a chain from C, via S, to A) and C will have a right to enforce the licence terms, which can be regarded as providing him or her with a benefit. (The benefit of the protection of an exemption clause is expressly recognised as falling

---

43   *Thompson v LM & S Rly* [1930] 1 KB 41. It would seem that a copy of the terms should be accessible before A contracts.

44   In *ibid, Thompson,* it was indicated that it was irrelevant that the passenger in question was illiterate. The reasonable person was to be presumed to be able to read English. The situation would be otherwise where the party seeking to incorporate the terms knew, or should, as a reasonable person, have known that the other party, or the group to which he or she belongs, was in some way less able to read or understand the notice (*Richardson, Spence & Co v Rowntree* [1894] AC 217; *Geier v Kujawa, Weston and Warne Bros (Transport)* [1970] 1 Lloyd's Rep 364).

45   But note the 'red hand rule' (above, fn 42).

46   *Hood v Anchor Line* [1918] AC 837, p 834.

47   [1940] 1 KB 532.

48   *Sugar v LM & S Rly* [1941] 1 All ER 172.

49   *Alexander v Rly Executive* [1951] 2 KB 882, p 886.

50   Section 1.

within the 1999 Act.)[51] An analogy might be made with the Scottish case of *Beta v Adobe*,[52] where, under Scottish law, the court did not have to contend with the privity rule and a third party could gain the benefit of a contract under the doctrine of *ius quaesitum tertio*.

Opening the envelope

The second possibility to consider is that of a second contract, separate from the acquisition contract, made when A opens the packet or clicks on the button on screen. The argument would be that the offer is made by C and A accepts by performing the stated act of opening the envelope. Acceptance of an offer normally requires communication, and communication may occur in the click wrap situation if the acquirer is online, but it is possible to have acceptance by conduct.[53] However, that conduct would have to be unequivocal and another explanation of the opening of the envelope may be possible. It could be argued that A may not be responding to C's offer of a licence, but, rather, that he or she is exercising a right already acquired. The contention would be that, at the time that the software was acquired from S, A also acquired certain basic rights to use it. Such rights might stem from the legislation implementing the EC Directive on the Protection of Computer Programs, from a common law licence, or from terms implied into the contract between S and A.

As was indicated above, Art 5(1) of the EC Directive on the Protection of Computer Programs provides the 'lawful acquirer' of software with a right to, *inter alia*, copy it, where such copying is necessary for its use 'in accordance with its intended purpose'. The reference to 'lawful acquirer' might well be seen as encompassing the person who buys software in a shop and as providing him, or her, with a right, which would explain the opening of the software packet as something other than an acceptance of the licence. However, as has already been indicated, what is now s 50C of the CDPA 1988, the provision intended as an implementation of Art 5(1), does not refer to the 'lawful acquirer' of software but, rather, to its 'lawful user', and also refers to 'lawful use' rather than 'intended purpose'. It seems doubtful whether, without using an implied term (considered below) or some such device, the acquirer of the software in the shop can be seen as a 'lawful user' unless the licence is effective. Certainly, that would seem to be the case on any natural construction of 'lawful user', but the point should be made that something other than a natural construction of the section may be required, if it is to be seen as a proper implementation of the Directive. In addition, as it stands, any natural interpretation of the reference to 'lawful user' in s 50C is open to the criticism of circularity.[54]

Another possible explanation for the opening of the envelope is that the common law provides a 'limited licence' for the acquirer of software so that the acquisition is not rendered pointless. An analogy with patent law might lead to such a conclusion.[55]

---

51 Section 1(6).
52 [1996] FSR 371.
53 *Brogden v Metropolitan Rly Co* (1877) 2 App Cas 666.
54 'Lawful user' is defined in s 50A(2). For criticism of the phrase see Sherwood-Edwards, 1993.
55 Smith, 1990 pp 140–41.

The point must be made, however, that it is, in any event, now unclear to what extent this analogy is still possible in the face of Art 5(1) of the EC Directive. That Article provides for the basic use of software in the absence of contractual provision. Certainly, it would seem that a non-contractual[56] implied licence should not provide a means to reduce an acquirer's rights below the level provided for by Art 5, and the impetus for non-contractual rights to be implied may not survive the Directive at all.

The final possibility to be considered here is that the opening of the software envelope was based not on acceptance of the licence, but on a right to use the software derived from an implied term in the contract under which the software was acquired (that is, the contract made in the shop with S, in our primary example). Certainly, in *Saphena Computing Ltd v Allied Collection Agencies Ltd*,[57] where software was supplied to the defendants for the purposes of their business as a debt collecting agency, the court regarded it as 'perfectly clear' that there had to be an implied term 'that the defendants should have a copyright licence to enable them to use the software for that purpose'.[58] Courts may well be reluctant to find that a supply of software is quite pointless because the acquirer has no right to use the software. They may be willing to imply a term in law giving a basic right to use the software on the basis that such a term is necessary in that type[59] of contract (see p 103). Of course, there are difficulties with the idea of an implied term, conferring rights to do what would otherwise be a breach of copyright, if the contract is not between the acquirer and the copyright holder. A chain of implied terms might be suggested, although such a chain would be vulnerable to the insertion of an express contrary term in the first contractual link between the copyright holder and the person to whom he or she supplies.[60]

Obviously, there are considerable hurdles in the way of finding that there were two effective contracts – the supply contract and the licence. It should also be noted that the two contract analysis was considered, and rejected, by the Scottish court in *Beta v Adobe*,[61] because of the difficulties which might ensue. If the situation was construed as one which could give rise to two distinct contracts, with S, the supplier, not being a party to any second licence or contract, Lord Penrose was concerned that A, the acquirer, might not be able to recover the purchase price of the software, or refuse to pay it, if A did not wish to accept the licence terms. Any statement on the packaging that A can recover the purchase price if the licence is unacceptable will not be contractually enforceable by A, against S, unless it has been properly incorporated into the contract between A and S (see p 115). However, A might be able to claim that S's

---

56 But note that s 50C, 'implementing Article 5(1)', merely refers to contrary agreement, without specifying that it must be contractual.

57 [1995] FSR 617.

58 Havery QC (Off Ref), p 637.

59 The argument here would seem to apply whether the transaction is a sale of the disk or merely a hiring of it (as may sometimes be argued to be the case) – in either situation, its acquisition is completely undermined if it cannot be used.

60 Even a term which would otherwise be implied in law will not be implied in the face of an express contrary term, although sometimes the express contrary term might be rendered ineffective, and the implication therefore allowed, under UCTA 1977 (*Johnstone v Bloomsbury HA* [1991] 2 All ER 293). See, also, UCTA 1977, s 3; Macdonald, 1992.

61 [1996] FSR 371.

supply was in breach of contract.[62] It might be argued that the supply of software
which, without further agreement with C, could not be used without infringing C's
copyright would be in breach of the term implied s 12 of the SGA 1979,[63] that the seller
has a right to sell the goods. In *Niblett Ltd v Confectioner's Materials Co Ltd*,[64] a breach of
that implied term was found when the sellers supplied tins of condensed milk which
were labelled in such a way as to infringe a third party's trademark.

The problem considered by Lord Penrose, outlined above, obviously arises if the
view is taken that A cannot use the software without accepting the licence terms.
However, Lord Penrose's other concern with the two contract analysis was in relation
to the possibility that C's attempt to create a licence with A would be ineffective but A
would nevertheless be able to use the software. He was concerned that S might be
liable to C, through a breach of the contract under which C supplied the software to S,
and, more significantly, that the position of C, as the copyright owner, would be
undermined (see below).

Pragmatism

The desire of the Scottish court in *Beta v Adobe* not to undermine the position of the
holder of the copyright was noted above, and it is also worth noting Lord Penrose's
statement that:[65]

> There is little doubt, in my mind, that the interests of the industry as a whole in the
> efficient and sensible management of transactions requires that effect should be given to
> the [licence] conditions if possible.

There may be an impetus to find shrink wrap licenses to be effective because that
result is viewed as being of practical benefit.[66] Something of this approach is also to be
found in the US case of *ProCD Inc v Mathew Zeidenberg and Silken Mountain Web Services
Inc*.[67] In that case, unlike the earlier *Step Saver* case,[68] the licence was held to be
effective against a background of the court's view of the benefits of such a conclusion.

In *ProCD v Zeidenberg*, ProCD used different licence terms to differentiate between
consumer and commercial purchases of its database. The consumer was charged $150
for the purchase, which was much less than the commercial buyer, but was also
authorised to do much less with the database than the commercial buyer. The court
took that the view that it was beneficial to both consumers and commercial buyers that

---

62 A restitutionary claim might also be made, but it would prove problematic to argue that a
    total failure of consideration had occurred when A had, technically, received title to the disk –
    see the approach taken in *Rowland v Divall* [1923] 2 KB 500.
63 If the contract is not one for the sale of goods, then it can be argued that an analogous term
    has been breached; see below, p 148.
64 [1921] 3 KB 387.
65 See below.
66 [1996] FSR 371, p 379.
67 But see Smith, 1990 pp 140–41.
68 *Step-saver Data Systems Inc v Wyse Technology and Software Link Inc* 939 F 2d 91 (3rd Cir 1991).

ProCD should take such an approach, which was obviously dependent on the effectiveness of the licence terms.

It should be noted that a statutory means of ensuring the validity of these licenses has now been decided upon in the US and is contained in the Uniform Computer Transactions Act.

CHAPTER 4

DEFECTIVE SOFTWARE – CONTRACT

INTRODUCTION

This chapter is concerned with the contractual supply of software and, in particular, liability for defective software. This may occur in relation to the acquisition of software by itself (a program) or of a system (software and hardware). Whether supplied by itself, or as part of a system, it is in general the software which raises questions unique to the area of information technology law, and which will be focused on here. Questions arise as to the obligations undertaken in the contract, and as to whether there has been a breach and the chapter starts by examining the question of the relationship of bugs to breaches. It will then look more fully at the contractual obligations, whether arising from express or implied terms, before considering the impact of exemption clauses. In considering implied terms, this chapter will address the question of whether one of the statutory regimes implying terms into certain types of contract can apply to a contract for the supply of software. The Sale of Goods Act (SGA) 1979, for example, implies terms that goods must correspond with their description (s 13) and sample (s 15), and that they should be of satisfactory quality (s 14(2)) and reasonably fit for the buyer's particular purpose (s 14(3)). Sections 8–10 of the Supply of Goods and Services Act (SGSA) 1982 imply similar terms into contracts for the hire of goods and s 13 implies a term into a contract for services that the services will be carried out with reasonable care and skill. (Obviously, if applicable, such terms could be very helpful to someone seeking damages for defects in a program). Finally, the chapter addresses exemption clauses and their control.

BUGS AND BREACHES

One of the fundamental issues in relation to system supply contracts is that of the relationship of bugs to breaches , that is, when will a bug (or bugs) constitute a breach. That point will be addressed below, and is the focus of this section. First, however, the point should briefly be made that it may be necessary to distinguish between a bug and something which the acquirer perceives as a problem with the software, but which is the absence of a function which the supplier did not set out to provide as it was never specified by the acquirer. The point was recognised in *Cooperative Group v ICL* [1]

> 197 … A bug is, when reduced to its essentials, a respect in which software does not perform as expected. In considering what was expected one has to have regard to what was specified as the functionality to be provided. Vagueness of wording of the relevant specification is the first area in which different assessors may reach different conclusions as to whether a supposed bug really is a bug or not. A conclusion that what it is said the software should do was not covered by the specification as written could lead to the view either that what was complained of was not a bug at all, or that it was really a request for the software to be modified to provide a different functionality, in other words, a change.

---

1   [2003] EWHC 1 (TCC). See further Macdonald, 2005.

However, as has been indicated, the primary focus here is on identifying when a bug will be a breach. The starting point is the comment of Steyn J in *Eurodynamic Systems Plc v General Automation Ltd.*[2] He said:

> ... The expert evidence convincingly showed that it is regarded as acceptable practice to supply computer programmes (including system software) that contain errors and bugs. ... Not every bug or error in a computer programme can therefore be categorised as a breach of contract ...

This makes the point that not every error or bug will be a breach, but does not tell us when a bug will be a breach. It raises the issue of the extent to which industry practice should help in determining when a breach will occur. These issues are raised further in the analysis the courts have developed in this area. *Saphena Computing v Allied Collection* Agencies,[3] *St Alban's City and District Council v International Computers* Ltd,[4] and *SAM Business Systems v Hedley & Co*[5] should be considered in this context.

Saphena Computing v Allied Collection Agencies
[1995] FSR 616, 652

The case was concerned with an attempt to provide an 'online' computer system for a debt collecting agency. The suppliers experienced difficulties in trying to make the software function as required. The time they spent in attempting to deal with the problems eventually led the acquirers to agree to a termination of the contract and they then called in a third party to deal with the problems. One of the issues raised was whether the bugs still left in the system when the contract was terminated meant that the suppliers were in breach.

> **Staughton LJ** But it is important to remember that software is not necessarily a commodity which is handed over or delivered once and for all at one time. It may well have to be tested and modified as necessary. It would not be a breach of contract at all to deliver software in the first instance with a defect in it. That seems to be confirmed in a passage in the expert report of Mr Larner, a witness called by the suppliers, dealing with the nature of the commodity. He said this:
>
> > Just as no software developer can reasonably expect a buyer to tell him what is required without a process of feedback and reassessment, so no buyer should expect a supplier to get his programs right first time. He, too, needs feedback on whether he has been successful. This is why the buyer needs to run acceptance tests using typical business transactions to ensure that each works correctly. Inevitably, though, some will not. This may be the supplier's fault but it is equally possible that the buyer may have got his requirements wrong, have expressed them badly or unwittingly have used terms which were open to different interpretations. Whatever the cause, the programs have to be modified and then retested until a correct result is achieved.
>
> We were told that there was no dispute as to that passage, although there was or may have been a dispute as to what acceptance tests there were. It seems to show in my judgment, as I have already said, that software is not a commodity which is delivered once, only once, and once and for all, but one which will necessarily be accompanied

---

2   (1988) unreported, 6 September. See further Macdonald, 2005.
3   [1995] FSR 616. On this and the cases below see further Macdonald, 2005.
4   [1996] 4 All ER 481.
5   [2003] 1 All ER (Comm) 465.

by a degree of testing and modification. Naturally it could be expected that the supplier will carry out those tasks. He should have both the right and the duty to do so. For somebody else to modify another person's software would necessarily, as the judge found in another connection, involve a degree of learning time.

So I conclude that it was part of the contract that the suppliers in this case should have the right and the duty to test and modify as necessary the software they supplied. No doubt there was a time limit for that purpose – a reasonable time is that which the law would ordinarily supply. The process was still continuing on February 11, 1986. No doubt it had continued for some time since the supply first started in September 1985. That, as I have said, may or may not have been due to changes required by the purchasers.

By February 11 the purchasers were becoming impatient and discontented, as appears from some letters to which we were referred. But the recorder did not find that a reasonable time had then expired. He merely finds that the defects still existed on that date.

The conclusion was reached that the termination agreement between the parties included an agreement that the suppliers were not liable for any defects unremedied at the point of termination. What is of interest here is the indication as to the conclusion that would have been reached in the absence of such an agreement. Clearly, two possible situations are identified as needing to be considered. First, that in which the acquirer has not made plain, and not made part of the contract, something which he, or she, wanted the software to do. Obviously, in that situation, failing to provide that function cannot be a breach of contract by the supplier. However, the second situation is where the software is not performing the functions specified in the contract. What should be emphasised here, is the indication by the court that, at the stage of the contract which had been reached prior to the termination agreement, the bugs would not, at that point, have led to the conclusion that the supplier was in breach. In addition, note should also be taken of the further reference to the expert witness's views in coming to that conclusion.

St Albans City and District Council v ICL
[1996] 4 All ER 481, 487

The case was concerned with a contract under which ICL contracted to provide the Council with software to implement the community charge. It was in the course of development, but prior to the date when it had to be used to implement the charge as such, it was used it to determine the number of charge payers, as required by legislation. *Inter alia*, ICL sought to rely on the approach indicated by Staughton LJ in *Saphena* (above) to argue that there was no breach as the software was still in development.

Nourse LJ   The basic submission of Mr Dehn as to the construction of the contract, advanced for the first time in this court, was that the defendant agreed to supply a system which was to be fully operative by the end of February 1990, when the amount of the community charge would have to be set. It was a system, as the contractual provisions recognised, which until then would still be in course of development. Thus, except where the defendant had acted negligently, the plaintiffs had impliedly agreed to accept the software supplied, bugs and all. Mr Dehn relied on observations of Staughton LJ in *Saphena Computing Ltd v Allied Collection Agencies Ltd* [1995] FSR 616, 652. Specifically, he submitted that the defendant was not contractually bound to provide software which would enable the correct figure to be extracted from the computer on 4 December 1989.

These submissions must be rejected. Parties who respectively agree to supply and acquire a system recognising that it is still in course of development cannot be taken, merely by virtue of that recognition, to intend that the supplier shall be at liberty to supply software which cannot perform the function expected of it at the stage of the development at which it is supplied. Moreover, and this is really an anterior point, the argument is concluded against the defendant by clause 1.1 of the plaintiffs' statement of user requirements which, having referred to the Bill that later became the Local Government Finance Act 1988, stated (I repeat):

> As the Bill has not yet received the Royal Assent, and a large number of Statutory Instruments/Regulations have still to be laid before Parliament, prospective suppliers will be expected to give a firm commitment to provide a system to cope with all the Statutory Requirements for registration, billing, collection and recovery and financial management of the Community Charge and Non-Domestic Rates; ... (emphasis added).

Mr Dehn sought to avoid the clear impact of that provision and others to the like effect by arguing that the statutory requirements there referred to were only those derived from the 1988 Act and any statutory instruments or regulations made under it. He pointed to the fact that the Secretary of State's requirement that all charging authorities should make returns of their relevant populations on Form CCR1 not later than 8th December 1989 derived from amendments to the 1988 Act made by the Local Government and Housing Act 1989. In my view that is to put an altogether too narrow construction on the provision. What it clearly contemplated was that the system must meet the statutory requirements, many of them still unknown, whatever they might prove to be. On a common sense interpretation of clause 1.1, it would be immaterial whether those requirements arose under the 1988 Act in its original form or as amended by the 1989 Act.

I therefore agree with the judge that the defendant was under an express contractual obligation in the terms stated by him. Accordingly, once the defendant knew, soon after 2nd November 1989, that the Secretary of State had notified all charging authorities of his intention to require them to make a return of relevant population on Form CCR1 not later than 8th December 1989, it became under an express contractual obligation to supply the plaintiffs with software which would enable them accurately to complete the return by that date.

Here there is an emphasis upon the limitations of Staughton LJ's views in *Saphena*.

SAM Business Systems v Hedley & Co
[2003] 1 All ER (Comm) 465

The case was concerned with a contract for the supply of a standard software package for use in Hedley's stockbroking business. It did not perform as required.

Judge Peter Bowsher QC   The point has frequently been made during the trial that InterSet works well elsewhere (and I have received evidence from stockbrokers, Hoodless Brennan to that effect) and accordingly it is said, if it did not work for Hedley's there must be something wrong with Hedley's method of working. That line of argument has prompted me to ask: (a) if it is a tried and tested system, why when supplied to Hedley's did it have admitted bugs? (b) what is the difference between a bug and a defect? Mr Peter Susman QC concealed any annoyance he may have felt when I returned to these questions more than once and he promised to answer them in his closing submissions but witnesses were not asked by him to deal with the questions, which I regard as questions of fact. In his closing speech, Mr Susman relied on some dicta of Staughton LJ *in Saphena Computing Ltd v Allied Collection Agencies Ltd* [1995] FSR 616 at 652. However, in that case, the court was dealing with an undeveloped system which was sold with bugs 'warts and all'. Staughton LJ referred to expert evidence that in a bespoke system bugs were inevitable. However, in another case of a bespoke system, *St Albans City and District Council v International Computers Ltd* [1996] 4 All ER 481 Nourse LJ said (at 487):

> Parties who respectively agree to supply and acquire a system recognising that it is still in the course of development cannot be taken, merely by virtue of that recognition, to intend that the supplier shall be at liberty to supply software which cannot perform the function expected of it at the stage of the development at which it is supplied.

> By contrast, InterSet was sold as a developed system allegedly already working well in other places. This is a much stronger case than the St Albans case against toleration of bugs. I am in no doubt that if a software system is sold as a tried and tested system it should not have any bugs in it and if there are any bugs they should be regarded as defects. Of course, if the defects are speedily remedied without charge, it may be that there will be no consequential damage.

Note here the contrast made between systems which are 'in development' and 'tried and tested' systems. Basically the contrasts between *St Alban's*, *Saphena* and the *SAM Business Systems* case make the point that whether a bug is a breach will depend upon what the parties contracted for, and even if a system is 'in development', it may have to satisfy certain requirements at certain stages of that process. However, that then raises the issue of establishing what the parties did contract for. That will be returned to below, when the terms of the contract are considered further. Here a few preliminary points can be made.

First, in relation to the point made in *SAM Business Systems*, about 'tried and tested systems' and bugs. Should the situation really be regarded as one in which the system should not have any bugs in it and if there are any bugs, they should be regarded' as breaches? In *Morgan and Stedman on Computer Contracts*,[6] the point is made as to the incidence of bugs in even 'the most widely used software'.[7]

> ... even the best designed and tested programs are liable to cough at totally unexpected data. Indeed some of the most best known and most widely used software is known to be subject to a large number of bugs, albeit few which have a material impact on the overall operation of the software. There is a well known fable about an American payroll package which worked well for years until two employees with identical names (it might have been Esme Brown) decided to marry each other – a contingency which the system designer (not unreasonably) had not envisaged. It may be said that there is no such thing as an absolutely perfect program... Having said this, it is obvious that there are ... eminently usable programs and appallingly unusable ones

It would seem that if the difficulty of eliminating bugs is taken into account, it would be unlikely that any software or system supplier will be found to have guaranteed an absence of bugs from its software, even if the system has been said to be 'tried and tested'. An analogy can be made with *Thake v Maurice*[8] where what was in question was whether a surgeon had guaranteed that a vasectomy would leave a patient sterile. The court concluded that there was no such absolute guarantee in the contract, but merely a term stating that the operation would be carried out with due care. In coming to that view, the court looked at what the surgeon had said and done from the viewpoint of the reasonable person in the position of the patient. Nourse LJ took the line that:[9]

---

6   Morgan and Burden, 2001.
7   At pp 6–7
8   [1986] 1 All ER 497. See further Macdonald, 2005.
9   At p 511

It does seem to me reasonable to credit him with the ... general knowledge that in medical science all things, or nearly all things are uncertain. That knowledge is part of the general experience of mankind ...

Similarly, here, the difficulty in eliminating bugs would seem to be well enough known to be credited as part of the 'general experience of mankind' at least for those living in modern states. Of course, if the issue is addressed through the eyes of the reasonable 'business person' (as should be the case in these business to business contracts) some such assertion is easier to make and the conclusion, that no guarantee of an absence of bugs would have been made, easier to draw, in the absence of the most explicit statement.

However, having referred to 'general knowledge' some consideration should now be given to the courts' use of 'expert evidence' of, for example, 'acceptable practice' (*Eurodynamic Systems v General Automation* above) or what 'necessarily' has to occur in the development of software (*Saphena Computing v Allied Collection Agencies* above).

In the absence of an (unlikely) guarantee of an absence of bugs, in determining whether there has been a breach, what will often be in question will be the meeting of some general standard by the software. (Although there may also be terms dealing with specific areas of the functionality of the program , for example, speed). That general standard is likely to be 'reasonable fitness for the buyer's particular purpose' whether that is arrived at under s 14(3) of the Sale of Goods Act (SGA) 1979, expressly, or by implication at common law. In any event, any 'general standard' is likely to have some dependence upon what is reasonable in the relevant circumstances, whether those circumstances are the 'buyer's particular purpose' or otherwise. It is understandable that in attempting to set such general objective level of performance, the courts should turn to the views of experts and industry practice. The concern must be, however, that low standard can thereby propagate themselves and enjoy the protection of a finding that following them will not produce a breach of contract. Although not being used in an attempt to drag standards down, something of these risks are evident in the comments of an expert in *Co-operative Group v ICL*.[10]

Co-operative Group v ICL
[2003] EWHC 1(TCC).

The case was concerned with the supply of software to CWS to deal with its electronic point of sale and back office needs, including the provision of a customer loyalty scheme. Ultimately, it was concluded that no contract was formed between ICL and CWS and there could be no question of breach by ICL in developing the GlobalStore software. Nevertheless, the judge considered whether, had there been a contract, there would have been a breach by ICL as to the quality of the software which they were developing. No such breach was found.

Judge Richard Seymour

264. The way in which Mr. Mawrey put the case for CWS as to the quality of the software delivered was to emphasise both the numbers of errors reported and their seriousness as perceived at the time of the initial report. ... I have already mentioned that it was common ground between CWS and ICL that some errors are to be

---

10   [2003] EWHC 1(TCC). See Macdonald, 2005.

expected in bespoke software. The only sensible enquiry, therefore, if an assessment has to be made as to whether the software delivered by ICL was of satisfactory quality, is what number of bugs is to be expected in bespoke software and what is the expected seriousness of those bugs? Dr Hunt expressed the conclusion in paragraph 5.109 of her report for the purposes of this action that:

> Research into the incidence of errors in bespoke software indicates typical error levels far higher than those revealed so far for GlobalSTORE. Research also confirms what is widely understood in the IT industry about the persistence of errors well beyond the testing stages into live operation, as stated in the axiom 'Testing reveals the presence of bugs, it cannot confirm their absence'.

Dr Hunt in her report proceeded to review the research data to which she referred. It is not necessary for the purposes of this judgment to set out that review. Suffice to say, that I accept the evidence of Dr Hunt on this point and I find that the data which she set out supports the conclusion which she reached. Mr. Mawrey did not really contest Dr Hunt's view, other than by suggesting that the software industry had unacceptably low standards. Dr Hunt emphasised that the research data to which she referred simply recorded what actually happened in practice. She said:

> This is not about buying software off the shelf. This is about having software developed for a specific purpose which is quite different. If you specify software to be developed as bespoke solution, then there is a process you go through and it is normal for errors. I believe that these numbers of errors (shown by the research) are actually rather too high and I have said so in my report. I think the numbers of errors quoted by these authorities is really a bit on the high side and that actually the numbers that we have arrived at for this project are much lower than that.

Pre-contractual statements: terms and misrepresentations

The consumer who wants software will either simply walk into a shop and purchase it 'off the shelf', select and purchase it through a mail order catalogue or purchase and download it from the web. Businesses may acquire hardware and software in the same way if all that is required is, for example, a straightforward word-processing package. However, if a business wants software which is tailored to its particular needs, it will contract for 'bespoke' software, to be written for it, or for standard software to be modified to meet its particular circumstances, and those circumstances might relate not only to the type of business, but also to the need for new software to be compatible with an existing system.

In any of the above situations, but particularly in relation to bespoke or modified standard software, there may be discussions between the supplier and the acquirer as to the needs of the acquirer and whether the software will fulfil them. If, after the acquisition, the acquirer is unhappy with the software, disputes may arise as to what was said about it and the legal effect of any such statements. The acquirer may claim that the supplier is liable, on the basis that the pre-contractual statements became terms or that they were misrepresentations, and such claims have occurred in relation to the acquisition of software and computer systems in, for example, *Micron Computer*

Systems Ltd v Wang[11] and *Mackenzie Patten & Co v British Olivetti Ltd*.[12] These two possible bases of liability should be considered.

Pre-contractual statements becoming terms

The question of whether a pre-contractual statement has become a term is often put in terms of whether the statement was a mere representation or a warranty.[13] The basic test for whether a pre-contractual statement became a term of the contract is the intention of the parties,[14] and that intention is objectively ascertained.[15] It is not easy to apply a test dependent upon the ascertainment of intention. However, certain indicators of the parties' intention have been focused on by the courts, such as the situation where it is clear to both parties that the statement in question is key to the decision to contract.[16] However, in the context of software contracts, the indicators which are most likely to be relevant are reliance and the relative expertise of the parties. This relates to the situation in which one party relies on the statements of the other party and that other party possesses the greater expertise. This can be illustrated by the contrasting cases of *Oscar Chess Ltd v Williams*[17] and *Dick Bentley Productions Ltd v Harold Smith (Motors) Ltd*.[18]

Oscar Chess Ltd v Williams
[1957] 1 All ER 325

The defendant sold a Morris car to the plaintiff car dealer. The dealer was familiar with the car and had been given lifts in it. The defendant innocently described the car as a 1948 model and produced the registration book ('log-book') which stated it to be a 1948 car. At some time before the defendant became the owner of the car, its registration book had been tampered with and the car was actually a 1939 model. There was no difference in appearance between a 1948 and a 1939 model and the plaintiff did not discover the truth until eight months after the purchase. The plaintiff took action to recover the difference between what he paid for the car and what he would have paid for a 1939 model. He claimed that it had been a term of the contract that the car was a 1939 model. His claim failed – no such term was found.

---

11   (1990) unreported, 9 May.
12   (1984) unreported, 11 January.
13   'Warranty' can be used in more than one sense. In this context, it is used simply to mean a term. It may also be used in contrast with conditions and innominate terms to designate a particular type of term, breach of which leads to specific consequences. Breach of a warranty gives rise only to a right to damages. Breach of a condition gives a right to damages and also a right to terminate the contract. Breach of an innominate term gives a right to damages but only gives a right to terminate if the breach substantially deprives the injured party of all the benefit which they were intended to derive from the contract. See Koffman and Macdonald, 2004, paras 8.18–8.46.
14   *Heilbut, Symons & Co v Buckleton* [1913] AC 30.
15   For a case which clearly shows the need for an objective approach see *Thake v Maurice* [1986] 1 All ER 497.
16   *Bannerman v White* (1861) 10 CBNS 844. See, further, Koffman and Macdonald, 2004, paras 7.11–7.16.
17   [1957] 1 All ER 325.
18   [1965] 2 All ER 65.

Denning LJ The material distinction here is between a statement which is a term of the contract and a statement which is only an innocent misrepresentation. This distinction is best expressed by the ruling of Holt CJ, 'Was it intended as a warranty or not?', using the word 'warranty' there in its ordinary English meaning; because it gives the exact shade of meaning required. It is something to which a man must be taken to bind himself.

In applying this test, however, some misunderstanding has arisen by the use of the word 'intended'. It is sometimes supposed that the tribunal must look into the minds of the parties to see what they themselves intended. That is a mistake ... The question whether a warranty was intended depends on the conduct of the parties, on their words and behaviour, rather than on their thoughts. If an intelligent bystander would reasonably infer that a warranty was intended that will suffice ...

It is instructive to take some recent instances to show how the courts have approached this question. When the seller states a fact which is or should be within his own knowledge and of which the buyer is ignorant, intending that the buyer should act on it and he does so, it is easy to infer a warranty: see *Couchman v Hill* [1947] 1 All ER 103, where a farmer stated that a heifer was unserved, and *Harling v Eddy* [1951] 2 All ER 212, where he stated that there was nothing wrong with her. So also if the seller makes a promise about something which is or should be within his own control; see *Birch v Paramount Estates Ltd* (1956) 16 EG 396, decided ... in this court, where the seller stated that the house would be as good as the show house. If, however, the seller when he states a fact, makes it clear that he has no knowledge of his own but has got his information elsewhere, and is merely passing it on, it is not easy to imply a warranty. Such a case was *Routledge v Mackay* [1954] 1 All ER 855, where the seller stated that a motor cycle combination was a 1942 model, and pointed to the corroboration of that statement to be found in the registration book, and it was held that there was no warranty.

Turning now to the present case, much depends on the precise words that were used. If the seller says, 'I believe that the car is a 1948 Morris. Here is the registration book to prove it', there is clearly no warranty. It is a statement of belief, not a contractual promise. If, however, the seller says, 'I guarantee that it is a 1948 Morris. This is borne out by the registration book, but you need not rely solely on that. I give you my own guarantee that it is', there is clearly a warranty. The seller is making himself contractually responsible, even though the registration book is wrong.

... What is the proper inference from the known facts? It must have been obvious to both that the seller himself had no personal knowledge of the year when the car was made. He only became owner after a great number of changes. He must have been relying on the registration book. It is unlikely that such a person would warrant the year of manufacture. The most that he would do would be to state his belief, and then produce the registration book in verification of it. In these circumstances the intelligent bystander would, I suggest, say that the seller did not intend to bind himself so as to warrant that the car was a 1948 model. If the seller was asked to pledge himself to it, he would at once have said 'I cannot do that. I have only the log-book to go by, the same as you' ...

Dick Bentley Productions Ltd v Harold Smith (Motors) Ltd
[1965] 2 All ER 65

DB asked the car dealer S to find him a 'well vetted' Bentley car. S found a car and showed it to DB. He told DB that it had only been driven 20,000 miles since a new engine had been fitted and that was the mileage shown on the odometer. DB purchased the car and had numerous problems with it. It was discovered that it had done a far greater mileage than

20,000 since the new engine had been fitted. DB sued on the basis that the mileage had become a.term of the contract – his claim was successful.

> **Lord Denning MR** Looking at the cases once more, as we have done so often, it seems to me that if a representation is made in the course of dealings for a contract, for the very purpose of inducing the other party to act on it, and it actually induces him to act on it by entering into the contract, that is *prima facie* ground for inferring that the representation was intended as a warranty ... Suffice it that the representation was intended to be acted on and was in fact acted on. But the maker of the representation can rebut this inference if he can show that it was an innocent misrepresentation, in that he was innocent of fault in making it, and that it would not be reasonable in the circumstances for him to be bound by it. In the *Oscar Chess* case the inference was rebutted ... [w]hereas in the present case it is very different. The inference is not rebutted. Here we have a dealer, Mr Smith, who was in a position to know, or at least to find out, the history of the car. He could get it by writing to the makers. He did not do so. Indeed it was done later. When the history of this car was examined, his statement turned out to be quite wrong. He ought to have known better. There was no reasonable foundation for it.

These cases illustrate that the courts regard the expertise of one party as relevant to the question of whether a statement has become a term. In the context of a software contract, the point can be further illustrated by *Mackenzie Patten & Co v British Olivetti Ltd*.[19] In that case, a solicitors' practice purchased hardware and software. The purchasers had no expertise or knowledge of computers and relied on the seller's statements as to its suitability for their needs and as to the functions it could perform. It proved unsuitable and could not perform one of the functions which the solicitors had wanted. The solicitors sued, claiming both breach of a term and misrepresentation. They succeeded on the basis that the seller's statements had become terms of the contract. The judge emphasised the purchasers' lack of expertise and reliance on that of the seller.[20] The remedy, as is usually the case for breach of contract, was damages.

Before leaving the question of whether a pre-contractual statement has become a term, some consideration should be given to the 'parol evidence rule'. This becomes relevant when, for example, there is a document recording contract terms but it does not include the contents of a pre-contractual statement which, it is being argued, became a term. It has been said that 'it is firmly established as a rule of law that parol evidence cannot be used to add to, vary or contradict a deed or other written document'.[21] In other words, where there is a contractual document, it might be argued that the 'parol evidence rule' prevented any evidence being brought that a pre-contractual statement furnished an additional term. However, the status of the so called parol evidence rule is doubtful. It may be nothing more than a presumption that, if there is a written agreement which looks like a complete contract, it is the complete contract. But that presumption can be rebutted if it is shown that there were intended to be other terms. Once looked at in this light, the 'rule' ceases to have much force. In addition, whilst taking the view of the 'rule' indicated here, the Law

---

19 (1984) unreported, 11 January.
20 The alternative claim, based on misrepresentation, was not addressed by the judge once he had found for the purchasers on the basis of a breach.
21 *Jacobs v Batavia and General Plantations Trust* [1924] 1 Ch 287, p 295, *per* Lawrence J.

Commission also concluded that even if it was, properly speaking, a rule of law, there were so many exceptions to it that it was unlikely to work injustice.[22]

However, a strictly working parol evidence rule would obviously have significant benefits in terms of certainty, so some contracts seek to produce the effects of such a rule by means of a terms of the contract – an 'entire' or 'whole agreement clause. This will be returned to below once pre-contractual statements as misrepresentations have been dealt with, as such clauses also often also set out to prevent there being liability for misrepresentations.

Pre-contractual statements as misrepresentations[23]

A misrepresentation requires a statement of existing or past fact by the misrepresentor, to the misrepresentee, which induces the misrepresentee to contract with the misrepresentor. In other words, what is needed is a pre-contractual statement of fact by one party to the other, which that other party relies upon in deciding to contract.[24] As has already been suggested, reliance may well be present where there is an imbalance of knowledge or expertise, as there often will be in the acquisition of software. The point which needs to be considered here, because of its particular relevance to the situation where advice is being given on the suitability of software, is the division between statements of opinion and statements of fact.

It has already been stated that, for a misrepresentation to be found, there must be a statement of fact. Statements of opinion or intention will not suffice.[25] However, in some situations, the courts have been willing to find statements of fact where at first sight, there is merely a statement of opinion or intention. That is obviously the case where what is stated to be one party's intention or opinion simply is not that party's intention or opinion – clearly, there is a misrepresentation that the party has that intention[26] or holds that opinion. Less obviously, the courts have also been willing to find statements of fact where what is, apparently, merely a statement of opinion is made by an expert or the person who is simply in the best position to assess the situation. So, for example, in *Smith v Land & House Pty Corp*,[27] the court was concerned with a statement in the sale particulars of a hotel that it was occupied by a 'most desirable tenant' for a term of 272 years. The tenant in question had not been paying his rent on time and Bowen LJ said:[28]

> ... if the facts are not equally known to both sides, then a statement of opinion by the one who knows the facts best involves very often a statement of material fact, for he impliedly states that he knows facts which justify his opinion.

---

22 Law Com 154, 1986. See Marston, 1986.
23 On misrepresentation generally see Koffman and Macdonald, 2004, Chapter 13.
24 *Smith v Chadwick* (1884) 9 App Cas 187.
25 *Bissett v Wilkinson* [1927] AC 177.
26 *Edgington v Fitzmaurice* (1885) 29 Ch D 459.
27 (1884) 28 Ch D 7.
28 *Ibid*, p 15. See, also, *Brown v Raphael* [1958] 1 Ch 636.

The court concluded that stating that the occupier was a 'desirable tenant' was not merely a statement of opinion. There was also a misrepresentation. Similarly, this type of argument might prove relevant in relation to a software contract. In that context, it is likely to be the statement of an expert which is in question and the implied statement of fact there would seem to be that the expert has properly used his or her expertise in forming his or her opinion.[29]

A misrepresentation makes a contract voidable, and so the contract can be rescinded provided that one of the bars to rescission is not operative.[30] Damages can also be claimed for misrepresentation. If the case is one where the misrepresentation involves fraud, the tort action for deceit can be used. Alternatively, damages may be available because the situation is covered by the tort action for negligent misstatement,[31] or because it falls within the ambit of s 2(1) of the Misrepresentation Act 1967. All of the actions for damages, including that under s 2(1),[32] will result in damages being calculated on the tortious, rather than the contractual, basis – they will put the injured party in the position he or she would have been in had the misrepresentation not occurred, that is, their pre-contractual position.[33]

The action under s 2(1) will normally be the most favourable of the actions for damages. Obviously, the common law action for negligent misstatement merely requires the injured party to prove negligence, rather than the fraud which has to be established for the action for deceit, although the action for negligent misstatement will also require proof of a duty of care. However, the action under s 2(1) is generally the easiest for the injured party to use. Under s 2(1), it is for the person who made the misrepresentation to prove that he or she reasonably believed in the truth of what was being asserted; that is, it is for the misrepresentor to disprove negligence under this action – reversing the burden of proof from that applicable under the action for negligent misstatement[34] – and, of course, no duty of care is required.

29 *Esso Petroleum Co Ltd v Mardon* [1976] QB 801.
30 The common law bars are: (a) *restitutio in integrum* has become impossible (ie, it is impossible to return the parties to their pre-contractual position); (b) third party rights (eg, a *bona fide* third party has acquired a proprietary interest in the goods which were the subject matter of the contract); (c) affirmation of the contract by the injured party, after he or she has acquired knowledge of the misrepresentation; (d) lapse of time. The Misrepresentation Act, s 2(2) is sometimes referred to as a 'statutory bar', since it allows the courts to prevent or undo rescission if it would be 'equitable so to do'. See, further, o Koffman and Macdonald, 2004, paras 13.68–13.83.
31 *Hedley Byrne and Co Ltd v Heller & Partners Ltd* [1964] AC 465.
32 *Royscott Trust Ltd v Rogerson* [1991] 3 All ER 294.
33 Contractual damages for breach will put the injured party in the position he or she would have been in had the contract not been breached, ie, the position he or she would have been in had the contract been performed (*Robinson v Harman* (1880) 5 App Cas 25, p 35, *per* Parke B).
34 A factor which was vital to the success of the injured party in *Howard Marine & Dredging Co Ltd v A Ogden & Sons (Excavations) Ltd* [1978] QB 574. (The absence of any need to establish a duty of care under s 2(1) was also of significance.) The action under s 2(1) also has the benefit of at least some of the rules applicable to the tort action based on fraud rather than negligence, such as the more lax remoteness test – *Royscott Trust Ltd v Rogerson* [1991] 3 All ER 294.

Entire agreement clauses

As was indicated above, a strictly working parol evidence rule would obviously have significant benefits in terms of certainty, so sometimes a contracting party will seek to produce the effects of such a rule by means of a term of the contract – an 'entire' or 'whole agreement' clause. Such clauses will set out to ensure that there are no terms additional to those contained in a specified contractual document or documents. In addition, they may well also set out to ensure that there is no potential for liability for misrepresentation in relation to any pre-contractual statements which have not become part of the terms stated in such documents. In the context of a software or system contract, particularly one dealing with software or a system which is to be developed or adapted for the acquirer, where the identification of the obligations undertaken, or representations made, by the supplier is particularly important, such clauses may well be used and play a key role. Their effect needs to be considered.

There have been some indications of a willingness to question whether these clauses produce the effect they set out to achieve. The Law Commission, for example, commented in relation to clauses attempting to prevent there being additional terms[35]

> [An entire agreement clause] may have a very strong persuasive effect but if it were proved that notwithstanding the clause, the parties intended some additional term to be of contractual effect the court would give effect to that term because that was the intention of the parties.

However, the trend in the recent case law has been to place emphasis upon the certainty achieved by such clauses and to see them as effective. This is illustrated in the context of 'terms' by an extract from *Inntrepreneur v East Crown* and, in relation to misrepresentations, by an extract from *Watford Electronics v Sanderson* (itself a contract for the supply of a bespoke computer system).

Inntrepreneur v East Crown
[2000] 2 Lloyd's Rep 61

Lightman J   The purpose of an entire agreement clause is to preclude a party to a written agreement from threshing through the undergrowth and finding in the course of negotiations some (chance) remark or statement (often long forgotten or difficult to recall or explain) on which to found a claim such as the present to the existence of a collateral warranty. The entire agreement clause obviates the occasion for any such search and the peril to the contracting parties posed by the need which may arise in its absence to conduct such a search. For such a clause constitutes a binding agreement between the parties that the full contractual terms are to be found in the document containing the clause and not elsewhere, and that accordingly any promises or assurances made in the course of the negotiations (which in the absence of such a clause might have effect as a collateral warranty) shall have no contractual force, save insofar as they are reflected and given effect in that document. The operation of the clause is not to render evidence of the collateral warranty inadmissible in evidence as is suggested in *Chitty on Contract*, 28th ed., vol. 1, par. 12-102: it is to denude what would otherwise constitute a collateral warranty of legal effect.

Entire agreement clauses come in different forms. In the leading case of *Deepak v.*

---

35   Law Com Rep No 154, para 2.15. On entire agreement clauses in system supply contracts see further Macdonald, 2005.

Imperial Chemical Industies plc [1998] 2 Lloyd's Rep 139, affirmed [1999] 1 Lloyd's Rep 387 the clause read as follows:

10.16 Entirety of Agreement

> This contract comprises the entire agreement between the PARTIES ... and there are not any agreements, understandings, promises or conditions, oral or written, express or implied, concerning the subject matter which are not merged into this CONTRACT and superseded thereby ...

Mr. Justice Rix and the Court of Appeal held in that case (in particular focusing on the words 'promises or conditions') that this language was apt to exclude all liability for a collateral warranty. In *Alman & Benson v. Associated Newspapers Group Ltd*, June 20, 1980 (cited by Mr. Justice Rix at p. 168), Mr. Justice Browne-Wilkinson reached the same conclusion where the clause provided that the written contract 'constituted the entire agreement and understanding between the parties with respect to all matters therein referred to' focusing on the word 'understanding'. In neither case was it necessary to decide whether the clause would have been sufficient if it had been worded merely to state that the agreement containing it comprised or constituted the entire agreement between the parties. That is the question raised in this case, where the formula of words used in the clause is abbreviated to an acknowledgement by the parties that the agreement constitutes the entire agreement between them. In my judgment that formula is sufficient, for it constitutes an agreement that the full contractual terms to which the parties agree to bind themselves are to be found in the agreement and nowhere else and that what might otherwise constitute a side agreement or collateral warranty shall be void of legal effect. That can be the only purpose of the provision. This view is entirely in accord with the judgment of Mr. John Chadwick, Q.C. (as he then was) sitting as a deputy High Court Judge in *McGrath v. Shah, (1987) 57 P. & C.R. 452*. .... It seems to me therefore that cl. 14.1 of the agreement provides in law a complete answer to any claim by Crown based on the alleged collateral warranty.

Watford Electronics v Sanderson
[2001] 1 All ER (Comm) 696

Chadwick LJ   The entire agreement clause–clause 14 in the Terms and Conditions of Sale, clause 15 in the Terms and Conditions of Software Licence–is also in two parts. The second part of the clause contains an acknowledgment by the parties that 'no statements or representations made by either party have been relied upon by the other in agreeing to enter into the contract'.

39 The effect of an acknowledgment of non-reliance, in terms which were sufficiently similar to those in the second part of the entire agreement clause in the present case as to be indistinguishable, was considered in this Court in *EA Grimstead & Son Ltd v. McGarrigan* (unreported, October 27, 1999). In a passage which was *obiter dicta* – but which followed full argument on the point – I said this (at p. 32A–C of the transcript):

> In my view an acknowledgement of non-reliance ... is capable of operating as an evidential estoppel. It is apt to prevent the party who has given the acknowledgement from asserting in subsequent litigation against the party to whom it has been given that it is not true. That seems to me to be a proper use of an acknowledgement of this nature, which, as Jacob J. pointed out in the Thomas Witter case (*Thomas Witter Ltd v TBP Industries Ltd [1996] 2 All ER 573*), has become a common feature of professionally drawn commercial contracts.

I went on, at p. 35A–C, to say this:

> There are, as it seems to me, at least two good reasons why the courts should not refuse to give effect to an acknowledgement of non-reliance in a commercial

contract between experienced parties of equal bargaining power—a fortiori, where those parties have the benefit of professional advice. First, it is reasonable to assume that the parties desire commercial certainty. They want to order their affairs on the basis that the bargain between them can be found within the document which they have signed. They want to avoid the uncertainty of litigation based on allegations as to the content of oral discussions at pre-contractual meetings. Second, it is reasonable to assume that the price to be paid reflects the commercial risk which each party–or, more usually, the purchaser–is willing to accept. The risk is determined, in part at least, by the warranties which the vendor is prepared to give. The tighter the warranties, the less the risk and (in principle, at least) the greater the price the vendor will require and which the purchaser will be prepared to pay. It is legitimate, and commercially desirable, that both parties should be able to measure the risk, and agree the price, on the basis of the warranties which have been given and accepted.

40 Those passages were not cited to the judge. He held that *Sanderson* could not rely on the acknowledgment of non-reliance contained in the second part of the entire agreement clause. He said this, at paragraph 107 of his judgment:

> ... the clause is, in substance, one that excludes liability rather than precludes liability from ever occurring. The clause states that no statement or representation has been relied on. It follows that the clause can only first bite once a statement or representation has been made that is capable of being relied on. The clause bites, therefore, on a potential misrepresentation that has been made. It is not preventing words that have been uttered from being a misrepresentation at all. Furthermore, the words that were used did, as a matter of fact, as I have found, induce the contract. Thus, this clause is one which is in substance an exclusion clause to which section 3 of the Misrepresentation Act is applicable

I confess to some difficulty in following the reasoning in that passage. It is true that an acknowledgment of non-reliance does not purport to prevent a party from proving that a representation was made, nor that it was false. What the acknowledgment seeks to do is to prevent the person to whom the representation was made from asserting that he relied upon it. If it is to have that effect, it will be necessary—as I sought to point out in *Grimstead v McGarrigan* – for the party who seeks to set up the acknowledgment as an evidential estoppel to plead and prove that the three requirements identified by this Court in *Lowe v Lombank Ltd [1960] 1 WLR 196* are satisfied. That may present insuperable difficulties; not least because it may be impossible for a party who has made representations which he intended should be relied upon to satisfy the court that he entered into the contract in the belief that a statement by the other party that he had not relied upon those representations was true. But the fact that, on particular facts, the acknowledgment of non-reliance may not achieve its purpose does not lead to the conclusion that the acknowledgment is 'in substance an exclusion clause to which section 3 of the Misrepresentation Act is applicable' ...

As can be seen, in the context of whether a pre-contractual statement becomes a term, a very mechanical approach is being taken. The entire agreement clause is being taken at face value without even any question of conflicting terms being raised. The certainty produced by this approach is emphasised. The approach in relation to misrepresentations is somewhat different, with 'evidential estoppel' being used to prevent any successful claim that, in addition to those specified, there was a (mis)representation which was relied on. Such an approach does have more potential for examination of the circumstances and a conclusion that there was a (mis)representation despite the clause. This is because of the requirements for an evidential estoppel. In this context, they can be identified as (i) that the statements (ie as to non-reliance on the (mis)representation) in the clause were clear and unequivocal, (ii) that the representee had intended that the representor act upon those statements (as to non-reliance), and (iii) that the representor had believed those statements (as to non-reliance) to be true and had acted upon them.[36] The difficulties which may arise in fulfilling those requirements are plain when it is emphasised that the 'statements' as to non-reliance which are in question will usually be in a standard form contract produced by the representor. They are being used to claim that the representee has so asserted his non-reliance that he is estopped from proving he relied on the representation. As has been seen, in *Watford Electronics v Sanderson*, Chadwick LJ, recognised that those requirements for an evidential estoppel 'may present insuperable difficulties, not least because it may be impossible for a party who has made representations which he intended should be relied upon to satisfy the court that he entered into the contract in the belief that a statement by the other party that he had not relied upon those representations was true'. Nevertheless, that case emphasises the need for certainty and of leaving the parties to their agreed allocation of risk. It may be that it will not be difficult to establish the evidential estoppel in a commercial contract, particularly with legally advised parties.

One final point to be considered here is as to the impact of legislation on such clauses. Firstly, their potential treatment as 'exclusion clauses'. They are, in one sense, preventing liability from arising. The possible application of the Unfair Contract Terms Act 1977 to an 'entire agreement' clause dealing with terms is contentious. Any such application would undermine the certainty generated by such a clause, but it is almost invited by an overeadiness to treat the clause at face value with no consideration given to the circumstance of the contested statement as sufficient to generate a contradictory term. However, because of the requirements for an evidential estoppel, there is less scope, and less need for, the application of s 3 of the Misrepresentation Act 1967 to a clause setting out to generate such an estoppel in relation to any (mis)representations. The situation will, however, encourage some such intervention if the requirements for an estoppel are found too easily because too much emphasis has been placed on certainty. Secondly, however, the Unfair Terms in Consumer Contracts Regulations 1999 (see below p 203) should be considered. They only relate to non-individually negotiated terms in contracts between consumers and sellers or suppliers but, in that consumer context, they are not restricted to a particular type of term, such as exemption clauses. In other words, entire agreement clauses are covered by the Regulations without any need to try to categorise them as exemption clauses. Many such terms will fall within the Regulations 'grey list' of terms which 'may be unfair' (Sched 2, para 1(n)) and in the first Office of Fair Trading Bulletin on the operation of the Regulations entire agreement clauses were identified as amongst the unfair terms most commonly encountered by the OFT.[37]

---

36   See Grimstead v McGarrigan 27th Octber, 1999 Chadwick LJ, basing his statements as to the requirements for an evidential estoppel on *Lowe v Lombank* [1960] 1 All ER 611.
37   *OFT Bulletin* 1, at p 19.

SYSTEM/SOFTWARE SPECIFICATIONS

The trend is away from bespoke software but contracts to develop software, or a computer system, for a particular business are still of some significance and they may create the most difficult problems in relation to the contents of the contract. A large part of the contract is likely simply to be the supplier's standard terms, encompassing, for example, their standard exemption clauses and entire agreement clauses (see p 133).

The latter were considered above and exemption clauses will be addressed below (see p 182).

Here we are concerned with the terms which will be more particular to the individual contract: the specification of the software/system. A particular difficulty with development contracts is identifying exactly what the acquiring party requires. As part of the contracting process, the parties should draw up a detailed functional specification, which then becomes part of the contract. This should state, in detail, what the proposed software will do. The importance of this was indicated above in the discussion of when bugs will amount to breaches as, ultimately, that will depend upon what the contract terms required. However, it may not be easy to draw up such specification – the software developer is an expert in software and what can be done with it, but he or she is not an expert in the acquirer's business, whatever that may be, and it is obvious that problems may arise from this information gap. The acquirer may end up with a system which does not do some of what he or she needed it to do because those needs have not been explained to the software developer. In *Micron Computer Systems Ltd v Wang (UK) Ltd*,[38] the purchaser of a system had expected the system to perform what he termed 'transaction logging'. It did not do so. It was found that that did not mean that the system was in breach of a term that it should be reasonably fit for the buyer's particular purpose. The buyer had never made known to the seller that 'transaction logging' was required. As was indicated above, when the software, or system, does not do what the acquirer expected, the question prior to whether a bug which is a breach, is whether there is a bug at all, that is whether those expectations of the acquirer were reflected in the contract specification (above p 121).

When development of software, or a system, is in question, what is required at any particular stage of the development may need to be considered. The relationship between the stage of development and the bugs remaining will need to be considered if the question of breach arises whilst the software /system is still 'in development'. The point was made above that in *Saphena Computing v Allied Collection Agencies*[39] no breach was found at the stage of development at which the parties agreed to terminate their contract (see p 123). However, as we have seen, in *St Albans City and DC v ICL*,[40] in dismissing submissions that the suppliers had not breached, which were based on the line taken by Staughton LJ in *Saphena*, Nourse LJ said:

38   (1990) unreported, 9 May.
39   [1995] FSR 616.
40   [1996] 4 All ER 481.

Parties who respectively agree to supply and acquire a system recognising that it is still in the course of development cannot be taken, merely by virtue of that recognition, to intend that the supplier shall be at liberty to supply software which cannot perform the function expected of it at the stage of development at which it is supplied.

Further, as at the time when a contract is made, it may be difficult for the parties to accurately define the software required, particularly when a development contract is in question, contracts may well need to be modified before their performance is completed. This was recognised in *Saphena Computing Ltd v Allied Collection Agencies Ltd*.[41] Havery QC regarded the contract as envisaging the modification of the content of the term that the goods should be reasonably fit for the acquirer's particular purpose. He said:[42]

> ... it was an implied term of each contract for the supply of software that the software would be reasonably fit for any purpose which had been communicated to the plaintiff's before the contract was made and for any purpose subsequently communicated, provided in the latter case that the plaintiffs accepted the defendant's instructions to make the relevant modifications. The making of the modifications constitutes or implies acceptance of the instructions ...

TERMS: CATEGORISING THE CONTRACT

Consideration is being given to the requirements of the contract. What should now be addressed is the application of one of the statutory regimes implying terms into certain types of contract. The Sale of Goods Act (SGA) 1979, for example, implies terms that goods must correspond with their description (s 13) and sample (s 15), and that they should be of satisfactory quality (s 14(2)) and reasonably fit for the buyer's particular purpose (s 14(3)). Sections 8–10 of the Supply of Goods and Services Act (SGSA) 1982 imply similar terms into contracts for the hire of goods and s 13 implies a term into a contract for services that the services will be carried out with reasonable care and skill. Obviously, if applicable, such terms could be very helpful to someone seeking damages for defects in a program, but, before the content and application of those terms is considered, there is a major issue to be addressed – the classification of contracts for the supply of software. Can a contract for the supply of software constitute a contract for the sale of goods? Even if software can be described as 'goods', would a contract for its supply be better classified as a contract for services? These are issues which should be addressed here. Once that has occurred consideration can be given to the content of these types of terms. However, first two initial points should be made. Firstly, even if a software contract is not seen to fit within one of the statutory regimes, software may well be found to be subject to the same type of implied terms at common law – particularly the requirement of reasonable fitness for the acquirer's particular purpose. Second, it would seem that a contract for the supply of a system involving both hardware and software will be categorised as one for the supply of goods[43] (unless the services element dominates the particular contract). These two

---

41   [1995] FSR 616.

42   At p 644. See further Macdonald, 2005.

43   *Toby Constructions Products Pty Ltd v Computa Bar (Sales) Pty Ltd* [1983] NSWLR 48. *St Albans City and DC v International Computers Ltd* [1996] 4 All ER 481.

latter points mean that the content of the implied terms should be considered even if software itself cannot be categorised as goods. Nevertheless the categorisation of the type of contract being looked at here should first be considered.

The central question addressed below is whether software can be 'goods', but some initial points should be made to clarify the discussion. Programs are most commonly supplied on a disk or other such medium and the focus will be on that method of supply. Unless otherwise indicated, references to 'software' will be to programs on disks. It will be made clear when what is being looked at is the treatment of any program which has been downloaded over a telephone line, or using some other such link.

An initial look at the court's approach.

In *St Albans City and DC v ICL*,[44] Sir Iain Glidewell stated that software could constitute goods. That case should be looked at before embarking on a more general discussion of the question of that categorisation. His comments were *obiter* and the issue requires full consideration.

St Albans City and DC v
International Computers Ltd
[1996] 4 All ER 481

This case was concerned with the sale of a computer and software, by ICL, to the local authority, which wanted the computer to deal with the introduction of the Community Charge and its finances generally. A defect in the program led to an overstatement of the population figure for the council's area and a consequent loss of revenue from central government and from the Community Charge itself (the rate was set too low for the smaller number of people from which the Community Charge would actually be collected), and also meant that the council had to pay a larger sum to the County Council by way of precept. The loss to the council was something in excess of £1.3 m. The question was whether this was recoverable from ICL. It was found that there was a breach of an express term. ICL claimed to rely upon a limitation clause to restrict this liability to £100,000 but Scott Baker J found that was ineffective under the Unfair Contract Terms Act 1977 and the local authority recovered. The Court of Appeal basically agreed with the decision of Scott Baker J, except that the sum recoverable by the council from ICL was reduced to take account of the fact that the loss of revenue from the Community Charge itself had, rightly, been claimed from charge payers the following year. However, what is important here is that it was considered whether terms could be implied by the Sale of Goods Act 1979 into contracts for software.

> **Sir Iain Glidewell** [Was] the contract between the parties subject to any implied term as to quality or fitness for purpose, and if so, what was the nature of that term? Consideration of this question during argument led to discussion of a more general question, namely: 'Is software goods?' To seek to answer this question, it is necessary first to be clear about the meaning of some of the words used in argument.

> In his judgment, Scott Baker J ([1995] FSR 686, p 698) adopted a description of a computer system which contains the following passage which I have found helpful:

By itself hardware can do nothing. The really important part of the system is the software. Programs are the instructions or commands that tell the hardware what to do. The program itself is an algorithm or formula. It is of necessity contained in a physical medium. A program in machine readable form must be contained on a machine readable medium, such as paper cards, magnetic cards, magnetic tapes, discs, drums ...

In relation to COMCIS, the property in the program, that is, the intangible 'instructions or commands', remained with ICL. Under the contract, St Albans was licensed to use the program. This is a common feature of contracts of this kind. However, in order that the program should be encoded in the computer itself, it was necessarily first recorded on a disk, from which it could be transferred to the computer. During the course of the hearing the term 'software' was used to include both the (tangible) disk onto which the COMCIS program had been encoded and the (intangible) program itself. In order to answer the question, however, it is necessary to distinguish between the program and the disk carrying the program.

In both the Sale of Goods Act 1979, s 61, and the Supply of Goods and Services Act 1982, s 18, the definition of goods includes 'all personal chattels other than things in action and money'. Clearly, a disk is within this definition. Equally clearly, a program, of itself, is not.

If a disk carrying a program is transferred, by way of sale or hire, and the program is in some way defective, so that it will not instruct or enable the computer to achieve the intended purpose, is this a defect in the disk? Put more precisely, would the seller or hirer of the disk be in breach of the terms as to quality and fitness for purpose implied by s 14 of the 1979 Act and s 9 of the 1982 Act? Mr Dehn QC, for ICL, argues that they would not. He submits that the defective program in my example would be distinct from the tangible disk, and thus that the 'goods' – the disk – would not be defective.

There is no English authority on this question ... We were referred as was Scott Baker J, to a decision of Rogers J in the Supreme Court of New South Wales, *Toby Constructions Products Pty Ltd v Computa Bar (Sales) Pty Ltd* [1983] NSWLR 48. The decision in that case was that the sale of a whole computer system, including both hardware and software, was a sale of 'goods' within the New South Wales legislation, which defines goods in similar terms to those in the English statute. That decision was in my respectful view clearly correct, but it does not answer the present question. Indeed Rogers J specifically did not answer it. In expressing an opinion I am therefore venturing where others have, no doubt wisely, not trodden.

Suppose I buy an instruction manual on the maintenance and repair of a particular make of car. The instructions are wrong in an important respect. Anybody who follows them is likely to cause serious damage to the engine of his car. In my view, the instructions are an integral part of the manual. The manual including the instructions, whether in book or video cassette, would in my opinion be 'goods' within the meaning of the 1979 Act, and the defective instructions would result in a breach of the implied terms in s 14.

If this is correct, I can see no logical reason why it should not also be correct in relation to a computer disk onto which a program designed and intended to instruct or enable a computer to achieve particular functions has been encoded. If the disk is sold or hired by the computer manufacturer, but the program is defective, in my opinion there would *prima facie* be a breach of the terms as to quality and fitness for purpose implied by the 1979 Act or the 1982 Act.

Some unease may be generated by the idea of treating an error in the instructions in a manual as a defect in goods that could constitute a breach of the terms implied by s 14 of the SGA 1979. Someone exercising professional expertise is normally only required to exercise due care and would not usually be subject to strict liability, such as that embodied in the implied terms. However, whatever the situation in relation to an instruction manual, there may be a stronger argument for characterising software as goods because of its functional nature, a point which will be returned to below (see p 144)

It should be emphasised that Sir Iain Glidewell's comments were *obiter*. There was an express term which covered the situation and, in any event, the case could not be one for the sale, or even hire, of goods, no matter what the characterisation of software. The disks containing the program were not supplied to the council; rather, a representative of ICL installed the program onto the council's computers and the council did not come into possession of the disks as such. The case is an important one, but the question of categorising software should now be addressed generally.

Goods: Definition and arguments

The starting point for considering whether software can be goods should be the statutory definition of goods. Section 61 of the SGA 1979 states:

> 'Goods' includes all personal chattels other than things in action and money ...

One argument is that a computer program cannot be goods, as it is, in nature, information and not a 'personal chattel'. Another is that it is intellectual property, and so is covered by the exclusion from the definition of 'things in action'. These two arguments should be considered and then further arguments will be addressed.

Software as information

The argument that a program is information and so cannot be goods is put forward by Scott.

> **Software as goods: *nullum simile est idem***
> **Andrew Scott**
> **(1987) 4 CL & P 133**
>
> The starting point in determining whether to classify software as goods or services must be the definition of 'goods' in s 61 of the Sale of Goods Act 1979. This defines 'goods' as including all personal chattels other than things in action and money. A personal chattel is a chose in possession, which is a form of personal property, that is, a thing in which a person has property rights.
>
> Software, since it is simply coded information, is altogether different in nature from personal property. In *Prince Albert v Strange* (1849) 1 Mac & G 25, however, Lord Cottenham LC held that the plaintiff could restrain the publication of copies of etchings made by the plaintiff, on the basis of the existence of property rights in those etchings. His Lordship stated:
>
> > The property in an author or composer of any work of literature, art or science, such work being unpublished and kept for his private use or pleasure, cannot be disputed.
>
> However, this proposition can no longer be considered good law. In *Fraser v Evans* [1969] 1 QB 349 Lord Denning MR stated that in proper circumstances the courts will restrain the publication or use of confidential information; but that the jurisdiction of the court to

do so was not based on the existence of property rights or contract, but on the duty of good faith. The existence of property rights in information has been repudiated by high authority. In *Boardman v Phipps* [1967] 2 AC 46 Lord Upjohn stated:

> In general information is not property at all. It is normally open to all who have eyes to read and ears to hear ... [C]onfidential information is often and for many years has been described as the property of the donor ... But in the end the real truth is that it is not property in any normal sense but equity will restrain its transmission to another if in breach of some confidential relationship.

Therefore rights with respect to information concern control over its use. It was this proposition which formed the basis of the decision of the stipendiary magistrate in *Oxford v Moss* [1978] 68 Cr App R 183, which was upheld on appeal. The defendant, who was an engineering undergraduate, was charged with the theft of confidential information from the senate of his university. This information consisted of the questions set for an examination. On appeal by the prosecutor, the Divisional Court held that confidential information was not 'property' within the meaning of s 4 of the Theft Act 1968, and therefore could not be appropriated.

Information, although not property, has value in itself. The courts recognise and protect this intrinsic value by permitting the author or donor control over its use. When information is recorded on some medium, that medium is then invested with the value of the information. Information, and therefore software, cannot be considered as 'goods' within the definition contained in s 61.

However, when a program is embodied on a computer disk or other such medium, the argument that it is simply information can be met from two perspectives – (a) the physical, and (b) the functional.

(a) Physical

The physical argument, that the program has physical form on the disk or other such medium, was recognised in the *St Albans* case.[45] It was also used in the criminal case of *R v Whiteley*,[46] where the question was whether the alteration and deletion of computer files by a 'hacker' could constitute criminal damage within s 1(1) of the Criminal Damage Act 1971. Additionally, it has been focused on by the US courts, for example, by the Supreme Court of Louisiana in *South Central Bell Telephone Co v Barthelemy*.[47] In considering whether the software Bell had acquired constituted 'tangible personal property' for the purposes of a New Orleans sales and use tax, it was said:

> South Central Bell argues that the software is merely 'knowledge' or 'intelligence', and as such is not corporeal and thus not taxable. We disagree with South Central Bell's characterisation. The software at issue is not merely knowledge but rather knowledge recorded in a physical form which has physical existence, takes up space on the tape, disk or hard drive, makes physical things happen and can be perceived by the senses ...

---

45   In the *St Albans* case, Sir Iain Glidewell recognised that a program, 'of itself', was not goods, but concluded that it could be such when embodied in a disk – see above.
46   (1991) *The Times*, 6 February. See, also, *Cox v Riley* [1986] CLR 460.
47   643 So 2d 1240 (La 1994).

R v Whiteley
(1991) 93 Cr App R 25

Lord Lane LCJ gave the opinion of the Court of Appeal.

The principle ground of the defence which has formed the basis of the appeal to this court was that a distinction had to be made between the disc itself and the intangible information held upon it which, it was contended, was not capable of damage as defined in law. The argument put before the court of trial and repeated here was as follows:

The computers and the disc cannot be damaged by the sort of interference performed by the appellant. They were designed to perform a particular function and, despite the appellants actions, they were still capable of performing that function. Neither the computers nor the discs suffered any physical damage at all. Any destruction or alteration of the information on a disc, or the writing of information to a disc, only affects information on the disk and does not damage or impair the usefulness of the disk itself ...

Section 10(1) of the Criminal Damage Act 1971, so far as material to the present case, defines 'property' as 'property of a tangible nature', whether real or personal ...

The evidence before the jury was that discs are so constructed as to contain upon them thousands, if not millions, of magnetic particles. By issuing commands to the computer, impulses are produced which magnetise or demagnetise those particles in a particular way. By that means it is possible to write data or information on the discs and to program them to fulfil a variety of functions. By the same method it is possible to delete or alter data, information or instructions which have previously been written on the disc. The argument advanced on behalf of the appellant when reduced to its essence seems to us to be this. That since the state of the magnetic particles on the disc is not perceptible by the unaided human senses, for instance sight or touch, the appellant's activities only affected the 'intangible information contained' on the disc itself even if the absence of such a perceptible change is not fatal to the prosecution, goes on the submission, interference with particles cannot amount to damage in law.

It seems to us that the contention contains a basic fallacy. What the Act requires to be proved is that intangible property has been damaged, not necessarily that the damage itself should be tangible. There can be no doubt that the magnetic particles upon the metal disc were part of the discs and if the appellant was proved to have intentionally and without lawful excuse altered the particles in such a way as to cause an impairment of the value or usefulness of the disc to the owner, there would be damage within the meaning of s 1. The fact that the alteration could only be perceived by operating the computer did not make the alterations any the less real, or the damage ...

It should be noted that the type of situation which was considered in *Whiteley* was taken outside the scope of the Criminal Damage Act 1971 by the Computer Misuse Act 1990, following the recommendations of the Law Commission.[48] The basic approach remains of interest here. It emphasises the physical embodiment of the program on the computer disk or other such medium.[49]

---

48 *Report on Computer Misuse*, No 186, 1989. See, further, below, Chapter 8.
49 But see *James Ashley v London Borough of Sutton* [1995] Tr L Rep 350.

(b) Functional

The second point to be raised, against the argument that software cannot be goods because it is information, is that based on its functional aspect. In the *South Central Bell* case (above), reference was made to the fact that the software is used to make a computer (that is, hardware) 'perform a desired function' and this aspect of software should now be considered.

It should be asked whether a program, embodied on a disk and ready to be fed into a computer, is merely information. Is it distinguishable from the exam paper in *Oxford v Moss*[50] which was referred to by Scott (above p 142). If a program is likened to a literary work, which is the categorisation applied to it to provide it with the protection of copyright, then it is most like an instruction manual or 'how to' book, which was the analogy made by Sir Iain Glidewell in *St Albans v ICL*. Certainly, software is not like a novel! However, a program differs from even an instruction manual. It does not simply tell the individual what to do. The software interacts directly, with the hardware. In *St Albans v ICL*,[51] at first instance, Scott Baker J was of the opinion that software 'is not simply abstract information like information passed by word of mouth. Entering software alters the contents of the hardware'. This may not be an entirely accurate view of the effect of software on hardware but the general idea is clear enough – software is not mere information, it has a direct effect on hardware. Another point can also be made, following on from this. If there is a defect in software, there may well not be a point at which an individual has an opportunity to exercise judgment, assess what is occuring and intervene to prevent some unexpected, and unwanted, result. Software may be information, but it is not simply information.

An analogy can be made here with the US case of *Winter v G P Puttnam & Sons*.[52] In that case, the question arose as to the applicability of product liability laws to a book on collecting and cooking mushrooms. It was held that the information contained in the book was not a product. What is of interest here is that, in coming to that conclusion, the court contrasted the situation before it with one involving software. It was indicated that software would be a product. The software was seen as something more than just information.[53] It can be contended that the functional aspect of software strengthens the case for the 'goods' categorisation to cover both a disk and the program embodied on it.

---

50 (1978) 68 Cr App R 183.

51 [1995] FSR 686, p 699.

52 938 F 2d 1033 (9th Cir 1991).

53 See, further, Saxby, (ed), 1990, p 7084. In fact, this type of distinction has been made in relation to US product liability laws in a way which might be used to argue that a program supplied as a written source code could constitute goods. In *Saloomey v Jeppesen* 707 F 2d 671 (1983), airline charts were not treated like other printed information. When a chart failed to show a mountain which was in the vicinity of an airport, it was held to be a defective product. Such information is relied on more automatically, and with less scope for assessment, than most information, and the analogy with a computer program can be made. For discussion of the question of product liability, see below, Chapter 5.

Intellectual property

As we have seen, the definition of 'goods' in the 1979 Act excludes 'things in action' and it might be argued that programs are covered by this exclusion and, therefore, are not goods. However, the program is not itself copyright; it is protected by copyright. This was recognised by Steyn J in *Eurodynamics Systems v General Automation Ltd*.[54] He said, 'Although the ideas and concepts involved in software remained [the defendants'] intellectual property, the reality of the transaction is that there has been the transfer of a product'. When there is a contract for the supply of a program, it is not simply an assignment of intellectual property rights. In fact, as has been indicated, in most cases there will not be an assignment of the copyright in a program, although licenses are normally granted. Properly identified, the problem is whether, when intellectual property rights are in question, they dominate the transaction to prevent the disk, with the program embodied in it, from being regarded as goods. Copyright restrictions are not seen as preventing a book, video tape or compact disc from being goods, but such items do not have a functional use in the way that software does, and that difference in use is not only noteworthy in itself, but also makes a considerable difference to the impact of intellectual property rights. Intellectual property rights impact upon the enjoyment of books and videos to a very much more limited extent than upon the enjoyment of software.[55] A book can be read or a video watched without any need for the purchaser to obtain a licence to avoid being in breach of copyright. In contrast, the use of software will entail copying it onto hardware, which, in the absence of a licence, would, *prima facie*, be in breach of copyright,[56] although the impact of the EC Directive on this must now be borne in mind.[57] In other words, the basic purpose for which a book or video is purchased can be fulfilled without any need for the purchaser to consider intellectual property rights. The same is not true of software. Indeed, the view has been taken that software cannot be likened to books or other such goods, but must be regarded as *sui generis*:[58]

> The analogy with a printed book is, in my opinion, false. Even if one considered the wider field of printed material, there would be no true analogy. A book typically is intended to be read, not copied, as a way of enjoying or using the object ... there are no limitations on accessing the information which affect readers generally ... In the case of software there is no possibility of accessing the information without copying it. In my opinion the only acceptable view is that the supply of proprietary software for a price is a contract *sui generis*.

However, the argument that software cannot be goods because of the intellectual property rights involved was considered by the US Court of Appeals for the Third Circuit in *Advent Systems Ltd v Unisys Corp*.[59] The court had to determine the

---

54 (1988) unreported, 6 September.
55 See *Beta Computers (Europe) Ltd v Adobe Systems (Europe) Ltd* [1996] FSR 387.
56 CDPA 1988, s 17(1).
57 See above, p 110, in relation to the impact of the EC Directive on the Legal Protection of Computer Programs (91/250/EC).
58 *Beta Computers (Europe) Ltd v Adobe Systems (Europe) Ltd* [1996] FSR 387, p 396, *per* Lord Penrose.
59 925 F 2d 670 (1991). But see *Conopco Inc v McCreadie* 826 F Supp 855 (1991). The argument was not considered, as such, in *Beta v Adobe*, but some support for it may be found in the approach there taken.

applicability of Art 2 of the Uniform Commercial Code to a contract under which Advent agreed to supply hardware and 'license software' to Unisys.[60] Weiss J, delivering the opinion of the court, said this:

> That a computer program may be copyrightable as intellectual property does not alter the fact that once in the form of a floppy disk or other medium, the program is tangible, movable and available in the marketplace.

The court emphasised the physical embodiment of the program in a disk or other such medium in concluding that it was goods, and not merely intellectual property, and fell within Art 2. This same approach could be taken to indicate that a program embodied on a disk would be goods under the SGA 1979. However, there is a further argument, based on the significance of the intellectual property rights in software, as to whether a contract for the provision of software is capable of being a contract for the sale of goods.

Section 2(1) of the SGA 1979 states that a contract of sale of goods is:

> ... a contract by which the seller transfers or agrees to transfer the property in goods to the buyer for a money consideration called the price.

The 'property in goods' is not the physical object but, basically, the ownership of the goods.[61] The person to whom a disk is supplied will take it subject to the restrictions of copyright and a licence will normally be involved. The question is whether those restrictions are sufficient to prevent that person acquiring the 'property' in the goods. Certainly, copyright restrictions are not seen as preventing there from being a sale of a book, video tape or compact disc, but, as has been indicated, such restrictions impact rather differently on books from their effect on software. However, if a disk with a program on it is classified as goods, it may be doubted whether this type of argument would prevail.

Of course, if there is clearly no transfer of the ownership, even of the disk or other such medium (which may well occur where non-standard software is in question), but a mere supply under an agreement that the disk will be returned when the program licence terminates, then the contract will not fall within the 1979 Act. However, it should be remembered that similar terms to those implied by the SGA 1979 are implied into contracts for the hire of goods by the SGSA 1982.

Further issues

Consideration has been given to the arguments that a program is information or copyright and so cannot constitute goods. Some arguments in favour of that classification have been indicated, but we should now consider two further arguments. One is pragmatic and the other relates to the appropriateness of classifying software as goods.

---

60   Article 2 applies to goods and intellectual property is outside the Uniform Commercial Code. See, generally, Rodau, A, 'Computer software: does Article 2 of the Uniform Commercial Code apply?' (1986) Emory LJ 853.
61   See, generally, Atiyah, Adams and MacQueen (eds) 2000, p 265 *et seq.*

Pragmatism

In the *St Albans* case, both Scott Baker J and Sir Iain Glidewell indicated that a program supplied on a disk or other such medium, but without any hardware, should be treated as 'goods'. Scott Baker J's reasoning was basically pragmatic. He took the view that otherwise no statutory regime would apply and the recipient would be unprotected in the absence of express terms. This type of pragmatic argument had already been seen as persuasive by Napier.

The future of information technology law
Brian Napier
[1992] CLJ 46

... we must first acknowledge the problem of knowing what software is in legal terms. When we acquire software, we acquire structured and coded information of a highly specialised nature. Software is of course protected by the law of intellectual property, but it is not itself intellectual property. It is essentially information, and as Lord Upjohn stated many years ago, information as such is generally not property. The law recognises its value by allowing restrictions on its use, not by bringing it within the realm of ownership. Information cannot be stolen and it would appear that it can be the subject of criminal damage only in so far as it is recorded on a physical storage medium. Thus it would seem to follow inexorably that no 'goods' within the meaning of the Sale of Goods Act 1979 are involved if a pure software transaction takes the form of a sale – though judges in England have hesitated to say so. When we buy pure software (ie structured information) we acquire the intellectual achievement of the individual who by his work has produced the information. But that is not all. In almost all cases such purchase of information is accompanied by the acquisition of the medium – such as a floppy disc or chip – on which it is recorded. We normally acquire title to that medium – at least when we buy the whole product in the shops. But when software is captured on a physical medium do we have, by *specificatio,* creation of a new thing, capable of constituting a 'good' ... ? If the answer is 'yes', as some have suggested then it might be objected that we have allowed the physical medium to dictate the legal message. But if we say 'no' we face a much greater evil – a flat contradiction between our commonsense expectations and legal analysis. Most consumers would be surprised, and rightly so, at the suggestion that the retailer from whom their software was bought guaranteed only the floppy disc and the system documentation (the handbook) – not the performance and quality of the programs recorded on it. The view that recorded software is 'goods' has recently been affirmed in the USA by a Court of Appeals considering the scope of Article 2 of the Uniform Commercial Code.

Appropriateness

However, even though there are undoubted attractions in finding software to be included in a well established legal category, it must be considered whether that is appropriate. The law may say that, henceforth, elephants are to be called mice, but the law cannot say that elephants are mice. Is software too unlike other things that are categorised as goods for the label to be appropriate? The goods which software is most akin to are books, music CDs and video tapes, but one of the factors used to indicate that software is not just information, its functional aspect, also makes it very different from those types of goods. Additionally, despite the comment of Scott Baker J in the *St*

Albans case,[62] it should be noted that programs are not always transferred using a disk or some other such medium. Could a program transferred down a telephone line constitute goods? That seems unlikely,[63] but, if it cannot, then a problem with the pragmatic argument arises. The 'goods' categorisation might provide an existing legal framework for consideration of some transactions involving computer programs but certainly not all. Would categorising as goods a program embodied, and transferred, on a disk or other such medium inappropriately divorce its legal categorisation from that of programs transferred without the use of such a medium?[64] In *Beta Computers (Europe) Ltd v Adobe Systems (Europe) Ltd*,[65] a Scottish case which dealt with the question of the effectiveness of a 'shrink wrap' licence (see above p 117), Lord Penrose, *obiter*, considered the contention that software should be regarded as goods. He said:

> This reasoning [that software is goods] appears to me to be unattractive, at least, in the context with which this case is concerned. It appears to emphasise the role of the physical medium and to relate the transaction in the medium to sale or hire of goods. It would have the somewhat odd result that the dominant characteristic of the complex product, in terms of value or the significant interests of the parties, would be subordinated to the medium by which it was transmitted to the user in analysing the true nature and effect of the contract.

The final point to be made here relates to Scott Baker J's concerns, in the *St Albans* case, that if the supply of software is not a supply of goods it will be 'something to which no statutory rules apply, thus leaving the recipient unprotected in the absence of express agreement'.[66] The SGA 1979 is largely based on the 1893 Act of the same name. Legislation covering other contracts dealing with goods occurred much later (for example, the SGSA 1982). However, prior to the existence of wider legislation, the common law proved capable of often implying the same, or similar, terms into contracts dealing with goods which did not fall within the Sale of Goods Acts.[67] Similarly, it would not be impossible for the court to find that the common law implied terms that programs should be of 'satisfactory quality' and 'reasonably fit' for the purchaser's 'particular purpose', even if, in all cases or some cases, software is not categorised as goods. When the Court of Appeal considered the *St Albans* case, Sir Iain

---

62 [1995] FSR 686, p 699.

63 It seems doubtful that such a contract could be considered as a contract for the sale of goods. Such a categorisation would seem contrary to an approach which emphasises the importance of the embodiment of the program in a disk or other such medium. However, it has been indicated that it is uncertain whether electricity can constitute goods (Guest, (ed) 1992 para 1-084) and, if it could be so treated, it could similarly be argued that a program supplied by downloading could be goods (see 'Computer programs as goods under the UCC' (1979) 77 Mich L Rev 1149). See also *Tamarind International Ltd v Eastern Natural Gas (Retail) Ltd* (2000) CLC 1397 – assumed agents acting in relation ot the sale or purchase of gas and electricity would fall with the Commercial Agents (Council Directive) Regulations 1993 on the basis that they were dealing with 'goods'.

64 And of some cases where such a medium was used but not delivered to the recipient of the program, as in *St Albans City and DC v ICL* [1995] FSR 686.

65 [1996] FSR 387.

66 [1995] FSR 686. There was an express term that the computer system would be reasonably fit for the buyer's purpose in the *St Albans* case.

67 Eg, *Dodd v Wilson* [1946] 2 All ER 691. See, generally, Atiyah, 2000.

Glidewell thought that, in the absence of an express term requiring the program to be fit for its purpose, one could have been implied at common law.[68]

As will be seen, when consideration is given to the terms implied by s 14 of the SGA 1979, those terms requiring the goods to be of 'satisfactory quality' and 'reasonable fitness' for the buyer's 'particular purpose' are flexible in their content, and similar terms dealing with the functioning of the program may be appropriate, generally, in contracts for the supply of programs. It is worthwhile considering the terms implied by the SGA 1979 not only because software may be categorised as goods in some cases but also because, even if that is not seen as appropriate in any case, the common law may imply the same or similar terms. In any event, they should be addressed as it would seem that a system involving both hardware and software will be treated as goods.[69]

Services

Even if software can be goods and ownership of the disk passes, it may still be argued that it is inappropriate that its supply should be categorised as a sale of goods. It may be argued that the transaction should be regarded as a contract for work and materials (or, more broadly, for 'services'), rather than for goods. Of course, there may well be found to be a contract for services if no goods are in question. However, what is of particular note here is the distinction between a contract for services, which also involves goods, and one that is simply for the sale of goods. The line between such contracts for services and contracts for the sale of goods has been one which the courts have attempted to draw in many different contexts and it has never proved an easy categorisation to make.[70] Nevertheless, it may be a very important distinction. If a contract for the supply of software is one for the sale of goods, then, subject to the possibility of their inapplicability, or of the effectiveness of an exemption clause, the software will have to comply with the statutory implied terms as to description (s 13 of the SGA 1979), satisfactory quality (s 14(2)) and reasonable fitness for the buyer's particular purpose (s 14(3)). Whilst the terms implied by s 14 set standards by reference to the 'reasonable person' (s 14(2)) or require 'reasonable fitness' (s 14(3)), they are all nevertheless strict. The seller cannot escape liability for their breach by proving that the problem with the goods was not due to any fault on his or her part.[71] In contrast, if what is in question is the provision of a service, then the relevant implied term stems from s 13 of the SGSA 1982, which merely requires that, where the supplier of a service acts in the course of a business, he or she should do so with due care. The strict terms, requiring goods to be, *inter alia*, of satisfactory quality, would apply only

---

68 [1996] 4 All ER 481, p 494. The implication envisaged would appear to have been one made 'in fact', but such an implied term might be found more generally, 'in law'. For the implication of terms at common law see above, p 103.

69 *Toby Constructions Products Pty Ltd v Computa Bar (Sales) Pty Ltd* [1983] NSWLR 48. *St Albans City and DC v International Computers Ltd* [1996] 4 All ER 481.

70 See, eg, Samek, RA, 'Contracts for work and materials' (1962) 36 ALJ 66.

71 *Kendall v Lillico* [1969] 2 AC 31; *Frost v Aylesbury Dairy Co* [1905] 1 KB 685.

to goods supplied incidentally to the service.[72] (It is possible for there to be additional terms which are either express or implied at common law, which impose stricter obligations in relation to what is produced by the services,[73] but here we are primarily concerned with the terms implied by statute.)

In the context of contracts concerned with software and the statutory regimes, the impact of a contract being for services rather than goods can be illustrated. If there is a contract to write a bespoke program, which is categorised as a contract for services, then the strict liability would seem only to apply to the fabric of the disk.[74] The content of the program would be the outcome of the services and the relevant statutorily implied term would simply be that requiring the services to be performed with due care. In other words, the strict liability terms would not apply to the product of the services; they would apply only to goods transferred to the other party incidentally to those services. A more complex problem might arise where the contract is for the supply and installation into the purchaser's system of an 'off the shelf' program. If such a contract was characterised as being one for services, because of the work involved in the installation, then it would seem that any aspect of the program adapted by that installation would only be covered by the requirement that the work should be carried out with due care. However, if the 'off the shelf' software was goods, then any defect in the program which was not caused by the installation would seem to be subject to the strict requirements of the statutorily implied terms as to fitness for purpose and satisfactory quality.[75]

Two basic approaches to distinguishing contracts for the sale of goods and contracts for the supply of services can be found. These can be seen in the cases of *Lee v Griffin*,[76] and *Robinson v Graves*.[77] *Lee v Griffin* was concerned with a contract made by a dentist to supply a set of false teeth, made to fit the individual patient. On appeal, that was concluded to be a contract for the sale of goods. In *Robinson v Graves*, a contract was made with an artist for a portrait of a particular individual and the Court of Appeal concluded that it was a contract for the services of the artist, rather than one for the sale of goods.

---

72 In *Dodd v Wilson* [1946] 2 All ER 691, the contract was for the services of a vet. He was strictly liable when a vaccine with which he inoculated a cow was not reasonably fit for its purpose. Of course, had the problem been with, eg, the way in which the injection was given, he would only have been liable in the absence of due care.

73 Eg, *Greaves & Co (Contractors) v Beynham Meikle and Partners* [1975] 3 All ER 99. An additional term implied at common law, that the software would be reasonably fit for its purpose, may be the explanation of the assumption in *Saphena Computing Ltd v Allied Collection Agencies Ltd* [1995] FSR 616 that it made no difference whether the contract was one for goods or services.

74 But see the assumption in *ibid*, *Saphena*, that it made no difference to the applicability of the strict liability terms as to quality whether the contract was characterised as being for goods or services (p 652, *per* Staughton LJ). See, also, above, fn 73; *St Albans City and DC v ICL* [1995] FSR 686, p 698, below, fn 75.

75 Could this provide, on the facts of the case, a justification for the odd assumption of Scott Baker J in *St Albans City and DC v ICL* [1995] FSR 686, p 698 that it made no difference to the implied terms whether the contract was characterised as being for goods or services?

76 (1861) 1 B & S 272.

77 [1935] 1 KB 579.

Lee v Griffin
(1861) 1 B & S 272

Crompton J The main question which arose at the trial was whether the contract ... could be treated as one for work and labour, or whether it was a contract for goods sold and delivered. The distinction between these two causes of action is sometimes very fine; but, where the contract is for a chattel to be made and delivered, it clearly is a contract for the sale of goods. There are some cases in which the supply of materials is ancillary to the contract, as in the case of a printer supplying the materials on which a book is printed. In such a case an action might perhaps be brought for work and labour done, and materials provided, as it could hardly be said that the subject matter of the contract was a sale of a chattel; perhaps it is more in the nature of a contract merely to exercise skill and labour ... I certainly do not agree to the proposition that the value of the skill and labour, as compared to that of the material supplied, is a criterion by which to decide whether the contract be for work and labour or for the sale of a chattel. Here however, the subject matter of the contract was the supply of goods. The case bears a strong resemblance to that of a tailor supplying a coat, the measurement of the mouth and fitting of the teeth being analogous to the measurement and fitting of the garment.

Blackburn J the question is whether the contract was one for the sale of goods or for work and labour. I think that in all cases, in order to ascertain whether the action ought to be brought for goods sold and delivered, or for work and labour done and materials provided, we must look at the particular contract entered into between the parties. If the contract be such that, when carried out, it would result in the sale of a chattel, the party cannot sue for work and labour; but, if the result of the contract is that the party has done work and labour which ends in nothing that can be the subject of a sale, the party cannot sue for goods sold and delivered. The case of an attorney employed to prepare a deed is an illustration of this latter proposition. It cannot be said that the paper and ink he uses in preparation of the deed are goods sold and delivered. The case of a printer printing a book would most probably fall within the same category ... In the present case, the contract was to deliver a thing which, when completed, would have resulted in the sale of a chattel; in other words, the substance of the contract was for goods sold and delivered. I do not think that the test to apply to these cases is whether the value of the work exceeds that of the materials used in its execution; for if a sculptor were employed to execute a work of art, greatly as his skill and labour, supposing it to be of the highest description, might exceed the value of the marble on which he worked, the contract would, in my opinion, nevertheless be a contract for the sale of a chattel.

Robinson v Graves
[1935] 1 KB 579

Greer LJ I can imagine that nothing would be more surprising to a client going to a portrait painter to have his portrait painted and to the artist who was accepting the commission than to be told that they were making a bargain about the sale of goods. It is, of course, possible that a picture may be ordered in such circumstances as will make it an order for goods to be supplied in the future, but it does not follow that that is the inference to be drawn in every case as between the client and the artist. Looking at the propositions involved from the point of view of interpreting the words in the English language, it seems to me that the painting of a portrait in these circumstances would not, in the ordinary use of the English language, be deemed to be the purchase and sale of that which is produced by the artist. It would, on the contrary, be held to be an undertaking by the artist to exercise such skill as he was possessed of in order to produce for reward a thing which would ultimately have to be accepted by the client. If that is so, the contract in this case was not a contract for the sale of goods.

... If you find as they did in *Lee v Griffin* that the substance of the contract was the production of something to be sold by the dentist to the dentist's customer, then that is a sale of goods. But if the substance of the contract, on the other hand, is that skill and labour have to be exercised for the production of the article and that it is only ancillary to that that there will pass from the artist to his client or customer some materials in addition to the skill involved in the production of the portrait, that does not make any difference to the result, because the substance of the contract is the skill and experience of the artist in producing the picture.

... For these reasons I am of opinion that in this case the substance of the matter was an agreement for the exercise of skill and it was only incidental that some materials would have to pass from the artist to the gentleman who commissioned the portrait. For these reasons I think that this was not a contract for the sale of goods

The Court of Appeal in *Robinson v Graves* attempted to argue that its approach was consistent with the line taken in *Lee v Griffin*, but it is clear that there are two different approaches operating.

In *Lee v Griffin*,[78] the basic approach was that if the services produced goods, the ownership of which the supplier transferred to the other party, there was a contract for the sale of goods. This line was mitigated only in the situation where the transfer of ownership of any goods could be regarded as relatively insignificant, as in the example of the solicitor drawing up the deed. Clearly, Blackburn J's references to the 'substance' of the contract were not intended to be taken any further than that.

Robinson v Graves takes an approach which allows much more scope for a contract to be characterised as one for services (or work and materials). It is a matter of looking for the dominant element in the contract – the end product or the skill and expertise of the person providing the services. This is commonly described as looking for the 'substance of the contract' but, as has already been indicated, this should not be confused with the line taken by Blackburn J in *Lee v Griffin*.

The supply of software

Obviously, the acquisition of bespoke software provides the strongest case for arguing that a contract for the supply of software must be regarded as one for services rather than goods. However, even then, the categorisation should not be assumed in every case. Two particular examples can be suggested where a contract for bespoke software might nevertheless be characterised as one for goods. The first example relates to the case in which, although the software is being written because it was requested by one particular company, the suppliers realise that there will be a market to supply it to other companies and intend to do so.[79] It might be argued that the intent to subsequently 'mass supply' the software could affect the characterisation of a contract to supply what was, at that stage, bespoke software, making it appropriate to characterise it as being for goods, rather than services. The other example concerns the 'turn key contract'. Even where goods are to be manufactured by a seller, it is possible for that seller to contract simply in relation to a result (the goods), rather than the manufacture and delivery of the goods. The former case may be argued to be one for

---

78   See, also, eg, *J Marcel (Furriers) Ltd v Tapper* [1953] 1 WLR 49.
79   This was the fact situation in *Saphena Computing Ltd v Allied Collection Agencies* [1995] FSR 616, which led to a dispute as to the ownership of copyright.

the sale of goods rather than the supply of services and this argument would seem to apply to the so called turn key contract. That is the type of contract where a complete system is installed and then simply handed over to the party to whom it is being supplied. (The name 'turn key contracts' stems from those cases where the acquirer is 'locked out' until the system is completed, only at that point being given access to it.) In such contracts, the way in which the supplier arrives at the completed product seems to be irrelevant to the other party. It is a contract purely concerned with results and a 'goods' rather than 'services' categorisation may be appropriate, even where what is in question is bespoke software.

After considering bespoke software, modified standard (or modified 'off the shelf') software should be looked at. The approach taken in *Robinson v Graves*,[80] could provide a strong argument in favour of the services classification where some modified standard software is in question, depending upon the extent and novelty of the modification.

At the other end of the spectrum from bespoke software is standard, or 'off the shelf', software. There seems to be little scope for an argument that, even if such software is goods, a contract for its supply must nevertheless be characterised as one for services.[81] In *Toby Constructions Products Ltd v Computer Bar Sales Pty Ltd*, where the contract was for the supply of a computer system composed of hardware and 'off the shelf' software, Rogers J concluded that he was dealing with a contract for goods and dismissed the argument that it was services that were in question. He said:[82]

> Whilst representing the fruits of much research work, [the software] was in current jargon, off the shelf, in a sense, mass produced. There can be no comparison with a one off painting. Rather is the comparison with a mass produced print of a painting.

IMPLIED TERMS: FITNESS FOR PURPOSE ETC

Sections 13–15 of the Sale of Goods Act imply terms into contracts for the sale of goods. They may prove very useful to the purchaser of defective software if such software is categorised as goods. However, as has been suggested, even if software by itself is not characterised as goods, a system involving both hardware and software may well be so labelled[83] and, in any event, even in relation to software the courts may imply similar terms at common law.[84] The value of examining these terms does not solely lie in the possibility that software will be construed as goods.

The possibility of excluding or restricting liability for breaches of the terms implied by ss 13–15 is restricted by s 6 of the Unfair Contract Terms Act (UCTA) 1977 (see p 194). The status of the implied terms should also be noted. They are conditions, and breach of a condition normally gives the injured party the right to reject the goods, as

---

80 See above, p 151.
81 But see *James Ashley v London Borough of Sutton* [1995] Tr L Rep 350.
82 [1983] 2 NSWLR 48, p 51.
83 *Toby Constructions Products Pty Ltd v Computa Bar (Sales) Pty Ltd* [1983] NSWLR 48. *St Albans City and DC v International Computers Ltd* [1996] 4 All ER 481.
84 *St Albans City and DC v ICL* [1996] 4 All ER 481; see above, p 148.

well as claim damages, no matter how trivial the breach. However, the effect of a breach of these conditions was modified by the Sale and Supply of Goods Act (SSGA) 1994.[85] Section 15A of the SGA 1979 now states:

(1) Where in the case of a contract of sale –

    (a) the buyer would, apart from this subsection, have the right to reject goods by reason of a breach on the part of the seller of a term implied by sections 13, 14, or 15 above; but

    (b) the breach is so slight that it would be unreasonable for him to reject them, then, if the buyer does not deal as consumer,

the breach is not to be treated as a breach of condition but may be treated as a breach of warranty.

(2) This section applies unless a contrary intention appears in, or is to be implied from, the contract.

(3) It is for the seller to show that a breach fell within subsection (1)(b) above.

This means that (subject to contrary intention), if the buyer does not 'deal as consumer',[86] then he or she has no right to reject the goods for a breach which is so trivial that it would be unreasonable to do so.[87]

However, there are now additional remedies to consider in relation to breach of the terms implied by ss 13–15. The Sale and Supply of Goods to Consumers Regulations 2002 (implementing EC Directive 1999/44/EC) have inserted sections 48A–48F into the Sale of Goods Act providing a consumer (that is, any natural person who is acting for purposes outside his trade, business or profession') with additional remedies in relation to goods which do not conform to the contract at the time of delivery. Goods do not so conform if there is a breach of an express term or a breach of a term implied by s 13, s 14, or s 15. The additional remedies are repair, replacement, reduction of purchase price or rescission of the contract. Replacement and repair take precedence.

The original rights to reject the goods and terminate the contract will remain but if the consumer has asked for repair or replacement under the new scheme he, or she, will have to give the seller a reasonable time to do so before exercising the original right to reject (s 48D).

---

85 SSGA 1994, s 4, following the recommendations of the Law Commission (Law Com No 160, Cmnd 137, 1987).

86 This phrase is taken from the Unfair Contract Terms Act 1977, where it is defined in s 12 (s 61(5A) Sale of Goods Act 1979). See above, p 194.

87 This innovation is analogous to the common law innominate term. However, when a term is innominate, rather than a condition or warranty, the right to terminate the contract for breach, or, in the language of the Sale of Goods Act 1979, the right to reject the goods, depends upon whether the injured party has been substantially deprived of all the benefit which he or she was intended to derive from the contract (*Hong Kong Fir Shipping Co Ltd v Kawasaki Kisen Kaisha* [1962] 2 QB 26). Ie, when a term is innominate, the right to reject is only present if the breach has very serious consequences. In contrast, s 15A means that rejection for breach of one of the terms implied by ss 13–15 is always available, except where the breach is trivial. Section 15A does not equate the implied terms with innominate terms but it is in keeping with their development. Both prevent a trivial breach from being used opportunistically, by the injured party, to escape from a contract which has simply become a bad bargain from that party's perspective. See Koffman and Macdonald, 2004 paras 8.27–8.32.

SALE BY DESCRIPTION – s 13

Section 13(1) of the SGA 1979 states:

> Where there is a contract for the sale of goods by description, there is an implied term that the goods will correspond with their description.

Two basic questions arise under the section: when is a sale 'by description' and what constitutes 'a description' for the purposes of s 13?

'By description'

Obvious examples will immediately spring to mind of situations in which there will clearly be a sale 'by description'. It would seem inevitable that there will be a sale by description when the contract is for unascertained goods (for example goods not identified when the contract is made, such as a contract for purely generic goods – say, 5,000 tons of coal). In relation to specific goods (that is, goods identified and agreed upon at the time that the contract is made), the obvious example of a sale by description is where buyer has not seen the goods before the contract is made.[88] However, it is clear that sale by description is not restricted to such cases. There may be a sale by description where goods are seen, and even selected, by the buyer. Section 13(3) states:

> A sale of goods is not prevented from being a sale by description by reason only that, being exposed for sale or hire, they are selected by the buyer.

This means that goods displayed in a shop and selected from the shelf by the buyer may still be sold by description. However, the emphasis here is on '*may*'. The question still arises as to when the goods involved in such sales, or other types of sales, are sold by description. In *Grant v Australian Knitting Mills*,[89] Lord Wright said:[90]

> ... a thing is sold by description though it is specific, so long as it is sold not merely as the specific thing but as the thing corresponding to a description.

In other words, the question is whether the parties were merely contracting about the thing in front of them (for example) or that thing as something corresponding to a description.[91] In the latter case, the sale is 'by description'. This was seen in terms of reliance by the Court of Appeal in *Harlingdon & Leinster Enterprises v Christopher Hull Fine Art*.[92]

Harlingdon & Leinster Enterprises v Christopher Hull Fine Art [1991] 1 QB 564

The defendant had two paintings for sale which had been described in a 1980 sale catalogue as the work of Gabrielle Munter, an artist of the German expressionist school.

---

88 *Varley v Whipp* [1900] 1 QB 513.
89 [1936] AC 85.
90 Ibid, at p 100.
91 See, also, *Beale v Taylor* [1967] 1 WLR 1193.
92 [1991] 1 QB 564.

The defendant telephoned the plaintiff, telling him that he had two Munters for sale. When the plaintiff came to the defendant's gallery, the defendant made it clear that he had no expertise in German expressionist painting. The plaintiff saw the paintings and bought one for £6,000. The invoice described the painting as being by Munter. The painting was discovered to be a fake and the plaintiff claimed, *inter alia*, that there was a breach of the term implied by the Sale of Goods Act 1979, s 13(1). The majority of the court, with Stuart-Smith dissenting, held that there had not been a sale by description.

Nourse LJ   Section 13(1) of the Sale of Goods Act 1979 is in these terms:

> Where there is a contract for the sale of goods by description, there is an implied condition that the goods will correspond with the description.

The sales to which the subsection is expressed to apply are sales 'by description'. Authority apart, those words would suggest that the description must be influential in the sale, not necessarily alone, but so as to become an essential term, ie a condition, of the contract. Without such influence a description cannot be said to be one by which the contract for the sale of the goods is made.

I think that the authorities to which we were referred are consistent with this view of section 13(1) ...

... It is suggested that the significance which some of these authorities attribute to the buyer's reliance on the description is misconceived. I think that that criticism is theoretically correct. In theory it is no doubt possible for a description of goods which is not relied on by the buyer to become an essential term of a contract for their sale. But in practice it is very difficult, and perhaps impossible, to think of facts where that would be so. The description must have a sufficient influence in the sale to become an essential term of the contract and the correlative of influence is reliance. Indeed, reliance by the buyer is the natural index of a sale by description. It is true that the question must, as always, be judged objectively and it may be said that previous judicial references have been to subjective or actual reliance. But each of those decisions, including that of Judge Oddie in the present case, can be justified on an objective basis. For all practical purposes, I would say that there cannot be a contract for the sale of goods by description where it is not within the reasonable contemplation of the parties that the buyer is relying on the description.

Slade LJ   While some judicial *dicta* seem to support the view that there can be no sale by description unless there is actual reliance on the description by the purchaser, I am not sure that this is strictly correct in principle. If a party to a contract wishes to claim relief in respect of a misrepresentation as to a matter which did not constitute a term of the contract, his claim will fail unless he is able to show that he relied on this representation in entering into the contract; in general, however, if a party wishes to claim relief in respect of a breach of a *term* of the contract (whether it be a condition or warranty) he need prove no actual reliance.

Nevertheless, where a question arises as to whether a sale of goods was one by description, the presence or absence of reliance on the description may be very relevant in so far as it throws light on the intentions of the parties at the time of the contract. If there was no such reliance by the purchaser, this may be powerful evidence that the parties did not contemplate that the authenticity of the description should constitute a term of the contract – in other words, that they contemplated that the purchaser would be buying the goods as they were. If, on the other hand, there was such reliance (as in *Varley v Whipp* [1900] 1 QB 513, where the purchaser had never seen the goods) this may be equally powerful evidence that it was contemplated by both parties that the correctness of the description would be a term of the contract (so as to bring it within section 13(1)).

Note the different degrees of reliance which Slade and Nourse LJJ referred to. Nourse LJ referred to sufficient reliance for the description to be an 'essential term' – a condition – whilst Slade LJ seems to have considered that sufficient reliance to make it a term will suffice. As we shall see, there is only very limited scope for a descriptive term to be the appropriate type of description to fall within s 13. The greater reliance indicated by Nourse LJ is in keeping with that.[93]

What constitutes a 'description' for the purposes of s 13?

At first sight, it might seem obvious what is being referred to when s 13 says that goods must correspond with their description. However, not everything which would be regarded as a description of the goods in everyday terms will constitute a 'description' for the purposes of s 13. In fact, modern case law takes a very restrictive view of which descriptions fall within s 13.

It has already become clear that only descriptions which are also terms of the contract in their own right can constitute 'descriptions' for the purposes of s 13. In other words, s 13 does not alter the balance between terms and representations.[94] However, not even all descriptive terms will now constitute 'descriptions' for the purposes of s 13.

In the past, in cases such as *Re Moore & Co and Landauer & Co*,[95] a very wide approach was taken in relation to which descriptive terms were capable of falling within s 13. In that case, there was a contract for the sale of Australian tinned fruit, packed in cases containing 30 tins each. The correct overall number of tins was delivered but some of them were packed in cases of 24 tins. The arbitrator found that it made no difference to the market value of the goods whether they were packed in cases of 24 or 30 tins. The Court of Appeal, nevertheless, held that there was a breach of the term implied by s 13. Bankes LJ stated that it was irrelevant whether the trade viewed such matters as important or whether they affected the market value of the goods if, on the face of the contract, they were part of the description of the goods.[96] However, the decision attracted criticism. As the implied term is a condition, this wide approach to s 13 meant that, at that time,[97] the buyer could have a right to reject the goods for trivial breaches. In order to avoid rejection of goods for trivial breaches, the courts developed the modern approach to the scope of the implied term – they could not take the alternative course of altering the status of the term, as that was dictated by statute.[98] The most significant case in considering the more modern, and narrower, approach to s 13 is *Ashington Piggeries v Christopher Hill*.[99]

---

93   But see *Beale v Taylor* [1967] 1 WLR 1193.
94   *Harlingdon & Leinster Enterprises v Christopher Hull Fine Art* [1991] 1 QB 564; *T & J Harrison v Knowles and Foster* [1918] 1 KB 608. See, further, below, p 161, in relation to what purpose is served by s 13 in the light of this.
95   [1921] 2 KB 519.
96   *Ibid*, p 523.
97   The SSGA 1994 amended the effect of the 'condition' classification (see above, p 154).
98   *Reardon Smith Line v Hansen Tangen* [1976] 1 WLR 989, p 998, *per* Lord Wilberforce.
99   [1972] AC 441.

Ashington Piggeries v Christopher Hill
[1972] AC 441

The appellants (Udall) had approached the respondents (Hill), who were animal food compounders, to mix mink food for them. The respondents knew nothing about mink but the appellants supplied them with the formula to be used. One of the ingredients in the formula was herring meal. The respondents supplied the appellants with the compounded mink food which was known as 'King Size'. However, they made up a quantity of 'King Size' using a batch of Norwegian herring meal. Unfortunately, the preservative in the meal had reacted, during its manufacture, to produce a chemical, dimethylnitrosamine (DMNA), which was poisonous to mink. The result was that the batch of 'King Size' made from Norwegian herring meal caused the death of some mink. The appellants claimed against the respondents on several bases. Their claim under s 13 was based on the argument that what had been used in the feed could not be described as 'herring meal' because of the DMNA. The respondents claimed, in turn, against the third party ('the Norwegians') who had supplied them with 'herring meal'. Their claim under s 13 was on the basis that the substance had been stated to be 'Norwegian herring meal. Fair average quality of the season' and that there was a breach of s 13 as it was not 'herring meal' and it was not 'fair average quality'. The description 'herring meal' was found to identify the goods and it fell within s 13 but there was no breach as the goods complied with that 'description', despite the DMNA. The descriptive words, 'fair average quality' did not identify the goods and so did not form part of the 'description' for the purposes of s 13.

Lord Diplock   Not all statements about the characteristics of goods which are the subject matter of a contract of sale form part of the 'description' by which they are sold. Sections 13 and 14 draw a distinction between the description by which goods are sold, on the one hand, and their fitness for the particular purpose for which they are required and their quality, on the other. Section 14(4) recognises that a contract for the sale of goods may contain an express statement about the fitness of the goods for a particular purpose or their quality which does not form part of the description by which they are sold but constitutes a separate stipulation in the contract which may be either a condition or warranty depending upon the construction of the contract (see s 11(1)(b)).

A contract for the sale of goods is one whereby the property in goods which have been physically identified is transferred from the seller to the buyer (see sections 1(1) and 16). But a contract may be made for the sale of unascertained goods before the actual goods in which the property is to be transferred are physically identified and agreed upon. At the time of making such a contract the kind of goods which are its subject matter can only be identified verbally and/or by reference to a sample. The 'description' by which unascertained goods are sold is, in my view, confined to those words in the contract which were intended by the parties to identify the kind of goods which were to be supplied. It is open to the parties to use a description as broad or narrow as they choose. But ultimately the test is whether the buyer could fairly and reasonably refuse to accept the physical goods proffered to him on the ground that their failure to correspond with that part of what was said about them in the contract makes them goods of a different kind from those he had agreed to buy. The key to section 13 is identification.

Udall bases his claim against Hill in the first instance on section 13 of the Act. The goods, he submits, did not correspond with the description by which they were sold. The contract was oral. The subject matter was unascertained goods, and it is common ground that the description by which they were sold was contained in Udall's formula, which set out in detail the ingredients of the feeding-stuff to be compounded by Hill. One of the described ingredients was 'herring meal' ...

DMNA was not an ingredient referred to in the formula. Milmo J, following the cases about the sale of 'copra cake' which was contaminated with castor seed, held that a feeding-stuff which contained DMNA in quantities which rendered it toxic to mink did not correspond with the description by which the goods were sold.

I agree with your Lordships and the Court of Appeal that this is not so. Udall's formula was commercial, not chemical. The ingredient described as 'herring meal' did not cease to comply with that description because it was manufactured from herrings to which a preservative had been added to prevent them from deteriorating. The most usual preservative is common salt (sodium chloride) but the evidence showed that another salt of sodium, sodium nitrite, had been used in Norway for several years before 1961. In certain conditions which can occur during the normal process of manufacture of herring meal the amino-acids naturally present in the herring break down into an organic chemical, dimethylsamine, which can react with sodium nitrite to form DMNA. The occurrence of this reaction may affect the quality of the meal. It does not alter its identity as 'herring meal' ...

So I come once more to section 13 of the Sale of Goods Act 1893, upon which Hill in turn founds his claim against the Norwegians. Since the contract was in writing the description by which the goods were sold must be determined by construing the words used by the parties in the contract. What the contract said about the goods was 'Norwegian herring meal, fair average quality of the season, expected to analyse not less than 70% protein, not more than 12% fat and not more than 40% salt'. I agree with your Lordships that the description by which the goods were sold is limited to the words 'Norwegian herring meal'. That is what identifies the subject matter of the contract. Where a contract contains an express statement about the quality of the goods to be supplied the *prima facie* inference is that this was intended by the parties not as an identification of the kind of goods that are alone the subject matter of the contract, but as an express stipulation as to the standard of quality to which goods of that kind supplied under the contract shall conform. Such an express stipulation may be intended as a condition or as a warranty. Which it is depends upon the construction of the contract.

Lord Wilberforce The question is whether the compound mink food sold by the respondents (under the name 'King Size') corresponded with the description. The appellants' case was that the food was to be made up according to a formula which identified generically the ingredients and specifically the chemical additives, quantifying precisely the proportions of each ingredient. One of these ingredients was herring meal. The food delivered in certain relevant months, it was claimed, did not correspond with the description because it contained a significant quantity of DMNA. The proposition is that 'King Size' made partly of herring meal which contains DMNA does not correspond with the description 'King Size'. This can be reduced to the proposition that the herring meal ingredient did not correspond with the description because it contained DMNA. The analogy was invoked, inevitably, by the appellants of copra cake with castor seed; the respondents invoked that of oxidised iron. The learned judge accepted the former, the Court of Appeal the latter.

Whether in a given case a substance in or upon which there has been produced by chemical interaction some additional substance can properly be described or, if one prefers the word, identified, as the original substance qualified by the addition of a past participle such as contaminated or oxidised, or as the original substance plus, or intermixed with, an additional substance, may, if pressed to analysis, be a question of an Aristotelian character. Where does a substance with a quality pass into an aggregate of substances? I do not think that it can be solved by asking whether the chemical interaction came about by some natural or normal process, eg, preservation by the addition of salt (sodium chloride), or by some alien intrusion by the production of DMNA from sodium nitrite through a heating effect. I cannot see any distinction in principle in this difference. Further, I do not believe that the Sale of Goods Act was designed to provoke metaphysical discussions as to the nature of what is delivered, in comparison with what is sold. The test of description, at least where commodities are concerned, is intended to be a broader, more common sense, test of a mercantile character. The question whether that is what the buyer bargained for has to be answered according to such tests as men in the market would apply, leaving more delicate questions of condition, or quality, to be determined under other clauses of the contract or sections of the Act. Perhaps this is to admit an element of impression into the decision, but I think it is more than impression which leads me to prefer the answer, if not all of the reasoning, of the Court of Appeal that the defect in the meal was a matter of quality or condition rather than of description. I think that buyers and sellers and arbitrators in the market, asked what this was, could only have said that the relevant ingredient was herring meal and, therefore, that there was no failure to correspond with description. In my opinion, the appellants do not succeed under section 13.

From *Ashington Piggeries*, the test for whether the relevant descriptive terms constitute 'descriptions' for the purposes of s 13 could be said to be that of 'identity', that is, only descriptions which identify the goods fall within the scope of s 13.[100] Although Lord Diplock referred to unascertained goods, the test can be regarded as a general one for specific and unascertained goods – he was adopting an approach previously indicated in relation to specific goods. Note should also be made of Lord Wilberforce's test for determining if the implied term has been breached – the 'men in the marketplace test'.[101]

However, what needs to be considered further here is the meaning of the 'identity test'. It would seem that s 13 covers descriptions which identify the goods in the sense that they indicate the 'kind' of goods with which the contract is concerned or that which is 'essential' about them. At this point, a philosophical discussion could be embarked upon as to the nature of identity and whether it is distinguishable from attributes. However, we should remember the context in which it has become necessary to consider the meaning of a test based upon identity and the way in which the courts are treating the test. Certainly, they do not seem concerned with the nature of goods in a metaphysical, or abstract, sense; rather, it is a question of whether the description relates to that which is essential about the goods in the eyes of the parties as reasonable people. Further assistance in understanding the 'identity test' can be gleaned from *Reardon Smith v Hansen Tangen*.[102]

Reardon Smith v Hansen Tangen
[1976] 1 WLR 989

A contract was made to charter a ship on which construction had not been commenced at the time of the contract. By the time the charter came to be fulfilled, the charter market had changed radically and the contract had become very costly to the charterers. The ship met the very detailed contract specifications but it was also stated in the contract that it was '354 Osaka', which would normally have indicated that it would be the 354th ship to be built at the Osaka shipyard. However, it was not built at the Osaka yard, as it was too large, but rather at a new yard, Oshima, and at that yard it was known as 004 Oshima.

---

100 For an interesting discussion of this see Coote, 1976.
101 Contrast the stricter approach in *Arcos Ltd v EA Ronaasen & Son* [1933] AC 470.
102 [1976] 1 WLR 989.

Throughout the documents dealing with its chartering and sub-chartering the ship had been referred to as '354 Osaka'. In order to escape from the costly contract the charterers alleged they had a right to repudiate the contract, as the ship was not 354 Osaka. They were arguing by analogy with sale of goods contracts that there was a breach of condition as the ship did not comply with its description. The House of Lords found that they had no right to reject the vessel because it was 004 Oshima.

Lord Wilberforce In my opinion the fatal defect in their argument consists in their use of the words 'identity' or 'identification' to bridge two meanings. It is one thing to say of given words that their purpose is to state (identify) an essential part of the description of the goods. It is another to say that they provide one party with a specific indication (identification) of the goods so that he can find them and if he wishes sub-dispose of them. The appellants wish to say of words which 'identify' the goods in the second sense, that they describe them in the first ... I can only read the words in the second sense.

The difference is vital. If the words are read in the first sense, then, unless I am right in the legal argument above, each element in them has to be given contractual force. The vessel must, as a matter of contract, and as an essential term, be built by Osaka and must bear their Yard Number 354 – if not, the description is not complied with and the vessel tendered is not that contracted for.

If in the second sense, the only question is whether the words provide a means of identifying the vessel. If they fairly do this, they have fulfilled their function. It follows that if the second sense is correct, the words used can be construed much more liberally than they would have to be construed if they were providing essential elements of the description.

The appellants at one time placed great stress on the yard no provision. They contended that by using it the 'owners' assumed an obligation that the vessel should bear a number which would indicate that it would be constructed in the yard, where that number was appropriate, in sequence after vessels bearing earlier yard numbers (350–53). But this argument broke down in face of the fact, certainly known to Sanko which used and introduced the number into the charter-parties, that the sequence through 354 was the sequence used at Osaka Shipbuilding Company's yard at Osaka, which yard could not construct the vessel. Thus the use of the yard no. for the contracted vessel must have had some other purpose than indicating construction at a particular yard. This turns the argument against the appellants – for it shows the words to be 'labelling' words rather than words creating an obligation.

Note Lord Wilberforce's two meanings of 'identity' and 'identification'. The court also considered whether it was vitally important that the ship was built at the Osaka yard because, for example, of the expertise available at that yard. Their consideration of whether '354 Osaka' 'identified' the ship was relative to the views of the parties. It was not based on the abstract nature of a tanker (there was no search for what constitutes 'essence of tanker'!).

Care is required in applying the identity test to distinguish which descriptive terms constitute 'descriptions' for the purposes of s 13. Only descriptive terms which state what is 'essential' about the goods, in the eyes of the parties, fall within s 13 and, in the light of *Ashington Piggeries*, it is clear that 'essential' has to be understood restrictively. In other words, the scope of the term implied by s 13 is very narrow. It would also seem that s 13 does very little. The older approach meant that s 13 had the role of giving all descriptive terms the status of conditions (converting at least some of them from the status of mere warranties). In contrast, if the modern approach only includes descriptive terms which state that which is essential about the goods, it would seem that such terms would be conditions in their own right. This might be seen as making s 13 irrelevant and unnecessary. However, the impact of s 6 of UCTA 1977 must be borne in mind. That section provides significant protection against the exclusion or restriction of liability for breach of the statutorily implied terms. Certainly, those who deal as consumers acquire greater protection against a clause exempting liability for breach of one of the terms implied by the SGA 1979 than for breach of a simple express term of the contract (see p 194).

In the context of software, questions relevant to s 13 of the 1979 Act might arise in relation to the statement that, for example, what was being supplied was a 'word-processing program suitable for office use'. Provided that the entire statement is part of the contract terms, the question of the scope of s 13 might become relevant. A number of examples can be considered:

- Section 13 might merely cover the statement that what was being supplied was a 'program'. If there was some defect in its functioning, the question would then arise (following Lord Wilberforce in *Ashington Piggeries*) as to whether that defect would affect the characterisation of it by 'the men in the marketplace' – would they still regard it as a 'program'?

- It seems more likely that the situation would be one in which it would be found to be essential to the parties that the program should be a 'word-processing program'. In this case, there would be a clear breach if what was supplied was not a word-processing program but a spreadsheet program. In the industry, these are clearly distinct types of program and are commonly advertised, and referred to, as such. In that context, the effect of the men in the marketplace test seems clear. However, if what has been supplied is a program which would be an efficient word-processor but for the defects in it, there seems less likely to be a breach (a merely defective program is still likely to be regarded as a word-processing program by the 'men in the marketplace', although it should depend upon the extent of the problems).

- The final possibility raised by the statement above is that the scope of s 13 extends to the statement that the word-processing program is for 'office use'. As Lord Diplock indicated in *Ashington Piggeries* (see above), there is no easy distinction to be made between quality and description. Words indicating the quality of the goods may be part of the 'description' for the purposes of s 13, but that will not usually be the case. They will usually merely be of relevance to the terms implied by s 14(2) and (3) or in their own right, as express conditions, warranties or innominate terms. However, the basic test must be applied in each case. What is important is the perceptions of the parties. It must be asked whether such a descriptive term 'identified' the goods in the relevant sense. If the statement that the program was for 'office use' was found to fall within s 13, then the 'men in the marketplace test' should be applied to the particular complaint, for example, that the program could not handle the integration of different documents well enough.

SATISFACTORY QUALITY

Section 14 implies a term that the goods are of satisfactory quality.

    (2)   Where the seller sells goods in the course of a business, there is an implied term that the goods supplied under the contract are of satisfactory quality.

(2A) For the purposes of this Act, goods are of satisfactory quality if they meet the standard that a reasonable person would regard as satisfactory, taking account of any description of the goods, the price (if relevant) and all other relevant circumstances.

(2B) For the purposes of this Act, the quality of goods includes their state and condition and the following (among other things) are in appropriate cases aspects of the quality of goods –

    (a) fitness for all the purposes for which goods of the kind in question are commonly supplied;

    (b) appearance and finish;

    (c) freedom from minor defects;

    (d) safety; and

    (e) durability.

(2C) The term implied by subsection (2) above does not extend to any matter making the quality of the goods unsatisfactory –

    (a) which is specifically drawn to the buyer's attention before the contract is made;

    (b) where the buyer examines the goods before the contract is made, which that examination ought to reveal; or

    (c) in the case of a contract for sale by sample, which would have been apparent on a reasonable examination of the sample.

(2D) If the buyer deals as consumer … the relevant circumstances mentioned in (2A) above include any public statements on the specific characteristics of the goods made about them by the seller, the producer or his representative, particularly in advertising or on labelling.

(2E) A public statement is not by virtue of subsection (2D) above a relevant circumstance for the purposes of subsection (2A) above in the case of a contract of sale, if the seller shows that –

    (a) at the time the contract was made, he was not, and could not reasonably have been, aware of the statement,

    (b) before the contract was made, the statement had been withdrawn in public or, to the extent that it contained anything which was incorrect or misleading, it had been corrected in public, or

    (c) the decision to buy the goods could not have been influenced by the statement.

(2F) Subsections (2D) and (2E) above do not prevent any public statement being a relevant circumstance for the purposes of subsection (2A) above (whether or not the buyer deals as consumer

… .) if the statement would have been such a circumstance apart from those subsections.

The SSGA 1994 substituted the term that goods should be of satisfactory quality for an older term which required goods to be of 'merchantable quality'. The statutory definition of 'merchantability' was somewhat different from that of the new term. What was then s 14(6) of the 1979 Act stated:

Goods of any kind are of merchantable quality within the meaning of subsection (2) above if they are as fit for the purpose or purposes for which goods of that kind are commonly bought as it is reasonable to expect having regard to any description applied to them, the price (if relevant) and all the other relevant circumstances.

Whilst there are some similarities with the basic definition of satisfactory quality in s 14(2A) (in the references to description and price), on the whole, this looks very different from the new term. The definition of 'merchantability' focused upon goods being reasonably fit for at least one of the purposes for which they were commonly supplied. However, in its application, it may not have been very different from what is required by the new term. Certainly, despite the emphasis on fitness for purpose in what was then s 14(6), the courts' interpretation of what was required for merchantability did not allow the term to be regarded as a simple requirement that the goods should function. A car might have been required to do more than simply get from A to B. It might have been required to do so with a degree of comfort, style and reliability, depending upon such factors as the price paid and the description of it.[103] In addition, the aspects of quality listed in what is now s 14(2B) are all matters which had been identified in the case law as relevant to the question of merchantability.[104] At the end of the day, the results arrived at in applying the new term may not be very different from those which would have resulted from requiring goods to be merchantable. However, the old case law should be considered with caution. Analogies will be appropriate in some cases but that will not always be so. The new term, requiring goods to be of satisfactory quality, should be applied as such and the basic test in s 14(2A) should be emphasised. It is a matter of what the reasonable person would regard as satisfactory. Of course, the reasonable person does not make the assessment in a vacuum, but against a background of 'any description of the goods, the price (if relevant) and all other relevant circumstances' and the assessment is also assisted by the list in s 14(2B) of 'aspects of the quality of goods'.

Before the test of satisfactory quality is addressed, the background factors to the implication of the term will be considered (for example, the term is implied where the contract was made 'in the course of a business'), as well as the situations identified in s 14(2C) in which there will not be a breach of the term requiring goods to be of satisfactory quality.

Sale 'in the course of a business'

For the term requiring goods to be of satisfactory quality to be implied by s 14(2), the seller must contract 'in the course of a business'. The same applies to the term implied by s 14(3) and it also applied to the term previously implied by s 14(2) (merchantability).

Section 61(1) tells us that 'business' includes 'a profession and the activities of any government department or local or public authority' but there is no further definition of 'business' or the phrase 'in the course of a business'. The phrase had, however, been given meaning under the Trade Descriptions Act 1968 and UCTA 1977. In that context, in *R & B Customs Brokers v United Dominion Trust*,[105] the Court of Appeal regarded a transaction as being in the course of a business if it was either integral to the business

---

103 See *Rogers v Parish Ltd* [1987] 1 QB 933, below.
104 'Appearance and finish' – *Rogers v Parish Ltd* [1987] 1 QB 933; *Bernstein v Pamson Motors (Golders Green) Ltd* [1987] 2 All ER 220. Minor defects – *ibid, Bernstein v Pamson Motors*. Safety – *Bartlett v Sydney Marcus Ltd* [1965] 2 All ER 753; *ibid, Bernstein v Pamson Motors*. Durability – *Business Applications v Nationwide Credit Corp* [1988] RTR 332.
105 [1988] 1 All ER 847; see above, p 194.

or, if merely incidental to the business, regularly occurring. The adoption of that approach can be criticised as inappropriate to the 1977 Act[106] and, in *Stevenson v Rogers*,[107] the Court of Appeal refused to follow it in the context of s 14 of the SGA 1979. In that case, the defendant had been a fisherman for some 20 years. He sold his boat, the *Jelle,* to the plaintiff in April 1988, intending to have a new boat built to his requirements. Shortly afterwards, he changed his mind and, in May, purchased another boat, the *Marilyn Jane.* He had previously owned and sold one other boat, the *Dolly Mopp.* The plaintiff claimed that the *Jelle* was not of merchantable quality within the term then implied by s 14(2) of the SGA 1979. However, a requirement of merchantability was only implied if the sale was made 'in the course of a business' (and that remains the case in relation to satisfactory quality). The meaning to be given to the phrase 'in the course of a business' came to be considered as a preliminary matter.

At first instance, the judge applied the test from *R & B Customs Brokers* and concluded that the defendant's sale of his fishing boat did not occur 'in the course of a business' and that no term as to the quality of the boat was implied by s 14(2). Clearly, there was no regular pattern of such sales by the defendant, and the question of whether a transaction is 'integral' to a business depends upon the transactions carried out by a business as such and not what it uses to facilitate those transactions. A car is key to the way in which a courier by car, or a taxi business, earns money, but the sale of a car is, in itself, integral to neither.[108] It is only if the business is buying and selling cars that the sale of a car is integral to the business; similarly, the sale of a ship by a fisherman is not integral to his business. However, the Court of Appeal in *Stevenson v Rogers* held that the judge had not applied the correct test in determining whether the sale was 'in the course of a business' within s 14(2) of the SGA 1979. The phrase had first appeared in the context of the implied term when it was amended by the Supply of Goods (Implied Terms) Act 1973. Until then, the SGA 1893 had implied the term as to merchantability only where goods were 'bought by description from a seller who deals in goods of that description'. The change to a requirement that the sale be made 'in the course of a business' was to broaden the availability of the implied term. It was made to ensure that 'every buyer from a business seller should have a right ... to receive goods of merchantable quality'.[109] The obligation was to be imposed on 'every trade seller no matter whether he is or is not habitually dealing in goods of the type sold'.[110] In other words, the reference to sales 'in the course of a business' in s 14(2) was not intended to be restrictive of the application of the implied term, but was supposed to remove any requirement of regularity of dealing in the goods sold. Potter LJ made the comment[111] that the phrase was there to 'distinguish between a sale made in the course of a seller's business and a purely private sale of goods outside the confines of the business (if any) carried on by the seller'.

106 Macdonald, 1999a.
107 [1999] 1 All ER 613.
108 *Davies v Sumner* [1984] 3 All ER 831; *Devlin v Hall* [1990] RTR 320.
109 Law Com No 24, 1969, para 46.
110 *Ibid*, para 31, n 29.
111 [1999] 1 All ER 613, p 623.

On the basis of the approach taken in *Stevenson v Rogers*, as long as a sale is even incidental to the seller's business and not a 'purely private sale', it should be in the course of a business for the purposes of s 14(2), and that is in keeping with the legislative history of the subsection.

'Goods supplied under the contract'

This seems to mean 'goods delivered in purported pursuance of the contract',[112] so that if the problem is something added to the goods contracted for, the seller cannot avoid liability simply by saying that there is nothing wrong with the contract goods themselves. In *Wilson v Rickett, Cockerell & Co Ltd*,[113] there was a contract for the sale of coalite but, unfortunately, what was supplied was not merely coalite. Added to it was an explosive substance which detonated when the coalite was put in a fire. The seller was unsuccessful in his argument that there was no breach of the implied term, as there was nothing wrong with the coalite, the contract goods, as such.[114] In the context of software, this type of argument might be raised if a virus had been added to the disk on which a program was supplied.

Exceptions

Subsection 14(2C) contains exceptions. If it applies, the buyer will not be able to claim that there has been a breach of the implied term. We are here concerned with the exceptions in s 14(2C)(a) and (b).[115] Subsection (a) refers to the situation where a matter which would otherwise have made the goods of unsatisfactory quality does not do so because it was drawn to the buyers attention before the contract was made. Subsection (b) deals with the situation where a matter which would have made the goods of unsatisfactory quality does not do so because, before contracting, the buyer examined the goods and that examination should have revealed the matter in question. As the reference is to 'that' examination, the exception should only relate to matters which should have been revealed by the examination actually made, however cursory, and not a 'reasonable examination'. However, in *Thornett and Fehr v Beer & Son*,[116] the buyer had seen the outside of the barrels of glue which he was purchasing but, through lack of time, he had not opened any of them. The defect would only have been discovered had he opened the barrels, but the examination made prevented a claim. The case seems to relate the exception to a 'reasonable examination' but it need cause us no difficulties now, as it was decided under an older version of the statutory provision dealing with merchantability, which referred to 'such examination' rather than 'that examination'. We are not now concerned with 'merchantability' and, in any event, as with the later provision dealing with merchantability, the reference now is to

---

112 *Wilson v Rickett, Cockerell & Co Ltd* [1954] 1 QB 598, p 607, *per* Denning LJ.
113 [1954] 1 QB 598.
114 See, also, *Geddling v Marsh* [1920] 1 KB 668.
115 Section 14(2C)(c) refers to the situation where a sale is by sample. See below, p 178.
116 [1919] 1 KB 486.

'that examination'. It should be emphasised that there is no obligation on the buyer to make any examination at all. In fact, odd as it may seem, given the presence of the exception in s 14(2C)(b), it may be argued that it is better for the buyer not to examine the goods.[117]

When software is in question, even a very detailed examination will not bring every 'bug' in the program to light and it should be emphasised that the exception should only relate to matters which should have been discovered by the examination actually made by the buyer. In addition, the point can be made that, for the exception in s 14(2C)(b) to apply, the buyer's examination will have to have been of 'the goods'. If software is purchased, it will often not have been the 'the goods' sold which were examined, but another copy, used for demonstration purposes. However, even if the exception will not technically apply, any difficulty revealed by an examination of another copy might affect what the reasonable person would regard as satisfactory – that is, it might affect the application of the basic test of satisfactory quality (see s 14(2A)).[118] In addition, the exception in s 14(2C)(a) is not restricted to matters drawn to the buyer's attention using 'the goods' sold to the buyer. Some limitation of the software sold to the buyer might be drawn to the buyer's attention by using another copy of that software.

There may be some difficulty with the exceptions where some matter which, but for the exceptions, would make the goods of unsatisfactory quality becomes known to the buyer prior to the contract of sale but it is reasonably believed to be unimportant and rectifiable and subsequently proves to be neither. This sort of situation might arise in relation to software which must be fitted into an existing system.[119] It arose in the context of the purchase of a car in *R & B Customs Brokers v United Dominion Trust* and was given some consideration by the Court of Appeal in the context of exception (b). In that case, R & B decided to purchase a Colt Shogun car and it was allowed to take possession of the car before the contract of sale was completed. Before the contract was made, R & B discovered that the car roof leaked. After the sale was completed, there were repeated, but unsuccessful, attempts to repair the leak and the upholstery became 'sodden with water, mouldy and evil-smelling'. When R & B brought an action, the defendant argued that the car was merchantable, despite the leak, because it was known about before the contract was made. The Court of Appeal did not have to decide upon that question, as they found for R & B on the basis that, in this climate, a car with a leaking roof was not reasonably fit for its purpose under s 14(3) of the SGA 1979. However, Neill LJ did not find himself 'persuaded' that merchantability was excluded as regards a defect which had come to light before contracting 'if, at the time the contract is made, the buyer is reasonably of the opinion that the defect can be, and will be, rectified quite easily at no cost to himself'.[120]

---

117 Unless the sale is by sample. See s 14(2C)(c).

118 The case would be inappropriate to be a sale by sample. See s 15, below.

119 In *Saphena Computing Ltd v Allied Collection Agencies Ltd* [1995] FSR 616, Staughton LJ said (p 652): 'It is important to remember that software is not necessarily handed over or delivered once and for all at one time. It may well have to be tested and modified as necessary.'

120 [1988] 1 All ER 847, p 856, *per* Neill LJ. See, also, *Bartlett v Sidney Marcus* [1965] 1 WLR 1013, p 1018, *per* Salmon LJ and p 1017, *per* Danckwerts LJ.

What constitutes satisfactory quality?

As we have seen, the basic test of satisfactory quality is set out in s 14(2A). It refers to the standard that 'a reasonable person would regard as satisfactory, taking account of any description, the price (if relevant) and all other relevant circumstances'. The reference to the standard of a reasonable person makes the test very flexible and able to encompass the vastly different types of goods to which the Act applies. The disadvantage of flexibility is that it makes it difficult to apply the term. There is some further assistance in the identification of certain 'aspects of the quality of goods' in s 14(2B). Where the buyer deals as consumer, subsections 14(2D) to (2F) give additional significance to any 'public statements' on the 'specific characteristics of the goods' by the 'seller, the producer, or his representative'[121]

Some idea of how the standard set by s 14(2A) may be applied may be gleaned from *Rogers v Parish Ltd*,[122] although the court was applying the old implied term of merchantability. It is worth noting the way in which the court used the description and price of the goods to decide whether the goods had complied with the standard required. (It should be remembered that, despite the focus in the definition of 'merchantability' on the goods' fitness for their common purpose, the court did not regard the mere basic functioning of the car as sufficient to render it merchantable.)

Rogers v Parish Ltd
[1987] QB 933

The case was concerned with the purchase of a new Range Rover which proved to have faulty oil seals and problems with the engine, gear box and bodywork. The Court of Appeal found that it was not merchantable.

Lord Mustill Starting with the purpose for which 'goods of that kind' are commonly bought, one would include in respect of any passenger vehicle not merely the buyer's purpose of driving the car from one place to another but of doing so with the appropriate degree of comfort, ease of handling and reliability and, one may add, of pride in the vehicles outward and interior appearance. What is the appropriate degree and what relative weight is to be attached to one characteristic of the car rather than another will depend on the market at which the car is aimed.

To identify the relevant expectation one must look at the factors listed in the subsection. First, the description applied to the goods. In the present case the vehicle was sold as new. Deficiencies which might be acceptable in a second hand vehicle were not to be expected in one purchased as new. Next, the description 'Range Rover' would conjure up a particular set of expectations, not the same as those relating to an ordinary saloon car, as to the balance between handling, comfort and reliability. The factor of price was also significant. At more than £14,000 this vehicle was, if not at the top end of the scale, well above the level of the ordinary family saloon.

The problems with the car rendered it unmerchantable when they were weighed against the reasonable expectations of the fitness of a passenger vehicle described as a 'new Range Rover' and for which the price charged was well above that of the

---

121 Those subsections were added by the Sale and Supply of Goods to Consumers Regulations 2002 (SI 2002/3045) – implementing EC Directive 1999/44/EC.
122 [1987] QB 933.

ordinary family saloon. Similarly, when considering whether goods are of the standard that a reasonable person would regard as satisfactory, it should be a matter of balancing the problems with the goods against the standard suggested by such matters as description and price. In relation to software, a program might be of unsatisfactory quality if it was so difficult to use that doing anything with it would take the average consumer an inordinate length of time. That would particularly be the case if the program was marketed as one which was easy to use by the average consumer.

In the light of the above discussion, it may seem odd that the reference to price in s 14(2A) is qualified by the phrase 'if relevant'. The immediate reaction to this may well be that the price must always be relevant. However, it is a factor over which care must be taken. It would not be relevant to set the standard for goods generally which were sold in, for example, the 'January sales' if the goods were not presented as 'seconds' or in any way 'shop soiled' or 'defective'.[123] In addition, the price factor may need to be treated with some care in relation to novel software. When a novel program is first put on the market, it will be expensive but it will have problems which have not yet come to light. Later versions will resolve the problems. It would seem that, despite the expense of a novel program when it is first put on the market, the reasonable person could nevertheless regard it as being of a satisfactory standard even though there were some problems with it.[124] Obviously, whether it is of satisfactory quality would be a matter of the number and extent of the problems. Lloyd makes a similar point on the relevance of price. His comment was made in the context of merchantability but it seems that it should still be valid.

Liability for defective software
I Lloyd
(1991) 32 Reliability Engineering and System Safety 193

In *Rogers* the court went on to point out that the price charged for a motor car would influence the level of quality required from it. Although this factor will normally be relevant in determining the acceptability of manufactured products it may be of less utility in relation to computer programs. Here, the cost of raw materials constitutes a fraction of the total value of the software and, on the basis that it is easier to emulate than to innovate, the costs of a company making a derivative version of an existing program should be lower. On this basis, the purchaser of a 'look alike' or 'cloned' version of a program should not be obliged to accept any significant lowering of standards.

Another point to be considered here is the use of 'expert evidence' of 'acceptable practice' in the industry to assist in establishing 'satisfactory quality'. In considering, above, when a bug is a breach, generally, it was noted that the courts referred to such evidence (see p 126) and the potential difficulties that might arise from doing so, in terms of industry acceptance of a low standard, were also indicated. In *Micron Computer Systems Ltd v Wang*[125] against the background of the industry norm, it was decided that the time taken by the system to 'back-up' did not make it

---

123 Price would also seem to be less directly significant if the purchase was in some sense a 'risk'. This would seem to provide the best explanation of why the price was seen as irrelevant to the question of the merchantability of the painting in *Harlingdon & Leinster Enterprises v Christopher Hull Fine Art* [1991] 1 QB 564.

124 But see *St Albans City and DC v ICL* [1996] 4 All ER 481.

125 (1990) unreported, 9 May.

unmerchantable, and neither did the failure of the hard disk after one year. That was regarded as normal and to be expected. As has been indicated, such references to industry norms could be used to lower the requirements of the implied term. However, although there were some *dicta* which might have raised concern that such a situation could occur in relation to merchantability[126] a similar argument was firmly rejected by the Court of Appeal in *Rogers v Parish*.[127]

After looking at the basic test of satisfactory quality, some consideration should also be given to the 'aspects' of quality identified in s 14(2B). Depending on the circumstances, they may be relevant to the reasonable person's assessment of what constitutes a satisfactory standard for the type of goods in question. As has already been indicated, the courts had identified these 'aspects' of satisfactory quality as relevant to the question of merchantability.[128] However, there is likely to be some difference in the treatment of the first aspect of quality – the fitness of the goods for all of the purposes for which goods of the kind sold are commonly supplied – and the way in which fitness for common purpose was treated in considering merchantability. The first point to be made is that 'purpose' is likely to be construed more narrowly now than when it provided the focus for the definition of merchantability. In the context of s 14(6), purpose had to be treated widely if merchantability was not to become a matter of whether the goods simply functioned. That impetus for a broad approach to 'purpose' is no longer present. 'Purpose' may now be regarded as referring to the mere functioning of the goods. In the context of a car, it may now be seen as merely referring to whether the car will get from A to B, without any requirement of a degree of style, comfort and reliability. Questions of style, comfort and reliability can now fall under other aspects of quality identified in s 14(2B) or could simply be encompassed within the general test of what a reasonable person would regard as satisfactory. The second point which should be made is that goods were merchantable if they were reasonably fit for one of their common purposes.[129] However, this change in the law must be treated with some care. The statutory reference to fitness for all the purposes for which goods of the kind in question are commonly supplied is a change in the law which provides a further impetus for the narrowing of the meaning of purpose. It is also likely to lead to careful consideration of what 'kind' of goods a contract is concerned with. This question arose in relation to merchantability.[130] However, the 'kind' of goods in question are likely to be more narrowly identified now that what is relevant is fitness for *all* the purposes for which goods of the kind in question are commonly supplied, not merely fitness for one of those purposes.[131] In relation to software, different versions of the same program may be supplied for home and office use. Provided that it was clear at the time of purchase that what was being bought was the version intended for home use, it would seem

---

126 Eg, *Bernstein Pamson Motors (Golders Green) Ltd* [1987] 2 All ER 220, pp 228–29, *per* Rougier J.
127 [1987] QB 933.
128 See above, p 164.
129 *Kendall v Lillico* [1969] 2 AC 31; *Aswan Engineering v Lupdine* [1987] 1 All ER 135.
130 See, eg, *Beecham v Francis Howard* [1921] VLR 428; *Brown v Craiks* [1970] 1 All ER 823.
131 It seems likely, eg, that the kind of goods would now be more narrowly construed in a case like *Aswan Engineering*.

that the 'kind' of goods would not be ones which were commonly supplied for office use. Under those circumstances, the aspect of quality identified by s 14(2B)(a) would not indicate that the software was of unsatisfactory quality if it was not reasonably fit for office use, provided that it was reasonably fit for home use.

Finally, before leaving consideration of this implied term, some thought can be given to the issues raised by the reaction of the judge in *Sam Business Systems v Hedley & Co*,[132] to the contention that the software was not in breach of contract as it was being used elsewhere. Judge Peter Bowsher QC said:[133]

> The 'use at other sites' is a continuing theme. I am no more impressed by it than if I were told by a garage that there were 1000 other cars of the same type as the one I had bought where there was no complaint of the defect that I was complaining of so why should I be complaining of a defect? We have all heard of Monday cars, so maybe this was a Monday software programme.

This raises two issues. The first is that some further thought should be given here to the appropriate borderline between the scope of the implied term as to satisfactory quality, and that addressed in the next section, as to reasonable fitness for the buyer's particular purpose. An argument that software is working well elsewhere may well be relevant to determine if it meets the general standard that is required by satisfactory quality, if the problem stems from something particular to the particular acquirer, such as integration with an existing unusual system. It should be emphasised that when fitness for purpose is referred to in this context as an 'aspect of quality', it is fitness for the purposes for which goods of the kind in question are 'commonly supplied'. Purposes which are beyond those for which the software is commonly supplied can only be relevant in so far as they have been expressly or impliedly made known to the supplier and are covered by the implied term dealing with fitness for the buyer's particular purpose.

The second point to be made here relates to the judge's reference to 'Monday cars' and the way in which defects in software occur. There might be a problem in relation to a particular copy of software. There might be some problem with the disk, for example, which was introduced during the manufacturing process and which might only affect that disk or a batch of disks. That sort of problem is likely to lead to software which is obviously defective and may well simply not run. However, in relation to software the problem is more likely to be part of the program. This will impact upon every copy of the program and there is no scope for 'Monday software' in relation to this type of problem. The point has been made by Lloyd:[134]

> If one copy of a software product exhibits defects it may be extremely likely that all products will be so tainted with manufactured products generally, most defects are introduced at the production stage and affect only a proportion of the products in question. A finding that one copy of a software package is [not of satisfactory quality] might, by way of contrast leave its producer liable to every purchaser.

---

132 [2003] 1 All ER (Comm) 465. See further Macdonald, 2005.
133 At [104].
134 Lloyd, (1997) p 455.

FITNESS FOR THE BUYER'S
PARTICULAR PURPOSE – s 14(3)

The implied term dealing with fitness for the buyer's purpose was originally dealt with by s 14(1) of the SGA 1893. An amended provision is now contained in s 14(3) of the SGA 1979, which states:

> Where the seller sells goods in the course of a business and the buyer, expressly or by implication, makes known –
>
> (a) to the seller; or
>
> (b) where the purchase price or part of it is payable by instalments and the goods were previously sold by a credit broker to the seller, to that credit broker,
>
> any particular purpose for which the goods are being bought, there is an implied obligation that the goods supplied under the contract are reasonably fit for that purpose, whether or not that is a purpose for which such goods are commonly supplied, except where the circumstances show that the buyer does not rely, or that it is unreasonable for him to rely, on the skill or judgment of the seller or credit-broker.

The implied term that the goods should be of 'satisfactory quality' sets a general standard for the goods. It is not a standard which relates to the buyer's intended use of the goods. In contrast, the term implied by s 14(3) may result in the seller guaranteeing that the goods are reasonably fit for the buyer's purpose. Of course, the seller should not be required to provide goods fit for some unusual and unknown purpose of the buyer and the term is restricted to the situation where the particular purpose has been expressly or impliedly made known to the seller and the buyer has reasonably relied on the skill or judgment of the seller. In addition, the term only requires *reasonable* fitness for the buyer's particular purpose and the standard thereby set for the goods will depend upon how broadly or narrowly the particular purpose has been made known to the seller. These points will be considered further below in looking at the specific elements of s 14(3).[135]

Particular purpose

It has already been indicated that the importance of s 14(3) lies in the fact that it requires the goods to be fit for the buyer's particular purpose. The reference to 'particular' does not mean that the purpose must be very narrow, it merely means 'specified'. A particular purpose may be very general,[136] but, whether it is wide or narrow, it must be expressly or impliedly made known to the seller.

---

135 Like 'satisfactory quality', the term here is only implied if the seller 'sells the goods in the course of a business'. We have already considered this requirement in the context of s 14(2) (see above, p 204). Similarly, the meaning of 'goods supplied under the contract' was also looked at above (see p 206). A point not looked at above, and which should be briefly explained here, is the reference in s 14(3) to 'credit broker'. The reference to the buyer making his purpose known to a credit broker is intended to cover the situation where a purchaser wishes to pay the purchase price of the goods in instalments and the original owner, the credit broker, arranges this by selling the goods to a finance house, which then sells them to the buyer on such terms. The reference to 'credit broker' in s 14(3) ensures that the person who sells the goods to the buyer cannot escape the requirements of the implied term on the basis that the buyer's purpose was made known not to him, but only to the original owner.

136 *Kendall v Lillico* [1969] 2 AC 31, p 114, *per* Lord Pearce.

In some cases, it will be easy to establish that the particular purpose has been impliedly made known. It will not be difficult, for example, to find that the buyer of a hot water bottle impliedly made known to the seller that her particular purpose was to fill it with hot water.[137] However, if the buyer's actual intended use of the goods is very specialised, or unusual, then it will have to be expressly brought to the seller's attention if the buyer is to gain the protection of the implied term. In *Micron Computer Systems Ltd v Wang*,[138] the buyers failed to make it known to the sellers that they wanted a system which would perform 'transaction logging'. The failure of the system to do this, therefore, did not mean that it was not reasonably fit for the buyer's particular purpose. A more general example is provided by *Griffiths v Peter Conway Ltd*.[139]

Griffiths v Peter Conway Ltd
[1939] 1 All ER 685

The sellers made a Harris tweed coat for the buyer. When she wore it an adverse skin reaction was provoked which induced dermatitis. The buyer claimed that there was a breach of the term implied by s 14(1), which was the subsection which then covered the term now implied by s 14(3), as the coat was not reasonably fit for her to wear. The court found that the dermatitis had been caused because she had unusually sensitive skin and that a similar effect would not have been produced on normal skin. On that basis there was no breach of the implied term. Her 'abnormal' particular purpose had not been made known to the sellers.

Sir Wilfred Greene MR   He says that the buyer, Mrs Griffiths, expressly made known to the defendants the particular purpose for which the coat was required, that is to say, for the purpose of being worn by her, Mrs Griffiths, when it was made. Once that state of affairs is shown to exist, Mr Morris says that the language of the section relentlessly and without any escape imposes upon the seller the obligation which the section imports.

It seems to me that there is one quite sufficient answer to that argument. Before the condition as to reasonable fitness is implied, it is necessary that the buyer should make known, expressly or by implication, first of all the particular purpose for which the goods are required.

The particular purpose for which the goods were required was the purpose of being worn by a woman suffering from an abnormality. It seems to me that, if a person suffering from such an abnormality requires an article of clothing for his or her use, and desires to obtain the benefit of the implied condition, he or she does not make known to the seller the particular purpose merely by saying: 'The article of clothing is for my own wear.' The essential matter for the seller to know in such cases with regard to the purposes for which the article is required consists in the particular abnormality or idiosyncrasy from which the buyer suffers. It is only when he has that knowledge that he is in a position to exercise his skill or judgment, because how can he decide and exercise skill or judgment in relation to the suitability of the goods that he is selling for the use of the particular individual who is buying from him unless he knows the essential characteristics of that individual? The fact that those essential characteristics are not known, as in the present case they were not known, to the

---

137 *Preist v Last* [1903] 2 KB 148.
138 (1990) unreported, 9 May.
139 [1939] 1 All ER 685. See, also, *Slater v Finning* [1996] 3 All ER 398.

buyer does not seem to me to affect the question. When I speak of 'essential characteristics', I am not, of course, referring to any variations which take place and exist within the class of normal people. No two normal people are precisely alike, and, in the 'matter of sensitiveness of skin', among people who would be described as normal their sensitiveness must vary in degree.

This does not mean that there is a line which it is the function of the court, or of a medical witness, to draw with precision, so as to define all cases where normality ceases and abnormality begins. The impossibility of drawing such a line by reference to some scientific formula or something of that kind does not mean that, for the present purpose, the difference between normality and abnormality is a thing that must be disregarded, cannot be ascertained. It is a question that no judge and no jury would have any real difficulty in deciding on the evidence in any particular case. In this particular case, the judge has found the existence of abnormality, and, that being so, it seems to me impossible to say that the seller here had the particular purpose pointed out to him so as to show that the buyer relied on his skill or judgment. After all, the object of that is to enable the seller to make up his mind whether or not he will accept the burden of the implied condition, and the effect of the argument addressed to us would be to impose that implied condition upon the seller without his having the opportunity of knowing the vital matter which would affect his mind.

One or two cases were referred to. The only one which I find it necessary to mention, and that for the purpose of distinguishing it, is *Manchester Liners Ltd v Rea Ltd* [1922] AC 74. That was a case where shipowners ordered from the defendants, who were coal merchants, 500 tons of South Wales coal for the bunkers of their steamship, the Manchester Importer. It so happened that, owing to the control of the coal trade that was in existence at that time, the supply of bunkering coal was very much restricted, and the defendants, having secured the right to a cargo through the coal controller, proceeded to supply bunker coal out of that cargo to the plaintiffs in satisfaction of the contract. It so happened that the coal so supplied was not suitable for the bunkering of that steamer, which was a natural draught steamer, and, as a consequence, she was obliged to return to port. The owners sued the coal merchants for damages, and relied upon the Sale of Goods Act 1893, s 14(1). It was held by the House of Lords that, on the facts of the case, the implication of the statutory warranty was not rebutted. The ground on which it was said that it was rebutted was connected with the coal control, which limited the source of supply available to the merchants for the purpose of fulfilling their contract. That was negatived. The important matter for the present purpose is that the House of Lords held that, by ordering bunker coal for that particular steamship, the buyer was making known to the seller the particular purpose for which the coal was required. Lord Buckmaster said:

> It then remains to be considered whether in the circumstances there was any warranty that the coal was suitable for the purpose for which it was required. It is plain that the order was expressed for the use of a particular steamship, and it must, therefore, be assumed that the respondents knew the nature of her furnaces and the character of the coal she used, for it was this coal they contracted to supply.

Mr Morris relies on that passage, and says that this coat was for the use of a particular individual. However, there is all the difference in the world between a case such as that and a case like the present. Steamships differ in types – and some of them have one kind of furnace and some another, and so forth, and the coal which is suitable for one is not necessarily suitable for another. That was a matter which would be within the knowledge of coal merchants.

In *Griffiths*, all that had been made known to the sellers was that the coat was to be worn by the purchaser. That was not sufficient to bring into play the term implied by what is now s 14(3). Her wearing of the coat was regarded as 'abnormal'. The situation would have been different had she informed the sellers that her skin was unusually sensitive and that she was relying on them to make her a coat which she could wear without skin problems arising. The situation should also be different where the goods are of a type which are known to have to be particularised to the user in relation to the relevant aspect of their use and that point provided the basis of the distinction made with the earlier case of *Manchester Liners Ltd v Rea Ltd*.[140] It was known in the trade that ships' boilers varied in the type of coal which they used. When the buyer stated the name of the ship, it was made clear to the seller that the buyer's particular purpose was to use the coal in boilers of the type on the ship specified.

It will often be clear what the buyer's general purpose is in buying software. A word-processing program will usually be purchased to word-process. However, if the buyer's purpose is a more specialised one, and if s 14(3) is to apply, that specialised purpose may well have to have been drawn specifically to the seller's attention. It may be that, for example, the software has to be compatible with an existing system. Sometimes, incompatibility with an existing system would make it a case analogous to *Griffiths*. On other occasions, if the software is such that it is normally used as a supplement to various systems, then the analogy would be with the *Manchester Liners* case. In more general terms, the test which was put in terms of 'abnormality' in *Griffiths* has been put in terms of whether the buyer's actual purpose was 'reasonably foreseeable';[141] for example, if a buyer just asks for a particular type of program, the applicability of s 14(3) to the question of compatibility depends upon whether it is reasonably foreseeable that the buyer's actual purpose is to use the software as part of a system so that he or she needs compatible software.

Another issue in relation to the different uses to which software may be put and the scope of s 14(3) is raised by Lloyd.

Liability for defective software
I Lloyd
(1991) 32 Reliability Engineering and System Safety 193

Under the Act, whilst a purchaser is obliged to inform the seller if he intends to put a product to an unusual purpose, no specific intimation is required in respect of normal usage. As in many other respects, the application of this provision to computer software raises difficult issues. The development of cheap personal computers has led to the marketing of cut down versions of programs intended for commercial use. Although these may be adequate for domestic purposes they may prove incapable of coping with the more extensive demands of a business user.

Whilst the distinction between business and domestic use is not a new one, novelty does lie in the fact that, with a computer program, any design limitations are not as transparent as those pertaining to a more tangible product. Thus, for example, it will normally be apparent whether the features present in an electric drill render it suitable for home or for

---

140 [1922] AC 74.
141 *Ashington Piggeries v Christopher Hill* [1972] AC 441, p 477; *Kendall v Lillico* [1969] 2 AC 31, p 91.

commercial use. This may face sellers with a dilemma. Given that the question whether a customer is obliged to give specific notice of an intended purpose is determined in large part by the seller's claim in respect of the product, the latter may be well advised to make clear the design limits to which the product is subject. However, this may reveal the fact that the product is an inferior version of a species program. Although this may be justified by reason of a lower selling price it would not constitute a compelling marketing feature.

It should be emphasised that, for the term to be implied, not only must the buyer rely upon the seller to provide goods which are reasonably fit for the buyer's particular purpose, but it must be reasonable for the buyer to so rely. Reliance can be partial, provided that it relates to the aspect of the goods' fitness, which is relevant to the buyer's claim.[142] Reliance may not exist, or may not be reasonable, if the buyer has the greater expertise or is in much the best position to make an assessment of the goods' suitability.[143]

In the context of the requirements of reasonable reliance and that the particular purpose of the buyer should be expressly or impliedly made known to the seller, some thought can be given to the suggestions for implied terms in system supply contracts in *Anglo Group v Winther Brown*.[144] In that case, HH Judge Tomlin suggested that in relation to a contract for the supply of a standard computer system, there should, *inter alia*, be implied terms that:

(a) the purchaser communicates clearly any special needs to the supplier;

(b) the purchaser takes reasonable steps to ensure the supplier understands those needs;

(c) the supplier communicates to the purchaser whether or not those precise needs can be met and if so how they can be met. If they cannot be met precisely the appropriate options should be set out by the supplier.

It can be seen that most of this is, in a sense, indirectly 'required' by the implied term under consideration here in that any 'special needs' will have to be made known to the seller if they are to be encompassed within the requirement of 'reasonable fitness for the buyer's particular purpose'. If they are so 'special' that they need to be explained, to be understood, then without such explanation, they may not have been sufficiently made known, and, in any event, reliance on the skill or judgment of the seller may well not be reasonable. In addition, once sufficient communication has been made to ensure that the implied term as to reasonable fitness encompasses the buyer's special needs, it is in the interests of the supplier to make plain any limits on what can they can achieve, or they will be liable if the software is not 'reasonably fit for the buyer's particular purpose'. This well known and established implied term, would seem to render unnecessary those set out above which were contended for in *Anglo Group v Winther Brown*. In addition, the point can also be made, that the judge there would seem to have been referring to implied terms which would operate during the negotiation of the contract – in other word, a situation in which there would normally be no contract and no basis to create contractual obligations to state 'special needs' etc. There is in contrast no difficulty in generating a need to state any such 'special needs'

---

142 *Cammell Laird & Co Ltd v Manganese Bronze and Brass Co Ltd* [1934] AC 402.
143 Eg, *Tehran Europe v ST Belton* [1968] 2 QB 545.
144 1 March 2000. See further Macdonald, 2005.

to ensure their inclusion in the scope of what will be an implied term of the contract once made.

There is a further point to be made here in relation to the fact that, as was indicated above (see p 138) at the time when a contract is made, it may be difficult for the parties to accurately define the software required, particularly when a development contract is in question and software development contracts may well need to be modified before their performance is completed. This was reflected in the view taken by Havery QC of the evolving nature of the coverage of the term that the software would be reasonably fit for the acquirer's purposes. In *Saphena Computing Ltd v Allied Collection Agencies Ltd* he said:[145]

> ... it was an implied term of each contract for the supply of software that the software would be reasonably fit for any purpose which had been communicated to the plaintiff's before the contract was made and for any purpose subsequently communicated, provided in the latter case that the plaintiffs accepted the defendant's instructions to make the relevant modifications. The making of the modifications constitutes or implies acceptance of the instructions ...

Obviously, what is normally envisaged under s 14(3) is that the goods should be reasonably fit for the buyer's purposes which were made known before, or at the time of, contracting. Contract obligations cannot change once the contract is made unless the contract is modified. Havery QC's version of the 'fitness for purpose' implied term, with its in-built expectation of variation, would seem to be a common law version of the normal statutory implied term.

However, even if the particular purpose has been expressly or impliedly made known to the seller and the buyer reasonably relied on the seller, the question still has to be asked whether the implied term has been breached. Where the particular purpose that is made known is a general purpose, the fact that the goods are not fit for the buyer's more specific, actual, purpose only means that they are not fit for part of the buyer's particular purpose. Being unfit for only part of the particular purpose does not necessarily mean that they are not *reasonably* fit for the particular purpose *as a whole*. The 'width of the [particular] purpose is compensated, from the seller's point of view, by the dilution of his responsibility'.[146] More generally, 'reasonable fitness for the buyer's particular purpose' will depend upon the seriousness of the problem with the goods and the proportion of the 'particular purpose' which is affected. Lord Pearce considered an example in *Kendall v Lillico*:[147]

> I would expect a tribunal of fact to decide that a car was reasonably fit for touring even though it was not well adapted for conditions in a heat wave: but not if it could not cope adequately with rain. If, however, it developed some lethal and dangerous trick in very hot weather I would expect it to be found unfit ... the rarity of the unsuitability would be weighed against the gravity of its consequences. Again if food was merely unpalatable or useless on rare occasions, it might well be reasonably suitable for food. But I should certainly not expect it to be held reasonably suitable if even on very rare occasions it killed the consumer.

---

145 [1995] FSR 616 at p 644.
146 *Ashington Piggeries v Christopher Hill* [1972] AC 441, p 497, *per* Lord Wilberforce.
147 [1969] 2 AC 31.

In addition, the point can be made that the implied term may be breached by an accumulation of smaller difficulties. In *Saphena Computing Ltd v Allied Collection Agencies Ltd*,[148] Havery QC (Off Ref) said:[149]

> ... its main problems were those which are evidence of a lack of tuning – principally slow operation and poor design of input and output procedures ... it is clear to me that on the evidence [these defects] represent a shortfall of the system below the standard required of fitness for its purpose.

SALE BY SAMPLE

Section 15 provides for implied conditions where the sale is by sample. Like s 13, and unlike s 14(2) and (3), there is no requirement that the sale should be 'in the course of a business', although other sales are unlikely to be 'by sample'. Section 15 states:

(1) A contract of sale is a contract for sale by sample where there is an express or implied term to that effect in the contract.

(2) In the case of a contract for sale by sample there is an implied term –

    (a) that the bulk will correspond with the sample in quality;

    (c) that the goods will be free from any defect, making their quality unsatisfactory, which would not be apparent on reasonable examination of the sample.[150]

A sample serves much the same purpose as a description of the goods. In *Drummond v Van Ingen*, Lord Macnaghten said:[151]

> The office of a sample is to present to the eye the real meaning and intention of the parties with regard to the subject of the contract which, owing to the imperfections of language, it may be difficult or impossible to express in words. The sample speaks for itself.

However, the mere fact that a small part of the goods was present at the time of contracting does not necessarily indicate that the sale is 'by sample' within s 15. The goods may have been displayed simply to provide a basic idea of the goods being offered. Under s 15(1), it is a matter of determining the parties' intention, as embodied in an express or implied term. The question is whether the parties contracted for goods which corresponded with a sample.

Section 15 seems unlikely to have much application in relation to the sale of software. Software will seldom be bought under circumstances which mean that there is provision of a sample from a larger bulk of goods. If a disk is supplied with a 'cut down' version of a program on it to encourage the purchase of the full program, in everyday terms, that may well be described as 'a sample', but it would seem that it should not be regarded as part of the 'bulk' (that is, the full program). It is a copy of part of it. The term would be apposite if there was a purchase of multiple disk copies of a particular program and one of the copies had been tested before the purchase.

---

148 [1995] FSR 616.

149 *Ibid*, p 644.

150 See, also, s 14(2C)(c), which prevents s 14(2) from being relied upon when the sample has not been inspected and the problem rendering the goods unsatisfactory would have been discoverable on a reasonable examination.

151 (1887) 12 App Cas 284, p 297.

RELEVANCE OF THE IMPLIED TERMS

The implied terms considered above deal with the situation where there is a sale of goods. It has already been pointed out that similar terms are implied if the goods are not sold but hired out[152] and that a contract involving the provision of software and hardware together would seem to be accepted as one under which goods are supplied[153]. The question does remains as to the classification of software (that is, whether it can it be goods). However, the statutory terms will have a broad compass in any event in system supply contract and it was also suggested above that these or similar terms may well be implied into software contracts by analogy at common law,[154] even if software is not regarded as goods but as something *sui generis*.

ACCEPTANCE TESTS

In looking at the performance required under the contract and the liability of the supplier for breach, consideration must be given to the contractual role of acceptance tests.

Acceptance tests are central to a contract for the development or significant customisation of software (or a system). They should be set out in the contract and would usually involve a set of tests designed to see how the software will work across the range of functions required of it. Successful completion of the acceptance tests will normally trigger payment, but what else will it do? It should be remembered that such testing may well not bring all bugs to light. As was stated above 'Testing reveals the presence of bugs, it cannot confirm their absence'. There are a number of points to consider here.

First, acceptance has an established meaning in sale of goods contracts. In relation to such contracts, under s 35 acceptance can occur in three ways:

when the buyer intimates to the seller that he accepts them;

when the goods have been delivered to the buyer and the buyer does an act inconsistent with the ownership of the seller;

when the buyer retains the goods beyond a reasonable time without intimating to the seller that he rejects them.

The effect of 'acceptance' within s 35 is that the buyer can no longer reject the goods. Even if a breach of condition subsequently comes to light, the buyer's remedy lies in damages. If the contract is one for the sale of goods, then the buyer's acknowledgement of successful completion of 'acceptance tests', could be seen as intimation of 'acceptance' in this technical sense. However, it is a technical sense and, even if the contract is seen as one for the sale of goods, may well not be being used in this way. Essentially what is in issue is the interpretation of the contract: what impact

---

152 SGSA 1982, ss 8–10.
153 *Toby Constructions Products Pty Ltd v Computa Bar (Sales) Pty Ltd* [1983] NSWLR 48. *St Albans City and DC v ICL* [1995] 4 All ER 481.
154 See *St Albans City and DC v ICL* [1996] 4 All ER 481; above, p 148.

did the parties (objectively) intend the acceptance tests to have. This can be considered further.

At the extreme, the supplier may want successful acceptance testing to mark the point at which any problems with the software/ system cease to be dealt with under the supply contract (or the supply part of a single contract) and are dealt with under the maintenance contract (or maintenance part). So, in *Morgan and Stedman on Computer Contracts*,[155] we find an example of a clause seeking to finish the supplier's liability under the supply contract.

> The licensee's acceptance of delivery of the software shall be conclusive evidence that the licensee has examined the software and found it to be complete, in accordance with the description in the specification, in good order and condition, fit for any purpose for which it may be required and in every way satisfactory ...

However, as we have seen, no matter how extensive the acceptance testing there are likely still to be bugs which will only subsequently reveal themselves. So what will the effect of such a clause be? Without the clause, some of those bugs would certainly be breaches for which the supplier would be liable. It seems unlikely that the court will accept such a clause at face value, as effectively defining the contractual obligations. Rather, it would seem that such a clause would normally be treated as an exemption clause and so subject to the Unfair Contract Terms Act 1977 and ineffective unless it satisfies the requirement of reasonableness.[156] In addition, in *Sam Business Systems Ltd v Hedley & Co*,[157] the point was made that even if an exemption clause is effective, it will not mean that it can make the remedying of bugs which constitute breaches something which the acquirer should have to pay for under a maintenance contract.

A less extreme approach by the supplier may be a more positive recognition of the likelihood of bugs being discovered after acceptance testing. There would be a basic ousting of rejection or a damages claim, but accompanied by a 'warranty' that any bugs which meant that the software did not comply with the contract would be rectified by the supplier. Obviously, any such 'warranty' would be stated to run for a limited period. Again, UCTA would be relevant, but with the supplier in an improved position, because of its 'warranty' when the application of the requirement of reasonableness arises.

Damages[158]

A software 'bug' can cause considerable losses to a business when its impact is felt. The potential scope of the losses which a bug can cause are graphically illustrated by what occurred when one affected AT & T's long distance telephone network. Within 10 minutes, 50% of calls were failing to get through and a day's telephone traffic was lost before software 'patches' could be installed to avoid the bug. The direct cost of the

---

155 Morgan and Burden, 2001.
156 see ss 3, 6 of UCTA 1977. See p 184.
157 [2003] 1 All ER (Comm) 465
158 See, generally, Koffman and Macdonald, 2004, Chapter 21.

day's lost traffic to AT & T was between $60 and $75 million and, obviously, losses would also have been made by AT & T's customers. Additionally, there were long term effects on AT & T through loss of confidence. It had been a company whose advertising had concentrated on its reliability to justify its pricing being higher than that of its competitors.[159]

Of course, the potential for losses caused by defective software will vary from business to business and the extent to which the business is dependent on the software, as well as the specific defect. It will also depend on the type of contract. The point has already been made as to the difficulties involved in drafting and performing a software development contract, for example (see above p 137). However, the damages recovered under contract law for any loss, no matter how large or small, depend upon the same basic rules. The basic principle on which an award of contractual damages is made is that damages should place the injured party in the position he or she would have been in had the contract been properly performed,[160] that is, the position he or she would have been in had there been no breach. This means that, when a contract is breached, the injured party can recover for the profits he or she would have made had the contract been performed. In other words, in contract, the injured party can recover his or her expectation loss. It is, of course, possible for an injured party merely to claim expenditure wasted because of the breach.[161] That party will not, however, be able to evade the basic principle by so doing. He or she will not recover any expenditure which the party in breach can establish would have been lost even if the contract been performed.[162] Claiming for wasted expenditure does not allow the injured party to recover more than he or she would have obtained had the contract been performed, that is, an award of damages does not relieve the injured party from the consequences of having made a bad bargain.

There are certain limitations on awards of damages made under the above basic principle. For example, the injured party will not recover for a loss which is too remote. This means that he or she will not recover for a loss which, at the time the contract was made, was not within the reasonable contemplation of the parties as liable to result from the breach.[163] This rule prevented recovery of some of the losses claimed in *Victoria Laundry (Windsor) Ltd v Newman Industries Coulson & Co Ltd*.[164] The case was concerned with the late delivery of a boiler to a laundry at a time when there was a shortage of laundry facilities. The laundry could recover for the loss of ordinary laundry business that it could have undertaken had it had the boiler on time, but it could not recover for the loss of an unusually profitable dyeing contract which it would have undertaken had the boiler not been delivered late. The second loss was too remote to be encompassed within the damages awarded.

---

159 See Davies, 1990.
160 *Robinson v Harman* (1880) 5 App Cas 25, p 35, *per* Parke B.
161 *Anglia TV v Reed* [1971] 3 All ER 690.
162 *CCC Films (London) Ltd v Impact Quadrant Films Ltd* [1984] 3 All ER 298; *C & P Haulage v Middleton* [1983] 3 All ER 94.
163 *Hadley v Baxendale* (1854) 9 Ex 341; *Koufos v Czarnikow Ltd* [1969] 1 AC 350; *Parsons (H) (Livestock) v Uttley Ingham & Co Ltd* [1978] 1 All ER 525.
164 [1949] 2 KB 528.

An award of damages may also be circumscribed by the duty to mitigate. This so called duty means that the injured party will not be able to recover for any loss that he or she could have avoided by behaving reasonably after the breach.[165] In *Salvage Association v CAP Financial Services Ltd*,[166] the question arose as to the damages recoverable when a system development contract had been terminated by SA because of CAP's inability to successfully complete the system. It would seem to have been with the duty to mitigate in mind that the judge commented that:[167]

> I am satisfied that SA's decision to abandon the CAP system altogether and start afresh was entirely reasonable ... CAP was not able to complete the system satisfactorily and there was no point in getting another software house to redesign and rebuild a discredited system. It was much more sensible to start afresh. The upshot was that the project to computerise SA's head office accounting with a system designed and developed by CAP had failed and SA's expenditure on that system had been wasted.

The injured party, SA, was able to recover all the money it had expended on the CAP system. Had it been found that the reasonable course was not to abandon the CAP system entirely but to contract with another company for its completion, then the duty to mitigate would mean that SA's recovery would not have encompassed any expenditure on the CAP system which would not have been wasted had that system been salvaged.[168]

In addition, the 'duty to mitigate' means that the cost of steps taken to deal with the breach by the acquirer will not be recoverable unless the actions were a reasonable response to the breach. In *SAM Business Systems Ltd v Hedley & Co*,[169] the suppliers of a system which did not function effectively argued that the acquirers had acted unreasonably in seeking the advice of a consultant on a replacement system. Their contention was based on the fact that no such consultation had taken place before acquisition of the supplier's system. Had the supplier's succeeded, the consultant's fees would not have been recoverable in damages, but the judge did not accept their view. He took the line that it was 'perfectly reasonable if a firm finds itself in a mess to go to a consultant for help in getting out of the mess whether or not they employed a consultant to take the course that got them into the mess'.[170]

EXEMPTION CLAUSES[171]

Exemption clauses are basically clauses which exclude or restrict, or appear to exclude or restrict liability for breach of contract or other liability arising through tort, bailment or statute. They may be aimed at totally excluding liability ('exclusion clauses') or

---

165 *British Westinghouse Electric and Manufacturing Co Ltd v Underground Electric Rlys Co of London* [1912] AC 673, p 689, *per* Lord Haldane.
166 [1995] FSR 654.
167 *Ibid*, p 680.
168 Obviously, in those circumstances, the cost of salvaging the system would have been recoverable – this is the other side of the duty to mitigate.
169 [2003] 1 All ER (Comm) 465.
170 At [155].
171 See Koffman and Macdonald, 2004, Chapters 9 and 10.

merely restricting or limiting it ('limitation clauses') by, for example, limiting the sum recoverable in damages.

To be effective in relation to contractual liability, an exemption clause must have been incorporated into the contract, it must be appropriately worded to cover the breach which occurred and it must not be rendered ineffective by legislation – basically, either UCTA 1977 or the Unfair Terms in Consumer Contracts Regulations 1999.[172] The question of incorporation of clauses into contracts has already been looked at. Brief consideration should be given to the construction of the contract (that is, interpreting it, or, more specifically, asking if the clause is appropriately worded to cover the breach), and the legislation must be looked at.

CONSTRUCTION

Traditionally, a strict approach is taken to the interpretation of exemption clauses and the *contra proferentem* rule is applied, which means that, if there is any ambiguity in the clause, it will be construed in the way which is least favourable to the party seeking to rely upon it. However, it is at present unclear as to the effect on the construction of exemption clauses of the movement in construction in general 'to assimilate the way in which [contracts] are interpreted by judges to the common sense principles by which any utterance would be interpreted in ordinary life'.[173] The traditional approach can be illustrated by *Houghton v Trafalgar Insurance Co.*[174]

Houghton (H) had insured his car with T. H had an accident and tried to claim on his insurance policy for the damage to his car. The policy excluded liability where 'loss, damage, and/or liability caused or arising whilst any car is involved in racing, pace making ... or is conveying any load in excess of that for which it was constructed'. When the accident occurred, there were six people in the car, instead of the five which it was designed to carry. The extra person had been sitting on the lap of one of the rear seat passengers. The insurers contended that they were not liable because of the exclusion dealing with conveyance of an excess 'load'. The Court of Appeal held that the insurers were liable. Whilst the first part of the exclusion clearly could relate to passenger vehicles, they interpreted the reference to a 'load' as relating to the situation where a vehicle, such as a lorry or van, has a specified 'load weight'. The clause was not regarded as sufficiently clear and unambiguous to remove the insurance company's liability for the accident to H's ordinary private car.

One particular aspect of the *contra proferentem* rule occurs in relation to liability for negligence[175] (for example, a negligent breach or negligence in tort). If a clause expressly refers to liability for negligence,[176] obviously, it will cover that liability. The difficulties arise where there is no express reference to negligence as such, but a widely

---

172 SI 1999/2083.

173 *Investors Compensation Scheme Ltd v West Bromwich Building Soc* [1998] 1 All ER 98 at 114.See above p 104.

174 [1954] 1 QB 247.

175 *Canada Steamship Lines Ltd v R* [1952] AC 192 (PC), p 208, *per* Lord Morton.

176 Eg, *Spriggs v Sotheby Parke Bernet & Co* [1986] 1 Lloyd's Rep 487.

worded general clause is used, which it is argued encompasses liability for negligence (for example, a clause referring to 'any liability'). In these circumstances, the courts have taken an approach which means that the clause is more likely to be construed as covering liability for negligence if there is no other liability for it to cover[177] and less likely to be construed as covering negligence if there is other, strict liability for it to cover.[178] The idea would seem to be that it is unlikely that the injured party would have accepted a clause covering the other party's liability in the event of negligence and, if there is other liability, the clause can be assigned a purpose without the need for it to be understood as covering negligence.

Prior to the enactment of UCTA 1977, the courts were apt to take an extreme approach to construction to prevent exemption clauses from being effective. In *Hollier v Rambler Motors Ltd*,[179] for example, they construed a clause as not covering liability based on negligence when there could be no breach in the absence of negligence – leaving the clause with no real role in the contract. Since the advent of the 1977 Act, it has been said that 'strained construction' should not be used.[180] It has also been indicated that the rules of construction should not be applied in 'their full rigour' to limitation clauses (in contrast with exclusion clauses).[181] However, this distinction does not seem justifiable in the extensive form envisaged. As the High Court of Australia said, in refusing to adopt the distinction, 'a limitation clause may be so severe in its operation as to be virtually indistinguishable from that of an exclusion clause'.[182] As has been indicated, it is at present unclear as to the impact in this area of developments in relation to construction in general.

UNFAIR CONTRACT TERMS ACT 1977

PART I

1   Scope of Part 1

    (1) For the purposes of this Part of this Act, 'negligence' means the breach –

        (a) of any obligation, arising from the express or implied terms of a contract, to take reasonable care or exercise reasonable skill in the performance of the contract;

        (b) of any common law duty to take reasonable care or exercise reasonable skill (but not any stricter duty);

        (c) of the common duty of care imposed by the Occupiers' Liability Act 1957 or the Occupiers' Liability Act (Northern Ireland) 1957.

    (2) This Part of the Act is subject to Part III; and in relation to contracts, the operation of sections 2 to 4 and 7 is subject to the exceptions made by Schedule 1.

---

177 Eg, *Alderslade v Hendon Laundry Ltd* [1945] 1 KB 189.
178 *White v John Warwick & Co Ltd* [1953] 2 All ER 1021.
179 [1972] 2 QB 71.
180 *Photo Production Ltd v Securicor* [1980] AC 827; *George Mitchell (Chesterhall) Ltd v Finney Lock Seeds Ltd* [1983] 2 AC 803.
181 *Ailsa Craig Fishing Co Ltd v Malvern Fishing Co Ltd* [1983] 1 WLR 964; *ibid, Finney Lock Seeds.*
182 *Darlington Futures Ltd v Delco Australia Pty* (1986) 68 ALR 385, p 391.

(3) In the case of both contract and tort, sections 2 to 7 apply (except where the contrary is stated in section 6(4)) only to business liability, that is liability to breach of obligations or duties arising –

  (a) from things done or to be done by a person in the course of a business (whether his own business or another's); or

  (b) from the occupation of premises used for business purposes of the occupier; and references to liability are to be read accordingly but liability of an occupier of premises for breach of an obligation or duty towards a person obtaining access to the premises for recreational or educational purposes, being liability for loss or damage suffered by reason of the dangerous state of the premises, is not a business liability of the occupier unless granting that person such access for the purposes concerned falls within the business purposes of the occupier.

(4) In relation to any breach of duty or obligation, it is immaterial for any purpose of this Part of this Act whether the breach was inadvertent or intentional, or whether liability for it arises directly or vicariously.

2 Negligence liability

(1) A person cannot by reference to any contract term or to a notice given to persons generally or to particular persons exclude or restrict his liability for death or personal injury resulting from negligence.

(2) In the case of other loss or damage, a person cannot so exclude or restrict his liability for negligence except in so far as the term or notice satisfies the requirement of reasonableness.

(3) Where a contract term or notice purports to exclude or restrict liability for negligence a person's agreement to or awareness of it is not of itself to be taken as indicating his voluntary acceptance of any risk.

3 Liability arising in contract

(1) This section applies as between contracting parties where one of them deals as consumer or on the other's written standard terms of business.

(2) As against that party, the other cannot by reference to any contract term –

  (a) when himself in breach of contract, exclude or restrict any liability of his in respect of the breach; or

  (b) claim to be entitled –

    (i) to render a contractual performance substantially different from that which was reasonably expected of him, or

    (ii) in respect of the whole or any part of his contractual obligation, to render no performance at all,

  except in so far as (in any of the cases mentioned above in this subsection) the contract term satisfies the requirement of reasonableness.

4 Unreasonable indemnity clauses

(1) A person dealing as consumer cannot by reference to any contract term be made to indemnify another person (whether a party to the contract or not) in respect of liability that may be incurred by the other for negligence or breach of contract, except in so far as the contract term satisfies the requirement of reasonableness.

(2) This section applies whether the liability in question –

  (a) is directly that of the person to be indemnified or is incurred by him vicariously;

  (b) is to the person dealing as consumer or to someone else.

5 'Guarantee' of consumer goods

(1) In the case of goods of a type ordinarily supplied for private use or consumption, where loss or damage –

(a) arises from the goods proving defective while in consumer use; and

(b) results from the negligence of a person concerned in the manufacture or distribution of the goods,

liability for the loss or damage cannot be excluded or restricted by reference to any contract term or notice contained in or operating by reference to a guarantee of the goods.

(2) For these purposes –

(a) goods are to be regarded as 'in consumer use' when a person is using them, or has them in his possession for use, otherwise than exclusively for the purposes of a business; and

(b) anything in writing is a guarantee if it contains or purports to contain some promise or assurance (however worded or presented) that defects will be made good by complete or partial replacement, or by repair, monetary compensation or otherwise.

(3) This section does not apply as between the parties to a contract under or in pursuance of which possession or ownership of the goods passed.

6 Sale and hire-purchase

(1) Liability for breach of the obligations arising from –

(a) section 12 of the Sale of Goods Act 1979 (seller's implied undertakings as to title etc);

(b) section 8 of the Supply of Goods (Implied Terms) Act 1973 (the corresponding thing in relation to hire-purchase),

cannot be excluded or restricted by reference to any contract term.

(2) As against a person dealing as consumer, liability for breach of the obligations arising from –

(a) sections 13, 14 or 15 of the 1979 Act (seller's implied undertakings as to conformity of goods with description or sample, or as to their quality or fitness for a particular purpose);

(b) sections 9, 10 or 11 of the 1973 Act (the corresponding things in relation to hire-purchase),

cannot be excluded or restricted by reference to any contract term.

(3) As against a person dealing otherwise than as consumer, the liability specified in subsection (2) above can be excluded or restricted by reference to a contract term, but only in so far as the term satisfies the requirement of reasonableness.

(4) The liabilities referred to in this section are not only the business liabilities defined by section 1(3), but include those arising under any contract of sale of goods or hire-purchase agreement.

7 Miscellaneous contracts under which goods pass

(1) Where the possession or ownership of goods passes under or in pursuance of a contract not governed by the law of sale of goods or hire-purchase, subsections (2) to (4) below apply as regards the effect (if any) to be given to contract terms excluding or restricting liability for breach of obligation arising by implication of law from the nature of the contract.

(2) As against a person dealing as consumer, liability in respect of the goods' correspondence with description or sample, or their quality or fitness for any

particular purpose, cannot be excluded or restricted by reference to any such term.

(3) As against a person dealing otherwise than as consumer, that liability can be excluded or restricted by reference to such a term, but only in so far as the term satisfies the requirement of reasonableness.

(3A) Liability for breach of the obligations arising under section 2 of the Supply of Goods and Services Act 1982 (implied terms about title etc in certain contracts for the transfer of the property in goods) cannot be excluded or restricted by reference to any such term.

(4) Liability in respect of –

   (a) the right to transfer ownership of the goods, or give possession; or

   (b) the assurance of quiet possession to a person taking goods in pursuance of the contract,

cannot (in a case to which subsection (3A) above does not apply) be excluded or restricted by reference to any such term except in so far as the term satisfies the requirement of reasonableness.

(5) This section does not apply in the case of goods passing on a redemption of trading stamps within the Trading Stamps Act 1964 or the Trading Stamps Act (Northern Ireland) 1965.

9 Effect of breach

(1) Where for reliance upon it a contract term has to satisfy the requirement of reasonableness, it may be found to do so and be given effect accordingly notwithstanding that the contract has been terminated either by breach or by a party electing to treat it as repudiated.

(2) Where on a breach the contract is nevertheless affirmed by a party entitled to treat it as repudiated, this does not of itself exclude the requirement of reasonableness in relation to any contract term.

10 Evasion by means of secondary contract

A person is not bound by any contract term prejudicing or taking away rights of his which arise under, or in connection with the performance of, another contract, so far as those rights extend to the enforcement of another's liability which this Part of this Act prevents that other from excluding or restricting.

11 The 'reasonableness' test

(1) In relation to a contract term, the requirement of reasonableness for the purposes of this Part of this Act, section 3 of the Misrepresentation Act 1967 and section 3 of the Misrepresentation Act (Northern Ireland) 1967 is that the term shall have been a fair and reasonable one to be included having regard to the circumstances which were, or ought reasonably to have been, known to or in the contemplation of the parties when the contract was made.

(2) In determining for the purposes of section 6 or 7 above whether a contract term satisfies the requirement of reasonableness, regard shall be had in particular to the matters specified in Schedule 2 to this Act; but this subsection does not prevent the court or arbitrator from holding, in accordance with any rule of law, that a term which purports to exclude or restrict any relevant liability is not a term of the contract.

(3) In relation to a notice (not being a notice having contractual effect), the requirement of reasonableness under this Act is that it should be fair and reasonable to allow reliance on it, having regard to all the circumstances obtaining when the liability arose or (but for the notice) would have arisen.

(4) Where by reference to a contract term or notice a person seeks to restrict liability to a specified sum of money, and the question arises (under this or any other Act) whether the term or notice satisfies the requirement of reasonableness, regard shall be had in particular (but without prejudice to subsection (2) above in the case of contract terms) to –

(a) the resources which he could expect to be available to him for the purpose of meeting the liability should it arise; and

(b) how far it was open to him to cover himself by insurance.

(5) It is for those claiming that a contract term or notice satisfies the requirement of reasonableness to show that it does.

12 'Dealing as consumer'

(1) A party to a contract 'deals as consumer' in relation to another party if –

(a) he neither makes the contract in the course of a business nor holds himself out as doing so; and

(b) the other party does make the contract in the course of a business; and

(c) in the case of a contract governed by the law of sale of goods or hire-purchase, or by section 7 of this Act, the goods passing under or in pursuance of the contract are of a type ordinarily supplied for private use or consumption.

But if the first party mentioned in subsection (1) is an individual paragraph (c) of that subsection must be ignored.

(2) But the buyer is not in any circumstances to be regarded as dealing as consumer –

(a) if he is an individual and the goods are second hand goods sold at public auction at which individuals have the opportunity of attending the sale in person ;

(b) if he is not an individual and the goods are sold by auction or by competitive tender.

(3) Subject to this, it is for those claiming that a party does not deal as consumer to show that he does not.

13 Varieties of exemption clause

(1) To the extent that this Part of this Act prevents the exclusion or restriction of any liability it also prevents –

(a) making the liability or its enforcement subject to restrictive or onerous conditions;

(b) excluding or restricting any right or remedy in respect of the liability, or subjecting a person to any prejudice in consequence of his pursuing any such right or remedy;

(c) excluding or restricting rules of evidence or procedure; and (to that extent) sections 2 and 5 to 7 also prevent excluding or restricting liability by reference to terms and notices which exclude or restrict the relevant obligation or duty.

(2) But an agreement in writing to submit present or future differences to arbitration is not to be treated under this Part of this Act as excluding or restricting any liability.

14   Interpretation of Part I

In this Part of the Act –

'business' includes a profession and the activities of any government department or local or public authority;

'goods' has the same meaning as in the Sales of Goods Act 1979;

'hire-purchase agreement' has the same meaning as in the Consumer Credit Act 1974;

'negligence' has the meaning given by section 1(1);

'notice' includes an announcement, whether or not in writing, and any other communication or pretended communication; and

'personal injury' includes any disease and any impairment of physical or mental condition.

PART II

[Deals with Scotland]

PART III

26   International supply contracts

(1)   The limits imposed by this Act on the extent to which a person may exclude or restrict liability by reference to a contract term do not apply to liability arising under such a contract as is described in subsection (3) below.

(2)   The terms of such a contract are not subject to any requirement of reasonableness under section 3 or 4: and nothing in Part II of this Act should require the incorporation of the terms of such a contract to be fair and reasonable for them to have effect.

(3)   Subject to subsection (4), that description of contract is one whose characteristics are the following –

(a)   either it is a contract of sale of goods or it is one under or in pursuance of which the possession or ownership of goods passes; and

(b)   it is made by parties whose places of business (or, if they have none, habitual residences) are in the territories of different States (the Channel Islands and the Isle of Man being treated for this purpose as different States from the United Kingdom).

(4)   A contract falls within subsection (3) above only if either –

(a)   the goods in question are, at the time of the conclusion of the contract, in the course of carriage, or will be carried, from the territory of one State to the territory of another; or

(b)   the acts constituting the offer and acceptance have been done in the territories of different States; or

(c)   the contract provides for the goods to be delivered to the territory of a state other than that within whose territory those acts were done.

27   Choice of law clauses

(1)   Where the law applicable to a contract is the law of any part of the United Kingdom only by choice of the parties (and apart from that choice would be the law of some country outside the United Kingdom) sections 2 to 7 and 16 to 21 of this Act do not operate as part of the law applicable to the contract.

(2) This Act has effect notwithstanding any contract term which applies or purports to apply the law of some country outside the United Kingdom, where (either or both) –

   (a) the term appears to the court, or arbitrator or arbiter to have been imposed wholly or mainly for the purpose of enabling the party imposing it to evade the operation of this Act; or

   (b) in the making of the contract one of the parties dealt as consumer, and he was then habitually resident in the United Kingdom, and the essential steps necessary for the making of the contract were taken there, whether by him or by others on his behalf.

SCHEDULE 1
SCOPE OF SECTIONS 2 TO 4 AND 7

1 Sections 2 to 4 of this Act do not extend to –

   (a) any contract of insurance (including a contract to pay an annuity on human life);

   (b) any contract so far as it relates to the creation or transfer of an interest in land, or to the termination of such an interest, whether by extinction, merger, surrender, forfeiture or otherwise;

   (c) any contract so far as it relates to the creation or transfer of a right or interest in any patent, trade mark, copyright, registered design, technical or commercial information or other intellectual property, or relates to the termination of any such right or interest;

   (d) any contract so far as it relates –

      (i) to the formation or dissolution of a company (which means any body corporate or unincorporated association and includes a partnership); or

      (ii) to its constitution or the rights or obligations of its corporators or members;

   (e) any contract so far as it relates to the creation or transfer of securities or of any right or interest in securities.

2 Section 2(1) extends to –

   (a) any contract of marine salvage or towage;

   (b) any charter-party of a ship or hovercraft; and

   (c) any contract for the carriage of goods by ship or hovercraft; but subject to this sections 2 to 4 and 7 do not extend to any such contract except in favour of a person dealing as consumer.

3 Where goods are carried by ship or hovercraft in pursuance of a contract which either –

   (a) specifies that as the means of carriage over part of the journey to be covered; or

   (b) makes no provision as to the means of carriage and does not exclude that means, then sections 2(2), 3 and 4 do not, except in favour of a person dealing as consumer, extend to the contract as it operates for and in relation to the carriage of the goods by that means.

4 Section 2(1) and (2) do not extend to a contract of employment, except in favour of the employee.

5 Section 2(1) does not affect the validity of any discharge and indemnity given by a person, on or in connection with an award to him of compensation for pneumoconiosis attributable to employment in the coal industry, in respect of any further claim arising from his contracting the disease.

SCHEDULE 2
'GUIDELINES' FOR APPLICATION OF REASONABLENESS TEST

The matters to which regard is to be had in particular for the purposes of sections 6(3), 7(3) and (4) ... are any of the following which appear to be relevant –

(a) the strength of the bargaining positions of the parties relative to each other, taking into account (among other things) alternative means by which the customer's requirements could have been met;

(b) whether the customer received an inducement to agree to the term, or in accepting it had an opportunity of entering into a similar contract with other persons, but without having to accept a similar term;

(c) whether the customer knew or ought reasonably to have known of the existence and extent of the term (having regard, among other things, to any custom of the trade and any previous course of dealing between the parties);

(d) where the term excludes or restricts any relevant liability if some condition is not complied with, whether it was reasonable at the time of the contract to expect that compliance with that condition would be practicable;

(e) whether the goods were manufactured, processed or adapted to the special order of the customer.

Scope of the Act

Despite its name, UCTA 1977 does not deal with 'unfair terms' as such. For the most part, the Act applies to clauses which 'exclude or restrict liability'.[183] It can, basically, be said that the Act applies to 'exemption clauses'. Of course, it does not apply to all exemption clauses, and the scope of the Act should be considered. It should, however, first be noted that it considerably overlaps with the Unfair Terms in Consumer Contracts Regulations 1999, which are considered below, and the Law Commissions are considering the substitution of a single unified and simplified piece of legislation.[184]

As has been indicated, the scope of the Act should now be addressed and basically, it applies to 'business liability' (s 1). However, certain contracts are excluded from its operation in whole, or in part (Sched 1). The important exclusion to consider here is that to be found in para 1(c) of Sched 1, which removes from the scope of ss 2 to 4 of the Act contracts insofar as they relate to the creation, transfer or termination of intellectual property rights. The scope of this ouster from the operation of the Act was considered in *The Salvage Association v CAP Financial Services Ltd*.

---

183 There is provision in it, most notably in ss 3(2)(b) and 13, to prevent it from being evaded by the redrafting of clauses to avoid its scope by avoiding the use of clauses in the form of exclusions or restrictions of liability.

184 *Unfair Terms in Contracts* Law Commission Consultation Paper No 166, Scottish Law Commission Discussion Paper No 119 – See E Macdonald (2004) 67 MLR 69. *Unfair Terms in Contracts* Law Commission Report No 292, Scottish Law Commission Report No 199 (2005).

The Salvage Association v
CAP Financial Services Ltd
[1995] FSR 654[185]

Judge Thayne Forbes (Off Ref) The use of the words '... any contract so far as it relates to ...' in subparagraph (c) shows clearly that the subparagraph is strictly limited in its application and that it does not necessarily extend to all the terms of a relevant contract. That is to be contrasted with the wording of paragraph 1(a) of Schedule 1 of the 1977 Act which provides that sections 2 to 4 do not extend to 'any contract of insurance ...' ie, the entire contract of insurance is excepted from the operations of sections 2 to 4, not just certain provisions of the contract: see *Micklefield v S A C Technology Ltd* [1990] 1 WLR 1002 at p 1008.

I agree with Mr Blunt's submission that paragraph 1(c) applies only to those provisions of a contract which deal with the creation or transfer of a *right or interest* in the relevant intellectual property. It does not extend generally to all the terms of a contract simply because the contract is concerned overall with the provision of a service, performance of which will result in a product to which the law affords the protection of one or more of the specified intellectual property rights. The individual terms of the contract in question have to be considered. Any term which is concerned with the creation or transfer of a right or interest in the intellectual property which attaches to the product will form part of the contract to which paragraph 1(c) applies ... On the other hand if a term is one which is concerned with aspects of the contract between the parties other than the creation or transfer of rights in the intellectual property attaching to the product, then paragraph 1(c) does not apply.

In my opinion, the terms of the two contracts out of which the issues in this action primarily arise are not concerned with the creation or transfer of any right or interest in the intellectual property rights which attach to the System, its programs and documentation. This action is principally concerned with the contractual terms as to the competence of CAP's staff, the quality of their performance, the quality of the subject matter of each contract, the time of completion of the System and the construction and application of terms which exclude or limit CAP's liability for breach of contract or negligence. In my judgment therefore, paragraph 1(c) of Schedule 1 to the 1977 Act does not apply to the provisions of the two contracts which deal with such matters, because contractual terms such as these do not relate to the creation or transfer of an interest in any relevant intellectual property either in the System or its documentation.

This takes a restrictive approach to the para 1(c) exclusion.

There are also provisions dealing with the application of the Act in relation to contracts with an international element (see ss 26, 27).

If the exemption clauses in question are capable of falling within the 1977 Act, it must be decided which, if any, of the 'active sections' is relevant. These are the sections which state that something is to happen to a certain exemption clause, that is, either that it is automatically ineffective or that it is effective only if it 'satisfies the requirement of reasonableness'. There are also 'definition sections' which assist in determining the scope of the 'active sections', and these will be looked at once the 'active sections' have been considered.

---

185 The facts are given above, p 182.

The active sections

Section 2 deals with liability arising from negligence.[186] Section 2(1) renders automatically ineffective clauses which 'exclude or restrict liability' for negligently caused death or personal injury. Such terms are 'black listed'. Their reasonableness or otherwise is irrelevant. Section 2(2) deals with clauses excluding or restricting any other sort of negligently caused loss or damage and renders them ineffective except insofar as they satisfy the 'requirement of reasonableness'. The section deals not only with contractual clauses, but also covers, for example, non-contractual disclaimers, which may be used to try to exclude or restrict such liability in tort.

Section 3 deals with the situation in which one party 'deals as consumer' or on the other party's 'written standard terms of business'. Contracts may come within both of the situations covered. Someone who deals as consumer may well contract on the other party's written standard terms of business. The meaning of 'deals as consumer' is dealt with by s 12 and is considered below (see p 194). There is no statutory definition of 'written standard terms of business'. Whether a party has a set of 'written standard terms' should depend upon the pattern and degree of usage of the relevant terms.[187] If the relevant party clearly has 'written standard terms of business', the question may arise as to whether the alterations of them in the instant case are such that the contract cannot be regarded as having been made on that party's written standard terms of business. Determining that should be a matter of the extent of alteration of the original terms, and also of which terms are altered (some terms in a set of standard terms being intended to be particularised to individual contracts).[188] One further point to be made is that what is required by s 3 is not merely that written standard terms of business be used, but that they should be the written standard terms of the relevant party. Should terms used throughout a particular trade and commonly used by the party in question be regarded as that party's 'written standard terms of business' for the purposes of s 3?[189]

Once it is determined that the contract in question falls within s 3, it should be noted that the scope of the section extends beyond terms which, in form, 'exclude or restrict liability'. Such terms are covered by s 3(2)(a) and are rendered ineffective unless they 'satisfy the requirement of reasonableness'. However, s 3(2)(b) extends the scope of the section beyond terms in the form of exclusions or restrictions of liability. It is one of the provisions of the Act which prevents its easy evasion by drafting which avoids those forms. Section 3(2)(b)(i), for example, extends the reasonableness test to terms under which the party who contracts on his own written standard terms of business, or who contracts with someone who deals as consumer, claims to render a performance substantially different from that which was reasonably expected of him.

---

186 Section 1(1) makes it clear that this covers the situation where there is a breach of the duty to take reasonable care or exercise reasonable skill arising under the contract or in tort or under the Occupiers' Liability Act 1957.

187 *Flamar Interocean Ltd v Denmac Ltd* [1990] 1 Lloyd's Rep 434; *Chester Grosvenor Hotel Co Ltd v Alfred McAlpine Management Ltd* (1992) 56 Build LR 115; *The Salvage Association v CAP Financial Services Ltd* [1995] FSR 654; *St Albans City and DC v ICL* [1995] FSR 686.

188 *Ibid, St Albans.*

189 For consideration of this case see *British Fermentation Products Ltd v Compair Reavell Ltd* [1999] 2 All ER (Comm) 389.

Section 6 covers exemption clauses dealing with the terms implied into contracts for the sale or hire purchase of goods. There are analogous provisions in s 7 dealing with other contracts under which possession or ownership of goods passes. Section 6(1)(a) renders automatically ineffective any term excluding or restricting liability in relation to the terms implied by s 12 of the SGA 1979. Section 6(2)(a) does the same in relation to the exclusion or restriction of liability for breach of the terms implied by ss 13–15 of the 1979 Act, provided that the buyer 'deals as consumer'. These are the other terms 'blacklisted' by the 1977 Act. However, if the buyer does not 'deal as consumer', liability for breach of the terms implied by ss 13–15 of the SGA 1979 can be excluded or restricted by a clause which satisfies the requirement of reasonableness.[190] Section 6 also contains analogous provisions dealing with exemptions of the terms implied into hire-purchase contracts.[191] Obviously, the question of whether the buyer 'deals as consumer' is very important in the context of s 6 (see below).

Unlike most of the other active sections, s 4 does not refer to terms which 'exclude or restrict liability'. It deals with terms under which someone who 'deals as consumer' has to indemnify the other party in relation to that other party's liability for negligence or breach of contract. Such clauses are ineffective unless they satisfy the requirement of reasonableness.

Section 5 of UCTA 1977 is of very limited application. It was enacted to deal with a very specific problem – that of manufacturers or distributors of goods attempting to remove their liability for goods which proved defective 'in consumer use' due to the negligence of the manufacturers or distributors. The relevant clause would be found in a 'guarantee', which also stated that the consumer had certain rights. This section does not apply between parties to a contract under which, or in pursuance of which, possession or ownership of goods passes (s 5(3)). It does not cover clauses in contracts between sellers and buyers of goods.

Section 10 deals with one of the ways in which the other sections of the Act might have been avoided. It prevents a term from being used in a second contract to achieve the exclusion or restriction of liability which the Act would prevent in a first contract.

Definitions – 'deals as consumer'

This phrase is dealt with by s 12. It is vital to the question of whether someone deals as consumer to determine whether they contract 'in the course of a business' and that was addressed in *R & B Customs Brokers v United Dominion Trust*.[192] The plaintiff company was in business as a freight forwarding agent. It purchased a car, on credit terms, for the use of its two directors and sole shareholders. The car proved to be defective and did not comply with the terms implied by s 14(3) of the Sale of Goods Act 1979, but there was an exemption clause. The question arose as to whether the buyer's dealt as consumer within s 12 of UCTA and that hinged upon whether they had contracted 'in the course of a business'. The Court of Appeal took the line that

190 Section 6(3).
191 On the terms implied by the SGA 1979, ss 13–15, see below, p 153.
192 [1988] 1 All ER 847

basically that depended upon whether the contract was integral to the business or, if merely incidental to it regularly occurring. The Contract was not integral to the buyer's business – their business was acting as freight forwarding agents, not buying and selling cars – and it was only the second or third such transaction undertaken so, it was incidental to the business and had not occurred regularly.[193]

Definitions – the 'requirement of reasonableness'

The requirement of reasonableness is a key feature of the Act, with the effectiveness of exemption clauses often depending on whether they can satisfy the test. Section 11(5) of UCTA 1977 places the burden of proving 'reasonableness' on the person seeking to use the clause. The assessment of reasonableness does not occur in the light of the actual breach which occurred, but on the basis of what was known, or should reasonably have been contemplated, at the time of contracting,[194] and that is very significant – a point which is illustrated by the outcome in *Stewart Gill Ltd v Horatio Myer & Co Ltd*.[195] In that case, the clause failed to satisfy the requirement of reasonableness, not because of the breach in the instant case, but because of the other situations which it could potentially cover. This means that there will be a greater possibility of a clause being effective if it is of narrow application and it would seem advisable to draft several clauses to cover different aspects of liability, rather than one wide one. In that way, at least some of the exemptions may be effective.[196]

Before considering the factors relevant to the 'requirement of reasonableness', the courts' approach to appeals in relation to the application of this test should be noted. In *George Mitchell Ltd v Finney Lock Seeds Ltd*,[197] Lord Bridge took the view that there could be legitimate differences of opinion on the reasonableness test and that:[198]

> ... when asked to review such a decision on appeal, the appellate court should treat the original decision with the utmost respect and refrain from interference with it unless satisfied that it proceeded upon some erroneous principle or was plainly and obviously wrong.

Decisions on the 'reasonableness' of a clause in one case are of limited precedent value.[199]

Consideration should now be given to the working of the test and it should be noted that Sched 2 contains guidelines as to its operation.[200] These guidelines are a

---

193 See Koffman & Macdonald, 2004, paras 10.63–10.69.
194 Section 11(1).
195 [1992] 2 All ER 257.
196 *Rees Hough Ltd v Redland Reinforced Plastics Ltd* [1985] 2 Con LR 109.
197 [1983] 2 AC 803.
198 *Ibid*, p 816.
199 But see Lord Griffiths' comments on future cases in *Smith v Bush*, below.
200 By s 11(2), these guidelines are relevant to the reasonableness test when applied under ss 6 or 7. However, they are the type of factors which are likely to be relevant, simply on the facts in many cases and will then be looked at on that basis (eg, *Phillips Products Ltd v Hyland* [1987] 2 All ER 620, p 628).

non-exhaustive list of relevant factors and that, in itself, is indicative of the functioning of the test, which, basically, involves a weighing of the relevant factors in each case. This can be seen through considering the House of Lords' decision in *Smith v Bush*.

Smith v Eric S Bush (A Firm)
[1990] 1 AC 831

The case was concerned with the liability of a surveyor for a negligent valuation of a house, which had been carried out for mortgage purposes. The valuation was paid for by the intending house purchaser, but the surveyor's contract was with the building society and the action by the house purchaser arose out of tort rather than contract. The question was whether the surveyor could rely upon a disclaimer to avoid liability to the house purchaser. The disclaimer fell to be considered under s 2 of the 1977 Act, the requirement of reasonableness had to be applied, and it was held that it was not satisfied. The disclaimer was ineffective. (Although the action was a tortious one, the comments on the reasonableness test are generally applicable.)

Lord Griffiths I believe that it is impossible to draw up an exhaustive list of factors that must be taken into account when a judge is faced with this difficult decision [that is, the application of the 'reasonableness' test]. Nevertheless, the following matters should in my view, always be considered.

(1) Were the parties of equal bargaining power? If the court is dealing with a one-off situation between parties of equal bargaining power the requirement of reasonableness would be more easily discharged than in a case such as the present where the disclaimer is imposed on the purchaser who has no effective power to object.

(2) In the case of advice, would it have been reasonably practicable to obtain the advice from an alternative source taking into account considerations of costs and time? In the present case it is urged on behalf of the surveyor that it would have been easy for the purchaser to have obtained his own report on the condition of the house, to which the purchaser replies that he would then be required to pay twice for the same advice and that people buying at the bottom end of the market, many of whom will be young first time buyers are likely to be under considerable financial pressure without the money to go paying twice for the same service.

(3) How difficult is the task being undertaken for which liability is excluded? When a very difficult or dangerous undertaking is involved there may be a high risk of failure which would certainly be a pointer towards the reasonableness of excluding liability as a condition of doing the work. A valuation, on the other hand, should present no difficulty if the work is undertaken with a reasonable skill and care. It is only defects which are observable by a careful visual examination that have to be taken into account and I cannot see that it places any unreasonable burden on the valuer to require him to accept responsibility for a fairly elementary degree of skill and care involved in observing, following up and reporting on such defects. Surely it is work at the lower end of the surveyor's field of professional expertise.

(4) What are the practical effects of the decision of the question of reasonableness? This must involve the sums of money potentially at stake and the ability of the parties to bear the loss involved, which in its turn, raises the question of insurance. There was once a time when it was regarded as improper even to mention the possible existence of insurance cover in a lawsuit. But those days are long past. Everyone knows that all prudent, professional men carry insurance, and the availability and cost of insurance must be a relevant factor when considering which of two parties should be required to bear the risk of a loss. We

are dealing in this case with a loss which will be limited to the value of a modest family house and against which it can be expected that the surveyor will be insured. Bearing the loss will be unlikely to cause significant hardship if it is borne by the surveyor but it is, on the other hand, quite possible that it will be a financial catastrophe for the purchaser who may be left with a valueless house and no money to buy another. If the law in these circumstances denies the surveyor the right to exclude his liability, it may result in a few more claims but I do not think so poorly of the surveyor's profession to believe that the floodgates would be opened. There may be some increase in surveyor's insurance premiums which will be passed on to the public, but I cannot think that it will be anything approaching the difference between the [building society's] offer of a valuation without liability and a valuation with liability discussed in the speech of my noble and learned friend Lord Templeman. The result of denying a surveyor, in the circumstances of this case, the right to exclude liability will result in distributing the risk of his negligence among all house purchasers through an increase in his fees to cover insurance, rather than allowing the whole of the risk to fall on the one unfortunate purchaser.

I would not, however, wish it to be thought that I would consider it unreasonable for professional men in all circumstances to seek to exclude or limit their liability for negligence. Sometimes breathtaking sums may turn on professional advice against which it would be impossible for the adviser to obtain adequate insurance cover and which would ruin him if he were to be held personally liable. In these circumstances it may indeed be reasonable to give the advice upon a basis of no liability or possibly of liability limited to the extent of the adviser's insurance cover ...

It must, however, be remembered that this is a decision in respect of a dwelling house of modest value in which it is widely recognised by surveyors that purchasers are in fact relying on their care and skill. It will obviously be of general application in broadly similar circumstances. But I expressly reserve my position in respect of valuations of quite different types of property ...

There will obviously be a variety of factors to be considered in each case and their importance will have to be assessed in the context of the particular case. The parties' relative bargaining powers may be relevant, as may the question of whether the party against whom the clause is being used knew its contents or had ample opportunity to ascertain them.[201]

However, although the application of the test is a weighing process and any factor is merely one indicator, some factors may be more significant than others. The existence, or otherwise, of an alternative to the particular contract has been important in some cases[202] and it was referred to by Lord Griffiths in *Smith v Bush*. The comment there was put in terms of whether or not the advice could have been obtained elsewhere, as advice was the commodity that the case was concerned with, but the availability of an alternative contract has been seen as generally relevant. It may be easier for a party to establish that his or her exemption clause is reasonable if it can also be established that he or she also offered an alternative, higher priced contract

---

201 Eg, *Singer Co (UK) Ltd v Tees and Hartlepool Port Authority* [1988] 2 Lloyd's Rep 164; *Stag Line Ltd v Tyne Ship Repair Group Ltd (The Zinnia)* [1984] 2 Lloyd's Rep 211.
202 *RW Green Ltd v Cade Bros Farms* [1978] 1 Lloyd's Rep 602; *Woodman v Photrade Processing Ltd* (1981) unreported.

which did not contain the exemption clause.[203] However, as the judgment of Lord Griffiths indicates, the court will consider not merely the existence of an alternative, but also its reality. In *Smith v Bush*, cost was the factor making the alternative unrealistic, but insufficiently drawing an alternative to the attention of the other party might also adversely affect the court's view of it.

However, it may be that the most generally significant factor is that of insurance. As we have seen, it was considered in *Smith v Bush*, and particular reference is made to it in s 11(4), in the context of determining the reasonableness of limitation clauses. The basic questions will be as to which party was in the best position to insure, and at what cost. That was considered by the House of Lords in *Photo Production Ltd v Securicor Ltd*.[204] In that case, the contract was for the provision of security services, which included periodic nightly visits to PP's factory by S's employees. On one visit, one employee of S decided to start a fire. The factory was burnt down. The question was whether S could rely upon an exemption clause in relation to its liability for the destruction of the factory. Because of the date when it was made, the contract was not one to which UCTA 1977 applied. However, having answered the construction question in S's favour, and obviously aware of the test in the 1977 Act, the House of Lords commented that the clause was 'reasonable'. The parties were of roughly equal bargaining power, the risk of fire damage had been allocated to the party best able to insure against it and S was providing a cheap service. PP had to insure its factory against fire damage in general and S could not have provided such a cheap service if it had needed to insure (even if it could have obtained such insurance).

However, as we have seen, in *Smith v Bush*, Lord Griffiths identified the fact that a difficult or dangerous task with a high risk of failure is involved may indicate the reasonableness of an exemption clause. In the context of system or software supply contracts, what is involved will not normally be a dangerous task but we have seen that it may be difficult to supply software without bugs. That is particularly so when the development of a system is in question, but may also be so when standard software is to be modified to meet the acquirer's requirements and even when what is in issue is the supply of standard software there may be difficulty in discerning the 'fit' between the software and the needs of the 'acquirer'. The significance of the 'risk' factor in considering the reasonableness of exemption clauses in software/system supply contracts can be seen in the two cases below, as can the need to look at, and weigh, all the relevant factors, such as the bargaining position of the parties, their awareness of the risk allocation, its relationship to the price, the extent of the clause, and the remedies left to the acquirer.

Watford Electronics Ltd v Sanderson CFL Ltd
[2001] 1 All ER (Comm) 696

The case was concerned with the sale of a computer system. The claimant purchasers, or customers, (Watford) were themselves suppliers of computer products, principally by mail order, and with particular expertise in the supply of personal computers. They had

203 *Ibid, Woodman.*
204 [1980] AC 827.

found the need for a computer system to deal with their mail order business and to perform accounting functions. They contracted with Sanderson for standard software ('Mailbrain' and 'Genasys') which was to be modified to meet their needs. There were three contractual documents which were seen as making up the contract – a sales 'contract' for equipment, a software licence for the standard software, and a software modification licence covering stated modifications. The three documents basically contained Sanderson's standard terms, but Watford had successfully negotiated for a price reduction and some modification of the terms. In the end, the total paid by Watford was £104,596. For our purposes, the significant term of the sales 'contract' (which was also reflected in the two licenses) was cl 7 – the exemptions clause. Clause 7(3) stated

> Neither the Company nor the Customer shall be liable to the other for any claims for indirect or consequential losses whether arising from negligence or otherwise. In no event shall the Company's liability under the Contract exceed the price paid by the Customer to the Company for the Equipment connected with any claim.

Watford had sought to have the exemption clause amended but Sanderson would only agree to an addendum to it under which Sanderson committed to 'their best endeavours in allocating appropriate resources to the project to minimise any losses that may arise from the contract'.

Chadwick LJ I turn, therefore, to consider whether the requirement of reasonableness is satisfied in relation to the term excluding indirect loss. It is important to keep in mind (i) that, as a matter of construction, the term does not seek to exclude loss resulting from pre-contractual statements in relation to which a claim lies (if at all) in tort or under the Misrepresentation Act 1967 and (ii) that the term is qualified by the addenda so that it does not exclude indirect or consequential loss resulting from breach of warranty unless Sanderson has used its best endeavours to ensure that the equipment and the software does comply with the warranty.

52 I accept that the court is required to have regard, in the present case, to the 'guideline' matters set out in Schedule 2 to the 1977 Act. There are factors, identified by the guidelines, which point to a conclusion that the term excluding indirect loss was a fair and reasonable one to include in this contract. The parties were of equal bargaining strength; the inclusion of the term was, plainly, likely to affect Sanderson's decision as to the price at which was prepared to sell its product; Watford must be taken to have appreciated that; Watford knew of the term, and must be taken to have understood what effect it was intended to have; the product was, to some extent, modified to meet the special needs of the customer. Other factors point in the opposite direction. The judge found that, although there were other mail order packages on the market, Mailbrain was the only one which appeared to fulfil Watford's needs (paragraph 126); and, further, that Watford could not reasonably have expected to have been able to have acquired a similar software package, if available, on better terms as to performance and as to the supplier's potential liability for non-performance.

53 I do not, for my part, accept that the term excluding indirect loss is a term to which section 11(4) of the 1977 Act applies. It is not, I think, properly to be regarded as a term by which a person (Sanderson) seeks to restrict liability to a specified sum of money; rather the term seeks to exclude liability for indirect or consequential loss altogether, in those circumstances in which it is intended to have effect. Nevertheless, it seems to me right to have regard, as part of the circumstances which were, or ought reasonably to have been, known to or in the contemplation of the parties when the contract was made, both to the resources which could be expected to be available to each party for the purpose of meeting indirect or consequential loss resulting from the failure of the equipment or software to

perform in accordance with specification, and to the possibility that such loss could be covered by insurance.

54 It seems to me that the starting point in an enquiry whether, in the present case, the term excluding indirect loss was a fair and reasonable one to include in the contract which these parties made is to recognise (i) that there is a significant risk that a non-standard software product, 'customised' to meet the particular marketing, accounting or record-keeping needs of a substantial and relatively complex business (such as that carried on by Watford), may not perform to the customer's satisfaction, (ii) that, if it does not do so, there is a significant risk that the customer may not make the profits or savings which it had hoped to make (and may incur consequential losses arising from the product's failure to perform), (iii) that those risks were, or ought reasonably to have been, known to or in the contemplation of both Sanderson and Watford at the time when the contract was made, (iv) that Sanderson was in the better position to assess the risk that the product would fail to perform but (v) that Watford was in the better position to assess the amount of the potential loss if the product failed to perform, (vi) that the risk of loss was likely to be capable of being covered by insurance, but at a cost, and (vii) that both Sanderson and Watford would have known, or ought reasonably to have known, at the time when the contract was made, that the identity of the party who was to bear the risk of loss (or to bear the cost of insurance) was a factor which would be taken into account in determining the price at which the supplier was willing to supply the product and the price at which the customer was willing to purchase. With those considerations in mind, it is reasonable to expect that the contract will make provision for the risk of indirect or consequential loss to fall on one party or the other. In circumstances in which parties of equal bargaining power negotiate a price for the supply of product under an agreement which provides for the person on whom the risk of loss will fall, it seems to me that the court should be very cautious before reaching the conclusion that the agreement which they have reached is not a fair and reasonable one.

55 Where experienced businessmen representing substantial companies of equal bargaining power negotiate an agreement, they may be taken to have had regard to the matters known to them. They should, in my view be taken to be the best judge of the commercial fairness of the agreement which they have made; including the fairness of each of the terms in that agreement. They should be taken to be the best judge on the question whether the terms of the agreement are reasonable. The court should not assume that either is likely to commit his company to an agreement which he thinks is unfair, or which he thinks includes unreasonable terms. Unless satisfied that one party has, in effect, taken unfair advantage of the other – or that a term is so unreasonable that it cannot properly have been understood or considered – the court should not interfere.

SAM Business Systems Ltd v Hedley & Co Ltd
[2003] 1 All ER (Comm) 465

The claimants, SAM, supplied software to the defendant stockbrokers, Hedley's for use in their business. SAM claimed money they alleged was due to them for the supply and maintenance of the software. Hedley's claimed damages for alleged defects in the software. The software was a ready made package for stockbrokers and others (such as banks) dealing in stocks and shares. SAM claimed that the package was tried and tested system which worked well elsewhere, nevertheless, it did not perform as Hedley's expected and breaches were found. The contract had provided a mechanism for Hedley's to terminate the contract and get their money back if the program failed to comply with the specified 'acceptance tests'. Hedley's had not taken that option and the question was whether or not they could recover the amounts claimed in the light of exemption clauses. The Judge considered the interpretation of the clauses and then the application of the requirement of reasonableness under UCTA.

Judge Peter Bowsher QC It is correct that the licence agreement does provide a detailed machinery of notices based on the acceptance criteria and if Hedley's had initiated that machinery and received an inadequate response they would have been entitled to reject the system and get their money back. They did not initiate the machinery. Does that mean that because they did not initiate the machinery they have no remedy for any defects in the software? As I understand Mr Susman's opening, he was submitting that the answer to that question is Yes. Clause 2.11 concludes with the words: 'This [that is, money back] shall be the sole and exclusive remedy available to client in the event of the application software not being accepted.' I interpret those words as referring to the only remedy available to the client on the software not being accepted under the machinery of cll 2.10 and 2.11. I do not read those words as restricting any remedy if the software is rejected for any reason outside that machinery, if that is possible.

[57] The licence agreement did however make a sweeping exclusion of warranties. By cl 3.2, SAM warranted that SAM had the right to licence the use of the application software and that use of the application software 'will not infringe any patent, copyright, design, trade or service mark or any intellectual property rights of any third party (whether British or foreign)'. The clause then continued: 'Except as set out in the preceding paragraphs of this section 3.2, there are no warranties, either expressed or implied, by this agreement. These include, but are not limited to, implied warranties of merchantability or fitness for a particular purpose, and all such warranties are expressly disclaimed to the extent permissible by law.

[58] By cl 3.3, the licence agreement continued: 'Except as provided in clauses 3.2 and 3.3, SAM will not be responsible for any direct, incidental or consequential damages such as, but not limited to, loss of profits resulting from the use of the software, even if SAM have been advised of the possibility of such damage:

Except as provided in clauses 3.2 and 3.3, any liability to which SAM might otherwise become subject shall, in aggregate, be limited to the licence fee paid.

[59] By cl 3.2, SAM sought to exclude liability for every form of liability likely as a matter of practice to arise (except for misrepresentation), but as the final words 'to the extent permitted by law' indicate, there was a lingering doubt that there was something that might not have been excluded, so by cl 3.3, remedies in damages were excluded. That exclusion excluded not only loss of profits and 'incidental or consequential damage' but also direct damage. If that were not enough, liability was limited in aggregate to the amount of the licence fee paid. The exclusion of liability in damages was expressed to relate to damages 'resulting from the use of the software'. That exclusion was not limited to breaches of warranty. It included damages resulting from the use of the software because it failed to come up to representation. So although I have found that the entire agreement clause was waived, subject to the issue of reasonableness of cl 3.3, there is no liability on SAM for misrepresentation.

...

[71] That evidence, together with the rest of Mr Tustain's written and oral evidence suggests that Hedley's choice was limited. The only way to get the software they needed was by contracting on terms that made rigorous exclusions of liability because those were the terms on which all suppliers were contracting. Moreover, the negotiating positions were not equal. Hedley's had to get a system in a short space of time that was Year 2000 compliant or go out of business. But that was a difficulty of their own making. If they had woken up to the problem earlier, as most people did, they would not have had a problem as to time. On the other hand, SAM no doubt

wanted the work to make a profit, but there is no evidence that they would have gone out of business if they did not get the work. However, although the agreements were signed by SAM on 12 October 1999 and sent to Hedley's, they were not signed and returned until 18 October 1999. In the interval, as Mr Tustain said, Hedley's asked no questions about the terms and made no attempt to negotiate any changes to the standard terms of SAM's contract. The only changes they requested were certain additional systems enhancements. If there had been any attempt to negotiate those terms SAM could perfectly easily have said 'take it or leave it' as both parties knew, or they might have agreed changes. As we now know from the oral evidence of Mr Tustain, he would probably have said: 'We cannot expose our business to that degree of risk. We cannot do that business.' As to the degree of risk, the counterclaim in this action is high enough, but it has been stressed on behalf of Hedley's that because of alleged defects in the software, Hedley's might have been closed down by the regulator. If that had happened, the counterclaim for loss of profits, costs of paying off staff, and indemnities against claims from clients could have been enormous. In that event, it is not unlikely that both companies (in the absence of insurance) would have been in liquidation, though I have to say that I have no detailed evidence about the funds available to either party beyond the evidence that they are both small companies. Although it has not been said in so many terms, SAM's attitude seems to be: 'We did not have to take on this contract. Having taken it on on our terms, why should the contract be rewritten to expose us to a huge risk and possibly put us out of business?' That is a freedom of contract attitude that would have been entirely acceptable in the nineteenth and early twentieth centuries. Can it survive since Parliament intervened at the behest of the Law Commission in 1977?

[72] Not forgetting my duty to look at each term individually, it is important to look at each in relation to the whole contract. Before contract, SAM says: 'We think our system is marvellous and will do everything you need, but if you are not satisfied you can ask for your money back.' The contract, signed by Hedley's after they have had a few days to think about it but without any attempt to negotiate on their part, says: 'So far as possible we exclude any liability for our system, but if you are not satisfied and you go through the right machinery, you can have your money back.' Having regard to the enormous potential liabilities, that seems to me to be a reasonable arrangement in the circumstances existing between the two parties. The big question is: not having gone through the contractual arrangements for getting their money back, can Hedley's none the less get their money back or recover any other damages?

[73] If SAM had not offered what Mr Tustain on 4 October 1999 called 'a standard money back guarantee on licence', I would have regarded the exclusion of liability and entire agreement clauses as quite unreasonable though I would have regarded the limitation of liability to the amount of money paid under the licence agreement as reasonable. But on the evidence before me and in all the circumstances to which I have referred (which would not necessarily exist with other contracts signed on the same terms) I find that all of the terms to which objection is taken in the contract were reasonable. The parties were of equal bargaining power in terms of their relative size and resources. Hedley's were in a difficult position of their own making because of their lateness in tackling the problem of Year 2000 compliance. The evidence from SAM is that other companies like theirs had similar exclusion clauses, but on the other hand, Hedley's did not even try to negotiate for terms more favourable to them.

[74] The effect of that finding is that SAM are under no liability to Hedley's for breach of contract or for misrepresentation.

Watford v Sanderson could be seen as indicating a generally non-interventionist approach in commercial contracts between parties of basically equal bargaining power.

However, *SAM v Hedley* notes the need to consider all the factors in each case and previous case law can be reflected on in that light. Obviously, in both of the above cases, the risk involved in the supply of software is plainly recognised.

Watford v Sanderson: **The requirement of reasonableness in**
system supply contracts and more generally
Elizabeth Macdonald
(2001) *Web Law Journal*

...the point can also be made that the particular facts of a case may show the need for the courts to intervene by finding an exemption clause unreasonable. So, for example, in the context of system, or software, supply contracts, *St Albans City and District Council v ICL Ltd* [1996] 4 All ER 481, has been seen as part of the 'high water mark against limited liability' (Harvey & Rudgard, 2001, p 25), and *Pegler v Wang* has been seen as part of 'the high water mark of judicial intervention in limitation provisions' (Barker, 2000, p 348), but there is a strong basis for contending that both would still be decided in the same way even after the decision of the Court of Appeal in *Watford v Sanderson*. In the *St Alban's* case, the clause in question set £100,000 as the limit of liability, but that limit had been used by mistake. When the particular contract was made, ICL's standard limit was £125,00 and through ICL's error a previous version of its standard terms, with the lower limit had been used. Under such circumstances it would certainly be difficult to argue that ICL had regarded the £100,000 limit as a fair allocation of the contract risk. In *Pegler v Wang*, Wang had misled Pegler as to the 'fit' between the standard software they could supply and Pegler's needs. As has been indicated, it is in trying to adapt software to meet the customer's needs that the risk in the supply and purchase of computer systems arises. In *Watford* it had indicated the reasonableness of the clause that both parties recognised the risk and the need to allocate responsibility for it (or insurance against it) and the reflection of that in the contract price. In *Pegler v Wang*, the misrepresentation of the degree to which the standard software, as such, fitted Pegler's needs led to the conclusion that it 'would be one thing for Wang to include in their contract standard terms intended to exclude liability in the event of some not readily foreseeable lapse on their part, but quite another to do so when they had so misrepresented what they were selling that breaches of contract were not unlikely'.

UNFAIR TERMS IN CONSUMER
CONTRACTS REGULATIONS 1999[205]

1   These Regulations may be cited as the Unfair Terms in Consumer Contracts Regulations 1999 and shall come into force on 1st October 1999.

Revocation

2   The Unfair Terms in Consumer Contracts Regulations 1994 are hereby revoked.

Interpretation

3   (1) In these Regulations –

'the Community' means the European Community;

'consumer' means any natural person who, in contracts covered by these Regulations, is acting for purposes which are outside his trade, business or profession;

---

205 SI 1999/2083. See Koffman and Macdonald, 2004, Chapter 11.

'court' in relation to England and Wales and Northern Ireland means a county court or the High Court, and in relation to Scotland, the Sheriff or the Court of Session;

'Director' means the Director General of Fair Trading;

'EEA Agreement' means the Agreement on the European Economic Area signed at Oporto on 2nd May 1992 as adjusted by the protocol signed at Brussels on 17th March 1993;

'Member State' means a State which is a contracting party to the EEA Agreement;

'notified' means notified in writing;

'qualifying body' means a person specified in Sched 1;

'seller or supplier' means any natural or legal person who, in contracts covered by these Regulations, is acting for purposes relating to his trade, business or profession, whether publicly owned or privately owned;

'unfair terms' means the contractual terms referred to in regulation 5.

(2) In the application of these Regulations to Scotland for references to an 'injunction' or an 'interim injunction' there shall be substituted references to an 'interdict' or 'interim interdict' respectively.

Terms to which these Regulations apply

4   (1) These Regulations apply in relation to unfair terms in contracts concluded between a seller or a supplier and a consumer.

(2) These Regulations do not apply to contractual terms which reflect –

(a) mandatory statutory or regulatory provisions (including such provisions under the law of any Member State or in Community legislation having effect in the United Kingdom without further enactment);

(b) the provisions or principles of international conventions to which the Member States or the Community are party.

Unfair terms

5   (1) A contractual term which has not been individually negotiated shall be regarded as unfair if, contrary to the requirement of good faith, it causes a significant imbalance in the parties' rights and obligations arising under the contract, to the detriment of the consumer.

(2) A term shall always be regarded as not having been individually negotiated where it has been drafted in advance and the consumer has therefore not been able to influence the substance of the term.

(3) Notwithstanding that a specific term or certain aspects of it in a contract has been individually negotiated, these Regulations shall apply to the rest of a contract if an overall assessment of it indicates that it is a pre-formulated standard contract.

(4) It shall be for any seller or supplier who claims that a term was individually negotiated to show that it was.

(5) Schedule 2 to these Regulations contains an indicative and non-exhaustive list of the terms which may be regarded as unfair.

Assessment of unfair terms

6   (1) Without prejudice to regulation 12, the unfairness of a contractual term shall be assessed, taking into account the nature of the goods or services for which the contract was concluded and by referring, at the time of conclusion of the contract, to all the circumstances attending the conclusion of the contract and to all the other terms of the contract or of another contract on which it is dependent.

(2) In so far as it is in plain intelligible language, the assessment of fairness of a term shall not relate –

to the definition of the main subject matter of the contract; or

to the adequacy of the price or remuneration, as against the goods or services supplied in exchange.

Written contracts

7 (1) A seller or supplier shall ensure that any written term of a contract is expressed in plain, intelligible language.

   (2) If there is doubt about the meaning of a written term, the interpretation which is most favourable to the consumer shall prevail but this rule shall not apply in proceedings brought under regulation 12.

Effect of unfair term

8 (1) An unfair term in a contract concluded with a consumer by a seller or supplier shall not be binding on the consumer.

   (2) The contract shall continue to bind the parties if it is capable of continuing in existence without the unfair term.

Choice of law clauses

9 These Regulations shall apply notwithstanding any contract term which applies or purports to apply the law of a non-Member State, if the contract has a close connection with the territory of the Member States.

Complaints – consideration by Director

10 (1) It shall be the duty of the Director to consider any complaint made to him that any contract term drawn up for general use is unfair, unless –

   (a) the complaint appears to the Director to be frivolous or vexatious; or

   (b) a qualifying body has notified the Director that it agrees to consider the complaint.

   (2) The Director shall give reasons for his decision to apply or not to apply, as the case may be, for an injunction under regulation 12 in relation to any complaint which these Regulations require him to consider.

   (3) In deciding whether or not to apply for an injunction in respect of a term which the Director considers to be unfair, he may, if he considers it appropriate to do so, have regard to any undertakings given to him by or on behalf of any person as to the continued use of such a term in contracts concluded with consumers.

Complaints – consideration by qualifying bodies

11 (1) If a qualifying body specified in Part One of Sched 1 notifies the Director that it agrees to consider a complaint that any contract term drawn up for general use is unfair, it shall be under a duty to consider that complaint.

   (2) Regulation 10(2) and (3) shall apply to a qualifying body which is under a duty to consider a complaint as they apply to the Director.

Injunctions to prevent continued use of unfair terms

12 (1) The Director or, subject to paragraph (2), any qualifying body may apply for an injunction (including an interim injunction) against any person appearing to the Director or that body to be using, or recommending use of, an unfair term drawn up for general use in contracts concluded with consumers.

   (2) A qualifying body may apply for an injunction only where –

(a) it has notified the Director of its intention to apply at least fourteen days before the date on which the application is made, beginning with the date on which the notification was given; or

(b) the Director consents to the application being made within a shorter period.

(3) The court on an application under this regulation may grant an injunction on such terms as it thinks fit.

(4) An injunction may relate not only to use of a particular contract term drawn up for general use but to any similar term, or a term having like effect, used or recommended for use by any person.

Powers of the Director and qualifying bodies to obtain documents and information

13 (1) The Director may exercise the power conferred by this regulation for the purpose of –

(a) facilitating his consideration of a complaint that a contract term drawn up for general use is unfair; or

(b) ascertaining whether a person has complied with an undertaking or court order as to the continued use, or recommendation for use, of a term in contracts concluded with consumers.

(2) A qualifying body specified in Part One of Sched 1 may exercise the power conferred by this regulation for the purpose of –

(a) facilitating its consideration of a complaint that a contract term drawn up for general use is unfair; or

(b) ascertaining whether a person has complied with –

(i) an undertaking given to it or to the court following an application by that body, or

(ii) a court order made on an application by that body,

as to the continued use, or recommendation for use, of a term in contracts concluded with consumers.

(3) The Director may require any person to supply to him, and a qualifying body specified in Part One of Sched 1 may require any person to supply to it –

(a) a copy of any document which that person has used or recommended for use, at the time the notice referred to in paragraph (4) below is given, as a pre-formulated standard contract in dealings with consumers;

(b) information about the use, or recommendation for use, by that person of that document or any other such document in dealings with consumers.

(4) The power conferred by this regulation is to be exercised by a notice in writing which may –

(a) specify the way in which and the time within which it is to be complied with; and

(b) be varied or revoked by a subsequent notice.

(5) Nothing in this regulation compels a person to supply any document or information which he would be entitled to refuse to produce or give in civil proceedings before the court.

(6) If a person makes default in complying with a notice under this regulation, the court may, on the application of the Director or of the qualifying body, make such order as the court thinks fit for requiring the default to be made good, and any such order may provide that all the costs or expenses of and incidental to the application shall be borne by the person in default or by any officers of a company or other association who are responsible for its default.

Notification of undertakings and orders to Director

14 A qualifying body shall notify the Director –

(a) of any undertaking given to it by or on behalf of any person as to the continued use of a term which that body considers to be unfair in contracts concluded with consumers;

(b) of the outcome of any application made by it under regulation 12, and of the terms of any undertaking given to, or order made by, the court;

(c) of the outcome of any application made by it to enforce a previous order of the court.

Publication, information and advice

15 (1) The Director shall arrange for the publication in such form and manner as he considers appropriate, of –

(a) details of any undertaking or order notified to him under regulation 14;

(b) details of any undertaking given to him by or on behalf of any person as to the continued use of a term which the Director considers to be unfair in contracts concluded with consumers;

(c) details of any application made by him under regulation 12, and of the terms of any undertaking given to, or order made by, the court;

(d) details of any application made by the Director to enforce a previous order of the court.

(2) The Director shall inform any person on request whether a particular term to which these Regulations apply has been –

(a) the subject of an undertaking given to the Director or notified to him by a qualifying body; or

(b) the subject of an order of the court made upon application by him or notified to him by a qualifying body,

and shall give that person details of the undertaking or a copy of the order, as the case may be, together with a copy of any amendments which the person giving the undertaking has agreed to make to the term in question.

(3) The Director may arrange for the dissemination in such form and manner as he considers appropriate of such information and advice concerning the operation of these Regulations as may appear to him to be expedient to give to the public and to all persons likely to be affected by these Regulations.

SCHEDULE 1
Regulation 3
QUALIFYING BODIES

PART ONE

1 The Data Protection Registrar.

2 The Director General of Electricity Supply.

3 The Director General of Gas Supply.

4 The Director General of Electricity Supply for Northern Ireland.

5 The Director General of Gas for Northern Ireland.

6 The Director General of Telecommunications.

7 The Director General of Water Services.

8　The Rail Regulator.

9　Every weights and measures authority in Great Britain.

10　The Department of Economic Development in Northern Ireland.

PART TWO

11　Consumers' Association.

SCHEDULE 2

Regulation 5(5)　Indicative and non-exhaustive list of terms which may be regarded as unfair

1　Terms which have the object or effect of

(a)　excluding or limiting the legal liability of a seller or supplier in the event of the death of a consumer or personal injury to the latter resulting from an act or omission of that seller or supplier;

(b)　inappropriately excluding or limiting the legal rights of the consumer *vis-à-vis* the seller or supplier or another party in the event of total or partial non-performance or inadequate performance by the seller or supplier of any of the contractual obligations, including the option of offsetting a debt owed to the seller or supplier against any claim which the consumer may have against him;

(c)　making an agreement binding on the consumer whereas provision of services by the seller or supplier is subject to a condition whose realisation depends on his own will alone;

(d)　permitting the seller or supplier to retain sums paid by the consumer where the latter decided not to conclude or perform the contract, without providing for the consumer to receive compensation of an equivalent amount from the seller or supplier where the latter is the party cancelling the contract;

(e)　requiring any consumer who fails to fulfil his obligation to pay a disproportionately high sum in compensation;

(f)　authorising the seller or supplier to dissolve the contract on a discretionary basis where the same facility is not granted to the consumer, or permitting the seller or supplier to retain the sums paid for services not yet supplied by him where it is the seller or supplier himself who dissolves the contract;

(g)　enabling the seller or supplier to terminate a contract of indeterminate duration without reasonable notice except where there are serious grounds for doing so;

(h)　automatically extending a contract of fixed duration where the consumer does not indicate otherwise, when the deadline fixed for the consumer to express this desire not to extend the contract is unreasonably early;

(i)　irrevocably binding the consumer to terms with which he had no real opportunity of becoming acquainted before the conclusion of the contract;

(j)　enabling the seller or supplier to alter the terms of the contract unilaterally without a valid reason which is specified in the contract;

(k)　enabling the seller or supplier to alter unilaterally without a valid reason any characteristics of the product or service to be provided;

(l)　providing for the price of goods to be determined at the time of delivery or allowing a seller of goods or supplier of services to increase their price without in both cases giving the consumer the corresponding right to cancel the contract if the final price is too high in relation to the price agreed when the contract was concluded;

(m) giving the seller or supplier the right to determine whether the goods or services supplied are in conformity with the contract, or giving him the exclusive right to interpret any term of the contract;

(n) limiting the seller's or supplier's obligation to respect commitments undertaken by his agents or making his commitments subject to compliance with a particular formality;

(o) obliging the consumer to fulfil all his obligations where the seller or supplier does not perform his;

(p) giving the seller or supplier the possibility of transferring his rights and obligations under the contract, where this may serve to reduce the guarantees for the consumer, without the latter's agreement;

(q) excluding or hindering the consumer's right to take legal action or exercise any other legal remedy, particularly by requiring the consumer to take disputes exclusively to arbitration not covered by legal provisions, unduly restricting the evidence available to him or imposing on him a burden of proof which, according to the applicable law, should lie with another party to the contract.

2 Scope of subparagraphs (g), (j) and (l)

(a) Subparagraph (g) is without hindrance to terms by which a supplier of financial services reserves the right to terminate unilaterally a contract of indeterminate duration without notice where there is a valid reason, provided that the supplier is required to inform the other contracting party or parties thereof immediately.

(b) Subparagraph (j) is without hindrance to terms under which a supplier of financial services reserves the right to alter the rate of interest payable by the consumer or due to the latter, or the amount of other charges for financial services without notice where there is a valid reason, provided that the supplier is required to inform the other contracting party or parties thereof at the earliest opportunity and that the latter are free to dissolve the contract immediately.

Subparagraph (j) is also without hindrance to terms under which a seller or supplier reserves the right to alter unilaterally the conditions of a contract of indeterminate duration, provided that he is required to inform the consumer with reasonable notice and that the consumer is free to dissolve the contract.

(c) Subparagraphs (g), (j) and (l) do not apply to: transactions in transferable securities, financial instruments and other products or services where the price is linked to fluctuations in a stock exchange quotation or index or a financial market rate that the seller or supplier does not control; – contracts for the purchase or sale of foreign currency, traveller's cheques or international money orders denominated in foreign currency;

(d) Subparagraph (l) is without hindrance to price-indexation clauses, where lawful, provided that the method by which prices vary is explicitly described.

The 1994 Regulations came into force on 1 July 1995 to implement the EC Directive on Unfair Terms in Consumer Contracts.[206] They have now been replaced by the 1999 Regulations on Unfair Terms in Consumer Contracts. The Regulations do not simply apply to exemption clauses; they apply a fairness test to non-individually negotiated terms in contracts between consumers and sellers or suppliers, with certain 'core' terms being exempted from the test, provided that they are in plain, intelligible language.

---

206 OJ 1993 L 95/29 – made under Art 100A on the basis that it is concerned with the establishment of an internal market.

The definition of 'consumer' is in reg 3. It is restricted to 'natural persons', which means that a company cannot be a consumer for the purposes of the Regulations. This differs from the category of those who 'deal as consumers' under UCTA 1977 and, in general, a mechanistic approach to the categorisation under the Regulations seems likely, with businesses simply being excluded from its protection without any consideration of how central the contract in question is to the operation of the business.[207]

The fairness test is applied to terms which have not been individually negotiated. Most such terms will be contained in standard form contracts but the category does not seem to be solely limited to such terms. Regulation 5(2) states that:

> ... a term shall always be regarded as not having been individually negotiated where it has been drafted in advance and the consumer has not been able to influence the substance of the term.

The exclusion of certain 'core' terms from the fairness test is covered by reg 6(2). It would seem to cover terms defining the main subject matter of the contract or stating the price and its exact scope is problematic,[208] but in *Director General of Fair Trading v First National Bank*,[209] the House of Lords made it clear that a restrictive approach should be taken to its coverage. It should only cover terms 'falling squarely within it'.[210] Further, it should be emphasised that it is restricted to cases in which the 'core' terms are in 'plain, intelligible language'. In any event, it would seem that the 'core' terms should always be taken into account in assessing the fairness of other terms.[211]

Regulation 5(1) states that a term shall be regarded as unfair if:

> ... contrary to the requirement of good faith it causes a significant imbalance in the parties' rights and obligations arising under the contract to the detriment of the consumer.

Like 'reasonableness' under the 1977 Act, this is assessed against the background of the circumstances at the time of contracting.[212] Looking for a significant imbalance in the parties' rights and obligations would seem to require a weighing of the rights and obligations of the two parties. Some consideration was given to the meaning of good faith in *Director General of Fair Trading v First National Bank*.[213] Lord Bingham saw it as a matter of 'fair and open dealing. He said:[214]

> The requirement of good faith in this context is one of fair and open dealing. Openness requires that the terms should be expressed fully, clearly and legibly, containing no concealed pitfalls or traps. Appropriate prominence should be given to terms which might operate disadvantageously to the customer. Fair dealing requires that a supplier should not, whether deliberately or unconsciously, take advantage of the consumer's necessity, indigence, lack of experience, unfamiliarity with the subject matter of the

---

207 Contrast the approach to 'deals as consumer' under the 1977 Act. See above, p 194.
208 Macdonald, 1994.
209 [2002] 1 All ER 97.
210 Lord Bingham [12].
211 See Recital 19 of the Directive.
212 Regulation 6(1).
213 [2002] 1 All ER 97.
214 [17]. See also Lord Steyn [36].

contract, weak bargaining position or any other factor listed in or analogous to those listed in Schedule 2 of the regulations.

Further assistance in determining which terms will be unfair can be found in Sched 2, which contains a non-exhaustive list of terms which 'may be regarded as unfair'.

The consumer can use the Regulations in the same way as someone can use UCTA 1977 against an exemption clause. An unfair term will not bind the consumer,[215] and the consumer can rely on this when in dispute with a seller or supplier. However, the Regulations also provide for a different form of attack on unfair terms. The Director General of Fair Trading has the power to, *inter alia*, obtain injunctions to prevent the use of unfair terms more generally[216] and, under the 1999 Regulations, that has been extended to certain qualifying bodies listed in Sched 1, such as the Consumers' Association.

---

215 Regulation 8(1).
216 Regulation 12.

CHAPTER 5

DEFECTIVE SOFTWARE –
PRODUCT LIABILITY AND TORT

INTRODUCTION

The liability for defective software arising out of contract has already been discussed in Chapter 4. As computer control becomes usual for many, if not most, applications, it becomes apparent that the failure of systems containing software may well have an impact on many people who are not a party to the contract to supply that software. They may suffer economic loss or physical injury.[1] One of the most highly publicised system failures of this type was that of the Computer Aided Despatch system of the London Ambulance Service in October and November 1992. The Report of the Inquiry into the incident[2] demonstrates a number of the difficult issues that may arise when attempting to apportion liability in an incident such as this. In contrast, more and more common domestic appliances are controlled by means of programmable devices. Unlike some of the other areas of law considered in this book, liability for defective software has no dedicated statutes to examine and no case law of significance to assist in predicting how existing legal principles might be applied to such situations. Some cases founded in contract have now come before the UK courts but these are a long way from answering some of the fundamental questions posed by such circumstances. There have, as yet, been no cases based in tort, although there has been much speculation as to how tortious principles should be applied. What follows is, therefore, an attempt to review and distil a number of the arguments that have been discussed into a coherent framework and to suggest how the law might move forward in this area. The case law cited has been chosen in an attempt to provide suitable analogies with other situations; many of these are favourites of other commentators but, where they make a useful point, no excuse should be needed for a re-examination. It must be remembered, though, that such cases can only be useful by way of analogy and some will perform this task rather better than others.

In the event of a system containing defective software failing, there may be liability in negligence and also, for cases of physical injury or damage, under the Consumer Protection Act (CPA) 1987.

The CPA 1987

Whilst it is not the purpose or function of this work to assess the rationale and philosophy underlying the introduction of the product liability regime introduced in the UK by the CPA 1987, a consideration of some of the debate surrounding the genesis of this statute is, necessarily, incidental. The 1987 Act was passed to implement the EC Product Liability Directive,[3] a document which had been some years in

---

1 For examples, see Rowland, 1991; Lloyd, 1991; Lannetti, 2000.
2 South West Thames RHA, 1993.
3 Council Directive 85/374/EEC of 25 July 1985 on the Approximation of the Laws, Regulations and Administrative Provisions of the Member States Concerning Liability for Defective Products OJ 1985 L 210/29.

gestation. Article 1 of the Directive provides, quite simply, that 'The producer shall be liable for damage caused by a defect in his product'. 'Product' is then further defined in Art 2 to include 'all movables ... even though incorporated into another movable or into an immovable'. This can be compared with the relevant section of the CPA,[4] which provides that '"product" means any goods or electricity and ... includes a product which is composed in another product, whether by virtue of being a component part or raw material or otherwise'. In theory, the effect of product liability legislation, for those situations in which it applies, is to eliminate the necessity to show negligence and, instead, replace it with the requirement to demonstrate a causal link between the defect in the product and the damage caused. This is often referred to as a type of strict liability on the grounds that the culpability of the producer in relation to the defect is not a relevant factor.

Is software a product?

Can computer software fall within this definition of 'product'? This question has stimulated much debate. Rusch points out that 'for anyone who has struggled with software that does not function as expected or causes unanticipated difficulties, the idea of a products liability regime applying to software is attractive. Not only that, given that software controls the functioning of many types of goods, malfunctioning software may create unreasonable risks of harm.'[5] Some of the arguments are, essentially, a reflection of the tangibility/intangibility debate already discussed in relation to software as goods and will not be repeated here,[6] but other arguments are inextricably linked with the concept of product and the underlying premises on which the Act and Directive are based.[7] The realisation that there might be problems with the categorisation of computer software had dawned prior to implementation of the Directive.

> **Implementation of the EC Directive on Product Liability**
> **DTI, November 1985, para 47**
>
> Special problems arise with those industries dealing with products concerned with information such as books, records, tapes and computer software ... It does not appear that the Directive is intended to extend liability in such situations. On the other hand, it is important that liability is extended to the manufacturer of a machine which contains defective software and is thereby unsafe ... the line between those cases may however not be easy to draw, particularly in the field of new technology where the distinction between hardware and software is becoming increasingly blurred.

This suggests that, even though software can be regarded as pure information in some respects, the development of technology, together with the way in which it might be used to control systems and apparatus, may conspire to make an apparently logical boundary indistinct. However, it appeared that, by the time of implementation, this issue had officially disappeared and the advice following implementation was that, in

---

4   Section 2(1).
5   Rusch, 2003, p 777.
6   See above, Chapter 4.
7   See Hirschbaeck, 1989; Lloyd, 1991; Rowland, 1991.

the event of a defect in software leading to physical damage, liability would rest with the producer of the complete system,[8] implicitly rejecting the notion of software as a product in its own right.

Predictably, this did not silence the academic debate and there is still a considerable divergence of views on the answer to the question. These differing approaches are now found, not only in specialist works, but also in standard texts on the law of tort: 'It is unclear whether books and computer software, which may endanger persons if they contain inaccuracies, fall within the definition of "products"'.[9] Compare, also, the following two views.

The Law of Torts
John G Fleming
8th edn, 1992, Sydney: Law Book Co, p 501

Products comprise 'any goods and electricity', including component parts. Presumably, however, not information contained in publications, however hardbound. Nor pure services: a designer is not liable unlike a producer of a defectively designed product. Misleading or inadequate warnings may make an accompanying product defective, but defective software instructions addressed to the computer, are not 'goods'.[10] What is the reason for drawing this distinction between goods and services, seeing that the rationale for the former – consumer protection – seems to apply equally to the latter? The distinction is doctrinally difficult to justify, seeing that the human element, albeit masked, is as much involved in the creation of products as is services and that the accident-preventive rationale necessarily targets human behaviour. The reasons are accidental and pragmatic. Foremost is the provenance of warranties attached to the sale of goods, from which the seminal American tort liability derived. More fundamental may be the fact that professional services are excluded because their product is furnished for one client at a time so that the cost of liability cannot be spread as widely as over a whole line of tangible products ...

Winfield and Jolowicz on Tort
WVH Rogers
15th edn, 1998, London: Sweet & Maxwell, p 342

It seems that information is not within the Act even though it is incorporated in tangible form in a book but the same may not be true of computerised information, where the line between 'software' and 'hardware' may be difficult to draw sensibly. If an airline crashes because a component in an automatic landing device fails above a certain temperature there is clearly a defective product within the Act. Can the position really be so different if it is programmed so that it simply does not operate in certain foreseeable conditions or if it gives the pilot a misleading indication? It has been said that, while software is not goods within the Sale of Goods Act, a disk containing a program is, and, when that is sold, the statutory implied terms apply to the software as well as the disk itself. Misleading instructions for use of a product are clearly not to be equated with 'pure' information, for they themselves render an otherwise perfect product defective.

A number of issues are raised in these two extracts: the 'pure information' theory, which is fatal to a classification of software as product; the goods/services distinction;

---

8   DTI, 1987, para 11.
9   Stanton, 1994, p 222.
10   Relying on Stapleton, 1989.

and the pragmatic approach, which considers the end result of the defect rather than its location. If the first of these is to be argued successfully, it is important that all the attributes of computer software are fully taken into account. In order to make the problem accessible, a number of writers have used quite simple analogies.

Textbook on Tort
David Howarth
1995, London: Butterworths, p 412

Instructions and warnings are words that deal with how to operate the object. But in recipes the words do not tell readers what to do with the book as a physical object; rather the physical object is the medium by which the words, which are the real product are delivered ...

Similar problems arise whatever the medium – a private letter, a video or a tape recording. Computer software may strike some people as different since the instructions it contains appear to be addressed in the first instance to a machine rather than a human. But the real difference between software and a recipe in a book is not the addressee of the instructions for in the end they are both instructions to human users, but simply the ease with which any mistake in the instructions may be identified. After all, computer programs are merely a form of complex recipe. The difference is that a mistake in a recipe will usually be easier to spot than a mistake in a computer program and so contributory negligence or even *novus acts interveniens* will be easier to establish.

Despite the apparent ease of spotting a mistake (or a defect?) in a recipe, there was no liability for breach of warranty in the US case of *Cardozo v True*,[11] in which a recipe book failed to point out that a particular ingredient in a recipe was poisonous unless cooked properly. Arguably the novice in either cookery or programming may have equal difficulty in detecting the defect in the relevant medium. A more useful distinction might be between choosing to rely on information and being compelled to so rely.[12] A further issue of the 'software as information' theory is explored in the next extract.

Three problems with the new product liability
Jane Stapleton
in *Essays for Patrick Atiyah*
Peter Cane and Jane Stapleton (eds)
1991, Oxford: OUP, Chapter 11

My suggestion that the reform focus on defective products may have been strengthened by a doomed attempt to shift attention away from human conduct and make the imposition of stricter liability more palatable, gains some support from the attitude of reformers to computer software. Some years ago I argued that software, being mere information, is not a 'good'[13] for the purposes of the UK law of supply of goods; and that were defective navigational software to cause a plane to crash or a heart-lung machine to cut out, those thereby injured might at first seem to have problems establishing a cause of action under the CPA which defines the 'product' in terms of 'goods'. But the CPA s 1(1) requires UK courts to construe its provisions to accord with the Directive which defines 'product' in terms of 'movables'. This might not seem to help much, but some commentators suggest that defective software may fall under the Directive, and that the

---

11　342 So 2d 1053 (Fla App 1977).

12　Rowland, 1991.

13　Relying on Stapleton, 1989.

European Court of Justice might take a 'flexible' attitude to the notion of 'product' which will allow it to be expanded more widely than 'goods' to allow in phenomena which, in policy terms, are 'like' defective goods. But what is it about defective software that suggests that it might be like defective goods? Is it like goods because, although it is a service, the human origin of errors in a program is less obvious than the human origin of most pure services? Is their human origin masked in a way that facilitates imposition of liability? Perhaps; but it should be noted that the masking characteristic is a variable. Suppose that the designer (A) of a navigational software program incorrectly enters the height of a mountain, causing a plane to crash. If the software package is to be a 'product' for the purposes of the Directive, is a map incorrectly drawn by B, which carries the identically incorrect information to the pilot also to be a product? If so, what about where the same information is conveyed to the pilot orally by an on-board navigator (C) – is he the supplier of a 'product'? ...

In deciding if 'defective software' is to be a 'defective product' within the Directive, the ECJ has to identify what it is about defective 'goods' which makes claims arising out of the injuries they cause special. The warranty origin of the focus on defective goods does not provide the answer. Nor does the fact that many goods are mass-produced, because liability under the Directive is not confined to mass-produced goods and, in any case, non-goods such as software and maps can be mass-produced and cause physical injury. For the same reasons, the complexity of some goods and their sophisticated production techniques do not provide the key. Nor can the reason be that the focus on defects in goods in the Directive eliminates the necessity to evaluate conduct: it does not.

Although the fact of inputting inaccurate data may result in a malfunction, which, in turn, produces certain adverse consequences, this is a gross simplification of both the nature and the function of computer control in most systems. The potential defects that are likely to give rise to the severest problems are errors in coding or logic that cause the mode of operation of the computer controlled system to depart from its specification. This may not be traceable to any particular human error as such, but instead may be due to a 'design error' in the software. This is, arguably, the point at which software begins to diverge from 'pure information'; although capable of reduction to written format, the program is designed to be a working entity and is 'engineered' in the true sense of the word, just as much as a more conventional control system might be. This suggests that the more accurate view is to consider a defect in the software as a design fault, and this argument can also take into account the more pragmatic approach suggested in the above extract from Winfield and Jolowicz.

The final issue raised is that of the goods vs services[14] debate – the extent to which the categorisation of the contract to supply software can be described in terms of a contract for goods or a contract for services and the impact that this categorisation might have on the boundaries of the definition of product. Whittaker, in supporting the division of software into the two categories of mass produced package and specialist bespoke software, finds assistance in the US approach.

European product liability and intellectual products
Simon Whittaker
(1989) 105 LQR 125, p 135

Should computer software be included as a product for the purposes of the Directive? ... English commentators in the specialist journals have merely raised the question of the

---

14   See the discussion above, Chapter 4.

application of the Directive to the area. The American materials are more helpful, although, somewhat surprisingly, there appears to be no American case decided specifically on the question whether computer software is a product for the purposes of its strict liability. However, American commentators agree that this issue should be determined by deciding whether the reasons for imposing strict liability apply to software. Prince, for example, sees the placing of the product into the 'stream of commerce', the producer's better position to control risks and his ability to spread the cost of accidents as the three rationales most commonly used by American courts considering the expansion of the scope of strict liability beyond chattels. He distinguishes two broadly different types of software: software which is specially designed for the needs and to the order of the consumer, and software which is a standard marketed package. Prince concludes that the reasons for strict liability do not apply to the specially designed computer program as it:

> ... is not really placed in the stream of commerce because it is distributed to only one customer. Also, because the program is only sold to one user, the supplier is not in a better position than the user to bear the costs. Since the supplier is not selling the product *en masse*, he cannot spread the cost of a defect over a number of consumers. Finally, the supplier may have more expertise and knowledge regarding the tailored program because the supplier wrote the program. However, in these situations, the user is normally very heavily involved in the design stage of the program because the user must tell the supplier what the program is to do.

On the other hand he considers that these same reasons do apply to 'ready to use software' as to any other product which is distributed *en masse*.

It is still the case that American courts have not extended product liability to software[15] so as yet there are no reliable indications of which of these interpretations of the nature of software the courts may choose to give effect to. In *Hou-Tex Inc v Landmark Graphic*, the court accepted that the particular software at issue was a product on the grounds that it was 'a highly technical tool used to create a graphic representation form technical data'. However it was at pains to point out that it was making no general assertion that all computer programs could be defined as products.[16] Evidence of the Commission's view of the intention of the Directive, if not necessarily of the logic of classifying software as a product, was illustrated in the answer to the following question asked in the European Parliament:[17] 'Does the EEC Directive on product liability also cover ... computer software?' The answer to this was unequivocal on the basis that, as the term 'product' was defined as all movables even though incorporated into another movable or into an immovable, the Directive also applied to software. Returning to the distinction between bespoke and mass produced software, Whittaker raises a further issue for interpretation of European Community law and the potential harmonisation of services.

European product liability and intellectual products
Simon Whittaker
(1989) 105 LQR 125, p 130

In the case of computer software a broad distinction should be drawn between the situations where it is made to a standard design for mass distribution ('off the peg') and

---

15 See eg, Rustad and Koenig, 2003, p 135. In Malaysia, the Consumer Protection Act 1999 excludes e-consumers from its ambit, see Jawahitha, 2004.
16. 26 SW 3d 103, 107 (Tex-App, Houston 14th Dist 2000).
17 Written Question 706/88 OJ 1989 C 114/42.

where it is composed specially to order for a particular purpose for a particular client ('made to measure'). In the former case, software packages circulate within the Community in very little different ways from other, manufactured goods and the arguments from competition and freedom of movement of goods would apply to the same extent. However, in the case of made to measure software, these arguments lose their force. Such programmes do not circulate in the market at all, whether within the Member State or within the Community. It is true that different liability rules would affect competition between software engineers of the Member States in question, but here it can be seen that we have strayed into the freedom of movement of services rather than of goods. This, of course, is also an important aspect of the common market and, moreover, the European Court has frequently taken the 'context of all the provisions establishing a common organisation of the market' into account in interpreting Community provisions.

Is there a defect?

If, indeed, computer software can be construed as a product, how is a defect in that software to be identified? This may raise practical as well as legal problems. Lloyd has remarked that 'The quest for perfect software has proved as successful as the hunt for the Loch Ness monster'.[18] In fact, the relevant issue may be not so much a question as to whether the sought after goal exists, but rather whether it is possible to demonstrate how far the search is from the target. The degree of complexity of most computer programs, creating manifold combinations and permutations, means that most computer software is impossible to test exhaustively for all foreseeable conditions. Comprehensive testing is therefore out of the question. Many faults will be discovered by routine testing but identifying defects that will compromise safety are more likely to be discovered by the testing of boundary conditions than by testing normal operating conditions. It is usual to assume that in any piece of software some residual 'bugs' will remain, but not all of these will give rise to 'defects; only those that could lead to damage.

'Defect' was defined in the Directive as follows:

Article 6

1   A product is defective when it does not provide the safety which a person is entitled to expect, taking all circumstances into account, including:

    (a) the presentation of the product;

    (b) the use to which it could reasonably be expected that the product would be put;

    (c) the time when the product was put into circulation.

2   A product shall not be considered defective for the sole reason that a better product is subsequently put into circulation.

This was implemented in s 3(1) of the CPA 1987 which provides that 'there is a defect in a product ... if the safety of the product is not such as persons generally are entitled to expect; and for those purposes "safety" in relation to a product, shall include safety with respect to products comprised in that product'.

---

18   Lloyd, 2004, p 613. See, also, similar comments in Lloyd and Simpson, 1994.

Basing the definition of defect on a safety standard that 'persons are entitled to expect' implies an objective assessment of 'defect'. This is in accordance with the commentary on the Strasbourg Convention.[19]

Commentary on the Strasbourg Convention
Paragraph 35

... the committee [of experts] formulated a definition of defect taking as the basic elements 'safety' and 'legitimate expectancy'.

This, however, does not involve the safety or expectancy of any particular person. The use of the words 'a person' and 'entitled' clearly shows that a product's safety must be assessed according to an objective criterion. The words 'a person' do not imply any expectation on the part of a victim or a given consumer. The word 'entitled' is more general than the word 'legally' (entitled); in other words, mere observance of statutory rules and rules imposed by authorities do not preclude liability.

The committee did not wish to use the word 'reasonably'. Such expression ... could diminish the consumer's rights, since it could include considering economic factors and assessing expediency which ought not to be taken into account in determining the safety of a product.

It is arguable whether, in fact, this is the standard which has survived the Directive and the 1987 Act, and there have been suggestions that, instead, reformers 'have seized on the ill-defined concept of a product "defect" which required the benefits of the product as they were at the time of circulation to be balanced against its costs'.[20] If it is this latter concept that has held sway, then the resultant effect is more akin to a negligence standard than one of strict liability. Moreover, the apparent decision, recorded above, not to employ a standard of reasonableness in the consideration of a safety issues is, itself, an interesting one when compared with the standards expected by other comparable legislation. The standard of safety for employees at work is governed primarily by the qualification 'as far as reasonably practicable',[21] which imports precisely the risk-benefit analysis that is purported to be excluded in the product liability regime envisioned under the Strasbourg Convention.

How, then, is the standard to be assessed in systems containing software? It has been suggested both that, 'in those more complex situations where modern tort liability also operates, eg cases of foreseeable misuse or complex design systems where the standard is neither agreed nor obvious, the "expectations test" is misleading and inadequate',[22] and also that '[t]he "consumer expectations" test for legal defectiveness ... has had limited appeal as an operational rule for complex design defect cases. Primarily this is because the consumer simply does not have adequate information to know what to expect'.[23] A comparison can be made with the situation for 'conventional' products, where the general safety record may have a particular relevance in ascertaining whether the product was defective. This is unlikely to be the

---

19 HMSO, 1977.
20 Stapleton, 1986.
21 See especially, in this context, the Health and Safety at Work Act 1974, s 6; *Edwards v NCB* [1949] 1 QB 704, *per* Lord Asquith.
22 Stapleton, 1994, p 235.
23 Terry, 1991.

case for systems involving computer software, where failure free operation in the past is not necessarily an indication of failure free operation in the future, especially for products that are likely to be used in different situations and conditions. In such circumstances, a fault could remain hidden for some time until triggered by a particular combination of inputs that may not have occurred before. In addition, the operative time at which a diagnosis of defectiveness needs to be made is the moment of supply. It is possible that the software may have been updated, modified or otherwise upgraded, making it difficult to assess the defectiveness of the original version, but, in the absence of such changes, software does not 'wear out' in the same way as hardware.

Causation

The final factor which has to be established is that the defect caused the damage. This may be difficult to prove, depending on the nature and type of software involved. It goes without saying that any physical damage will always be inflicted by hardware, and so a causal link has to be established between the apparently defective software instructions, their effect on the hardware and the consequence to the victim. Such observations perhaps highlight the difference between software and pure information; once computer software has commenced giving instructions to the system under its control, it may activate an inevitable sequence of events which becomes difficult to interrupt.[24]

It may be difficult to establish causation if there has also been some human input or intervention. In so called fly-by-wire aircraft, such as the Airbus A320 (now being superseded by the A330 and A340), the pilot flies the plane not directly, but by means of a joystick connected to the appropriate mechanisms via a computer.[25] The presence of the computer allows for intelligent control of the aircraft, which should be able to compensate for both malfunctions and pilot error. The role of the pilot (or, indeed, the operator/controller of other computerised systems) often only becomes crucial in the event of failure of the normal operating system. What is the situation if defective software causes such a malfunction and the pilot is unable to land the plane safely? What was the cause of the accident? Clearly, each case will hinge on its particular circumstances, but there are a number of general observations which can be made. There will be appropriate procedures which should be carried out in the event of a failure and, if the pilot fails to carry these out, there may be a break in the chain of causation and the accident may be put down to 'pilot error'. However, the danger with human intervention being confined to abnormal cases can mean that there is very little opportunity to practise and become proficient in such skills.[26] In addition, it is entirely

---

24 Details and discussions of a number of software failures and near-failures can be found in the newsgroup comp.risks, available also at www.catless.ncl.ac.uk/Risks/. These include reports of the circumstances of some of the Airbus A320 accidents and reports of the incidents involving the Therac 25 radiotherapy machine.

25 In fact, the A320 has five on-board computers, some of which are back-ups designed to switch into use if a fault is detected in the operational computer.

26 Apparently, human error is involved in about 60% of all aircraft accidents. Although this does not necessarily indicate 'pilot error', it does show that human factors are also a relevant consideration. See, eg, Storey, 1996.

possible that a situation could arise where the computer would 'not allow' the pilot to take corrective action or, alternatively, that the back-up system of control provided was inadequate to land the plane safely, especially in adverse weather conditions, even for an expert pilot. Although the root cause of the mishap might be the defective software, at least some of these elements would qualify as a *novus actus interveniens*, sufficient to break the chain of causation.

Some of the possibilities are illustrated by the facts revealed in *Airbus Industrie v Patel and Others*.[27] On 14 February 1990, an Airbus A320 crashed on landing at Bangalore. In December 1990, the report of the Indian Board of Inquiry found that when the aircraft struck the ground it had been in 'idle/open descent' mode, which allowed the aircraft to descend in a glide with the engines idling. The investigation concluded that this was because the pilots had mistakenly instructed the aircraft to descend to 700 ft altitude instead of descending at a rate of 700 ft/min. Apparently, the altitude and vertical speed controls in A320s were, at that time, similar and adjacent to each other. The report further concluded both that the pilots failed to observe their error until it was too late to gain any thrust from the engines and that there was no evidence of any failure of any part of the aircraft, its controls or its engines. The accident was therefore held to be the result of pilot error coupled with lack of training. The airline, IAL, was criticised as employer, as was the airport authority at Bangalore – Hindustan Aeronautics Ltd – whose failure to have suitable accident arrangements exacerbated the outcome of the incident.

Despite the finding that there was no fault with the aircraft itself, a number of passengers and their relatives began proceedings in Texas, where the liability for defective products was strict and it is relatively easy to establish personal jurisdiction. On what basis might such an incident reveal a defect? Could ergonomic problems such as a confusing instrumentation layout compromise safety sufficiently to produce a finding of defectiveness? Does this not, in many ways, raise similar issues to confusing and inadequate instructions which are explicitly included in the law on product liability? As was pointed out following the Bangalore incident, 'assuming that the systems *are* working properly, when does it stop being "human error" and become poor ergonomics? ... [T]he very way the pilot *interacts* with the aircraft is also a safety issue'.[28] Whether or not such problems would be sufficient to render a product defective in law, it is interesting to note that, following the above crash, it was reported that certain changes were made to the Airbus A320 control software to enable the engines to spool up faster if the pilot had to advance the throttle suddenly.[29] Had this been in place at the time of the Bangalore incident, it would have enabled the pilots to rectify the situation once they had realised their mistake.

In the mid-1980s, defects in the software controlling the Therac-25 radiotherapy machine[30] resulted in substantial overdoses of radiation being administered to several patients, with resulting injury, illness and death in some cases. Conceptually, this appears to be an example of where it is easier to accept the link between the defective

---

27 The facts are set out in [1997] 2 Lloyd's Rep 8 (CA); [1998] 2 All ER 257 (HL), but the legal issue in this particular case actually concerned a conflicts of law point as to which was the appropriate forum to bring the action.
28 Dorsett, R, 1990; Neumann, 1990. See also, Bott, et al, 2000, s 10.5.6.
29 Moxon, 1991, p 20.
30 For further details see Leveson, 1995, Appendix A.

software and the damage. Suppose, instead, that the software error had resulted in an underdose of radiation, with the result that patients died, not from the effects of the radiation, but from the cancer for which they were supposedly being treated.[31] In this scenario, the damage would be the result of the original disease, that is, it would not be caused by the radiotherapy machine, which could not, therefore, be classed as 'legally defective'.[32]

The development risks defence

Notwithstanding the label of 'strict liability' applied to the products liability regime introduced by the EC Directive and the CPA 1987, it is possible for producers to escape liability if they can avail themselves of the so called 'development risks' defence contained in Art 7(e) of the Directive, 'that the state of scientific and technical knowledge at the time when he put the product into circulation was not such as to enable the existence of the defect to be discovered'. This is a controversial defence and the Member States were given the choice as to whether to include it in their implementing legislation. Interestingly, it had not been included in the Strasbourg Convention, for the reasons given below.

Commentary on the Strasbourg Convention
Paragraphs 39–40[33]

Some experts maintained that 'development risks' should be a ground for exclusion of liability in the case of technically advanced products. Any stipulation to the contrary might discourage scientific research and the marketing of new products.

Against this opinion it was argued that such an exception would make the convention nugatory since it would reintroduce into the system of liability established by the convention the possibility for the producer to prove the absence of fault on his part. Exclusion of liability in cases of 'development risks' would also invite the use of the consumer as a 'guinea-pig'.

In conclusion the committee considered that the problem was one of social policy, the main question being whether such risks should be borne by the consumer of the producer and/or, in whole or in part, by the community.

The committee considered that, as insurance made it possible to spread risk over a large number of products, producers' liability, even for development risks, should not be a serious obstacle to planning and putting into circulation new and useful products.

The committee therefore decided that development risk should not constitute an exception to producers' liability.

Despite criticisms over both the use of the defence as such and the change in wording from that supplied in the Directive,[34] the UK included the defence in s 4(1)(e) of the 1987 Act:

---

31 A similar situation arose in relation to a radiotherapy device at a North Staffordshire hospital, although not as a result of a error in the software.

32 See, also, below, p 231 in relation to negligent designs.

33 HMSO, 1977.

34 *Hansard* (Lords) Vol 485 Cols 848–55, 9 March 1987; *Hansard* (Lords) Vol 487 Col 784, 14 May 1987.

... that the state of scientific and technical knowledge at the relevant time was not such that a producer of products of the same description as the product in question might be expected to have discovered the defect if it had existed in his products while they were under his control.

The emphasis of this defence appears to be rather different and refers to a comparison with other producers, that is, a negligence-type test, whereas the Directive implies an obligation to consider the available knowledge in the world at large.[35] Thus, in relation to the UK defence, Reed[36] suggests that, given the practice in the industry, 'it is arguable that a software producer who failed to discover a quite serious defect in his software would nevertheless be able to take advantage of the defence, so long as the defect is not in an area of the program that would be tested as a matter of course by others in the industry'.

The apparent divergence in the scope of Art 7(e) of the Directive and s 4(1)(e) led to the Commission bringing proceedings against the UK for failure to implement the Directive satisfactorily. In the absence of relevant case law, both the Advocate General and the European Court of Justice were of the view that there was no evidence that a UK court would not interpret the wording of s 4(1)(e) in the light of the arguably narrower scope of Art 7(e). The Commission's application was, therefore, dismissed, but the Advocate General made some useful comments about the nature of the development risks defence.

Case C-300/95 *Commission v UK* [1997] ECR I-2649

19   ... the Directive ... opted for a system of strict liability which was no longer absolute but limited, in deference to a principle of the fair apportionment of risk between the injured person and the producer, the latter having to bear only quantifiable risks, but not development risks, which are by their nature unquantifiable. Under the Directive, therefore, in order for the producer to be held liable for defects in the product, the injured party is required to prove the damage, the defect in the product and the causal relationship between defect and damage, but not negligence on the part of the producer.

The producer, however, may exonerate himself from liability by proving that the 'state of the art' at the time when he put the product into circulation was not such as to cause the product to be regarded as defective. This is what Art 7(e) of the Directive provides.

20   It should first be observed that, since that provision refers solely to the 'scientific and technical knowledge' at the time when the product was marketed, it is not concerned with the practices and safety standards in use in the industrial sector in which the producer is operating. In other words, it has no bearing on the exclusion of the manufacturer from liability that no one in that particular class of manufacturer takes the measures necessary to eliminate the defect or prevent it arising if such measures are capable of being adopted on the basis of available knowledge.

Other matters which likewise are to be regarded as falling outside the scope of Art 7(e) are aspects relating to the practicability and expense of measures suitable for eliminating the defect from the product. Neither from this point of view, can the fact that the producer did not appraise himself of the state of scientific knowledge or does

---

35   Newdick, 1991.
36   Reed and Welterveden, 2003 p. 115.

not keep up to date with developments in this area as disclosed in the specialist literature, be posited as having any relevance for the purposes of excluding liability on his part. I consider, in fact, that the producer's conduct should be assessed using the yardstick of the knowledge of an expert in the sector.

21 Some additional considerations need to be explored, however, in order to tie down the concept 'state of knowledge'.

The progress of scientific culture does not develop linearly in so far as new studies and new discoveries may initially be criticized and regarded as unreliable by most of the scientific community, yet subsequently after the passage of time undergo an opposite process of 'beatification' whereby they are virtually unanimously endorsed. It is therefore quite possible that at the time when a given product is marketed, there will be isolated opinions that it is defective, while most academics do not take that view. The problem at this juncture is to determine whether in such a situation, that is to say, where there is a risk that is not certain and will be agreed to exist by all only *ex post*, the producer may still rely on the defence provided in Art 7(e) of the Directive.

In my view, the answer to this question must be in the negative. In other words, the state of scientific knowledge cannot be identified with the views expressed by the majority of learned opinion, but with the most advanced level of research which has been carried out at a given time.

22 That interpretation, which coincides with that suggested by the Commission ... is closest to the *ratio legis* of the Community rules: the producer has to bear the foreseeable risks, against which he can protect himself by taking either preventative measures by stepping up experimentation and research investment or measures to cover himself by taking out civil liability insurance against any damage caused by the defects in the product.

Where in the whole gamut of scientific opinion at a particular time there is also one isolated opinion (which, as the history of science shows, might become with the passage of time *opinio communis*) as to the potentially defective and/or hazardous nature of the product, the manufacturer is no longer faced with an unforeseeable risk, since, as such, it is outside the scope of the rules imposed by the Directive.

23 The aspect which I have just been discussing is closely linked with the question of availability of scientific and technical knowledge in the sense of the accessibility of the sum of knowledge at a given time to interested persons. It is undeniable that the circulation of information is affected by objective factors, such as, for example, its place of origin, the language in which it was given and the circulation of the journals in which it was published ...

24 ... More generally, the 'state of knowledge' must be construed so as to include all data in the information circuit of the scientific community as a whole, bearing in mind, however, on the basis of a reasonableness test the actual opportunities for the information to circulate.

Even with the proviso expressed in para 24, it should be noted that this view puts a very great burden on manufacturers to stay abreast of developments in their field which could be considered to be even higher than that imposed by the law of negligence (discussed below).

A number of commentators have discussed the various possible combinations envisaged by the defence.[37] The two outer extremes are those where the defect is either

---

37 See, eg, Newdick, 1991; 1988; Hodges, 1993.

unknown and undiscoverable or known and discoverable. In the former there will be no liability, whereas there will always be liability in the latter case. In between these two extremes are the situations where the defect is either known but undiscoverable or, conversely, unknown but discoverable. The latter is, arguably, the usual position, and one in which it is incumbent on the producer to utilise the current state of knowledge to uncover the defect. The former is more difficult to rationalise but is, perhaps, the one which best describes the position with respect to potential defects in software. It is never possible to provide assurance that any software is free from error and such errors are capable of becoming defects if they compromise the safety of the system. Techniques used to develop software for use in safety-critical systems take this fact into account by starting from the premise that such software is bound to contain errors. The use of the definite article in the wording of the defence seems to indicate that it refers to a specific defect. Such a concept is difficult to apply to software development and, based on this, the use of the defence appears problematic. On the other hand, if we start from the presumption of the presence of a defect, it may be that the situation is accurately represented by the phrase 'known but undiscoverable'. It has been suggested that where the danger is known but science has not developed a means of eliminating the danger, then it would be open to the manufacturer to argue that the product is not defective instead of pleading a defence of development risks.[38] In relation to defective software, though, the view has also been expressed that 'the argument that a software producer could not be expected to discover his own mistakes is not a compelling one'.[39] Since software is developed by human ingenuity, any faults should be regarded as introduced, rather than inherent. Neither is it clear how all of these factors affect, or are affected by, the question of resource allocation for research. Stapleton[40] points out that the full pre-circulation screening test for some defects, including bugs in complex software, would be 'astronomically expensive', but suggests also that, '[t]o give the defence substance then it must protect in cases of defects which could only be discovered, if at all, by extraordinary means'. It is plain that testing cannot be carried on forever, but when should a producer stop testing? Does this, necessarily, entail a comparison with the behaviour of the 'reasonable' producer?

It is also important to note that the issue of when knowledge becomes available is crucial – the defence is unavailable after the date at which the existence of the defect could have been discovered. This may be especially pertinent for non-research-based industries (this market is becoming increasingly relevant as increasing numbers of domestic appliances contain software) for which it is likely that there will be a lapse in time before the requisite information concerning the defect is available to the producer.

It is difficult to assess how important the availability of a development risks defence might be to the software industry. An argument that was advanced at the time of the Strasbourg Convention,[41] albeit unsuccessfully, was that technically advanced industries needed a development risks defence if innovation and progress were not to

---

38 McKendrick, 1990, but compare Newdick's view that the defence cannot be available once the possibility of a defect has been foreseen (*ibid*).
39 Lloyd, 1991.
40 Stapleton, 1994.
41 Above, p 223.

be stifled. This was the primary reason for including it within the UK legislation. Nonetheless, a number of other Member States have chosen not to include the defence and producers exporting to those countries will need to take responsibility for their own development risks, even though this is unnecessary in relation to the domestic market. In addition, there is no similar defence in contract where liability is imposed when a defect would not be able to be detected even by the 'utmost skill and judgment on the part of the seller'.[42]

Some other statutory systems impose a much stricter standard. A case frequently referred to in this connection, by way of analogy, is that of *Smedley v Breed*,[43] decided under the Food and Drugs Act 1955. The case arose out of a caterpillar in a tin of peas. The salient facts for comparison are that a stringent system of inspection had been instigated, the success of which was evidenced by the fact that there were only four complaints out of a total of 3.5 million tins, despite the fact that the caterpillars were difficult to detect, being of similar shape, size and colour to the peas themselves. So, even though the particular 'defect' might be difficult to discover, there was ample evidence that the defendant had taken steps to ensure that the number of such defects was minimised. Nonetheless, the court found that, under the strict liability scheme contained in the relevant statute, the only possible defence for the presence of extraneous matter was where this was 'an unavoidable consequence of the process itself'. Although the court accepted that the system was as good as reasonable skill and diligence could make it, this could only go to mitigation and the fact that in any commercial process, however well managed, some failures are statistically predictable was irrelevant. Interestingly, the observed failure rate of four out of 3.5 million was clearly viewed as excellent by the court at the time; it is a moot point as to whether this would be an acceptable failure rate for safety-critical software for which probability of failure rates demanded are typically of the order of 10^{-8} and 10^{-9}.

In contrast, s 6 of the Health and Safety at Work Act 1974, which imposes requirements on those who manufacture 'articles for use at work', utilises a standard of 'as far as reasonably practicable', as referred to earlier,[44] but also includes a positive duty to arrange for testing and examination to ensure safe design and construction, together with a duty to arrange for research to discover and hence eliminate or minimise risks.[45]

Negligence

Whether or not the CPA 1987 can ever be said to apply to systems containing software, there will always be some situations involving defects in software where the regime is inappropriate, either because of the nature of the software at issue or because of the nature of the damage. In such cases, potential liability will be determined by the principles of negligence. Even then, there have been suggestions that negligence will not be capable of founding liability. It was suggested in *Ministry of Housing and Local*

---

42 *Henry Kendall and Son Ltd v William Lillico* [1969] 2 AC 44, p 84, *per* Lord Reid.
43 [1974] AC 839.
44 Above, p 220.
45 See, further, Rowland, 1991; Bott *et al*, 2000.

Government v Sharp, a case concerning an inaccurate land certificate, that, due to the likelihood of computerisation of the Land Registry, the Registrar's absolute statutory duty of care should be held to exist independently of negligence, since 'Computers might produce an inaccurate certificate without negligence on the part of anyone'.[46] It might be supposed that the average person (and even the average judge!) now has a greater general understanding of computing, at least to the extent of realisation that computers can only be as accurate as the person who wrote the program, input the data or interpreted the output made them. Nonetheless, there is still some truth in Tapper's assertion that 'It is common experience that computer systems do malfunction without any negligence on anyone's part, just because they are so complicated, and exhaustive testing in all possible situations in which they might be used is impossible'. The challenge is to distinguish the failures that are due to negligence from those that are not.

Where the loss generated as a result of a defect in software is purely economic, then, if there is no remedy available in contract, the only possibility will be to consider liability for negligent misstatement, the operative principles for which were set out in *Hedley Byrne v Heller*.[47] In order to limit the class of potential claimants, a special relationship is required between the parties, plus evidence of reliance on the statement. This test for liability could be appropriate when the loss is a consequence of relying on the output of the software[48] – unless the act of reliance on the output can itself be construed as negligent. Such an approach might be suitable when considering the potential liability for artificial intelligence and expert systems, as it can be argued that diagnostic expert systems are tools to 'aid' professionals in making their diagnoses. They should not be relied on absolutely, as they are no substitute for intelligent thought but merely a useful pointer to a particular course of action. This could also be the case where the output is accurate but insufficient by itself.[49] It has also been suggested that, given the problems with the intangible nature of software, the tort of negligent misstatement might have more general application in relation to computer software, in that the program instructions are 'relied upon' by the computer to attain the relevant result.

In the case of bespoke software, which, being categorised as the provision of services, is unlikely to fall within the ambit of product liability legislation, it will be necessary to show that the system was designed negligently.

Product Liability
Jane Stapleton
1994, London: Butterworths, p 251

... claims relating to the inadequate design of products can be made in negligence. There may well be practical reasons why such claims were in the past less often made than were claims for manufacturing errors but the propriety of such claims in negligence is without doubt. Many past negligence cases rested on a plaintiff's complaint that her predicament

---

46 [1970] 2 QB 223, p 275, *per* Salmon LJ.
47 [1964] AC 465.
48 See, also, Sookman, BB, 1989.
49 Cf the situation in *The Lady Gwendolen* [1965] P 294, cited in, eg, Reed.

was made worse by the negligence of the defendant in relation to the design ... The highly publicised Thalidomide litigation of the late 1960s and early 1970s was a classic example in the UK of a negligent design and R & D allegation, yet it was never challenged as being outside the realm of *Donoghue v Stevenson* negligence liability. A number of other UK design cases can be found typically focusing on the inadequacy of R & D or failure to warn [cites cases]. Moreover in recent years UK appellate courts have clearly confirmed manufacturer liability in negligence for the design condition of products. Although the issues raised on appeal in *Lambert v Lewis* did not focus on the trial judge's finding of liability against the manufacturer of a towing hitch on the basis of negligent design both the Court of Appeal and the House of Lords expressly accepted that finding.

The House of Lords in *IBA v EMI* and *BICC*,[50] could have found liability for negligent misstatement, as certain assurances were given concerning the efficacy of the design, but they equally found negligence in the design itself, which Lord Fraser regarded as 'a distinct and sufficient reason for imposing liability'. How is the negligence of a designer of software systems to be judged? By what criteria should the achievements and failures of software engineers be assessed? It is clear that the individuals in question possess, or should possess, special expertise, and one area of law that has developed to examine the achievements of those professing a particular expertise is that of professional negligence. There have, as yet, been no cases which have had to consider the role of software engineer as designer or the status of software engineer as a 'professional'. Could such a person be construed as coming within this latter category? Jackson and Powell[51] refer to the four attributes which are deemed to be necessary characteristics of professions, namely, the nature of the work, the moral aspect, collective organisation and status. Thus the nature of the work is expected or presumed to be of high intellectual content, requiring particular study and qualifications; professionals are expected to have some moral commitment to the community at large; they are expected to be governed by an organisation that sets the standards for, and regulates the conduct of, its members; and there should be evidence that they are accorded a particular status by the community. How far do these factors pertain to software engineers?

The extent to which software engineering may be regarded as a profession is debatable,[52] but, where the work undertaken is of a safety-critical nature, the relevant factors are becoming increasingly pertinent. Many transport systems, particularly air and rail, rely on computer control, as do major hazard installations such as nuclear reactors and chemical plants. Failure of such systems is likely to result in disaster such that it seems inconceivable that persons designing the software for those applications would not be cognisant of their duty to the public at large. The 'profession' is governed by two professional organisations, the Institution of Electrical Engineers (IEE) and the British Computer Society (BCS), which together have considered the entry qualifications and continuing professional development necessary for those engaged on such work. Both organisations create standards and codes of conduct, to

---

50   (1980) 14 BLR 1 and see below, p 235.
51   Jackson and Powell, 1997.
52   See, eg, Rowland 1999; Rustad and Koenig 2003, p 137, note that: 'as the field of information technology matures, it is likely that software developers, web site designers and Internet security specialists will begin to professionalise by developing industry standards of care.'

which their members are expected to adhere.[53] Of particular relevance in this context is the following definition of competence from the IEE's professional brief on safety-related systems.[54]

> Competence requires the possession of qualifications, experience and qualities which include:
>
> - such theoretical training as would ensure acquisition of the necessary knowledge of the field in which they are required to work;
> - a thorough knowledge of the hazards and failure of the equipment for which they are responsible;
> - an understanding and detailed knowledge of the working practices used in the organisation for which they work, as well as a general knowledge of the working practices in other establishments of a similar type;
> - a detailed working knowledge of all statutory provisions, approved codes of practice, other codes of practice, guidance material and other information relevant to their work, and an awareness of legislation and practices, other than those which might affect their work;
> - the ability to give advice to others;
> - the calibre and personality to enable them to communicate effectively with their peers, any staff working under their supervision, and their own supervisors;
> - an awareness of current developments in the field in which they work;
> - an appreciation of their own limitations, whether of knowledge, experience, facilities, resources, etc, and a preparedness to declare any such limitation.

The status of such engineers in the wider community is uncertain, as, arguably, is the status of a number of other branches of engineering that, nevertheless, have been considered as professions by the courts. It is certainly clear from the documentation of the relevant professional organisations that they feel they have the attributes of a profession, so would presumably expect their members to reach the standard that the law requires of a professional. The above definition of 'competence' has recently been developed even further[55] to define specific competences for a wider range of safety-related tasks, although the extent to which these correlate with the standard that the law might expect from a 'reasonably competent practitioner' is by no means clear.

In any case, where the software engineer has contracted to design specialist bespoke software, the Supply of Goods and Services Act 1982 will imply a term that 'reasonable care and skill' will be used in the performance of the contract. It is submitted that such a term will, in any case, require a similar level of competence as that appropriate to the professional in negligence. Nonetheless, in negligence there will not necessarily be a duty of care towards all those who might be affected by the failure of the software. It is clear that there is a very different range of foreseeable claimants in relation to defects in the design of a radiotherapy machine as compared with a fly-by-wire aircraft, for instance. There are policy considerations which may pull in either direction and the dividing line may not be easy to draw. There may be such potential

---

53 IEE/BCS 1989.
54 IEE 1992, 1995.
55 For further details see www.iee.org.uk/pab/hands/comp_pes.htm.

for damage that it may be considered unjust to hold the designer liable, but, equally, both contractor and client may have their own particular knowledge and expertise about the system such that an apportionment of liability may be more appropriate.

There will again be the necessity to show causation. Returning to the example of the radiotherapy machines,[56] although an arguable case of negligence might be made out in relation to the overdose, because of the problems with proving causation, a claim of negligence might, again, be difficult to substantiate where the software fault resulted in an underdose. If a design standard was mandated for the design of the equipment and was not adhered to in either case, it is difficult to support the conclusion that the designer in the one instance is less culpable than the other. Similar issues were raised in a case involving the decision of a coroner's court not to hold an inquest on the death of an asthmatic after an ambulance was delayed, on the basis that she did not die an 'unnatural' death. Coincidentally, this case was heard around the time of the failure of the London Ambulance Service computer system and, although, this was not the cause of the delay in this case, the court was clearly aware of the implications.

R v Poplar Coroner ex p Thomas
[1993] 2 WLR 547, p 552
Court of Appeal

Dillon LJ it is easy to think of a variety of different scenarios as a result of which an ambulance could have arrived too late to save a patient who had suffered a severe attack of asthma like Miss Thomas', eg: (i) the distance from the ambulance centre to the patient's home was too great for there to have ever been any chance of the ambulance arriving in time to save the patient; (ii) there was much more traffic than normal in the locality and so the ambulance was delayed and arrived just too late; (iii) the ambulance was diverted on its journey and had to take a much longer route because of flooding caused by a burst water main, which may have been due to lack of proper maintenance by the water company; (iv) a newly installed computer installed by the ambulance service to handle emergency calls more efficiently malfunctioned, as newly installed computers are prone to; or (v) the ambulance came late because the ambulance crew were inefficient and the management was slack.

I do not suggest that any of these scenarios actually fits the facts of Miss Thomas's case. I do not know what the cause of delay was. But in each of these scenarios common sense indicates that what caused the patient's death was, on Lord Salmon's test in *Alphacell Ltd v Woodward* [1972] AC 824, p 847, the asthmatic attack, not the congestion of the traffic, the bursting of the water main, the malfunction of the computer or the inefficiency of the ambulance service.

Although the court was not charged with any assessment of civil liability, the causation issue is set out in very plain terms. As to the existence of a duty of care, it does not seem unreasonable that, if someone is contracted to write software for an ambulance despatch system, then they might have in their contemplation the likely effect on a patient in the event of a system failure. Although agreeing with Dillon LJ as to the outcome of this case on the facts, Simon Brown LJ took a rather more circumspect view of the causation issue, especially as it might affect a negligence claim.

R v Poplar Coroner ex p Thomas
[1993] 2 WLR 547, p 554
Court of Appeal

Simon Brown LJ I do not find the question of causation in this context susceptible of quite the same sort of robust approach that the House of Lords advocated in a very different context in cases such as *McGhee v National Coal Board* [1973] 1 WLR 1. The question arising there was: can the court properly infer, in the absence of a provable direct link, that one particular state of affairs caused or contributed to another. In those cases the possibility of there being more than one cause was immaterial. Indeed courts often find there to have been several different causes of a given eventuality. Take this very case: can it really be doubted that if an action was brought in respect of Miss Thomas's death, whatever the court found regarding negligence it would certainly find the death to have been caused at least in part by the late arrival of the ambulance?

A similar line of reasoning was taken by Kennedy LJ in *Kent v London Ambulance Service*, another case involving the delay of an ambulance called to attend an asthmatic patient, whose condition was severely exacerbated by its late arrival. Unlike the previous case, this was a negligence case, and so issues not only of causation but also of the existence of a duty of care were of central importance.

Kent v London Ambulance Service
[1999] Lloyd's Rep Med 58, p 63
Court of Appeal

Kennedy LJ That leaves only the question of whether it is fair, just and reasonable that a duty of care should be imposed ... I acknowledge that the Ambulance Service operates in a difficult area, with cash limits, competing claims on limited sources, difficulty in deciding between competing calls from different locations, and the ever present problems of traffic hazard.

... an important consideration in relation to the ambulance service is demonstrated by the facts of this case. That is that if the ambulance service undertakes to attend, the person who has been promised that assistance, and those acting on his or her behalf normally abandon the search for other possible means of transport to the hospital ... I ... recognise that if a duty of care does exist it must make allowance for those factors to which I have just referred but I consider ... that a court might well find not only sufficient proximity but also that it is just, fair and reasonable that a duty of care should be imposed.

Although neither of these cases involve software failures, they may nevertheless provide important pointers as to whether a duty of care might be adjudged to arise in safety-critical cases. Kennedy LJ implied, albeit indirectly, that the reliance on the emergency services was a factor. In cases where software controls a safety-critical function, there is clearly no option but to rely on the correct operation of that software, which is the responsibility of those who created it. Also in *Kent*, Schiemann LJ was inclined to find sufficient proximity between the parties to give rise to a duty of care merely from the fact that the degree of foreseeability of harm was high,[57] a condition which will inevitably be satisfied in relation to safety-critical systems. However, although a relevant factor, it is clear from a number of other cases that the mere foreseeability of harm may not, of itself, give rise to a duty of care. As pointed out by

---

57   *Kent v London Ambulance Service* [1999] Lloyd's Rep Med 58, p 64.

Lord Bridge, 'It is never sufficient to ask simply whether A owes B a duty of care. It is always necessary to determine the scope of the duty by reference to the kind of damage from which A must take care to save B'.[58] Nonetheless, in safety-critical cases, the likelihood of severe harm cannot be ignored and must surely be an essential factor in the equation.

Assuming that there are no problems in respect of causation, the standard of care required of a professional is that of the ordinarily competent member of that profession, as set out by McNair J in *Bolam v Friern HMC*:

> When you get situations which involve the use of some special skill or competence, then the test as to whether there has been negligence or not, is not the test of the man on the top of the Clapham Omnibus, because he has not got that special skill. The test is the standard of the ordinary skilled man exercising and professing that special skill. A man need not possess the highest expert skill; it is well established law that it is sufficient if he exercises the ordinary skill of an ordinary competent man exercising that particular art.[59]

This basic test, then, has been refined in relation to different professions taking note of the fact that professions can be divided into two groups: those who cannot guarantee the results of their labour and those who could be said to impliedly warrant to produce a particular result.[60] Engineers are likely to fall into the latter category, as noted by Lord Scarman in *IBA v EMI and BICC*: 'In the absence of any terms (express or implied) negating the obligation, one who contracts to design an article for a purpose made known to him undertakes that the design is reasonably fit for the purpose.'[61] This can be construed as requiring a higher standard than the basic *Bolam* test.[62]

A number of facets of the standard of care required of the emerging profession of the software engineer have been identified,[63] but, of these, some are of particular concern to this discipline. The first is: on whom does the duty fall to identify the system as safety-related? Whereas it might be thought that the procurer would be in the best position to make this assessment, it cannot necessarily be assumed that the procurer is aware that safety-critical applications require design and implementation procedures that are any different from those used for 'normal' computer systems. This may be especially pertinent for systems for which the safety connection is not immediately obvious.[64] However, neither can it be assumed that the software engineer is likely to be in a better position to make this assessment.

A common measure of the standard of care is provided by adherence to relevant standards and codes of practice[65] and there is no reason why this should be any different for the software engineer.

This can include compliance not only with externally approved standards, but also with generally accepted practice in the industry. As pointed out by Viscount Simonds,

---

58 *Caparo Industries plc v Dickman and Others* [1990] 2 AC 605, p 627; see, also, Rowland, 1999.
59 [1957] 1 WLR 582, p 586.
60 Rowland and Rowland, 1993.
61 (1980) 14 BLR 1 and see below, p 235.
62 *Greaves & Co v Baynham Meikle* [1974] 1 WLR 1261, p 1269, affirmed [1975] 1 WLR 1095.
63 See, further, Rowland and Rowland, 1993; Cooke 1991.
64 See Geake, 1992.
65 *Bevan Investments v Blackhall and Struthers (No 2)* [1973] 2 NZLR 45.

'it would be unfortunate if an employer who has adopted a practice, system or set-up ... which has been widely used without complaint could not rely on it as at least a *prima facie* defence to an action of negligence'.[66] However, the fact of general acceptance of a particular practice does not automatically mean that the practice is a good one or that it should not be modified and reviewed in the light of technical developments.

Negligence, professional competence and computer systems
Diane Rowland
[1999] 2 JILT

... the courts have not fought shy of declaring common practice to be negligent. In general this is the result of application of objective tests of the reasonable man variety (see, eg, *General Cleaning v Christmas* (1953)). What should be regarded as reasonable in technical specialisms where knowledge is advancing all the time? Is there a duty to keep up to date? How far does this extend? What effect should new information have on an existing general practice? ... Some guidance can be found in *Stokes v GKN (Bolts and Nuts) Ltd* (1968):

> ... where there is a recognised and general practice which has been followed for a substantial period in similar circumstances without mishap, he is entitled to follow it, unless in the light of common sense or newer knowledge it is clearly bad; but, where there is developing knowledge, he must keep reasonably abreast of it and not be too slow to apply it, and where he has in fact greater than average knowledge of the risks, he may be thereby obliged to take more than the average or standard precautions.

An example of the application of these principles can be seen in the cases relating to liability for noise-induced hearing loss where the above dictum of Swanwick J was quoted with approval in *Thompson v Smiths Shiprepairers (North Shields) Ltd* (1984) ... The crucial factor was not when the knowledge (in this case that excessive exposure to noise resulted in hearing loss) was discovered in the absolute sense but when it should be deemed to be known in the industry. The clear implication is that if the industry is at the forefront of research and development then it will be expected to take technological advances into account very quickly. Clearly the salient issue is not just one of the actual knowledge of the producer or designer but also of his or her constructive knowledge.

With regard to externally imposed standards, reference has already been made to the definition of 'competence' in various professional and industry codes. There are also a number of standards laid down for specific industry sectors, such as defence and the aircraft industry.[67] Until relatively recently, there were no widely accepted standards for the development of safety-critical software, other than a general acceptance that the usual practices of software development for non safety-related applications are inadequate for safety-related systems. However, after a long period of gestation, a generic international standard, IEC 61508, was adopted in 1999. The fundamental tenet of this standard is that there is a relationship between the level of competence required of a software engineer and the integrity required of the design. Given that the latter increases with the level of safety required, it is here that an awareness of the standard of care becomes paramount.

---

66 *Cavanagh v Ulster Weaving Ltd* [1960] AC 145, p 158.
67 See, further, Bott *et al*, 2000, Chapter 10.

Competence and legal liability in the development
of software for safety-related applications
D Rowland and JJ Rowland
(1993) 2 Law, Computers and Artificial Intelligence 229, p 233

At present, safety-critical practitioners seem to divide into three groups:

1   Those who are aware in general of the problems raised by safety-critical software development and are striving to adjust their working practices so as to produce software of what they consider to be an adequate quality.

2   Those who are attempting to follow, and where possible do better than, the emerging standards.

3   Those who are developing safety-critical systems and yet are not aware that there are special problems.

The first of these probably most accurately reflects what can be described as the ordinarily competent safety-critical practitioner, whilst a growing number of specialists fall into the second category. It is widely suspected that a significant proportion of companies producing safety-related software belong in the third category ...

An important consideration for a technologically advanced industry such as the software industry is the legitimate concern that innovation should not be stifled by legal rules. Designs for systems that are 'at the cutting edge of technology' may not have been tried and tested in the same way as a more pedestrian project, and the industry owes its success to its ability to create and market new methods of control or new systems and products. Nonetheless, where there are safety implications in a design, the law has not shied away from requiring the highest consideration of the safety factors, as evidenced in the case of *IBA v EMI and BICC*[68] concerning the collapse of the Emley Moor television transmitter in 1969. The defendants, BICC, argued vigorously that a finding of negligence would be likely to stifle innovation and inhibit technological progress. They produced evidence that there was neither any available source of empirical knowledge nor agreed practice; they were 'both at and beyond the frontier of professional knowledge'.

Competence and legal liability in the development of
software for safety-related applications
D Rowland and JJ Rowland
(1993) 2 Law, Computers and Artificial Intelligence 229, p 238

In view of the potentially catastrophic consequences of collapse of the mast, the House of Lords were agreed that it would have been necessary for BICC to exercise a high degree of care. By applying standard principles of negligence Lord Edmund-Davies deduced:

The graver the foreseeable consequences of failure to take care, the greater the necessity for special circumspection ... The project may be alluring. But the risks of injury to those engaged in it, or to others, or to both, may be so manifest and substantial, and their elimination may be so difficult to ensure with reasonable certainty that the only proper course is to abandon the project altogether ... The law requires even pioneers to be prudent.

---

68   (1980) 14 BLR 1. For a more detailed consideration of this case see, eg, Stanton and Dugdale, 1981.

It was found that the cause of the collapse was due to a combination of vortex shedding and asymmetric icing on the stays, which would be likely to cause problems at even relatively low wind velocities. The House of Lords unanimously agreed that these factors could reasonably have been foreseen and the fact that the project was at the forefront of knowledge at the time was no excuse. It was foreseeable that large quantities of ice might be deposited on the stays and that this was likely to be asymmetric, but that the resultant stresses would be exacerbated by vortex shedding had never been considered by BICC whose design was therefore held to be negligent.

The behaviour that the law expects of the reasonably competent professional who is operating at the frontiers of knowledge at the time can be inferred from this statement of Lord Edmund-Davies:

> Justice requires that we seek to put ourselves in the position of BICC when first confronted by their daunting task, lacking all empirical knowledge and adequate expert advice in dealing with the many problems awaiting solution. But those very handicaps created a clear duty to identify and to think through such problems, including those of static and dynamic stresses, so that the dimensions of the 'venture into the unknown' could be adequately assessed and the ultimate decision as to its practicality arrived at.

The power of software arises principally from the relative ease with which highly complex systems can be created and changed. There is a consequent temptation to undertake development without adherence to appropriate engineering principles and to quite readily undertake a 'venture into the unknown'; after all, software can be changed easily and it is tempting to think that any faults can be corrected easily. However, unless software is designed very carefully a seemingly simple change can have an unexpected side effect that may not become apparent for some considerable time afterwards, so that any departure from strict quality assurance procedures during development almost certainly becomes another 'venture into the unknown'. In the case of software the 'dimensions' of such ventures are not readily assessed, so that departure from established methods can be particularly risky.

Finally, what is the standard that can be expected if the client requests (and pays for) the services of an acknowledged expert? Is the expertise of such a person to be judged by reference to the standards of the 'ordinarily competent practitioner'? It seems reasonable to suggest that the standard of such individuals should, instead, be assessed by reference to a more limited class of those with specialist knowledge. This might create problems where the class is small such that the general or accepted standard is difficult to determine, but it has been confirmed that even a small number of specialists can constitute a reasonable body of opinion; the question is one of quality, not quantity.[69] In any event, if the specialist is in possession of actual knowledge that might not be possessed by the general body of that profession, then he or she is under a duty to make use of that actual knowledge.[70]

Thus, although there may be a number of possible causes of action which could be pursued in the event of defective software which resulted in damage, there is considerable uncertainty about the scope and boundaries of liability and also about those on whom liability might fall. Modern technology relies extensively on software and it is perhaps surprising that there has been little activity in the courts as yet.

---

69   *De Freitas v O'Brien* [1995] 6 Med LR 108, p 115, *per* Otton LJ.
70   See, eg, *Wimpey Construction v Poole* [1984] 2 Lloyd's Rep 499.

Neither does this seem to be due to the excellence of the software: Hatton[71] points out that 'An explosion in the volume of software would not be a cause for concern if software quality was improving at the same rate proportionately. Unfortunately the plain truth is that software is simply not getting much better'. Given these concerns, it is, perhaps, surprising that the judiciary have not been called upon to decide some of the issues raised in this chapter.

71 Hatton, 1997.

PART II

THE CHALLENGES OF
COMPUTER NETWORKS

CHAPTER 6

E-COMMERCE

INTRODUCTION

Scope

'Definitions of e-commerce vary considerably.'[1] However, consideration of two brief definitions raises some basic issues. Thus, it has been said that:

> Electronic commerce is a broad concept that covers any commercial transaction that is effected via electronic means and would include such means as facsimile, telex, EDI, internet and telephone. For the purposes of this report the term is limited to those trade and commercial transactions involving computer to computer communications whether utilising an open or closed network.[2]

In addition, it has also been said that:

> Electronic commerce could be said to comprise commercial transactions, whether between private individuals or commercial entities, which take place in or over electronic networks. The matters dealt with in the transactions could be intangibles, data products, or tangible goods. The only important factor is that the communication transactions take place over an electronic medium.[3]

These definitions raise issues in relation to the form of communication, the subject matter of the transactions and the contracting parties.

The first of the above definitions emphasises that e-commerce, in a broad sense, could encompass trading carried out by any means of communication that can be labelled 'electronic'. However, it emphasises computer to computer transactions and the concern here is basically email and web-based communication, which are sufficiently different from the more traditional means of communication to raise significant issues for the law. The second definition includes some recognition of the different types of subject matter of electronic contracts. Such contracts may simply be concerned with traditional goods or services to be delivered in the traditional way. However, e-commerce does not simply provide a new means of making contracts. In some situations, it also provides a new method of performance:

> Certain products, such as software, video, books, music and even newspapers and magazines no longer have to be physically delivered in hard copy format to the purchaser. Suppliers can instead send the products in digital form over the internet, providing both time and cost saving.[4]

As we have seen, this type of supply challenges the traditional categorisation of goods and services (see p 138) and the use of the law which evolved around them, for

---

1   OECD, 1997, p 20.
2   Report of the Electronic Expert Group to the Attorney General (Australia), 1998.
3   Davies, 1998.
4   Chissick and Kelman, 2000, para 3.0.

example, the application of the quality terms implied into contracts for the sale of goods (see p 138). The final point to be made here, and which is again raised by the second definition, relates to the parties contracting by email or over the web. A substantial number of such contracts will be business to business, but consumers are now also making use of the technology and this raises issues of the application of consumer protection regimes in the e-commerce context.

Global nature

By its nature, e-commerce is not restricted by geographical boundaries in the same way as more traditional business forms. Obviously, contracts have always been made between parties in different jurisdictions and have led to disputes involving elements from different countries, and the rules about the jurisdiction and the substantive law to be applied in such cases will be considered below. However, email and web-based contracting make it very easy for businesses to contract with businesses in other jurisdictions and, even more radically, those methods allow for a significant amount of consumer contracting outside of the consumer's home country. In this context, a considerable impetus is generated to consider the differences between the legal regimes in different countries. It is recognised that measures relating to e-commerce cannot be efficiently taken by a single regime. The European Community (EC) already provides for measures dealing with a group of States and the need for such an approach in the e-commerce area has been recognised, as has the fact that the EC itself will not contain e-commerce within its borders – an even broader approach will be required.

The Recitals to the EC Directive on Electronic Commerce state:

59   Despite the global nature of electronic communications, co-ordination of national regulatory measures at European level is necessary to avoid fragmentation of the Internal Market, and for the establishment of an appropriate European regulatory framework; such coordination should also contribute to the establishment of a common and strong negotiating position in international fora.

60   In order to allow the unhampered development of electronic commerce, the legal framework must be clear and simple, predictable and consistent with the rules applicable at international level so that it does not affect the competitiveness of European Industry or impede innovation in that sector.

61   If the market is actually to operate by electronic means in the context of globalisation, the European Union and the major non-European area need to consult each other with a view to making laws and procedures compatible.

62   Co-operation with third countries should be strengthened in the area of electronic commerce, in particular with applicant countries, the developing countries and the European Union's other trading partners.

This chapter will refer not only to EC measures, but also to the work of even more broadly international bodies, such as the United Nations Commission on International Trade Law (UNCITRAL).

Electronic data interchange (EDI)

EDI is a particular form of e-commerce, representing 'one of the earliest forms'.[5] Its distinguishing feature is that it is highly structured, and so it is more secure than simple email. There will be protocols for message formats, data storage logs, acknowledgments of messages and confirmation of their content. It would be normal for parties trading together using EDI to have first established a regime for their communications under an interchange agreement. Such an agreement will not deal with the substance of a trading contract but, rather, will provide the basis for the parties to use EDI to make those contracts.[6] The degree of structure means that it can be used for automated ordering by computerised stock systems without any need for direct human involvement, and that can be carried through to the generation of invoices and even payment by electronic means. The removal of the paper element and the automation of such transactions may provide considerable cost savings.[7] However, the focus here is on email and simple web-based contracting. They now provide the more significant part of e-commerce.

Regulation

At a domestic level, we are used to some regulation of commerce, particularly, but not exclusively, where consumers are involved. Liability for breach of the statutorily implied terms as to the quality of goods[8] cannot be excluded or restricted if the buyer 'deals as consumer',[9] for example; but, even if the buyer does not deal as consumer, that liability can only be excluded or restricted by a reasonable term.[10] There are obviously difficulties in regulating e-commerce – it is simply not geographically, or jurisdictionally, restricted in the same way as more traditional forms – and there are competing pressures to regulate or not to regulate. Some consideration is given to this in the extracts below.

**Borderless trade and the consumer interest: protecting
the consumer in the age of e-commerce
James P Nehf
(1999) Colum J Transnat Law 457**

Governments continually struggle to balance the consumer interest against economic growth. The two priorities often find themselves at odds: more consumer protection usually means more restrictions on the freedom of sellers to manufacture, market and sell as they please. Conversely, policies designed to encourage business activity often do so at the expense of the consumer interest. Successful consumer protection regimes should result in a net benefit increase in social welfare, however measured, even if some business opportunities and profits are curtailed along the way.

---

5   Lloyd, 2000, p 233.
6   The EC has adopted a Model Interchange Agreement – 94/820/EC OJ L338/98 (28 December 1994).
7   Lloyd, 2000, p 233.
8   SGA 1979, s 14. See above, p 162.
9   UCTA 1977, s 6(2). See above, p 193.
10   *Ibid*, s 6(3). See above, p 193.

This principle holds true in domestic, even local, transactions within any country, State or city. National laws, State initiatives, and town ordinances can restrict business activity in an effort to increase the quality of life for the citizenry. In the current age of multilateral trade pacts such as GATT, NAFTA, EU and ASEAN, however, the trade-offs between encouraging international commerce and respecting the consumer interest are being re-examined in a new light. Government regulations within a country that have set strict consumer protection standards – for example, rules governing advertising and marketing claims – may strike an acceptable balance for domestic businesses and consumers, but they can also discourage or surprise foreign firms that wish to advertise and penetrate the market there.

A model for internet regulation
Lars J Davies
www.scl.org/content/ecommerce, s 1.3.2
(Report funded by the Society for Computers and Law)

... two dangers need to be avoided. The first is to under regulate. The second is to over regulate. The threat posed by over regulation is easy to see. It would result in too rigid a market, stifling it of the flexibility of operation, potentially its best feature, and so stifle development of electronic commerce, and could easily lead to commercial entities setting up in jurisdictions with less rigid controls. The formation of electronic commerce havens of a reduced or minimal control is a distinct possibility. Overly strong control could also lessen the financial attractiveness of conducting electronic commerce. Economic development would suffer as the benefits offered by this new activity would be lost to other markets with less rigid structures.

Though it would seem incongruous that it would be possible to under regulate in a market driven economy, which is essentially what the electronic market place appears to be, insufficient regulation can have several consequences. The lack of sufficient controls could also lead to the perception that electronic commerce is an activity that contains an unacceptably high element of risk and so prevent parties from engaging in the activity regardless of whether they are commercial entities or consumers.

One difficulty, which is not directly referred to in the above extracts, is how far the scope of a particular state's regulation should extend. Should it apply to businesses that are, in some sense, 'based' in another state but which conduct business with consumers or businesses in the particular state? How is to be determined where a business is 'based'? The geographic factors, which often naturally determined the scope of regulation, are usually simply inappropriate when e-commerce is in question. One example of extra-state legislation attempting to produce an appropriate balance point between a number of states in relation to the regulation of a particular area of e-commerce is provided by the EC Directive on Certain Legal Aspects of Electronic Commerce in the Internal Market (2000/31/EC). It deals with certain areas of law, 'the co-ordinated field', in relation to 'information society services'. It recognises the difficulties in businesses having to take account of different legal regimes in different countries and, within bounds, takes a home country approach, allowing a business 'established' in a Member State to rely on compliance with the requirements of that State.[11] It contains requirements for information society service providers to make

---

11   Article 3.

certain information available.[12] (For implementation in the UK see The Electronic Communications (EC Directive) Regulations 2002 and the Electronic Communications Act 2000).

EC Directive on Electronic Commerce

CHAPTER I

Article 1
Objective and Scope

1   This Directive seeks to contribute to the proper functioning of the Internal Market by ensuring the free movement of Information Society services between Member States.

2   This Directive approximates, to the extent necessary for the achievement of the objective set out in paragraph 1, certain national provisions on Information Society Services relating to the Internal Market, the establishment of service providers, commercial communications, electronic contracts, the liability of intermediaries, codes of conduct, out of court settlements, court actions and co-operation between Member States.

3   This Directive complements Community Law applicable to Information Society services without prejudice to the level of protection for, in particular, public health and consumer interests, as established by Community Acts and national legislation implementing them insofar as this does not restrict the freedom to provide Information Society services.

4   This Directive does not establish additional rules on private International law nor does it deal with the jurisdiction of Courts.

5   This Directive shall not apply to –

(a)   the field of taxation;

(b)   questions relating to Information Society services covered by Directive 95/46/EC and 97/66/EC;

(c)   questions relating to agreements or practices governed by cartel law;

(d)   the following activities of Information Society services:

   –   the activities of notaries or equivalent professions to the extent that they involve a direct and specific connection with the exercise of public authority;

   –   the representation of a client and defence of his interests before the courts;

   –   gambling activities which involve wagering a stake with monetary value in games of chance, including lotteries and betting transactions.

6   This Directive does not affect measures taken at Community or national level in respect of Community Law, in order to promote cultural and linguistic diversity and to ensure the defence of pluralism.

---

12   See Art 7. It also deals with some other barriers to e-commerce, providing some clarification of the contracting process and requiring Member States to deal with formality requirements (for example, the requirement of 'writing') that might impede e-commerce. (These latter issues are considered below). Other areas which it addresses are beyond the scope of this chapter such as the liabilty of ISPs.

Article 2
Definitions

For the purpose of this Directive, the following terms shall bear the following meanings:

(a) 'Information Society services': services within the meaning of Article 1(2) of Directive 98/34/EC as amended by Directive 98/48/EC;

(b) 'service provider': any natural or legal person providing an Information Society service;

(c) 'established service provider': a service provider who effectively pursues an economic activity using a fixed establishment for an indefinite period. The presence and use of the technical means and technologies required to provide the service do not, in themselves, constitute an establishment of the provider;

(d) 'recipient of the service': any natural or person who, for professional ends or otherwise, uses an Information Society service, in particular for the purposes of seeking information or making it accessible;

(e) 'consumer': any natural person who is acting for purposes which are outside his trade or profession;

(f) 'commercial communication': any form of communication designed to promote, directly or indirectly, the goods, services or image of a company, organisation or person pursuing a commercial, industrial or craft activity or exercising a regulated profession. The following do not in themselves constitute commercial communications:

   – information allowing direct access to the activity of the company, organisation or person, in particular a domain name or an electronic email address;

   – communications relating to the goods, services or image of the company, organisation or person compiled in an independent manner, particularly when this is without financial consideration;

(g) 'regulated profession':

(h) 'coordinated field': requirements laid down in Member States legal systems applicable to Information Society service providers or Information Society services, regardless of whether they are general in nature or specifically designed for them.

   (i) The coordinated field contains requirements with which the service provider has to comply in respect of:

      – the taking up of the activity of an Information Society service, such as requirements concerning qualifications, authorisation or notification;

      – the pursuit of the activity of an Information Society service, such as requirements concerning the behaviour of the service provider, requirements regarding the quality or content of the service including those applicable to advertising and contracts, or requirements concerning the liability of the service provider.

   (ii) The coordinated field does not cover requirements such as:

      – requirements applicable to goods as such;

      – requirements applicable to the delivery of goods;

      – requirements applicable to services not provided by electronic means.

Article 3
Internal Market

1   Each Member State shall ensure that the Information Society provided by a service provider established on its territory comply with the national provisions applicable in the Member State in question which fall within the coordinated field.

2   Member States may not, for reasons falling within the coordinated field, restrict the freedom to provide Information Society services from another Member State.

3   Paragraphs 1 and 2 shall not apply to the fields referred to in the Annex.

4   Member States may take measures to derogate from paragraph 2 in respect of a given Information Society service if the following conditions are fulfilled:

(a) the measures shall be:

(i)   necessary for one of the following reasons:

    –   public policy, in particular the prevention investigation, detection and prosecution of criminal offences, including the protection of minors and the fight against any incitement to hatred on the grounds of race, sex, religion or nationality, and violations of human dignity concerning individual persons;

    –   the protection of public health;

    –   public security, including the safeguarding of national security and defence;

    –   the protection of consumers, including investors;

(ii) taken against a given Information Society service which prejudices the objectives referred to in point (i) or which presents a serious and grave risk of prejudice to those objectives;

(iii) proportionate to those objectives before taking the measures in question and without prejudice to court proceedings, including preliminary proceedings and acts carried out in the framework of a criminal investigation, the Member State has:

    –   asked the Member State referred to in paragraph 1 to take measures and the latter did not take such measures, or they were inadequate;

    –   notified the Commission and the Member State referred to in paragraph 1 of its intention to take such measures.

5   Member States may, in the case of urgency derogate from the conditions stipulated in paragraph 4(b). Where this is the case, the measures shall be notified in the shortest possible time to the commission and to the Member State referred to in paragraph 1, indicating the reasons for which the Member State considers there is urgency.

6   Without prejudice to the Member State's possibility to proceed with the measures in question, the commission shall examine the compatability of the notified measures with Community Law in the shortest possible time; where it comes to the conclusion that the measure is incompatible with community law, the Commission shall ask the Member State in question to refrain from taking any proposed measures or urgently to put an end to the measures in question.

CHAPTER II

PRINCIPLES

Section 1: Establishment and Information Requirements

Article 4
Principle excluding Prior Authorisation

1   Member States shall ensure that the taking up and pursuit of the activity of an Information Society service provider may not be made subject to prior authorisation or any other requirement having equivalent effect.

2   Paragraph 1 shall be without prejudice to authorisation schemes which are not specifically targeted at Information Society services, or which are covered by Directive 97/13/EC of the European Parliament and of the Council of 10 April 1997 on a common framework for general authorisations and individual licenses in the field of telecommunication services.

Article 5
General Information to be Provided

1   In addition to other information requirements established by Community Law, Member States shall ensure that the service provider shall render easily, directly and permanently accessible to the recipients of the service and competent authorities, at least the following information:

(a) the name of the service provider;

(b) the geographic address at which the service provider is established;

(c) the details of the service provider, including his electronic mail address which allow him to be contacted rapidly and communicated with in a direct and effective manner;

(d) where the service provider is registered in a trade or similar public register, the trade register in which the service provider is entered and his registration number, or equivalent means of identification in the register;

(e) where the activity is subject to an authorisation scheme, the particulars of the relevant supervisory authority;

(f) as concerns the regulated professions:

–   any professional body or similar institution with which the service provider is registered;

–   the professional title and the Member state where it has been granted,

a reference to the applicable professional rules in the Member State of establishment and the means to access them;

(g) where the service provider undertakes an activity that is subject to VAT, the identification number.

2   In addition to other information requirements established by Community Law, Member States shall at least ensure that, where Information Society services refer to prices these are to be indicated clearly and unambiguously and, in particular, must indicate whether they are inclusive of tax and delivery costs.

Section 2: Commercial Communications

Article 6
Information to be Provided

In addition to other information requirements established by Community Law, Member States shall ensure that commercial communications that are part of, or constitute, an Information Society service comply at least with the following conditions:

(a) the commercial communication shall be clearly identifiable as such;

(b) the natural or legal person on whose behalf the commercial communication is made shall be clearly identifiable;

(c) promotional offers, such as discounts, premiums and gifts, where permitted in the Member State where the service provider is established, shall be clearly identifiable as such, and the conditions which are to be met to qualify for them shall be easily accessible and presented clearly and unambiguously;

(d) promotional competitions and games, where permitted in the Member State where the service provider is established, shall be clearly identifiable as such, and the conditions for participation shall be easily accessible and must be presented clearly and unambiguously.

Article 7
Unsolicited Commercial Communications

1 In addition to other requirements established by Community Law, Member States which permit unsolicited commercial communication by a service provider established in their territory shall be identifiable clearly and unambiguously as such as soon as it is received by the recipient.

2 Without prejudice to Directive 97/7/EC and Directive 97/66/EC, Member States shall take measures to ensure that service providers undertaking unsolicited commercial communications by electronic mail consult regularly and respect the opt out registers in which natural persons not wishing to receive such commercial communications can register themselves.

Article 8
Regulated Professions

1 Member States shall ensure that the use of commercial communications which are part of, or constitute, an Information Society service provided by members of a regulated profession is permitted, subject to compliance with the professional rules regarding, in particular, the independence, dignity and honour of the profession, professional secrecy and fairness towards clients and other members of the profession.

2 Without prejudice to the autonomy of professional bodies and associations, Member States and the Commission shall encourage professional associations and bodies to establish codes of conduct at Community level in order to determine the types of information that can be given for the purposes of commercial communication in conformity with the rules referred to in paragraph 1.

3 When drawing up proposals for Community initiatives which may become necessary to ensure the proper functioning of the internal market with regard to the information referred to in paragraph 2, the Commission shall take due account of codes of conduct applicable at Community level and shall act in close co-operation with the relevant professional associations and bodies.

4 This Directive shall apply in addition to Community Directives concerning access to, and the exercise of, activities of regulated professions.

Basically, the Directive is concerned with information society services[13] and the provisions dealing with such services which fall within the Directive's 'co-ordinated field'[14]. The references to 'information society services' cover 'any service normally provided for remuneration, at a distance by electronic means and at the individual request of a recipient of services'.[15] This spans 'a wide range of economic activities which take place online'.[16] These 'activities can ... consist of selling goods online'. Activities 'such as the delivery of goods as such or the provision of services off-line are

---

13   Article 2, Recital 18.
14   Article 2, Recital 21.
15   Recital 18.
16   Recital 19.

not covered'.[17] If 'a contract is made electronically for the for the supply of goods or the provision of services off-line, the Directive will apply to the making of the contract ... but not to the performance (or non-performance) of the obligation to supply goods or provide the service'.[18] Further explanation is to be found in Recital 18:

> Information services also include services consisting of the transmission of information via a communications network, in providing access to a communication network or in hosting information provided by the recipient of the service; television broadcasting ... and radio broadcasting are not Information Society services because they are not provided at individual request; by contrast, services which are transmitted point to point, such as video on demand or the provision of commercial communications by electronic mail are Information Society services; the use of electronic mail or equivalent individual communications for instance by natural persons acting outside their trade, business or profession including their use for the conclusion of contracts between such persons is not an Information Society service; the contractual relationship between an employer and employee is not an Information Society service; activities which by their very nature cannot be carried out at a distance and by electronic means, such as the statutory auditing of company accounts or medical advice requiring the physical examination of a patient, are not Information Society services.

The Directive's reference to its 'co-ordinated field' refers to requirements in the legal systems of Member States which are applicable to information society services, or their providers, in relation to the 'taking up of the activity of an Information Service' or the 'pursuit of an activity of Information Service provider'.[19] It covers requirements 'relating to online activities such as online information, online advertising, online shopping, online contracting and does not concern Member States' legal requirements relating to goods, such as safety standards, labelling obligations, or liability for goods, or Member States' legal requirements relating to the delivery or the transport of goods'.[20]

As has been indicated, potential barriers to the growth of e-commerce stem from the different requirements of different legal systems. A trader may be reluctant to do business with those from other jurisdictions out of concern for the need to comply with a legal system with which he or she is unfamiliar. It has been said that 'the problem of the modern law abiding merchant with international ambitions is figuring out how to tailor its selling practices to the laws of each national market'.[21] To some extent, this concern is met in the E-Commerce Directive by the 'home country' approach of Article 3.

Article 3 requires a Member State to ensure compliance with relevant national provisions by information society service providers 'established' within its territory, and also requires other Member States not to 'restrict the freedom to provide information society services from another Member State.'[22] This has been characterised as the 'home country'[23] or 'country of origin' approach and, as indicated,

---

17 Recital 18.
18 Susman, 2000 p 30.
19 See Art 2.
20 Recital 21.
21 Nehf, 1999.
22 For implementation of this in the UK see regs 4 and 7 of the The Electronic Commerce (EC Directive) Regulations 2002
23 Eg, Calleja 2000 p 28.

within its limited scope, enables a business to place some reliance on compliance with the rules of its own State as sufficient. However, the Directive recognises that there are other interests to be protected than simply those who wish to do business in the electronic environment, such as 'public health and consumer interests' (Art 1) and, for example, 'contractual obligations concerning consumer contracts' are included in the specific exemptions from the application of Art 3(1) and (2) in the Annex to the Directive.[24] Within limits, 'establishment' is a key concept. To be established within a Member State requires the pursuit of an economic activity using a fixed establishment for an indefinite period.[25] The mere location of server is not sufficient to constitute a business' 'place of establishment':

> The place of establishment of a company providing services via an internet website is not the place at which the technology supporting its website is located or the place at which its website is accessible.'[26]

It is instead the 'place where it pursues its economic activity'.[27] The point has been made that 'the country of origin principle is only possible because of the large degree of harmonisation which has already taken place in fields such as consumer protection, and because the Directive's other provisions on commercial communication (Arts 6 and 7) and the provision of information about the business (Art 5) introduce common controls on potentially controversial aspects of these activities. How far the principle will be adopted on a global scale depends very much on the degree to which the economic pressures exerted by e-commerce result in convergence of these aspects of the laws of other jurisdictions'[28]. It can be questioned as to how far such an approach could be extended.

Scope of the chapter

In a chapter on e-commerce, it would be impossible to include consideration of everything falling within 'commercial law' and 'consumer law' in the context of electronic communication. In other words, in a single chapter, comprehensive coverage of everything that might fall within the e-commerce category is impossible. Some particular issues, raising particular concerns in the electronic context, will be addressed:

- jurisdiction/the governing law;
- aspects of contracting by electronic means;
- requirements of writing and signature;

In addition, it should be noted that the matters that are relevant here have been dealt with elsewhere. Exemption clauses will be used in e-commerce as in every other kind

---

24 See, also, Art 3(3).
25 Recital 19. It is made clear that 'establishment' is to be determined in conformity with the case law of the Court of Justice.
26 Recital 19.
27 Of course, the technology may be located in the place where a business 'pursues its economic activity', in which case the technology will be located in the business' place of establishment.
28 Reed and Slatter , 2003.

of contracting and they are dealt with in Chapter 3, as are the Regulations on Unfair Terms in Consumer Contracts. Similarly, sale of goods contracts made electronically will raise issues as to the statutory implied terms (for example, as to satisfactory quality and reasonable fitness for the buyer's particular purpose).[29]

JURISDICTION AND THE GOVERNING LAW

One of the significant impacts of e-commerce lies in the increase in trading involving more than one country. For example, an Englishman contracts with a Frenchman (each remaining in their respective countries) for the purchase of goods to be delivered from Spain. If a dispute arises, then the international element of the transaction will raise questions as to which court is to have jurisdiction and which country's laws are to be applied to resolve the dispute. These can be described as the jurisdiction question and the governing law question.

JURISDICTION

As the principal determinant of jurisdiction within the EU in relation to commercial matters is now the Brussels Regulation, that will be considered here. It came into force on 1 March 2002, replacing the Brussels Convention. The Regulation was in part introduced to take account of 'new forms of commerce.'[30]

EC Regulation No 44/2001 on jurisdiction and the recognition and enforcement of judgments in civil and commercial matters

Chapter 1

SCOPE

Article 1

1   This Regulation shall apply in civil and commercial matters whatever the nature of the court or tribunal. It shall not extend, in particular, to revenue, customs, or administrative matters.

2.   This Regulation shall not apply to:

   (a) the status or legal capacity of natural persons, rights in property arising out of a matrimonial relationship, wills and succession;

   (b) bankruptcy, proceedings relating to the winding up of insolvent companies or other legal persons, judicial arrangements, compositions and analogous proceedings;

   (c) Social Security;

   (d) Arbitration.

---

29 SGA 1979, s 14. See above, p 162.
30 COM (1999).

3. In this Regulation, the term 'Member State' shall mean Member States with the exception of Denmark.

Chapter II

JURISDICTION

Section 1

GENERAL PROVISIONS

Article 2

1. Subject to this Regulation, persons domiciled in a Member State shall whatever their nationality, be sued in the courts of that Member State.
2. Persons who are not nationals of the Member State in which they are domiciled shall be governed by the rules of jurisdiction applicable to nationals of that State.

Article 3

1. Persons domiciled in a Member State may be sued in the courts of another Member State only by virtue of the rules set out in Sections 2 to 6 of this Chapter.
2. In particular the rules of national jurisdiction set out in Annex 1 shall not be applicable as against them.

Article 4

1. If the defendant is not domiciled in a Member State, the Jurisdiction of the courts of each Member State shall subject to Articles 22 and 23, be determined by the law of that Member State.
2. As against such a defendant, any person domiciled in a Member State may, whatever his nationality, avail himself in that State of the rules of jurisdiction there in force, and in particular those specified in Annex 1 in the same way as nationals of that State.

SECTION 2

SPECIAL JURISDICTION

Article 5

A person domiciled in a Member State may, in another Member State, be sued –

1   (a) In matters relating to a contract, in the courts for the place of performance of the obligation in question;

    (b) for the purpose of this provision and unless otherwise agreed, the place of performance of the obligation in question shall be:

        –   in the case of sale of goods, the place of performance in a Member State where, under the contract, the goods were delivered or should have been delivered,

        –   in the case of the provision of services, the place in a Member State where, under the contract, the services were provided or should have been provided,

    (c) if subparagraph (b) does not apply then subparagraph (a) applies;

...

3   In matters relating to tort, delict or quasi delict, in the courts for the place where the harmful event occurred.

4   As regards a civil claim for damages or restitution which is based on an act giving rise to criminal proceedings, in the court seized of those proceedings to the extent that that court has jurisdiction under its own law to entertain civil proceedings.

5   As regards a dispute arising out of the operation of a branch, agency or other establishment, in the courts for the place in which the branch, agency or other establishment is situated.

...

Article 6

A person domiciled in a Member State may also be sued:

1   where he is one of a number defendants, in the courts for the place where any one of them is domiciled, provided the claims are so closely connected that it is expedient to hear and determine them together to avoid the risk of irreconcilable judgments from separate proceedings;

2   as a third party in an action on a warranty or guarantee or in any other third party proceedings, in the courts seized of the original proceedings, unless these were instituted solely with the object of removing him from the jurisdiction of the court which would be competent in his;

3   on a counter claim arising from the same contract or facts on which the original claim was based, in the court in which the original claim is pending;

4   in matters relating to a contract, if the action may be combined with an action against the same defendant in matters relating to rights in *rem* in immoveable property, in the court of the Member State in which the property is situated.

...

SECTION 3

JURISDICTION IN MATTERS RELATING TO INSURANCE

...

SECTION 4

JURISDICTION OVER CONSUMER CONTRACTS

Article 15

1.   In matters relating to a contract concluded by a person, the consumer, for a purpose which can be regarded as being outside his trade or profession, jurisdiction shall be determined by this section, without prejudice to Article 4 and point 5 of Article 5, if:

    (a) it is a contract for the sale of goods on instalment credit terms; or

    (b) it is a contract for a loan repayable by instalments, or for any other form of credit, made to finance the sale of goods; or

    (c) in all other cases, the contract has been concluded with a person who pursues commercial or professional activities in the Member State of the consumer's domicile or, by any means, directs such activities to that Member State or to several States including that Member State, and the contract falls within the scope of such activities.

2. Where a consumer enters into a contract with a party who is not domiciled in a Member State but has a branch, agency or other establishment in one of the Member States, that party shall, in disputes arising out of the operations of the branch, agency or establishment, be deemed to be domiciled in that State.

3. This Section does not apply to a contract of transport other than a contract which, for an inclusive price, provides for a combination of travel and accommodation.

Article 16

1. A consumer may bring proceedings against the other party to a contract either in the courts of the Member State in which that party is domiciled or in the courts of the Contracting State in which the consumer is domiciled.

2. Proceedings may be brought against a consumer by the other party to the contract only in the courts of the Member State in which the consumer is domiciled.

3. This Article shall not affect the right to bring a counter claim in the court in which, in accordance with this Section, the original claim is pending.

Article 17

The provisions of this Section may be departed from only by an agreement:

which is entered into after the dispute has arisen; or

which allows the consumer to bring proceedings in courts other than those indicated in this Section; or

which is entered into by the consumer and the other party to the contract, both of whom are at the time of conclusion of the contract domiciled or habitually resident in the same Member State, and which confers jurisdiction on the courts of that Member State, provided that such an agreement is not contrary to the law of that Member State.

SECTION 6

EXCLUSIVE JURISDICTION

Article 22

The following courts shall have exclusive jurisdiction, regardless of domicile:

1 In proceedings which have as their object rights in rem in immoveable property or tenancies of immoveable property, the courts of the Member State in which the property is situated. However, in proceedings which have as their object tenancies of immoveable property concluded for temporary private use for a maximum period of six consecutive months, the courts of the Member State in which the defendant is domiciled shall also have jurisdiction, provided that the tenant is a natural person and that the landlord and tenant are domiciled in the same Member State.

2 In proceedings which have as their object the validity of the constitution, the nullity or the dissolution of companies or other legal persons or associations of natural or legal persons, or of the validity of the decisions of their organs, the courts of the Member State in which the Company, legal person or association has its seat. In order to determine the seat, the court shall apply its rules of private international law.

3 In proceedings which have as their object the validity of entries in public registers, the courts of the Member State in which the register is kept.

4 In proceedings concerned with the registration or validity of patents, trade marks, designs, or other similar rights required to be deposited or registered, the courts of

the Member State in which the deposit or registration has been applied for, has taken place or is under the terms of a community instrument or an international convention deemed to have taken place.

Without prejudice to the jurisdiction of the European Patent Office under the Convention on the Grant of European Patents, signed at Munich on 5 October 1973, the courts of each Member State shall have exclusive jurisdiction, regardless of domicile, in proceedings concerned with the registration or validity of any European Patent granted for that State;

5   In proceedings concerned with the enforcement of judgments, the courts of the Contracting State in which judgment has been or is to be enforced.

SECTION 7

PROROGATION OF JURISDICTION

Article 23

1.   If the parties, one or more of whom is domiciled in a Member State, have agreed that a court or the courts of a Member State are to have jurisdiction to settle any disputes which have arisen or which may arise in connection with a particular legal relationship, that court or those courts shall have jurisdiction. Such jurisdiction shall be exclusive unless the parties have agreed otherwise. Such an agreement conferring jurisdiction shall be either –

    (a) in writing or evidenced in writing; or

    (b) in a form which accords with practices which the parties have established between themselves; or

    (c) in international trade or commerce, in a form which accords with a usage of which the parties are or ought to have been aware and which in such trade or commerce is widely known to, and regularly observed by, parties to contracts of the type involved in the particular trade or commerce concerned.

2.   Any communication by electronic means which provides a durable record of the agreement shall be equivalent to 'writing'.

3.   Where such an agreement is concluded by the parties, none of whom is domiciled in a Member State, the courts of other Member States shall have no jurisdiction over their disputes unless the court or courts chosen have declined jurisdiction.

...

Article 24

Apart from the jurisdiction derived from other provisions of this Regulation, a court of a Member State before which a defendant enters an appearance shall have jurisdiction. This rule shall not apply where appearance has been entered solely to contest the jurisdiction, or where another court has exclusive jurisdiction by virtue of Article 22.

Annex 1

Rules of Jurisdiction referred to in Article 3(2) and Article 4(2)

....

– in the United Kingdom: rules which enable jurisdiction to be founded on:

(a) the document instituting the proceedings having been served on the defendant during his temporary presence in the United Kingdom; or

(b) the presence within the United Kingdom of property belonging to the defendant; or

(c) the seizure by the plaintiff of property situated in the United Kingdom.

The scope of the Regulation depends upon the subject matter of disputes.[31] It applies in 'civil and commercial matters' but does not extend to 'revenue, customs or administrative matters' and further exclusions are set out in Art 1, such as bankruptcy proceedings. Otherwise, the starting point for consideration of the application of the Regulation is the domicile of the defendant (the meaning of 'domicile' is considered below – see p 262).The basic rule, in Art 2, is that persons domiciled in a Member State 'shall, whatever their nationality, be sued in the courts of that Member State' and may be sued in the courts of another Member State only by virtue of the rules in ss 2–6 of Chapter II (Arts 5–22).[32] However, subject to certain exceptions, if the defendant is not domiciled in a Member State, then the jurisdiction of a Member State is determined by the law of that Member State (for example, the common law in England).[33] Article 22 sets out certain 'exclusive jurisdiction' rules which apply 'regardless of domicile' (for example, where what is in question are rights *in rem* in immovable property situated in a Member State, then it is basically that State which has exclusive jurisdiction). In Art 24, subject to the exclusive jurisdiction provisions of Art 22, there is a recognition of jurisdiction for the courts of a Member State through submission to jurisdiction by the defendant entering an appearance in response to an action commenced by the other party. However, probably one of the most significant provisions in the e-commerce context is Article 23. That provides that where one of the parties is domiciled in a Member State, there is jurisdiction for courts of the Member State agreed upon by the parties (exclusive jurisdiction unless they agree otherwise) – the agreement must comply with one of the alternative requirements there set out. One of the alternative means of making such an agreement effective is for it to be 'in writing or evidenced in writing'.[34] As is discussed elsewhere (see p 284), such requirements of form can provide barriers to e-commerce and the Regulations have here an addition to what was previously found in the Brussels Convention to 'take account of the development of new communication techniques'[35]. Article 23(2) provides that:

> Any communication by electronic means which can provide a durable record of the agreement shall be deemed to be in writing.

However, although inserted to deal with e-commerce, this provision is by no means easy to understand in that context. The issue arises as to what can constitute a 'durable record' in the electronic context.

As has been indicated, with limited exceptions, where the defendant is domiciled in a Member State, that State has jurisdiction. However, the Convention provides for alternative 'special jurisdictions' (at the choice of the claimant) in some cases. Article 5 allows for an alternative jurisdiction derived from a connection to the basis of the action. So, for example, under Art 5(5), where there is a 'dispute arising out of the

---

31 Article 1.
32 Article 3.
33 Article 4.
34 Article 23.
35 COM (1999), para 18.

operations of a branch, agency or other establishment' of the defendant, a person domiciled in a Member State may be sued 'in the courts for the place in which the branch, agency or other establishment is situated'. In the e-commerce context, this raises the issue of whether a server or website could constitute a 'branch, agency or other establishment' to give jurisdiction in its location. This will be returned to below, as the same phrase is also used in the context of additional jurisdictions provided to consumers. Under Art 5(1), 'in matters relating to contract', there is jurisdiction 'in the courts for the place of performance of the obligation in question'. Difficulties may arise in determining the place of performance but, now unless the parties agree otherwise, for these purposes, in Article 5, the Regulation gives the 'place of performance ... an autonomous definition in two categories of situation'.[36]

- in the case of sale of goods, the place in a Member State where, under the contract, the goods were delivered or should have been delivered;
- in the case of the provision of services, the place in a Member State where under the contract the services were provided or should have been provided.

Of course, in the context of e-commerce, the idea of 'place' can be highly problematic and the additional provisions are not necessarily helpful. Certainly in relation to 'pure' e-commerce contracts, where even the performance is provided electronically, with, for example the supply of music or software electronically, the first question to arise is whether the contract in question is one for the provision of goods or services or should be given its own characterisation (see above p 138). If, that initial question can be resolved the place of delivery or, particularly, of the supply of services, is still by no means certain. However, where the contract made electronically is for a more traditional supply then identifying the place where the goods should have been delivered, or services provided, as a possible jurisdiction may be of assistance to some e-commerce contractors. (Where the purchaser is a consumer, see below).

Article 6 provides for some situations in which there are multiple defendants or actions, allowing all of them to be addressed in one jurisdiction. So, for example, provided the claims are sufficiently connected, where he or she is one of a number of defendants, a person domiciled in a Member State 'may also be sued in the courts of the place where one of them is domiciled'.[37]

The Convention makes special provision in relation to a number of types of contract where one party may require some protection of their interests because of inequality of bargaining power – namely, consumer contracts,[38] employment contracts and contracts of insurance.[39] In relation to some consumer contracts, for example, Arts 15-17 basically provide that, where the other party is domiciled in a Member State, a consumer can *sue* in either that other party's or consumer's domicile, but can only *be sued* in the consumer's domicile (Art 16). This is additionally extended somewhat if the other party has a branch, agency or other establishment in a Member State and the dispute arises out of the operation of that branch, agency or other establishment. In those circumstances, the other party is deemed to be domiciled in that State (Art 15(2)).

---

36   COM (1999), para 4.2.
37   Article 6(1).
38   Section 4. Art 15 ff.
39   Section 3.

In the consumer context, a jurisdiction agreement will only be effective in limited circumstances. It is necessary to determine which contracts are covered by these provisions. A 'consumer' is someone who contracts 'for a purpose which can be regarded as being outside his trade or profession' and the consumer contracts covered are set out in Art 15, including, in Art 15(1)(c) the situation in which:

> The contract has been concluded with a person who pursues commercial or professional activities in the Member State of the consumer's domicile or, by any means, directs such activities to that Member State or to several States including that Member State, and the contract falls within the scope of such activities.

This provision has been considerably changed from that in the Brussels Convention, which was very problematic in the e-commerce context. However, despite the impetus behind the Regulation to provide clarification in the e-commerce context, its impact in that context is by no means clear. The effect of Art 15(1)(c) needs further consideration here.

First, the point can be made that Art 15(1)(c) encompasses two possibilities, that is the consumer contracts with someone whom either:

pursues commercial or professional activities in the Member State of the consumer's domicile or

by any means, directs commercial activities to that Member State, or to several States including that Member State,

provided, in both cases, that the contract falls within the scope of such activities.

The scope of each of these possibilities in the e-commerce context can be raised. It has been contended that 'pursues refers to commercial activities of some substance' on the basis of the overtones of the other language versions of the Regulation and also in contrast with 'directs' which is seen as 'more comprehensive and less precise'.[40] It has further been argued that the requirement that the relevant activities be pursued 'in' the Member State of the consumer's domicile may necessitate physical presence and if it does so it would prevent this part of Art 15(1)(c) from encompassing 'pure' e-commerce.[41] The additional point has, however, been made that if such an interpretation is avoided then it might encompass the situation where 'the vendor over a long period of time has operated a web shop particularly established and designed for the inhabitants of one Member State, or operates by an electronic agent on a strictly national electronic marketplace'. In such circumstances the situations are seen as such that 'it seems natural to claim that the vendor is pursuing commercial activities *in* that state'.[42]

The second part of Art 15(1)(c), with its idea of 'directing' activities to a Member State, seems more specifically designed to attempt to deal with e-commerce, although of course, it could also deal with more traditional trading activities and the overall effect of traditional and electronic activities may well need to be considered together.

---

40 St Oren (2003) p 676.
41 Ibid, p 677.
42 Ibid, p 677.

However, the focus here is on e-commerce and a number of issues arise as to when commercial activities will be directed to a Member State.

E-mail sent to an individual might initially be seen as an obvious case of directed activity. However, 'an e-mail address is not necessarily associated with a specific state in the same way as geographical addresses' are. Is commercial activity directed to France when an individual domiciled in France has an e-mail address ending with the indicia for the United Kingdom (that is, .uk) or ending with neutral indicia such as .com?[43] In relation to websites, and whether they are directed at a Member State, Joakim St Oren identifies a 'natural starting point' and its limitations.

Jurisdition over Consumer Contracts in e-Europe
Joakim St Oren
(2003) 52 ICLQ 665, 676

When assessing the question to which geographical area a website is directed a natural starting point could be the existence of country-specific indicia occurring on the website. This could for instance be national indicia in the domain name, the language used on the website, the offered product(s), the currencies accepted for payment, the use of geographically limited credit cards or guarantors, the vendor's stated account number, etc. These are usually easy to identify and especially if all the indicia point to the same State(s), this will usually create an impression to the surrounding world that the vendor is directing his activities to this geographical area. However, the significance of this should not be exaggerated. Such indicia will often be misleading, and in many situations will not provide any guidance at all. For instance, domain names containing suffixes like .com, .net, .org are nationally neutral and in *crossborder* e-commerce it is obvious that the vendor often will operate his web shop under a domain name of his own state of domicile, and not under a domain name of the State to which he is directing his business. Neither is language always a strong connecting factor. Certain languages are spoken in several different countries, and when it comes to the internet, it can be maintained that English in particular is used as a universal and common language often irrespective of which States the website is intended for. On the other hand, if a web shop is presented in a language with a narrow and clear geographical spread, typically one Member State, this could indicate that the vendor is directing his business to that State. But then another question arises; is the vendor only directing his activities to that geographical area or to every person speaking that language irrespective of State of domicile? And lastly, with the introduction of the Euro, currency is no longer a particularly strong guide in relation to the Jurisdiction Regulation. Based on this, it is obvious that the weight and significance of national indicia will vary considerably with different situations. They are not particularly suitable in creating predictability for the parties, and must therefore be no more than a starting point in the overall assessment necessary in order to decide whether the 'directing test' in Article 5(1)(c) of the Jurisdiction Regulation is fulfilled or not.

St Oren goes on to suggest that some predictability may be achieved by vendors adopting 'ring fencing mechanisms' that is, adopting mechanisms to make it clear that they are only directing their activities to certain areas. Such mechanisms could include statements on websites that the vendor only intends to contract with consumers

---

43   Ibid, p 689.

domiciled in certain states, or a registration process requiring the consumer to state his, or her domicile coupled with a technical device preventing the transaction progressing when the consumer states their domicile as a State which the vendor would not wish to be sued in. The impact of a mere statement by the vendor may not be sufficient, but would certainly need to be made plain to the consumer and the effect of any method would seem to depend upon the vendor acting within his stated policy and not actually contracting with consumers domiciled in an 'excluded' Member State.[44] In the alternative, certainty could be generated if the mere accessibility of a website was enough. However, the point has been made that businesses would be concerned by such an approach. 'Since an internet website is accessible anywhere in the world, [it] would subject an electronic trader to the jurisdiction of the courts of any Member State where a consumer who chose to contract with him resided even though he had no intention of targeting consumers in that State.'[45] Such an approach would also seem to largely negate the requirement in Art 15(1)(c) that the business activity be 'directed' to a Member State.[46]

However, what must now be considered is a further point of interest in the e-commerce context which arises both in relation to the jurisdiction provided to consumers and the special jurisdictions provided under Art 5. Article 5(5) provides for deemed domicile, and thus a right to sue in that party's 'deemed domicile' in relation to disputes arising out of the 'operations of a branch agency or other establishment', and the possible places in which a consumer can sue is similarly extended by Art 15(2). The question arises as to whether a website or server could bring a particular party within the scope of these provisions. The location of a server would seem to be too fortuitous, and almost certainly unknown to someone contracting with the relevant party, to be a determining factor here.[47] It is the question of a website which requires further consideration. A website may be automated so that, in effect, contracts can be made through it and the point has been made that 'Functionally a website can play much the same role as a branch or agency – particularly if it utilises advanced intelligent agent software to process and execute customer orders' and continuous operation through one unique domain name can provide a an element of 'permanency'.[48] The argument for a website to be recognised as a 'branch, agency or other establishment' can be made, but should it be, when it requires a physical location to be given to something that essentially has none? The limitations of looking for country specific indicia to provide, in some sense, a location, for a website were indicated above. Nevertheless, Foss and Bygrave argue that there could be seen to be sufficient connection to provide jurisdiction for the consumer.[49] They use the example of www.amazon.de which has its domain name ending in .de, its sole use of the German language, and its best seller list for the German market and conclude:

---

44   Ibid, pp 692–693 and see p 271.
45   Susman, 2000 p 30.
46   St Oren (2003) p 691.
47   And see Art 2(c) E-Commerce Directive – above p 246.
48   Foss and Bygrave, 2000, pp 127 –128.
49   Ibid.

A German consumer purchasing goods products through [the site] would have almost, if not equally as great an expectation of being able to litigate in German Courts in the event of a legal dispute with the vendor as he/she would have were he/she to purchase the book at an ordinary store established by Amazon in Germany. There can be little doubt that these expectations would be reasonable in the circumstances.

However, whilst they see the recognition of such a possibility as fulfilling the purpose of the consumer provisions of 'ensuring fairness to consumers', with the reasonable expectations of the consumer being key to that,[50] they also make the point that the same justification does not arise for taking an expansive view of the 'location' of a website in relation to the special jurisdiction provision in Art 5(5). The rationale for that extended jurisdiction is seen as the 'interests of the due administration of justice' and they identify the relevant factors for the extension of jurisdiction to the site of the 'branch, agency or administration' as being 'primarily of a practical nature'.

> Given that the dispute must have arisen out of the operations of the branch/agency, the staff of the latter will tend to be amongst those persons who know the details of the dispute best. As a result they will tend to be called before the court as witnesses or representatives of the defendant. In addition, much of the relevant evidence (documentation etc) will be found at the branch/agency. When a local court is given jurisdiction, the costs and delays involved in sending persons and evidence to another country are avoided.[51]

However, 'when one considers litigation arising out of the operations of a website, it is very difficult to see how the factors identified above can have much relevance'.[52]

There are a few, final general points to be made in relation to the Regulation. In many cases, it is possible for the courts of more than one forum to have jurisdiction. Section 9 contains measures that are aimed at preventing conflicting judicial decisions in different States in basically the same case, or in relation to related issues. Basically, precedence is given to the court 'first seised'.

The last point to consider here is the meaning of 'domicile'. As will have been obvious from the above this is key to the application of the Regulation. In relation to individuals, under Art 59, whether an individual is domiciled in a State whose courts are seised of a matter is determined by the 'internal law of that State'. In order to determine whether the individual is domiciled in another Member State, the law of that State is applied. For the purpose of the Regulations domicile is dependent upon 'residence' and 'the nature and circumstances of [the] residence' indicating a 'substantial connection' with the UK. Three months' residence raises a presumption of substantial connection.[53] (And similarly for a particular part of the UK.) In relation to legal persons, the Regulations set a uniform rule. Under Article 60, a company is domiciled where it has its statutory seat, central administration, or principal place of business.

---

50   *Ibid.,* p 129.
51   *Ibid,* p 132.
52   *Op cit* p 132–133.
53   Civil Jurisdiction and Judgments Order 2001 (SI 2001/3929) Sch 1, para 9.

THE GOVERNING LAW

An English company may agree with a French company to purchase goods that are to be delivered from Spain. Questions arise as to which law is to apply in the event of a dispute – the contract law of England, France, Spain or even somewhere else – and the questions occur across the entire contractual spectrum, from formation to performance, breach and remedies. Obviously, the potential for such contracts is markedly increased with the advent of e-commerce, and what must be considered here are the rules which are used to determine which law will apply in the event of a dispute. Of course, no such issue would arise if each jurisdiction applied the same substantive law to a particular problem and there is, for example, a UN Convention on Contracts for the International Sale of Goods (the Vienna Convention 1980), but that has not yet been ratified by the UK. However, within the EC, the 1980 Rome Convention on the Law Applicable to Contractual Obligations has provided considerable harmonisation of the choice of law rules and, in the UK, the law applied in relation to most contractual disputes will now be determined by that Convention. This was implemented in the UK by the Contracts (Applicable Law) Act 1990. In 'ascertaining the meaning or effect of any provision' of the Rome Convention, the official Report on it by Guiliano and Lagarde[54] may be considered.[55] Under Art 1, the rules of the Convention apply to all disputes coming before the UK courts, whether or not it is the laws of contracting States which are involved. Article 1 also contains certain ousters from the scope of the rules (for example, obligations arising under bills of exchange or contracts of insurance (but not re-insurance)). The point should also be made that e-commerce may well prove to be the significant means for the supply of software, but the Guiliano-Lagarde Report interprets the Convention as also excluding intellectual property. However, this interpretation is made on the basis that, 'since the law is only concerned with the law applicable to contractual obligations, property rights and intellectual property are not covered by these provisions'.[56] This 'exclusion most likely only concerns proprietary rights, not contracts licensing or selling copies of intellectual property'.[57] Some of the more relevant provisions of the Rome Convention are set out below.

Rome Convention on the Law Applicable to Contractual Obligations

Article 3
Freedom of Choice

1 A contract shall be governed by the law chosen by the parties. The choice must be express or demonstrated with reasonable certainty by the terms of the contract or the circumstances of the case. By their choice the parties can select the law applicable to the whole or only part of the contract.

2 The parties may at any time agree to subject the contract to a law other than that which previously governed it, whether as a result of an earlier choice under this

---

54 Reproduced in OJ C, 31 October 1980.
55 Contracts (Applicable Law) Act 1990, s 3(2).
56 In relation to Art 1.
57 Chissick and Kelman, 2004, para 4.23.

article or of other provisions of this Convention. Any variation by the parties of the law to be applied made after the conclusion of the contract shall not prejudice its formal validity under Article 9 or adversely affect the rights of third parties.

3   The fact that the parties have chosen a foreign law, whether or not accompanied by the choice of a foreign tribunal, shall not, where all the other elements relevant to the situation are connected with one country only, prejudice the application of rules of the law of that country which cannot be derogated from by contract, hereinafter called 'mandatory rules'.

4   The existence and validity of the consent of the parties as to the choice of the applicable law shall be determined in accordance with the provisions of Articles 8, 9 and 11.

Article 4
Applicable Law in the absence of Choice

1   To the extent that the applicable law has not been chosen in accordance with Article 3, the contract shall be governed by the law of the country with which it is most closely connected. Nevertheless, a severable part of the contract which has a closer connection with another country may by way of exception be governed by the law of that other country.

2   Subject to the provisions of paragraph 5 of this Article, it shall be presumed that the contract is most closely connected with the country where the party who is to effect the performance which is characteristic of the contract has, at the time of conclusion of the contract, his habitual residence or, in the case of a body corporate or unincorporated, its central administration. However, if the contract is entered into in the course of that party's trade or profession, that country shall be the country in which the principal place of business is situated or, where under the terms of the contract the performance is to be effected through place of business other than the principal place of business, the country in which that other place of business is situated.

3   Notwithstanding the provisions of paragraph 2 of this Article, to the extent that the subject matter of the contract is a right in immoveable property or a right to use immoveable property it shall be presumed that the contract is most closely connected with the country where the property is situated.

4   A contract for the carriage of goods shall not be subject to the presumption in paragraph 2. In such a contract if the country in which, at the time the contract is concluded, the carrier has his principal place of business is also the country in which the place of loading or the place of discharge or the principal place of business of the consignor is situated, it shall be presumed that the contract is most closely connected with that country. In applying this paragraph single voyage charterparties and other contracts the main purpose of which is the carriage of goods shall be treated as contracts for the carriage of goods.

5   Paragraph 2 shall not apply of the characteristic performance cannot be determined, and the presumptions in paragraphs 2, 3, and 4 shall be disregarded if it appears from the circumstances as a whole that the contract is more closely connected with another country.

Article 5
Certain Consumer Contracts

1   This article applies to a contract the object of which is the supply of goods or services to a person ('the consumer') for a purpose which can be regarded as outside his trade or profession, or a contract for the provision of credit for that object.

2   Notwithstanding the provisions of Article 3, a choice of law made by the parties shall not have the result of depriving the consumer of the protection afforded to him by the mandatory rules of the law of the country in which he has his habitual residence –

-   if in that country the conclusion of the contract was preceded by a specific invitation addressed to him or by advertising, and he had taken in that country all the steps necessary on his part for the conclusion of the contract, or
-   if the other party or his agent received the consumers order in that country, or
-   if the contract is for the sale of goods and the consumer travelled from that country to another country and there gave his order, provided that the consumer's journey was arranged by the seller for the purpose of inducing the consumer to buy.

3   Notwithstanding the provisions of Article 4, a contract to which this article applies shall in the absence of choice in accordance with Article 3, be governed by the law of the country in which the consumer has his habitual residence if it is entered into in the circumstances described in paragraph 2 of this Article.

4   This article shall not apply to –

(a) a contract of carriage;

(b) a contract for the supply of services where the services are to be supplied to the consumer exclusively in a country other than that in which he has his habitual residence.

5   Notwithstanding the provisions of paragraph 4, this Article shall apply to a contract which, for an inclusive price, provides for a combination of travel and accommodation.

Article 6
Individual Employment Contracts

...

Article 7
Mandatory Rules

1   When applying under this Convention the law of a country, effect may be given to the mandatory rules of the law of another country with which the situation has a close connection, if and in so far as, under the law of the latter country, those rules must be applied whatever the law applicable to the contract. In considering whether to give effect to these mandatory rules, regard shall be had to their nature and purpose and to the consequences of their application or non-application.

2   Nothing in this Convention shall restrict the application of the rules of the law of the forum in a situation where they are mandatory irrespective of the law otherwise applicable to the contract.

Article 8
Material Validity

[See below, p 283]

Article 9
Formal Validity

[See below, p 298]

Article 10
Scope of the Applicable Law

1   The law applicable to a contract by virtue of Articles 3 to 6 and 12 of this Convention shall govern in particular –

(a) interpretation;

(b) performance;

(c) within the limits of the powers conferred on the court by its procedural law, the consequences of breach, including the assessment of damages in so far as it is governed by the rules of law;

(d) the various ways of extinguishing obligations, and prescription and limitation of actions;

(e) the consequences of nullity of contract.

2   In relation to the manner of performance and the steps to be taken in the event of defective performance regard shall be had to the law of the country in which performance takes place.

...

Article 16
'Ordre Public'

The application of a rule of the law of any country specified by this Convention may be refused only if such an application is manifestly incompatible with the public policy ('ordre public') of the forum.

...

Basic scope of the applicable law

Articles 3–6 are concerned with determining the 'applicable' law, and issues of 'substance'[58] are determined by the 'applicable law'.[59] It encompasses questions of construction,[60] the discharge of the contract,[61] (for example, frustration and termination for breach), performance generally,[62] and the consequences of breach (such as whether a particular type of loss is recoverable), although the procedural aspects of calculation of damages will require reference to the law of the forum.[63]

The applicable law – basic rule and limits

Under Art 3, the basic starting point for determining the applicable law is that of the parties' choice. The choice may be express or 'demonstrated with reasonable certainty by the terms of the contract or the circumstances of the case'. This reflects the idea of freedom of contract and, if an express choice is made, it is a means of promoting certainty. The suggestion has been made that:

---

58   Clarkson and Hill, 1997, p 236.
59   Article 10.
60   Article 10(1)(a).
61   Article 10(1)(d).
62   But note Art 10(2).
63   Articles 1(2)(h), 10(1)(c).

... e-commerce vendors are advised always to make a choice of law in their standard terms and conditions ... Express choice of law solidifies the governing law in nearly all cases, including, surprisingly enough, consumer contracts (subject to a few restrictions).[64]

If no 'choice' of law can be found to have been made by the parties, Art 4 applies the 'law of the country with which the contract is most closely connected' and supplies presumptions for determining that connection in some cases. It should be noted that there is also recognition that legal systems other than the applicable law may have an interest in a contract and the Convention provides some scope for the application of certain 'mandatory rules' from systems other than that of the applicable law.[65] In addition, special provision is made for certain contracts where the parties' 'agreement' to the use of a particular law may be affected by inequality of bargaining power – in, for example, consumer contracts[66] and contracts of employment.[67]

Country of closest connection

When the parties have not made a choice under Art 3, then, under Art 4, the country of closest connection is sought to determine the 'applicable law'. In relation to most contracts,[68] there is a presumption that refers to the country relating to the party who is to effect the 'performance which is characteristic of the contract'.[69] According to Giuliano and Lagarde:

> [In] bilateral (reciprocal) contracts ... the counterperformance by one of the parties in a modern economy usually takes the form of money. This is not, of course, the characteristic performance of the contract. It is the performance for which the payment is due, that is, depending on the type of contract, the delivery of goods ... the provision of a service.[70]

So, for example, if the contract is entered into in the 'course of' the 'trade or profession' of the party rendering the characteristic performance, the country will be that in which that party's 'principal place of business is situated or where under the terms of the contract the performance is to be effected through a place of business other than the principal place of business, the country in which that other place of business is situated'. In the e-commerce context, the question has been raised as to whether the supplier could artificially generate a 'place of business' through the location of his or her web server[71] – the supply of an information service could occur through the server. However, the physical location of the server has no necessary link of any substance to the supplier's business. Its arbitrary nature should mean that it is not sufficient to constitute a 'place of business'.[72] The 'characteristic performance' presumption will

---

64 Chissick and Kelman, 2000, para 4.31. On the situation in relation to consumers see below, p 269.
65 Articles 3(3), 7 – but note that the UK has derogated from the application of Art 7(1).
66 Article 5.
67 Article 6.
68 For the presumptions dealing with contracts 'the subject matter of which is immoveable property' and contracts for the carriage of goods, see Art 4(3) and (4) respectively.
69 Article 4(2).
70 Guiliano-Lagarde Report OJ 1980 C 282/1.
71 See Chissick and Kelman, 2000, para 4.31.
72 *Ibid*, para 4.31; Schu, R, 1997, p 221. See Art 2(c) EC Directive on Electronic Commerce above p 246.

not apply if the 'characteristic performance cannot be determined' and, in any event, the presumption is disregarded 'if it appears from the circumstances as a whole that the contract is more closely connected with another country'.[73]

Mandatory rules

The contracting parties might agree to an 'applicable law' in order to avoid particular rules of the more obvious legal system applying to their agreement. Some account of this is taken by Art 3(3), under which the fact that the parties have chosen a particular legal system does not prejudice the application of the 'mandatory rules' (that is, those which cannot be derogated from by contract) of a country in which are situated 'all the other elements relevant to the situation at the time of choice'. The test is objective – there is no requirement that the choice be made to avoid the application of the relevant law. In addition, Art 7 deals with a more limited class of mandatory rules, that is, those that apply 'irrespective of the law otherwise applicable to the contract'. (The terminology 'overriding rules' has been suggested to describe this subset of mandatory rules.[74]) Article 7(1), which does not apply in the UK, provides for the application of the mandatory (overriding) rules of a State with which 'the situation has a close connection'. More significantly, as it does apply in the UK, Art 7(2) provides for the application of the mandatory (overriding) rules of the forum. 'Whether a rule is optional, mandatory or overriding is a question of interpretation to be resolved by the law of the country of which the rule forms a part.'[75] When a statute is in question, its application in situations with extraterritorial elements may be made clear. For example, consider s 27 of the Unfair Contract Terms Act 1977, which states:

(1) Where the law applicable to a contract is the law of any part of the United Kingdom only by choice of the parties (and apart from that choice would be the law of some country outside the United Kingdom) sections 2 to 7 and 16 to 21 of this Act do not operate as part of the law applicable to the contract.

(2) This Act has effect notwithstanding any contract term which applies or purports to apply the law of some country outside the United Kingdom, where (either or both) –

(a) the term appears to the court or arbitrator or arbiter to have been imposed wholly or mainly for the purpose of enabling the party imposing it to evade the operation of the Act; or

(b) in the making of the contract one of the parties dealt as consumer, and he was then habitually resident in the United Kingdom, and the essential steps necessary for the making of the contract were taken there whether by him or by others on his behalf.

It will be noted that s 27(1) is self-denying, ousting the operation of the Act where the applicable law is that of part of the UK 'only' by the choice of the parties. The question of a connection to the law stated should not be affected merely by the location of a web server, which need have no substantial connection to the transaction.[76] However, it is s

---

73   Article 4(5).
74   Clarkson and Hill, 1997, p 216.
75   *Ibid*.
76   Schu, 1999, p 208.

27(2) which is primarily of interest here, as, in the circumstances specified in (a) and (b), it provides for the operation of the Act even where there is a term applying the law of some other country. In other words, in the circumstances specified, it makes the operation of the 1977 Act 'overriding'. Although the position is 'not entirely made clear', it would seem that the application of s 27(2)(b) only requires the consumer's 'steps necessary for the making of the contract' to have taken place in the UK, and not the conclusion of the contract as such.[77] A standard internet consumer transaction seems to be caught by s 27(2), at least where the consumer is resident in the UK and uses a terminal there.[78] A similar provision to s 27(2) is also to be found in reg 9 of the Unfair Terms in Consumer Contracts Regulations 1999,[79] which provides:

> These Regulations shall apply notwithstanding any contract term which applies or purports to apply the law of a non-Member State, if the contract has a close connection with the territory of the Member States.

(The references to the laws of non-Member States follows from the fact that the Regulations are the UK implementation of the EC Directive on Unfair Terms in Consumer Contracts and should have been implemented in all Member States.) The final point to note here is the possibility, under Art 16, of refusing to apply the law otherwise determined by the Convention on the basis of 'public policy'. However, the point has been made that 'it is intended that, under the Convention, public policy should have a very narrow scope'[80] and it should also be emphasised that the need to refer to public policy is diminished by the scope given to 'overriding rules', indicated above.[81]

Consumers

Within a limited sphere, Art 5 ensures that, in contracting, a consumer will not lose the benefit of the mandatory rules of his or her habitual residence and may find that the applicable law is that of his or her habitual residence. When Art 5 applies, 'a choice of law by the parties shall not have the result of depriving the consumer of the protection afforded to him by the mandatory rules of' his habitual residence.[82] In addition, if there is no choice of law under Art 3, the reference to the country of closest connection in Art 4 does not apply; rather, the applicable law will be that of the consumer's habitual residence. However, it should be emphasised that the application of Art 5 is considerably circumscribed. The person to whom the supply is being made will be a consumer if the supply is 'for a purpose which can be regarded as outside his trade or profession'.[83] It applies to contracts 'the object of which is the supply of goods or

---

77   *Ibid.*
78   *Ibid.*
79   Replacing the 1994 Regulations – see above, p 203.
80   Clarkson and Hill, 1997, p 223.
81   *Ibid*, pp 224–25.
82   Article 5(2).
83   Article 5(1).

services' to a consumer or to contracts 'for the provision of credit for that object',[84] but there is an exception to its application where the contract is for the supply of services and 'the services are to be supplied to the consumer exclusively in a country other than that in which he has his habitual residence'.[85] In addition, for Art 5 to apply, the contract must have been made in certain specified circumstances – the consumer's habitual residence must have been relevant to the contract in one of a number of specified ways. That is, the rules in Art 5 apply:

(a) if, in that country, the conclusion of the contract was preceded by a specific invitation addressed to him or by advertising, and he had, in that country, taken all the steps necessary on his part for the conclusion of the contract; or

(b) if the other party or his agent received the consumer's order in that country; or

(c) if the contract is for the sale of goods and the consumer travelled from that country to another country and there gave his order, provided that the consumer's journey was arranged by the seller for the purpose of inducing the consumer to buy.

These specified circumstances, in particular, raise certain issues in the e-commerce context. Several points should be addressed in relation to point (a). First, the point is made elsewhere that it may be open to debate as to where a contract made using email or the web is made. However, the words 'steps necessary on his part' were 'expressly adopted ... in order to avoid the classic problem of determining the place where the contract was concluded'.[86] It should be a matter of where the consumer does what he or she has to do in order to conclude a contract – in this context, tapping out the necessary message on his or her computer. Secondly, consideration should be given to the requirement of a 'specific invitation' to the consumer. It would seem that this has to take place in the consumer's habitual residence and, whilst an email can easily be envisaged as a specific invitation to the consumer to whom it is sent, a question may be raised as to whether that requires the consumer to receive it in that country and, if so, what is meant by 'receipt'. An email message could be regarded as received when it reaches the server used by the consumer, and that server need not be geographically close to the consumer – it need not be in the place of the consumer's habitual residence. The location of a mail server can be purely fortuitous. To avoid the arbitrary element, an email message should be regarded as received where the consumer accesses it from (see p 282) – which should usually be their habitual residence.

The final point which will be considered here relates to website advertisements. Clearly, such communications are not 'specific invitations' to the individual consumer, so the question is whether they are advertisements falling within Art 5. In relation to paper-based publication, the line taken is shown by the following example:[87]

> ... if a German makes a contract in response to an advertisement published by a French company in a German publication, the contract is covered by the special rule. If, on the other hand, the German replies to an advertisement in American publications, even if

---

84 *Ibid.*

85 Article 5(4)(b). It does, however, apply to a contract 'which, for an inclusive price, provides for a combination of travel and accommodation' (Art 5(5)).

86 Guiliano-Lagarde Report, OJ 1980 C282/1.

87 *Ibid.*

they are sold in Germany, the rule does not apply unless the advertisement appeared in special editions of the publication intended for European countries. In the latter case, the seller will have made a special advertisement intended for the country of the purchaser.

This carries with it some idea that the advertisement has to be 'directed' at consumers in the country in question if it is to fall within the bounds of Art 5. On this basis, the mere fact that a website can be accessed by a consumer in a particular country would not be sufficient for Art 5. However, mere accessibility could be regarded as sufficient and as a website can be accessed from anywhere, such an approach might cause anxiety to businesses about being potentially subject to at least the mandatory rules of every country where a consumer is habitually resident. They might try to avoid this by including a disclaimer in the website, stating that the business will only contract with consumers in certain specified jurisdictions. The effectiveness of such a clause is open to doubt – under English law, if a contract was nevertheless made with a consumer from a non-specified State, the line might be taken that, by contracting, the business had thereby shown that it was not so restricting itself in the instant case.[88] In addition, in the context of a similar rule in relation to jurisdiction (see p 261), the point has been made that:[89]

> ... the fragmentary effect on the Internal Market of this [disclaimer] solution, as well as its incongruence with the 'without frontiers' and innovative basis on which the internet is founded, seems likely to detract from the appeal of this approach and may even constitute an infringement of EU principles of competition and free movement.

Particular issues

It has been indicated that many contractual issues are dealt with by the applicable law, but there are questions which are referred to another law. Matters of material validity, for example, are specifically dealt with by Art 8. That article encompasses issues of formation – offer, acceptance, consideration, intention to create legal relations and matters affecting consent, such as duress. (It is considered further below in relation to offer and acceptance – see p 283). Formal validity in dealt with under Art 9, and that is considered when issues such as writing and signature are addressed generally (see p 298).

SOME ASPECTS OF CONTRACTING
BY ELECTRONIC MEANS

Introduction

The basic requirements of the contracting process have been considered (see above p 114). Here, consideration is given to a number of aspects of contract formation which raise particular issues in the e-commerce context.

---

88 Compare the type of situation in, eg, *Harling v Eddy* [1951] 2 KB 739; *Couchman v Hill* [1947] KB 554. See discussion of those cases in Macdonald, 1999b, pp 428–31.
89 Seaman, 1999–2000, p 30.

'Automated contracting'

The point has been made that 'one of the advantages of e-commerce is the automation of tasks which previously required human involvement'.[90] In attempting to make a contract by email or on the web, an individual's communication may be met by the purely programmed response of a computer, without any immediate human knowledge or intervention. Is it possible for a contract to be formed in such circumstances? The issue is discussed by Glatt.[91]

Comparative issues in the formation of electronic contracts
Christopher Glatt
(1998) 6 Int JLIT 34

In an electronic environment email may be sent or answered by computers. Interactive websites enable users to transmit information directly by filling in an electronic form. The response will be generated by software. Where EDI is used, contract processes are likely to be fully automated: computers exchange offer and acceptance without any human participation. This raises the question of whether such interactions create valid contracts. Can it be said that they express the parties' *intention*?

The problem is not entirely new. Courts have dealt with the lack of direct intention in cases where automatic machines were involved in contract formation. In these transactions machines are reacting automatically to the customer's conduct ... The machines cannot express intention and there is no real communication between offeror and acceptor. As Lord Denning put it in *Thornton v Shoe Lane Parking*: '... he [the customer] may protest to the machine even swear at it. But it will remain unmoved.' Nevertheless, the courts had little difficulty in translating these situations into offer and acceptance. The physical involvement of a machine had no legal consequences because it was held to be only the result of prior human intention. Thus, automated declarations of offer and acceptance are valid.

Some argue that this reasoning is not applicable to electronic communications: prior intentions are not relevant because the principal has no influence on the single transaction directed by a complex program. This is not convincing. Even the most sophisticated software does not make autonomous decisions, but operates according to previous programming. The responsibility therefore remains with the principal, who decides to use such software with the intention of being bound by its 'declarations'. The single transaction has to be seen in the context of the established communications system and its purpose.

The purpose of an EDI link, for instance, will be, *inter alia*, the formation of contracts. The parties clearly intend to be bound by the 'declarations' exchanged between their computer systems. Interactive web pages which are designed for commercial purposes are put on the world wide web in order to create binding agreements ... Therefore as in the case of automated machines, it is of no legal consequences that a computer program completes a contract.

The idea that an automatically generated message can have legal effect because of the prior involvement of the relevant parties is embodied in the UNCITRAL[92] Model Law on Electronic Commerce. Paragraph 35 of its Guide to Enactment states:

---

90 Chissick and Kelman, 2000, para 3.35.
91 See, also, Nicholl, [1998] ; Chissick and Kelman, 2000, paras 3.35–3.36.
92 United Nations Commission on International Trade Law.

... Data messages that are generated automatically by computers without human intervention should be regarded as 'originating' from the legal entity on behalf of which the computer is operated.

However, the impact of the communication by one side being a purely computerised response will need to be considered further in relation to the issue of whether a communication is an offer or merely an invitation to treat (see p 274).

Offer or invitation to treat?

As has been indicated, contract formation will normally be analysed in terms of offer and acceptance (see p 114). However, the question may arise as to whether a particular communication constituted an offer or was merely an 'invitation to treat'.[93] When an offer is made, there will be an intention on the part of the offeror to be bound by its terms if the other party accepts them. The other party can accept them and thereby create a contract. An invitation to treat is merely an attempt to engage in negotiations or to elicit an offer, and it can be differentiated from an offer because of the lack of an intention to be bound.[94] Although the question must always be as to the presence or absence of an intention to be bound, in the non-electronic context it has become established that certain communications will normally only amount to an invitation to treat. Thus, shop window displays[95] and advertisements[96] will normally only amount to invitations to treat, not offers.

In the e-commerce context, the question may arise as to the effect of a web-based advertisement and whether such an advertisement will normally be merely an invitation to treat. There are considerable arguments for the conclusion that such an advertisement will normally be an invitation to treat. In *Grainger & Son v Gough*,[97] in the context of a distributed paper price list, the point was made that a supplier will not want to become bound to sell more of a particular item than he can supply, which could occur if the price list (or advertisement) was construed as an offer. Lord Herschell said:[98]

> The transmission of such a price list does not amount to an offer to supply an unlimited quantity of the wine described at the price named so that, as soon as an order is given, there is a binding contract to supply that quantity. If it were so, the merchant might find himself involved in any number of contractual obligations to supply wine of a particular description which he would be quite unable to carry out, his stock of wine of that description being necessarily limited.

---

93 See, eg, *Gibson v Manchester CC* [1979] 1 WLR 294.
94 *Ibid.*
95 Eg, *Fisher v Bell* [1961] 1 QB 394.
96 Eg, *Partridge v Crittenden* [1968] 2 All ER 421. Note that the situation is different where the advertisement is setting out how a reward may be earned or is an analogous case; in that context, the advertisement may well be seen as an offer of a unilateral contract – see, most famously, *Carlill v Carbolic Smoke Ball Co* [1893] 1 QB 256.
97 [1896] AC 325.
98 *Ibid*, p 334.

This argument will also often apply in the e-commerce context, but the point has been made that, 'if the contract deals with the supply of data, the limited stock argument might fail. Software, information and other data is available in an unlimited number of copies'.[99] However, it has also been noted that 'copyright law ... could restrict reproduction and so, again, a supplier cannot be held bound to an unforeseeable number of acceptances'.[100] In addition, there are other reasons for arguing that suppliers will not normally intend their websites to constitute an offer – just as in the paper-based world, they may well not intend to be bound to contract with whomsoever responds. That may be, for example, because they wish to limit their contracts to certain jurisdictions, in order to avoid those where the law is in some way unfavourable to them.[101]

On the above reasoning, a web-based advertisement will normally amount to an invitation to treat, rather than an offer. However, some separate consideration is required of the situation where an order is placed through a website and is dealt with by an automated response, without any immediate human intervention. The general possibility of a contract being concluded by an automated response was considered above (see p 272). The point to be examined here is whether the website will constitute an offer or an invitation to treat. The mechanism for the making of a contract when money is put into a vending or similar machine was outlined by Lord Denning MR in *Thornton v Shoe Lane Parking*.

Thornton v Shoe Lane Parking
[1971] 2 QB 163

Lord Denning MR The customer pays his money and gets a ticket. He cannot refuse it. He may protest to the machine, even swear at it; but it will remain unmoved. He is committed beyond recall. He was committed at the very moment that he put his money in the machine. The contract was concluded at that time. It can be translated into offer and acceptance in this way. The offer is made when the proprietor of the machine holds it out as being ready to receive the money. The acceptance takes place when the customer puts his money into the slot.

An analogy might be drawn between the situation considered above, in *Thornton*, and automatic response systems which are linked to orders made through websites. If such an analogy is accepted, then the website linked to automated ordering would be viewed as an offer. However, the system dealing with web-based orders may be much more sophisticated than Lord Denning's vending machine type of case. The system may have a function for examining certain elements of the order. It might, for example, be programmed to reject orders requiring goods to be delivered to a specified jurisdiction. In such cases, there would be every reason to say that the web page was not intended as an offer but merely an invitation to treat. There may be reasons not to follow Lord Denning's vending machine analogy in the context of an automated web-based system.

---

99   Glatt, 1998, p 50.

100   *Ibid*.

101   There may be, eg, import/export restrictions, consumer protection legislation, regulation of the activity provided by an online service (eg, financial services). See Chissick and Kelman, 2000, para 3.17 *et seq*.

The above discussion indicates a general approach, which regards website advertisements as invitations to treat rather than offers. This would lead to a situation in which the offer was made by the customer and accepted (or otherwise) by the supplier. Such an approach would be in keeping with the EC Electronic Commerce Directive (2000/31/EC). In the context of 'information society services', Art 11(1)[102] states:

> Member States shall ensure, except where otherwise agreed by parties who are not consumers, that in cases where the recipient of the service places his order through technological means, the following principles apply:
>
> – the service provider has to acknowledge the receipt of the recipient's order without undue delay and by electronic means;
>
> – the order and the acknowledgment of receipt are deemed to be received when the parties to whom they are addressed are able to access them.

The second point will be returned to below in the context of the timing of the conclusion of a contract made electronically (see below). The first point 'shall not apply to contracts concluded exclusively by exchange of electronic mail or by equivalent individual communication',[103] but here we are concerned with web-based contracting and the point can be made that, on the above analysis, the 'recipient's order' would constitute the offer and the 'acknowledgment of receipt' the acceptance – the 'order' and 'acknowledgment of receipt' would very naturally be part of the contracting process. In addition, in such circumstances, there is every reason for service providers to send an 'acknowledgment'. However, although this is a convenient analysis, 'order' under the Directive is not necessarily to be equated with 'offer' in the technical sense.[104]

Acceptance – effective on receipt or on posting?

Electronic communication will normally occur at a distance and questions can arise as to when, where and if a contract has been made. The situation may arise in which an acceptance is lost.[105] More commonly, the question may simply be as to the time at which an acceptance became effective or where the contract was made. The general rule is that acceptance is only effective once it has been communicated to the offeror.[106] However, when something other than simple face to face communication has been used between the parties, the question has often arisen as to whether that rule should apply. The 'postal rule' is well known and it means that, normally, a posted acceptance will be effective on posting,[107] although that will not be the case if it goes astray because the acceptor has not addressed it properly[108] or is otherwise at fault. In addition, it should be noted that the postal rule will not apply if the offeror has made it

---

102 See Reg 13, Electronic Commerce (EC Directive) Regulations 2002.

103 Article 11(3).

104 This is explicit in Reg 14 of the implementing legislation – the Electronic Commerce (EC Directive) Regulations 2002.

105 Or damaged so that it is unintelligible.

106 *Entores v Miles Far East Corp* [1955] 2 QB 327.

107 *Adams v Lindsell* (1818) 1 B & Ald 681. On the application of the postal rule in the electronic context see further MacDonald and Poyton, 2005.

108 *Household Fire Insurance v Grant* (1879) 4 Ex D 216.

clear that it will not, by, for example, requiring actual receipt of acceptance.[109] However, the postal rule has not been applied in the context of messages sent by telex machines, and we must consider the approach which should be taken to an offer and acceptance made using email or the web. It should be noted that, 'except when agreed otherwise by the parties who are not consumers' and prior to an order being placed, Art 10 of the EC Electronic Commerce Directive provides that the service provider must specify, *inter alia*, 'the different technical steps to follow to conclude the contract'.[110] That requirement does not apply in the context of 'contracts concluded exclusively by exchange of electronic mail or by equivalent individual communication',[111] but, where it is required, or occurs, in specifying the 'technical steps', there may also be an express or implied specification of what is to amount to an offer and an acceptance. However, in the absence of some specification of what is to amount to an acceptance, the question remains to be asked as to whether the normal rule or the postal rule should apply. Some guidance on this may be found in considering the line taken by the courts in relation to acceptance sent by telex.

Entores Ltd v Miles Far Eastern Corp
[1955] 2 QB 326

The plaintiffs, in London, made an offer by telex to the agents of the defendant corporation, in Holland. This was accepted by a telex which was received on the plaintiff's telex machine in London. The relevant issue was whether the contract was made in England. If it was, that would provide a basis for the plaintiffs to serve a writ on the defendant corporation outside of the jurisdiction. The court held that the contract was made in London.

Denning LJ   When a contract is made by post it is clear law throughout the common law countries that the acceptance is complete as soon as the letter is put into the post box, and that is the place where the contract is made. But there is no clear rule about contract made by telephone or by Telex. Communications by those means are virtually instantaneous and stand on a different footing.

The problem can only be solved by going in stages. Let me first consider the case where two people make a contract by word of mouth in the presence of one another. Suppose for instance that I shout an offer to a man across a river or a courtyard but I do not hear his reply because it is drowned by an aircraft flying overhead. There is no contract at that moment. If he wishes to make a contract, he must wait till the aircraft is gone and then shout back his acceptance so that I can hear what he says. Not until I have his answer am I bound ...

Now take the case where two people make a contract by telephone. Suppose, for instance, that I make an offer to a man by telephone and, in the middle of his reply, the line goes 'dead' so that I do not hear his words of acceptance. There is no contract at that moment. The other man may not know the precise moment when the line failed. But he will know that the telephone conversation was abruptly broken off: because people usually say something to signify the end of the conversation. If he wishes to make a contract he must therefore get through again to make sure that I heard. Suppose next, that the line does not go dead, but is nevertheless so indistinct

109 *Holwell Securities v Hughes* [1974] 1 All ER 161.
110 Article 10(1). See Reg 11(1).
111 Article 10(4). See Reg 11.

that I do not catch what he says and I ask him to repeat it. He then repeats it and I hear his acceptance. The contract is made, not on the first time when I do not hear, but only on the second when I do hear. If he does not repeat it there is no contract. The contract is only complete when I have his answer accepting the offer.

Lastly, take the Telex. Suppose a clerk in a London Office taps out on the teleprinter an offer which is immediately recorded on a teleprinter in a Manchester office, and a clerk at that end taps out an acceptance. If the line goes dead in the middle of the sentence of acceptance, the teleprinter motor will stop. There is then obviously no contract. The clerk at Manchester must get through again and send his complete sentence. But it may happen that the line does not go dead, yet the message does not get through to London. Thus the clerk at Manchester may tap out his acceptance and it will not be recorded in London because the ink at the London end fails or something of that kind. In that case, the Manchester clerk will not know of the failure but the London clerk will know of it and will immediately send back a message – 'not receiving'. Then, when the fault is rectified, the Manchester clerk will repeat his message. Only then is there a contract. If he does not repeat it there is no contract. It is not until the message is received that the contract is complete.

In all the instances I have taken so far, the man who sends the message of acceptance knows that it has not been received or he has reason to know it. So he must repeat it. But, suppose he did not know that his message did not get home. He thinks it has. This may happen if the listener on the phone does not catch the words of acceptance, but nevertheless does not trouble to ask for them to be repeated: or the ink on the teleprinter fails at the receiving end, but the clerk does not ask for the message to be repeated: so that man who sends an acceptance reasonably believes an acceptance has been received. The offeror in such circumstances is clearly bound, because he will be stopped from saying that he did not receive the message of acceptance. It is his own fault that he did not get it. But if there should be a case where the offeror without any fault on his part does not receive the message of acceptance – yet the sender of it reasonably believes it has got home when it has not – then I think there is no contract.

My conclusion is that the rule about instantaneous communication between the parties is different from the rule about the post. The contract is only complete when the acceptance is received by the offeror: and the contract is made at the place where the acceptance is received.

Brinkibon Ltd v Stahag Stahl und Stahlwarenhandelgesellschaft mbH
[1982] 1 All ER 293

The parties negotiated the sale of a quantity of steel bars. The buyers, an English company, accepted by telex sent from London to Vienna. The relevant question was whether the contract was made in England, allowing service out of the jurisdiction. The court held that the contract was made in Vienna.

Lord Wilberforce In this situation, with a general rule covering instantaneous communication *inter praesentes* or at a distance, with an exception applying to non-instantaneous communication at a distance, how should communication by telex be categorised? In *Entores Ltd v Miles Far Eastern Corp* the Court of Appeal classified them with instantaneous communications. Their ruling, which has passed into the textbooks ... appears not to have caused either adverse comment, or any difficulty to businessmen. I would accept it as a general rule.

Since 1955 the use of Telex communication has been greatly expanded, and there are many variations on it. The senders and the recipients may not be the principals to the contemplated contract. They may be servants or agents with limited authority. The message may not reach, or be intended to reach, the designated recipient immediately: messages may be sent out of office hours, or at night, with the intention, or on the assumption, that they will be read at a later time. There may be some error or default at the recipient's end which prevents receipt at the time contemplated and believed in by the sender. The message may have been sent and/or received through machines operated by third persons. And many other variations may occur. No universal rule can cover all such cases, they must be resolved by reference to the intentions of the parties, by sound business practice, and in some cases by a judgment where the risk should lie ...

Lord Fraser   I wish only to add a comment on the subject of *where* a contract is made when it is accepted by telex between parties in different countries. The question is whether acceptance by telex falls within the general rule that it requires to be notified to the offeror in order to be binding, or within the exception of the postal rule whereby it becomes binding when (and where) it is handed over to the Post Office. The postal rule is based on considerations of practical convenience, arising from the delay that is inevitable in delivering a letter. But it has been extended to apply to telegrams sent through the Post Office, and in strict logic there is much to be said for applying it also to telex messages sent by one business firm directly to another. There is very little, if any, difference in the mechanics of transmission between a private telex from one business to another and a telegram sent through the Post Office, especially one sent from one large city to another. Even the element of delay will not be greatly different where the operator of the recipient's telex is a clerk with no authority to conclude contracts, who has to hand it to his principal. In such a case a telex message is not in fact received instantaneously by the responsible principal. I assume that the present case is a case of that sort.

Nevertheless, I have reached the opinion that, on balance, an acceptance sent by telex directly from the acceptor's office should be treated as if it were an instantaneous communication between the principals, like a telephone conversation. One reason is that the decision to that effect in *Entores v Miles* seems to have worked without leading to serious difficulty or complaint from the business community. Secondly, once the message has been received on the offeror's telex machine, it is not unreasonable to treat it as delivered to the principal offeror, because it is his responsibility to arrange for the prompt handling of messages within his own office. Thirdly, a party (the acceptor) who tries to send a message by telex can generally tell if his message has been received on the other party's (the offeror's) machine, whereas the offeror, of course, will not know if an unsuccessful attempt has been made to send an acceptance to him. It is therefore convenient that the acceptor, being in the better position, should have the responsibility for ensuring that his message is received. For these reasons, I think that it is right in the ordinary simple case, such as I take this to be, the general rule and not the postal rule should apply. But I agree ... that the general rule will not cover all the many variations that may occur in telex messages.

In asking the question whether the normal rule – requiring acceptance to be received – or the postal rule should apply, it is common to focus on whether the method of communication was 'instantaneous'. This has become the point which is commonly emphasised from the above cases. However, it can be argued that such a focus is misconceived. In *Entores*, Denning LJ's survey of the problem primarily dealt with situations in which one party should have known that a message had not arrived. Under those circumstances, the answer as to whether or not there has been an effective acceptance seems self-evident. It is obvious, for example, that there should not have been an effective acceptance if the acceptor knew, or should have known, that his or her message had not arrived on the offeror's telex. The more difficult situation is where the message is not received on the offeror's machine and neither party is at fault, or should have known that it had not arrived. In that situation, what is required is a rule which allocates the risk that the message will not be received without either party having been in a position to know of that non-arrival, or being at fault in the non-arrival. In effect, Denning LJ chose the normal rule, rather than the postal rule, to allocate that risk. This will be returned to below.

In any event, acceptance telexes are generally only effective once received, but a brief clarificatory point should be made. In *Brinkibon*, Lord Fraser suggests that receipt of a telex should be taken to occur when it arrives on the offeror's machine, 'as it is his responsibility to arrange for the prompt handling of messages in his own office'. It would seem to be a commercially acceptable practice, and in keeping with the generally objective approach to contract, that the telex should be taken to have been received when it is printed on the telex of the offeror, rather than requiring the offeror actually to read it. However, a qualification should be placed on this where a telex arrives on the offeror's machine outside of normal office hours. In that case, the better approach would seem to be that a message which arrives on the machine outside of office hours should only be effective once office hours have resumed.[112]

Against the above background, consideration should now be given to acceptance by email and on the web. The first situation to consider is where the parties are communicating by email. There are obvious analogies to be made with the situation in which the postal rule is applied. Although at first sight email might look like an 'instantaneous' method of communication, it soon becomes clear to users that that is not the case. There may be a delay of hours, or even days, before a message arrives. However, the point was made above that the question of whether a communication is 'instantaneous' was not the real question being asked in deciding if the postal rule should be applied. Before that is addressed further, brief consideration should be given to another traditional contention made in relation to the postal rule. The point has been made that the postal rule applies to allocate risk where the message is entrusted to a third party and that, therefore, the question of its application, or otherwise, in the context of email should be dependent upon the 'communication topography', that is, whether the communication is seen as simply between two computers, as in the case of simple email between two computers linked to the internet, or communications via a common server, as with email sent through an online service provider to someone else using the same service (involving one third party) or via several servers.[113] The appropriateness of these categorisations could be contested.[114] However, it has been noted that, although the early case law on the postal rule placed some emphasis on the role of the post office as 'agent' – explaining the effectiveness of acceptance on posting on the basis that the post office was the offeror's agent to receive the communication of acceptance – the myth is not a current one (clearly, the Post Office is not empowered to receive the content of a communication on anyone's behalf).[115] The analogy does not provide a basis for determining the point of effectiveness of an emailed

112 In *Mondial Shipping and Chartering BV v Astarte Shipping Ltd* [1995] CLC 1011, Gatehouse J took this approach to the question of when a notice of withdrawal of a ship became effective. For discussion of the case see Haslam, 1996.
113 Davies, in Edwards, and Waelde, (eds), 1997.
114 Downing and Harrington, 2000.
115 *Ibid.*

communication as an acceptance, that is, for making that determination dependent upon the 'communication topography' and whether one or more third parties were significantly involved in 'conveying' the communication. In addition, the point can be made that an approach which is dependent upon the communication topography is simply impractical. Most parties would not be aware of the 'communication topography' being used. Even commercial parties may often operate on the basis of relative ignorance of the legal background to their transactions, and the need for technological awareness should not be added to the difficulties they face when wishing to determine the legal impact of their communications.

However, if neither of the usual points raised in relation to the scope of application of the postal rule is very helpful, what must be considered is risk allocation. It can be contended that there are basically two issues to consider. First, whether the acceptor or offeror is more likely to have been at fault if an acceptance is delayed or does not arrive. Secondly, if there is no fault involved, who should bear the risk of the acceptance being lost or delayed. Each of these issues should be explained and considered in turn.

As has already been indicated, much of Denning's discussion in *Entores* is concerned with the situation in which one party is at fault in the message not being received, and in such situations, it is obvious which party should bear the risk of acceptance being lost or delayed. However, it would make the rule cumbersome in its application if it relied too heavily on identifying fault and that issue is less likely to arise if the rule which operates without proof of fault allocates the risk to the party most likely to be at fault. It is contended that this is really what Denning's discussion of the nature of the communication as instantaneous is about. It is about, in effect, identifying the sender of the message as the person most likely to be at fault in its delay or loss and so as indicating the postal rule as inappropriate. With face to face communication, it is very unlikely that there will be a lack of communication of which both parties are not aware but certainly the speaker should be. As one moves away from that face to face communication, through communication over the phone and by fax, the risk increases that a communication will not be received and also that that may occur without it being realised, but the acceptor who 'sends' the message is arguably the person most likely to realise it has been delayed or lost. Relevant to that, is the factor of how close to truly instantaneous the method of communication is, but as was indicated in *Brinkibon* the notion of 'instantaneous' was a very artificial one when applied to a telex. Nevertheless, once the question which should be asked is identified, it can be seen why the issue of whether or not the communication was instantaneous was arrived at. It was, in effect, a substitute for the first question identified here, and was also intuitively persuasive of the way in which it should be answered, that is, once a communication could be classified as 'instantaneous', no matter how artificial the classification, intuitively it pointed to the person making the communication as the one most likely to know if it had not arrived and, more generally, to be at fault in it not arriving. In the context of telex, once it was labelled as an instantaneous form of communication, the perception of probability pointed towards the acceptor being more likely to be at fault and so towards the acceptor bearing the risk of the delay of loss of the acceptance, that is, it pointed towards the postal rule not being applied.

The second question deals with the issue of where the risk of delay or loss of the acceptance should lie when there is no fault. This can be put in a slightly expanded form, that is, the question is whether the offeror should be assigned the risk of being contractually bound without their knowledge, or a reasonable opportunity of becoming aware of it, or whether the acceptor, should, without their knowledge, or a reasonable opportunity of becoming aware of it, find themselves not in a contractual relationship when they thought they were. It is contended that, once put in this expanded form, the answer to where the loss should lie is plain. It is better that someone be at risk of not being in a contract when they thought they were, than that someone should be at risk of being subject to obligations they are unaware of. In other words, the simple question of where the loss should lie when there is no fault, points away from the application of the postal rule.

What then of the possible application of the postal rule in the e-commerce context? The answer to the second question indicates against its application. What of the first? Even if the first pointed towards the postal rule being applied, what would be in issue would then be the relative strength of the competing pulls and it is contended that the pull of the answer to the second question should prevail. Where fault is established, the risk will follow it, the first question is there merely to limit the number of occasions on which fault will be raised. However, it is contended that the perception is likely to be that the sender of the message is more likely to be at fault in its loss or delay and it is likely to be that perception, rather than any actual statistical likelihood which would determine the approach to the first question. If that is so, then both questions would pull towards the non-application of the postal rule in relation to email.

As was indicated above in relation to telex communication, the courts did not favour extension of the postal rule and, whatever the analysis used, it would seem that it is unlikely to be revived in the context of email and, if it is not, then the emailed acceptance will only be effective once received. Of course, that raises the issue of what amounts to 'receipt'. 'Is receipt when the acceptance arrives at the offeror's mail server, when it is downloaded onto the computer, or when the offeror reads it?'[116] The generally objective nature of contract law should prevent any claim that actual communication is required, and we have seen that, in the context of telex communication, all that was required was arrival on the offeror's machine (see above p 279). That was, of course, qualified if a telex arrived outside of office hours, but the timing of receipt was only then delayed until the recommencement of office hours. However, is arrival on the offeror's mail server sufficient, or does it have to be downloaded to the offeror's machine? It has been contended that it is the point of downloading from server that is the relevant moment.[117] However, in *Brinkibon* (above p 278) Lord Fraser viewed arrival at the telex machine as sufficient because it was the offeror's 'responsibility to arrange for the prompt handling of messages in his own office' and an analogy could be made with the arrival of the message at the offeror's

---

116 Chissick and Kelman, 2000, para 3.43.

117 *Ibid*, para 3.45. The suggestion has been made that it is dependent upon the offeror's control; ie, if the offeror uses an internet service provider, there is no receipt of acceptance until it is downloaded, as it is, until that moment, still 'in transit'. But, if the offeror operates his or her own mail server, acceptance would have been received when it arrived at that server, the 'transit' of the message then being complete.

server. In addition, Art 11 of the EC Directive on E-Commerce[118] provides for an 'order' and an 'acknowledgment of receipt' of the order and that:

> ... an order and the acknowledgment of receipt are deemed to be received when the parties to whom they are addressed are able to access them.

This could be seen as indicating that it is sufficient when the communications arrive on the server of the offeree, although the point can be made that it is at that point that the offeree can *normally* access them – who has not, at times had problems connecting with their server to collect their e-mail. However, even if a contract is concluded when the acceptance arrives at the mail server used by the offeree, the contract should not be taken as concluded where the relevant mail server is located. That location may well be in a country which is otherwise unconnected with the parties or the contract. The contract should be taken as concluded at the location of the offeror's computer. This avoids potentially arbitrary places of contracting. It can be seen as not out of keeping with Art 11, above, with its reference to the ability of the parties to access the orders and acknowledgments. It merely requires an emphasis upon the place from which acceptances can be accessed, rather their arbitrary, intermediate location, and, under Art 15(4) of the UNCITRAL Model Law, 'unless otherwise agreed between the originator and addressee, a data message ... is deemed to be received where the addressee has its place of business'. Of course, there is no difficulty with this if the point in time at which acceptance occurs is when it is downloaded to the offeror's computer form the server. In those circumstances, plainly it would be the location of the offeror's computer which would be the place of contracting.

Some brief consideration should also be given to the situation where the parties are contracting via the web. The suggestion has been made that:[119]

> The world wide web exhibits the features of a method of instantaneous communication (interactive and real-time), the sender has almost immediate feedback, and errors or faults are readily apparent. As a result the receipt rule will probably apply to web contracts.

The point was made above that the question as to whether communication is 'instantaneous' should not be perceived as the basis of the application or non-application of the postal rule. What should be emphasised here is that the receipt rule was contended for above, in the context of email, and any arguments against the receipt rule are even weaker in this context. (Email, at least, has some superficial similarity to ordinary mail.)

Law governing formation

The above discussion deals with the question of what approach English law will take to when and where an electronic contract will be taken to have been made. In relation to contracts involving communications between different countries, logically, the first

---

118 See above, p 275 *et seq*. And see reg 13(2) Electronic Commerce (EC Directive) Regulations 2002.
119 Chissick and Kelman, 2004, para 3.47.

question to ask is which country's law governs that issue (the conflicts question). Under the Rome Convention (see p 263) many contractual issues are referred to the 'applicable law' (see p 266). However, issues of material validity, such as whether there has been an effective offer and acceptance, are dealt with by Art 8. This states:

(1) The existence and validity of a contract, or of any term of a contract, shall be determined by the law which would govern under this Convention if the contract or term were valid.

(2) Nevertheless a party may rely upon the country in which he has his habitual residence to establish that he did not consent if it appears from the circumstances that it would not be reasonable to determine the effect of his conduct in accordance with the law specified in the preceding paragraph.

Article 8 generally refers such issues to the law which would govern if the contract were valid – the putative applicable law.[120] Additionally, Art 8(2) provides an exception which may be used to find that there is no binding contract. A party may rely upon the law of his habitual residence to show that he did not consent if 'it would not be reasonable to determine the effect of his conduct' by the putative applicable law. The general rule is illustrated, in the context of posted communication, by an example given by Clarkson and Hill:[121]

> Suppose a Swiss seller sends by post an offer to sell goods to an English buyer, who posts back an acceptance which is lost in the post. By English law there is a contract, because acceptance is effective on posting; by Swiss law there is no contract, because acceptance is effective only on receipt. Which law is to decide whether a contract was made? The putative applicable law approach adopted by the Convention requires the court to determine which law would be the applicable law on the assumption that a contract was made.

Under such circumstances, if there was no choice of law by the parties, the putative proper law would be determined under Art 4 on the basis of the country with which the contract, if it existed, would be most closely connected.[122] There is a presumption in Art 4(2) in favour of the country which is appropriately connected with the party who is to render the performance which is 'characteristic of the contract'. In this case, that will be the Swiss seller (the English buyer's performance being merely the payment of money) and, assuming that the seller entered into the contract in the course of his trade or business, the appropriate connection will be to his 'principal place of business'.[123] So, unless the presumption is rebutted on the basis that 'it appears from the circumstances as a whole that the contract is more closely connected with another country',[124] the alleged contract is governed by Swiss law and, therefore, does not exist.[125]

---

120 The material validity of a choice of law clause is referred to the law which would govern if the clause was valid – see Art 3(4).
121 Clarkson and Hill, 1997, p 229.
122 Assuming that the buyer is not a consumer – see above, p 269.
123 Article 4(2).
124 Article 4(5).
125 Clarkson and Hill, 1997, p 229.

Formalities

Making a contract may involve formalities; for example, it may be required to be in writing. Requirements such as a signature or writing may provide obstacles to efficient electronic contracting. Formalities are considered below in the context of requirements such as writing and signature more generally (see below).

WRITING, SIGNATURE, ETC

Introduction

On occasion, there are legal requirements that information be conveyed in a certain way, such as 'in writing' or by a 'document' (so that a paper-based communication might be seen as necessary), or that the information be authenticated by 'signature'. These types of requirements have been perceived as barriers to efficient e-commerce. As the Guide to the Enactment of the UNCITRAL Model Law on Electronic Commerce states:

> 2   ... The communication of legally significant information in the form of paperless messages may be hindered by legal obstacles to the use of such messages, or by uncertainty as to their legal effect or validity ...
>
> 3   ... in a number of countries, the existing legislation governing communication and storage of information is inadequate or outdated because it does not contemplate the use of electronic commerce. In certain cases, existing legislation imposes or implies restrictions on the use of modern means of communication, for example, by prescribing the use of 'written', 'signed' or 'original' documents.

English law has few requirements of form in relation to the making of contracts, but 'legally significant information' extends far beyond the contract as such. Requirements exist for a great variety of 'documents' and 'notices', and also for record keeping. In considering the legislative references to such requirements, a basic principle has gained widespread acceptance, even if there is not the same level of similarity of approach to its implementation. The UNCITRAL Model Law, for example, has as one of its objectives the provision of 'equal treatment to users of paper-based documentation and electronic information'[126] and this idea of such 'equal treatment' has also been expressed as one of 'functional equivalence', or 'technology neutrality'.[127] The steps being taken in the UK to deal with this issue in the Electronic Communications Act 2000 will be dealt with below, as will the need for UK law to

---

126 Guide to the Enactment of the UNCITRAL Model Law on Electronic Commerce, 1996, para 6.
127 DTI, 1999a, para 16: '... ensuring that, as far as possible, the law does not discriminate between traditional and electronic ways of doing business, ie, that the law should be technology neutral in its application.' It should be noted, however, that the terminology 'technology neutrality' has been given a different meaning elsewhere. In the Summary of the (Australian) Electronic Transactions Act 1999, para 4, it is stated that 'Technology neutrality means that the law should not discriminate between different forms of technology – eg, by specifying technical requirements for the use of electronic communications that are based upon an understanding of the operation of a particular form of electronic communication technology'. It has also been used in this sense in the UK, eg, DTI, 1999b, para 32.

comply with the EC measures in this area. 'Writing' and related issues will be considered before 'signature' is addressed.

Writing, documents and notices

Initial consideration will be given to the situation in which references to, for example, 'writing', a 'document' or 'notice' might be seen as requiring a paper-based communication. English law frequently makes reference in statutes and regulations to 'writing' or communications in 'written' form, for example, and in most cases the individual pieces of legislation do not define such terminology. There is, however, a definition in the Interpretation Act 1978 which defines 'writing' as including:

> ... typing, printing, lythography, photography and other modes of representing or reproducing words in a visible form ...

It has been contended that this definition, 'by placing emphasis on visibility, rules out electronic "writing", which is, in essence, a series of electronic impulses'.[128] In contrast, it has been argued that 'visibility' on the computer screen is sufficient,[129] even though it is the non-visible electronic charges by which the information is transmitted and recorded.[130] The Law Commission takes the view that in general email communications and web based communications will satisfy a requirement of writing because of their dual form, that is, 'first their display on a screen; secondly, their transmitted/stored form as files of binary (digital) information'. On that basis, whilst the 'latter alone cannot satisfy the Interpretation Act definition', they regard the visibility on a computer screen as sufficient to do so.[131] Their further conclusion from this approach is that EDI messages will not generally fulfil any requirement of writing.

> The aim of EDI is to improve business efficiency. One way in which this is achieved by an EDI system is to remove (or reduce) the need for human involvement in business transactions. EDI messages are exchanged between computers according to their programming. It is not intended that the EDI message itself should be read by any person. The EDI message is not therefore in a form (or intended to be in a form) in which it can be read (other than by another computer system operating to the same EDI protocol). Because the parties are not able to view the EDI message, the interpretation Act requirement of visibility will not be satisfied and such a message will not, in our view, be capable of satisfying a statutory requirement of writing.[132]

In relation to requirements for a 'document', it can be argued that they can generally be fulfilled electronically by information in a digital form 'because the essential feature

---

128 DTI, 1999a. See, also, Lloyd, 1997, p 139.
129 Eg, Bainbridge, 2000, p 266; Arden 1999, p 1686.
130 In addition, it can be suggested that perception of the need for separate treatment of 'electronic impulses' may gain strength from the transitory nature of the visible production of the electronic pulses on a computer screen. Note the UNCITRAL Model Law, Art 6(1), with its references to accessibility for future reference: 'Where the law requires information to be in writing, that requirement is met by a data message if the information contained therein is accessible so as to be usable for future reference.'
131 Law Commission, 2001, para 3.8.
132 *Ibid*, paras 3.19–3.20.

of a document is that it conveys information'.[133] However, in some cases, the focus may be on the medium of storage of the information – the physical 'document' – rather than the information as such, and an electronic communication might not then be found to be appropriate.[134]

So, whilst it may be contended that many requirements of form can be met by electronic communications, there will be some specific legislative requirements which it will not be possible to meet in this way. In addition, even uncertainty as to the legal effectiveness of an electronic communication provides a barrier to efficient e-commerce. Section 8 of the Electronic Communications Act 2000 provides a means of dealing with such requirements and uncertainties:

8   (1) Subject to subsection (3), the appropriate Minister may by order made by statutory instrument modify the provisions of –

(a) any enactment or subordinate legislation; or

(b) any scheme, licence, authorisation or approval issued, granted or given by or under any enactment or subordinate legislation,

in such manner as he may think fit for the purpose of authorising or facilitating the use of electronic communications or electronic storage (instead of other forms of communication or storage) for any purpose mentioned in subsection (2).

(2) Those purposes are –

(a) the doing of anything which under any such provisions is required to be or may be done or evidenced in writing or otherwise using a document notice or instrument;

(b) the doing of anything which under any such provisions is required to be or may be done by post or other specified means of delivery;

(c) the doing of anything which under any such provisions is required to be or may be authorised by a person's signature or seal, or is required to be delivered as a deed or witnessed;

(d) the making of any statement or declaration which under any such provision is required to be made under oath or to be contained in a statutory declaration;

(e) the keeping, maintenance or preservation, for the purposes or in pursuance of any such provisions, of any account, record, notice instrument or other document;

(f) the provision, production or publication under any such provisions of any information or other matter;

(g) the making of any payment that is required to be or may be made under any such provisions.

(3) The appropriate Minister shall not make an order under this section authorising the use of electronic communications or electronic storage for any purpose unless he considers that the authorisation is such that the extent (if any) to which records of things done for that purpose will be available will be no less satisfactory in cases where use is made of electronic communications or electronic storage than in other cases.

133 Reed, 1996, p 288.
134 *Ibid*, pp 285–89.

(4) Without prejudice to the generality of subsection (1), the power to make an order under this subsection shall include power to make an order containing any of the following provisions –

(a) provision as to the electronic form to be taken by any electronic communications or electronic storage the use of which is authorised by an order under this section;

(b) provision imposing conditions subject to which the use of electronic communications or electronic storage is so authorised;

(c) provision, in relation to cases in which any such conditions are not satisfied for treating anything for the purposes of which the use of such communications or storage is so authorised as not having been done;

(d) provision, in connection with anything so authorised, for a person to be able to refuse to accept receipt of something in electronic form except in such circumstances as may be specified in or determined under the order;

(e) provision in connection with any use of electronic communications so authorised for intermediaries to be used, or to be capable of being used, for the transmission of any data or for establishing the authenticity or integrity of any data;

(f) provision in connection with any use of electronic storage so authorised, for persons satisfying such conditions as may be specified in or determined under the regulations to carry out functions in relation to the storage;

(g) provision, in relation to cases in which the use of electronic communications or storage is so authorised, for the determination of any of the matters mentioned in subsection (5), or as to the manner in which they may be proved in legal proceedings;

(h) provision, in relation to cases in which fees or charges are or may be imposed in connection with anything for the purposes of which the use of electronic communications or electronic storage is so authorised, for different fees or charges to apply where use is made of such communications or storage;

(i) provision, in relation to any criminal or other liabilities that may arise (in respect of the making of false or misleading statements or otherwise) in connection with anything for the purposes of which the use of electronic communications or electronic storage is so authorised, for corresponding liabilities to arise in corresponding circumstances where use is made of such communications or storage;

(j) provision requiring persons to prepare and keep records in connection with the use of electronic communications or storage which is so authorised;

(k) provision requiring the production of the contents of any records kept in accordance with an order under this section;

(l) provision for a requirement imposed by virtue of paragraph (j) or (k) to be enforceable at the suit or instance of such persons as may be specified in or determined in accordance with the order;

(m) any such provision in relation to electronic communications or electronic storage the use of which is authorised otherwise than by an order under this section as corresponds to any provision falling within any of the preceding paragraphs that may be made where it is such an order that authorises the use of the communications or storage.

(5) The matters referred to in subsection 4(g) are –

(a) whether a thing has been done using an electronic communication or electronic storage;

     (b) the time at which or the date on which a thing done using any such communication or storage was done;

     (c) the person by whom such a thing was done; and

     (d) the contents authenticity or integrity of any electronic data

(6) An order under this section –

     (a) shall not (subject to paragraph (b)) require the use of any electronic communications or electronic storage for any purpose; but

     (b) may make provision that a period of notice specified in the order must expire before effect is given to a variation or withdrawal of election or other decision which –

          (i) has been made for the purposes of such an order; and

          (ii) is an election or decision to make use of electronic communications or electronic storage.

(7) The matters in relation to which provision may be made by an order under this section do not include any matter under the care and management of the Commissioners of Inland Revenue or any matter under the care and management of the Commissioners of Customs and Excise.

(8) In this section references to doing anything under the provisions of any enactment include references to doing it under the provisions of any subordinate legislation the power to make which is conferred by that enactment.

Section 8 of the Electronic Communications Act 2000 does not, in itself, amend any provision, but allows the 'appropriate Minister'[135] to do so by means of statutory instruments 'for the purpose of authorising or facilitating the use of electronic communications or electronic storage for any purpose mentioned in subsection (2)'. Subsection (2) is broadly drafted to deal with many situations where legislative references might be seen as requiring, or allowing, paper-based communication or record keeping. It has references not only to 'writing', 'document', 'notice' and 'instrument', but also to related situations, such as where there is a requirement that information be posted (para (b)) or for the 'provision, production or publication' of information (para (f)). Subsection (4) makes it clear that the statutory instruments do not simply have to provide for a blanket conversion of such paper-based references. The statutory instruments may impose certain conditions on the use of the electronic medium. For example, under para (a), conditions may be imposed as to the form of electronic communication or storage to be used and, likewise, under para (j), as to record keeping. In addition, under para (g) and subsection (5), the statutory instrument may provide for the determination of certain matters or the manner in which they may be proved in court: whether a thing has been done using electronic communication or storage; the time at which it was so done; the person by whom it was done; and the contents, authenticity and integrity of any electronic data.

    Section 8(3) makes it clear that 'the appropriate Minister' cannot make an order under s 8 unless sure that the availability of records will be no less satisfactory when electronic communications or storage is used than in other cases. This can be contrasted with the UNCITRAL Model Law, where the substitution of a 'data message'

---

135 As defined in s 9.

for the more traditional 'writing' is dependent upon the 'accessibility' of the information so as to be 'usable for subsequent reference'. Article 6(1) states:

> Where the law requires information to be in writing, that requirement is met by a data message if the information contained therein is accessible so as to be usable for future reference.

This was criticised as 'introducing a new requirement that [electronic] communications wishing to be regarded as writing must be retained', which, desirable as it may be evidentially, is not a 'pre-requisite for the validity of a contract constituted in ordinary "hard copy"'.[136] Section 8(3) is not stated as an absolute requirement, but is relative to the situation in relation to 'hard copy'.

It is made clear in s 8(6) that, even when an order has been made under the section allowing for the use of electronic communications, it will not generally require it. However, if an election has been made to use electronic communication or storage, provision can be made for a period of notice to expire before such electronic means cease to be used.[137]

The general approach taken in s 8 is worthy of some consideration. As has been indicated, it does not itself make any necessary changes in the law – it merely allows for them to be made by statutory instrument. This means that many further decisions have to be made in 'updating of the law to reflect what is technologically possible'.[138] Consideration should be given to the factors affecting the appropriateness of the amendment of any particular piece of legislation.

In determining the appropriateness of enabling the replacement of paper-based communication by electronic means, the function of the paper-based communication should be considered. Addressing that issue may indicate that permitting electronic communication would be inappropriate or should only be permitted when certain conditions are complied with. Formalities in the contracting process may be required for a number of reasons,[139] for example, promoting certainty through requiring clear evidence of the terms, encouraging the parties to fully consider the legal obligations being undertaken or to provide protection to the person in the weaker bargaining position.[140]

The relevance of the function of paper-based communications is illustrated by the Guide to the Enactment of the UNCITRAL Model Law on Electronic Commerce. In considering this, it should be remembered that s 8 of the Electronic Communications Act 2000 is wide ranging, encompassing what are identified in the Model Law as different levels of paper-based communication by the references merely to 'writing' or

136 Lloyd, 1997, p 139.
137 Section 8(6)(b).
138 DTI, 1999a, para 3.
139 Fuller (1941); Law Com, 1987, No 164.
140 Eg, the requirements of the Consumer Credit Act 1974.

'documents' (Art 6) or to 'originals' (Art 8).[141] The power, in s 8, to impose conditions on the use of electronic communications should also be borne in mind:

48   In the preparation of the Model Law, particular attention was paid to the functions traditionally performed by the various kinds of 'writings' in a paper-based environment. For example, the following non-exhaustive list indicates reasons why national laws require the use of 'writings': (1) to ensure that there would be tangible evidence of the existence and nature of the intent of the parties to bind themselves; (2) to help the parties be aware of the consequences of their entering into a contract; (3) to provide that a document would be legible at all; (4) to provide that a document would remain unaltered over time and provide a permanent record of a transaction; (5) to allow for the reproduction of a document so that each party would hold a copy of the same data; (6) to allow for the authentication of data by means of a signature; (7) to provide that a document would be in a form acceptable to public authorities and courts; (8) to finalise the intent of the author of the 'writing' and provide a record of that intent; (9) to allow for the easy storage of data in a tangible form; (10) to facilitate control and subsequent audit for accounting, tax or regulatory purposes; and (11) to bring legal rights and obligations into existence in those cases where a writing was required for validity purposes.

49   However, in the preparation of the Model Law, it was found that it would be inappropriate to adopt an overly comprehensive notion of the functions performed by writing. Existing requirements that data be presented in written form often combine the requirement of a 'writing' with concepts distinct from writing, such as signature and original. Thus when adopting a functional approach attention should be given to the fact that the requirement of a writing should be considered as the lowest layer in a hierarchy of form requirements which provide distinct level of reliability, traceability and unalterability with respect to paper documents. The requirement that data be presented in written form (which can be described as a 'threshold requirement') should thus not be confused with more stringent requirements such as 'signed writing', 'signed original' or 'authenticated legal act' ... In general notions such as 'evidence' and 'intent of the parties to bind themselves' are to be tied to more general issues of reliability and authentication of data and should not be included in a definition of a 'writing'.

50   The purpose of Article 6 is not to establish a requirement that, in all instances, data messages should fulfil all conceivable functions of a writing ... Article 6 focuses on the basic notion of information being reproduced and read. That notion is expressed in

---

141 Article 8 states:

(1)   Where the law requires information to be presented or retained in its original form, that requirement is met by a data message if:

     (a)   there exists a reliable assurance as to the integrity of the information from the time when it was first generated in its final form, as a data message or otherwise; and

     (b)   where it is required that information be presented, that information is capable of being displayed to the person to whom it is to be presented ...

     For the purposes of subparagraph (a) of paragraph (1):

     (a)   the criteria for assessing integrity shall be whether the information has remained complete and unaltered apart from the addition of any endorsement and any change which arises in the normal course of communication, storage and display; and

     (b)   the standard of reliability required shall be assessed in the light of the purpose for which the information was generated and in the light of all the relevant circumstances ...

The use of cryptography to ensure the integrity of an electronic communication is considered below in relation to 'electronic signature' – see below, p 319.

Article 6 in terms that were found to provide an objective criterion, namely that the data message must be accessible so as to be usable for subsequent reference. The use of the word 'accessible' is meant to imply that information in the form of computer data should be retained. The word 'usable' is not intended to cover only human use but also computer processing. As to the notion of 'subsequent' reference, it was preferred to such notions as 'durability' or 'non-alterability', which would have established too harsh standards, and to such notions as 'readability' or 'intelligibility', which might constitute too subjective criteria ...

...

62 If original were defined as a medium on which information was fixed for the first time, it would be impossible to speak of 'original' data messages, since the addressee of a data message would always receive a copy thereof. However, Article 8 should be put in a different context. The notion of 'original' in Article 8 is useful since in practice many disputes relate to the question of originality of documents, and in electronic commerce the requirement of presentation of originals constitutes one of the main obstacles that the Model Law attempts to remove ...

63 Article 8 is pertinent to documents of title and negotiable instruments, in which the notion of uniqueness of an original is particularly relevant. However, attention is drawn to the fact that the Model Law is not intended only to apply to documents of title and negotiable instruments, or to such areas of law where special requirements exist with respect to registration or notarization of 'writings', eg family matters of real estate. Examples of documents that might require an 'original' are trade documents such as weight certificates, agricultural certificates, quality or quantity certificates, inspection reports, insurance certificates, etc. While such documents are not negotiable or used to transfer rights or title, it is essential that they be transmitted unchanged, that is in their 'original' form, so that other parties in international commerce may have confidence in their contents. In a paper-based environment, these documents are only accepted if they are 'original' to lessen the chance that they be altered, which would be difficult to detect in copies. Various technical means are available to certify the contents of a data message to confirm its 'originality' ...

...

65 Article 8 emphasises the importance of the integrity of the information for its originality and sets out criteria to be taken into account when assessing integrity by reference to systematic recording of the information, assurance that the information was recorded without lacunae and protection of the data against alteration. It links the concept of 'originality' to a method of authentication and puts the focus on the method of authentication to be followed in order to meet the requirement ...

The use of cryptography to ensure that an electronic communication has not been altered is considered below in relation to 'electronic signatures'.

As has been indicated, the approach taken in s 8 of the Electronic Communications Act 2000 means that further action is required to actually amend paper-based legislative references. The basic alternative would have been an '"opt out" approach, by means of a general validity law with a few specific exceptions to it (for example, transfers of land, wills, etc)'.[142] It is this latter type of approach which is adopted, within a limited ambit, by the EC Directive on Electronic Commerce. Article 9 states:

---

142 DTI, 1999b, para 17.

1   Member States shall ensure that their legal system allows contracts to be concluded by electronic means. Member States shall in particular ensure that the legal requirements applicable to the contractual process do not create obstacles for the use of electronic contracts or result in such contracts being deprived of legal effectiveness and validity on account of their having been made by electronic means.

2   Member States may lay down that paragraph 1 shall not apply to all or certain contracts falling into one of the following categories:

(a) contracts that create or transfer rights in real estate, except for rental rights;

(b) contracts requiring by law the involvement of the courts, public authorities or professions exercising public authority;

(c) contracts of suretyship granted and collateral securities furnished by persons acting for purposes outside their trade, business, or profession;

(d) contracts governed by family law or the law of succession.

3   Member States shall indicate to the Commission the categories referred to in paragraph 2 to which they do not apply paragraph 1. Member States shall submit to the Commission every five years a report on the application of paragraph 2 explaining the reasons why they consider it necessary to maintain the category referred to in paragraph 2(b) to which they do not apply paragraph 1.

It should be noted that this only relates to the making of contracts. As has been indicated, s 8 has a much wider scope, making it capable of encompassing communications and storage unrelated to contracting as such. Article 9 would obviously apply to requirements for contracts to be made in writing or evidenced in writing (or signed), but such requirements are limited to a few specific types of contract in English law. Of course, the reference in Art 9 to the 'contractual process' would makes it more widely applicable than simply in relation to the concluded contract, covering, for example, a requirement that a party be notified of specified information before a particular type of agreement can be effective as a contract. The Law Commission considered compliance with Art 9 and took the view that:

> Requirements that a contract (or any steps required to be taken under or in relation to a contract) be in writing, evidenced in writing, or signed, or signed are very rare in English Law.

> In those rare cases, except where the statutory context otherwise dictates, the form requirements are, in our view, capable of being satisfied by e-mails or website trading but not by EDI.[143]

Further, 'An order under s 8 may ... be used to deal with any statutory form requirements which conflict (or which may conflict) with Article 9'.[144] This will be returned to below p 296.

Signature

The previous section was headed 'writing, documents, notices' and dealt with those terms and related references in legislation which could provide a barrier to

---

143 Law Commission, 2001, para 3.48.
144 *Ibid*, para 3.55.

e-commerce. Similarly, references to 'signature' might provide such a barrier and, as we have seen (see p 292) in the context of 'legal requirements applicable to the contractual process', Art 9 of the Directive on E-Commerce requires that to be addressed. In addition, as with 'writing', there may be other, more administrative requirements when signature could provide a 'barrier'. Further, the positive facilitation of e-commerce, rather than the mere removal of 'barriers', means that consideration should be given more broadly to the role of the signature. The common law gives significance to signature in situations in which there is no requirement for it. This latter type of case can be exemplified by the situation in relation to the making of a contract which does not require any formalities but where signature is the simplest (and surest) method of establishing contractual agreement to standard terms (see p 103). These issues should be considered. First some general consideration will be given to 'electronic signatures' before the legislation is addressed.

A typed in version of a name, or an electronically stored facsimile of an individual's manuscript signature could be termed electronic signatures when added to an e-mail or other document. However, what should initially be explained here is the idea of an electronic signature which does not reproduce anything which looks like a manuscript or even typed signature. A functional equivalent of a signature can be produced cryptographically. This will be referred to here as a 'digital signature'. Cryptography can provide a form of electronic signature, serving the purposes of identifying the sender of a message (authenticating it) and also of ensuring that it has not been altered (ensuring its integrity).[145] One cryptographic method of dealing with the needs for authentication and integrity (and security) is through the use of two 'keys', as described in *Building Confidence in Electronic Commerce – A Consultation Document*:[146]

> One way of providing electronic signatures is to make use of what is known as *public key*, or *asymmetric, cryptography*. Public key cryptography uses two keys, also known as a *key pair*. (These keys are both large numbers with special mathematical properties.) When this technique is used for signatures, the *private key* (which as the term suggests is known only to its owner) is used to transform a data file, by scrambling the information contained in it. The transformed data is the electronic signature and can be checked against the original file using the *public key* of the person who signed it. Anyone with access to the public key (which might, for example, be available on a website) can check the signature, so verifying that it could only have been used by someone with access to the private key. If the only one with access to the *private key* is its owner, then the owner must have signed the message ... If a third party had altered the message, the fact they had done so would be easily detectable.

This describes one method of producing an electronic signature, but it should be borne in mind, in relation to both this technology and others in the area of e-commerce, that one aim of any relevant legislation will be 'technology neutrality', in the sense that it is not specific to the current technology but is flexible enough to deal with fresh technological advances. However, the point to be made here is that cryptography can

---

145 The further use of cryptography is to provide security for messages (ie, to keep them confidential to the relevant persons).
146 DTI, 1999.

produce something which could be regarded as an 'electronic signature' and it can provide both an authenticating and a security function.

However, having explained some forms of electronic signature, consideration should now be given to how they might be received by the courts, when statutory requirements of signature are in question. The meaning of 'signature' has been considered by the courts in the context of various statutes. In the absence of any definition, on the whole, a wide approach has been taken. In *Goodman v J Eban Ltd*,[147] the use of a rubber stamp that contained a facsimile of the firm's ordinary signature was held to be sufficient to comply with the requirement of signature in the Solicitors Act 1932.

Goodman v J Eban Ltd
[1954] 1 QB 550

Romer LJ   It is stated in Stroud's *Judicial Dictionary* (3rd edn) under the title 'Signed; signature' that 'speaking generally a signature is the writing or otherwise affixing, a person's name, or a mark to represent his name, by himself or by his authority with the intention of authenticating a document as being that of, or as binding on, the person whose name or mark is so written or affixed'. This statement appears to me to be in accordance with the authorities, and, in my opinion, Mr Goodman's letter was 'signed' within this formula. The letter was typewritten and concludes with the words (also typed) 'Yours faithfully Goodman, Monroe and Company'. This was immediately followed by a repetition of the firm name, in a form which at first sight looks as though it had been written by hand, but which in reality was impressed by Mr Goodman through the medium of a rubber stamp. This repetition would plainly be otiose were it merely intended to repeat the typed name of the firm; and the obvious intention of Mr Goodman was that it should be regarded as a signature for the purposes of authenticating the letter. If, in fact, his clients entertained any doubt as to the authenticity of the letter, nothing could be easier than to ask him, by telephone or letter, to confirm it. A manual signature is not necessary either for a will (which is at least as solemn a document as a solicitor's bill of costs) or to satisfy the Statute of Frauds; and provided that affixing of a name by a rubber stamp complies in other respects with the definition in Stroud to which I have already referred, I see no reason why it should not be sufficient for the purposes of s 65 of the Solicitors Act 1932 ...

Printing or typewriting the relevant name can also be sufficient, and this type of approach could be seen as encompassing a broad range of electronic signatures, in the absence of any contrary indication in the specific statute.[148] The Law Commission take the view 'the principal function of a signature is to indicate that the 'signatory' had an authenticating intention. What is required therefore is something which is not purely oral and which evidences that authenticating intention'.[149] On this basis, the Law Commission further conclude that generally a digital signature, using public key encryption and a certification authority, a scanned electronic manuscript signature, and the typing of a name, will all satisfy any requirement of signature. In addition, they considered the situation where website trading 'involves the purchaser entering onto the website details of the goods which they wish to purchase, confirming

---

147 [1954] 1 QB 550.
148 For further discussion see Reed, 1996, p 300.
149 Law Comm, 2000, para 3.28

payment and personal details, and clicking on a button to confirm the order'.[150] In relation to that type of communication, they took the view that:

> We do not believe that there is any doubt that clicking on a website button to confirm an order demonstrates the intent to enter into that contract. That will satisfy the principal function of a signature: namely demonstrating an authenticating intention. We suggest that the click can reasonably be regarded as the technological equivalent of a manuscript 'X' signature. In our view, clicking is therefore capable of satisfying a statutory signature requirement (in those rare cases in which such a requirement is imposed in the contract formation context).

However, barriers to efficient e-commerce are raised by uncertainty as to whether electronic communication can constitute 'writing', 'notice' or a 'document', and this point can similarly be made in relation to uncertainty as to the effectiveness of 'electronic signature'. Although the Law Commission concluded that 'the principal function of a signature is to indicate that the 'signatory' had an authenticating intention and therefore came to their broad view on the effectiveness of wide range of electronic signatures, the courts might decide that a particular statutory requirement of signature has further functions which cannot be so easily fulfilled. 'The courts may well consider that in some ... statutory contexts (for example contracts of guarantee under s 4 of the Statute of Frauds) either "writing" or "signature" should not be interpreted as broadly as the Law Commission generally propose, in the interests of the protection of the person to be bound thereby ... Article 9 of the Electronic Commerce Directive ... does allow a Member State to make an exception for contracts of suretyship but only where undertaken by persons "acting outside their trade business or profession".[151] The legislation in this area must now be considered.

As has been seen, s 8 of the Electronic Communications Act 2000 allows the 'appropriate Minister' to amend legislation by statutory instrument for 'purposes of facilitating the use of electronic communications' for any of the purposes 'mentioned in subsection (2)'. Included in subsection (2)(c) is the 'doing of anything which under any such provisions is required to be or may be authorised by a person's signature'.[152] This encompasses the possible amendment of legislative references to 'signature' in order to allow electronic communication to be used. The statutory instrument may contain 'provision ... for intermediaries to be used ... for establishing the authenticity or integrity of any data'.[153] Thus, it allows for provision to be made for third parties to provide certificates as to the authorship of an electronic signature or the integrity of the data[154] and the Electronic Signatures Regulations 2002 (SI 2002/318) provide for the

---

150 *Ibid*, para 3.36. For criticism of the approach see Macdonald and Poyton, 2005.

151 Beale (ed), 2004, para 4-006.

152 Subsection (2)(c) also encompasses deeds.

153 Section 8(4)(e).

154 In addition, s 8(4)(g) allows for the statutory instrument to provide for the 'determination of any of the matters mentioned in subsection (5)', which includes '(d) the contents, authenticity or integrity of any electronic data'. It should be noted, however, that s 14 provides that the Act does not confer any general power to require the deposit of a cryptographic 'key' with another person. Section 8 cannot be used to meet the problem of criminal activities being facilitated by encrypted communications by requiring the deposit of 'keys' for code breaking. Under s 14(2), the deposit of a key with the intended recipient of electronic communications can be required or there can be a requirement to otherwise prevent data from becoming inaccessible through the loss of a key or its becoming unusable. See, also, s 8(3).

supervision and liability of 'certification-service-providers'. *Inter alia*, Section 8 would seem to provide the means to fulfil the requirement of Art 9 of the Electronic Commerce Directive, where the statutory requirements are not simply found to be fulfilled by the wide band of electronic signatures suggested by the Law Commission.[155]

Section 7 of the Electronic Communications Act 2000 provides a basis for the broader recognition of the effective use of electronic signatures. It states:

(1) In any legal proceedings –

    (a) an electronic signature incorporated into or logically associated with a particular electronic communication or particular electronic data, and

    (b) the certification by any such person of such a signature,

shall each be admissible in evidence in relation to any question as to the authenticity of the communication or data as to the integrity of the communication or data.

(2) For the purposes of this section an electronic signature is so much of anything in electronic form as –

    (a) is incorporated into or otherwise associated with any electronic communication or electronic data; and

    (b) purports to be so incorporated or associated for the purpose of being used in establishing the authenticity of the communication or data, the integrity of the communication or data, or both.

(3) For the purposes of this section an electronic signature incorporated into or logically associated with a particular electronic communication or particular electronic data is certified by any person if that person (whether before or after the making of the communication) has made a statement confirming that –

    (a) the signature,

    (b) a means of producing, communicating or verifying the signature, or

    (c) a procedure applied to the signature,

is (either alone or in combination with other factors) a valid means of establishing the authenticity of the communication or data, the integrity of the communication or data, or both.

This section has a definition of 'electronic signature' (s 7(2)) and provides that it is admissible as evidence of the 'authenticity' or 'integrity' of the relevant communication or data (s 7(1)). 'Integrity' refers to 'whether there has been any tampering with or other modification of the communication or data' (s 15(2)(b)). If the signature is being used as evidence of 'authenticity', then, under s 15(2)(a), it is being used as evidence of one or more of the following:

(a) whether the communication or data comes from a particular person or source;

(b) whether it is accurately timed and dated;

(c) whether it is intended to have legal effect.

With its reference to the origin of the communication and 'whether it is intended to have legal effect', this would seem to allow for, for example, the possibility of an

---

155 For Art 9, see above, p 292 and note the exceptions in Art 9(2).

electronic signature on a contractual document having the same recognition as the common law gives to a more traditional signature to show that the document contains the terms of a contract to which the electronic signatory is a party; that is, in the absence of fraud, misrepresentation or *non est factum*, to make those terms binding upon the relevant party, whether he or she has read them or not.[156] However, what does this encompass as an 'electronic signature'? Certainly unless a very broad scope is given to 'associated with any electronic communication' the 'click button' type of signature identified by the Law Commission does not seem to be covered. The typed in signature at the bottom of an email, or the electronically inserted facsimile of a manuscript signature might well do. They are 'incorporated into' the electronic communication in a way that the 'click button' response would not seem to be and, although they would not seem to help in establishing the 'integrity of the communication', arguably they fulfil the identified alternative function of an electronic signature of 'being used in establishing the authenticity of the communication' (albeit they might not do so very well). However, obviously better evidence of authenticity and integrity would be provided by a cryptographically generated digital signature and that is further enhanced by third party certification (The Electronic Signatures Regulations 2002 (SI 2002/318) provides for the supervision and liability of 'certification-service-providers'). The EC Directive on a Community Framework for Electronic Signatures provides for the greater recognition for 'an advanced electronic signature', than others. [157]

---

156 *L'Estrange v Graucob Ltd* [1934] 2 KB 394. See above, p 103.

157 The EC Directive on a Community Framework for Electronic Signatures provides a greater recognition of different levels of security which may be provided by different types of electronic signature. (It does not 'cover aspects related to the conclusion and validity of contracts or other legal obligations where there are requirements of form prescribed by national or community law – Art 1). Article 5 provides:

(1) Member States shall ensure that advanced electronic signatures which are based on a qualified certificate and which are created by a secure-signature-creation device:

    (a) satisfy the legal requirements of a signature in relation to data in electronic form in the same manner as a handwritten signature satisfies those requirements in relation to paper-based data; and

    (b) are admissible as evidence in legal proceedings.

(2) Member States shall ensure that an electronic signature is not denied legal effectiveness and admissibility as evidence in legal proceedings solely on the grounds that it is:

    – in electronic form, or

    – not based on a qualified certificate, or

    – not based upon a qualified certificate issued by an accredited certification-service-provider, or

    – not created by a secure signature-creation device.

Definitions are dealt within in Art 2, so that 'electronic signature' means:

... data in electronic form which are attached to or logically associated with other electronic data and which serve as a method of authentication.

And an 'advanced electronic signature' is:

... an electronic signature which meets the following requirements:

(a) it is uniquely linked to the signatory;

(b) it is capable of identifying the signatory;

(c) it is created using means that the signatory can maintain under his sole control; and

(d) it is linked to the data to which it relates in such a manner that any subsequent change of the data is detectable.

continued over page

Formalities – governing law

There has been some discussion above of formal requirements for the validity of a contract. In the context of a contract which involves more than one country, the conflicts question will need to be asked; that is, with which country's laws does the contract have to comply to be formally valid? The question of the governing law relating to formalities is dealt with by Art 9 of the Rome Convention:[158]

Formal Validity

1. A contract concluded between persons who are in the same country is formally valid if it satisfies the formal requirements of the law which governs it under this Convention or of the law of the country where it is concluded.

2. A contract concluded between persons who are in different countries is formally valid if it satisfies the formal requirements of the law which governs it under this Convention or of the law of one of those countries.

3. Where a contract is concluded by an agent, the country in which the agent acts is the relevant country for the purposes of paragraphs 1 and 2.

4. An act intended to have legal effect relating to an existing or contemplated contract is formally valid if it satisfies the formal requirements of the law which under this Convention governs or would govern the contract or of the law of the country where the Act was done.

5. The provisions of the preceding paragraphs shall not apply to a contract to which Article 5 applies, concluded in the circumstances described in paragraph 2 of Article 5. The formal validity of such a contract is governed by the law of the country in which the consumer has his habitual residence.

6. Notwithstanding paragraphs 1 to 4 of this Article, a contract the subject matter of which is a right in immoveable property or a right to use immoveable property shall be subject to the mandatory requirements of form of the law of the country where the property is situated if by that law those requirements are imposed irrespective of the country where the contract is concluded and irrespective of the law governing the contract.

---

157 *continued*

In addition, a 'secure-signature-creation device' means 'a signature-creation device which meets the requirements laid down in Annex III'. 'Certificate' means 'an electronic attestation which links signature-verification data to a person and confirms the identity of that person' and a 'qualified certificate' is one which 'meets the requirements laid down in Annex I and is provided by a certification-service-provider who fulfils the requirements laid down in Annex II'.

Article 5 refers to different 'types' of electronic signature. However, whilst providing for some recognition of electronic signatures generally, it gives a specific role to 'advanced electronic signatures', based on a 'qualified certificate' and created by a 'secure-signature-creation device' (see also the UNCITRAL Model Law on Electronic Signatures). The former cannot be denied 'legal effectiveness' and admissibility as evidence in legal proceedings solely on the grounds that it is' eg 'in electronic form or not based on a qualified certificate. However, the 'advanced electronic signature' must 'satisfy the legal requirements of a signature in relation to data in electronic form in the same manner as a handwritten signature satisfies those requirements un relation to paper based data. Of the types of electronic signature referred to above, it is cryptographically generated digital signature which are capable of being 'advanced electronic signatures'.

158 On the Rome Convention generally, see above, p 263 *et seq*.

CHAPTER 7

PROTECTING THE PRIVATE INDIVIDUAL

INTRODUCTION

Since time immemorial, information has been collected and exchanged about individuals at many levels of society. In the words of Earl Ferrers, 'The collection of personal data is as old as society itself. It may not be the oldest profession but it is one of the oldest habits'.[1] Such activities range from the collection and storage of personal information by government for a multitude of reasons and purposes to the gossip exchanged at local meeting places. Apart from the fact that increasing computerisation has facilitated the collection and storage of such data, the much used phrase, 'the global village', encompasses the notion that exchange of information can now take place on a worldwide scale. This is converted into practical reality by the growth of the internet and world wide web, predicted to have up to 200 million users over the next few years. These users come from diverse backgrounds, encompassing domestic, educational, governmental and commercial sectors. Indeed, the growth of e-commerce has, itself, posed problems in relation to privacy protection which are in urgent need of solution if the projected growth of this section of the economy is to be realised. As has been pointed out:

> On the one hand modern society increasingly depends on the collection, storage, processing and exchange of information of all kinds, including personal information. On the other hand it is important to ensure that where information about individuals is used their interests, including their privacy, are properly respected.[2]

This chapter is devoted to a consideration of the way in which the law is able to deal with abuses of the global information infrastructure insofar as this relates to information about individuals, whether true or false. This will involve a study of whether, and in what manner, increasing computerisation can compromise an individual's privacy or facilitate acts which threaten the individual's reputation or integrity, together with an analysis of the legal response to these issues.

DATA PROTECTION: THE NATURE OF THE PROBLEM

Prior to the so called information revolution, information and data held on individuals would only be kept in traditional filing cabinets or their equivalent. Not only might these be accessed only relatively infrequently, perhaps, by the holder of the data, but it would be difficult for other users of similar information or information about the same individual to gain access. The ease with which computers can store and manipulate data has caused a dramatic change in this respect and has made it a simple matter for information about particular individuals held in a number of places to be correlated.

---

1   HL Debs Vol 349, Col 37, 11 October 1993.
2   Cm 3725, 1997, para 1.9.

Indeed, a whole industry has arisen out of the operation referred to as 'data matching', whereby a profile of a particular individual is assembled from data held at a number of sources. Such profiles are used extensively for marketing purposes and lists of those with similar profiles form a commodity which is, itself, traded to businesses to enable selective targeting of a particular sector of the market. This process need not, however, be confined to business use, as pointed out succinctly by Browne-Wilkinson VC:

> If the information obtained by the police, the Inland Revenue, the social security services, the health service and other agencies were to be gathered together in one file, the freedom of the individual would be greatly at risk. The dossier of private information is the badge of the totalitarian State.[3]

This not only describes the phenomenon of data matching, but also highlights the dangers to individual rights and liberties and is indicative of some of the fears which surround the storage of personal data on computer systems. These fears have been voiced for some time[4] and, even as far back as 1975, a significant amount of information about identifiable individuals was already kept on computer by central government.[5] Such anxieties were exacerbated as industry and commerce also began to rely on the use of computers to such an extent that it is today impossible to imagine business being carried on without them. In the words of Perri: 'personal information has become the basic fuel on which modern business and government run'.[6]

The particular features which were likely to be the cause of concern were identified by the Younger Committee on Privacy.

Report of the Committee on Privacy[7]
Paragraph 581

> We attempted to identify the various aspects of this alleged threat which were raised by computerised personal information stores and seemed to distinguish such stores in the public mind from others kept by traditional methods. We found that the computer's facility to store, link, manipulate, and provide access to information gave rise to suspicions that complete personal profiles on a great number of people could be compiled; that information could be used for a purpose for which it was not initially collected; that some information could be inaccurate; that it facilitated access to confidential information by many people scattered over a wide area; that its powers of correlation were so superior to traditional methods that it made practicable what had hitherto been impracticable; and that it encouraged the growth on an entirely new scale of information gathering and of organisations to do it. Others feel that there is a danger of information emanating from a computer being thought to be free from human error.

---

3   *Marcel v Metropolitan Police Comr* [1992] Ch 225, p 240.
4   See, e.g., Ashdown, House of Commons Debates, Col 86, 30 January 1984; *Eighth Report of the Data Protection Registrar*, 1992, London: HMSO, Appendix 1, quoting the above comment of Browne-Wilkinson VC.
5   For details see *Computers: Safeguards for Privacy*, Cmnd 6354, 1975, London: HMSO, Tables 1 and 2, further updated in *Report of the Committee on Data Protection*, Cmnd 7341, 1978, London: HMSO, Appendix 6.
6   Perri, 1998, p 23.
7   Cmnd 5012, 1972, London: HMSO.

The Committee thus concentrated on three particular areas of concern: the use of computers to compile personal profiles; their capacity to correlate information; and the ease with which unauthorised access to data could be obtained.

The extract above was written in 1972 but, even as rules were being formulated and developed to deal with the issues raised, the nature of the threat was undergoing a subtle change as the technology continued to progress. In the 1970s and early 1980s, the focus was on the development of large, centralised databases held on mainframe computers. Technological advancement then abruptly changed direction and, instead of even larger machines being developed, the advent of the microcomputer resulted in computers rapidly becoming a common tool, both at work and in the home, rather than being confined to large institutions. Further, the creation of computer networks on a global scale[8] moved the emphasis from centralised systems to increasingly decentralised systems, typified by the internet and world wide web. These give rise to qualitatively different problems.

Anonymity on the Internet[9]
Working Party on the Protection of Individuals with
regard to the Processing of Personal Data
Recommendation 3/97

... it has become apparent that one of the greatest threats to this fundamental right to privacy is the ability for organisations to accumulate large amounts of information about individuals, in a digital form which lends itself to high speed (and now very low cost) manipulation, alteration and communication to others ...

A feature of telecommunications networks and of the Internet in particular is their potential to generate a huge quantity of transactional data (the data generated in order to ensure the correct connections). The possibilities for interactive use of the networks (a defining characteristic of many Internet services) increases the amount of transactional data yet further. When consulting an on-line newspaper, the user 'interacts' by choosing the pages he wishes to read. These choices create a 'clickstream' of transactional data. By contrast more traditional news and information services are consumed much more passively (television for example), with interactivity being limited to the off-line world of newspaper shops and libraries ...

As on-line services develop in terms of their sophistication and their popularity, the problem of transactional data will grow. Everywhere we go on the Internet, we leave a digital trace. As more and more aspects of our daily activities are conducted on-line, more and more of what we do, our choices, our preferences, will be recorded.

But the risks to our personal privacy lie not only in the existence of large amounts of personal data on the Internet, but also in the development of software capable of searching the network and drawing together all the available data about a named person.

A later document from the Art 29 Working Party was to explain the perceived threat in more detail.

---

8   Computer networks actually had their genesis in the 1960s with the creation of the ARPANET, but it was not until the mid-1980s that the internet began to be used on a regular, day-to-day basis outside the research community.

9   Available at: www.europa.eu.int/comm/internal_market/en/media/dataprot/wpdocs/ wp6en.htm.

Anonymity on the Internet[10]
**Working Party on the Protection of Individuals with
regard to the Processing of Personal Data
Recommendation 1/99**

Presently it is almost impossible to use the Internet without being confronted with privacy-invading features which carry out all kinds of processing operations of personal data in a way that is invisible to the data subject. In other words, the Internet user is not aware of the fact that his/her personal data have been collected and further processed and might be used for purposes that are unknown to him/her. The data subject does not know about the processing and has no freedom to decide on it.

An example of this type of technique is the so called cookie, which can be defined as a computer record of information that is sent from a web server to a user's computer for the purpose of future identification of that computer on future visits to the same web site.

Browsers are software programs designed to, among other things, graphically display material that is available on the Internet. Browsers communicate between the user's computer (client) and the remote computer where information is stored (Web server). Browsers often send more information to the Web server than strictly necessary for establishing the communication. Classical browsers will automatically send to the Web server visited the type and language of the browser, the name of other software programs installed on the user's PC and operating system, the referring page, cookies, etc. Such data can also be transmitted systematically to third parties by the browser software, in an invisible way.

These techniques allow the creation of clicktrails about the Internet user. Clicktrails consist of information about an individual's behaviour, identity, pathway or choices expressed while visiting a website. They contain the links that a user has followed and are logged in the Web server.

... Cookies or browsers can contain or further process data allowing the direct or indirect identification of the individual internet user.

Thus, the possibility of retaining and collating trace information from successive web searches may prove very useful for personal profiling purposes, even though the individual in question may be completely unaware that the data has been collected. Access/service providers may hold personal details about their clients, transactional information such as the types of site visited, connection times, etc, and even, perhaps, the content of private communications such as email, which can also be used for data matching processes. The problem was summed up succinctly by the then Data Protection Registrar (this role is now subsumed within that of the Information Commissioner):

Every time you access a service [on the internet] whether it is to make a contribution to a newsgroup or to make a commercial transaction, you are at risk of leaving an electronic trace which can be used to develop a profile of your personal interests and tastes.[11]

More recently, a report from the Electronic Privacy Information Center (EPIC) concluded that:

---

10 Available at www.europa.eu.int/comm/internal_market/en/media/dataprot/wpdocs/wp17en.htm.

11 *Eleventh Report of the Data Protection Registrar*, 1995, London: HMSO, Appendix 6.

... the current practices of the on-line industry provide little meaningful privacy protection for consumers ... On balance, we think that consumers are more at risk today than they were in 1997. The profiling is more extensive and the marketing techniques are more intrusive.[12]

A US Federal Trade Commission Report presenting results of a survey of frequently used websites spelt out the threat more explicitly, pointing out that, 'when the traffic of all sites surveyed is taken into account, there is a 99% chance that, during a one month period, a consumer surfing the busiest sites on the web will visit a site that collects personal identifying information'.[13]

DATA PROTECTION AND PRIVACY

It will have been apparent that many of the extracts cited in the previous section refer to both privacy and 'privacy-invading features' in the context of data protection. Nevertheless, the relationship between the terms 'data protection' on the one hand and 'privacy' on the other have not always been easy to reconcile. Data protection is often viewed as a technical term relating to specific information management practices, the preferred stance of those who would see data protection primarily as an aspect of business regulation. In contrast, privacy is more likely to be considered as a fundamental human right and accorded specific protection under human rights conventions or constitutions. It is, however, possible to discuss privacy issues in the terminology of risk and risk assessment, concepts which are, perhaps, more familiar in a business environment. Three risk factors can be identified which could be considered to be elements of privacy.[14] The first of these is the risk of injustice due to significant inaccuracy in personal data, unjust inference, 'function creep' (the gradual use of data for purposes other than those for which it was collected) or reversal of the presumption of innocence, as seen in data matching when correlation of information from disparate sources may produce an impression which is greater than the sum of the parts. The second risk is to one's personal control over the collection of personal information as a result of excessive and unjustified surveillance (which would presumably include monitoring the use of particular websites) collection of data without the data subject's consent and also the prohibition or active discouragement of the means to remedy these risks, such as the use of encryption and anonymising software. Finally there is a risk to dignity as a result of exposure or embarrassment due to an absence of transparency in information procedures, physical intrusion into private spaces, unnecessary identification or absence of anonymity, or unnecessary or unjustified disclosure of personal information without consent. Many of these have echoes of data protection issues and, in the technical sense, data protection measures may be considered as risk management devices which need to balance the risk to the individual from unnecessary invasion of privacy with the measures necessary to

---

12 *Surfer Beware III: Privacy Policies without Privacy Protection*, December 1999, available at www.epic.org/reports/surfer-beware3.html.
13 *Privacy Online: Fair Information Practices in the Electronic Marketplace*, May 2000, available at www.ftc.org/reports/privacy2000/privacy2000text.pdf, p 9. See, also, below.
14 See Perri, 1998, p 40.

control that risk.[15] It may be that such differences in terminology are not so disparate as they might appear at first sight.

Nonetheless, an agreed definition of privacy remains elusive. Ever since the seminal article of Warren and Brandeis[16] at the end of the 19th century, academic writers have been analysing the multi-faceted concept of privacy. Westin suggested that 'Privacy is the claim of individuals, groups or institutions to determine for themselves when, how and to what extent information about them is communicated to others', a definition based on the right of self-determination that may be placed at particular risk by the practice of data matching, made so simple by modern information technology.[17] This notion was supported by Miller,[18] in the specific context of this technology, who considered privacy as 'the individual's ability to control the circulation of information relating to him'. Gavison,[19] on the other hand, is critical of the ability to control personal information as being a determinant of the definition of privacy precisely because a dependence on subjective choice makes both a realisation of the scope of the concept and the provision of legal protection problematic. In a quest for a more neutral approach, she attempts to deconstruct privacy into three components: secrecy, anonymity and solitude. The definitional difficulties are exacerbated by the fact that whether or not privacy is considered to have been invaded is a very subjective issue, which will depend not only on the view of the person whose privacy is being invaded, but also on who is the invader and what information they are uncovering. Even using the apparently neutral approach of Gavison, the question of whether there has, in fact, been an invasion of privacy is likely to remain a subjective one.

Perri has submitted that the reason why there is no consensus over definition is that 'as a society we do not and cannot agree on what it is about private life and privacy that we value',[20] while Feldman comments that: 'The problem is that privacy is controversial. The very breadth of the idea and its tendency to merge with the idea of liberty itself produces a lack of definition which weakens its force in moral and political discourse'.[21]

Whether or not there is an accepted and acceptable definition of privacy, there is undeniably a tension between the rights of all those who would seek to exert control over personal information. It is possible to consider that personal information should be under the control of the person to whom it refers, whereas it may be claimed that, insofar as personal data arises from information which may have been recorded and/or processed in a particular way, the data user should be able to exert right over the use of such data. Thus, competing interests, although often a reflection of the conflict between the individual and the State, may equally well refer to a balancing of the right of individuals to privacy and control over the use of their own information

---

15 See, also, Raab in Kooiman (ed), 1993, pp 89–103; Bott, *et al*, 2000.
16 Warren and Brandeis, 1980.
17 Westin, 1967. See, also, Poullet in Kaspersen and Oskamp (eds), 1990, p 161.
18 Miller, 1971.
19 Gavison, 1980.
20 Perri, 1998, p 21.
21 Feldman, 1991.

with the right of other individuals or organisations to use that same information, which they may have compiled and processed, to the best commercial effect.

Whilst, in upholding a general right to privacy, civil libertarians might tip this balance in favour of the right of individuals to control data concerning themselves, this may not be an automatic or obvious result.

Data protection between property and liberties
Yves Poullet
in *Amongst Friends in Computers and Law*
HWK Kaspersen and A Oskamp (eds)
1990, The Hague: Kluwer, p 174

The individual is not the owner of data that concerns him, not even the bearer towards it of a right close to a real right. An individual projects a certain image of himself spontaneously upon society, which image may be precisely captured by another. Coupled with other information, it then takes shape in the eyes of the person who is processing it. There can be no question of *a priori* denying to another the use of an image of me which I myself have given him. My liberty is opposed to his, which is that of freedom of association within the framework of data systems operated by a union, of religious liberty in the framework of processing undertaken by a religious authority, or more frequently, the liberty to do business in the case of companies. This conflict should resolve itself by the balance of interests method, by which the authority charged with deciding the conflict takes into account the respective legitimate interests expressing the liberty of each party.

... a number of legislative rulings foresee an exception for certain data or certain types of processing. Thus it is easy to justify, that legislation should forbid the processing of philosophical, trade union or religious data, because, *a priori*, the processing of such data imperils my religious, political or philosophical liberty. With reference to the same data, the same legislations exempt precisely such religious associations, trade unions and the press from this very prohibition, which can be explained as the desire to affirm the freedom of association and the freedom of the press above individual liberties. As we can observe from these limited examples, recording of the same nominative data my be limited, regulated or free, according to the liberties put into question by its being recorded. There is certainly a debate between liberties and the necessity of appreciating, with regard to the interests of society, the weight accorded to each of them.

Particularly in the context of the freedom of the holder of the file to do business, beyond the limits imposed with regard to certain data which characterize, in an immediate way, such recognised constitutional liberties as freedom of opinion, of religion or association, may we admit that legislation, in defining the file holder's right to information also defines the limit of that right? Should not the principle of the holder of the file's right to collect data be affirmed as such, even if, *a posteriori*, certain abuses must be decided *in casu* by the judge? In other words, should data protection legislation intervene in the private sector other than by providing for the right of access ... should it rule on the contents and limits of private processing?

As mentioned above, Gavison defines three components of privacy as secrecy, anonymity and solitude, while Feldman uses the words 'secrecy, dignity, autonomy'. In both of these formulations, the word 'secrecy' is used to encompass the idea of informational privacy, reflecting the desire of individuals to be able to place checks on what is known about them, not only in the sense of data released, but also in control over subsequent use and reuse. Does this concept of informational privacy equate with data protection or overlap with it? In 1978, the Lindop Committee was established to look exclusively at the issue of data protection in the UK. Although referring to the definitions of both Westin and Miller, quoted above, the Lindop Report,[22] was at pains to distinguish privacy and data protection, perhaps to reassure those who were concerned about the introduction or what could be regarded as privacy legislation.

Report of the Committee on Data Protection
Cmnd 7341, 1998

The concept of data privacy

2.03   There are aspects of privacy which have no immediate connection with the handling of personal data in information systems, such as intrusion into the home, powers of entry and search, and embarrassing publicity in the media. There are also aspects of data protection which have no immediate connection with privacy. For example, the use of inaccurate or incomplete information for taking decisions about people is properly a subject for data protection, but it may not always raise questions of privacy.

2.04   The Younger Committee had to deal with the whole field of privacy. Our task has been to deal with that of data protection. In fact, the two fields overlap, and the area of overlap can be called 'information privacy' or, better, 'data privacy'. It is an important area, and we have a good deal to say about it in this Report. But it is not by itself the whole field of data protection, and we have had to consider some matters which do not directly raise questions of privacy. However, we found it useful to examine the concept of data privacy, and its implications and consequences. For this purpose we have used the term data privacy to mean the individual's claim to control the circulation of data about himself.

'Private' data

2.05   There is wide variation in what data about themselves people regard as 'private'. Such variations exist between one individual and another, between different sections of society, between societies in different countries, and between different periods of time in the same society.

2.06   Some people are willing to allow more to be known about themselves than others. Differences of age, personality, temperament, views and beliefs all have a part to play. Variations in social and cultural mores account for variations between different sectors of the same society; variations in institutions, cultures and traditions, and in the style and political characteristics of government, account for variations between different societies. Changes in attitude in the same society are related to many factors such as its economic development, changing educational standards, social conventions, and opportunities for self determination.

2.07   'Privateness' is clearly not an attribute of data themselves, for the same data may be regarded as very private in one context and not so private, or not private at all, in another. Equally, when data are regarded as private, that does not mean that they are, or should be, known only to the individual to whom they refer: rather it means that he wants them to be known only to him and to those others who he agrees should know them. There are many ways in which such agreements are established. In the simplest case the individual gives the data directly to another party; this may be a quite voluntary act or it may be an obligation entered into as

---

22   For details see *Computers: Safeguards for Privacy*, Cmnd 6354, 1975, London: HMSO, Tables 1 and 2, further updated in *Report of the Committee on Data Protection*, Cmnd 7341, 1978, London: HMSO, Appendix 6.

part of a commercial contract. At the other extreme, the agreement may be made on his behalf by Parliament enacting legislation which requires him to provide the data to someone. One cannot judge such agreements, however they are reached, without taking a view of the purposes for which the data are to be used, and the conditions under which they are to be applied to those purposes.

Notwithstanding this attempt at semantic differentiation, other sources and commentators have often used the words interchangeably or appear to assume the link between the two. Gellman, for instance, refers to 'the slice of privacy known as "data protection"'[23] and goes on to suggest that:

> This is a useful European term referring to rules about the collection, use and dissemination of personal information. One major policy objective of data protection is the application of fair information practices, an organized set of values and standards about personal information defining the rights of record subjects and the responsibilities of record keepers. This is an important subset of privacy law.

As acknowledged by Gellman, the term 'data protection' originated in Europe, but few would dispute the contention that it has become a globally recognised term. However, it could be argued that the coining of this specific term has, itself, been the root of the problem – suggesting or being indicative of separate strands of meaning where, perhaps, none exist. Although recent initiatives seem more likely to stress the link between data protection and privacy, even in 1980 both the Organisation for Economic Co-operation and Development (OECD) and the Council of Europe were in no doubt that data protection was a facet of privacy. In the context of the automatic processing of personal data, the Council of Europe considered that 'it is desirable to extend the safeguards for everyone's rights and fundamental freedoms, and in particular the right to the respect for privacy',[24] while the OECD commented in its *Guidelines on the Protection of Privacy and Transborder Flows of Personal Data*,[25] that 'privacy protection laws have been introduced ... to prevent what are considered to be violations of fundamental human rights such as the unlawful storage of personal data or the abuse or unauthorised disclosure of such data'. The now ubiquitous term 'data protection' was reserved for the explanatory memorandum accompanying the *Guidelines*.

The link between data protection and privacy has increasingly been recognised in the UK as well as internationally. In 1994, the then Data Protection Registrar said in his Final Report that 'data protection legislation is about the protection of individuals rather than the regulation of industry. It is civil rights legislation rather than technical business legislation'.[26] Even though the Data Protection Act 1984 never used the word 'privacy', Lord Hoffman in *R v Brown* remarked that 'English common law does not know a general right of privacy and Parliament has been reluctant to enact one. But there has been some legislation to deal with particular aspects of the problem. The Data Protection Act 1984 ... is one such statute'.[27] The decision of the Data Protection

---

23 Gellman, in Agre and Rotenberg 1998, p 194.
24 Council of Europe Convention for the Protection on Individuals with regard to the Automatic Processing of Personal Data, available at: www.conventions.coe.int/treaty/EN/cadreprincipal.htm.
25 Available at www.oecd.org/dsti/sti/it/secur/prod/PRIV-EN.HTM.
26 *Tenth Annual Report of the Data Protection Registrar*, 1994, London: HMSO.
27 *R v Brown* [1996] 1 All ER 545, p 555.

Tribunal in *British Gas Trading Ltd v Data Protection Registrar* was more specific, stating that 'an underlying purpose of the data protection principles is to protect privacy with respect to the processing of personal data',[28] a view which looks both back to the Council of Europe Convention and forward to Directive 95/46/EC.[29] Following implementation of this Directive, the Deputy Data Protection Registrar asserted that:[30]

> If the 1998 Act satisfies the Directive, then it serves to protect the rights of individuals to privacy, at least in respect of the processing of personal data. If the 1998 Act fails to protect personal privacy in accordance with the Directive, then the UK is in breach of its Community obligations. I do not assert that data protection legislation is comprehensive privacy legislation protecting every aspect of that right, but I do ask how it can be doubted that, as a matter of law, data protection is a form of privacy protection.

Notwithstanding that such comments and pronouncements originate from a variety of sources, the historic lack of legal protection for privacy *per se* in the UK has meant that there is still resistance, and even suspicion in some quarters, towards any legislation which purports to protect or which could be regarded as protecting privacy. Proponents of such views seek to divorce the concepts of data protection and privacy. This has resulted in warnings against data protection law bringing in privacy law surreptitiously by the 'back door'. Those who espouse such views concentrate, instead, on the business regulation aspects of data protection and its role in promoting the free flow of personal data. Thus, Viscount Astor stated that:

> ... the Bill which implements the Directive is designed to improve the free movement of personal data throughout the Community
>
> ... we need to protect the rights of individuals but we do not want a back door privacy law.[31]

In the same debate, Lord Wakeham was to suggest that the Data Protection Bill (now the Data Protection Act 1998, implementing Directive 95/46/EC) was 'an excellent piece of legislation which avoids all the perils of a privacy law. It is entirely in line with the Government's stated commitment to self-regulation and their opposition to a privacy law'.

Both sides of this debate have always recognised that the reliance by business on the increased use of computers and computer networks, both internally and externally to the enterprise, creates the tension between business needs and individuals' right of privacy.

Report of the Committee on Data Protection[32]

2.09   In the use that is made of personal data, the interests of the individual and the interests of society may conflict and need to be resolved in the same way as in the context of individual liberty. With data protection the solution must take the same form: a balance must be found between the interests of the individual and the

---

28   *British Gas Trading Ltd v Data Protection Registrar* (1998); See *Fourteenth Annual Report of the Data Protection Registrar*, 1998, London: HMSO, Appendix 6, available at www.wood.ccta.gov.uk/dpr/dpdoc.nsf.

29   See below, p 322.

30   Aldhouse, 1999, p 11.

31   *Hansard*, Col 445, 2 February 1998.

32   Cmnd 7341, 1978, London: HMSO.

interests of the rest of society, which include the efficient conduct of industry, commerce and administration. But, as with our liberties, it is not a single point of balance which must be established. There are cases, for example with regard to religious and political beliefs, where the right balance will preserve the individual's freedom to adhere to his beliefs and will deny to society, and to particular institutions within it such as government departments or commercial enterprises, the opportunity to interfere with that freedom. At the other extreme the maintenance of national security and of law and order in society may require the balance to be struck at a point where the interests of society are given a far higher value than those of the individual. Between these extremes there is a wide spectrum, and the balance for a particular use of personal data may be established differently in different cases. It may also be settled differently in different societies, and may shift within the same society with changes, for example, in its political climate or institutional structures.

2.10 The means by which the balances are struck, and the conditions under which the agreements between data subjects and data users are reached, are of great importance. Where the agreement is voluntary, the result will not be fair unless each party fully understands the requirements of the other, and there is a clear understanding of what data are to be provided, and for what purposes they will be used. Fairness requires openness in such dealings and it also requires that no advantage should be taken of any disparities in bargaining power.

2.11 But there are many cases where these conditions for fairness cannot exist. Data users cannot always be expected, or even be able, to appreciate fully the requirements of data subjects. Even less can data subjects be expected to appreciate fully the requirements of data users, let alone the relevant technicalities of information handling. In many cases, especially where the relationship is between the government and the governed, there can be no question of equal bargaining power; in yet others it may turn out that agreement simply cannot be reached. In all such cases, only an independent third party can fairly weigh all the interests involved – those of the data subject, the data user and society at large – and determine the best point of balance.

Whereas it is accepted that civil liberties and human rights cannot be absolute and unfettered, this extract illustrates how difficult it may be to achieve an acceptable balance between the competing rights of those involved. It is the Herculean task of data protection regulation to achieve that balance.

REGULATORY APPROACHES AND INITIATIVES

Identification of these competing needs, together with pressure from a variety of intergovernmental organisations such as the OECD and the Council of Europe, have led to regulation of this area in a number of jurisdictions. However, as yet, there has not been any global consensus on either the most appropriate way of achieving and maintaining the balance between the competing objectives or the provision of a suitable regulatory framework. The discussion above indicates that it is axiomatic that data protection regulation is required to protect privacy of individual data subjects, suggesting that the central issue is merely the problem of reaching agreement on the method of achieving this result. But the counter-argument is that data protection laws impede the free flow of data, stifle rapid innovation and generally restrict the free market. There is also a considerable compliance burden related to the cost of implementation. On this argument, only minimal, external regulation is likely to be tolerated and the advantages of market-driven, self-regulatory practices espoused. In other words, strong data protection will, inevitably, hinder commercial activity. Moderating this view, some legal and economic analyses have apparently demonstrated that the reality may not be so simple and that a strong legal infrastructure may actually encourage commerce. Whichever side of the argument is supported, it does seem to be generally recognised that privacy regulation may be more apt and relevant in relation to business-consumer transactions than for business-business ones.[33]

If it is taken as a given that some regulation is necessary for the protection of individuals, what is the most suitable method? A clear division in approach is evident between the US on the one hand, which favours a sectoral, self-regulatory system, and Europe, which has a long history of legislative intervention.[34] Indeed, as already pointed out, the very concept of data protection appears to be a European creation. In order to be able to appreciate the nature of the debate which has unfolded surrounding the regulation of data protection in different jurisdictions, especially in the US and Europe, it is prudent to examine some of the advantages and disadvantages of these apparently opposing philosophies.

Self-regulation is arguably a much maligned and frequently misunderstood term. It should not be confused with non-regulation,[35] but can reasonably be equated with non-governmental regulation, although a number of self-regulatory regimes do in fact operate within a statutory framework. At its most reduced form, it suggests the propensity of individuals to provide rules for themselves, although these may include, of course, compliance with external, central regulation. Within the business and commercial sector, the term is usually used to denote a much more formal regulatory framework which may be established by the industries, trade and professional associations themselves, in response to the need to be accountable for their members' activities or in response to a statutory framework, imposed for the control of a particular activity, as noted above. This latter system is sometimes referred to as 'enforced self-regulation'. Self-regulatory schemes of this nature have become an increasingly familiar aspect of the regulation of commercial activity in many jurisdictions and it is in reference to such schemes that the majority of academic scrutiny and comment has occurred.[36]

Rethinking self-regulation
Anthony I Ogus
(1995) 15 OJLS 97

What then are the advantages traditionally claimed for self-regulation over public regulation? First, since self-regulatory agencies (hereafter SRAs) can normally command a greater degree of expertise and technical knowledge of practices and innovatory possibilities within the relevant area than independent agencies, information costs for the formulation and interpretation of standards are lower. Secondly, for the same reasons,

---

33 For further discussion see Swire and Litan, 1998, Chapter 4.
34 See also, Charlesworth, 2000.
35 See further, Page, 1986.
36 See generally, Baldwin, and Cave, 1999; Ogus, 1994; Baldwin, 1987.

monitoring and enforcement costs are also reduced, as are the costs to practitioners of dealing with regulators, given that such interaction is likely to be fostered by mutual trust. Thirdly, to the extent that the processes of, and rules issued by, SRAs are less formalised than those of public regulatory regimes, there are savings on the costs (including those attributable to delay) of amending standards. Fourthly, the administrative costs of the regime are normally internalised in the trade or activity which is subject to regulation; in the case of independent, public agencies, they are typically borne by taxpayers ... Lawyers and economists have been equally scathing in their criticisms of self-regulation. From a legal perspective, it is seen as an example of modern 'corporatism', the acquisition of power by groups which are not accountable to the body politic through the conventional constitutional channels. The capacity of an SRA to make rules governing the activities of an association or profession may itself constitute an abuse if it lacks democratic legitimacy in relation to members of the association or profession. The potential for abuse becomes intolerable if, and to the extent that, the rules affect third parties. Further, if – as often occurs – the SRA's functions cover policy formulation, interpretation of the rules, adjudication and enforcement (including imposition of sanctions) as well as rule-making, there is a fundamental breach of the separation of powers doctrine. Finally, irrespective of theoretical considerations, SRAs are claimed to have a poor record of enforcing their standards against recalcitrant members.

Thus, self-regulation provides a particular type of regulatory regime, whose flexibility and relative informality is often appreciated by the business community. In practice, it may be difficult to assess how well the regime has been implemented or performs its functions, but this is a criticism which can also be directed at some statutory regimes. For the purposes of the present discussion, the major question is whether it can be as effective in protecting individual rights as a statutory scheme.

In Europe, there has been little consideration of the use of self-regulatory regimes as the primary method of regulation. In the UK, the origins of data protection legislation can be traced back to the Younger Committee on Privacy, referred to above. This Committee was established in response to growing concerns during the 1960s about the amount of personal information kept by various organisations, to which the individuals concerned had no right of access. Its terms of reference were:

> To consider whether legislation is needed to give further protection to the individual citizen and to commercial and industrial interests against intrusion into privacy by private persons and organisations or by companies and to make recommendations.

A statutory framework was thus what was in contemplation. Although, at this time, the use of computers was still comparatively novel and was largely confined to big commercial and educational institutions, the potential for the problems identified earlier in the use of computer systems for these purposes had already been identified, and one chapter of the Younger Report[37] concentrated on this perceived threat to privacy. Although the Report concluded that the threat to privacy from computers was not sufficient at that time to warrant legislation,[38] nevertheless 10 principles were formulated which were suggested as providing a guide for the use of computers that manipulated personal data.

---

37 Cmnd 5012, 1972, London: HMSO.
38 But note that, around this time, some of these fears had been identified as a reality in the US – see, e.g., Miller, 1971, Chapter 2.

Report of the Committee on Privacy
Paragraphs 592–600

There could be an incentive to cover the cost of acquisition and recording of the information by using it for purposes additional to that for which it was originally collected. For example, a computerised record of subscribers to a trade publication might well prove useful to the manufacturers of certain products advertised therein. The situation could be a clear breach of privacy in so far as it could be held that private information (a name and address) given solely for the purpose of receiving a magazine is passed on without the authority of the originator. Therefore:

1   Information should be regarded as held for a specific purpose and should not be used without appropriate authorisation for other purposes.

2   Access to information should be confined to those authorised to have it for the purpose for which it was supplied.

Furthermore, because it is often cheaper to collect all available information in one operation and because computers have the capacity to store it, there could be a double incentive for the owners of the computers to hoard large amounts of information, some of which, though not essential now, might prove useful at some later date. We believe that:

3   The amount of information collected and held should be the minimum necessary for achievement of a specified purpose.

A great deal of personal information is acquired to provide statistics to assist planning and other research, or is acquired for some other purpose and subsequently adapted to a form suitable for such ends. Planners and researchers, however, rarely need to know identities of individuals. Therefore:

4   In computerised systems handling information for statistical purposes, adequate provision should be made in their design and programs for separating identities from the rest of the data.

... While we do not think that a printout should automatically be supplied [of the information held about individuals in a computerised record] we think that every system should be so designed that in situations where printout is appropriate an individual can on request be told of the contents of the record. Therefore:

5   There should be arrangements whereby the subject could be told about the information held concerning him.

We are not convinced that considerations of privacy are at present sufficiently in the minds of computer users and we think that more regard should be paid to such considerations than is the case now. Therefore:

6   The level of security to be achieved by a system should be specified in advance by the user and should include precautions against the deliberate abuse or misuse of information.

... A security system would be incomplete, however, if it did not include provision for the detection of an irregularity. Therefore:

7   A monitoring system should be provided to facilitate the detection of any violation of the security system.

There are three further principles of only marginal relevance to privacy which we feel we should put forward for consideration alongside the seven we enumerate above. Computers have the capacity to retain information in effect indefinitely so that it is occasionally stored ... with little regard to a time limit. Therefore:

8   In the design of information systems, periods should be specified beyond which the information should not be retained.

Private sector computer users usually have a commercial interest in ensuring the accuracy of an up-to-dateness of information and protecting it from corruption during processing. There are at present, however, no procedures in general use for dealing quickly with inaccuracies. Therefore:

9   Data held should be accurate. There should be machinery for the correction of inaccuracy and the updating of information.

The coding of the subjective judgments often entails the loss of shades of meaning and emphasis. For example, a numeral; indicating 'fair' in evaluating an employee's performance is capable of wide interpretation. In such cases it would be preferable to refer the interrogator of the computer to a more detailed report. Therefore:

10   Care should be taken in coding value judgments.

Similar principles enunciating fair information practices have since formed the backbone of legal instruments for the regulation of data protection, at both the national and international level. The OECD *Guidelines* of 1980,[39] formulated principles of good data management, identified by a description of the content, and which covered essentially the same ground. Again, a statutory regime was envisaged, the OECD recommending that these *Guidelines* be taken into account in the member countries' domestic legislation on privacy.

Guidelines on the Protection of Privacy and
Transborder Flows of Personal Data
OECD, 1980

Part Two: Basic Principles of National Application

Collection Limitation Principle

7   There should be limits to the collection of personal data and any such data should be obtained by lawful and fair means and, where appropriate, with the knowledge or consent of the data subject.

Data Quality Principle

8   Personal data should be relevant to the purposes for which they are to be used, and, to the extent necessary for those purposes, should be accurate, complete and kept up to date.

Purpose Specification Principle

9   The purposes for which personal data are collected should be specified not later than at the time of data collection and the subsequent use limited to the fulfilment of those purposes or such others as are not incompatible with those purposes and as are specified on each occasion of change of purpose.

Use Limitation Principle

10   Personal data should not be disclosed, made available or otherwise used for purposes other than those specified in accordance with Paragraph 9 except:

(a) with the consent of the data subject; or

(b) by the authority of law.

---

39   Available at www.oecd.org/dsti/sti/it/secur/prod/PRIV-EN.HTM.

Security Safeguards Principle

11 Personal data should be protected by reasonable security safeguards against such risks as loss or unauthorised access, destruction, use, modification or disclosure of data.

Openness Principle

12 There should be a general policy of openness about developments, practices and policies with respect to personal data. Means should be readily available of establishing the existence and nature of personal data, and the main purposes of their use, as well as the identity and usual residence of the data controller.

Individual Participation Principle

13 An individual should have the right:

   (a) to obtain from a data controller, or otherwise, confirmation of whether or not the data controller has data relating to him;

   (b) to have communicated to him, data relating to him

       – within a reasonable time;

       – at a charge, if any, that is not excessive;

       – in a reasonable manner; and

       – in a form that is readily intelligible to him;

   (c) to be given reasons if a request made under subparagraphs (a) and (b) is denied, and to be able to challenge such denial; and

   (d) to challenge data relating to him and, if the challenge is successful to have the data erased, rectified, completed or amended.

Accountability Principle

14 A data controller should be accountable for complying with measures which give effect to the principles stated above.

Around the same time, the Council of Europe adopted the Convention for the Protection of Individuals with regard to Automatic Processing of Personal Data, which has its own version of these principles. Article 4(1) of this Convention also seemed to envisage an approach that would be primarily legislative, providing that 'Each Party shall take the necessary measures in its domestic law to give effect to the basic principles for data protection'.

Council of Europe Convention for the Protection of Individuals with regard to Automatic Processing of Personal Data 1981[40]

Chapter II – Basic principles for data protection

Article 5
Quality of data

Personal data undergoing automatic processing shall be:

   (a) obtained and processed fairly and lawfully;

---

40 Treaty No 108; Full text available at: www.conventions.coe.int/treaty/EN/cadreprincipal.htm.

(b) stored for specified and legitimate purposes and not used in a way incompatible with those purposes;

(c) adequate, relevant and not excessive in relation to the purposes for which they are stored;

(d) accurate and, where necessary, kept up to date;

(e) preserved in a form which permits identification of the data subjects for no longer than is required for the purpose for which those data are stored.

Article 6
Special categories of data

Personal data revealing racial origin, political opinions or religious or other beliefs, as well as personal data concerning health or sexual life, may not be processed automatically unless domestic law provides appropriate safeguards. The same shall apply to personal data relating to criminal convictions.

Article 7
Data security

Appropriate security measures shall be taken for the protection of personal data stored in automated data files against accidental or unauthorised destruction or accidental loss as well as against unauthorised access, alteration or dissemination.

Article 8
Additional safeguards for the data subject

Any person shall be enabled:

(a) to establish the existence of an automated personal data file, its main purposes, as well as the identity and habitual residence or principal place of business of the controller of the file;

(b) to obtain at reasonable intervals and without excessive delay or expense confirmation of whether personal data relating to him are stored in the automated data file as well as communication to him of such data in an intelligible form;

(c) to obtain, as the case may be, rectification or erasure of such data if these have been processed contrary to the provisions of domestic law giving effect to the basic principles set out in Articles 5 and 6 of this Convention;

(d) to have a remedy if a request for confirmation or, as the case may be, communication, rectification or erasure as referred to in paragraphs (b) and (c) of this article is not complied with.

It was international activity of this type which was to lead many of the signatories to these agreements to produce legislation for the regulation of this area – among them the UK, whose first data protection legislation, the Data Protection Act 1984, was enacted as a direct result of the perceived need to ratify the Council of Europe Convention.

Parliamentary Debates (Commons)
11 April 1983

William Whitelaw ... I draw attention to the European dimension. In January 1981, the Council of Europe Convention on Data Protection was opened for signature. Together with the guidelines on privacy protection of the OECD, the Convention offers an international standard for data protection. This has provided us with a yardstick against which to measure our own proposals. Our intention is to ratify the Council of Europe Convention, and we have kept its provisions firmly in mind in drafting the Bill.

With the Convention now widely accepted as setting a necessary standard, we shall find increasingly a division between those countries with data protection, and those without. The latter will be more and more at risk of action from countries determined to prevent the undermining of their own data protection laws by the export of personal data to countries without protection. We must not allow any excuse for sanctions against the United Kingdom. That is what makes it imperative that we legislate without delay. Even if we were not already convinced of the rightness of legislation in this field, we should be compelled by this consideration to bring ourselves into line with European practice.

As well as showing awareness of the propensity for conflict between different regulatory schemes, this extract shows the influence of these international guidelines in leading to legislation in the UK. A similar phenomenon could be observed in other European States. Indeed, Mayer-Schönberger has commented that, in Europe, 'almost all the national norms enacted after 1981 reflected the spirit if not the text of the OECD Guidelines.' However the legislative approach has not remained static and Mayer-Schönberger has further traced this development in terms of a succession of generations of data protection legislation. Of these, the first generation represents those laws passed in the early 1970s, the second generation emerged in the late 1970s, the third during the 1990s and the fourth, of which a key example is Directive 95/46/EC, in the 1990s.

Generational development of data protection in Europe
Viktor Mayer-Schönberger[41]
First generation: data protection norms

The first data protection laws were enacted in response to the emergence of electronic data processing within government and large corporations. They represent attempts to counter dim visions of an unavoidably approaching Brave New World exemplified by plans discussed in the 1960s and 1970s to centralize all personal data files in gigantic national data banks ...

Most of the first-generation data protection norms do not focus on the direct protection of individual privacy. Instead they concentrate on the function of data processing in society ... the first-generation data protection norms take a functional look at the phenomenon of data processing ... The first generation statutes avoid using well-known words such as 'privacy', 'information', and 'protection of intimate affairs'; instead they employ rather technical jargon : 'data', 'data bank', 'data record', data base', 'data file' ...

The second generation: warding off more and different offenders

Data protection in the second generation focused on individual privacy rights of the citizen. Well-known sources of privacy, such as the right to be let alone and the right to delimit one's own intimate space, were brought back into the discussion. Data protection was now explicitly linked to the right of privacy, and was seen as the right of the individual to ward off society in personal matters ...

... all norms of data protection always included rights of the individual to access and correct his or her personal data. But during the first generation of norms these individual rights were interpreted functionally. They were seen as supporting the accuracy of the personal data stored and processed. Individuals could not decide on whether their data

41   Agre and Rotenberg, 1998, Chapter 8.

was processed at all; they could merely rectify misleading or inaccurate data about themselves.

In the second generation of data protection rights, individuals obtained a say in the process. Their consent was sometimes a precondition to the data processing; in other instances, individual consent might overwrite a legal presumption that prohibited processing ...

This reorientation of data protection from technology regulation to individual liberty and freedom linked it rhetorically with old legal categories of personal privacy. But the noble ideals of negative liberty and individual freedom remained largely political wishful thinking. Their transformation into black-letter law was bound to fail. It is impossible to realise individual informational liberty and privacy without endangering the functioning of the complex European social welfare states. In real life the individual rarely had the chance to decide between taking part and remaining outside society ...

The third generation: the right to informational self-determination

These and similar ideas have led to a third major reform of data protection laws. Individual liberty, the right to ward off invasions into personal data, was transformed into a much more participatory right to informational self-determination ...

... The individual cannot only, as in second generation data protection norms, once and for all decide in an 'all-or-nothing' choice to have his or her personal data processed, but has to be – at least in principle – continuously involved in the data processing ...

The revisions and replacement of the technical first generation data protection terms necessitated by the change in technology were part of the second generation. During the third generation of data protection, information technology developed even further away from centralized information-processing models.

... data protection norms of the third generation are characterised by the concentration on – not to call it retreat from – the individual right of informational self-determination and the belief that citizens would exercise this right ...

The third generation emphasised informational participation ...

But reality turned out to be different again. Even when empowered with new and extended participatory rights, people were not willing to pay the high monetary and social cost they would have to expend when rigorously exercising their right of informational self-determination ...

Consequently data protection, despite deliberate attempts to broaden access and streamline enforcement remained largely a privilege of minorities, who could economically and socially afford to exercise their rights ...

The fourth generation: holistic and sectoral perspectives

... The legislators realised the generally weak bargaining position of the individual when exercising his or her right. Fourth generation norms and amendments try to rectify this through two rather distinct approaches.

On the one hand, they try to equalise bargaining positions by strengthening the individual's position vis-à-vis the generally more powerful informational gathering institutions. In essence, such attempts preserve the belief in the ability of the individual to bring about data protection through individual self-determination if the bargaining balance is reestablished.

On the other hand, legislators take away parts of the participatory freedom given to the individual in second and third generation data protection norms and subject it to mandatory legal protection. Such an approach reflects the understanding that some areas of informational privacy must be absolutely protected and cannot be bargained for individually.

Each of these approaches has found a way into the fourth generation data protection norms ...

In addition, under fourth generation developments general data protection norms are supplemented by specific sectoral data protection regulations ...

Conclusion

Since 1970, European data protection norms have evolved into a dynamic and changing legal framework. While data protection turned into an accepted concept, its content shifted and adjusted to address technological changes and challenges and to take into account philosophical and ideological transformations. Data protection is no longer seen as a purely functional construct to be used to directly shape and influence the use of information-processing technology. Instead, the focus has shifted to the individual. Citizens' rights feature prominently in all European data protection systems. The individual rights approach has tended away from simplistic versions of informational privacy as a negative liberty and toward broad participatory rights of informational self-determination, supported and enhanced by a renaissance of direct regulatory involvement ...

Thus, the adoption of a statutory regulatory regime does not, and need not, automatically imply uniformity of provisions, notwithstanding the central influence of the various principles of good data management formulated in the OECD *Guidelines* and the Council of Europe Convention. There is clearly room for variation in the scope of protection provided and, despite the categorisation into generations, not all jurisdictions within Europe have, as yet, embraced the later generations of norms to the fullest extent.

Reliance on the provision of principles of good data management is not confined to legislation and such principles are also a feature of the primarily self-regulatory regime in use in the US. The following extract describes the rationale behind the US approach to the regulation of informational privacy.

An analysis of the informational privacy protection afforded by the European Union and the United States
Tracie B Loring
(2002) 37 Tex Int'l LJ 421

Unlike the European Union's omnibus, centralized approach to informational privacy, which reflects the notion that data protection must be ensured by comprehensive legislation, data protection regulation in the United States is decentralized, fragmented, ad hoc, and narrowly tailored to target specific sectors. While the European Union enacts legislation to counter market forces, the United States, in comparison, focuses less on government intervention in the private sector and, instead, places a greater emphasis on market constraints. Furthermore, through the utilization of control mechanisms for oversight, the European Union has adopted a proactive, preventative approach to guard against data protection privacy violations. In contrast, the United States relies on a patchwork of laws, namely the Constitution, federal and state legislation, and the common law of torts to regulate the right to privacy. Consequently, federal and state privacy legislation is largely reactive as it targets specific sectors where problems have arisen. ...

A critical component underlying US privacy protection involves the gravity attached to maintaining an unrestricted flow of information. The premise is that openness of information advances privacy interests as it enables citizens to obtain affordable access to data about themselves and, consequently, promotes the correction of erroneous information. Since attempts to increase privacy protection often exact costs on the free flow of information, efforts to enhance privacy protection may lead to undesirable consequences such as facilitating the dissemination of false information; protecting the withholding of relevant information; and interfering with the collection, organization, and storage of information upon which businesses rely in making prompt, informed decisions.

Historically, the United States' approach to data privacy protection has depended upon industry self-regulation. To some degree, this policy can be attributed to the American public's traditional disfavor for centralized government. While the federal government remains largely responsible for regulating privacy, its role in safeguarding privacy in the private sector is restricted to facilitating individual action. As a result, a wide range of actors, including federal and state legislatures, agencies and courts, industry associations, individual companies, and market forces, are in charge of executing data protection standards and enforcement.

This is not, necessarily, to say that the basic tenets differ substantially. The 1998 Report of the Federal Trade Commission (FTC), *Privacy Online: A Report to Congress*,[42] discussed five core principles of privacy protection by reference to the corresponding OECD guidelines, namely: notice/awareness; choice/consent; access/participation; integrity/security and enforcement/redress. Beyond this apparent similarity, however, the regulatory regimes in Europe and the US diverge markedly. The emphasis on individual rights in Europe appears to have been the prime catalyst to the legislative approach to data protection, whereas business needs have been set much more centre stage in the US. The FTC noted consumer concern about privacy issues in its 1998 Report but nevertheless felt that these concerns could be resolved by the encouragement of self-regulation, even though it recognised that, at that time, there were severe deficiencies in the extent of regulatory protection.

Privacy Online: A Report to Congress
FTC, 1998

Conclusions

... The Commission has encouraged industry to address consumer concerns regarding online privacy through self-regulation. The internet is a rapidly changing marketplace. Effective self-regulation remains desirable because it allows firms to respond quickly to technological changes and employ new technologies to protect consumer privacy. Accordingly, a private-sector response to consumer concerns that incorporates widely-accepted fair information practices and provides for effective enforcement mechanisms could afford consumers adequate privacy protection. To date, however, the Commission has not seen an effective self-regulatory system emerge.

As evidenced by the Commission's survey results, and despite the Commission's three-year privacy initiative supporting a self-regulatory response to consumers' privacy concerns, the vast majority of online businesses have yet to adopt even the most fundamental fair information practice (notice/awareness). Moreover, the trade association guidelines submitted to the Commission do not reflect industry acceptance of the basic fair information practice principles. In addition, the guidelines, with limited exception, contain none of the enforcement mechanisms needed for an effective self-regulatory regime. In light of the lack of notice regarding information practices on the

---

42   Available at www.ftc.gov/reports/privacy3/toc.htm.

World Wide Web and the lack of current industry guidelines adequate to establish an effective self-regulatory regime, the question is what additional incentives are required in order to encourage effective self-regulatory efforts by industry.

A further Report in July 1999,[43] reiterated the philosophy of the previous Report: that 'self-regulation is the least intrusive and most efficient means to ensure fair information practice, given the rapidly evolving nature of the internet and computer technology'. It noted that, although there were still observable problems with compliance, there had been significant developments reflecting 'industry leaders' substantial effort and commitment to fair information practices'. This fact, together with other initiatives to protect individual privacy, suggested to the FTC that legislation to address online privacy was not appropriate at that time.

These brief details of the contrasting approaches to regulation of data protection in Europe and the US illustrate some of the points of conflict, but it would be misleading to imagine that these apparently opposing mechanisms are entirely mutually exclusive. The view is expressed in the recitals of the OECD's 1998 Ministerial Declaration on the Protection of Privacy on Global Networks[44] that, although there are different approaches to privacy in member countries, these methods can, nevertheless, 'work together to achieve effective privacy protection on global networks'. Although self-regulatory mechanisms are frequently invoked as a substitute for, or an avoidance of, legislation, they may also play a valuable role in both implementing and supplementing framework legislation by providing particular rules for specific sectors and/or purposes. Compare, for instance, how a general framework for maintaining privacy might be put into effect in relation to direct marketing as opposed to the management of health records. In each of these cases, the risks and consequences of inappropriate processing are very different. Codes of Practice (a common form of self-regulation) can be very effective at filling in the necessary detail to enable the framework requirements and guidance to be complied with in specific cases. The disadvantage, of course, is that too great a reliance on self-regulatory codes may result in divergence between the sectors, which, in turn, can lead to fragmentation at the implementation level.

Despite the possibilities for reconciliation, the two conflicting approaches in the US and Europe appear entrenched within the existing regulatory frameworks and it was apparent that there was likely to be a time when these would clash or would, alternatively, each have to find ways of accommodating the other. This eventually became an imperative with the adoption and implementation of Directive 95/46/EC, which has provisions requiring the adequacy of data protection in third countries to be assessed before transborder data flows will be allowed.[45] In May 2000, the European Union (EU) Member States approved an agreement with the US concerning arrangements to safeguard individual privacy in transborder data flow which, in effect, attempt to reconcile the self-regulatory regime in the US with the legislative

---

43   *Self-Regulation and Privacy Online,* available at www.ftc.gov/os/1999/9907/privacy99.pdf.
44   SG/EC (1998) 14 final, available at www.oecd.org//dsti/sti/it/consumer/prod/cpguidelines_final.pdf.
45   See the discussion on Arts 25 and 26 below, p 333.

approach in the EU (the so called 'Safe Harbor Agreement', discussed in more detail below). Surprisingly, perhaps, in view of the content of the previous reports and the sometimes acrimonious nature of the safe harbor discussions, the FTC coincidentally published a further Report,[46] calling for statutory intervention in the US to safeguard individual privacy.

Privacy Online: Fair Information Practices in the Electronic Marketplace
FTC, May 2000

The Commission has long encouraged industry to address consumer concerns regarding online privacy through self-regulation ... In its 1998 testimony before Congress, the Commission stated that is was 'hopeful that self-regulation [would] achieve adequate online privacy protections for consumers'. The Commission, however, also 'recognize[d] that there [were] considerable barriers to be surmounted for self-regulation to work'. Specifically, the Commission noted that 'an effective enforcement mechanism is crucial' to the success of self-regulation, and that 'it [would] be difficult for self-regulatory programs to govern all or even most commercial Web sites'. Nevertheless, in light of industry efforts at that time, the Commission recommended that Congress refrain from passing legislation. The Commission noted, however, that unless industry could demonstrate that it had developed and implemented broad-based and effective self-regulatory programs, additional government authority in this area might be necessary. In its 1999 Report, a majority of the Commission again determined that legislation was not then appropriate, but noted the 'substantial challenges' that industry continued to face in implementing widespread self-regulation.

The Commission recognizes the magnitude of the public policy challenge presented by Internet privacy and applauds the significant accomplishments of the private sector in developing self-regulatory initiatives to date. The improved statistics regarding the number of Web sites with privacy disclosures and the development of online seal programs are a tribute to industry's ongoing efforts in this area. The Commission also applauds the industry leaders who have adopted fair information practices. The 2000 Survey data, however, demonstrate that industry efforts alone have not been sufficient. Because self-regulatory initiatives to date fall far short of broad-based implementation of self-regulatory programs, the Commission has concluded that such efforts alone cannot ensure that the online marketplace as a whole will follow the standards adopted by industry leaders ...

Ongoing consumer concerns regarding privacy online and the limited success of self-regulatory efforts to date make it time for government to act to protect consumers' privacy on the Internet. Accordingly, the Commission recommends that Congress enact legislation to ensure adequate protection of consumer privacy online. In doing so, however, the Commission recognizes that industry self-regulation, as well as consumer and business education, should still play important roles in any legislative framework, as they have in other contexts.

Whether or not legislation will be forthcoming in the US remains to be seen, but, if there is statutory intervention in this area, it will represent a significant step towards global harmonisation of the legal regulation of one aspect of activity on the internet.

---

46   Available at www.ftc.org/reports/privacy2000/privacy2000text.pdf.

THE DATA PROTECTION DIRECTIVE (95/46/EC)

In view of the Council of Europe Convention on the Processing of Personal Data, it was not surprising that the legislation of those Member States of the EU who regulated this area would be couched in similar terms. It was, nevertheless, perceived that the discrepancies between them were sufficient to warrant further harmonisation between the Member States. Despite the Convention, by the end of the 1980s, some Member States still had no appropriate legislation and a further concern was that any differences in the protection afforded to data in each Member State might lead to restrictions on transborder data flow from those countries with a higher level of protection. This would obviously impede the functioning of the internal market, a crucial factor in the wake of the date of 31 December 1991 set by the Single European Act 1986 for the completion of the Single European Market. Accordingly, in 1990, a proposal for a Directive on the Protection of Individuals with regard to the Processing of Personal Data and on the Free Movement of such Data was published.[47]

The foregoing might suggest that a primary reason was business efficacy and the facilitation of free movement of data, but the competing interests endemic in this area are strongly represented in the preamble to the original proposal, which refers not only to transborder data flows, but also to the importance of protecting the right of privacy. In the event, the final version was to be a long time in gestation – one problem was to devise legislation which would both ensure a high level of protection and yet not compromise that already in place in some Member States. In view of the different interpretations put on the various concepts in the different jurisdictions, the Economic and Social Committee were particularly concerned as to whether the proposal actually increased the level of protection or merely accentuated the differences between Member States. An amended proposal was published in 1992,[48] but, although this was debated by the European Parliament and approved subject to amendments,[49] progress then seemed to come to a halt. Action was eventually precipitated by activity in a related area, in the shape of the Recommendations to the European Council from the High Level Group on the Information Society (the Bangemann Report). This Report, initiated by the European Council in December 1993 and produced for the Corfu Summit in 1994, looked at all facets of the Information Society. Chapter 3, 'Completing the agenda', contains reference to those provisions which will need to be taken into account if the full benefit of the new era is to be realised without any risk of consequent damage and disadvantage. These include, *inter alia*, a consideration of privacy issues:

> The demand for the protection of privacy will rightly increase as the potential of the new technologies to secure (even across national frontiers) and to manipulate detailed information on individuals from data, voice and image sources is realised. Without the legal security of a Union-wide approach, lack of consumer confidence will certainly undermine rapid development of the information society.

> Europe leads the world in the protection of the fundamental rights of the individual with regard to personal data processing. The application of new technologies potentially

---

47 COM (1990) 314 final, SYN 287 [1990]; OJ 1990 C 277/3.
48 COM (1992) 422 final, SYN 287 [1992]; OJ 1992 C 311/30.
49 OJ 1992 C 94/198.

affects highly sensitive areas such as those dealing with the images of individuals, their communication, their movements and their behaviour. With this in mind, it is quite possible that most Member States will react to these developments by adopting protection, including trans-frontier control of new technologies and services.

Disparities in the level of protection of such privacy rules create the risk that national authorities might restrict free circulation of a wide range of new services between Member States in order to protect personal data.

The Group believes that without the legal security of a Union-wide approach, lack of consumer confidence will certainly undermine the rapid development of the information society. Given the importance and sensitivity of the privacy issue, a fast decision from Member States is required on the Commission's proposed Directive setting out general principles of data protection.

This recommendation, from such an eminent source, proved the necessary boost to revive the proposed Directive. In the period between the original proposal and the Bangemann Report, new legislative procedures had been adopted following the Treaty on European Union and the proposed Directive had become subject to the co-decision procedure under the new Art 189b of the EC Treaty (now Art 251, following the entry into force of the Treaty of Amsterdam 1999). In pursuance of this process, the Council adopted a common position early in 1995[50] and, following the decision of the Parliament,[51] the final Directive was published in October 1995.[52] The adopted Directive is a much amended and augmented version of the original 1990 proposal and contains a total of 72 recitals in the preamble. However, it is an indication of the general agreement between Parliament and the Council on this issue that the final text exhibits only very minor changes to that of the common position.

PROVISIONS OF DIRECTIVE 95/46/EC

Article 1 sets out the objectives of the Directive. First, and fundamentally, this Article refers to the protection of privacy, signalling that, even though limited, data protection is part of the fundamental right of privacy, albeit within a specifically defined area:

Article 1
Object of the Directive

1   In accordance with this Directive, Member States shall protect the fundamental rights and freedoms of natural persons, and in particular, their right to privacy with respect to the processing of personal data.

However, this is immediately followed by an important counterbalancing provision:

2   Member States shall neither restrict nor prohibit the free flow of personal data between Member States for reasons connected with the protection afforded under paragraph 1.

---

50   OJ 1995 C 93/1.

51   OJ 1995 C 166/80 and 105.

52   European Parliament and Council Directive 95/46/EC on the Protection of Individuals with regard to the Processing of Personal Data and on the Free Movement of Such Data, 24 October 1995, OJ 1995 L 281/31, available at www.europa.eu.int/eur-lex/en/lif/dat/1995/en_395L0046.html.

Thus, as far as the Member States of the EU are concerned, the free flow of personal data is envisaged for whatever purpose and this flow cannot be restricted, assuming that there is compliance with the provisions of the Directive. This is, of course, a necessary consequence of the harmonisation of data protection law throughout the EU and the situation is, as we shall see below, rather different for transborder data flow to third countries.

The scope of the Directive is independent of the mode of storage of the data or information:

Article 2
Definitions

...

(c) 'personal data filing system' ('filing system') shall mean any structured set of personal data which are accessible according to specific criteria, whether centralized, decentralized or dispersed on a functional or geographic basis ...

Article 3
Scope

1 This Directive shall apply to the processing of personal data wholly or partly by automatic means, and to the processing otherwise than by automatic means of personal data which form part of a filing system or are intended to form part of a filing system.

Although the foregoing discussion has concentrated on the technological threat to privacy, this provision makes it clear that so called 'manual data' are also included within the ambit of the Directive, albeit that there are clear limits to the application of the Directive to manual data, as can be inferred from the definition above and from Recital 27:

... as regards manual processing, this Directive covers only filing systems, not unstructured files; whereas, in particular, the content of a filing system must be structured according to specific criteria relating to individuals, allowing easy access to personal data; whereas, in line with the definition in Art 2(c), the different criteria for determining the constituents of a structured set of personal data, and the different criteria governing access to such a set, may be laid down by each Member State; whereas files or sets of files as well as their cover pages, which are not structured according to specific criteria, shall under no circumstances fall within the scope of this Directive.

The UK expressed some disquiet over the inclusion of manual records in this way and a derogation was negotiated, allowing manual records which predated the Directive a period of 12 years before compliance by Member States was required, subject to the provision that, if they were subjected to further manual processing in the interim, they should be brought into conformity at that time (Art 32(2) and Recital 69).

The Directive does not apply to the processing of data outside the scope of Community competence:

Article 3

2 This Directive shall not apply to the processing of personal data:

in the course of an activity which falls outside the scope of Community law, such as those provided for by Titles V and VI of the Treaty on European Union and in any case to processing operations concerning public security, defence, State security (including the economic well being of the State when the processing operation relates to State security matters) and the activities of the State in areas of criminal law ...

There has been some debate over what is intended to be encompassed by this requirement. Presumably, it includes all areas of economic and business activity which the Community has competence to regulate, but it will then be for individual Member States to decide whether or not to include other activities within the protection afforded by their legislation. Nonetheless, the Directive refers to the 'activities of the State' – it is clear that there is not a general prohibition on the processing of records relating to crime, since this is further governed by Art 8(5) referring to sensitive data.[53]

Definitions of the salient terms are found in Art 2, of which those concerning the meaning of 'personal data' and 'processing' are expressed in particularly wide terms:

Article 2

... 'personal data' shall mean any information relating to an identified or identifiable natural person ('data subject'); an identifiable person is one who can be identified, directly or indirectly, in particular by reference to an identification number or to one or more factors specific to his physical, physiological, mental, economic, cultural or social identity;

'processing of personal data' ('processing') shall mean any operation or set of operations which is performed upon personal data, whether or not by automatic means, such as collection, recording, organization, storage, adaptation or alteration, retrieval, consultation, use, disclosure by transmission, dissemination or otherwise making available, alignment or combination, blocking, erasure or destruction ...

The data protection principles

In common with many other international and national instruments on this topic, the Directive lays down principles of good data management. Article 6 appears to give only five principles, but some matters, such as subject access and security, which are often included in some other versions (compare the OECD *Guidelines*) are dealt with elsewhere in the Directive:

Article 6
Principles relating to data quality

1   Member States shall provide that personal data must be:

(a) processed fairly and accurately;

---

53 In this context, there is potential for conflict between the data protection regime and that introduced for criminal records by the Police Act 1997, Pt V, as amended by the Protection of Children Act 1999, administered by the Criminal Records Bureau. Compare the Data Protection Act, s 56 and see, also, *Better Regulation Taskforce: Review of Fit Person Criteria*, available at www.cabinet-office.gov.uk/regulation/1999/task_force/fitpersons.pdf; the Report prepared for the Office of the Data Protection Registrar by the Personnel Policy Research Unit on the *Use and Abuse of Personal Data in the Employment Situation*, available at www.dataprotection.gov.uk/ppru.htm. The website of the Criminal Records Bureau is available at www.crb.gov.uk/index.htm.

(b) collected for specified, explicit and legitimate purpose and not further processed in a way incompatible with those purposes. Further processing of data for historical, statistical or scientific purposes shall not be considered as incompatible provided that Member States provide appropriate safeguards;

(c) adequate, relevant and not excessive in relation to the purposes for which they are collected and/or further processed;

(d) accurate, and where necessary, kept up to date; every reasonable step must be taken to ensure that data which are inaccurate or incomplete, having regard to the purposes for which they were collected or for which they are further processed, are erased or rectified;

(e) kept in a form which permits identification of data subjects for no longer than is necessary for the purposes for which the data were collected or for which they are further processed. Member States shall lay down appropriate safeguards for personal data stored for longer periods for historical, statistical or scientific use.

In the definitions set out in Art 2, the Directive distinguishes between the 'controller' and the 'processor' of data, the latter being merely one who processes data on behalf of the controller. The 'controller' is the one (whether alone or jointly with others) who 'determines the purposes and means of processing personal data'. All controllers of personal data in the areas covered by the Directive will be required to adhere to the principles,[54] even if they are subject to exemption from notification (see below).

Criteria for lawful processing

The general standard for lawful processing of non-sensitive personal data is contained in Art 7:

Article 7
Criteria for making data processing legitimate

Member States shall provide that personal data may be processed only if:

(a) the data subject has unambiguously given his consent; or

(b) processing is necessary for the performance of a contract to which the data subject is party or in order to take steps at the request of the data subject prior to entering into a contract; or

(c) processing is necessary for compliance with a legal obligation to which the controller is subject; or

(d) processing is necessary in order to protect the vital interests of the data subject; or

(e) processing is necessary for the performance of a task carried out in the public interest or in the exercise of official authority vested in the controller or in a third party to whom the data are disclosed; or

(f) processing is necessary for the legitimate interests pursued by the controller.

Article 6(1)(c) and Arts 7(c) and (e) were held to be directly effective in Case C-465/00 *Rechnungshof v Österreichischer Rundfunk* on the basis that they were unconditional obligations and so were sufficiently precise to be relied on by individuals and applied in the national courts.[55] This suggests that the other provisions in Arts 6(1) and 7,

---

54   See, also, Directive 95/46/EC, Recital 51.
55   [2003] ECR I-4989, [2003] 3 CMLR 10, para. 100.

although not at issue in this case, will also have direct effect as they are couched in similarly unconditional language.

Separate provision is made for the processing of so called 'sensitive' data in Art 8, which appears to start from the premise that such information should not be processed at all:

Article 8
The processing of special categories of data

1   Member States shall prohibit the processing of personal data revealing racial or ethnic origin, political opinions, religious of philosophical beliefs, trade-union membership, and the processing of data concerning health or sex life.

However, subsequent paragraphs provide for certain occasions when such processing will be allowed subject to appropriate safeguards, examples of which are given below:

2   Paragraph 1 shall not apply where:

 (a) the data subject has given his explicit consent to the processing of those data, except where the laws of the Member State provide that the prohibition referred to in paragraph 1 may not be lifted by the data subject's giving his consent; or

 (b) processing is necessary for the purposes of carrying out the obligations and specific rights of the controller in the field of employment law in so far as it is authorized by national law providing for adequate safeguards; or

 (c) processing is necessary to protect the vital interests of the data subject or of another person where the data subject is physically or legally incapable of giving his consent; or

 (d) processing is carried out in the course of its legitimate activities with appropriate guarantees by a foundation, association or any other non-profit-seeking body with a political, philosophical, religious or trade-union aim and on condition that the processing relates solely to the members of the body or to persons who have regular contact with it in connection with its purposes and that the data are not disclosed to a third party without the consent of the data subjects; or

 (e) the processing relates to data which are manifestly made public by the data subject or is necessary for the establishment, exercise or defence of legal claims.

3   Paragraph 1 shall not apply where processing of the data is required for the purposes of preventive medicine, medical diagnosis, the provision of care or treatment or the management of health-care services, and where those data are processed by a health professional subject under national law or rules established by national competent bodies to the obligation of professional secrecy or by another person also subject to an equivalent obligation of secrecy.

Taking the provisions of Arts 7 and 8 together, it is clear that, unless the specific exceptions apply, and assuming that Member States have not outlawed the processing of sensitive personal data entirely, the processing of both sensitive and non-sensitive data can only be legitimised by the consent of the data subject. Such consent is qualified by the adjective *unambiguous* with respect to non-sensitive data and by *explicit* with respect to sensitive data. Consent is defined in Art 2(h) as 'any freely given specific and informed indication of his wishes by which the data subject signifies his agreement to personal data relating to him being processed'. What is the significance of the different qualifications placed on consent in these two Articles? Clearly, if consent is to be construed as unambiguous, then there must be no room for doubt, but explicit consent suggests a higher standard of proof, in which the consent is distinctly stated and cannot be implied, however unequivocal the implication. Before the adoption of the Directive, it was common to construe consent from the absence of objection, but, even for non-sensitive data, it seems that the Directive may require more positive action to legitimise processing of personal data. The presumption is thus changed from one in which further processing is permitted unless a contrary indication is notified, to one in which it is not permitted unless there is definite evidence of consent. At a minimum, it would appear that even the qualification 'unambiguous' 'strengthens the argument that the consent must entail a clear indication of the agreement of the individual',[56] whereas the use of the qualification 'explicit' suggests that the fact that consent has been given must be established beyond doubt.

With respect to non-sensitive data, the alternative criteria in Art 7 are all qualified by the use of the word *necessary*, which imports a strict construction and an objective standard beyond mere convenience and desirability for the data controller. In respect of sensitive data, it can be seen that, by and large, the exceptions are targeted at very specific situations where there are other legitimate objectives to be attained by the processing of the data in question.

Rights of data subjects

From the inception of the provisions in Art 1(1), the Directive places individual rights firmly within its ambit. The express reference to the right of privacy in relation to the processing of personal data is amplified by the more detailed rights set out in Sections IV, V and VII. These rights can be divided, loosely, into the right of access, the right to information and the right to object. These are then reinforced and supplemented by provisions relating to compensation and judicial remedies.

Information to be given to the data subject

Article 10
Information in cases of collection of data
from the data subject

Member States shall provide that the controller or his representative must provide a data subject from whom data relating to himself are collected with at least the following information, except where he already has it:

(a) the identity of the controller and of his representative, if any;

(b) the purposes of the processing for which the data are intended;

(c) any further information, such as:

  – the recipients or categories of recipients of the data,

  – whether replies to the questions are obligatory or voluntary, as well as the possible consequences of failure to reply,

  – the existence of the right of access to and the right to rectify the data concerning him,

---

56   Jay and Hamilton, 2003, p 94.

in so far as such further information is necessary, having regard to the specific circumstances in which the data are collected, to guarantee fair processing in respect of the data subject.

Article 11
Information where the data have not been obtained
from the data subject

1   Where the data have not been obtained from the data subject, Member States shall provide that the controller or his representative must at the time of undertaking the recording of personal data or if a disclosure to a third party is envisaged, no later than the time when the data are first disclosed provide the data subject with at least the following information, except where he already has it:

  (a) the identity of the controller and of his representative, if any;

  (b) the purposes of the processing;

  (c) any further information, such as:

     – the categories of data concerned,

     – the recipients or categories of recipients,

     – the existence of the right of access to and the right to rectify the data concerning him,

    in so far as such further information is necessary, having regard to the specific circumstances in which the data are processed, to guarantee fair processing in respect of the data subject.

2   Paragraph 1 shall not apply where, in particular for processing for statistical purposes or for the purposes of historical or scientific research, the provision of such information proves impossible or would involve a disproportionate effort or if recording or disclosure is expressly laid down by law. In these cases Member States shall provide appropriate safeguards.

The data subject's right of access to data

Article 12
Right of access

Member States shall guarantee every data subject the right to obtain from the controller:

  (a) without constraint at reasonable intervals and without excessive delay or expense:

     – confirmation as to whether or not data relating to him are being processed and information at least as to the purposes of the processing, the categories of data concerned, and the recipients or categories of recipients to whom the data are disclosed,

     – communication to him in an intelligible form of the data undergoing processing and of any available information as to their source,

     – knowledge of the logic involved in any automatic processing of data concerning him at least in the case of the automated decisions referred to in Article 15(1);

  (b) as appropriate the rectification, erasure or blocking of data the processing of which does not comply with the provisions of this Directive, in particular because of the incomplete or inaccurate nature of the data;

  (c) notification to third parties to whom the data have been disclosed of any rectification, erasure or blocking carried out in compliance with (b), unless this proves impossible or involves a disproportionate effort.

The Directive provides no general right to object to processing of personal data, as this would be likely to be disproportionate to the objective of maintaining the free flow of personal data. It does, however, provide a limited right in two particular situations which are perceived as having the potential to severely prejudice individuals.

The data subject's right to object

Article 14
The data subject's right to object

Member States shall grant the data subject the right:

(a) at least in the cases referred to in Article 7(e) and (f), to object at any time on compelling legitimate grounds relating to his particular situation to the processing of data relating to him, save where otherwise provided by national legislation. Where there is a justified objection, the processing instigated by the controller may no longer involve those data;

(b) to object, on request and free of charge, to the processing of personal data relating to him which the controller anticipates being processed for the purposes of direct marketing, or to be informed before personal data are disclosed for the first time to third parties or used on their behalf for the purposes of direct marketing, and to be expressly offered the right to object free of charge to such disclosures or uses.

Member States shall take the necessary measures to ensure that data subjects are aware of the existence of the right referred to in the first subparagraph of (b):

Article 15
Automated individual decisions

1   Member States shall grant the right to every person not to be subject to a decision which produces legal effects concerning him or significantly affects him and which is based solely on automated processing of data intended to evaluate certain personal aspects relating to him, such as his performance at work, creditworthiness, reliability, conduct, etc.

2   Subject to the other Articles of this Directive, Member States shall provide that a person may be subjected to a decision of the kind referred to in paragraph 1 if that decision:

(a) is taken in the course of the entering into or performance of a contract, provided the request for the entering into or the performance of the contract, lodged by the data subject, has been satisfied or that there are suitable measures to safeguard his legitimate interests, such as arrangements allowing him to put his point of view; or

(b) is authorized by a law which also lays down measures to safeguard the data subject's legitimate interests.

Article 14(a) refers to processing in connection with the exercise of official authority vested in the controller, tasks carried out in the public interest or the purposes of the legitimate interests pursued by the controller. In this case, it is possible for this right to be overridden by national legislation. The right to object to the use of personal data for direct marketing contained in Art 14(b) would, arguably, arise from a combination of other provisions, such as the need for unambiguous consent and the principle of fair processing. But, in view of the depth of feeling on this matter, an expressly stated right is welcome.

Notification

Some of the first generation data protection statutes were based on a concept of universal registration, but this had been criticised as unnecessarily bureaucratic and cumbersome to administer. The Directive replaces the concept of registration with one of notification:

Article 18
Obligation to notify the supervisory authority

1   Member States shall provide that the controller or his representative, if any, must notify the supervisory authority ... before carrying out any wholly or partially automatic processing operation or set of such operations intended to serve a single purpose or several related purposes.

Article 19
Contents of notification

1   Member States shall specify the information to be given in the notification. It shall include at least:

 (a) the name and address of the controller and of his representative, if any;

 (b) the purpose or purposes of processing;

 (c) a description of the category or categories of the data subject and of the data or categories of data relating to them;

 (d) the recipients or categories of recipient to whom the data might be disclosed;

 (e) proposed transfers of data to third countries;

 (f) a general description allowing a preliminary assessment to be made of the appropriateness of the measures taken ... to ensure security of processing.

It is open to Member States to simplify the notification process, or to exempt from notification in certain circumstances specified in further parts of Art 18, or to extend any aspects of the notification process to non-automatic processing operations (Art 18(5)).

The purpose of the notification and related provisions is to ensure transparency, rather than to create a method of control, but the Directive recognised that there may be situations where further investigation is both relevant and desirable:

Article 20
Prior checking

1   Member States shall determine the processing operations likely to present specific risks to the rights and freedoms of data subjects and shall check that these processing operations are examined prior to the start thereof.

2   Such prior checks shall be carried out by the supervisory authority following receipt of notification from the controller or by the data protection official, who, in cases of doubt, must consult the supervisory authority.

3   Member States may also carry out such checks in the context of preparation either of a measure of the national parliament or of a measure based on such a legislative measure, which define the nature of processing and lay down appropriate safeguards.

Exemptions

As already mentioned, limiting the scope of the Directive to matters within the competence of the Community to legislate (as detailed in Art 3(2)) effectively means that processing for certain purposes will, in any case, fall out with the provisions of the Directive. Further, Art 3(2) also provides that the Directive does not apply to processing of personal data 'by a natural person in the course of a purely personal or household activity'. However, there are also other areas which may attract exemption from some or all of the provisions. Exemptions for the purpose of controlling information are a common feature of statutes, be it personal information, as here, or public information, which may also be controlled by freedom of information legislation. Such exemptions arise in recognition of the fact that there may be overriding reasons which will mitigate against disclosing what would otherwise be public information, or allowing access to what would otherwise be protected as personal.

Some of the reasoning behind allowing exemptions was discussed by the UK Data Protection Registrar in *Questions to Answer: Paper 9 – The Exemptions*:

> ... exemptions should only be permitted in limited circumstances. Broadly, these are the circumstances where achieving the 'right' balance of interests requires the data protection rule to be disapplied. What is meant by the 'right' balance will vary according to the particular circumstances ... it may be that the balance, for example, favours the public interest whereas in others it favours the individual data subject or another individual ... the balance may require safeguarding the privacy of third parties at the expense of individuals' subject access rights by removing information identifying third parties when responding to a subject access request. What is meant by the 'rule' will also vary. It may, for example, be withholding information in response to a subject access request where provision of the information would be likely to prejudice the prevention of detection of crime in that particular case: a very narrow exemption applying to only one area of data protection regulation.

The Council of Europe Convention requires that any exemptions from the data protection rules must be:

> ... a necessary measure in a democratic society in the interests of:
>
> (a) protecting State security, public safety, the monetary interests of the State or the suppression of criminal offences;
>
> (b) protecting the data subject or the rights and freedoms of others.

It appears that the exemptions provided in the Directive are capable of a wider construction than those of the Convention.

Article 13
Exemptions and restrictions

1   Member States may adopt legislative measures to restrict the scope of the obligations and rights provided ... when such a restriction constitutes a necessary measure to safeguard:

   (a) national security;

   (b) defence;

   (c) public security;

(d) the prevention, investigation, detection and prosecution of criminal offences, or of breaches of ethics for regulated professions;

(e) an important economic or financial interest of a Member States or of the EU, including monetary, budgetary and taxation matters;

(f) a monitoring, inspection or regulatory function connected, even occasionally, with the exercise of official authority in cases referred to in (c), (d) and (e);

(g) the protection of the data subject or of the rights and freedoms of others.

As well as the exemptions expressly referred to in Art 13, there are other limitations on the application of the Directive, such as the permissible derogations from the obligation to notify, referred to above. It also appears, from Recital 29 and Art 6(1)(e), that it is expected that there will be exemption provided, in relation to length of time, for storage of personal data used for historical and statistical purposes.

A further exemption is contained in Art 9:

Article 9
Processing of personal data and freedom of expression

Member States shall provide for exemptions or derogations ... for the processing of personal data carried out solely for journalistic purposes or the purpose of artistic or literary expression only if they are necessary to reconcile the right to privacy with the rules governing the freedom of expression.

Behind the provision of derogations for these so called special purposes is the tacit assumption that the media should be treated differently, although on what basis is not explicitly stated.[57]

Whether or not the media are a special case, it is axiomatic that upholding a right of privacy may at the same time be breaching the right to freedom of expression, and vice versa. Where the protection of one fundamental right may impinge on the enjoyment of another right, the problem of achieving a satisfactory balance is never amenable to easy solution. The Directive leaves it to Member States to achieve an appropriate balance in this context, a process which needs to be viewed within the wider debate of press freedom and privacy[58] but which will, inevitably, be influenced by the distinctive cultures and legal traditions of the individual Member States.

Transborder data flows

In the discussion of individual rights, it must not be forgotten that the Directive, in common with other data protection regulation,[59] has the dual objective of both safeguarding privacy in relation to processing of personal data and facilitating

---

57 Perri, 1998.

58 See, e.g., *Review of Press Regulation*, Cm 2135, 1993, London: HMSO; Consultation Paper of the Lord Chancellor's Department, *Infringement of Privacy*, 1993, London: Scottish Office; Wacks, 1995.

59 Compare, e.g., the Council of Europe Convention, which attempts, *inter alia*, to reconcile the notion of effective data protection with the ideal of free flow of information, as set out in the European Convention on Human Rights, Art 10. In pursuance of this, Art 12 of the Convention, on automatic processing of data, contains provisions allowing restriction of transborder data flows 'except where the regulations of the other Party provide an equivalent protection [for the personal data]'.

transborder data flow (Art 1). The importance of the free flow of such data is further underlined by part of the first sentence of Recital 56: '... cross-border flows of personal data are necessary for the expansion of international trade ...'. Thus, there are no grounds for restricting the free flow of data, provided that the appropriate safeguards are in place. Indeed, it is the very necessity referred to in Recital 56 which makes protection of the individual so vital. Given the expected harmonisation of protection created by the Directive, cross-border data flow between individual Member States would not be expected to create an additional threat to the privacy of individuals. The situation could be very different, though, in relation to transfer of data to third countries which may not have data protection to the same extent, or at all. For this reason, Arts 25 and 26 are of extreme importance and their inclusion within the Directive has led many commentators to speculate on the potentially wide reaching effect of the Directive. Thus, Bennett[60] has suggested that the 'Data Protection Directive now constitutes the rules of the road for the increasingly global character of data processing operations' and Mayer-Schönberger[61] predicts that the Directive will assist the drive to homogeneity of approach on a global scale.

Transfer of data to third countries

Article 25
Principles

1   The Member States shall provide that the transfer to a third country of personal data which are undergoing processing or are intended for processing after transfer may take place only if, without prejudice to compliance with the national provisions adopted pursuant to the other provisions of this Directive, the third country in question ensures an adequate level of protection.

The question of whether or not personal data had actually been transferred to a third country was considered by the ECJ in Case C-101/01 *Bodil Lindqvist*.[62] Mrs Lindqvist had developed an internet home page as part of a course she was following. She published on this site the personal data of a number of people who worked with her on a voluntary basis in a parish of the Swedish Protestant church for which she was a catechist. This included not just names and addresses but also family circumstances, health issues and other comments. Her colleagues were not informed of this and neither did she notify the relevant supervisory authority. She was subsequently charged with a number of offences relating to breaches of data processing rules and a number of questions were referred to the ECJ. One of these asked 'whether there is any transfer [of data] to a third country ... where an individual loads personal data onto an internet page which is stored on an internet site on which the page can be consulted and which is hosted by a natural or legal person ... thereby making those data accessible to anyone who connects to the internet, including people in a third country.' The question also went on to ask whether it made any difference to the answer if no one from a third country actually accessed the page.

---

60   Bennett, 1998, p 111.
61   Mayer-Schönberger, 1998, p 223.
62   [2004] 1 CMLR 20, [2004] QB 1014.

Bodil Lindqvist
[2004] 1 CMLR 20
European Court of Justice

58. Information on the internet can be consulted by an indefinite number of people living in many places at almost any time. The ubiquitous nature of that information is a result, *inter alia*, of the fact that the technical means used in connection with the internet are relatively simple and becoming less and less expensive.

59 Under the procedures for use of the internet available to individuals ... the author of a page intended for publication on the internet transmits the data making up that page to his hosting provider. That provider manages the computer infrastructure needed to store those data and connect the server hosting the site to the internet. That allows the subsequent transmission of those data to anyone who connects to the internet and seeks access to it. The computers which constitute that infrastructure may be located, and indeed often are located, in one or more countries other than that where the hosting provider is established, without its clients being aware or being in a position to be aware of it.

60 ... in order to obtain the information appearing on the internet pages on which Mrs Lindqvist had included information about her colleagues, an internet user would not only have to connect to the internet but also personally carry out the necessary actions to consult those pages. In other words, Mrs Lindqvist's internet pages did not contain the technical means to send that information automatically to people who did not intentionally seek access to those pages.

61 It follows that, in circumstances such as those in the case in the main proceedings, personal data which appear on the computer of a person in a third country, coming from a person who has loaded them onto an internet site, were not directly transferred between those two people but through the computer infrastructure of the hosting provider where the page is stored. ...

The court then went on to discuss the extent to which the Directive was intended to apply to publication on the internet or could be interpreted as applying to publication of personal data on the internet.

68 Given, first, the state of development of the internet at the time Directive 95/46 was drawn up and, second, the absence, in Chapter IV, of criteria applicable to use of the internet, one cannot presume that the Community legislature intended the expression transfer [of data] to a third country to cover the loading, by an individual in Mrs Lindqvist's position, of data onto an internet page, even if those data are thereby made accessible to persons in third countries with the technical means to access them.

69 If Art.25 of Directive 95/46 were interpreted to mean that there is transfer [of data] to a third country every time that personal data are loaded onto an internet page, that transfer would necessarily be a transfer to all the third countries where there are the technical means needed to access the internet. The special regime provided for by Chapter IV of the directive would thus necessarily become a regime of general application, as regards operations on the internet. Thus, if the Commission found, pursuant to Art.25(4) of Directive 95/46, that even one third country did not ensure adequate protection, the Member States would be obliged to prevent any personal data being placed on the internet.

70 Accordingly, it must be concluded that Art.25 of Directive 95/46 is to be interpreted as meaning that operations such as those carried out by Mrs Lindqvist do not as such constitute 'a transfer [of data] to a third country'. ...

71 The reply to the fifth question must therefore be that there is 'no transfer [of data] to a third country' within the meaning of Art 25 of Directive 95/46 where an individual in a Member State loads personal data onto an internet page which is stored with his hosting provider which is established in that State or in another Member State, thereby making those data accessible to anyone who connects to the internet, including people in a third country.

This is perhaps not a surprising judgment given the potential impact, noted in para 69, that a contrary finding could have. Conceptually it can be likened to a finding that, in the virtual world, individuals accessing an internet page containing personal data 'visit' that page rather than the data is sent to them. This is not dissimilar to the approach taken by Jacob J in *Euromarket Designs Inc v Peters*,[63] in relation to trade mark infringement, in which he likened browsing on commercial sites on the internet to looking into the shop or 'visiting' it. On the other hand, the approach taken in some defamation cases, discussed later in this chapter,[64] equates publication on the internet with publication to the world; i.e. something rather more active.

Assuming that, in a particular case, there has actually been a transfer of personal data, the more difficult issue raised by Art 25 is the interpretation of 'adequate'. Should 'adequate protection' mean 'in conformity with the Directive'? Or 'functional similarity'? Or some lesser standard? How should, or can, this be assessed? The second paragraph of Art 25 sets out some of the factors to be taken into account:

2   The adequacy of the level of protection afforded by a third country shall be assessed in the light of all the circumstances surrounding a data transfer operation or set of data transfer operations; particular consideration shall be given to the nature of the data, the purpose and duration of the proposed processing operation or operations, the country of origin and country of final destination, the rules of law, both general and sectoral, in force in the third country in question and the professional rules and security measures which are complied with in that country.

3   The Member States and the Commission shall inform each other of cases where they consider that a third country does not ensure an adequate level of protection ...

4   Where the Commission finds ... that a third country does not ensure an adequate level of protection ... Member States shall take the measures necessary to prevent any transfer of data of the same type to the third country in question.

Art 25(2) is of little help in providing any indication of clear priority amongst the criteria to be applied in assessment of adequacy and does not explicitly create a reference point by which adequacy may, or should, be determined. It was envisaged that there would be practical problems encountered in the assessment of adequacy and a number of possible methodologies were explored. One report[65] prepared for the Commission used the concept of 'functional similarity', noting that Europe should not seek the direct transposition of its own principles and systems of protection into other countries. Instead, adequacy might be determined in the presence of any element in the regulation of a third country providing the relevant requirements, even if this was accomplished in a completely different way. Such an approach permits better respect

63 [2001] FSR 20 and see further discussion in Chapter 9.
64 See e.g. *Dow Jones & Co v Gutnick* [2002] HCA 56.
65 Poullet *et al*, 1998.

for local legal structures than the requirement for equivalent protection inherent in complete juristic similarity. The particular technique employed was to reduce the elements of data protection to 'risk factors', namely, loss of control, reuse, non-proportionality and inaccuracy, and assess the way in which they were protected. A further report[66] referred to the problem of 'cultural and institutional non-equivalence', pointing out that judgments of adequacy must appreciate and remain sensitive to important cultural differences. Despite the apparent convergence of data protection rules, privacy is still a variable concept and different legal traditions still place different emphasis on protection and apportionment of rights. The report also submitted that 'assessment of adequacy will be incomplete to the extent that it cannot assess actual practices and the realities of compliance' and that 'a more empirical analysis of policies and practices, as well as rules, serves both to advance the debate and to anticipate the specific problems that will be encountered in the implementation of the Directive'.

The Directive provides for two particular groups which, *inter alia,* have a role to play in relation to determination of adequacy. These are referred to as a 'Working Party' and a 'Committee':

Article 29
Working Party on the Protection of Individuals with regard to the Processing of Personal Data

1   A Working Party on the Protection of Individuals with regard to the Processing of Personal Data, hereinafter referred to as the 'Working Party', is hereby set up.

   It shall have advisory status and act independently.

2   The Working Party shall be composed of a representative of the supervisory authority or authorities designated by each Member State and of a representative of the authority or authorities established for the Community institutions and bodies, and of a representative of the Commission.

Article 30

1   The Working Party shall:

   (a) examine any question covering the application of the national measures adopted under this Directive in order to contribute to the uniform application of such measures;

   (b) give the Commission an opinion on the level of protection in the Community and in third countries;

   (c) advise the Commission on any proposed amendment of this Directive, on any additional or specific measures to safeguard the rights and freedoms of natural persons with regard to the processing of personal data and on any other proposed Community measures affecting such rights and freedoms;

   (d) give an opinion on codes of conduct drawn up at Community level.

3   The Working Party may, on its own initiative, make recommendations on all matters relating to the protection of persons with regard to the processing of personal data in the Community.

4   The Working Party's opinions and recommendation shall be forwarded to the Commission and the committee referred to in Article 31.

---

66   Raab *et al*, 1998.

Article 31
The Committee

1   The Commission shall be assisted by a committee composed of the representatives of the Member States and chaired by the representative of the Commission.

2   The representative of the Commission shall submit to the committee a draft of the measures to be taken. The committee shall deliver its opinion on the draft ...

The opinion shall be delivered by the majority laid down in Article 148(2) [now Article 205(2)] of the Treaty ...

The Commission shall adopt measures that shall apply immediately ...

The provisions above illustrate some of the important differences between these two bodies, in terms of both membership and functions. The differing membership is, of itself, suggestive of potential conflicts of interest as a result of different objectives and priorities. The key words in relation to the Working Party are 'advisory' and 'independent'. In this capacity, the Working Party has produced a large number of Opinions and Recommendations, a number of which have been referred to in this text.[67] The Art 31 Committee, on the other hand, clearly has a much more formal role in the legislative and oversight process. With specific reference to the assessment of adequacy, the formal outcome is made according to the procedure in Art 31(2) (see Art 25(4)–(6)) and, by virtue of Art 30(1)(b), the Working Party is specifically required to give an Opinion to the Commission on the level of protection in third countries. This is to be forwarded to the Art 31 Committee (Art 30(4)). Although, by Art 30(5), the Commission is under a duty to inform the Working Party of action taken in response to its Opinions and Recommendations, there appears to be no duty, as such, on the Commission to act on, or to take account of these.

The following extract explains the view of the Working Party on the issue of adequate protection.

Transfers of personal data to third countries:
Applying Arts 25 and 26 of the EU Data Protection Directive
Opinion 12/98[68]

Chapter One: Assessing Whether Protection Is Adequate

(1) What constitutes 'adequate protection'?

The purpose of data protection is to afford protection to the individual about whom data are processed. This is typically achieved through a combination of rights for the data subject and obligations on those who process data, or who exercise control over such processing. The obligations and rights set down in directive 95/46/EC build upon those set down in Council of Europe Convention No 108 (1981), which in turn are not dissimilar from those included in the OECD guidelines (1980) or the UN guidelines (1990). It would therefore appear that there is a degree of consensus as to the content of data protection rules which stretches well beyond the fifteen states of the Community.

However, data protection rules only contribute to the protection of individuals if they are followed in practice. It is therefore necessary to consider not only the content of rules

---

67   For a full list see www.europa.eu.int/comm/internal_market/en/media/dataprot/wpdocs/index.htm.

68   Available at www.europa.eu.int/comm/internal_market/en/media/dataprot/wpdocs/wp12en.htm.

applicable to personal data transferred to a third country, but also the system in place to ensure the effectiveness of such rules. In Europe, the tendency historically has been for data protection rules to be embodied in law, which has provided the possibility for non-compliance to be sanctioned and for individuals to be given a right to redress. Furthermore such laws have generally included additional procedural mechanisms, such as the establishment of supervisory authorities with monitoring and complaint investigation functions. These procedural aspects are reflected in directive 95/46/EC, with its provisions on liabilities, sanctions, remedies, supervisory authorities and notification. Outside the Community it is less common to find such procedural means for ensuring compliance with data protection rules. Parties to Convention 108 are required to embody the principles of data protection in law, but there is no requirement for additional mechanisms such as a supervisory authority. The OECD guidelines carry only the requirement that they be 'taken into account' in domestic legislation and provide for no procedural means to ensure that the guidelines actually result in effective protection for individuals. The later UN guidelines, on the other hand, do include provisions on supervision and sanctions, which reflects a growing realisation worldwide of the need to see data protection rules properly enforced.

Against this background it is clear that any meaningful analysis of adequate protection must comprise the two basic elements: the content of the rules applicable and the means for ensuring their effective application.

Using directive 95/46/EC as a starting point, and bearing in mind the provisions of other international data protection texts, it should be possible to arrive at a 'core' of data protection 'content' principles and 'procedural/enforcement' requirements, compliance with which could be seen as a minimum requirement for protection to be considered adequate. Such a minimum list should not be set in stone. In some instances there will be a need to add to the list, while for others it may even be possible to reduce the list of requirements. The degree of risk that the transfer poses to the data subject will be an important factor in determining the precise requirements of a particular case. Despite this proviso, the compilation of a basic list of minimum conditions is a useful starting point for any analysis.

The Working Party is thus clearly of the view that, due to the convergence of data protection rules, it is possible to specify a base level of protection which can be defined as adequate and which, because of its origin in a number of international Conventions, ought not to be too contentious for third countries. The Art 31 Committee arguably appears not to be so rigid:

> ... adequate protection is not, according to our interpretation or the interpretation of the Member States, equivalent protection, so we are not trying to use the precise standards of the Directive for establishing this standard, but nevertheless we do have to make it a relatively tough standard in order to protect the high levels of data processing which have been established in the Community itself.[69]

Nevertheless, it is clear that these two positions can amount to the same thing, as the Art 31 Committee went on to suggest that:

> Our approach is to look at our own Directive, to look at a number of important existing international standards such as the Council of Europe Convention, the OECD guidelines and so on, and try to distil out of that what are the fundamental principles which a decent data protection regime needs to protect. We would not expect that standard to be as high

---

69   Available at www.europa.eu.int/comm/internal_market/en/media/dataprot/backinfo/euus.htm.

and demanding as that of the Directive or as detailed, but it would contain the core principles ... We were not asked to apply equivalent protection or the same protection, but adequate protection.

The interaction of the Working Party and the Art 31 Committee can be observed in a number of the negotiations, which have already taken place or are ongoing, associated with assessment of the adequacy of the data protection in third countries. One of the first examples was the case of Switzerland, for example, in which the Working Party issued an Opinion on 7 June 1999.[70] This concluded that both federal and cantonal legislation in that jurisdiction was broadly in accordance with the Council of Europe Convention and that Switzerland could be considered to be ensuring an adequate level of protection. On 26 July 2000, the Commission issued a Decision[71] to that effect, which acknowledges (in Recital 12) that this opinion of the Working Party has been taken into account. More recently the level of data protection in Argentina has also been judged to be adequate using a similar process.[72]

In contrast, discussions concerning the adequacy of the primarily self-regulatory regime in the US proved to be not so simple or straightforward. The EU and US have been discussing data protection issues and privacy since before the entry into force of Directive 95/46/EC, with a view to trying to create a bridge between the EC legislative approach and the mainly self-regulatory approach in the US. So that the US would not be seen as a 'data haven', the adopted approach has been to attempt to define a 'safe harbor' for personal data, a set of principles that US companies would sign up to on a voluntary basis but to which they would then be bound. As explained by the EC Commission Information Society Directorate General:

> Safe harbor is a mechanism which, through an exchange of documents, enables the EU to certify that participating US companies meet the EU requirement for adequate privacy protection. Participation in the safe harbor is voluntary. Organisations will need to agree to adhere to the privacy requirements laid out in the safe harbor documents for all data received from the EU. The safe harbor is, figuratively, a place where US companies can find shelter from potentially damaging crosswinds caused by different privacy regimes in the US and EU.[73]

The advantage of this approach is that, whilst respecting the different regulatory culture on both sides of the Atlantic, it is able to provide legal certainty for EU data controllers exporting data to 'safe harbor' participants, it does not impose a too onerous administrative burden and it provides guidance to US companies and other organisations who wish to meet the 'adequate protection' standard specified in the Directive. It is these principles which have been examined for 'adequacy' against the Directive's provisions. The, at times, turbulent history of the 'safe harbor' negotiations can be charted by an examination of successive documents of the Working Party[74]

---

70   Available at www.europa.eu.int/comm/internal_market/en/media/dataprot/wpdocs/ wp22en.htm.
71   Commission Decision 2000/518 [2000] OJ L 215/1.
72   Working Party Opinion 4/2002 and Commission Decision 2003/1731 [2003] OJ L168. For details of other findings see www.europa.eu.int/comm/internal_market/privacy/ adequacy_en.htm.
73   Available at www.ispo.cec.be/ecommerce/epolicy/2000-06.html.
74   Six separate Opinions and a Working Document have been published since the beginning of 1999. For details see www.europa.eu.int/comm/internal_market/en/media/dataprot/ wpdocs/index.htm.

which expose the tension between the objectives of the various players involved. Given the commercial power of the US, there are clearly political motivations driving those who are directly participating in the discussions to work towards a negotiated, albeit inevitably compromised, settlement. On the other hand, the Working Party, with its independent yet only advisory status, has shown itself keen to uphold standards, suggesting a potential criticism that it is trying to equate the term 'adequate' with the protection afforded under the Directive.

At the inception of the discussions, the Working Party was of the view that 'the current patchwork of narrowly focused sectoral laws and voluntary self-regulation cannot at present be relied upon to provide adequate protection in all cases for personal data transferred from the EU'. It confirmed its view of the importance of international agreements, specifically the OECD *Guidelines*, which the US has, ostensibly, adopted:

> The Working Party considers that the standard set by the OECD guidelines of 1980 cannot be waived as it constitutes a minimum requirement for the acceptance of an adequate level of protection in any third country.

Nevertheless, it appeared to be generally in favour of the 'safe harbor' concept, referring to it as an 'agreed benchmark standard' and a 'useful approach'. As the proposed principles have developed through successive drafts, there are signs that the consensus which was being worked towards, which has now culminated in an agreement between the Commission and the US, was not completely shared by the Working Party. At the end of 1999 a further Opinion,[75] deplored the fact that 'most of the comments made in its previous position papers do not seem to be addressed in the latest version of the US documents' and confirmed both its general concerns and its view that the OECD *Guidelines* should represent a minimum requirement. Following the agreement, a further Opinion invited the Art 31 Committee to 'ensure that the final steps of this important process are taken only in the light of the final opinion of the Working Party'. This final Opinion confirmed the previous opinions and detailed the issues which were, in the view of the Working Party, of continuing cause for concern.

Agreement was eventually reached in the summer of 2000 and confirmed by a Commission Decision.[76] The rationale of 'safe harbor' is that organisations wishing to accept personal data from EU or EEA countries can agree to comply with the Safe Harbor principles by a self-certification method.[77] The level of protection offered to that data will then be deemed to be adequate for the purposes of Arts 25 and 26. They consist of seven principles issued by the US Department of Commerce and contained in Annex 1 to Decision 2000/520.

Decision 2000/520/EC – *Annex 1*
Safe Harbor Privacy Principles
NOTICE

An organization must inform individuals about the purposes for which it collects and uses information about them, how to contact the organization with any inquiries or

---

75 Opinion 7/99, available at www.europa.eu.int/internal_market/en/media/dataprot/wpdocs/wp27en.htm.
76 Decision 2000/520/EC of 26 July 2000, [2000] OJ L215/7.
77 For further details see www.export.gov/safeharbor/index.html.

complaints, the types of third parties to which it discloses the information, and the choices and means the organization offers individuals for limiting its use and disclosure. ...

CHOICE

An organization must offer individuals the opportunity to choose (opt out) whether their personal information is (a) to be disclosed to a third party or (b) to be used for a purpose that is incompatible with the purpose(s) for which it was originally collected or subsequently authorized by the individual. Individuals must be provided with clear and conspicuous, readily available, and affordable mechanisms to exercise choice. ...

ONWARD TRANSFER

To disclose information to a third party, organizations must apply the Notice and Choice Principles. ...

SECURITY

Organizations creating, maintaining, using or disseminating personal information must take reasonable precautions to protect it from loss, misuse and unauthorized access, disclosure, alteration and destruction.

DATA INTEGRITY

Consistent with the Principles, personal information must be relevant for the purposes for which it is to be used. An organization may not process personal information in a way that is incompatible with the purposes for which it has been collected or subsequently authorized by the individual. To the extent necessary for those purposes, an organization should take reasonable steps to ensure that data is reliable for its intended use, accurate, complete, and current.

ACCESS

Individuals must have access to personal information about them that an organization holds and be able to correct, amend, or delete that information where it is inaccurate, except where the burden or expense of providing access would be disproportionate to the risks to the individual's privacy in the case in question, or where the rights of persons other than the individual would be violated.

ENFORCEMENT

Effective privacy protection must include mechanisms for assuring compliance with the Principles, recourse for individuals to whom the data relate affected by non-compliance with the Principles, and consequences for the organization when the Principles are not followed. ...

It has been pointed out by Ewing that these principles conform, in the main, to those articulated in the Council of Europe Convention and the OECD *Guidelines*, but not to the more detailed requirements of the Directive.[78] 'Safe Harbor' has had a mixed reception. Immediately after the Commission decision was adopted, the European Parliament expressed concerns that the Commission had exceeded its powers in reaching its agreement with the US. It suggested that it 'go back to the negotiating table and change the agreement in such a way that the individual right of appeal to an independent body is recognised where the principles of data protection are alleged to have been violated'.[79] Neither were American companies initially queuing to join.

---

78 Ewing, 2002.
79 *European Parliament Session News*, available at www.europarl.eu.int/dg3/sdp/pointses/en/ps000703_ens.htm#19.

Schriver reports that after six months only 12 companies had signed up. This number slowly rose – by March 2002, there were 168 organisations in the Safe Harbor.[80] This number has steadily increased, and by June 2005, 738 companies had signed up.[81]

The detailed rules in Art 25 can be ameliorated to a certain extent by derogations provided in Art 26(1). These are not dissimilar to those provided in Arts 7 and 8 and are based primarily on the data subject's consent, the data subject's interest or where transfer is from publicly available registers or documents. In addition, Art 26(2) provides another route whereby adequate protection can be assured:

Article 26
Derogations

2. ... a Member State may authorize a transfer or a set of transfers of personal data to a third country which does not ensure an adequate level of protection within the meaning of Article 25(2), where the controller adduces adequate safeguards with respect to the protection of the privacy and fundamental rights and freedoms of individuals and as regards the exercise of the corresponding rights; such safeguards may in particular result from appropriate contractual clauses.

This provision has resulted in a further Commission Decision on standard contractual clauses for the transfer of personal data to third countries.[82] Annex 1 of this decision sets out standard clauses for the protection of personal data which will conform to the requirements of the Directive.

DATA PROTECTION IN THE UK

The Data Protection Directive was implemented in the UK by the Data Protection Act 1998,[83] which was finally brought into force on 1 March 2000. The structure of this statute follows that of the previous enactment, the Data Protection Act 1984. Both statutes are rather different from most other UK statutes. In relation to the 1984 Act, Stallworthy suggests that this arose because the main provisions followed the Council of Europe Convention and were, therefore, influenced by principles of statutory draftsmanship which are more usually associated with civil law systems.[84] The view of Aldhouse is that: 'the Data Protection Act is unprecedented. Even the black letter criminal provisions make use of new concepts'.[85] Both statutes are based on the premise of compliance with principles of good data management – the 'data protection principles' – which are contained in a Schedule appended to the Act. The earlier statute was based on the notion of universal registration but, unfortunately, the

---

80 Schriver, 2002.
81 Although not all of these are still current there is a requirement to renew the notification every 12 months, see list at web.ita.doc.gov/safeharbor/shlist.nsf/webPages/safe+harbor+list.
82 Decision 2001/497/EC of 15 June 2001 [2001] OJ L181/19.
83 See www.legislation.hmso.gov.uk/acts/acts1998/19980029.htm.
84 Stallworthy, 1990.
85 Aldhouse, 1991, p 184.

manner of drafting meant that these principles could only be enforced against those registered. This created a lacuna whereby the only action which could be taken against those not registered was a prosecution for non-registration, regardless of the degree to which the principles had apparently been flouted. This is no longer the case, as registration has now been superseded by a notification requirement and the principles can be enforced against all users regardless of whether notification has, in fact, taken place. The Information Commissioner, the role of the Data Protection Commissioner created by the 1998 Act having been subsumed in the office of Information Commissioner following the Freedom of Information Act 2000, is given powers to enforce the principles with the aid of a range of enforcement notices. A number of criminal offences and individual remedies are also created in the body of the statute.

Basic definitions are included in s1 of the Act which includes, *inter alia*, the following:

Data Protection Act 1998
Section 1
Basic interpretative provisions

In this Act, unless the context otherwise requires –

'data' means information which –

(a) is being processed by means of equipment operating automatically in response to instructions given for that purpose,

(b) is recorded with the intentions that it should be processed by means of such equipment,

(c) is recorded as part of a relevant filing system or with the intention that it should form part of a relevant filing system, …

'data controller' means … a person who (either alone or jointly or in common with other persons) determines the purposes for which and the manner in which any personal data are, or are to be, processed;

'data processor', in relation to personal data, means any person (other than an employee of the data controller) who processes the data on behalf of the data controller;

'data subject' means an individual who is the subject of personal data;

'personal data' means data which relate to a living individual who can be identified –

(a) from those data, or

(b) from those data and other information which is in the possession of, or is likely to come into the possession of, the data controller, and includes any expression of opinion about the individual and any indication of the intentions of the data controller or any other person in respect of the individual;

'processing', in relation to information or data, means obtaining, recording or holding the information or data or carrying out any operation or set of operations on the information or data, including –

(a) organisation, adaptation or alteration of the information or data,

(b) retrieval, consultation or use of the information or data,

(c) disclosure of the information or data by transmission, dissemination or otherwise making available, or

(d) alignment, combination, blocking, erasure or destruction of the information or data.

'relevant filing system' means any set of information relating to individuals to the extent that, although the information is not processed by means of equipment operating automatically in response to instructions given for that purpose, the set is structured, either by reference to individuals or by reference to criteria relating to individuals, in such a way that specific information relating to a particular individual is readily accessible.

Of these definitions, two have been the subject of judicial discussion in *Durant v FSA*.[86] The case arose out of a dispute between Durant and Barclays Bank which eventually led to Durant making a subject access request under s 7 of the DPA 1998, discussed later, to obtain personal data about him held by the Financial Services Authority which had been adjudicating his complaint with the bank. The FSA refused to provide all the information to which Durant believed he was entitled, on the basis that it did not all constitute 'personal data' as defined or that, if it did, it was not contained within a 'relevant filing system'. As discussed later, the basic entitlement in s 7 is to information constituting personal data which means that the precise scope of this definition is vital in the assessment of the data subject's entitlement under the section. In addition, to the extent that some of the information may be contained in a 'relevant filing system' rather than on computer, the specific meaning of this phrase is also of significance. The court acknowledged the importance of interpreting the provisions of the Act in the light of the Directive which contains a definition of personal data in Art 2.

Data Protection Directive
Article 2
Definitions

For the purposes of this Directive:

(a) 'personal data' shall mean any information relating to an identified or identifiable natural person ('data subject'); an identifiable person is one who can be identified, directly or indirectly, in particular by reference to an identification number or to one or more factors specific to his physical, physiological, mental, economic, cultural or social identity.

The argument for Durant was that both definitions suggested a 'wide and inclusive definition of "personal data"' and one which 'covered any information retrieved as a result of a search under his name, anything on file which had his name on it or from which he could be identified or from which it was possible, to discern a connection with him.'[87] However the court came to the conclusion that the definition was much narrower than that.

Durant v Financial Services Authority
[2004] FSR 28
Court of Appeal

28. ... not all information retrieved from a computer search against an individual's name or unique identifier is personal data within the Act. Mere mention of the data subject in a document held by a data controller does not necessarily amount to his personal data. Whether it does so in any particular instance depends on where it falls in a continuum of relevance or proximity to the data subject as distinct, say, from transactions or matters in which he may have been involved to a greater or lesser degree. It seems to me that there are two notions that may be of assistance. The first is whether the information is biographical in a significant sense, that is, going beyond the recording of the putative data

---

86 [2004] FSR 28.
87 *Ibid*, para 24.

subject's involvement in a matter or an event that has no personal connotations, a life event in respect of which his privacy could not be said to be compromised. The second is one of focus. The information should have the putative data subject as its focus rather than some other person with whom he may have been involved or some transaction or event in which he may have figured or have had an interest, for example, as in this case, an investigation into some other person's or body's conduct that he may have instigated. In short, it is information that affects his privacy, whether in his personal or family life, business or professional capacity.

Auld LJ went on to distinguish information about Durant and information about his complaints and the objects of them which he was of the view could not fall within the definition of 'personal data.' He was also of the view that this narrow interpretation of personal data went 'hand in hand with a narrow meaning of 'relevant filing system".[88] Having considered the provisions and objectives of the Act, and also of both the Directive and the Council of Europe Convention which preceded them, he was extremely influenced by the fact that, notwithstanding the Convention's provision permitting extension to manual data, the provisions of all the instruments were substantially focused on computerised data.

48. It is plain from the constituents of the definition considered individually and together … that Parliament intended to apply the Act to manual records only if they are of sufficient sophistication to provide the same or similar ready accessibility as a computerised filing system. That requires a filing system so referenced or indexed that it enables the data controller's employee responsible to identify at the outset of his search with reasonable certainty and speed the file or files in which the specific data relating to the person requesting the information is located and to locate the relevant information about him within the file or files, without having to make a manual search of them. To leave it to the searcher to leaf through files, possibly at great length and cost, and fruitlessly, to see whether it or they contain information relating to the person requesting information and whether that information is data within the Act bears … no resemblance to a computerised search. … The statutory scheme for the provision of information by a data controller can only operate with proportionality and as a matter of common-sense where those who are required to respond to requests for information have a filing system that enables them to identify in advance of searching individual files whether or not it is 'a relevant filing system' for the purpose. …

50. … I conclude … that a 'relevant filing system' for the purpose of the Act is limited to a system:

(1) in which the files forming part of it are structured or referenced in such a way as clearly to indicate at the outset of the search whether specific information capable of amounting to personal data of an individual requesting it under s 7 is held within the system and, if so, in which file or files it is held; and

(2) which has, as part of its own structure or referencing mechanism, a sufficiently sophisticated and detailed means of readily indicating whether and where in an individual file or files specific criteria or information about the applicant can be readily located.

The decision in *Durant* has subsequently been applied and approved in *Johnson v Medical Defence Union*,[89] and has necessitated the Office of the Information

---

88   *Ibid*, para 27.
89   [2004] EWHC 347 and see later discussion.

Commissioner publishing revised guidance to data controllers and has resulted in some adverse academic comment. However it may not be the last word on the subject as, in May 2004, Durant submitted a complaint to the European Commission that this interpretation of the statute was not compatible with the Directive. This has instigated an investigation by the Commission, apparently focusing on the definition of 'personal data' rather than 'relevant filing system'.[90] This may lead to infringement proceedings in the European Court if, as a result of the investigatory process, the Commission reaches the conclusion that the Directive is not being adequately implemented.

THE DATA PROTECTION PRINCIPLES

The eight data protection principles are listed in Pt I of Sched 1 to the 1998 Act and some guidance on their interpretation in contained in Pt II of that Schedule. A number of the basic requirements contained in the 1998 data protection principles remain unchanged so, there will be case law under the 1984 Act which remains relevant.

Principle 1

1   Personal data shall be processed fairly and lawfully and, in particular, shall not be processed unless –

   (a) at least one of the conditions in Schedule 2 is met, and

   (b) in the case of sensitive personal data, at least one of the conditions in Schedule 3 is also met.

The definition of processing in s 1(1) gives a wide meaning, encompassing the majority of acts which could be applied to data, including the initial obtaining, a process which was treated as distinct from actual processing in the 1984 Act.[91] An interesting question has arisen as to whether the act of making data anonymous constitutes processing of that data and is therefore subject to the requirements of the first principle. The problem is well illustrated by the facts of *R v Department of Health ex p Source Informatics*.[92] Source Informatics provided software to pharmacists to record prescribing patterns of certain drugs by GPs, which could then be used by drug companies for marketing purposes. This was intended to be done with the consent and involvement of the GPs and the information was all made anonymous before being collated in this way. However, as a result of advice from the Department of Health that this information was subject to a duty of confidence, notwithstanding the fact that it had been made anonymous, many pharmacists and GPs refused to participate. Source Informatics therefore sought judicial review of the decision of the Department of Health that the use of the data in this way would constitute a breach of confidence.

---

90   see e.g. www.itspublicknowledge.info/newsletter8.htm, www.twobirds.com/english/ publications/legalnews/EU_Commission_investigation_UK_data_protection_legislation.cfm where it is suggested that other issues such as the lack of a definition of consent may also be scrutinised by the European Commission.

91   The 1984 version of the first data protection principle reads: 'The information to be contained in personal data shall be obtained and the personal data shall be processed, fairly and lawfully.'

92   [2000] 1 All ER 786, and see discussion in Rowe, 2000, pp 248 *et seq*.

At first instance, Latham J was of the view both that the information was subject to a duty of confidence, whether or not it had been made anonymous before being passed on, and that, in the absence of consent from the patient, there would be an offence under the 1984 Act for unauthorised use of data. He specifically rejected the 'sophistry' of a two stage test.[93] The precise nature of the relationship between data protection and breach of confidence and, indeed, between personal data and confidential data has still to be fully explored, but a number of relevant points were made by the Court of Appeal which were in conflict with Latham J's reasoning concerning the potential application of the 1998 Act. They considered the likely impact of the implementation of the 1995 Directive, even though this post-dated the relevant policy information, and, specifically, whether making the data anonymous could be considered processing. If the answer was yes, then all the conditions for lawful processing would apply, which might include the consent of the patients concerned; if the answer was no, then no consent or other conditions would be required. In the following extract, Simon Brown LJ considers the arguments for and against including making data anonymous within the definition of processing.

R v Department of Health ex p Source Informatics Ltd
[2000] 1 All ER 786, p 798

Simon Brown LJ ... [the] argument put at its simplest is that the proposed anonymisation of the information contained in a prescription form will – under the very wide definition of 'processing' set out in Art 2(b) – constitute the processing of data concerning the patient's health, and that this is impermissible under Art 8.1, such processing not being required for any of the stipulated purposes allowed for by Art 8.3 ... [The] best answer to this submission [for the GMC and Source] is that the Directive can have no more application to the operation of anonymising data than to the use or disclosure of anonymous data (which, of course, by definition is not 'personal data' and to which, therefore, it is conceded that the directive has no application). [Counsel for the GMC] points to the several recitals emphasising the right to privacy as the principal concern underlying this directive, and he places great reliance on recital 26:

> Whereas the principles of protection must apply to any information concerning an identified or identifiable person; whereas, to determine whether a person is identifiable, account should be taken of all the means likely reasonably to be used either by the controller or by any other person to identify the said person; whereas the principles of protection shall not apply to data rendered anonymous in such a way that the data subject is no longer identifiable; whereas codes of conduct within the meaning of Art 27 may be a useful instrument for providing guidance as to the ways in which data may be rendered anonymous and retained in a form in which identification of the data subject is no longer possible ...

Although this is clearly not the appropriate occasion to attempt a definitive ruling on the scope of the Directive – and still less of the impending legislation – I have to say that common sense and justice alike would appear to favour the GMC's contention. By the same token that the anonymisation of data is in my judgment unobjectionable here under domestic law, so too, I confidently suppose, would it be regarded by other Member States. Of course the processing of health data requires special protection and no doubt the 'erasure or destruction' of such data is included in the definition of processing for good reason: on occasion it could impair the patient's own health requirements. It by no means

---

follows, however, that the process envisaged here should be held to fall within the definition: on the contrary, recital 26 strongly suggests that it does not.

Assuming that there is processing as defined, then, by virtue of the first principle, this must be carried out both fairly and lawfully. 'Lawful' is not a term defined in either the 1998 Act or its predecessor.

Ninth Report of the Data Protection Registrar, June 1993[94]

4 Determining the Meaning of the Law: Lawfulness in the First and Second Data Protection Principles

The First Principle not only refers to fairness but also to lawfulness. It requires that personal data shall be processed lawfully. This term also arises in the Second Principle which requires that personal data shall be 'held only for ... lawful purposes' ...

No interpretation of the term 'lawful' is provided in the Act. Therefore, it has to be interpreted in accordance with the normal rule, which is that a word must be given its ordinary meaning unless the context in which it is used shows another intention. There is nothing in the Data Protection Act to suggest that the term should be given other than its normal meaning.

Lawfulness was considered in a House of Lords case in 1991[95] and in that case 'unlawful' was held to mean:

> ... something which is contrary to some law or enactment or is done without lawful justification or excuse.

This is a broad definition; it applies equally to the public and the private sectors and it applies both to those breaches of the law which can be punished by criminal penalties and those which are dealt with by the civil courts.

The effect of this broad definition is that a data user must comply with all relevant rules of law in relation to the purposes for which he holds personal data, and the ways in which he obtains and processes it. So, for example, it seems to me that information which is obtained by theft or in breach of an enforceable contractual agreement is likely to be unlawfully obtained under the First data protection principle. Data users may only lawfully hold personal data for purposes for which they have adequate powers, otherwise the data will be held for unlawful purposes under the Second data protection principle.

The Registrar also suggested certain areas for concern which might be fertile ground for breaches of the first and second data protection principles:

(i) Confidentiality

There are circumstances where an obligation of confidence arises between a data user and a data subject. This may flow from a variety of circumstances or in relation to different types of information. Examples might occur in respect of medical information or banking procedures. An obligation of confidence gives the data subject the right not to have his information used for other purposes or disclosed without his permission unless there are other overriding reasons in the public interest for this to happen.

Where an obligation of confidence arises it is unlawful for a data user to use the information for a purpose other than that for which it was provided. Where such a use involves the processing of the personal data, then this may entail unlawful processing within the meaning of the First Principle. This is important for those who hold and process information which may be subject to an obligation of confidence. ...

---

94 See, also, *Data Protection Registrar's Guidelines: Third Series*, November 1994, guideline 4.
95 *R v R* [1991] 3 WLR 767, p 775, *per* Lord Keith of Kinkel.

(ii) The *ultra vires* rule

... The *ultra vires* rule is a rule of law which states that those vested with statutory powers are only able to do those things that Parliament has allowed them to do by statute. This includes doing things that are reasonably necessary to allow them to fulfil their primary functions. It follows, therefore, that a statutory body which obtains, processes or holds personal data for a purpose for which it has no statutory authority will be acting *ultra vires* and, therefore, unlawfully in holding, obtaining and processing those data.

(iii) Excess of delegated powers

The rules applying to Crown bodies are similar in effect although technically different in law. Where a particular activity is covered by a statutory scheme, for example the payment of benefits, then the Secretary of State and government agency dealing with that area have to follow the rules laid down in the statute in order to act lawfully. If they do not do so they may be acting unlawfully. Even where there is no detailed specific law dealing with an area and it is dealt with under executive powers then those powers will be defined either expressly or implicitly. ...

(iv) The concept of legitimate expectations

... there is a continuing, firm, majority belief that government agencies can be trusted to keep and use information in a responsible way. It is within this context of the expectations of individuals that the concepts of legitimate expectation fall to be considered.

In essence this means that in some circumstances an individual who will be adversely affected by a decision of a public body will be entitled to be notified of or consulted about such a decision before it is made. ..... Failure to comply with a legitimate expectation may render unlawful any holding or processing of personal data associated with the proposed alteration in information practices.

It is clear here that the Data Protection Registrar was calling on established legal principles to suggest the likely interpretation of the terms at issue,[96] a practice which, as we shall see, may need to be continued in relation to other terms in the Act, such as consent.

The previous first data protection principle separated fair and lawful obtaining from fair and lawful processing. A number of appeals against notices served by the Data Protection Registrar under the 1984 Act relating to the concepts of both fair obtaining and fair processing of data led to the Data Protection Tribunal considering both of these issues. Since the absorption of 'obtaining' into the definition of 'processing', this distinction appears no longer current but, nonetheless, the guidance on interpretation of the principles given in the second part of Sched 1 refers to these two concepts separately. In the light of both the existing case law and the guidance in the 1998 Act, it is therefore convenient to consider these two aspects individually.

(a) Information shall be obtained fairly[97]

Some of the factors to be taken into account in the decision as to whether information has been obtained *fairly* came before the Tribunal as a consequence of a notice served

---

96 See, also, in this context, Jay and Hamilton, 2003, Ch. 5.
97 For the statutory guidance on interpretation of fair obtaining see the Data Protection Act 1998, Sched 1, Pt II.

on the mail order company, Innovations Ltd. As well as supplying goods mail order, this firm derived a significant amount of its income by trading in lists of customer names and addresses and making these lists available to other companies for direct marketing purposes (so called 'list rental'). Direct marketing practices are now, of course, explicitly referred to in the Directive in relation to the right to object to processing. At the time of this incident, the whole area of direct marketing[98] and trading in customer details was already a concern for those seeking to regulate data management in response to the fact that customer data had become a commodity in its own right. In 1985, a Council of Europe Recommendation[99] suggested that:

> The collection of data from an individual for any reason other than normal customer or contributor relations should be permissible for direct marketing purposes only on condition that this has been expressly stated at the time of collection.

The Recommendation further suggested that the customer should have rights to refuse to allow their data to be included on lists, to have the lists transmitted to third parties and to have data removed from lists. The same view had been taken by the Registrar – that individuals should be notified of the likelihood of their personal details being used for list rental before, or at the time of, obtaining the relevant data if that data were to be deemed to be *fairly* obtained. There was evidence that this had been generally accepted, as it was included in the British Code of Advertising Practice,[100] which included the stipulation that customers should be given the opportunity to object at the time of data collection and should be advised if the purposes for which the data were to be used changed subsequently. However, in contrast, there had also been a strong lobby from a sector of the industry during the draft stages of the EC Directive on Data Protection against the requirement that the data subject be informed of the purposes of the intended processing.[101]

It was against this background that a notice was served on Innovations Ltd. The enterprise obtained its custom by orders from their catalogues and in response to advertisements placed in the media. Customers ordering directly from the catalogues were advised of the possibility of their details being made available for other purposes, but those responding to the advertisements did not receive this information until after they had placed an order, that is, after they had supplied their personal details in response to the advertisement. The company argued that it was not practicable to provide notice of this practice in all other media advertisements, because of time and space constraints, and that later notification was more appropriate, as it would allow customers to be given more choice over the potential use of their information. The Registrar, on the other hand, argued that, if the obtaining was to be fair, the customer had to be aware of all the potential uses of personal details at the time that the order was made. The company appealed against the notice.

---

98 That this remained a concern is reflected in the introduction of Directive 95/46/EC and, hence, in the 1998 Act of a right to object to processing for the purposes of direct marketing, see below p 367.
99 Council of Europe Recommendation No R (85) 20 1985.
100 On rules for direct marketing, including list and database management, see, e.g., *Encyclopedia of Data Protection* paras 5-419–5-437. See bibliography.
101 This lobby was not successful and the final Art 10 of Directive 95/46/EC has evolved from a right of the data subject to be informed to a duty on the data user to inform.

Innovations (Mail Order) Limited v Data Protection Registrar[102]
Case DA/92 31/49/1

30   We have reached a conclusion that the words 'fairly obtained' in the first data protection principle direct attention to the time of obtaining, not to a later time. We do not ignore the facts and circumstances of what happens thereafter. They may provide evidence of the purpose or purposes for which the data was in fact obtained and may provide evidence of the intention of the data user when he has sought, received, collected and obtained the personal information. We conclude in the facts and circumstances of this case that a purpose for which personal information is obtained, namely, list trading, is not obvious, unless clearly stated before it is obtained. The purpose that is obvious is the supply of goods. We conclude the personal information will not be fairly obtained unless the data subject is so told of the non-obvious purpose before the information is obtained. We have taken into account that many advertisers give notice in ordinary language in their advertisements that they may trade in names and addresses. Many give prospective customers the option to order without having their names and addresses traded. We do not have to decide whether the absence of such a choice may in certain circumstances, for example, with a monopoly supplier, result in unfair obtaining. What the enforcement notice seeks to achieve is that each advertisement should warn that trading in personal information may result if the name and address is supplied. Many traders are likely to incorporate choice for the customer as to whether to have his name list traded or not in order to avoid loss of trade. It may also assist those to whom the lists are traded since it will remove from the lists those who are unlikely to be interested in such direct mail. The fact that many advertisers currently give, notice in their advertisements where they trade in personal information makes it more likely that the absence of such a warning, where there is nonetheless a general purpose to list trade, increases the risk that members of the public will be misled.

31   We conclude that a later notice may be a commendable way of providing a further warning, but whether it does so or not, we conclude that the law requires in the circumstance we have here that when possible the warning must be before the obtaining. This can best be done by including the warning in the advertisement itself. Where it may not be possible (eg, the use of existing names for a new purpose) we consider that the obligation to obtain the data subject's positive consent for the non-obvious use of their data falls upon the data user.

In order to ensure compliance with the original form of the first data protection principle, the most frequent practice engaged in by companies who participate in list rental was to provide an 'opt out' box in their order form or advert to enable customers to indicate if they did not wish their data to be used in this way. The scope of fair obtaining was returned to in the later case of *Linguaphone Institute Ltd v Data Protection Registrar*.[103] Here, the Data Protection Tribunal confirmed the decision in *Innovations* and drew attention to the fact that it could equally be a violation of the first data protection principle if the opt out box was not clearly positioned and/or was in such minute typeface that it could not be regarded as putting customers on notice of the potential use of their data.[104]

---

102 *Encyclopedia of Data Protection*, paras 6-176–6-178.

103 Case DA/94 31/49/1.

104 The courts have, of course, taken a similar approach in relation to disclaimers and trade descriptions: 'To be effective, any such disclaimer must be as bold, precise and compelling as the trade description itself and must be as effectively brought to the notice of any person to whom the goods may be supplied.' (*Norman v Bennett* [1974] 1 WLR 1229, p 1232 *per* Lord Widgery.) Compare, also, cases on incorporation of contractual terms: see, eg, the reasoning advanced in *Roe v RA Naylor* [1917] 1 KB 712, *per* Bailhache J.

19   ... we are concerned that the opt out box appears in minute print at the bottom of the
     order form. In the Tribunal's view the position, size of print and wording of the opt
     out box does not amount to a sufficient explanation to an enquirer that the company
     intends or may wish to hold use or disclose that personal data provided at the time
     of enquiry for the purpose of trading in personal information ... [105]

It is a moot point whether the arguably more stringent requirements of consent,
already discussed in relation to the Directive and expanded upon below in relation to
the Act, are met by the use of the opt out box. An opt in box would be capable of
providing a more unequivocal indication of the view of the data subject. We shall
return to this point during the discussion of fair processing.

(b) Information shall be processed fairly

Any assessment of whether processing is fair will need to take into account the
purposes of processing, the type of processing and the consequences to the data
subject. Consideration of some of the issues involved in the determination of fair
processing arose out of a number of appeals against enforcement notices served
against certain credit reference agencies. In each case, the important fact was that the
method of processing was too wide – typically by address rather than by name,
resulting in persons being judged to be bad credit risks on the basis of another person's
record. This was illustrated, by what was agreed to be a representative complaint, in
the case of *CCN Systems Ltd and CCN Credit Systems Ltd v Data Protection Registrar*. J
had bought a house from W. Three years later, J applied for a cheque guarantee card
but was refused and was told that CCN had provided the credit reference. A copy of
his file (obtained under s 158 of the Consumer Credit Act 1974) showed a judgment
against W. The only connection between J and W was that they had, at separate times,
lived at the same address. This led to a further consideration of the interpretation of
fair processing.

*CCN Systems Ltd and CCN Credit Systems
Ltd v Data Protection Registrar*[106]
Case DA/90 25/49/9

Fairness

48   We now come to the crucial question whether the processing that we have described
     may be said to be unfair ...

...

51   The word 'fairly' in the first principle is not defined in the Act, and no guidance is
     given as to its interpretation. In determining its meaning we must have regard to the
     purpose of the Data Protection Act. It is quite clear, from the Act as a whole and in
     particular from the data protection principles set out in Sched 1, that the purpose of
     the Act is to protect the rights of the individual about whom data is obtained, stored,
     processed or supplied, rather than those of the data user.

---

105 The decisions in *Innovations* and *Linguaphone* resulted in the Registrar publishing revised
    guidelines concerning list and database management in relation to direct marketing.
    Following the Data Protection Directive, data subjects now have an absolute right to object to
    use of their data for direct marketing purposes.
106 *Encyclopedia of Data Protection*, paras 6-055–6-056.

52 In our view, in deciding whether the processing we have described is fair we must give the first and paramount consideration to the interests of the applicant for credit- the 'data subject' in the Act's terms. We are not ignoring the consequences for the credit industry of a finding of unfairness, and we sympathise with their problems, but we believe that they will accept that they must carry on their activities in accordance with the principles laid down in the Act of Parliament.

53 Having taken due account of the evidence we have heard and the considerations urged upon us we have come to the clear conclusion that it is unfair for a credit reference agency, requested by its customers to supply information by reference to a named individual, so to program the extraction of information as to search for information about all persons associated with a given address or addresses notwithstanding that those persons may have no links with the individual the subject of the enquiry or may have no financial relationship with that individual. We believe this to be so even if the customer has requested address-based information and notwithstanding what is said to be its predictive value. We reject the notion that an organisation like CCN, with its wide specialist knowledge of and experience in credit reference and credit scoring, is a mere 'conduit pipe.' We believe the sort of processing carried out in this case is the very sort of activity at which the Act is aimed. We think it right to say that we accept that CCN did not intend to process data unfairly, and did not believe itself to be acting unfairly. But it is necessary to determine the question of fairness objectively, and in our view the case of unfairness has been made out.

Two important points are made here: first, in relation to the purpose of the legislation in protecting the rights of the individual; and, secondly, in relation to the fact that the standard is one of objective fairness – therefore, the matter of whether or not the data user had the motive or intention to breach the data protection principles is irrelevant. A further case, that of *Infolink Ltd v Data Protection Registrar*, discussed the 'extraction of information constituting the data', a rather obscure facet of processing which is no longer a part of the definition. In addition, it clarified the position in relation to balancing the competing interests of the individual and the processor. It was noted that the fact that in *CCN* the needs of the individual had been referred to as paramount did not mean that the applicant's interests prevailed over all other interests. It was necessary to weigh the various considerations but, in so doing, the Tribunal was entitled to give more weight to the interests of the individual, in line with the objectives of the legislation. Given the increased emphasis on individual rights in the Directive and the 1998 Act, it is unlikely that this approach will be modified in any material way.

In addition to the general requirement of fair and lawful processing, the first principle further stipulates that personal data shall not be processed unless one of the conditions in Sched 2 are met.

Data Protection Act 1998

SCHEDULE 2

Conditions Relevant for Purposes of the First Principle:
Processing of any Personal Data

1 The data subject has given his consent to the processing.

2 The processing is necessary –

(a) for the performance of a contract to which the data subject is a party, or

(b) for the taking of steps at the request of the data subject with a view to entering into a contract.

3   The processing is necessary for compliance with any legal obligation to which the data controller is subject, other than an obligation imposed by contract.

4   The processing is necessary in order to protect the vital interests of the data subject.

5   The processing is necessary –

(a) for the administration of justice,

(b) for the exercise of any functions conferred on any person by or under any enactment,

(c) for the exercise of any functions of the Crown, a Minister of the Crown or a government department, or

(d) for the exercise of any other functions of a public nature exercised in the public interest by any person.

6   (1) The processing is necessary for the purposes of legitimate interests pursued by the data controller or by the third party or parties to whom the data are disclosed, except where the processing is unwarranted in any particular case by reason of prejudice to the rights and freedoms or legitimate interests of the data subject.

In addition, for sensitive personal data, there must be compliance with at least one of the conditions in Sched 3. 'Sensitive personal data' is defined by s 2 as:

... personal data consisting of information as to –

(a) the racial or ethnic origin of the data subject,

(b) his political opinions,

(c) his religious beliefs or other beliefs of a similar nature,

(d) whether he is a member of a trade union (within the meaning of the Trade Union and Labour Relations (Consolidation) Act 1992,

(e) his physical or mental health or condition,

(f) his sexual life,

(g) the commission or alleged commission by him of any offence, or

(h) any proceedings for any offence committed or alleged to have been committed by him, the disposal of such proceedings or the sentence of any court in such proceedings.

SCHEDULE 3

Conditions Relevant for Purposes of the First Principle: Processing of Sensitive Personal Data

1   The data subject has given his explicit consent to the processing of the personal data.

2   (1) The processing is necessary for the purposes of exercising or performing any right or obligation which is conferred or imposed by law on the data controller in connection with employment ...

3   The processing is necessary –

(a) in order to protect the vital interests of the data subject or another person, in a case where –

(i)   consent cannot be given by or on behalf of the data subject, or

(ii) the data controller cannot reasonably be expected to obtain the consent of the data subject, or

(b) in order to protect the vital interests of another person, in a case where consent by or on behalf of the data subject has been unreasonably withheld.

4   The processing –

(a) is carried out in the course of its legitimate activities by any body or association which –

(i) is not established or conducted for profit, and

(ii) exists for political, philosophical religious or trade-union purposes,

(b) is carried out with appropriate safeguards for the rights and freedoms of data subjects,

(c) relates only to individuals who either are members of the body or association or have regular contact with it in connection with its purposes, and

(d) does not involve disclosure of the personal data to a third party without the consent of the data subject.

5   The information contained in the personal data has been made public as a result of steps deliberately taken by the data subject.

6   The processing –

(a) is necessary for the purpose of, or in connection with, any legal proceedings (including prospective legal proceedings),

(b) is necessary for the purpose of obtaining legal advice, or

(c) is otherwise necessary for the purposes of establishing, exercising or defending legal rights.

7   (1) The processing is necessary –

(a) for the administration of justice,

(b) for the exercise of any functions conferred on any person by or under an enactment, or

(c) for the exercise of any functions of the Crown, a Minister of the Crown or a government department ...

8   (1) The processing is necessary for medical purposes and is undertaken by –

(a) a health professional, or

(b) a person who in the circumstances owes a duty of confidentiality which is equivalent to that which would arise if that person were a health professional.

(2) In this paragraph 'medical purposes' includes the purposes of preventative medicine, medical diagnosis, medical research, the provision of care and treatment and the management of healthcare services.

9   (1) The processing –

(a) is of sensitive personal data consisting of information as to racial or ethnic origin,

(b) is necessary for the purpose of identifying or keeping under review the existence or absence of equality of opportunity or treatment between persons of different racial or ethnic origins, with a view to enabling such equality to be promoted or maintained, and

(c) is carried out with appropriate safeguards for the rights and freedoms of data subjects.

The constraints on processing contained in Scheds 2 and 3 mirror those in Arts 7 and 8 of the Directive (see above) and are based on a requirement of consent, unless the processing falls within one of the listed categories for which the process or its purpose is deemed *necessary*. An interesting difference is that the qualification 'unambiguous' in Art 7 has been omitted, although the presumably higher standard of explicit consent in Art 8 has been retained. Further the word 'consent', although defined in the Directive, has not been given a definition in the Act,[107] possibly because it is a word which has been much discussed in both civil and criminal case law. A comprehensive exploration of the issues surrounding consent in relation to data protection is given by Jay and Hamilton who note that 'consent is an area in which there is a variety of case law drawn from different areas of law'.[108] The extent to which the same standard of consent might be appropriate in different circumstances is debatable, but some interesting points were made in a case under the Landlord and Tenant Act 1954 on the distinction between consent and acquiescence. These seem to be of particular relevance to the scope of consent, which has erstwhile been implied from a failure to complete the 'opt out' box.

Bell v Alfred Franks & Bartlett Co Ltd
[1980] 1 All ER 356

Shaw LJ   ... If acquiescence is something passive in the face of knowledge, what does 'consent' mean? In the context of the contrast implicit in the subsection, the only practical and sensible distinction that can be drawn is that if acquiescence can arise out of passive failure to do anything, consent must involve a positive demonstrative act, something of an affirmative kind. It is not to be implied, because the resort to implication betokens an absence of express affirmation. The only sense in which there can be implied consent is where a consent is demonstrated, not by language but by some positive act other than words which amounts to an affirmation of what is being done and goes beyond mere acquiescence in it. It may lead, in this context, to a false conclusion to speak of 'implied consent', which is what the learned judge said was the proper inference to be drawn from the long history of acquiescence. I would prefer for myself to say 'consent' involves something which is of a positive affirmative kind ...

Waller LJ   ... but acquiescence is something which has to be contrasted with consent and, in my judgment, consent requires some positive action on the part of the landlord or his predecessor, usually no doubt in words, perhaps in writing, possibly, if gestures were absolutely clear, it could conceivably be by gesture but, in my view, careful proof of such an intention would be required. Normally one would look for some express statement, either in writing or orally ...

Thus, a positive 'opt in' rather than an 'opt out' box might conform to Shaw LJ's requirement of a 'positive act' as a necessary prerequisite of a demonstration of consent. Although consent to process was not an overt feature of the 1984 Act, nonetheless it was discussed in a number of proceedings of the Data Protection Tribunal as a necessary ingredient of fair processing, and so should be not be regarded as an entirely new ingredient. In *Innovations*, the Tribunal pointed out that, if there was use of data for a further purpose to that for which it had been provided and which was non-obvious to the data subject, then it was incumbent on the data user (now controller) to obtain the data subject's positive consent. This issue was discussed

---

107 The lack of a definition of consent is understood to be one of the reasons for the European Commission investigating the UK's implementation of the data protection directive following the complaint of Durant, see above fn. 90.

108 Jay and Hamilton, 2003.

further in the later case of *British Gas Trading Ltd v Data Protection Registrar*.[109] British Gas customers were sent circulars allowing them to opt out of processing for other purposes, specifically marketing purposes for products and services which were not, necessarily, related to the supply of gas. Many customers did not return the circular and subsequently brought complaints about the non-obvious further use of their data. The Tribunal considered both the role of consent as a part of fair processing and the view of the Registrar, based on the previous Tribunal decisions, that 'any intended use must be clear to the data subject at the time at which the information in collected by the data user, unless it can be shown that there has been subsequent consent and that consent cannot be inferred from a lack of response to a circular offering an opt out'. This led the tribunal to the conclusion that 'processing, without consent, for wider uses than could reasonably have been expected from a monopoly gas supplier and which are not obvious uses, is unfair'.

Principle 2

> Personal data shall be obtained only for one or more specified and lawful purposes, and shall not be further processed in any manner incompatible with that purpose or those purposes.

This principle essentially combines the ingredients of both the second and third principles in the 1984 Act. It was seen in relation to the first principle that use beyond the purpose for which the data was collected can be an aspect of fair processing, but this principle puts it beyond doubt that processing must relate only to the original purpose of collection. A case under the 1984 Act provides an illustration. In *Macgregor v Procurator Fiscal of Kilmarnock*,[110] the neighbour of a police officer was concerned about the man with whom his 18-year-old daughter was living and asked the police officer if he could find out any information for him. Certain information about the man in question was obtained from both the Police National Computer and the Scottish Criminal Records Computer and the police officer communicated some of this to the daughter in a telephone call, with the intention of trying to persuade her to return to her father. He was found to have used the information for a purpose other than that for which registration had been made, and appealed on the basis that, as he was seeking to maintain law and order and was concerned for the girl's welfare, he had used the information for policing purposes. According to the terms of registration under the 1984 Act, 'policing purposes' included the protection of life and property, the maintenance of law and order and the rendering of assistance to the public. Whilst the court accepted that the police officer's motives were undoubtedly humanitarian, the purpose of his action could not be equated with a policing purpose as defined and his appeal was dismissed.

Principle 3

> Personal data shall be adequate, relevant and not excessive in relation to the purpose or purposes for which they are processed.

---

109 See 14th Annual Report of the Data Protection Registrar, 1998, London: HMSO, Appendix 6.
110 22 June 1993; see *Encyclopedia of Data Protection* para 6-513.

This wording is identical to that of the fourth principle in the previous Act, although its application may now need adjustment in the light of the wider definition of 'processing'. The interpretation of this principle has been discussed in a number of tribunal decisions prior to the 1998 Act. During the existence of the short lived Community Charge, or 'poll tax', a number of complaints were received that information required by those administering the tax was in excess of that needed. The task of compiling and maintaining the register of those who were subject to the charge was the duty of the Community Charge Registration Officers (CCROs) in each area. In relation to the fourth data protection principle, the Registrar had already produced guidelines suggesting that data users should establish the minimum amount of information they could hold which was compatible with their intended purposes and, as a result, a number of CCROs modified their requests. A number of officers did not comply and applications to register were refused on this basis, in accordance with the old s 7(2)(b). The CCROs appealed. Three of these appeals were heard together, as they all concerned the gathering of information concerning the type of property inhabited, a factor which was argued to have no relevance to the levying of a *per capita* tax.

Community Charge Registration Officers of Runnymede BC, South Northamptonshire DC and Harrow BC v Data Protection Registrar
Cases DA/90 24/49/3, 4 and 5

Having concluded that property type information was personal data we had to consider whether we were satisfied that the holding of such data infringed the fourth data protection principle that the data should be adequate relevant and not excessive for the purposes for which it was held by the CCRO ... We considered the duty to maintain the register could properly include the obtaining and holding of at least some additional information on the computer database ... The appellant submitted that we should not take a very restrictive view of the discretion that a particular CCRO might exercise as to the amount of additional information he considered should be held to assist him to carry out his statutory duty. While there may be some force in the argument that what is judged to be excessive should not in some circumstances be too strictly construed we concluded that it could not be decisive where the issue is whether a wide class of data such as property type information should be held without any kind of limitation as to the extent of what was held ...

We were referred in the course of the hearing to the Guideline booklet Number 4 issued by the Data Protection Registrar, entitled *The Data Protection Principles*. Paragraph 4.2 relating to the fourth principle advises that data users should seek to identify the minimum amount of information about each individual which is required in order properly to fulfil their purpose and that they should try to identify the cases where additional information will be required and seek to ensure that such information is only collected and recorded in those cases. We endorse this general guidance for those wishing to have a test to apply to answer the question whether personal data is adequate, relevant and no excessive for the purposes for which it is held. We find that the appellants held on database a substantial quantity of property type information obtained from voluntary answers on the canvass forms or from other sources. It was established that in holding such information, the appellants were holding far more than was in fact necessary for their purposes ...

We find and the appellants appear to accept, that it is not relevant and would be excessive to hold wide classes of data merely on he ground that future changes in the law may in remote and uncertain future circumstances require further property types to be added to the existing exceptions identified by the Data Protection Registrar.

A further case considered a similar question, this time in relation to the gathering of information regarding dates of birth. It was accepted by the Registrar that it might, on occasion, be necessary to hold dates of birth in relation to certain categories of person, such as those who were almost 18, students, etc, and, subject to these exceptions, the majority of CCROs removed any reference to date of birth for other individuals. However, the CCRO for Rhondda did not comply and alleged, *inter alia*, that the information required was necessary because holding dates of birth provided a useful method of distinguishing between people in an area in which many had both surnames and given names in common.

Community Charge Registration Officer of
Rhondda BC v Data Protection Registrar
Case DA/90 25/49/2

There was evidence before us that nationally less than one per cent of households contained persons with the same surname and the same first name. There was no evidence before us as to percentages applying within the area of Rhondda Borough Council, although it was probable that they were greater than the national figure. We approached the question of whether the information was irrelevant and excessive without taking too restrictive a view of the discretion that a particular CCRO might exercise as to the amount of information he considered would assist him to carry out his statutory duties. We found that it was established that the Appellant held and wished to continue holding dates of birth information on as many as possible. The information was to be obtained from answers voluntarily given on canvass forms. We found that the Appellant did not seek to limit the information to be held on his database to those who would shortly attain the age to become charge payers or to identify persons living at the same address with identical names. The information as to dates of birth was personal data and was to cover persons generally at least insofar as the information had been voluntarily provided. We find that the information the Appellant wishes to hold on database concerning individuals exceeds substantially the minimum amount of information which is required in order for him to fulfil the purposes for which he has sought registration namely to fulfil his duty to compile and maintain the Community Charges Register ... We are satisfied by the evidence before us that the wide and general extent of the information about dates of birth is irrelevant and excessive.

Principle 4

Personal data shall be accurate and, where necessary, kept up to date.

Guidance on the interpretation of this principle, which is identical in wording to the previous fifth principle, is contained in Part II of Sched 1:

The fourth principle is not to be regarded as being contravened by reason of any inaccuracy in personal data which accurately record information obtained by the data controller from the data subject or a third party in a case where –

(a) having regard to the purpose or purposes for which the data were obtained and further processed, the data controller has taken reasonable steps to ensure the accuracy of the data, and

(b) if the data subject has notified the data controller of the data subject's view that the data are inaccurate, the data indicate that fact.

This seems to have been inserted in order to close an apparent loophole relating to accuracy in the 1984 Act. As was pointed out in the parliamentary debates prior to the

1984 Act, 'Where a data user records inaccurate information supplied by someone else, the data are accurate. They are an accurate record of what someone else said'. Whilst this is still a pertinent point, it can have unfortunate consequences for a data subject. This guidance and corresponding amendments to the right of rectification (see below) have sought to remedy this problem.

Principle 5

Personal data processed for any purpose or purposes shall not be kept for longer than is necessary for that purpose or those purposes.

There appears to be no specific guidance on this principle, which has the same wording as the previous sixth principle, but the purpose of the processing will clearly be a very relevant factor. The objective is clearly to encourage data to be reviewed and destroyed at appropriate intervals, removing the possible temptation to process for further purposes, which might also fall foul of principles 1 and 2. One of the complaints in *Pal v General Medical Council & ors* was that personal data had been kept longer than was justified. The case arose out of complaints made by Dr Pal to the GMC about the treatment of elderly patients in the spring of 2000. The complaint was closed in October 2000 but correspondence continued between the defendants in which views were expressed that Dr Pal was perhaps acting irrationally, or even might have a mental health problem. At no time was any complaint made about her by other doctors or by patients but nevertheless, papers concerning the issue were not destroyed, indeed relevant correspondence was still occurring in 2002. The evidence was that the GMC had a retention policy which required that, where a doctor had not been informed of a complaint, all papers should be destroyed after 6 months. In this case not only had the doctor not been informed, no complaint had been made, and yet the papers were still in existence some 4 years after the initial incident. At a preliminary hearing, the argument that this was because the GMC was reconsidering its policy on document retention, and was therefore absolved from its duties under the Act, received short shrift from the court.

Pal v General Medical Council & ors
2004 WL 1476683
High Court

31 ... [counsel for defence] argues that the papers must not be disposed of because the GMC is reconsidering its policy and has indeed been doing so for some four years. There is a draft new policy document, which also contains a six-month retention period. It is argued that since such an important body as the GMC is still considering its retention policy, it cannot be right to order it to dispose of documents until it has made its mind up.

32 This strikes me as a very curious and ambitious submission. Its policy must be in accordance with the law and the law is that contained in the Data Protection Act. It is not open to the GMC to arrive at a policy which runs contrary to the requirements of the Act: either it is acting in compliance with the legislation or it is not. The fact that it may be spending several years deciding when, whether and how to comply cannot excuse or justify non-compliance. Far from the claimant's case having no real prospect of success in this aspect, it seems that her prospects of success might be quite promising.

Principle 6

The previous seventh principle, to which the new sixth principle is a direct parallel, was designed to require those in control of data to take the rights of individual data subjects into account, specifically, the right of access to the data and the right to have the data corrected or erased where appropriate. The reformulated principle is expressed in more general terms:

> Personal data shall be processed in accordance with the rights of data subjects under this Act.

It is clear from the guidance on interpretation in Pt II of the Schedule that this principle will be complied with as long as data controllers comply with ss 7 and 10–12 of the Act itself. These deal with the right of access, the right to prevent processing likely to cause damage or distress, the right to prevent processing for the purposes of direct marketing and rights in relation to automated decision making.

Principle 7

The seventh data protection principle is concerned with the security of data, as was the previous eighth principle, but the new version specifically refers to both technical and organisational factors, something which was merely implicit in the former version:

> Appropriate technical and organisational measures shall be taken against unauthorised or unlawful processing of personal data and against accidental loss or destruction of, or damage to, personal data.

The following guidance on interpretation is given in Pt II of the Schedule:

> Having regard to the state of technological development and the cost of implementing any measures, the measures must ensure a level of security appropriate to –
>
> (a) the harm that might result from such unauthorised or unlawful processing or accidental loss, destruction or damage as are mentioned in the seventh principle, and
>
> (b) the nature of the data to be protected.
>
> The data controller must take reasonable steps to ensure the reliability of any employees of his who have access to the personal data.

The specific reference to the state of technological development is an interesting one, as it is unclear to what extent technical solutions to privacy protection, such as the use of encryption, can be specifically required by the law on data protection. Where personal data is particularly sensitive or confidential, it may be that the seventh data protection principle will not be deemed to be complied with without the use of cryptography or other technical mechanism.[111]

---

111 For further discussion of the role of cryptography in data protection see, e.g., Price, 1999, p 108 *et seq*. It should also be noted that the use of cryptography raises a number of other concerns relating to law enforcement and the detection of crime, as well as to rights of access to the keys to the encrypted messages. See further the provisions of the Regulation of Investigatory Powers Act 2000, below p 390 and see also, Chandrani, 2000.

Under the 1984 Act, the security principle was the only one which had to be complied with by the so called 'data bureaux'. This concept has been replaced in the 1998 Act by the term 'data processor', which is defined in s 1(1) as 'a person (other than an employee of the data controller) who processes the data on behalf of the data controller'. Even in this case there is an overriding duty on the data controller to ensure that there is compliance with the security requirement in the seventh data protection principle, and the relevant obligations are also detailed in the guidance in Pt II of Sched 1:

> Where processing of personal data is carried out by a data processor on behalf of a data controller, the data controller must in order to comply with the seventh principle –
>
> (a) choose a data processor providing sufficient guarantees in respect of the technical and organisational security measures governing the processing to be carried out, and
>
> (b) take reasonable steps to ensure compliance with those measures.
>
> Where processing of personal data is carried out by a data processor on behalf of a data controller, the data controller is not to be regarded as complying with the seventh principle unless –
>
> (a) the processing is carried out under a contract –
>
>   (i) which is made or evidenced in writing, and
>
>   (ii) under which the data processor is to act only on instructions from the data controller, and
>
> (b) the contract requires the data processor to comply with obligations equivalent to those imposed on a data controller by the seventh principle.

Principle 8

A new eighth principle deals with transborder data flow:

> Personal data shall not be transferred to a country or territory outside the European Economic Area unless that country or territory ensures an adequate level of protection for the rights and freedoms of data subjects in relation to the processing of personal data.

The problems with the interpretation of adequacy have already been discussed in relation to Arts 25 and 26 of the Directive.

Rights of the data subject

The rights of the data subject under the 1984 Act were far less extensive than those required by the Directive and were confined to the right of access, together with a limited right of rectification and erasure. These rights were supplemented, subject to certain provisos, by the ability to claim compensation for inaccuracy and loss or unauthorised disclosure.

In line with the Directive, the 1998 Act now includes, in s 7(1), a right of access, which is spelt out more comprehensively than that in s 21 of the 1984 Act.

Data Protection Act 1998

Section 7 Right of access to personal data

(1) Subject to the following provisions of this section and to ss 8 and 9, an individual is entitled –

    (a) to be informed by any data controller whether personal data of which that individual is the data subject are being processed by or on behalf of that data controller,

    (b) if that is the case, to be given by the data controller a description of –

        (i) the personal data of which that individual is the data subject,

        (ii) the purposes for which they are being or are to be processed, and

        (iii) the recipients or classes of recipients to whom they are or may be disclosed,

    (c) to have communicated to him in an intelligible form –

        (i) the information constituting any personal data of which that individual is the data subject, and

        (ii) any information available to the data controller as to the source of those data …

(2) A data controller is not obliged to supply any information under subsection (1) unless he has received-

    (a) a request in writing, and

    (b) except in prescribed cases, such fee (not exceeding the prescribed maximum) as he may require.

(3) A data controller is not obliged to comply with a request under this section unless he is supplied with such information as he may reasonably require in order to satisfy himself as to the identity of the person making the request and to locate the information which that person seeks.

(4) Where a data controller cannot comply with the request without disclosing information relating to another individual who can be identified from that information, he is not obliged to comply with the request unless –

    (a) the other individual has consented to the disclosure of the information to the person making the request, or

    (b) it is reasonable in all the circumstances to comply with the request without the consent of the other individual.

(5) In subsection (4) the reference to information relating to another individual includes a reference to information identifying that individual as the source of the information sought by the request; and that subsection is not to be construed as excusing a data controller from communicating so much of the information sought by the request as can be communicated without disclosing the identity of the other individual concerned, whether by the omission of names or other identifying particulars or otherwise.

(6) In determining for the purposes of subsection (4)(b) whether it is reasonable in all the circumstances to comply with the request without the consent of the other individual concerned, regard shall be had, in particular, to –

    (a) any duty of confidentiality owed to the other individual,

    (b) any steps taken by the data controller with a view to seeking the consent of the other individual,

    (c) whether the other individual is capable of giving consent, and

(d) any express refusal of consent by the other individual.

...

(9) If a court is satisfied on the application of any person who has made a request under the foregoing provisions of this section that the data controller in question has failed to comply with the request in contravention of those provisions, the court may order him to comply with the request.

Compliance with this section is not necessarily a simple matter. The first issue is the definition of personal data, since it is only that to which the data subject has a right of access. As discussed above, this definition has been construed narrowly by the Court of Appeal in *Durant v FSA* whereas no significant questions were raised as to its ambit by the ECJ in *Bodil Lindqvist* (discussed earlier in relation to transborder data flow). Beyond this, subsections 4–6 potentially raise considerable uncertainty for the controller as to the circumstances in which personal data can be revealed when to do so might reveal data about a third party. Further guidance on when a third party could be identified is given in s 8(7).

(7) For the purposes of section 7(4) and (5) another individual can be identified from the information being disclosed if he can be identified from that information, or from that and any other information which, in the reasonable belief of the data controller, is likely to be in, or to come into, the possession of the data subject making the request.

Disclosure is clearly legitimised by the consent of the third party, but uncertainty arises when such consent cannot be obtained. In such a case an assessment has to be made of whether, nevertheless, it is 'reasonable in all the circumstances' to comply with the subject access request. The balancing of interests that this entails was discussed by Auld LJ in *Durant*.

Durant v Financial Services Authority
[2003] EWCA Civ 1746, [2004] FSR 28
Court of Appeal

55 There are two basic points to make about the scheme of ss.7(4)-(6), and 8(7), for balancing the interests of the data subject seeking access to his personal data and those of another individual who may be identified in such data. The first is that the balancing exercise only arises if the information relating to the other person forms part of the "personal data" of the data subject, as defined in s.1(1) of the Act. The second is that the provisions appear to create a presumption or starting point that the information relating to that other, including his identity, should not be disclosed without his consent. The presumption may, however, be rebutted if the data controller considers that it is reasonable 'in all the circumstances', including those in s.7(6), to disclose it without such consent.

56 It is important to note that the question for a data controller posed by s.7(4)(b) is whether it is reasonable to *comply* with the request for information notwithstanding that it may disclose information about another, not whether it is reasonable to *refuse* to comply. The distinction may be of importance, depending on who is challenging the data controller's decision, to the meaning of 'reasonable' in this context and to the court's role in examining it. The circumstances going to the reasonableness of such a decision, as I have just noted, include, but are not confined to, those set out in s.7(6), and none of them is determinative. It is important to note that s.7(4) leaves the data controller with a choice whether to seek consent; it does not oblige him to do so before deciding whether to disclose the personal data sought or, by redaction, to disclose only part of it. However, whether he has sought such consent and, if he has done so, it has been refused, are among the circumstances mentioned in the non-exhaustive list in s.7(6) going to the reasonableness of any decision under s.7(4)(b) to disclose, without consent ...

61 ... the right to privacy and other legitimate interests of individuals identified in or identifiable from a data subject's personal data are highly relevant to, but not determinative of, the issue of reasonableness of a decision whether to disclose personal data containing information about someone else where that person's consent has not been sought. The data controller and, if necessary, a court on an application under s.7(9), should also be entitled to ask what, if any, legitimate interest the data subject has in disclosure of the identity of another individual named in or identifiable from personal data to which he is otherwise entitled, subject to the discretion of the court under s.7(9). ...

64 It is important for data controllers to keep in mind the two stage thought process that s.7(4) contemplates and for which s.7(4)-(6) provides.

65 The first is to consider whether information about any other individual is *necessarily* part of the personal data that the data subject has requested. I stress the word 'necessarily' for the same reason that I stress the word 'cannot' in the opening words of s.7(4), 'Where a data controller *cannot* comply with the request without disclosing information about another individual who can be identified from the information'. If such information about another is not necessarily part of personal data sought, no question of s.7(4) balancing arises at all. The data controller, whose primary obligation is to provide information, not documents, can, if he chooses to provide that information in the form of a copy document, simply redact such third party information because it is not a necessary part of the data subject's personal data.

66 The second stage, that of the s.7(4) balance, only arises where the data controller considers that the third party information necessarily forms part of the personal data sought. In that event, it is tempting to adopt Mr Sales's submission that, where the status of an individual is obvious and his or her identity is immaterial or of little legitimate value to the data subject, it would normally be reasonable to withhold information identifying that person in the absence of his consent. However, it is difficult to think in the abstract of information identifying another person and any other information about him which would be so bound up with the data subject as to qualify as his personal data, yet be immaterial or of little legitimate value to him. Much will depend, on the one hand, on the criticality of the third party information forming part of the data subject's personal data to the legitimate protection of his privacy, and, on the other, to the existence or otherwise of any obligation of confidence to the third party or any other sensitivity of the third party disclosure sought. Where the third party is a recipient or one of a class of recipients who might act on the data to the data subject's disadvantage s.7(1)(b)(iii), his right to protect his privacy may weigh heavily and obligations of confidence to the third party(ies) may be non-existent or of less weight. Equally, where the third party is the source of the information, the data subject may have a strong case for his identification if he needs to take action to correct some damaging inaccuracy, though here countervailing considerations of an obligation of confidentiality to the source or some other sensitivity may have to be weighed in the balance. It should be remembered that the task of the court in this context is likely to be much the same as that under s.7(9) in the exercise of its general discretion whether to order a data controller to comply with the data subject's request (see para. [74] below). In short, it all depends on the circumstances whether it would be reasonable to disclose to a data subject the name of another person figuring in his personal data, whether that person is a source, or a recipient or likely recipient of that information, or has a part in the matter the subject of the personal data. Beyond the basic presumption or starting point to which I referred in para.[55] above, I believe that the courts should be wary of attempting to devise any principles of general application one way or the other.

Rather than laying down any guidelines for the anxious data controller, this judgment serves to underline the potential difficulties in deciding whether it is 'reasonable in all the circumstances' to disclose the information.

A further difficulty arises with the potential clash between a putative duty of confidentiality and the data subject's right of access. This is illustrated most clearly by the issue of when a reference given in 'confidence' nevertheless may be disclosed to the data subject. References given by a data controller 'in confidence' are exempt from the subject access provisions by virtue of the miscellaneous exemption in Sched 7(1) but this appears to have no effect on the exercise of the subject access right to the data controller who receives such a reference. Can such references remain confidential? Briefly, the general requirement at common law is that an obligation of confidence will arise if the information is confidential in the sense that it is not known to others and is given in circumstances in which the receiver is made aware that there is an expectation of confidentiality. A party to whom information is given in confidence may not divulge it unless there are specific grounds for doing so. These are the consent of the confider, legal compulsion or overriding public interest. The only relevant one here would be consent which, as in s 7(4), will obviously legitimise disclosure. Where third party data might be revealed, what role does this obligation play in the balancing act required by s 7(4)–(6)? One construction of s 7(6)(1) would be that a confidence is not overridden merely by the right of subject access. On the other hand, s 27(5) which provides that, but for the provisions on exemptions, the 'subject information provisions shall have effect notwithstanding any enactment or rule of law prohibiting or restricting the disclosure, or authorising the withholding, of information' could be construed as suggesting the opposite. In summary, consent will always validate the disclosure of third party information, but in other cases data controllers may be faced with a complex balancing exercise.[112]

In line with the Directive, the 1998 Act now includes specific rights to prevent processing likely to cause damage or distress (s 10), to prevent processing for purposes of direct marketing (s 11) and in relation to automated decision making (s 12). The right in s 11 was a central issue in *Robertson v Wakefield Metropolitan District Council*. Robertson wished to have his name withheld from the electoral register because he objected to the practice of selling the register for use for direct marketing purposes. The electoral registration officer refused on the grounds that it was a legal requirement for electors to complete the requisite form and be included in the register. The court considered the provisions in Art 14(b) of the Directive, and its implementation in s 11 of the DPA 98. It found that s 11 implemented the requirement in Art 14(b) and that, even if it did not, Art 14(b) had direct effect so that it could be relied on by an individual. It was therefore held that the legal rules concerning representation of the people must be construed 'in a manner which is Directive-compliant and consistent with the Data Protection Act 1998.'[113]

---

112 There are certain cases where consent is deemed to be given by virtue of the third party's professional status. See e.g. Data Protection (Subject Access Modification) (Health) Order 2000 SI 2000/413, Data Protection (Subject Access Modification) (Education) Order 2000 SI 2000/414 and Data Protection (Subject Access Modification) (Social Work) Order 2000 SI 2000/415.
113 [2002] QB 1095, para 24.

The rights in ss 10–12 may all be exerted by application to court. The ability to claim compensation is no longer restricted merely to cases of inaccuracy, loss or unauthorised disclosure.

Data Protection Act 1998
Section 13 Compensation for failure to comply with certain requirements

(1) An individual who suffers damage by reason of any contravention by a data controller of any of the requirements of this Act is entitled to compensation from the data controller for that damage.

(2) An individual who suffers distress by reason of any contravention by a data controller of any of the requirements of this Act is entitled to compensation from the data controller for that distress if –

  (a) the individual also suffers damage by reason of the contravention, or

  (b) the contravention relates to the processing of personal data for the special purposes.

(3) In proceedings brought against a person by virtue of this section it is a defence to prove that he had taken such care as in all the circumstances was reasonably required to comply with the requirement concerned.

In cases of inaccuracy, s 14 also gives the court the power to order rectification, blocking, erasure and destruction of the relevant data.

Administration of the Act

The Data Protection Directive refers to a 'supervisory authority' but is not prescriptive about the way in which its requirements should be enforced and administered. Most Member States have set up a specific Commission and Commissioner for this purpose.[114] In the UK, the role of Data Protection Commissioner established in the 1998 Act, and continuing the role of Data Protection Registrar under the 1984 Act, has now been subsumed within the role of Information Commissioner. The functions and duties of the Commissioner are detailed in Part VI of the Act. They include: promoting good practice and observance of the Act by data controllers (s 51); reporting annually to Parliament (s 52); providing assistance to individuals who are bringing proceedings under certain sections of the Act (s 53); and participating in international cooperation (s 54). The Commissioner also has a role in enforcement and, *inter alia*, is empowered by s 40 to issue enforcement notices where he 'is satisfied that a data controller has contravened or is contravening any of the data protection principles.' This was described in relation to the parallel duty in the 1984 Act as a 'potentially onerous duty [since] in combination with his other functions, [it] puts the Registrar into the position of being lawgiver, policeman, judge and jury at the lowest level of enforcement'.[115]

There is clear potential for a conflict of interests when so many roles need to be combined, but the government of the day was quite clear as to the rationale behind it.

114 See http://europa.eu.int/comm/internal_market/privacy/links_en.htm.
115 *Encyclopedia of Data Protection*, para. 1-042.

Parliamentary Debates (Commons)
11 April 1983

William Whitelaw ... We have made compliance with these principles enforceable through the medium of the registrar, so establishing a single authority on the subject who can consult, advise and negotiate before taking action. A vital feature of the scheme is his capacity to use his discretionary powers to tailor his response to the circumstances in each case. This flexibility of approach, we believe, is much preferable to any scheme in which, say, a user collecting data unfairly or holding inaccurate data is directly liable to criminal prosecution.

We have gone for a single registrar rather than a multimember authority for positive reasons. We see it as by far and away the most economic use of resources. Since the scheme will be funded by data users themselves, that is of particular importance to them. We believe that an individual registrar will be able to act more rapidly, authoritatively and consistently in this complex and infinitely varied field than could a committee. His interpretation of the principles, and determination of what in particular circumstances constitutes contravention of the principles, will place a premium on consistency and the kind of build-up of understanding and expertise that an individual can best achieve. Because of the variety of cases that will arise, we think that a registrar who is able to look for and accept advice from wherever he sees fit in the special circumstances that he faces will be better equipped than a committee representing an inevitably incomplete range of interests ...

In providing for a registrar with a supervisory function of this kind we have had to strike a delicate balance. On the one hand, there is the risk of setting up a cumbersome bureaucracy, continuously at the heels of legitimate business activity and impeding technological developments. On the other hand, we must guard against the registrar being ineffective, lacking the powers and resources to give any teeth to the legislation. The Government do not want some vast new quango that will jeopardise efficiency in every area of national life: thus we have gone for a compact Organisation which will not interfere unnecessarily. The burdens on law-abiding data users will be kept to a minimum. On the other hand, it is nonsense to suggest that the registrar will be ineffective when the need for action arises.

The extent to which the combination of roles is successful is a moot point – although both Data Protection Acts merge these roles into the person of the Registrar, now Commissioner, neither enactment has provided the means to fulfil them all efficiently. Thus, there is a policing function, but this is not supported by any real powers of investigation. This combination of responsibilities at the primary enforcement level is common to a number of other regulatory regimes; however, it is rare to have one individual responsible for such a range of activities.

Whatever the conflicts between the varying roles of the Commissioner,[116] the enforcement function is, arguably, of central importance, with other duties, such as dissemination of information, being ancillary to this. This is in contrast with Data Protection Commissioners in some other jurisdictions, whose role can be likened more to that of an Ombudsman.

---

116 Since the enactment of the Freedom of Information Act 2000, the role of Information Commissioner now encompasses responsibility for both ensuring rights of access to government information and ensuring privacy for individuals' personal data. .

UK Data Protection – where are we in 1991?
FGB Aldhouse
(1991) 5 LCT Yearbook 180

Registrar's Role

... The United Kingdom Registrar has the power to prosecute and to serve supervisory notices. He has a duty to consider complaints and he has certain limited investigatory powers such as the ability to obtain search warrants. In that respect the Registrar is a classic UK enforcing authority. Although his status of independence and reporting to Parliament is akin to that of the Parliamentary Commissioner, he does not have the decision making role of an ombudsman.

That is distinctly not the case with officials such as the Federal German Data Protection Commissioner of the Canadian Federal Privacy Commissioner. Their jurisdiction is limited to the public sector. They have an audit role and their sanction is principally publicity rather than the use of classic enforcement measures.

This distinction has consequences for the political role of data protection officials. The ombudsman-type commissioners see an important part of their task as promoting political debate about data protection and privacy issues, commenting on those issues and indeed campaigning for a particular viewpoint. On the other hand those officials such as the Irish Commissioner and the United Kingdom Registrar, who are authorities enforcing a legal sanction and are cast much more in the role of policemen, are considerably more circumspect in commenting on these general contentious issues. This is perhaps in part a matter of political culture, but it is undoubtedly in large part a consequence of the distinct role of these officials.

The Commissioner also has powers to bring criminal proceedings in relation to the commission of the offences created by the legislation. Most of these are regulatory offences of strict liability. Thus, s 21 of the 1998 Act makes it an offence not to register particulars with the Commissioner or to fail to notify any changes in these particulars and s 47 creates an offence for failure to comply with a notice. The 1998 Act makes all of these offences subject to a defence of due diligence. Section 55, on the other hand, creates a number of other offences.

Data Protection Act 1998
Section 55 Unlawful obtaining etc of personal data

(1) A person must not knowingly or recklessly, without the consent of the data controller –

   (a) obtain or disclose personal data or the information contained in personal data, or

   (b) procure the disclosure to another person of the information contained in personal data.

(2) Subsection (1) does not apply to a person who shows –

   (a) that the obtaining, disclosing or procuring –

     (i) was necessary for the purpose of preventing or detecting crime, or

     (ii) was required or authorised by or under any enactment, by any rule of law or by the order of a court,

   (b) that he acted in the reasonable belief that he had in law the right to obtain or disclose the data or information or, as the case may be, to procure the disclosure of the information to the other person,

   (c) that he acted in the reasonable belief that he would have had the consent of the data controller if the data controller had known of the obtaining, disclosing or procuring and the circumstances of it, or

    (d) that in the particular circumstances the obtaining, disclosing or procuring was justified as being in the public interest.

(3) A person who contravenes subsection (1) is guilty of an offence.

(4) A person who sells personal data is guilty of an offence if he has obtained the data in contravention of subsection (1).

(5) A person who offers to sell personal data is guilty of an offence if –

    (a) he has obtained the data in contravention of subsection (1), or

    (b) he subsequently obtains the data in contravention of that subsection.

(6) For the purposes of subsection (5), an advertisement indicating that personal data are or may be for sale is an offer to sell the data.

The offences created by this section are all based on obtaining, disclosing or procuring disclosure 'knowingly or recklessly', a phrase which also qualified similar offences in s 5(5) of the 1984 Act. It is accepted that recklessness may be used in either a subjective or objective ('*Caldwell*') sense in the criminal law. Subjective recklessness refers to the conscious taking of an unjustified risk,[117] whereas objective recklessness may arise when either no thought has been given as to the existence of an obvious risk or there has been recognition of the risk but it has been ignored. This definition was first expounded in the cases of *Caldwell* and *Lawrence*.[118] The use of *Caldwell* recklessness has largely been restricted to statutory offences containing the word 'reckless' or 'recklessly' but is not invariably applied to such offences, and it appeared that it was confined to cases under the Criminal Damage Act 1971 (such as *Caldwell*) and cases of reckless driving (such as *Lawrence* and, more recently, *Reid*[119]). In which sense should 'recklessly' be used in the Data Protection legislation?

In *Data Protection Registrar v Amnesty International (British Section)*,[120] Amnesty was charged under both s 5(2)(b) and (d) of the 1984 Act in relation to two offences of trading in and disclosure of personal information for purposes and to persons not described in the Register. At first instance, Amnesty was acquitted, on the basis that the relevant factor was foreseeability of harm, rather than whether or not the user had been reckless as to the management of the data in a manner incompatible with the registration. Using this test, as the outcome of the action was merely an unsolicited mailing, it was held that Amnesty had not been reckless. On appeal to the Divisional Court by way of case stated, it was held that the seriousness of the consequences of the breach had been confused with the breach itself. In ruling that the appropriate definition of 'recklessness' for s 5 was the objective definition found in *Lawrence*, Rose LJ said:

> ... The particular sensitivity of a person about whom data was released was unlikely to be in the knowledge of the holder of the data and it would be wrong if criminal liability were to be determined by reference to a factor outside the knowledge of the holder or discloser
> ...
> ... in order for the prosecution to prove the necessary element of recklessness in s 5 it had to show:

---

117 See, eg, *R v Cunningham* [1957] 2 QB 396.

118 *R v Caldwell* [1982] AC 341; *R v Lawrence* [1982] AC 510.

119 *R v Reid* [1992] 3 All ER 673.

120 (1994) *The Times*, 23 November.

1   that there was something in the circumstances that would have drawn the attention
     of the ordinary prudent individual to the possibility that his act was capable of
     causing the kind of mischief that s 5(2) and (5) were intended to prevent and that the
     risk of those mischiefs occurring was not so slight that the ordinary prudent
     individual would justifiably treat it as negligible; and

2   that before doing the act the defendant either failed to give any thought to the
     possibility of any such risk or, having recognised the possibility, nevertheless went on
     to do it.

In other words, the recklessness required is foresight of serious harmful consequences.
This decision has been criticised[121] on the basis that the need for such foresight 'seems
entirely inappropriate in the context' and that to 'insist on the foreseeability of serious
consequences to constitute recklessness would be to make that the more serious form
of the offence', that is, more serious than knowingly disclosing personal data in
contravention of the legislation.

The later case of *Information Commissioner v Islington London Borough Council*,[122] also
related to events which occurred when the 1984 Act was in force. Islington Borough
Council had been registered in respect of a number of purposes for the use of personal
data but had let some of these registrations lapse without renewal. Reminders had
been issued which had not been acted upon, and personal data had continued to be
processed in connection with purposes for which there was no longer a current
registration. The Council was charged with the unauthorised use of personal data
contrary to s 5 of the DPA 1984 and, as in the *Amnesty* case above, it had to be
established that the Council had been reckless. One difficulty was that it was the
Council as a body which should have been registered but that the use of the personal
data was by individual employees. The charge was dismissed in the magistrates' court
and there was an appeal by way of case stated. In the statement of the case, one of the
questions asked was how, in applying the test of recklessness, the 'actions and inferred
responsibilities of the Council as a body through its servants or agents past and
present' should have been approached, and whether an omission to ensure registration
was enough to constitute recklessness. In essence, the decision suggested that in order
to find the requisite recklessness in the use of the data, it was possible to aggregate the
acts of employees in using the data with the recklessness of the Council in failing to
renew the registration. This was summed up by Kennedy LJ in the following extract.

Information Commissioner v Islington London Borough Council
[2002] EWHC 1036
High Court

28. ... if a corporate body such as this council fails to renew a registration it can
reasonably be inferred that it is aware of its omission, and that inference is re-inforced
when, as in this case, the council, through the medium of its relevant official, is
specifically reminded of the need to renew and subsequently of the failure to do so. If
thereafter the council, as a result of the actions of some other officer, acting within the
normal course of his or her employment, uses data which should not be used when
unregistered then, as it seems to me, the council must be found to have knowingly or
recklessly contravened the prohibition on such user.

---

121 [1995] Crim LR 633, p 634.
122 [2002] EWHC 1036.

Exemptions

There is a long list of exemptions to some or all of the requirements of the Act. The fact that a topic is apparently covered by an exemption does not necessarily imply that the exemption is from the requirements of the Act *in toto* and the precise terms of the exemption will need to be studied in each case. The so called 'primary exemptions' are to be found in ss 28–36. They include: national security; four separate categories of crime; taxation; health; education and social work; regulatory activity; research, history and statistics; special purposes (that is, artistic, literary and journalistic purposes); information made available to the public by law; disclosures required by law or in connection with legal proceedings; and domestic purposes. These broadly mirror the provisions of the Directive in Arts 3(2) and 13. In addition, Sched 7 contains certain, more specific, 'miscellaneous exemptions' including provisions relating to preparation of confidential references; armed forces; judicial appointments; Crown employment; management forecasts; negotiations; corporate finance; examination scripts and marks; legal professional privilege; and self-incrimination.

The exemption on the grounds of national security found in s28 is a broad exemption with the potential to exclude from data protection law all processing of personal data which could be construed to come under this head.

Data Protection Act 1998

Section 28 National Security

Personal data are exempt from any of the provisions of –

    (a) the data protection principles,

    (b) Parts II, III and V, and

    (c) section 55,

if the exemption from that provision is required for the purpose of safeguarding national security.

(2) Subject to subsection (4), a certificate signed by a Minister of the Crown certifying that exemption from all or any of the provisions mentioned in subsection (1) is or at any time was required for the purpose there mentioned in respect of any personal data shall be conclusive evidence of that fact.

    ...

The potential ambit of this exemption is very wide since Part II of the Act deals with the rights of data subjects, Part III with notification requirements and Part V with enforcement. Given that the data protection principles are not applicable to personal data processed for national security purposes, there can be no assurance that the processing will be fair or that other guarantees will be provided related, for instance, to adequacy and relevancy. Accepting that there might be corresponding problems with enforcement and the provision of remedies, it is difficult to see what would be lost by requiring adherence to the principles, especially those relating to fair and lawful processing for the purposes for which the data were collected. Removing the need to comply with the principles allows users to be cavalier with the personal data of others. However, the wording of the exemption does suggest that exemption should not be granted if compliance with the Act is possible without prejudicing national security. In theory, therefore, there is no automatic blanket exemption. In contrast, the crime exemption in s 29 exempts only from the first data protection principle (except to the extent that it requires compliance with the conditions in Scheds 2 and 3 and s 7 which provides for the rights of subject access. Further, this exemption only applies to the extent that the application of those provisions would be likely to prejudice the prevention or detection of crime. So, in many cases, the full force of the Act will apply, and, in all cases, the police will be required to process personal data in conformity with the majority of the principles. Remedies are also available to those whose rights have been compromised.

Section 28(4) and (5) give a person 'directly affected' by a certificate issued under s 28(2) the right to appeal to the Information Tribunal which may allow the certificate to be quashed if it is satisfied that the Minister did not have reasonable grounds for issuing it. The scope and effect of s 28 was considered in *Norman Baker MP v Secretary of State for the Home Department*.[123] The case arose out of a subject access request by the MP Norman Baker for all the information held on him by the Security Services. A certificate, as detailed in s 28(2), had been issued by the Home Secretary which was both 'detailed and carefully drafted'.[124] Although there were differences between the treatment of personal data in different categories, the overall effect of the certificate could 'fairly be described as a blanket exemption for "any personal data that is processed by the Security Service" in the performance of its statutory functions'.[125] In particular, this meant that there was an exemption from s 7(1)(a) relating to subject access which supported the use of a 'neither confirm nor deny' policy whereby data subjects would not be informed whether or not data was, in fact, held. Accordingly, Baker was informed that the Security Services would notify of processing of personal data for staff administration, building security CCTV and commercial agreements, but that it held no information on him in those categories and that all other processing was exempt from the requirements of DPA 1998. Baker subsequently appealed against this decision and, in its consideration of the matter, the Tribunal itemised a number of general considerations that applied to the work of the security services and the need for some of its work to remain secret. In particular, there was agreement that it was a necessary policy objective that some of this work should remain secret, even to the extent of not revealing that files existed, and that in some cases at least, a 'neither conform nor deny' policy was justifiable.[126] However, the point was made that the blanket exemption absolved the Security Services from any need to consider individual cases on either their particular merits, or whether they actually do pose any threat to national security.

In its decision, the Tribunal, accepting that national security was a legitimate aim, considered that 'the concept of proportionality is the key issue'[127] especially where individual rights were at stake and there was discretion in the review process. Having considered the relevant case law, notably the decisions of the Privy Council in *De Freitas v Permanent Secretary of Ministry of Agriculture, Fisheries, Land and Housing*,[128]

---

123 Information Tribunal (National Security Appeals) 1 October 2001 available from www.lcd.gov.uk/foi/bakerfin.pdf.
124 *Ibid*, para 25.
125 *Ibid*.
126 *Ibid*, para 35.
127 *Ibid*, paras 69–70.
128 [1999] 1 AC 69.

and the House of Lords in *R(Daly) v Secretary of State for the Home Department*,[129] the Tribunal concluded that 'where convention rights are engaged, judicial review principles may require a more intrusive judicial attitude'.[130] This would always be sensitive to the context of the subject matter of the review.

Norman Baker v Secretary of State for the Home Department
Information Tribunal (National Security Appeals)
1 October 2001

76.   ... this Tribunal must remain sensitive to the issue underlying these proceedings; when does national security take precedence over human rights? Where the context is national security judges and tribunals should supervise with the lightest touch appropriate; there is no area (foreign affairs apart) where judges have traditionally deferred more to the executive view than that of national security; and for good and sufficient reason. They have no special expertise; and the material upon which they can make decisions is perforce limited. That the touch should be lightest in comparative terms does not, of course, assist in weighing up how light that should be in absolute terms ... our exercise of quasi-judicial power ultimately is limited, as well as created, by the language of s 28(4). We must apply judicial review principles in a manner appropriate to the national security context: no less, but no more.

Having considered all the issues the Tribunal concluded that:

113. ...

(A) the blanket exemption ... is wider that is necessary to protect national security;

(B) it is common ground that some personal data relating to individuals is processed (held) by the Service which could be released to them without endangering national security;

(C) we have no evidence as to the number of requests received or likely to be received or as to the proportion of them which could lead to a decision to release personal data, if individual consideration was given to each request. We have no reason to suppose that the burden of dealing with them individually would be unduly onerous for the Service or that the proportion falling within (B) would be negligible or small;

(D) the blanket exemption relieves the Service of any obligation to give a considered answer to individual requests;

(E) we can conceive of no positive reason for giving a blanket exemption to all processing by the Service in respect of all its activities until such a time as personal data is released to the Public Record Office ... ;

(F) the statutory functions of the Service, since 1989, have included matters which may, but do not necessarily overlap its task of safeguarding national security. ...;

(G) the safeguards and other remedies available to individuals who are aggrieved by conduct of or on behalf of the Service are insufficient to make reasonable the otherwise unreasonable issue of such a certificate;

(H) it has not been represented to us that it would be impossible or difficult to revise the wording of the Certificate, or to modify the internal procedures of the Service or of the Home Office so as to achieve a situation where each request is considered on its merits and either acceded to or refused accordingly. That, it seems to us, would be

129 [2001] 2 WLR 1622.
130 *Ibid*, para 73.

a proportionate and reasonable response, given the right to respect for their private lives which individuals now enjoy;

(I) limited evidence as to the practice in other countries did not identify anywhere where an identical unchallengeable exemption was permitted. Notably the practice in the USA was more considerate of individual rights than the practice in the United Kingdom exemplified in these proceedings;

(J) the Certificate as drafted defines the exemption by reference to the purposes for which and the circumstances in which personal data is processed by the Service, rather than the consequences for national security if the data is released or even its existence is acknowledged at the time of the request.

The Tribunal quashed the certificate providing blanket exemption. It pointed out that this did not, inevitably, mean that all s 7 requests had to be acceded to, but that it would be open to the Secretary of State to issue a new certificate taking into account the points detailed in the decision.

The other exemption which has received judicial consideration is that relating to the special purposes contained in s 32 of the DPA 1998. This represents the implementation of Art 9 of the Data Protection Directive relating to data protection and freedom of expression. To the extent that data protection is a facet of privacy, there is always going to be a tension between the rights guaranteed under the data protection legislation and the right to freedom of expression in as far as that might involve discussion of an individual's personal details.

Data Protection Act 1998
Section 32 Journalism, Literature and Art

32. - (1) Personal data which are processed only for the special purposes are exempt from any provision to which this subsection relates if –

(a) the processing is undertaken with a view to the publication by any person of any journalistic, literary or artistic material,

(b) the data controller reasonably believes that, having regard in particular to the special importance of the public interest in freedom of expression, publication would be in the public interest, and

(c) the data controller reasonably believes that, in all the circumstances, compliance with that provision is incompatible with the special purposes.

Where this applies, s 32(2) provides an exemption from the data protection principles (other than principle 7 relating to organisational and technical measures), from the right of subject access (s 7), the right to prevent processing likely to cause damage or distress (s 10), rights in relation to automatic decision-making (s 12) and the rights relating to rectification, blocking, erasure and destruction contained in s 14(1)–(3).

The application of this exemption was considered in *Campbell v MGN*. The case arose as a result of photographs published by the *Daily Mirror* of the model, Naomi Campbell, arriving at meetings of Narcotics Anonymous. The ensuing litigation was based on breach of confidence, privacy and also the right in s 13 of the DPA 1998 to receive compensation for processing likely to cause damage or distress. Central to the adjudication was whether publication was in the public interest. In the High Court,[131]

---

131 [2002] EWHC 499.

Morland J found that it was not. In relation to the Data Protection Act claim, he held that the published information constituted 'sensitive personal information' and that the newspaper had therefore failed to comply with the first data protection principle as none of the relevant conditions in Schedules 2 and 3 had been satisfied. The newspaper was not allowed to rely on s 32 on the basis that the exemption applied up to, but not on or after, publication. The Court of Appeal, after an extensive exploration of the relevant provisions,[132] took a different view.

Campbell v Mirror Group Newspapers
[2003] QB 633
Court of Appeal

87 Morland J held that the defendants had failed to comply with the first data protection principle in the following respects. (i) The processing was not 'fair'. The photographs had not been fairly obtained. They had been taken covertly, giving no opportunity to Miss Campbell to refuse to be photographed. (ii) The processing was unlawful, in that it was in breach of confidence. (iii) None of the conditions in Schedule 2 were satisfied. (iv) The information published constituted sensitive personal data. None of the specific conditions in Schedule 3 were satisfied. Nor did the defendants satisfy the conditions in the Data Protection (Processing of Sensitive Personal Data) Order 2000.

...

89 The major issue before the judge was whether the defendants could rely upon the exemption contained in section 32 of the Act. The judge was persuaded by [counsel for Miss Campbell] ... that they could not. His reasoning, which the judge accepted, can be summarised as follows. Section 32 draws a clear distinction between processing and the subsequent publication: see the references in subsections (1)(a) and (4)(b) to processing 'with a view to the publication' and in subsections (1)(b) and (3) to belief that publication 'would be' in the public interest. We continue in the judge's own words:

In my judgment Mr White's submission is clearly right. The wording of the section is in my judgment dealing only with pre-publication processing. It is aimed at limiting a disproportionate restraint on freedom of expression by publication such as the granting of injunctions to stop publication ...

90 The judge's conclusions were, thus, that while journalists were protected by section 32 from being prevented, by interim injunction, from proceeding with the processing of information with a view to publication, they enjoyed no special protection from claims for compensation once publication had taken place.

91 [Counsel for MGN] ... argued compellingly both in his skeleton argument and before us that Morland J's conclusions had surprising results. Without the consent of the data subject, a newspaper would hardly ever be entitled to publish any of the information categorised as sensitive without running the risk of having to pay compensation. Indeed, it would be difficult to establish that the conditions for processing any personal information were satisfied. If this were correct, it would follow that the Data Protection Act had created a law of privacy and achieved a fundamental enhancement of Article 8 rights, at the expense of Article 10 rights, extending into all areas of media activity, to the extent that the Act was incompatible with the Human Rights Convention.

92 In answer to this unsatisfactory scenario [Counsel for MGN] submitted that, if the section 32 exemption did not apply to publication, this was because the Act itself had no application to the publication of newspapers.

93 If this submission is correct, it must apply to the publication of any hard copy documents, created through the processing of data. ...

94 ... journalists ... have cause for concern if Morland J was correct to conclude that section 32 applies only pre-publication. In the present case, Miss Campbell has limited her complaint to the publications themselves of the processed data. Had she complained both of the processing and of the publication it would not have availed the defendants to argue that the Act had no application to publication. They would have needed the protection of section 32.

95 Thus, this area of the case raises three important, interrelated issues: (1) Does the Act apply to publication of newspapers and other hard copies containing information that has been subjected to data processing? (2) Does the section 32 exemption only apply up to the moment of publication? (3) Does the section 32 exemption apply to publication, in so far as this falls within the scope of the Act?

The court went on to consider the answer to these questions. In answer to the first question, an examination of the objectives of the legislation and the Directive which it implements, the competing balance between the rights of privacy and freedom of expression given in the ECHR and referred to in the recitals to the Directive, and the general scope of both the Directive and the Act, resulted in the finding that 'the publication forms part of the processing and falls within the scope of the Act.'[133] An assessment of the relevant provisions did not, however, lead to the conclusion that s 32 only applied pre-publication.

111 We accept that these provisions must inform the interpretation of section 32. They do not, however, suggest that exemptions will only be appropriate if their application is limited to the period prior to publication.

...

117 Subsections (1) to (3), on their face, provide widespread exemption from the duty to comply with the provisions that impose substantive obligations upon the data controller, subject only to the simple conditions that the data controller reasonably believes (i) that publication would be in the public interest and (ii) that compliance with each of the provisions is incompatible with the special purpose – in this case journalism. If these provisions apply only up to the moment of publication it is impossible to see what purpose they serve, for the data controller will be able to obtain a stay of any proceedings under the provisions of subsections (4) and (5) without the need to demonstrate compliance with the conditions to which the exemption in subsections (1) to (3) is subject.

...

119 Furthermore, it would seem totally illogical to exempt the data controller from the obligation, prior to publication, to comply with provisions which he reasonably believes are incompatible with journalism, but to leave him exposed to a claim for compensation under section 13 the moment that the data have been published.

120 For these reasons we have reached the conclusion that, giving the provisions of the subsections their natural meaning and the only meaning that makes sense of them, they apply both before and after publication.

133 *Ibid*, paras 96–106.

121 It seems to us that there are good reasons for subsections (1) to (3) to mean what they say. The overall scheme of the Directive and the Act appears aimed at the processing and retention of data over a sensible period. Thus the data controller is obliged to inform the data subject that personal data about the subject have been processed and the data subject is given rights, which include applying under section 14 for the rectification, blocking, erasure or destruction of the data on specified grounds. These provisions are not appropriate for the data processing which will normally be an incident of journalism.

...

128 Because the exemption provided by section 32(1) depends upon the processing being undertaken with a view to publication the door was open to the argument advanced on behalf of Miss Campbell that the processing could not include the publication itself. The result of this argument is an absurdity. Exemption is provided in respect of all steps in the operation of processing up to publication on the ground that publication is reasonably believed to be in the public interest – yet no public interest defence is available to a claim for compensation founded on the publication itself. ...

Having decided, unequivocally, that s 32 could be relied on at all stages of the publication process, the Court went on to consider whether or not the provisos in s 32(1) could be relied on in this particular case. In the High Court, Morland J had accepted the editor of the *Daily Mirror's* evidence as to why he had decided to publish. This was deemed sufficient to satisfy the public interest test in s 32(2), based on the fact that Campbell was a role model for young people, she had nevertheless been involved in the use of drugs over a period of time, despite public denials. She had now 'admitted to drug addiction, chosen to seek help for it, and had demonstrated real commitment to tackling her problem by regular attendance at Narcotics Anonymous over a prolonged period'. The reason why it was not possible to comply with the data protection legislation was that Campbell had 'made it plain that there was no consent to the publication'. On this basis, the Court decided that the public interest justified the publication of the article without Miss Campbell's consent'.[134]

The decision of the Court of Appeal in favour of publication was subsequently reversed by a divided House of Lords which considered the balance between the rights guaranteed in Arts 8 and 10 of the ECHR. It concluded that: 'looking at the publication as a whole and taking account of all the circumstances the claimant's right pursuant to Art 8 to respect for her private life outweighed the newspaper's right pursuant to Art 10 to freedom of expression; and that, accordingly, publication of the additional information and the accompanying photographs constituted an unjustified infringement of the claimant's right to privacy'.[135] There was no discussion of the interpretation of the Data Protection Act, as such, and it seems reasonable to assume, therefore that the judgment of the Court of Appeal with respect to publication stands.

The Court of Appeal's decision was referred to with favour by the High Court in *Douglas v Hello* No. 5 as making 'an understanding of the Act easier than do the unvarnished provisions of the Act itself'.[136] This much publicised case concerned the unauthorized publication of the wedding of Michael Douglas and Catherine Zeta-Jones by *Hello!* magazine when exclusive coverage had been granted to a rival

---

134 *Ibid*, para 132.
135 [2004] 2 AC 457.
136 [2003] EMLR 31, para 230.

publication. In that case *Hello!* was not able to rely on the s 32 exemption as there was 'no credible evidence' that the publication of the photographs could be in the public interest.

FURTHER ASPECTS OF DATA PROTECTION

With data protection, as with other aspects of computer law, there is continual discussion as to whether the law is sufficiently flexible to keep pace with technological change. Even prior to the 1998 Act, this was reflected in successive Reports of the Data Protection Registrar, which included assessments as to how the existing regime might be applied to technological advances.[137] The need to keep abreast of developments was also referred to in Recital 14 of the preamble to Directive 95/46/EC:

> Whereas, given the importance of the developments under way, in the framework of the information society, of the techniques used to capture, transmit, manipulate, record, store or communicate sound and image data relating to natural persons, this Directive should be applicable to processing involving such data.

This reflects the fact that advances in the technology have now made it possible not only for personal data, as such, to be transmitted, manipulated and processed, but also for visual and audio material to be used in such ways. As discussed at the beginning of this chapter, one major advance which is also capable of including these features is the growth in the size and volume of traffic on the internet – the global network. It will be recalled that the original fears expressed about the potential for the abuse of personal data were based on the existence of separate computer networks, a fraction of the size of the internet. Although quantification of such matters cannot be exact, it is presumed that the magnitude of the risk is likely to increase supra-linearly with the size of the network.

Eleventh Report of the Data Protection Registrar 1995
Appendix 6
Data Protection and the Internet

> ... perhaps the most important thing to understand about the Internet is that its whole purpose is to facilitate the exchange of information. It grew up in an academic and research environment where the ready and open exchange of information is the norm, indeed is the lifeblood. It is an open environment; it exists to publicise information; it encourages browsing.

> Today, commercial traffic on the Internet exceeds academic traffic, but the intrinsically insecure nature of the Internet environment has not changed. Protecting information runs counter to the culture. Furthermore, the features which make the Internet so attractive to genuine users and to those whose motive is mere idle curiosity also attract those whose interest is far from innocent. The prospect of being able to roam around the world without leaving your desk, with access to, potentially, a million or more computer systems is an exciting one for any hacker.

---

137 See, eg, 10th Report of the Data Protection Registrar, 1994, London: HMSO, referring to the application of the Act to, *inter alia*, calling line identification, teleworking, smart cards, document image processing and the internet.

Any proposal to use the Internet to provide access to personal data or to communicate personal data from one user to another therefore need to be regarded with caution. Merely connecting a system to the Internet poses a risk for personal data on the system, even if there is no intention to use the Internet to access or communicate those data.

There are risks too for individuals who access services on the Internet. Every time you access a service whether it is to make a contribution to a newsgroup or to make a commercial transaction, you are at risking of leaving an electronic trace which can be used to develop a profile of your personal interests and tastes. And who knows through which countries your data has passed and by whom the data might have been captured in transit?

The internet and, in particular, the growth of the world wide web, with home pages inviting the browser to 'sign the visitors' book', provides many more opportunities for the capture, retention and subsequent processing of personal data. Photographs may be made available on the web, identifying particular persons; such images can then be viewed or downloaded across the world. That such data is personal is indisputable, but does it render meaningless the restriction of transborder data flows where there are no guarantees of appropriate safeguards? How can the originator of the material know in which jurisdiction the resultant data might be used? When such information is placed on the web by an organisation or institution, how should that organisation's registration be framed? If the information is made available on an individual's home page, does that mean that the processing attracts an exemption on the grounds of personal and domestic use? In short, can legislation on data protection cope with this phenomenon? Even if the capability is there, does enforcement and supervision become such a gargantuan task that it becomes impossible, for all practical purposes, to locate and deal with contraventions?

Some of these issues were touched upon in *Bodil Lindqvist*. In that case, Advocate General Tizzano suggested that including personal data about others on an individual's website could not be regarded as purely personal and domestic use but that any consequent processing nevertheless fell outside the scope of the Directive on the grounds that it was not processing for economic gain and therefore could not be linked to the functioning of the internal market.[138] This was not the view of the ECJ. It noted that Art 3(2) of the directive excludes from its scope data processing:

> in the course of an activity which falls outside the scope of Community law, such as those provided for by Titles V and VI of the Treaty on European Union and in any case to processing operations concerning public security, defence, State security ... and the activities of the State in areas of criminal law,
>
> by a natural personal in the course of a purely personal or household activity.

The ECJ decided that charitable and religious activities were not equivalent to the activities in the first paragraph[139] but neither did they fall within the second as 'that exception must ... be interpreted as relating only to activities which are carried out in the course of private or family life of individuals, which is clearly not the case with the processing of personal data consisting in publication on the internet so that those data are made accessible to an indefinite number of people'.[140] Instead, as discussed

---

138 [2004] 1 CMLR 20, paras AG34-36, AG44.
139 *Ibid*, Judgment, para 45.
140 *Ibid*, para. 47.

previously, the ECJ decision was based upon the fact that putting personal data on a home page should not be equated with transferring that data to a third country, and that the Directive had not been drafted to apply to the internet.[141] Although providing a solution in the particular case, the facts and judgment serve to highlight the questions raised above.

The internet is also now a common medium for commercial transactions. The increasing amount of commercial traffic on the open network (rather than an EDI network developed for and dedicated to business use) is a reflection of the enhanced access of consumers to the network, resulting in consumer transactions as well as purely business-business contracts, and a consequent escalation in the transfer of personal data. The use of computer networks for commercial transactions, that is, e-commerce, is growing fast. Recent figures suggest a market worth $3.5 trillion in North America and $1.5 trillion in Europe for 2004. It is often suggested that the reason why e-commerce is not growing even faster, particularly for business-consumer transactions, is due to a perceived lack of trust and confidence and, specifically, concern about privacy protection. That this is not an unreasonable perception is underlined by a consideration of the available technology. The following extract explains the potentially insidious effect of browsing trails and cookies, but to this should be added the privacy invading aspects of 'sniffers' which can be used to capture data in transit on a network; 'intelligent agents' which can be used to retrieve required information;[142] and the use of spyware and adware.[143]

Personal Privacy on the Internet: Should it be a Cyberspace Entitlement
Brian Keith Groemminger
(2003) 36 Ind L Rev 827

A. Dissection of an Internet Transaction

Without burrowing too deeply into the technological nuances of Internet architecture, it is important to understand the mechanics involved in a typical Internet transaction in order to understand how one's privacy can be so easily surrendered in cyberspace. Basically, Internet activities are composed of electronic requests for information and subsequent electronic fulfillment of those requests. In other words, a surfer's mouse 'click' initiates a submission of an electronic request to view data on a Web site, the site's computer receives the electronic request, and finally, the site sends the requested data to the specific computer making the request. In order to send the information to the correct computer among the millions logged onto the Internet, the Web site must be able to distinguish the computer requesting data from all other online computers. An Internet protocol (IP) address, which is basically a specific machine address assigned by the Web surfer's Internet service provider (ISP) to a user's computer, accomplishes this task. Hence, every time a transaction requesting or sending data occurs on the Web this unique IP address accompanies the data. Furthermore, both the ISP and the Web site typically log these transactions to the detriment of users' personal privacy and anonymity on the Web, however, the uniqueness of the IP address may allow someone in possession of another user's IP address to find detailed personal facts about the user, such as the user's name, address, birth date, social security number, and e-mail address, within minutes.

---

141 See paras 68–71 extracted above at p 335.
142 For further details see, eg, Van Overstraten and Szafran, 2001.
143 See, eg, Schwarz, 2004.

B. Cookies and Clickstreams

Another common method of surreptitiously collecting data from users is through the use of small text files commonly known as cookies. Web sites place these files on the computer hard drives of Web site visitors during Internet transactions. A cookie file contains a unique identification number which allows a Web site to recognize and distinguish the user in subsequent visits to the site. Cookies also typically store information such as user preferences, the type of browser software or operating system used, installed plug-ins, and password or login information which allow for easier Web site browsing by the user in future visits. However, cookies have a dual-personality potential because they can abrogate an individual's privacy in cyberspace by collecting information regarding the user and his or her behavior.

Cookies accomplish their darker-sided agenda in several ways. First, a Web site can retrieve cookies at a future time. When the Web site does this, the cookie can disclose a detailed list of all Web sites that a specific computer visited within a particular time frame. Embedded within these cookie files may be telltale information that can identify a user personally, such as a user's name, password, e-mail address, and other personal information. In the past, only the Web site that placed the cookie could read the file; however, now the use of cookie sharing between sites or the use of placement ads by the same ad agency allows cookies from multiple Web sites to be aggregated to create a comprehensive personal profile of an individual user. Second, some cookies have the capability to record the Web site from which a user came, the links accessed at the site, and any personal information entered at the site. A Web site may also use these types of cookies in concert with a more efficient, and yet more intrusive, technique for gathering personal data known as 'clickstreams.' A clickstream is basically a recording of all Web sites a user visits during the same session or connection. Clickstream collections not only gather a list of sites visited, but also the duration spent on each site, purchases made, advertisements viewed, and data entered. Internet service providers usually perform clickstream monitoring, because users have essentially rented a line from the provider to connect to the Internet. Lastly, some cookies may be able to identify the IP address of the computer, which could lead to the ultimate disclosure of the location of the computer used to access the site.

Notwithstanding the inevitable difficulties, these more insidious and secretive ways of collecting personal data should not be immune from application of accepted legal rules and principles merely because they take place on global networks. As pointed out by the Art 29 Working Party:

> The Internet is not a legal vacuum. Processing of personal data on the Internet has to respect data protection principles just as in the off-line world. This does not constitute a limitation of the uses of the Internet, but is on the contrary part of the essentials aiming at ensuring trust and confidence of users in the functioning of the Internet and the services provided over it. Data protection on the Internet is thus an indispensable condition for the take-up of electronic commerce.[143]

When first adopted, the 1995 Directive could have reasonably been regarded as the 'state of the art' as far as data protection legislation is concerned, but it has not proved a panacea to all privacy concerns raised by the use of computers, especially, computer networks, or provided a completely suitable privacy protection framework for e-commerce. The difficult issues are not so much the cases where the data subject is aware that data has been collected and used, or even where this information is made

---

144 Working Document, *Processing of Personal Data on the Internet,* available at www.europa.eu.int/comm/internal_market/en/media/dataprot/wpdocs/wp16en.htm.

available on the internet, since this is, arguably, the type of activity for which data protection law was designed. Rather, the problems arising as a consequence of the traceability of operations online will be in situations where the potential data subject may not be aware that data is being collected and retained.

How should the Directive and implementing legislation be applied in such cases? Although this collection and retention of data may be an inevitable consequence of the use of the internet for many purposes, the correlation of that data with a specific identifiable individual may not be straightforward. Whether such a correlation can be made at all may be crucial for the application of the Directive. Although directives are legally binding as to the result to be achieved, they leave the choice of form and method for achieving that result to the individual Member State. Notwithstanding the fact that the Data Protection Directive is intended to harmonise data protection provisions throughout all Member States, there is thus the propensity for a certain divergence of approach. Given that the Directive is not explicit in regard to its application to the internet, the manner in which data protection law has developed in the different jurisdictions may be crucial.

One anomalous area which has already been identified is in the interpretation of what constitutes 'personal' or 'nominative' data. Many jurisdictions, including the UK, require a close link between the data and the individual for data protection law to apply. However, the definition of 'nominative data' has been construed rather wider in France, for example, than most other jurisdictions in the EU.[145] This difference in scope may be sufficient to bring, for example, the information gathered by 'cookies' within the ambit of data protection law in France, whereas this seems unlikely elsewhere because the connection between the data and an identifiable individual in such a case may be tenuous. Given that the objectives of the Directive include not only the protection of the individual but also the removal of obstacles to the free flow of information and the harmonisation of the relevant national provisions, this is clearly a problem which cannot be ignored.

As already discussed, central to the requirements of the 1995 Directive is the need for the consent of the data subject, except in a restricted number of specific situations. A valid consent needs more than an affirmative response; it necessitates the data subject being made aware, at the time that the consent is given, of the intended purposes of processing, likely use of the data, possible disclosures, etc. Even where the collected data can be correlated with a specific identifiable individual, the invisibility of the collection leaves little opportunity for informed consent. Some of these issues have been addressed in Directive 2002/58/EC of 12 July 2002 concerning the processing of personal data and the protection of privacy in the electronic communications sector.[146] This Directive supplements Directive 95/46 and attempts to clarify how the provisions of that directive can be applied to later developments. Its provisions are intended to be as technology neutral as possible so that it is applicable to a wide range of communications technologies. The provisions of most relevance to privacy protection on the internet include Art 5(3) which can be applied to 'cookies'

---

145 See *Online Services and Data Protection and the Protection of Privacy Vol 1*, 1999, DG Internal Market and Financial Services Annex to the Annual Report 1998 (XV D/504(98)) of the Working Party established by Art 29 of Directive 95/46/EC.
146 [2002] OJ L201/37.

etc. and Art 15(3) which regulates unsolicited commercial e-mails (sometimes referred to as UCE or, more popularly, 'spam'). The Directive has been implemented in the UK in the Privacy and Electronic Communications (EC Directive) Regulations 2003.[147] The provisions on both cookies and spam are premised on the need for information and consent.

Directive 2002/58/EC
Article 5
Confidentiality of the Communications

3. Member States shall ensure that the use of electronic communications networks to store information or to gain access to information stored in the terminal equipment of a subscriber or user is only allowed on condition that the subscriber or use concerned is provided with clear and comprehensive information in accordance with Directive 95/46/EC, *inter alia* about the purposes of the processing, and is offered the right to refuse such processing by the data controller. This shall not prevent any technical storage or access for the sole purpose of carrying out or facilitating the transmission of a communication over an electronic communications network, or as strictly necessary in order to provide an information society service explicitly requested by the subscriber or user.

This should be read in conjunction with Recital 25.

(25) ...devices, for instance so-called 'cookies' can be a legitimate and useful tool, for example, in analyzing the effectiveness of website design and advertising, and in verifying the identity of users engaged in on-line transactions. Where such devices, for instance, cookies, are intended for a legitimate purpose, such as to facilitate the provisions of information society services, their use should be allowed on condition that users are provided with clear and precise information in accordance with Directive 95/46/EC about the purposes of cookies or similar devices so as to ensure that uses are made aware of information being placed on the terminal equipment they are using. Users should have the opportunity to refuse to have a cookie or similar device ... This is particularly important where users other than the original user have access to the terminal equipment and thereby to any data containing privacy-sensitive information stored on such equipment. Information and the right to refuse may be offered once for the use of various devices to be installed on the user's terminal equipment during the same connection and also covering any further use that may be made of those devices during subsequent connections. The methods of giving information, offering a right to refuse or requesting consent should be made as user-friendly as possible. Access to specific website content may still be made conditional on the well-informed acceptance of a cookie or similar device, if it is used for a legitimate purpose.

Spam has proved to be something of an intractable problem for internet users all over the globe. As one commentator writes:

Unsolicited Commercial e-mail: Implementing the EU Directive
Abu Bakir Munir
(2004) 10 CTLR 105

Email is viewed by many as one of the 'killer applications' for the growth of the internet. It has become a powerful medium for communication, idea and information exchange as

---

well as e-commerce. Unsolicited commercial e-mail, or 'spam' however can pose a threat to the security and reliability of internet communications. Large volumes of spam can interfere with critical computer infrastructure and endanger public safety. Spam may also be used maliciously as a denial of service attack. Most important of all, spam can create distrust among internet users in the digital economy, which could have an adverse impact on the development of e-commerce. Spam can lead to consumer reluctance to participant on the internet, which may prove to be a threat to the usefulness of e-mail.

However this does not mean that all are in favour of spam being regulated or penalties imposed on those who introduce spam.

Spam after CAN-SPAM: How inconsistent thinking has made a hash out of unsolicited commercial e-mail policy
Jeffrey D Sullivan and Michael B De Leeuw
(2004) 20 Santa Clara Computer & High Tech LJ 887, 906

The Internet has long had a reputation as a haven for individualists and experimenters. Many Internet pioneers and experts have been vociferous in their opposition to most forms of governmental incursion into the realm of electronic communication or commerce. Some reach this anti-regulatory standpoint from either a libertarian or classical liberal economic viewpoint, and some from a more left-leaning concern with freedom of speech and communication. It thus perhaps comes as no surprise that many proponents of a minimally-regulated Internet have not lined up behind any governmental approach to UCE control. Indeed, some have looked with skepticism on any broad treatment of UCE as a problem to be quashed, believing that such approaches may suppress the presumptively-favorable maximization of information exchange and threaten to legitimize other governmental intrusions on personal and economic liberty. Some, indeed, wax elegiac about the liberating democratic potential of completely unregulated e-mail. The ability to send anonymous, untraceable e-mails, using such spammer-beloved tactics as return address spoofing or anonymous 'remailers' has even been specifically touted as a signal benefit of the electronic age ...

But these authors go on to point out that this view 'ignores the harsh realities of spam and the independent dangers that it poses to Internet culture and Internet infrastructure':

Even Internet veterans, who might in other respects espouse the rugged individualist view of the Internet as a medium whose potential best thrives when left to the grassroots ingenuity of its atomistic, distributed participants, seem less than convinced about the benefits of a totally unregulated Internet and e-mail regime. Some believe that bad information (such as spam) threatens to drive out the good information whose free exchange was one of the exciting, and potentially-liberating, promises of the Internet frontier. A vigorous liberal economics-based embrace of the Internet and e-mail as liberating, and profit enhancing, tools in a free market of information, ideas, and goods and services does not imply wholesale acceptance of a rule-free marketplace. Even ardent free market theorists may accept that not all markets are purely efficient, and that less-than-efficient markets are subject to failure.

From this perspective, rational regulation of the e-mail 'market' is entirely appropriate. How that regulation would occur, however, and the extent of that regulation would depend on the perceived cause of the market breakdown.

As mentioned above, Article 13 of Directive 2002/58 is intended to deal with the problem in the EU.

Article 13
Unsolicited communications

1. The use of automated calling systems without human intervention (automatic calling machines), facsimile machines (fax) or electronic mail for the purposes of direct marketing may only be allowed in respect of subscribers who have given their prior consent.

2. Notwithstanding paragraph 1, where a natural or legal person obtains from its customers their electronic contact details for electronic mail, in the context of the sale of a product or a service, in accordance with Directive 95/46/EC, the same natural or legal person may use these electronic contact details for direct marketing of its own similar products or services provided that customers clearly and distinctly are given the opportunity to object, free of charge and in an easy manner, to such use of electronic contact details when they are collected and on the occasion of each message in case the customer has not initially refused such use.

3. Member States shall take appropriate measures to ensure that, free of charge, unsolicited communications for purposes of direct marketing, in cases other than those referred to in paragraphs 1 and 2, are not allowed either without the consent of the subscribers concerned or in respect of subscribers who do not wish to receive these communications, the choice between these options to be determined by national legislation.

4. In any event, the practice of sending electronic mail for purposes of direct marketing disguising or concealing the identity of the sender on whose behalf the communication is made, or without a valid address to which the recipient may send a request that such communications cease, shall be prohibited.

5. Paragraphs 1 and 3 shall apply to subscribers who are natural persons. Member States shall also ensure, in the framework of Community law and applicable national legislation, that the legitimate interests of subscribers other than natural persons with regard to unsolicited communications are sufficiently protected.

The problems caused by spam have led to legislative activity not only in the EU but in a number of other jurisdictions.[148] In the US, the CAN-SPAM Act (Controlling the Assault of Non-solicited Pornography and Marketing Act of 2003, 15 USC §§ 7701-7713 and 18 USC § 1037) was passed at the end of 2003. In contrast to the perceived relationship between UCEs, direct marketing and intrusions into personal privacy evident in Directive 2002/58,[149] this statute arose in response to the perceived threat to the convenience and efficiency of electronic mail, additional costs etc., together with concerns about, for example, the increasing use of misleading subject headers and the nature of the content of some UCEs. The statute makes it an offence, *inter alia*, not to give recipients information about how not to receive further communications, but it nevertheless puts the onus on the recipient to opt out before any cause of action arises. The use of an opt out rather than an opt in approach,[150] together with the fact that the enterprise which adheres carefully to the statute can still lawfully send out unsolicited emails until an objection is received, has been severely criticised.[151] It may be that a

148 For possible legal responses in the absence of bespoke legislation see, e.g. Edwards, L. 2000.
149 See, e.g. Recital 40.
150 Cf. Directive 2002/58 Article 13 above and also the Australian Spam Act 2003 which contains a much clearer prohibition on UCEs together with strict rules concerning those commercial emails that are permitted.
151 See, e.g. Sullivan and De Leeuw, 2004; Alongi, 2004.

technological solution to the problem of spam is likely to be both more effective and more appropriate, or that a combination of techniques is required,[152] whether the objective is the protection of privacy or wider concerns about the effects of spam.

Whether or not European data protection law is capable of fully protecting privacy rights on global networks is still a moot point, but an interesting development is the recommendation of anonymity as a privacy protection measure. It is certainly clear that anonymity would effect such protection during commercial transactions on the open network and, as such, resolve some of the consumer protection issues raised by the increased, and increasing, use of e-commerce. Anonymity is therefore being espoused and promoted by a number of intergovernmental and supranational organisations which are active in this area.

Anonymity on the Internet[153]
Working Party on the Protection of Individuals with regard to the Processing of Personal Data Recommendation 3/97

Transactional data are only a threat to individual privacy if the data relate to an identifiable person. Clearly one way of addressing privacy concerns would therefore be to seek to ensure that wherever feasible the data traces created by using the Internet do not permit the identification of the user. With anonymity guaranteed, individuals would be able to participate in the Internet revolution without fear that their every move was being recorded and information about them accumulated which might be used at a later date for purposes to which they object.

The OECD has recommended[154] that the privacy principles enshrined in the 1980 OECD *Guidelines* on data protection should be taken into account, subject to the 1998 Ministerial Declaration on the protection of privacy on global networks. This Declaration reaffirms the continuing applicability of the 1980 *Guidelines*, which are considered to 'provide a foundation for privacy protection on global networks'. These guidelines do articulate principles of good data management but the problems that have already been outlined, those of application to invisible data collection, will still apply. In addition, they were formulated before the development of computer networks and Kirby,[155] amongst others, has called for a 'second generation of information privacy principles in harmony with the development of the Internet'. The 1998 OECD Declaration makes further specific recommendations such as the 'encouragement of privacy enhancing technologies'. This is presumably in accordance with the statement in the recitals that users should be 'assisted to maintain their anonymity'. The Declaration notes that further encouragement should be given to the adoption of privacy policies, whether implemented by legal, self-regulatory or other means. There have been many suggested solutions based on self-regulatory mechanisms. Thus, the Platform for Privacy Preferences Project (P3P) is based on the idea that measures to deal with privacy and data protection are to be agreed between the 'client' and the website collecting the data. The supposition is that clients will only

152 *Ibid* at p. 931, but compare also the views of Mossoff, 2004.
153 See www.europa.eu.int/comm/internal_market/en/media/dataprot/wpdocs/wp6en.htm.
154 See www.oecd.org//dsti/sti/it/consumer/prod/cpguidelines_final.pdf.
155 Kirby, 1998.

consent to collection of their data if the website has an appropriate privacy policy. Setting aside the fact that many websites either do not have a privacy policy or, apparently, do not adhere to the policy they do have,[156] other dangers inherent on relying on this concept as primary protection rather than a useful addition have been identified.

Platform for Privacy Preferences (P3P)
and the Open Profiling Standard (OPS)
Working Party on the Protection of Individuals with
regard to the Processing of Personal Data
Opinion 1/98

A technical platform for privacy protection will not in itself be sufficient to protect privacy on the Web. It must be applied within the context of a framework of enforceable data protection rules, which provide a minimum and non-negotiable level of privacy protection for all individuals. Use of P3P and OPS in the absence of such a framework risks shifting the onus primarily onto the individual user to protect himself, a development which would undermine the internationally established principle that it is a 'data controller' who is responsible for complying with data protection principles ... Such an inversion of responsibility also assumes a level of knowledge about the risks posed by data processing to individual privacy that cannot realistically be expected of most citizens.

The clash between legal regulation and industry self-regulation has already been discussed extensively in the context of transborder data flow and the negotiations on the safe harbour principles. In addition, the contents of the EPIC Report (discussed above) make it clear that, in relation to privacy, there is greater polarisation of views in the US than appears to be the case in Europe. The speculation is that this is due to the familiarity with the effects of legal regulation of data protection which has been present in Europe for some time and has been strengthened by the adoption of the 1995 Directive.

The Council of Europe has also made a Recommendation[157] in this area which states in its preamble that there is 'a need to develop techniques which permit the anonymity of data subjects ... while respecting the rights and freedoms of others and the values of a democratic society'. The Recommendation later comments that 'anonymous access to and use of services, and anonymous means of making payments, are the best protection of privacy' and submits, but does not expand upon this point, that, in some cases, 'complete anonymity may not be appropriate because of legal constraints' and suggests pseudonymity in such cases.

The Electronic Commerce Directive (Directive 2000/31/EC), adopted in May 2000 to provide a legal framework for e-commerce in the EU, requires full compliance with the Data Protection Directive, but does suggest in one of the recitals that anonymous use cannot be prevented by invoking the 2000 Directive. Anonymity as such is not a feature or requirement of existing data protection law and it is interesting that it has been promoted in this way, given the down side of fostering anonymous use. It must

---

156 See, eg, *Surfer Beware III*, www.epic.org/reports/surfer-beware3.html; FTC Report, *Privacy Online: A Report to Congress*, available at www.ftc.gov/reports/privacy3/toc.htm.
157 Recommendation No R (99) 5, available at www.coe.fr/DataProtection/elignes.htm.

not be forgotten that measures which foster anonymity in order to protect privacy may, incidentally, facilitate or even encourage antisocial and illicit behaviour. This calls not so much for a balancing of rights, perhaps, as a balancing of the relative risk from different threats. Other interests are also fuelling the discussion. Prior to about 1996, the prevailing commentary seemed to suggest that, on balance, allowing, not to mention favouring, anonymity had the propensity to turn cyberspace into the ungovernable space prophesied in the popular press. The subsequent rapid expansion of e-commerce and, therefore, the increasing presence on the internet of large corporate actors, together with the desire of individual governments to promote this type of activity, seemed to have the effect of reversing the debate. The general perception was that consumer protection issues, including privacy concerns, relating to commercial transactions over the internet had eclipsed other threats. In the words of the EPIC Report, 'it appears that commercial activity on the internet is driving the increased collection of personal data'.

The following extract from a Commission Report which considered some case studies on methods of assessing adequacy, provides a final, telling comment:

> Compliance with fair information practices for the 6 electronic commerce transfers studied is almost wholly dependent on whether the jurisdiction has a comprehensive data protection law. Where no law applies general fair information practices to electronic commerce activities, e-commerce is virtually unregulated for data protection. Voluntary industry codes exist in the jurisdictions without applicable laws, but the extent to which those codes address all elements of fair information practices let alone meet the standards of the data protection directive, is highly variable.[158]

The discussion thus far has described regulatory activity at national and international level. This has the objective of providing a suitable framework within which to safeguard users privacy on the internet. However, in 2000, the UK passed the Regulation of Investigatory Powers Act. This statute gives the government wide ranging powers, allowing them to monitor all UK internet traffic in the name of law enforcement and national interest. Internet service providers (ISPs) will be obliged to put in place appropriate technology to intercept email and other communications.[159] There has been significant criticism of this statute which can be viewed as a clumsy tool when considering the delicate and diplomatic task of balancing rights and interests.[160]

Before the full effects of implementation of this statute could be appreciated, the UK, in common with a number of other jurisdictions in Europe and elsewhere, responded to the atrocities of 11 September 2001 by enacting legislation with the objective of addressing terrorist activities. The Anti-terrorism, Crime and Security Act 2001 Act contains provisions on a wide range of topics including, for example immigration and asylum issues, the security of the pathogens and toxins, aviation security and police powers but, in relation to this discussion, chapter 11 includes provisions on retention of communications data. These allow communications service

---

158 Raab *et al*, 1998.
159 For further details of the statutory regime see www.homeoffice.gov.uk/crimpol/crimreduc/ regulation/index.html.
160 See, eg, Jarvie, 2003; Akdeniz *et al*, 2001.

providers to retain data about their customers' communications for national security purposes. The Secretary of State is also given powers to make orders connected with the retention of communications and a Code of Practice on Data Retention was brought into effect in December 2003.[161] Data retention in certain circumstances, over and above retention for declared business purposes, is permitted in some situations by Article 15 of Directive 2002/58 but potentially raises significant privacy concerns. The extent to which this marks an erosion in the data protection rights which have been developed over two or three decades, is open to debate and will depend on the approach to practical implementation of these powers.[162]

DEFAMATION

It is not only a person's private information that may be compromised by the escalating use of computer networks. Indeed, many reviews of privacy protection in the UK have cited the action for defamation as a central ingredient of privacy protection,[163] and a number of commentators have concurred with the notion that defamation actions can be viewed as a facet of privacy.[164] Computer networks provide ample opportunity for propagating scurrilous material about others, which may range from the irritating to that which is potentially defamatory or even a form of harassment. This is especially true of the internet, where such activity, known as 'flaming', has been raised almost to an art form, with its own brand of rules and etiquette.[165] The growth of news groups and bulletin boards have really facilitated this kind of activity. Easy communication across the globe naturally spawned discussion groups of people interested in similar topics, ranging from the serious and scholarly to the frivolous and bizarre. These have been variously organised into newsgroups, electronic bulletin boards and electronic mailing lists, for the exchange of views and experiences and the dissemination of information. Although the way in which they are set up and operated varies, they provide similar scope for the promulgation of defamatory material.[166]

Whatever their subject matter, both bulletin boards and newsgroups may be moderated or unmoderated, with a corresponding variation in the integrity of the material available. In particular, those intended for an academic or professional readership are likely to be moderated, so that some editorial control is retained. In contrast, it can be the norm for the language used in some unmoderated groups to be somewhat intemperate. The difference being that the normal readership is so different that the use of excessive language does not provoke an avalanche of claims in

---

161 Text available from www.legislation.hmso.gov.uk/si/si2003/draft/5b.pdf and see Retention of Communications Data (Code of Practice) Order 2003 SI 2003/3175.

162 For further discussion see, eg, Rowland, 2004.

163 See, eg, the Younger Report on *Privacy*, Cmnd 5012, 1972, London: HMSO; the Calcutt Report on *Privacy and Related Matters*, Cmnd 1102, 1990, London: HMSO.

164 See, eg Gibbons, 1996, p 589.

165 See, eg Inman and Inman, 1996 and references cited therein.

166 See, eg Braithwaite, 1995.

defamation. In such an environment, Dooley,[167] suggests that 'defamation has been elevated to the status of a spectator sport on the information superhighway, with entire bulletin boards being devoted to flaming'.

However, what may be viewed as acceptable by some protagonists may be experienced as 'vituperative literary battles'[168] by those on the receiving end, for which, if they believe their reputation to have been diminished thereby, they may wish to seek redress in a court of law. This should be distinguished from invasion of privacy – what is at stake here is the individual's standing in the eyes of his or her peers and the way in which the law can protect it. As in the discussion of privacy, this necessitates balancing the protection of an individual's reputation against the right of others to pass comment on that person's words and actions. Even in a country like the UK, which has no written constitution, the law has identified the public interest in the freedom of speech in the defences available to an action for defamation such as fair comment, absolute and qualified privilege, etc.

The Australian case of *Rindos v Hardwick*,[169] was the first libel action to arise as a consequence of information posted to a newsgroup. Rindos, an anthropologist, had been refused tenure at the University of Western Australia. A comment, in support of his work was placed on ANTHRO-L, an electronic bulletin board subscribed to by anthropologists. In response, the defendant sent a vitriolic missive about Rindos to the newsgroup, sci.anthropology, another forum frequently accessed by academic anthropologists. Since this first case, there have been many other instances of alleged defamation committed, and even facilitated, by this medium of communication which have given rise to litigation in a number of jurisdictions. Some of these will feature in the subsequent discussion as the necessary ingredients for an action for defamation are explored in more detail. *Rindos v Hardwick* established that, in principle, libel could be committed via electronic media, but the case did not really have to address any of the difficult issues which might arise.

Is it libel or slander?

It is important to establish whether defamation by electronic means falls within the category of libel or slander, because libel is actionable *per se*, whereas slander requires proof of damage. It is generally accepted that defamation which is written and permanent will be libel, but that which is audible and purely transient, such as the spoken word, will constitute slander. However, these represent the most clear cut examples and some examples will fall between the two extremes. Most commentators seem to believe that defamation over the internet should be viewed as libel and the judgment of Ipp J in *Rindos v Hardwick* assumes that the criteria for libel are made out. There has been some discussion, however, as to whether the medium provides

---

167 Dooley, 1995.
168 Braithwaite and Carolina, 1994.
169 No 1994 of 1993, unreported judgment 940164, 31 March 1994, Supreme Court of Western Australia, unverified text available at www.mark.law.auckland.ac.nz/cases/Rindos.html. See also, Arnold-Moore, 1994; Auburn, 1995.

sufficient permanence.[170] What constitutes permanence? *Monson v Tussauds Ltd,*[171] concerned an exhibition of waxworks in which an effigy of the plaintiff was placed in the entrance to the Chamber of Horrors. Lopes LJ, discussing the various forms that libel could take, pointed out that, although writing or printing was the most usual medium, any other permanent form could suffice, including 'a statue, a caricature, an effigy, chalk marks on a wall, signs or pictures'. Clearly, there is no general standard of permanence exhibited in these examples – chalk marks can easily be erased and, in this particular case, it was the positioning of the waxwork, a factor which is clearly not inherently permanent, rather than its content, that gave rise to a finding of libel. To what extent can information made available over computer networks be viewed as permanent? Braithwaite and Carolina explain the answer as follows:[172]

> Electronic messages, although seemingly transitory, can be both stored for future reference and redisseminated far more readily than the printed word. Their transience and ease of alteration can be overstated, while their damaging effects may be much harder to eradicate.

This not only assesses the level of permanence but also suggests a policy reason why electronic communication should give rise to actions in libel rather than slander as a result of the potential for damage.

In 1975, the Faulks Committee on Defamation recommended that the distinction between libel and slander be abolished.[173] This was never acted upon but it may be that there is a need for statutory clarification in respect of electronic communication. If that were to be the case, it would not be the first time that the law has intervened in this way. Section 166(1) of the Broadcasting Act 1990 provides that, for the purposes of libel and slander, 'the publication of words in the course of any programme included in a programme service shall be treated as publication in permanent form'.[174]

Is the offending material defamatory?

Although there is no global harmonisation, as such, of the laws of defamation, most jurisdictions provide a remedy for injury to a person's reputation or integrity,[175] although there are likely to be differences of substance and degree, depending on legal form and tradition. Old authority in the UK says that a defamatory statement is one 'which is calculated to injure the reputation of another by exposing him to hatred, contempt or ridicule'.[176] This is a rather narrow view of the nature of defamation and an alternative test is to consider the effect of the offending statement within the boundaries of the space in which the reputation is enjoyed, whether geographical or social. This has been expressed in the somewhat archaic sounding formulation of Lord Atkin as to whether the statement was one which would tend 'to lower the [claimant]

---

170 See, Arnold-Moore, 1994; Dooley, 1995; Shillito, 1994.
171 [1894] 1 QB 671.
172 Braithwaite and Carolina, 1994.
173 Cmnd 5909, 1975.
174 See, also, the Theatres Act 1968, s 4.
175 See Carter-Ruck and Starte, 1997, Chapters 27–31.
176 *Parmiter v Coupland* (1840) 6 M & W 105, p 108, *per* Parke B.

in the estimation of right thinking members of society generally'.[177] Gibbons makes
the point that the use of this test 'reflects the idea that an external assessment has been
made of the person's behaviour and characteristics, and that it represents the views of
a group or a community or interests, for example, neighbours, colleagues, clientele,
customers or the public at large'.[178] The case law on defamation in more traditional
media is not particularly helpful in defining the relevant society for these purposes,
but this may be a crucial issue in relation to defamation on the internet and world
wide web. Despite the global nature of this medium, it would clearly be erroneous to
suppose that, in the majority of cases, reputations were, themselves, also global.

There are a number of potential delimitations on the scope of societal boundaries in
cyberspace. These may be geographical, or perhaps linguistic: a person's reputation
may only subsist in a particular physical location. Thus, even though material
published on the internet may be accessible outside this area (see, further, below),
there may be no damage arising as a result of the alleged defamation if, in fact, there is
no reputation to be impugned. Even within the apparently anarchic, amorphous and
disorganised world of cyberspace, individuals will consciously or unconsciously
impose their own limits on use and these may serve to delineate the areas in which
their reputations are likely to subsist. A range of geographical jurisdictions may be
encompassed but this need not, necessarily, imply that all potential users in those
jurisdictions are included. Thus, habitual contributors to particular bulletin boards,
newsgroups, etc, may enjoy a certain reputation among other users in those groups
but not within the jurisdiction at large. As already discussed, there are a vast range of
newsgroups, ranging from the staid and sober to the scurrilous and seditious. A
description of an unmoderated chat forum and the language typically employed can
be seen in *Global Telemedia International Inc v Doe 1*:

> Unlike many traditional media, there are no controls on the postings. Literally anyone
> who has access to the Internet has access to the chat-rooms. The chat-rooms devoted to a
> particular company are not sponsored by that company, or by any other company. No
> special expertise, knowledge or status is required to post a message, or to respond. The
> postings are not arranged by topic or by poster. The vast majority of the users are, because
> of the 'handles,' effectively anonymous. ... The messages range from relatively
> straightforward commentary to personal invective directed at other posters and at the
> subject company to the simply bizarre. ... For example, one exchange includes 'joemeat,
> you are one of the stupidest suckers that ever posted here' to which 'joemeat' responded
> 'akita ... that means so much coming from a degenerate who speaks regularly from his
> lower orifice.' ... The statements were posted anonymously in the general cacophony of
> an Internet chat-room in which about 1,000 messages a week are posted ... The postings
> at issue were anonymous as are all the other postings in the chat-room. They were part
> of an on-going, free-wheeling and highly animated exchange ... the postings are full of
> hyperbole, invective, short-hand phrases and language not generally found in fact-based
> documents ... .[179]

In those fora where the common mode of expression is immoderate or even
vituperative, it may be that defamation becomes more difficult to establish, as there

---

177 *Sim v Stretch* [1936] 2 All ER 1237, p 1240.
178 Gibbons, 1996, p 589.
179 132 F Supp 2d 1261, 1264 (CD Cal 2001).

may be little evidence that the allegedly offending statement actually damaged the reputation amongst the members of that society. Clearly, the way in which the relevant society is defined and constituted may be crucial and, as yet, there is little guidance from the courts.

Given that defamation is an intrinsically personal wrong providing a remedy for injury to reputation, it is essential that there must be no confusion as to whom the statement refers. Although a definitive test has proved elusive, it does not mean that the statement need be 'about' the targeted person as such. In *Lunney v Prodigy Services Co*,[180] which concerned emails to bulletin boards apparently posted by Lunney, the New York State Court of Appeals had to decide whether statements which were not directly about the plaintiff but were ascribed to him could be regarded as defamatory. The first instance court had inclined to the view that in such cases there was no defamation because, although the statements in question purported to have been written by Lunney, they were not 'of or concerning' him. Although the majority of the argument in both courts centred on the issue of publication (see below), the view of the Court of Appeals was that Lunney was 'defamed by being portrayed as the author of the foul material'.

Publication

The purpose of the tort of defamation is to protect reputation rather than injury to feelings caused by insults addressed only to the claimant/plaintiff, for instance. Thus, there will only be a cause of action where there is *publication* of the libel to a third party.[181] One of the dangers of participation in electronic discussion groups for the unsuspecting defendant is that it can, at times, appear very like a one-to-one interchange; it can be easy to forget that the contents may be mailed to others or available to others who choose to access a particular newsgroup. It is also true that newsgroups and bulletin boards aimed at academics and professional users are increasingly specialised in content and may attract a significant proportion of readers amongst that particular interest group. Thus, the potential for damaging an individual reputation in the eyes of others working in the same field can be high. In the words of Braithwaite and Carolina:

> ... bulletin boards are often the chosen method of correspondence in certain fields of study. Scurrilous bulletin board messages, even if not widely disseminated by conventional mass media standards, may be nicely targeted to achieve maximum damage to professional or business reputations.[182]

They also have this to say in relation to the fact of publication itself:

> When does publication occur? Is information published when data are copied to or stored on individual host computers or is it only when the information is actually communicated to the end user? Principle suggests that the actual communication is

---

180 94 NY 2d 242 (NY 1999).

181 But, for offensive and insulting email intended only for the recipient, a charge under the Malicious Communications Act 1988 may be possible.

182 Braithwaite and Carolina, 1994.

necessary, not mere availability, since the gist of defamation is actual or presumed damage to reputation flowing from publication. On the other hand, it would be onerous to expect a plaintiff to prove that stored information had been accessed.

There is old authority which suggests that actual *communication* to the third party may not be necessary to show publication.

R v Burdett
(1820) 4 B & Ald 95, p 126

It is assumed that publication means a manifestation of the contents. I deny that such is the meaning of the word publication. In no part of the law do I find that it is used in that sense. A man publishes an award, but he does not read it. Again, he publishes a will, but he does not manifest its contents to those to whom he makes the publication; he merely desires the witnesses to take notice at the paper to which they affix their different attestations is his will. So in the case of a libel, publication is nothing more than doing the last act for the accomplishment of the mischief intended by it. The moment a man delivers a libel from his hands his control over it is gone; he has shot his arrow, and it does not depend upon him whether it hits the mark or not. There is an end of the *locus pœnitentiæ*, his offence is complete, all that depends upon him is consummated, and from that moment, upon every principle of common sense, he is liable to be called upon to answer for his act. Suppose a man wraps up a newspaper and sends it into another county by a boy; who is the publisher? The boy who perhaps cannot read or is ignorant of its contents, or the man who has put it in the envelope? The boy who carries it is merely an innocent instrument; there can be no other publisher but the person who sent it, and who publishes when he delivers it to the boy. If the sending of a letter by the post be not a publication in the county from whence it is sent, how is a libeller to be punished who sends his libel by the post to some foreign country for circulation?

In contrast, in the light of the current technological environment, the question has arisen as to whether the mere fact that publications via computer networks are accessible globally is equivalent to publication in all jurisdictions simultaneously for the purposes of defamation law. In the Australian case of *Macquirie Bank v Berg*,[183] Simpson J in the New South Wales Supreme Court denied interlocutory relief on the basis that any effects of the injunction could not be restricted to New South Wales, but would also impact on the rest of the world, since, 'once published on the internet, material can be received anywhere, and it does not lie within the competence of the publisher to restrict the reach of the publication'.

Macquirie Bank v Berg
[1999] NSWSC 526
Supreme Court of New South Wales

13 The consequence is that, if I were to make the order sought (and the defendant were to obey it) he would be restrained from publishing anywhere in the world via the medium of the internet.

The difficulties are obvious. An injunction to restrain defamation in NSW is designed to ensure compliance with the laws of NSW, and to protect the rights of plaintiffs, as those rights are defined by the law of NSW. Such an injunction is not designed to superimpose the law of NSW relating to defamation on every other state, territory and country of the world. Yet that would be the effect of an order restraining

183 [1999] NSWSC 526; see www.austlii.edu.au/au/cases/nsw/supreme_ct/1999/526.htm.

publication on the internet. It is not to be assumed that the law of defamation in other countries is coextensive with that of NSW, and indeed, one knows that it is not. It may very well be that, according to the law of the Bahamas, Tazhakistan or Mongolia, the defendant has an unfettered right to publish the material. To make an order interfering with such a right would exceed the proper limits of the use of the injunctive power sought.

This view has been doubted on the basis that it is an oversimplification and arguably misunderstands the technology – the alternative is that the nature and operation of this medium of communication is such that mere accessibility should not automatically be equated with publication in this medium.

Defamation on the internet –
a duty free zone after all?
Uta Kohl
(2000) 22 Sydney L Rev 119, pp 126–27

The tort of defamation occurs where the defamatory imputation is published. This in turn raises the issues as to what amounts to 'publication' and how this applies to the medium of the Internet. Does world-wide accessibility equate with world-wide publication and, if not, where is the material put on the Internet actually published? In defamation, the defamatory imputation is published if it is communicated to some person or persons other than the plaintiff himself. With the emphasis being on communication or the making known of the defamatory imputation, it is not enough merely to write defamatory words and it is not even enough to deliver a defamatory statement to another if the other person does not become aware of the defamatory words. Similarly, publication is generally not equivalent to the mere posting of a message, but only becomes complete when the communication reaches the addressee. While it is not necessary for the plaintiff in all cases to prove directly that the defamatory matter was brought to the actual knowledge of anyone, publication is only established if the plaintiff makes it a matter of reasonable inference that such was the case ... it must be probable or a matter of reasonable inference that someone actually read the defamatory imputation after it was sent. Therefore, the question in the Internet context is, how probable is it that a particular website is being accessed by someone other than the plaintiff, in the absence of positive evidence of such access? And for those who assume putting a website on the Internet equates with worldwide publication, it must not merely be probable that someone accessed the site but that someone in every jurisdiction accessed it. While this may at first not appear to be difficult to prove, it must be appreciated that there are more than 14.8 million domain names registered world-wide and it can be assumed that the number of individual web pages must be in the 100 millions. Given the sheer number of websites the Internet must be distinguished from television and radio broadcasts. Mere accessibility of these media has been held to equate with publication of their programmes, that is, publication is presumed to occur in all areas to which their waves are transmitted. This is because (given the relatively limited number of radio or TV channels and the great number of viewers and listeners) it is highly probable that someone in each area will actually switch on and view or listen to the particular programme. In contrast, with the Internet it is not at all probable that every website will be accessed in every jurisdiction where it can theoretically be accessed. Some states have clearly a much greater Internet presence than others. This may make it probable that even an obscure site is accessed in a state such as the United States but not necessarily in one which is hardly connected to the Internet. So, if as a matter of reasonable inference, it cannot be assumed that any site put on the Internet and theoretically accessible from anywhere is in fact accessed everywhere, where then can publication be assumed? This is a question of fact which will depend on the circumstances of each particular case.

This analysis suggests that some statistical evaluation of the likelihood of communication in any specified jurisdiction will be required to raise a presumption that publication has in fact occurred. A presumption that there had been no publication in a particular jurisdiction could, however, be rebutted by evidence of actual access. Support for the view that publication can be equated with actual access can be found in the judgment of Morland J in *Godfrey v Demon Internet*, when he remarked that:

> In my judgment, the defendant, whenever it transmits and whenever there is transmitted from the storage of its news server a defamatory posting, publishes that posting to any subscriber to its ISP who accesses the newsgroup containing that posting. Thus, every time one of the defendant's customers accesses 'soc.culture.thai' and sees that posting defamatory of the plaintiff, there is a publication to that customer.[184]

Although, arguably, this approach may represent a more realistic evaluation of the fact of publication at first sight, it is likely to be beset by evidential difficulties. In reality, the method might be assisted by two factors. The first is technical: many websites have facilities for recording 'hits' and such records may give an indication of the jurisdictions where access has occurred and, *prima facie*, the material has been published. Also, as discussed above, it is not possible to damage a reputation where none exists and the nature of many reputations in this medium is that they may be parochial in either the physical (reputation enjoyed in a particular location) or virtual (reputation confined to those who use a particular newsgroup, etc) sense.

The question of where publication occurs was considered by the Australian courts again in *Dow Jones & Co. Inc v Gutnick*.[185] The case concerned material posted on the internet in New Jersey but accessible in Victoria where the plaintiff resided. The High Court of Australia was unpersuaded by the argument that the place of publication should be deemed to be New Jersey and that an action for defamation could only be defended there. For the most part, this decision was arrived at by considering traditional principles and was not based on any novel claims for the internet as a medium to which different rules should be applied.

Dow Jones & Co Inc v Gutnick
High Court of Australia
[2002] HCA 56

Gaudron J:

38   In the course of argument much emphasis was given to the fact that the advent of the World Wide Web is a considerable technological advance. So it is. But the problem of widely disseminated communications is much older than the Internet and the World Wide Web. The law has had to grapple with such cases ever since newspapers and magazines came to be distributed to large numbers of people over wide geographic areas. Radio and television presented the same kind of problem as was presented by widespread dissemination of printed material, although international transmission of material was made easier by the advent of electronic means of communication.

39   It was suggested that the World Wide Web was different from radio and television because the radio or television broadcaster could decide how far the signal was to be broadcast. It must be recognised, however, that satellite broadcasting now

permits very wide dissemination of radio and television and it may, therefore, be doubted that it is right to say that the World Wide Web has a uniquely broad reach. It is no more or less ubiquitous than some television services. In the end, pointing to the breadth or depth of reach of particular forms of communication may tend to obscure one basic fact. However broad may be the reach of any particular means of communication, those who make information accessible by a particular method do so knowing of the reach that their information may have. In particular, those who post information on the World Wide Web do so knowing that the information they make available is available to all and sundry without any geographic restriction.

40   Because publication is an act or event to which there are at least two parties, the publisher and a person to whom material is published, publication to numerous persons may have as many territorial connections as there are those to whom particular words are published. It is only if one starts from a premise that the publication of particular words is necessarily a *singular* event which is to be located by reference *only* to the conduct of the publisher that it would be right to attach no significance to the territorial connections provided by the several places in which the publication is available for comprehension.

44   In defamation, the same considerations that require rejection of locating the tort by reference only to the publisher's conduct, lead to the conclusion that, ordinarily, defamation is to be located at the place where the damage to reputation occurs. Ordinarily that will be where the material which is alleged to be defamatory is available in comprehensible form assuming, of course, that the person defamed has in that place a reputation which is thereby damaged. It is only when the material is in comprehensible form that the damage to reputation is done and it is damage to reputation which is the principal focus of defamation, not any quality of the defendant's conduct. In the case of material on the World Wide Web, it is not available in comprehensible form until downloaded on to the computer of a person who has used a web browser to pull the material from the web server. It is where that person downloads the material that the damage to reputation may be done. Ordinarily then, that will be the place where the tort of defamation is committed.

Callinan J:

180   A publisher, particularly one carrying on the business of publishing, does not act to put matter on the Internet in order for it to reach a small target. It is its ubiquity which is one of the main attractions to users of it. And any person who gains access to the Internet does so by taking an initiative to gain access to it in a manner analogous to the purchase or other acquisition of a newspaper, in order to read it.

181   The appellant contends that the Internet is not 'pushed' into any particular jurisdiction. The contention ignores the commercial and social realities that greater publication produces both greater profit and broader persuasion. ... Publishers are not obliged to publish on the Internet. If the potential reach is uncontrollable then the greater the need to exercise care in publication.

182   ... The most important event so far as defamation is concerned is the infliction of the damage, and that occurs at the place (or the places) where the defamation is comprehended. Statements made on the Internet are neither more nor less 'localized' than statements made in any other media or by other processes. Newspapers have always been circulated in many places. The reach of radio and television is limited only by the capacity of the technology to transmit and hear or view them, which already, and for many years, has extended beyond any one country. ...

185   The Court was much pressed with arguments about the ubiquity of the Internet. That ubiquity, it was said, distinguished the Internet from practically any other form of human endeavour. Implicit in the appellant's assertions was more than a

suggestion that any attempt to control, regulate, or even inhibit its operation, no matter the irresponsibility or malevolence of a user, would be futile, and that therefore no jurisdiction should trouble to try to do so. I would reject these claims. … There is nothing unique about multinational business, and it is in that that this appellant chooses to be engaged. If people wish to do business in, or indeed travel to, or live in, or utilise the infrastructure of different countries, they can hardly expect to be absolved from compliance with the laws of those countries. The fact that publication might occur everywhere does not mean that it occurs nowhere. …

198   The appellant's submission that publication occurs, or should henceforth occur relevantly at one place, the place where the matter is provided, or first published, cannot withstand any reasonable test of certainty and fairness. If it were accepted, publishers would be free to manipulate the uploading and location of data so as to insulate themselves from liability in Australia, or elsewhere …

Although concurring in the result, one of the four judges, Kirby J, felt that this was not a 'wholly satisfactory outcome'. After an extensive review of the arguments for and against regarding the internet and the world wide web as a special case requiring different or novel solutions, he suggested that both national legislative attention and international consideration of the issues might be warranted.

164   … Intuition suggests that the remarkable features of the Internet (which is still changing and expanding) makes it more than simply another medium of human communication. It is indeed a revolutionary leap in the distribution of information, including about the reputation of individuals. It is a medium that overwhelmingly benefits humanity, advancing as it does the human right of access to information and to free expression. But the human right to protection by law for the reputation and honour of individuals must also be defended to the extent that the law provides.

165   The notion that those who publish defamatory material on the Internet are answerable before the courts of any nation where the damage to reputation has occurred, such as in the jurisdiction where the complaining party resides, presents difficulties: technological, legal and practical. It is true that the law of Australia provides protections against some of those difficulties which, in appropriate cases, will obviate or diminish the inconvenience of distant liability. Moreover, the spectre of 'global' liability should not be exaggerated. Apart from anything else, the costs and practicalities of bringing proceedings against a foreign publisher will usually be a sufficient impediment to discourage even the most intrepid of litigants. Further, in many cases of this kind, where the publisher is said to have no presence or assets in the jurisdiction, it may choose simply to ignore the proceedings. It may save its contest to the courts of its own jurisdiction until an attempt is later made to enforce there the judgment obtained in the foreign trial. It may do this especially if that judgment was secured by the application of laws, the enforcement of which would be regarded as unconstitutional or otherwise offensive to a different legal culture.

166   However, such results are still less than wholly satisfactory. They appear to warrant national legislative attention and to require international discussion in a forum as global as the Internet itself. In default of local legislation and international agreement, there are limits on the extent to which national courts can provide radical solutions that would oblige a major overhaul of longstanding legal doctrine in the field of defamation law. Where large changes to settled law are involved, in an area as sensitive as the law of defamation, it should cause no surprise when the courts decline the invitation to solve problems that others, in a much better position to devise solutions, have neglected to repair.

The reasoning employed in *Dow Jones v Gutnick* was referred to in *Lewis v King*,[186] where, after quoting various paragraphs from the Australian judgment, there was reference to 'the court's vindication of traditional principles relating to publication and jurisdiction in defamation cases'.[187] Although by no means proposing a 'free-for-all for claimants libelled on the Internet', the court pointed out that a global publisher should not be too fastidious as to the part of the globe where he is made a libel defendant'.[188] A rather different approach has since been taken in *Dow Jones v Jameel*.[189] In March 2003, Dow Jones had published an article in the *Wall Street Journal* on-line, via servers in New Jersey, about the so-called 'Golden Chain'; individuals and organisations who were alleged to provide financial support to Osama bin Laden and al Qaeda. A hyperlink in this article enabled readers of the article to access a list of donors; the fourth name was that of the claimant, a Saudi national. He alleged that the material was defamatory in that it suggested, either naturally or inferentially, that he had been among the first financial supporters of Osama bin Laden and al Qaeda, and that there were reasonable grounds to suspect that he had continued to provide financial support for such terrorism including, in particular, for those who had been responsible for the attacks on 11 September 2001.[190] Further, this had led to him falsely being suspected of association with Osama bin Laden and al Qaeda. As a result, he brought a number of actions and, on the basis that the website was accessible in the UK, one of these was in the English courts. The evidence was that only five individuals had accessed the article in the UK. Of these three were connected with the claimant (his solicitor and two business associates) and there was no evidence that the other two knew the claimant. The Court of Appeal did not find that this was sufficient to allow an action for libel to be brought – 'the five publications that had taken place in this jurisdiction did not, individually or collectively, amount to a real and substantial tort'.[191] This represents a considerable departure from the reasoning in *Dow Jones v Gutnick* discussed above.

Notwithstanding their obvious differences, the above cases can be further contrasted with the US case of *Young v New Haven Advocate*.[192] In this case, two local newspapers published in Connecticut were alleged to carry material which defamed a resident of Virginia. The issue was whether the action could be pursued in Virginia, where the plaintiff had a reputation to protect, when the only basis for publication in that State was via the internet. The court did not consider where the plaintiff's reputation had suffered damage, but looked for an intention to direct the publication at Virginia, demonstrated by something more than mere accessibility, or passive availability, of the information. The court found that not only was the general information, advertisements etc, not relevant to an audience in Virginia, but also that the specific articles complained of were focused on Connecticut interests. The court concluded that the websites were maintained to 'expand the reach of their papers in local markets' and there was no manifest intent to target readers elsewhere. So, although publication

---

186 [2004] EWCA Civ 1329 (CA).
187 *Ibid,* para. 30.
188 *Ibid,* para. 31.
189 [2005] EWCA Civ 75; *The Times,* 14 February 2005.
190 *Ibid,* paras 7–11.
191 *Ibid,* para 70.
192 315 F 3d 256 (4th Cir 2002).

on the web inevitably had the result that the newspapers could be accessed in other states, this did not inevitably result in a finding that a Virginia court could exercise jurisdiction. [193] This is clearly entirely different reasoning to that in either of the *Dow Jones* cases. However, whatever the eventual outcome or consensus, the question of whether publication on the internet can equate to effective publication in all jurisdictions will only be of real significance to those who actually have a global reputation to protect.

Who is liable for the publication?

It is not only the author of a libel who may be liable, but anyone who participates in the publication of the defamatory matter; this might include the publisher, editor, printer and distributor. It may be that mere distributors have no cause to suspect the existence of a libel in the material in question and, in such a case, they may be able to avail themselves of the defence of innocent dissemination. This was originally established in the case of *Emmens v Pottle*,[194] and applies where the defendant had no reason to believe that the publication in question contained a libel and this ignorance did not arise from negligence on the part of the defendant. A particular concern for networked information is the extent of the liability of the bulletin board operator (BBO) or the ISP. Are they akin to distributors, so that the defence of innocent dissemination could be applied, or are they, in reality, more like editors or publishers? Two cases from the US, where a similar defence is available, illustrate the two sides of the coin.

Cubby Inc v CompuServe Inc,[195] concerned an online service provider which provided access to a bulletin board, monitored by an independent company which exerted editorial control. A newsletter called *Rumorville* was available via the bulletin board. The case arose as a consequence of the development by the plaintiff of a news database which would be likely to be in competition with *Rumorville*. When certain allegedly defamatory remarks were then made about the plaintiff in the newsletter, a libel action was brought against, *inter alia*, CompuServe, the service provider:

> The requirement that a distributor must have knowledge of the contents of a publication before liability can be imposed for distributing that publication is deeply rooted in the First Amendment, made applicable to the states through the Fourteenth Amendment. '[T]he constitutional guarantees of the freedom of speech and of the press stand in the way of imposing' strict liability on distributors for the contents of the reading materials they carry ... In [*Smith v California* (1959)] ... the court reasoned that 'Every bookseller would be placed under an obligation to make himself aware of the contents of every book in his shop. it would be altogether unreasonable to demand so near an approach to omniscience'.

---

193 Compare also the earlier Canadian case of *Braintech Inc v Kostiuk* [1999] 171 DLR (4th) 46 in which the CA for British Columbia held that a more specific connection with the other jurisdiction had to be established other than that 'someone in that jurisdiction might have reached out to cyberspace to bring the defamatory material to a screen'. See also discussion in Ludbrook, 2004.

194 (1885) 16 QBD 354.

195 776 F Supp 135 (SDNY 1991).

... Technology is rapidly transforming the information industry. A computerised database is the functional equivalent of a more traditional news vendor, and the inconsistent application of a lower standard of liability to an electronic news distributor such as CompuServe than that which is applied to a public library, book store or news-stand would impose an undue burden on the free flow of information. Given the relevant First Amendment considerations, the appropriate standard of liability to be applied to CompuServe is whether it knew or had reason to know of the allegedly defamatory *Rumorville* statements.

The court went on to find that CompuServe were not liable for the defamation, because they 'neither knew nor had reason to know of the allegedly defamatory *Rumorville* statements'. The issue of whether a database operator exercising editorial control over content might be construed as a publisher rather than a distributor and, in consequence, be unable to avail themselves of this 'distributor's defence' was left open.

In contrast, the circumstances in *Stratton Oakmont Inc v PRODIGY Services Co*,[196] were to lead to a different result. Derogatory comments and accusations about the plaintiff company were posted on a bulletin board made available by PRODIGY and an action was taken against them for libel:

A distributor, or deliverer of defamatory material, is considered a passive conduit and found liable in the absence of fault ... However, a newspaper, for example, is more than a passive receptacle or conduit for news, comment and advertising ... The choice of material to go into a newspaper and the decisions made as to the content of the paper constitute the exercise of editorial control and judgment ... and with this increased control comes increased liability. In short, the critical issue to be determined by this court is whether the ... evidence establishes a *prima facie* case that PRODIGY exercised sufficient editorial control over its computer bulletin boards to render it a publisher with the same responsibilities as a newspaper.

The court found that Prodigy not only held itself out as controlling the contents of its bulletin boards but also that it implemented this control through an automatic software screening program. The court was therefore 'compelled to conclude that ... PRODIGY is a publisher rather than a distributor' and was therefore liable for the defamatory remarks. The court did, however, point out that they fully agreed with the decision in *Cubby* and that 'computer bulletin boards should generally be regarded in the same context as bookstores, libraries and network affiliates'.

Although these two decisions can be reconciled on the basis of the extent of editorial control, concentrating on this aspect alone masks a vigorous debate over the extent to which ISPs should be held liable[197] for the content of material to which they provide access. This is a debate which, as we shall see, has not been resolved and to which different answers pertain in different jurisdictions.

In the US, cases such as *Cubby* and *Stratton* were superseded by statutory intervention in the form of s 230 of the Telecommunications Act of 1996.[198]

---

196 1995 NY Misc Lexis 229.

197 See, also, below, p 405.

198 Also referred to as the Communications Decency Act. For discussion of other provisions of this statute see below, p 461.

Telecommunications Act of 1996
104th Congress

Title II of the Communications Act of 1934 (47 USC 201 *et seq*) is amended by adding at the end the following new section:

SEC 230 (47 USC 230)

Protection for private blocking and screening of offensive material

(a) Findings – The Congress finds the following:

    (1) The rapidly developing array of Internet and other interactive computer services available to individual Americans represent an extraordinary advance in the availability of educational and informational resources to our citizens.

    (2) These services offer users a great degree of control over the information that they receive, as well as the potential for even greater control in the future as technology develops.

    (3) The Internet and other interactive computer services offer a forum for a true diversity of political discourse, unique opportunities for cultural development, and myriad avenues for intellectual activity.

    (4) The Internet and other interactive computer services have flourished, to the benefit of all Americans, with a minimum of government regulation.

    (5) Increasingly Americans are relying on interactive media for a variety of political, educational, cultural, and entertainment services.

(b) Policy – It is the policy of the United States:

    (1) to promote the continued development of the Internet and other interactive computer services and other interactive media;

    (2) to preserve the vibrant and competitive free market that presently exists for the Internet and other interactive computer services, unfettered by Federal or State regulation;

    (3) to encourage the development of technologies which maximize user control over what information is received by individuals, families, and schools who use the Internet and other interactive computer services;

    (4) to remove disincentives for the development and utilization of blocking and filtering technologies that empower parents to restrict their children's access to objectionable or inappropriate online material; and

    (5) to ensure vigorous enforcement of Federal criminal laws to deter and punish trafficking in obscenity, stalking, and harassment by means of computer.

(c) Protection for 'Good Samaritan' Blocking and Screening of Offensive Material

    (1) Treatment of publisher or speaker – No provider or user of an interactive computer service shall be treated as the publisher or speaker of any information provided by another information content provider.

    (2) Civil liability – No provider or user of an interactive computer service shall be held liable on account of –

        (A) any action voluntarily taken in good faith to restrict access to or availability of material that the provider or user considers to be obscene, lewd, lascivious, filthy, excessively violent, harassing, or otherwise objectionable, whether or not such material is constitutionally protected; or

        (B) any action taken to enable or make available to information content providers or others the technical means to restrict access to material described in paragraph (1).

(e) Definitions – As used in this section:

(1) Internet – The term 'Internet' means the international computer network of both Federal and non-Federal interoperable packet switched data networks.

(2) Interactive computer service – The term 'interactive computer service' means any information service, system, or access software provider that provides or enables computer access by multiple users to a computer server, including specifically a service or system that provides access to the Internet and such systems operated or services offered by libraries or educational institutions.

(3) Information content provider – The term 'information content provider' means any person or entity that is responsible, in whole or in part, for the creation or development of information provided through the Internet or any other interactive computer service.

(4) Access software provider – The term 'access software provider' means a provider of software (including client or server software), or enabling tools that do any one or more of the following:

(A) filter, screen, allow, or disallow content;

(B) pick, choose, analyze, or digest content; or

(C) transmit, receive, display, forward, cache, search, subset, organize, reorganize, or translate content.

Section 230(a) and (b) provide the context within which s 230(c)(1) gives ISPs an immunity from suit in relation to material provided by others. The application of this provision in cases of online defamation was first discussed in *Zeran v America Online*,[199] a case arising out of the imputation to Zeran of offensive and tasteless slogans related to the Oklahoma bombings. The US Court of Appeals for the Fourth Circuit was in little doubt as to the effect of s 230(c)(1):

> By its plain language, § 230 creates a federal immunity to any cause of action that would make service providers liable for information originating with a third party user of the service. Specifically, § 230 precludes courts from entertaining claims that would place a computer service provider in a publisher's role. Thus, lawsuits seeking to hold a service provider liable for its exercise of a publisher's traditional editorial functions – such as deciding whether to publish, withdraw, postpone or alter content – are barred.

The court considered the context within which the provision was intended to operate. It cited s 230(a)(4) and pointed out that, whilst vigorous enforcement might be necessary against those who introduced illicit material (s 230(b)(5)), Congress had made a policy choice 'not to deter harmful online speech through the separate route of imposing tort liability on companies that serve as intermediaries for other parties' potentially injurious messages'. A major reason for this is the immense practical difficulty for ISPs, given the sheer volume of traffic for which they could be held responsible, coupled with the potentially restrictive effects on freedom of speech if ISPs were to take an unduly restrictive approach in order to ensure the avoidance of liability. The court noted also that a further purpose in forbidding the imposition of publisher liability was to encourage self-regulation.

The issue in *Zeran* was whether such immunity extended also to the liability of distributors. Zeran contended that the terms 'publisher' and 'distributor' were legally distinct and that s 230 left distributor liability intact. On this reasoning, AOL would still be liable if they had actual knowledge of the defamatory statements. The court

---

199 129 F 3d 327 (4th Cir 1997).

could not concur with this argument and neither did it believe that its view was necessarily out of line with the decisions reached in *Cubby* and *Stratton*.

Zeran v America Online Inc
129 F 3d 327, 332
US Court of Appeals (4th Cir 1997)

The terms 'publisher' and 'distributor' derive their legal significance from the context of defamation law ... Because the publication of a statement is a necessary element in a defamation action, only one who publishes can be subject to this form of tort liability ... Publication does not only describe the choice by an author to include certain information. In addition, both the negligent communication of a defamatory statement and the failure to remove such a statement when first communicated by another party ... constitute publication ... In fact, every repetition of a defamatory statement is considered a publication.

In this case, AOL is legally considered to be a publisher. '[E]very one who takes part in the publication is charged with publication.' Even distributors are considered to be publishers for purposes of defamation law.

Those who are in the business of making their facilities available to disseminate the writings composed, the speeches made, and the information gathered by others may also be regarded as participating to such an extent in making the books, newspapers, magazines, and information available to others as to be regarded as publishers. They are intentionally making the contents available to others, sometimes without knowing all of the contents – including the defamatory content – and sometimes without any opportunity to ascertain, in advance, that any defamatory matter was to be included in the matter published. AOL falls squarely within this traditional definition of a publisher and, therefore, is clearly protected by § 230's immunity.

Zeran contends that decisions like *Stratton Oakmont* and *Cubby Inc v CompuServe Inc* 776 F Supp 135 (SDNY 1991) recognize a legal distinction between publishers and distributors. He misapprehends, however, the significance of that distinction for the legal issue we consider here. It is undoubtedly true that mere conduits, or distributors, are subject to a different standard of liability. As explained above, distributors must at a minimum have knowledge of the existence of a defamatory statement as a prerequisite to liability. But this distinction signifies only that different standards of liability may be applied within the larger publisher category, depending on the specific type of publisher concerned ... To the extent that decisions like *Stratton* and *Cubby* utilize the terms 'publisher' and 'distributor' separately, the decisions correctly describe two different standards of liability. *Stratton* and *Cubby* do not, however, suggest that distributors are not also a type of publisher for purposes of defamation law.

Zeran simply attaches too much importance to the presence of the distinct notice element in distributor liability. The simple fact of notice surely cannot transform one from an original publisher to a distributor in the eyes of the law. To the contrary, once a computer service provider receives notice of a potentially defamatory posting, it is thrust into the role of a traditional publisher. The computer service provider must decide whether to publish, edit, or withdraw the posting. In this respect, Zeran seeks to impose liability on AOL for assuming the role for which § 230 specifically proscribes liability – the publisher role ...

Zeran next contends that interpreting § 230 to impose liability on service providers with knowledge of defamatory content on their services is consistent with the statutory purposes outlined in Part IIA. Zeran fails, however, to understand the practical implications of notice liability in the interactive computer service context. Liability upon notice would defeat the dual purposes advanced by § 230 of the CDA.

Later cases have largely followed the same line of reasoning, although some notes of concern have been voiced in relation to the issue of notice (*Doe v AOL*)[200] and the actual or potential behaviour of ISPs, as shown in the following extract.

Blumenthal and Blumenthal v Drudge and America Online Inc
992 F.Supp 44, 51
DDC (1998)

If it were writing on a clean slate, this Court would agree with plaintiffs. AOL has certain editorial rights with respect to the content provided by Drudge and disseminated by AOL, including the right to require changes in content and to remove it; and it has affirmatively promoted Drudge as a new source of unverified instant gossip on AOL. Yet it takes no responsibility for any damage he may cause. AOL is not a passive conduit like the telephone company, a common carrier with no control and therefore no responsibility for what is said over the telephone wires. Because it has the right to exercise editorial control over those with whom it contracts and whose words it disseminates, it would seem only fair to hold AOL to the liability standards applied to a publisher or, at least, like a book store owner or library, to the liability standards applied to a distributor. But Congress has made a different policy choice by providing immunity even where the interactive service provider has an active, even aggressive role in making available content prepared by others. In some sort of tacit *quid pro quo* arrangement with the service provider community, Congress has conferred immunity from tort liability as an incentive to Internet service providers to self-police the Internet for obscenity and other offensive material, even where the self-policing is unsuccessful or not even attempted ... While it appears to this Court that AOL in this case has taken advantage of all the benefits conferred by Congress in the Communications Decency Act, and then some, without accepting any of the burdens that Congress intended, the statutory language is clear: AOL is immune from suit, and the Court therefore must grant its motion for summary judgment.

Further, in *Lunney v PRODIGY Services*, the lower court found PRODIGY not to be liable by applying common law principles and believed this outcome to be 'in complete harmony with current Federal statutory law contained in the Communications Decency Act (47 USC § 230 *et seq*)'. There was thus no need to decide 'the essentially academic question of whether this Federal statute would apply to all or part of the allegations'.[201] Lunney's appeal was dismissed with the court stating that 'the public would not be well served by compelling an ISP to examine and screen millions of email communications, on pain of liability for defamation',[202] but, nevertheless, declined to come down on either side of the debate set out in *Zeran* in relation to the immunity afforded by 47 USC s 230. In the later case of *Barrett v Rosenthal* the trial court, following *Zeran*, ruled that the CDA gave internet content providers immunity but, on the facts of the case, this finding was reversed by the Californian Court of Appeal for the First District.[203] The judgment in the higher court contained an extensive critique of the decision in *Zeran* citing both case law and

---

200 718 So.2d 385 (Fla.App. 4 Dist 1998).

201 683 NYS 2d 557, 563 (NYAD 1998).

202 94 NY 2d 242, 249 (NY 1999) and the Supreme Court subsequently denied a certificate of certiorari to review this case, 146 L Ed 2d 776.

203 9 Cal Rptr 3d 142 (Cal App 1 Dist 2004).

academic comment. It found that 'the court ascribed to Congress an intent to create a far broader immunity than that body actually had in mind or is necessary to achieve its purposes'.[204] In particular, the court was unwilling to conclude that Congress had necessarily, or inevitably, intended the common law rules on distributor liability to be superceded by the CDA and that 'survival of knowledge-based liability under the common law would not render section 230 nugatory'.[205] Such arguments allow liability to be imposed where, as in this case, there has been actual knowledge or notice of offending material. This decision attracted as much criticism as that of *Zeran* and the Californian Supreme Court is in the process of reviewing the decision at the time of writing.[206] The criticisms of a wide approach to the construction and application of s 230 are based on individual rights and the difficulties in obtaining a suitable remedy, whereas those in favour of the broad construction cite arguments based on freedom of expression and the unnecessary chilling effect which could occur if total immunity were not available. Such a balance of rights is a perennially delicate matter[207] and it will be interesting to see the contribution of the Californian Supreme Court when it gives its judgment.

A quite different situation pertains in the UK, although, as yet, there has been little action in the courts. The Defamation Act 1996 includes a statutory version of the innocent dissemination defence.

Defamation Act 1996
1 Responsibility for publication

(1) In defamation proceedings a person has a defence if he shows that –

    (a) he was not the author, editor or publisher of the statement complained of;

    (b) he took reasonable care in relation to its publication; and

    (c) he did not know, and had no reason to believe, that what he did caused or contributed to the publication of a defamatory statement.

(2) For this purpose 'author', 'editor' and 'publisher' have the following meanings ...

    'author' means the originator of the statement, but does not include a person who did not intend that his statement be published at all;

    'editor' means a person having editorial or equivalent responsibility for the content of the statement or the decision to publish it; and

    'publisher' means a commercial publisher, that is, a person whose business is issuing material to the public, or a section of the public, who issues material containing the statement in the course of that business.

This suggests that ISPs may escape liability if they act purely as distributors and, to an extent, this is clarified in the subsequent subsections.

---

204 *Ibid*, p. 154.
205 *Ibid*, p. 166.
206 For petition for review see www.caspnet/sc_pet1.html, and for various briefs see www.eff.org/Censorship/SLAPP/Defamation_abuse/Barrett_v_Clark/20041124_BarrettAm icusFinal.pdf and www.law,berkeley.edu/cenpro/samuelson/papers/briefs/Barrett-CalSup-2004.pdf.
207 See further Rowland, 2005.

Defamation Act 1996

1 Responsibility for publication

(3) A person shall not be considered the author, editor or publisher of a statement if he is only involved ...

    (c) In processing, making copies of, distributing or selling any electronic medium in or on which the statement is recorded, or in operating or providing any equipment, system or service by means of which the statement is retrieved, copied, distributed or made available in electronic form ...

(5) In determining for the purposes of this section whether a person took reasonable care, or had reason to believe that what he did caused or contributed to the publication of the defamatory statement, regard shall be had to –

    (a) the extent of his responsibility for the content of the statement or the decision to publish it;

    (b) the nature or circumstances of the publication; and

    (c) the previous conduct or character of the author, editor or publisher.

The effect of this is clearly quite different from the operation of 47 USC § 230 and its subsequent interpretation. The Defamation Act 1996 causes liability not to fall on those who are not deemed to be publishers, whereas the US statute provides actual immunity from suit for all those who fall within the ambit of the term 'publisher'. Whereas it might be supposed that the majority of ISPs would not generally be acting as 'publishers', the situation is complicated further by the fact that an 'internet service provider' may act in many capacities over and above the mere provision of connection to the internet. Tiberi and Zamboni[208] point out that ISPs may be company, university or government bodies, may offer any combination of a range of services and may act in a variety of capacities including as network operator, access provider, host provider, bulletin board operator, information location toll provider and content provider.

Although pure distributors may escape liability, the situation is much less clear with respect to BBOs and similar activities. Where there is editorial control over the content, then the defence would fall at the first hurdle, in s 1(1)(a). The situation would presumably be similar for a moderated newsgroup. This does not automatically mean that it would be safer to operate an unmoderated bulletin board or newsgroup (in any case, this might be undesirable for other reasons) because a presumption may arise that such a BBO should be aware of the likely traffic on the board to which they provide access and it could be that they would be unable then to satisfy s 1(1)(b) and/or (c).[209] For an unmoderated newsgroup, in particular, it may, in any case, be difficult to identify any appropriate defendant. This might suggest that there could be policy reasons for allowing liability to fall on the service provider in certain cases.

The application of these provisions of in a case of alleged defamation on an internet newsgroup arose in *Godfrey v Demon Internet*.[210] As in *Lunney*, this case concerned a 'squalid and obscene' email posting which purported to come from the

---

208 Tiberi and Zamboni, 2003.

209 Consider in this context the facts of George Robertson's case against the *Sunday Herald* in relation alleged defamatory comments on the newspaper's unmoderated online forum for which a settlement was reached in September 2004. See Vass, 2004, www.sundayherald.com/44642 and discussion in Ludbrook 2004, Part II.

210 [1999] 4 All ER 342.

claimant. At the interlocutory hearing, there was no argument that this could not constitute defamation and, indeed, the hearing proceeded on the basis that the offending material was defamatory. The discussion centred instead on whether the ISP, Demon, could rely on the defence provided in s 1 of the Defamation Act 1996, given that Godfrey had notified Demon that the posting was a forgery for which he was not responsible and had asked that they remove it from the news server. In Morland J's opinion, Demon was 'clearly not the publisher of the posting defamatory of the [claimant] within the meaning of s 1(2) and (3) and incontrovertibly can avail itself of s 1(1)(a)'. Section 1(1)(b) and (c) were to prove more problematic for Demon and the fact that it knew of the defamatory posting but chose not to remove it from its Usenet news servers was deemed to place it 'in an insuperable difficulty so that it cannot avail itself of the defence provided by s 1'.

The court compared this outcome with that in a much older case, that of *Byrne v Dean*.[211] In this case, the person who was in control of the contents of a physical noticeboard in a private club was held to be responsible for the publication of a defamatory notice posted by someone else, on the grounds of her failure to remove the offending notice.

Byrne v Dean
[1937] 1 KB 818, p 837

Greene LJ ... publication, of course, is a question of fact and it must depend on the circumstances in each case whether or not publication has taken place. It is said that as a general proposition where the act of a person alleged to have published a libel has not been any positive act, but has merely been the refraining from doing some act, he cannot be guilty of publication. I am quite unable to accept any such general proposition. It may very well be that in some circumstances a person, by refraining from removing or obliterating the defamatory matter, is not committing any publication at all. In other circumstances he may be doing so. The test it appears to me is this: having regard to all the facts of the case is the proper inference that by not removing the defamatory matter the defendant really made himself responsible for its continued presence in the place where it had been put?

Greene LJ went on to explain that there might be certain cases in which it would be difficult for someone in the position of the defendant to remedy the matter, but:

On the other hand, you have a case such as the present where the removal of this particular notice was a perfectly simple and easy thing to do, involving no trouble whatsoever. The defendants, having the power to remove it, and being able to do it without any difficulty at all, and, knowing that members of the club when they came into the room would see it, I think must be taken to have elected deliberately to leave it there. The proper inference, therefore, in those circumstances, it seems to me, is that they were consenting parties to its continued presence on the spot where it had been put up. That being so, it seems to me that they must be taken to have consented to its publication to each member who saw it.

Would ISPs be in the first or second of Greene LJ's categories? How difficult is it for them to remedy such a matter on notice? It is clear that ISPs have the power to remove an offending message, but other factors may nevertheless conspire to make removal a less than simple matter. Compare the view of this issue taken by the court in *Zeran*.

---

211 [1937] 1 KB 818.

Zeran v America Online Inc
129 F 3d 327, 333
US Court of Appeals 4th Cir (1997)

... liability upon notice reinforces service providers' incentives to restrict speech and abstain from self-regulation. If computer service providers were subject to distributor liability, they would face potential liability each time they receive notice of a potentially defamatory statement from any party, concerning any message. Each notification would require a careful yet rapid investigation of the circumstances surrounding the posted information, a legal judgment concerning the information's defamatory character, and an on-the-spot editorial decision whether to risk liability by allowing the continued publication of that information. Although this might be feasible for the traditional print publisher, the sheer number of postings on interactive computer services would create an impossible burden in the Internet context ... Because service providers would be subject to liability only for the publication of information, and not for its removal, they would have a natural incentive simply to remove messages upon notification, whether the contents were defamatory or not ... Thus, like strict liability, liability upon notice has a chilling effect on the freedom of Internet speech.

Similarly, notice-based liability would deter service providers from regulating the dissemination of offensive material over their own services. Any efforts by a service provider to investigate and screen material posted on its service would only lead to notice of potentially defamatory material more frequently and thereby create a stronger basis for liability. Instead of subjecting themselves to further possible lawsuits, service providers would likely eschew any attempts at self-regulation. More generally, notice-based liability for interactive computer service providers would provide third parties with a no-cost means to create the basis for future lawsuits. Whenever one was displeased with the speech of another party conducted over an interactive computer service, the offended party could simply 'notify' the relevant service provider, claiming the information to be legally defamatory.

In light of the vast amount of speech communicated through interactive computer services, these notices could produce an impossible burden for service providers, who would be faced with ceaseless choices of suppressing controversial speech or sustaining prohibitive liability.

Further developments occurred in Europe relating to ISP liability in the E-commerce Directive[212] which included a number of relevant provisions.

Directive 2000/31/EC
Section 4
Liability of Intermediate Service Providers

Article 12

'Mere conduit'

1. Where an information society service is provided that consists of the transmission in a communication network of information provided by a recipient of the service, or the provision of access to a communication network, Member States shall ensure that the service provider is not liable for the information transmitted, on condition that the provider:

(a) does not initiate the transmission;

---

212 Directive 2000/31/EC of the European Parliament and of the Council of 8 June 2000 on certain legal aspects of information society services, in particular electronic commerce, in the Internal Market [2000] OJ L178/1.

(b) does not select the receiver of the transmission; and

(c) does not select or modify the information contained in the transmission.

2. The acts of transmission and of provision of access referred to in paragraph 1 include the automatic, intermediate and transient storage of the information transmitted in so far as this takes place for the sole purpose of carrying out the transmission in the communication network, and provided that the information is not stored for any period longer than is reasonably necessary for the transmission.

...

Article 13

'Caching'

1. Where an information society service is provided that consists of the transmission in a communication network of information provided by a recipient of the service, Member States shall ensure that the service provider is not liable for the automatic, intermediate and temporary storage of that information, performed for the sole purpose of making more efficient the information's onward transmission to other recipients of the service upon their request, on condition that:

(a) the provider does not modify the information;

(b) the provider complies with conditions on access to the information;

(c) the provider complies with rules regarding the updating of the information, specified in a manner widely recognised and used by industry;

(d) the provider does not interfere with the lawful use of technology, widely recognised and used by industry, to obtain data on the use of the information; and

(e) the provider acts expeditiously to remove or to disable access to the information it has stored upon obtaining actual knowledge of the fact that the information at the initial source of the transmission has been removed from the network, or access to it has been disabled, or that a court or an administrative authority has ordered such removal or disablement.

...

Article 14

Hosting

1. Where an information society service is provided that consists of the storage of information provided by a recipient of the service, Member States shall ensure that the service provider is not liable for the information stored at the request of a recipient of the service, on condition that:

(a) the provider does not have actual knowledge of illegal activity or information and, as regards claims for damages, is not aware of facts or circumstances from which the illegal activity or information is apparent; or

(b) the provider, upon obtaining such knowledge or awareness, acts expeditiously to remove or to disable access to the information.

2. Paragraph 1 shall not apply when the recipient of the service is acting under the authority or the control of the provider.

3. This Article shall not affect the possibility for a court or administrative authority, in accordance with Member States' legal systems, of requiring the service provider to terminate or prevent an infringement, nor does it affect the possibility for Member States of establishing procedures governing the removal or disabling of access to information.

It is made clear in Recitals 42 and 43 that these exemptions provided in the Directive are limited to those cases where 'the information society service provider has neither knowledge of nor control over the information which is transmitted or stored' and, further, that there is no modification of the information transmitted of manipulations of a technical nature.

Article 15

No general obligation to monitor

1. Member States shall not impose a general obligation on providers, when providing the services covered by Articles 12, 13 and 14, to monitor the information which they transmit or store, nor a general obligation actively to seek facts or circumstances indicating illegal activity.

2. Member States may establish obligations for information society service providers promptly to inform the competent public authorities of alleged illegal activities undertaken or information provided by recipients of their service or obligations to communicate to the competent authorities, at their request, information enabling the identification of recipients of their service with whom they have storage agreements.

The application of the Defamation Act 1996 and the Electronic Commerce (EC Directive) Regulations 2002 (implementing Directive 2000/31/EC) to ISPs has been reviewed by the Law Commission which made a number of proposals for reform.

Defamation and the Internet: A Preliminary Investigation
Law Commission Scoping Study No. 2
December 2002

2.65 There is a strong case for reviewing the way that defamation law impacts on internet service providers. While actions against primary publishers are usually decided on their merits, the current law places pressure on secondary publishers to remove material without considering whether it is in the public interest, or whether it is true. These pressures appear to bear particularly harshly on ISPs, which are seen as tactical targets for those wishing to prevent the dissemination of material on the internet. There is a possible conflict between such pressure to remove material, even if true, and the emphasis placed upon freedom of expression under the European Convention of Human Rights. Although it is a legitimate goal of the law to protect the reputation of others, it is important to ask whether this goal can be achieved through other means.

2.66 Several reforms have been suggested. It would not be appropriate, in a short project of this type, to reach a conclusion on the relative merits of the various proposals. One possibility would be to exempt ISPs from liability, as in the USA. Another is to extend the innocent dissemination defence, which could be done in a variety of ways. Any extension would need to be accompanied by clearer guidance to ISPs on how to deal with the practicalities of receiving and responding to complaints. Guidance could be provided through an industry code, negotiated with interested parties. There may also be a case for including some form of independent adjudication within such a code, so that the decision on whether material could be justified was taken out of the hands of ISPs.

The Court of Appeal in *Lewis v King*, however, noted that it was rather less troubled than the Law Commission about the legal liability attached to ISPs and declined to make any recommendations for reform.[213]

Advances such as the internet and the world wide web have made electronic publishing a very accessible operation,[214] often without the need for any participation

---

213 [2004] EWCA 1329, para 32.
214 See, eg, comments in *Dendrite International v John Doe* 775 A 2d 756, 761 (2001).

by a publishing company, as such. It is entirely possible that the situation could arise where, unlike traditional forms of publishing, only the original author could be liable if the circumstances were such that the service provider could avail themselves of this defence. This could be an undesirable outcome, not least because it may make it difficult to bring an action against the author, if he or she happens to be in a different jurisdiction (see below). In cases such as these, it is very likely that, as in *Godfrey v Demon Internet* (above), the actual author may well be anonymous. This is as likely to be the case in situations where individuals might wish to make genuine critical comment without fear of reprisals, as those in which they wish to engage in gratuitous criticism or denigrating remarks, for example so-called cyber-smearing. The US has seen a steady rise in cases that attempt to unmask anonymous posters – the so-called 'CyberSLAPP' cases. SLAPP stands for Strategic Lawsuits against Public Participation. A consequence of the strong constitutional protection for free speech in the US is that the Supreme Court has upheld a right to anonymous speech in a number of cases.[215] Many states actually have anti-SLAPP statutes drafted to deter such actions in traditional fora which are now being applied to electronic communications. There has been significant debate on Cybersmearing and CyberSlapps, particularly amongst US commentators,[216] but in the absence of a *prima facie* case of defamation, the courts in the US have leaned towards a presumption of safeguarding anonymity to 'foster open communication and debate'. [217]

In the UK there has been little comparable activity in the courts but the facts of *Totalise plc v Motley Fool Ltd*[218] did show certain similarities to the CyberSlapp cases and resulted in an order to an ISP to reveal the identity of a pseudonymous poster on the basis of a prima facie finding that the comments posted were defamatory.

In *R v Griffiths*, the distributors of a contempt of court were found liable on the basis that they were 'the only persons who can ... be made amenable in the courts of this country'.[219] What is the situation in respect of cross-border libel? Where can the claimant bring an action? The decision as to whether the English courts will have jurisdiction depends on matters of some complexity, some of which have been reviewed above, but one factor may be the existence of agreements between the countries in question. Following *Shevill and Others v Presse Alliance SA*,[220] the situation has been clarified, so far as those countries which are signatories to the Brussels and Lugano Conventions are concerned.[221] The case concerned a French newspaper, *France Soir*, published by Presse Alliance, that had its major circulation in France but also had a small circulation in England. An article in this newspaper suggested that Ms Shevill, who had worked temporarily at a bureau de change in Paris, together with her

---

215 See eg, *Talley v California* 4 L Ed 2d (1960) *McIntyre v Ohio* 131 L Ed 2d (1996) and *Watchtower Bible v Stratton* 153 L Ed 2d (2002).

216 See eg, Rowland, 2003; Rowland, 2005 and references cited therein.

217 *John Doe v 2theMart.com Inc* 140 F Supp 2d 1088, 1092 *and see also eg, Columbia Insurance Company v Seescandy.com* 185 FRD 573 (1999) and *Dendrite International v John Doe* 775 A 2d 756 (2001).

218 *The Times*, 15 March 2001.

219 [1957] 2 All ER 379; however the *Griffiths* case shows that there is a rather stricter view of the liability of distributors in the context of contempt of court.

220 Case C-68/93 [1995] All ER (EC) 289.

221 Incorporated into domestic law by the Civil Jurisdiction and Judgments Acts 1982 and 1991. See, also, above, p 256.

employers and others, was implicated in the laundering of the proceeds of drug trafficking. As the plaintiff was English and domiciled in England, an action was brought in England, claiming damages for the publication of the libel there.

Article 5(3) of the Convention on Jurisdiction and the Enforcement of Judgments in Civil and Commercial Matters 1968 (the Brussels Convention) allows a claimant/plaintiff to bring an action in 'the place where the harmful event occurred'. The defendants, Presse Alliance, argued that the court had no jurisdiction to hear the case as the harmful event had taken place in France and no damage had actually been shown in England. The English law of libel presumes damage once publication has been demonstrated. The Court of Appeal held that the matter of the damage being presumed was not an issue of jurisdiction as such and that 'the place where the harmful event occurred' could be construed as referring to both the place where the tortious act occurred and the place where the damage was suffered.[222] Thus, where an act was done in one State which caused damage in another, the plaintiff could choose to bring an action in either State.

On appeal, the House of Lords referred several questions to the European Court of Justice (ECJ).

Shevill and Others v Presse Alliance SA
[1995] All ER (EC) 289

1   In a case of libel by a newspaper article, do the words 'the place where the harmful event occurred' in Article 5(3) of the Convention mean: (a) the place where the newspaper was printed and put into circulation; or (b) the place or places where the newspaper was read by particular individuals; or (c) the place or places where the plaintiff has a significant reputation?

2   If and in so far as the answer to the first question is (b), is 'the harmful event' dependent upon there being a reader or readers who knew (or knew of) the plaintiff and understood those words to refer to him?

3   If and in so far as harm is suffered in more than one country (because copies of the newspaper were distributed in at least Member State other than the Member State where it was printed and put into circulation), does a separate harmful event or harmful events take place in each Member State where the newspaper was distributed, in respect of which such Member State has separate jurisdiction under Article 5(3), and if so, how harmful must the event be, or what proportion of the total harm must it represent?

4   Does the phrase 'harmful event' include an event actionable under national law without proof of damage, where there is no evidence of actual damage or harm?

5   In deciding under Article 5(3) whether (or where) a 'harmful event' has occurred is the local court expected to answer the question otherwise than by reference to its own rules and, if so, by reference to which other rules or substantive law, procedure or evidence?

6   If, in a defamation case, the local court concludes that there has been an actionable publication (or communication) of material, as a result of which at least some damage to reputation would be presumed, is it relevant to the acceptance of jurisdiction that other Member States might come to a different conclusion in respect of similar material published within their respective jurisdictions?

---

222 [1992] 1 All ER 409.

7   In deciding whether it has jurisdiction under Article 5(3) of the Convention, what
     standard of proof should a court require of the plaintiff that the conditions of Article
     5(3) are satisfied: (a) generally; and (b) in relation to matters which (if the court takes
     jurisdiction) will not be re-examined at the trial of the action?

These questions would clearly have relevance in cases where the libel had been
perpetrated by electronic means, provided that the relevant ingredients, such as
publication in a particular Member State, had been established. The ECJ divided the
questions into two, according to whether they concerned questions of jurisdiction or
assessment of damage.

Shevill and Others v Presse Alliance SA
[1995] All ER (EC) 289, p 317

33   ... the answer to the first, second, third and sixth questions referred by the House of
     Lords must be that, on a proper construction of the expression 'place where the
     harmful event occurred' in Article 5(3) of the Convention, the victim of a libel by a
     newspaper article distributed in several Contracting States may bring an action for
     damages against the publisher either before the courts of the Contracting State where
     the publisher of the defamatory publication is established, which have jurisdiction to
     award damages for all the harm caused by the defamation, or before the courts of
     each Contracting State in which the publication was distributed and where the victim
     claims to have suffered injury to his reputation, which have jurisdiction to rule solely
     in respect of the harm caused in the State of the court seised.

In respect of the remaining questions, referring to the assessment of damage, the court
felt that the matter was one that should be decided by the rules pertaining in the
particular Member State in which the action was brought, assuming that the
provisions of the Convention were not compromised.

Application of the principles expounded above in relation to newspaper
publishing to electronic fora presumes that there has been identification of those
responsible for propagating the libel. This may be no easy task in relation to media
such as the world wide web, even where the individuals are named on the page. The
computer hosting the pages may not readily be discerned and may be in a completely
different jurisdiction from the person producing the web pages. Where a defendant
can be isolated and is in a convenient jurisdiction, to what extent are they deemed to
be accountable for all the information which can be accessed from their pages? A
particular feature of 'hypertext mark-up language' (HTML), which is used for
preparing information to be made available on the world wide web, is that embedded
links can be incorporated which will provide access to other related sites when the
user 'points and clicks'. Suppose that the home site is not itself defamatory but
provides links to other sites which contain libellous material. Is the host of the home
page liable for the publication of this material?

Hird v Wood,[223] concerned an individual who pointed continually at a placard so
that all who passed by were made aware of the writing on it. The person who had
written the placard or placed it in position was unknown. It was held that the act of
pointing to the contents was enough to constitute evidence of publication. This seems

---

223 (1894) 38 SJ 235.

to provide a remarkably good analogy for the situation occurring when readers of a home page are directed to a page hosted by a third party which may provide further information of interest. The matter is not quite so simple as that, however, because, of course, the process does not stop there and there may then be further links to other pages creating the 'web'. It seems unlikely that any court would find liability for defamatory material hosted on a site which could not be reached directly from the defendant's home pages. The situation is further complicated by the fact that, unlike traditionally produced works, the information on web pages (or other networked information) is not static but is continually being refined and updated. If a direct link is provided from one page to another provided by a third party, then whether or not there is liability for material will undoubtedly depend on the particular circumstances of the case. Nonetheless, proprietors of home pages might be prudent to check their embedded links at intervals, not only to ensure they are still operative, but also to ensure that they would continue to be happy to point their readers in that direction.[224]

---

224 See further discussion on the legality of hyperlinks in Chapter 9.

CHAPTER 8

POLICING 'CYBERSPACE'

INTRODUCTION

Recent estimates suggest that computer crime may cost as much as $50 billion per year and that each year there may be almost six million intrusions into computer systems by outside hackers.[1] Denial of service attacks and the introduction of computer viruses and worms have been proved similarly costly for users. Indeed the ILOVEYOU virus which was estimated to have infected some 45 million computers in 2000 and caused billions of dollars worth of damage has even been described as 'the most devastating crime in history'.[2] In the last few years, there have been prosecutions for the possession and publication of child pornography both in the UK and the US, this being material that was available either on computer networks or on other electronic media.[3] Such examples serve to illustrate how the computer can be used to assist the perpetration of crime and other anti-social activity. Neither is this a new phenomenon. During the 1980s, a number of cases came to court in a number of jurisdictions that could, perhaps, be regarded purely as examples of antisocial behaviour, but caused problems for the law in trying to locate the behaviour within existing legal provisions. A number of these were cases of computer hacking and the outcomes were often inconsistent, even in relation to ostensibly similar facts. In some cases, there might be an acquittal because the charge chosen was deemed to be inappropriate or, alternatively, because the law was interpreted in novel ways in order to found a conviction.[4] Although computer hacking is often what comes to mind when computer misuse and abuse is referred to, there is a whole spectrum of activity that may be referred to as computer crime[5] or computer-related crime that began to become apparent as the so called computer or information revolution progressed.[6]

Thus, August Bequai, writing in the preface to an early Council of Europe Recommendation on Computer-Related Crime,[7] suggests that, 'In the information society, power and wealth are increasingly becoming synonymous with control over our data banks ... The computer revolution has provided tools with which to steal

---

1 Source: www.intergov.org/public_information/general_information/latest_web_stats.html.
2 Katyal, (2001) and see also, for example, Sprinkel, 2002; Cesare, 2001, p 145.
3 See below, p 474.
4 Compare, eg, *R v Gold and Schifreen* and *R v Whiteley*, discussed below, p 433 et seq.
5 The use of this term has itself led to some controversy. Tapper, 1987, describes the phrase as 'ungrammatical and inelegant', although other writers are rather more dismissive of any perceived semantic difficulties: 'Clearly it is easy to argue over a definition of computer crime. Such an argument seems fruitless, and will not be engaged in here.' (*Encyclopedia of Information Technology Law*, London: Sweet & Maxwell, Vol II, para 12.03.) This writer is clearly of a much more pragmatic persuasion: 'The notion of computer crime is retained here merely because it serves as a useful umbrella under which to address a range of quite new and difficult criminal law problems ...'
6 For an anecdotal account of some of the more high profile cases and examples see Clough and Mungo, 1993.
7 Council of Europe Recommendation R (89) 9 on Computer-Related Crime, 1990, p 4.

with impunity, control and manipulate the thoughts and movements of millions, and hold an entire society hostage'. In his report for the COMCRIME study in 1998, Sieber referred to international computer networks as 'the nerves of the economy, the public sector and society' such that any attack or intrusion could have a devastating effect on the functioning of the information society.[8] Sieber underlines the potential for a particular type of abuse of computer systems, and to this may be added a number of 'traditional' crimes that may be facilitated by the use of computer systems such as offences of theft, deception and fraud; offences related to obscenity and indecency; criminal breaches of copyright arising from intentional distribution and commercial exploitation of copyright works; and criminal damage aimed at the computer system itself. That these are different in kind, both from each other and from the 'new' offences related to or relying on computer hacking, goes without saying, but together they make up a body that has come to be referred to, however inaccurately, as computer crime and, in varying degrees, has caused problems for the interpretation and development of the law in this area. It is not the purpose of this chapter to examine the accuracy of the phrase 'computer crime': whatever the shortcomings of this term, it has become accepted terminology for a particular species of activity that has the common ingredient of computer use.

A coherent response to these problems is difficult, however, because of an absence of homogeneity in the subject matter, demonstrated by a lack of consensus both in the definition of and in the severity of the offences, and also in identifying the jurisdiction in which the offence occurred. Discrepancies in the type of regulation because of the former, together with the confusion raised by the latter, may inevitably lead to the likelihood of 'forum shopping' in the hope of a favourable hearing in situations where an offence can be deemed to have taken place in one of a number of jurisdictions. An explanation for the apparent increase in computer crime is difficult, although the suspicion is that, like the advent of the motor car, the advent of the computer created more opportunities for crime. This difficulty has been identified by Wasik:[9]

> ... the sheer diversity of behaviour within the context of computer misuse, where the computer may figure at one moment as the instrument of crime, and at the next as the target for crime, and given the importance of non-economic motives in some forms of computer misuse, such as the unauthorised access of computer systems purely for intellectual challenge and some cases of computer sabotage, makes any monolithic explanation of this phenomenon quite implausible.

This diversity has been reflected more recently in the Cybercrime Convention which makes provision for acts based on illegal access, illegal interception, data interference, system interference, misuse of devices, computer-related fraud, computer-related forgery, offences related to child pornography and offences related to copyright and related rights. Whatever the origin and type of behaviour at issue, it is clear that the law has had to respond to these activities, and it has done so with varying degrees of consistency and success. This chapter will consider the response of the law and will draw conclusions as to the consistency of approach.

8   Sieber, 1998.
9   Wasik, 1990, p 33.

COMPUTER FRAUD

Many considerations of the phenomenon of computer crime begin with a study of computer fraud, defined by the Audit Commission[10] as: 'Any fraudulent behaviour connected with computerisation by which someone intends to gain dishonest advantage'. Fraudulent schemes are usually devised to create some pecuniary benefit or to relieve the perpetrator of a financial burden. Although the level of reported computer fraud as a percentage of all reported computer misuse is falling, this is more to do with the increase of other types of abuse, such as the introduction of viruses and denial of service attacks. Nevertheless, the average value of detected computer fraud was estimated at £36,000 in 2001.[11] Most studies in this area, in common with the Audit Commission, have identified three species of computer fraud, namely, input fraud, output fraud and program fraud, of which the latter is less common, as it requires considerably more knowledge and expertise. Thus, input fraud might include the misuse of cash cards or the creation of accounts for 'ghost employees', whereas theft of pre-signed cheques is an example of an output fraud. Program frauds are necessarily rather more elaborate and include the so called salami type, in which a program is written which automatically 'slices off' small amounts from a number of accounts and transfers them to another account created for the purpose. A small deficit may not be noticed or reported on one account, but, if the process is repeated on a vast number of accounts, a considerable sum can be accrued in the illicit account. Salami and other program frauds can also be activated at a later date, creating consequent problems in detection of both the fraud and the perpetrator.

How has the law responded to the issue of computer fraud? In its first consideration of the problem, the Law Commission concluded that, in general, the existing criminal law was adequate to deal with cases of computer fraud.[12] The exception to this was identified as those offences that have proof of deception as an element, since this raised the vexed question of whether it is possible to deceive a machine or whether this is an act that can only be performed on humans. A further complication may be that, although an appropriate offence can be identified, the nature of computer technology may make it more difficult to identify both when and where the offence occurred, both of which factors may have important ramifications for the final outcome of the case.

The potential difficulties that may arise in such situations are illustrated by the facts of *Thompson*.[13] Thompson was a computer programmer, employed by a bank in Kuwait. He identified five accounts that were both substantial and dormant, that is, no transactions had been made into or out of them for a long time. He then opened five accounts in his name at various branches of the bank and transferred money into these accounts from the dormant accounts.

To cover his tracks, the program did not execute until he had left the bank's employment and was returning to the UK. The intention was that the program would erase itself and all records of the transfers after executing. Once in the UK, Thompson

---

10   Audit Commission, 1985, p 9.
11   Audit Commission, 2001.
12   Law Commission, Cmnd 819, 1989.
13   [1984] 1 WLR 962.

opened accounts in UK banks and wrote to the Kuwaiti bank manager, asking him to transfer the money now in the five accounts held in his own name. This led to him being found out and he was charged and convicted of obtaining property by deception, contrary to s 15 of the Theft Act 1968, which states:

(1) A person who by any deception dishonestly obtains property belonging to another, with the intention of permanently depriving the other of it, shall on conviction on indictment be liable to imprisonment for a term not exceeding ten years.

(2) For the purposes of this section a person is to be treated as obtaining property if he obtains ownership, possession or control of it, and 'obtain' ... includes obtaining for another or enabling another to obtain or to retain it.

Section 4(1) of the same Act provides:

'Property' includes money and all other property, real or personal, including things in action and other intangible property.

The issue in the case itself was not so much a question of whether or not this offence had been committed, but, rather, when and where and, in consequence, whether or not the English courts had jurisdiction to hear the case. Section 15(2) of the Theft Act 1968 defines 'obtaining property' for the purposes of the offence of obtaining by deception in s 15(1) as obtaining *ownership, possession or control*. The argument for the Crown was that the offence had occurred in England when the credit balance in the fraudulently created accounts was transferred to the accounts in England, as this was the moment at which Thompson obtained *ownership, possession or control*. The defence argued that, on the contrary, control was obtained in Kuwait, at the time when the manipulation of the balances in the respective accounts was made. The Court of Appeal, although recognising the points raised, was anxious not to treat the fraud in any different manner to a similar case of fraud perpetrated by more traditional means.

R v Thompson
[1984] 1 WLR 962, p 967

May LJ We think, however, that one may legitimately ask: of what property did this appellant in that way obtain control in Kuwait? What was the nature of that property? .... Discard for the moment the modern sophistication of computers and programmes and consider the old days when bank books were kept in manuscript in large ledgers. In effect all that was done by the appellant through the modern computer in the present case was to take a pen and debit each of the five accounts in the ledger with the relevant sums and then credit each of his own five savings accounts in the ledger with corresponding amounts. On the face of it his savings accounts would then have appeared to have in them substantially more than in truth they did have as the result of his forgeries; but we do not think that by those forgeries any bank clerk in the days before computers would in law have thus brought into being a chose in action capable either of being stolen or of being obtained by deception contrary to section 15 of the Theft Act 1968.

Insofar as the customers whose accounts had been fraudulently debited and who had to be reimbursed by the bank, as Mr Caplan submitted, are concerned, we prefer the approach of Mr Walsh. He submitted that properly considered it was not a question of reimbursement: it was merely a question of correcting forged documents, forged records, to the condition in which they ought to have been but for the fraud.

In those circumstances and for those reasons we agree with the judge in the court below that the only realistic view of the undisputed facts in this case is that the six instances of obtaining charged in the indictment each occurred when the relevant sums of money were received by the appellant's banks in England. Further it seems to us quite clear ...

that those sums of money were obtained as the result of the letters which the appellant wrote to the bank in Kuwait. The only proper construction to be put upon those letters is that they contain the representations pleaded in the particulars of offences in the indictment.

In this case, the decision was arrived at by applying exactly the same principles as would be applied in a more conventional case and, although the use of the computer clearly facilitated the fraud, the existing law was still capable of application. This does not automatically mean that all cases of computer fraud present no problems. The prosecution in *Thompson* was able to identify a human mind which had been deceived by the acts of the accused, namely, the bank manager in Kuwait, at the time of receiving the letter of instruction from Thompson. Would the result have been the same if no such person could have been identified? The Scottish Law Commission[14] suggested that there was, in this respect, a distinction in relation to offences involving fraudulent activity between the law in Scotland and that in England and Wales:

> ... in Scotland such activities, even where they involved computers, would be adequately dealt with by the common law crimes of fraud, or in some cases, theft. Referring to the classic definition of fraud given by Macdonald,* we did question whether it could be said that there had been a false pretence if no other human being was involved and the pretence was made solely to a computer. However, we concluded that the concept of 'false pretence' is probably sufficiently flexible to cope even with that sort of case. In this respect, we noted, Scots law may have an advantage over English law, which, in the Theft Act 1968 and elsewhere, uses the concept of 'deception' which, it has been held, requires a human mind to be deceived. Under both systems of law, of course, there will be many cases involving computers where it will nonetheless be perfectly possible to say that a false pretence has been made to a person, or that a person has been deceived.
>
> * *Criminal Law of Scotland*, 5th edn, p 52: fraud 'involves a false pretence made dishonestly in order to bring about some definite practical result'.

This difference highlights the fact that the applicability of existing legislative provisions to otherwise 'traditional' offences committed with the aid of computers may depend on the vagaries of language and the capability of that language of being interpreted in such a way as to take into account any special features of computer crime. The nuances of the relevant language were spelled out by Buckley J in *Re London and Globe Finance Corp Ltd*.

> To deceive is, I apprehend, to induce a man to believe that a thing is true which is false, and which the person practising the deceit knows or believes to be false. To defraud is to deprive by deceit: it is by deceit to induce a man to act to his injury. More tersely it may be put, that to deceive is by falsehood to induce a state of mind; to defraud is by deceit to induce a course of action.[15]

Thus, use of the concepts of false pretence and fraud may result in there being no need to wrestle with the thorny question of whether a machine (that is, a computer) can be deceived on occasions where there has been no communication or intervention by humans.

---

14 Scottish Law Commission, Cmnd 174, 1987, para 2.4.
15 [1903] 1 Ch 728, p 732.

One recent cause for concern has been the phenomenon of so called phantom withdrawals from automatic teller machines at banks. An early example was the case of *R v Munden*,[16] involving a policeman who alleged that money had been extracted from his account even though he had made no withdrawals. He was prosecuted for attempted fraud and eventually acquitted. However, for computer law, this is arguably more correctly described as an issue of evidence than one of fraud.

Although the whole area of so called computer crime was reviewed by the Law Commissions for both Scotland and England and Wales, it was generally concluded that most cases of computer fraud could be dealt with adequately by the existing provisions, except on those rare occasions on which the case might rest on the 'deception' of a machine. In recognition of this, the Law Society made the suggestion that the definition in the Theft Act 1968 should be extended by introduction of the wording 'inducing a machine to respond to false representations which the person making them knows to be false as if they were true'.

This proposal was not acted upon and it remains the position that 'the prevailing opinion is that it is not possible in law to deceive a machine'.[17] It is suggested in the next extract, however, that, as technology develops, this situation need not necessarily remain the same, although the use of the concept of 'false representations' is still preferred.

Arlidge and Parry on Fraud
Anthony Arlidge, Jacques Parry and Ian Gatt
2nd edn, 1997, London: Sweet and Maxwell, p 143
Non-human minds

Whatever the precise nature of the state of mind which must be induced, it cannot exist unless there is a mind for it to exist in ...

A more difficult question is whether it is possible to deceive a machine ... The question is likely to be one of increasing importance in the context of computer fraud. If a person enters false data into a computer, or gains access to confidential files by using someone else's password, is he deceiving the computer? ... One would hardly say, other than metaphorically, that the computer *believes* the input to be accurate. On the other hand it might be argued that here again the notion of belief may be misleading, since it is not expressly used in the legislation. The question is not whether computers can have beliefs, but whether they can be deceived; and the more 'intelligent' they become, the more arguable it must be that they can. But this may be a rare case where the change from the terminology of false pretences to that of deception assists the defence, since it might be easier to establish that the defendant made a *false representation* to a computer than that the computer was thereby deceived.

In some situations, cases might now be enabled to proceed by virtue of certain changes introduced by s 1(1) of the Theft (Amendment) Act 1996.

---

16 See www.cl.cam.ac.uk/~mk623/phantom/phantoms.html which also catalogues a number of other examples of phantom withdrawals from ATMs.
17 Smith, 1997, p 97.

Theft Act 1968 (as amended)

15A Obtaining a money transfer by deception

(1) A person is guilty of an offence if by any deception he dishonestly obtains a money transfer for himself or another.

24A Dishonestly obtaining a wrongful credit

(1) A person is guilty of an offence if –

    (a) a wrongful credit has been made to an account kept by him or in respect of which he has any right or interest;

    (b) he knows or believes that the credit is wrongful; and

    (c) he dishonestly fails to take such steps as are reasonable in the circumstances to secure that the credit is cancelled …

...

(3) … A credit to an account is wrongful if it is the credit side of a money transfer obtained contrary to s 15A …

Section 15A does not refer to electronic transfer, other than to say in sub-s (4) that 'it is immaterial whether the money transfer is effected on presentment of a cheque or by another'. Crucially, though, the need for deception, which unsurprisingly retains the same meaning (s 15B(2)), has not been eliminated from the provision. This is due to the amendments being introduced to rectify the situation following the House of Lords' decision in *R v Preddy*.[18] This case arose as a result of false statements made to obtain mortgage advances and which were credited electronically, leading to a charge of obtaining property by deception. As the building society representatives could be identified as the target of this deception, the salient issue in the particular case was whether any property as such had been transferred. The House of Lords was of the view that the creation of a new chose in action could not be equated with obtaining property, precipitating swift action by the Law Commission[19] and Parliament to resolve the situation. In the consequent haste, the opportunity for a more comprehensive overhaul of the legislation, which could have taken into account the difficulties with the concept of deception and computerised accounting methods, was missed. A case which depends solely on the 'deception' of a machine may lead to a similar 'knee jerk' reaction unless, as suggested by Arlidge and Parry, above, the computer has become sufficiently advanced to be deemed deceivable. Otherwise, it appears likely that there will be a range of conduct which could result in an acquittal on a charge based on deception and which might not fit comfortably into any of the other offences in the Theft Act 1968. In the words of Chapman:

> If it is essential that criminal offences attach liability to the wrong conduct itself, rather than to some peripheral activity associated with the same, then it is equally important to identify accurately the conduct that attracts moral obloquy.[20]

---

18 [1996] AC 815.
19 Law Commission, 1996.
20 Chapman, 2000, p 96.

The Law Commission returned to the issue of computer fraud as part of a more general consideration of the law of fraud at the end of the 1990s[21] and summed up the difficulties surrounding the issues related to deceiving a machine in their report of 2002:

Law Commission Report No. 276 on Fraud
Cm 5560, 2002
Computers and machines

3.34 A machine has no mind, so it cannot believe a proposition to be true or false, and therefore cannot be deceived. A person who dishonestly obtains a benefit by giving false information to a computer or machine is not guilty of any deception offence. Where the benefit obtained is property, he or she will normally be guilty of theft, but where it is something other than property (such as a service), there may be no offence at all.

3.35 This has only become a problem in recent years, as businesses make more use of machines as an interface with their customers. There are now many services available to the public which will usually be paid for via a machine. For example, one would usually pay an internet service provider by entering one's credit card details on its website. Using card details to pay for such a service without the requisite authority would not currently constitute an offence. As the use of the internet and automated call centres expands, this gap in the law will be increasingly indefensible.

The Report went on to suggest that one option would be to 'extend the concept of deception so as to include the giving of false information to a machine as well as a person,'[22] but this was rejected as being too artificial and instead:

8.4 ... We are persuaded that we should tackle the problem head on. Rather than requiring deception but diluting its meaning, we need to accept that deception should not be essential at all. This is because, where a person dishonestly obtains a service by giving false information to a machine, the gravamen of that person's conduct is not the provision of the false information but the taking of a valuable benefit without paying for it.

Accordingly:

8.8 ... We are therefore proposing that it should be an offence to obtain a service dishonestly – whether by deceiving a person, giving false information to a machine, manipulating a machine without giving it false information, or by any other dishonest means. This offence would be more analogous to theft than to deception, because it could be committed by "helping oneself" to the service rather than dishonestly inducing another person to provide it.

This proposal was qualified by two provisos that 'it should not be possible to commit the offence by omission alone'[23] and that 'the offence could be committed *only* where the dishonesty lies in an intent *not to pay* for the service.'[24]

---

21 Law Commission, 1999.
22 See Law Commission, 2002, para 8.4.
23 *Ibid*, para 8.11.
24 *Ibid*, para 8.12.

As a response to the Law Commission's proposals the Home Office issued a consultation paper seeking views on the proposal to 'create a general offence of fraud with 3 different ways of committing it.'[25] One of the ways will be by obtaining services dishonestly and will include the case where services are obtained from a machine, thus dealing with the problem that a machine cannot be deceived.[26]

Aside from the potential problems with deception, which may be resolved if legislative action follows the above consultation process, the existing law seemed sufficiently adaptable to deal with instances of computer fraud. This certainly seems to be the case where the methods used for perpetrating the fraud broadly correlate with those which would have been used before the advent of computers. However, we cannot leave this topic without a consideration of another type of 'fraud', incidences of which have apparently become the source of the most frequent complaints of monetary loss via computer networks; the phenomenon of online auction fraud.[27] The online auction phenomenon began in 1995 with the establishment of ebay.com and has since expanded dramatically to the extent that there may now be approaching one and a half million transactions a day on internet auction sites.[28] The number of providers have proliferated as a simple web search will confirm. A typical internet auction obviously has similarities with a traditional auction in that the items are offered for sale and potential buyers make bids; the sale being concluded with the person who has offered the highest bid at the pre-determined time when bidding is concluded (analogous to the fall of the hammer). The website can therefore be likened to the sale room, but without providing the chance to see or examine the goods. The bidder must act purely in response to the details and description provided on the website. With the exception of the case in which the website operates as a business providing the merchandise, the auction site will facilitate consumer-consumer transactions so that, when the auction is over and a bid has been accepted, the seller deals directly with the buyer in relation to payment and delivery. Although there are many satisfied auction site users worldwide, the system provides much scope for the less than honest buyer or seller.[29] There is considerable scope for fraudulent activity which may include auctioning of intentionally substandard[30] or even fictitious goods, or operating illicit bidding arrangements.

What is the best method of regulating these activities? Can the existing law be applied satisfactorily? A number of the problem issues are more accurately and appropriately analysed in contractual terms, but the discussion in this chapter will be confined to those areas in which the criminal law does, or may have, a role to play. Most jurisdictions have laws which govern the conduct of auctions and/or which create offences in certain situations of fraudulent dealing. Can these be applied directly or by analogy? In a study which is mainly focused on business auctions online, rather

---

25 *Fraud Law Reform: Consultation on proposals for legislation*, Home Office 2004, para 12.

26 *Ibid*, para 33. The proposals also refer (in para F) to the provisions of the Council of Europe's Cybercrime Convention on fraud (for further discussion of the provisions of the Convention see below p 480.

27 See successive reports from the Internet Fraud Complaint Center available from www.ifccfbi.gov/strategy/statistics.asp; Selis, *et al* 2001, an update of a report originally published in 2001 and available from the same source.

28 *Ibid*.

29 For a comprehensive summary of the possibilities see eg, Albert, 2002.

30 See, eg, the facts of *US v Gajdik* 292 F 3d 555 (7th Cir 2002).

than the consumer interactions which are the subject of this section, Ramberg discusses some of the difficulties which a national legislature might face in regulating these activities.

Internet Marketplaces: The law of auctions and exchanges online
Christina Ramberg
Oxford: OUP 2002 p. 27

The future ability of the national legislature to prescribe mandatory legislation affecting the inner life of Internet marketplaces will probably be limited. This is due to the problems for the national state in monitoring activities conducted in cyberspace. An additional explanation is that a single national State can hardly claim to have any authority over an autonomous Internet marketplace. Examples of legislation not likely to prevail in the Internet environment are the French and German requirements of authorization for selling new goods in an auction and the French law that auction sales of second-hand goods may only be conducted by public officers.

However that is not to say that there is no pre-existing law which might be capable of application. Conventional auctions are an old established method for the sale of goods and as such are the subject of a well developed body of law. The first issue to consider is the extent to which this existing law might be applicable to and suitable for online and internet auctions. There is no authoritative or comprehensive definition of an auction in English law, but the essential element is generally agreed to be sale to the highest bidder in a public competition.[31] There are a number of different types of auction. Arguably, the most common model is the so-called English or 'ascending bid' auction, but there are a number of other possible variants;[32] the one that most closely represents the online situation is a now obsolete form in conventional auction houses where a time limit is placed on the bidding, either by the burning of a candle or the use of another timing device. A feature of a conventional auction is the presence of an auctioneer whose activities are governed in the UK by the Auctioneers Act 1845, s 7 of which requires that the name and place of residence of the auctioneer should be displayed prominently to all those attending the auction. In some jurisdictions auctioneers still require a licence to operate, but this provision in the 1845 Act was repealed by the Finance Act 1949. The auctioneer is technically an agent of the seller, but will have duties and responsibilities in relation to both parties to the sale which may provide a remedy for some of the possibilities for improper action which are possible on online auction sites.

The very nature of a sale by auction lends itself to fraudulent activity by rigging the bidding. Sellers can arrange to artificially inflate the bidding by either alone, or in collusion with others, making bids on their own items. This is sometimes referred to, especially in the US, as 'shill bidding'. Unscrupulous buyers, on the other hand, either alone or in collusion with others, can place multiple bids of differing values for an item, some of which will be high to deter other potential purchasers; a practice sometimes referred to as 'bid shielding'. In the final minutes of the auction, the buyer then removes all the high bids leaving only their own low bid at which the item must be sold. A detailed consideration of the law relating to bidding is beyond the scope of this chapter, but criminal sanctions can be invoked in relation to certain illicit bidding

---

31   See, eg, Harvey and Franklin, 1995.
32   *Ibid*, p. 3, Ramberg, 2002.

arrangements. In the UK, the Sale of Goods Act 1979 s 57(4) generally proscribes bidding on behalf of the seller and subsection (5) goes on to provide that any such sale may be treated as fraudulent by the buyer:

> Section 57(4) Where a sale by auction is not notified to be subject to a right to bid by or on behalf of the seller, it is not lawful for the seller to bid himself or to employ any person to bid at the sale, or for the auctioneer knowingly to tale any bid from the seller or any such person.

Further, certain types of collusion between bidders are regulated by the Auctions (Bidding Agreements) Act 1927 as amended by the Auctions (Bidding Agreements) Act 1969. The 1927 Act, as amended, is generally aimed at dealers who contrive to obtain goods on a low bid by offering a consideration, in some form, to a bidder in return for abstention from bidding. Any resultant sale can be regarded as having been induced by fraud.

Auctions (Bidding Agreements) Act 1927

Section 1 Certain bidding agreements to be illegal.

(1) If any dealer agrees to give, or gives, or offers any gift or consideration to any other person as an inducement or reward for abstaining, or for having abstained, from bidding at a sale by auction either generally or for any particular lot, or if any person agrees to accept, or accepts, or attempts to obtain from any dealer any such gift or consideration as aforesaid, he shall be guilty of an offence ...

(2) Any sale at an auction, with respect to which any such agreement or transaction as aforesaid has been made or effected, and which has been the subject of a prosecution and conviction, may, as against a purchaser who has been a party to such agreement or transaction, be treated by the vendor as a sale induced by fraud ...

The Auctions (Bidding Agreements) Act 1969 s 3 provides further rights for the seller of goods by auction where an agreement subsists that some person shall abstain from bidding for the goods, but these are basically confined to the provision of contractual remedies and relate to the situation in which one of the parties to the collusion is a dealer as defined in the 1927 Act. However this statute has been so rarely used that it has been suggested that its lack of application must be a deliberate policy.[33]

Does it appear that situations in the UK legislation where the auction contract can be regarded as fraudulent are confined to traditional auctions as defined? Or could they be extended to online auctions? In a traditional auction, if the auctioneer sells items of which the seller is not the true owner, then a purchaser who was subsequently pursued by the true owner could both seek to recover from the auctioneer, and possibly sue the auctioneer personally for their part in any fraudulent activity. In an online auction, a purchaser of such goods would not have this option. The question would then be whether the website would be held to have played any part in the perpetration of the fraud. Despite fulfilling the requirements of sale to the highest bidder in a competitive sale, most consumer to consumer auction sites are at pains to point out in their conditions of use that they are not true auctions, but merely provide a 'venue' within which the buying and selling of goods to the highest bidder can be facilitated. The better analogy is therefore with a bazaar rather than a conventional

---

33   See discussion of *R v Jordan* [1981] CLY 131 cited in Harvey and Franklin, 1995, p. 209.

auction.[34] This issue has not yet been directly addressed by the courts, as such, but there may be some circumstances in which they could operate in similar ways.

Chambre Nationale des Commissaires Priseurs v Nart SAS
[2001] ECC 24, paras 21 – 28
Tribunale de Grande Instance, Paris

... the defendants argue that such sales cannot be considered as public auctions and that the Internet is not an auction house in Paris. The defendants also argue that the sales should not be treated as auctions because they do not create the pressure to bid more provoked by the heat of the auction and the simultaneity of the bidding. In reality, an online auction presents all the characteristics of a public auction because it is open to all interested Internet users as long as they register beforehand and agree to the contractual clause governing online sales. The registration has as its sole object the identification and individualisation of the bidder. This object is necessary and achieved, albeit in another way, in traditional sales in an auction room. Furthermore, for the purpose of organising and carrying out an auction, the Internet consists of a vast auction room extending to infinity and able to change in order to take account of the changes in physical space in which the offers of auctions are distributed. ... Finally despite the defendants' arguments, online auctions do create the same atmosphere and heat in the bidding as traditional auctions. The bids are simultaneous in that the participant knows how much has already been offered and can make a higher bid ... it follows from the above that the online auctions organised by the defendants possess all the characteristics of public auctions.

However, this case involved a business with a conventional auction house operating an auction via its website, in other words there was both control and management of the auction process, and it would perhaps be dangerous to extend this view directly to some other forms of online auctions. On the other hand, it is clear that the primary characteristics of competitive bidding and sale to the highest bidder are fulfilled, and the points about the need for identification of bidders in ways which are appropriate to the situations are also relevant in making the parallel between the two activities.

An alternative view is that, in considering the volume of transactions on online auction sites, there is more similarity with an ISP for which the liability issues have been well rehearsed by both courts and academics and have also been the subject of legislative intervention in some jurisdictions.[35] There is an argument that, given that the major role of auction sites is one of facilitation rather than active interaction, there should be no liability in the absence of actual knowledge of fraudulent activity or collusion in the same. In the UK, auctioneers can also be criminally liable under the Trade Descriptions Act 1968 s 1 for any false or misleading descriptions of the goods.[36]

As mentioned above, one scam which is used by the unscrupulous vendor is to instigate fictitious bids in order to artificially inflate the price which the eventual buyer has to pay to secure the desired item. In the old case of *Heatley v Newton*,[37] a property was being sold by auction. The prospective buyer believed that it was about to be sold

---

34 See, eg, para. 3 e-bay user agreement available at www.ebay.co.uk.
35 See, eg, discussion of *Prodigy, Zeran* and the CDA immunity in Chapter 7, p 402 et seq, and of the DMCA in Chapter 9, p 494 et seq.
36 See, eg, *May v Vincent* (1990) 154 JP 997.
37 (1881) 19 ChD 326.

to a *bona fide* bidder for £12,950 and so offered £13,000 to clinch the sale. The reality was far different.

Heatley v Newton
(1881) 19 ChD 326, 327

... the fact is, that not only was the alleged bid for £12,950 an entirely fictitious bidding, but that almost, if not quite, all the preceding biddings were also fictitious, and that the apparently brisk and eager competition herein before mentioned was occasioned by the vendors and their agents, or some of them, bidding against each other, and running up the price so as to induce the Plaintiff and the other bona fide attendants at the said auction to believe that there were many persons desirous of purchasing the premises at a far higher price than was actually the fact. There was no bona fide bidding within five or six thousand pounds of the sum of £12,950. All the numerous biddings or alleged biddings after the sum of £ 8,000 or thereabouts were either biddings by the vendors or their agents or some of them, bidding one against another, or were no biddings at all, and were merely announced by the auctioneers without any bidding having been made. More than one person bid at such auction on behalf of the vendors.

Murdoch discusses the view of the Court of Appeal in the action for recovery and goes on to analyse the reasons for the illegality.

Law of Estate Agency and Auctions 4th ed
John Murdoch
London: Estates Gazette 2003 p. 187

First there can be no doubt that inducing someone to buy property by pretending that others have made offers for it is a misrepresentation; if this is done knowingly it is fraud. Second, ... unlawful conduct by vendor or auctioneer is no less unlawful where it takes place below the reserve because it may continue to influence bidding above this figure. Third, provided the necessary element of 'dishonesty' can be established there seems no reason to doubt that 'calling' a bid which the auctioneer knows has not been made will constitute the criminal offence of obtaining (or attempting to obtain) property by deception.

Similar arguments can be applied to damping the bids for fraudulent reasons.

By analogy with the situation above, it might be expected that it would be a criminal conspiracy for bidders to collude to depress the hammer price, by bid shielding for example, as referred to above, but it appears that this is not the case.[38] Harvey and Meisel explain the reasons for and against allowing auction rings to operate.

Auctions Law and Practice 2nd ed
Brian Harvey and Franklin Meisel
Oxford: OUP 1995 p. 215

There is an argument of policy that auction rings should be recognised as legal. Provided the seller fixes a realistic reserve, this is his primary insurance in not parting with his goods at a gross undervalue. Furthermore, the fact that a ring is operating does not necessarily mean that a satisfactory price was not obtained. It must be a matter of fortune as to whether there is a rival ring, an individual dealer or a private collector who is prepared to bid the goods up. Furthermore, dealers must be allowed to exploit their

---

38 Murdoch, 2003, p 196.

expertise and recognition of a valuable piece lying undiscovered by the experts is all part of the trade.

On the other hand, it can be argued, the existence of auction rings threatens to bring the auction process into considerable disrepute when private sellers subsequently find their goods resold at a hugely inflated price. Also, new entrants to a saleroom may be permanently discouraged by the predatory behaviour of existing rings. It is patently in the auctioneer's interest that this practice is at least regulated.

The former argument highlights one of the points of distinction between traditional and online auctions namely that traditional auctions, although attended by private persons, are dominated by dealers and professional collectors and the law may then be reluctant to interfere in what has become widely accepted as custom and practice in the trade. In contrast, consumer-consumer transactions, where neither party is either expert or professional, are very much more common in online auctions. It may be, therefore, that similar activity on online auctions would not be so acceptable and would much more correspond with the second argument put forward above.

In the US, the operation of auctions is governed by the Uniform Commercial Code (UCC) §2-328, and para 4 is a parallel provision to that in the Sale of Goods Act s 57(4) namely

(4) If the auctioneer knowingly receives a bid on the seller's behalf or the seller makes or procures such a bid, and notice has not been given that liberty for such bidding is reserved, the buyer may at his option avoid the sale or take the goods at the price of the last good faith bid prior to the completion of the sale. This subsection shall not apply to any bid at a forced sale.

This provision merely provides contractual remedies and any criminal activity which has taken place is left to be dealt with by, for instance, generic fraud offences. Two provisions which have proved to be of practical use in apprehending fraudsters on online auctions have proved to be the provisions on mail fraud and wire fraud found in 18 USC §§ 1341 and 1343.

Sec. 1341. Frauds and swindles

Whoever, having devised or intending to devise any scheme or artifice to defraud, or for obtaining money or property by means of false or fraudulent pretenses, representations, or promises, or to sell, dispose of, loan, exchange, alter, give away, distribute, supply, or furnish or procure for unlawful use any counterfeit or spurious coin, obligation, security, or other article, or anything represented to be or intimated or held out to be such counterfeit or spurious article, for the purpose of executing such scheme or artifice or attempting so to do, places in any post office or authorized depository for mail matter, any matter or thing whatever to be sent or delivered by the Postal Service, or deposits or causes to be deposited any matter or thing whatever to be sent or delivered by any private or commercial interstate carrier, or takes or receives therefrom, any such matter or thing, or knowingly causes to be delivered by mail or such carrier according to the direction thereon, or at the place at which it is directed to be delivered by the person to whom it is addressed, any such matter or thing, shall be fined under this title or imprisoned ... or both. ...

Sec. 1343. Fraud by wire, radio, or television

Whoever, having devised or intending to devise any scheme or artifice to defraud, or for obtaining money or property by means of false or fraudulent pretenses, representations, or promises, transmits or causes to be transmitted by means of wire, radio, or television communication in interstate or foreign commerce, any writings, signs, signals, pictures, or sounds for the purpose of executing such scheme or artifice, shall be fined under this title or imprisoned ... or both. ...

These provisions are similar in essence. Both require that there be a scheme or plan for obtaining money or property by the use of false statements which would reasonably influence someone to part with the money or property, that the statements were known to be false and that there was an intention to defraud. In the first section, the offence is complete when the statements are made via the mail, and in the second case by the transmission of wire, radio etc. Charges under these sections have been used successfully in a number of cases where the relevant medium was an online auction, and where the prospective vendors either did not possess, or did not intend to deliver, the items for which bidders had offered payment.[39]

A number of defendants in a bidding ring involving shill bidding for a fake painting, have also been successfully prosecuted under these provisions. The activities took place on the ebay auction site in the period 1998–2000 and the three defendants concealed their identities by providing false names, addresses and telephone numbers. They also created multiple user ids in order to make the false bids appear legitimate to other ebay users. Two of the perpetrators were apprehended and prosecuted in 2001 for, *inter alia*, mail fraud and wire fraud and the final defendant was prosecuted in 2003 resulting in custodial sentences.[40]

COMPUTER MISUSE ACT 1990

The discussion above has shown that some existing criminal offences could be applicable to certain cases of computer fraud and online auction fraud, but, as far as other types of activity were concerned, the application of the criminal law was by no means so certain. This was particularly true in relation to the phenomenon of 'computer hacking', which produced some particular headaches for the courts in many jurisdictions prior to the passing of bespoke statutes designed to compensate for the failure of existing law to deal with the situation. In the UK, one of the most celebrated cases prior to the enactment of specific legislation in the Computer Misuse Act 1990 was *R v Gold and Schifreen*.[41]

Gold and Schifreen hacked for a hobby and had managed to obtain the password for the Prestel System operated by BT, which provided subscribers with both email facilities and access to a number of database services. The password they obtained was in fact that issued to BT engineers, so not only did it not charge them for use, but it also gave widespread access to all parts of the system (note, however, that it was not a particularly complex password: 22222222 followed by the user ID 1234). By this means, they were even able to leave messages in the email box of the Duke of Edinburgh! Their activities eventually aroused suspicion and they were tracked down

---

39 See eg, *US v Hartman* 74 Fed Appx 159 (3rd Cir. (Pa.) 2003), *US v Jackson* 61 Fed Appx 851 (4th Cir (Va) 2003), *US v Blanchett* 41 Fed Appx 181 (10th Cir 2002).

40 See www.usdoj.gov/criminal/cybercrime/ebayplea.htm and www.usatoday.com/tech/news/2004-05-27-ebay-art-fraud_x.htm.

41 [1988] AC 1063; [1988] Crim LR 437 (HL). See, also, Kwiatkowski, 1987.

by monitoring their telephone usage. The question then arose as to what could be an appropriate charge. A prosecution was brought under s 1 of the Forgery and Counterfeiting Act 1981, which provides that: 'A person is guilty of forgery if he makes a false instrument with the intention that he or another shall use it to induce somebody to accept it as genuine and by reason of so accepting it do or not do some act to his own or any other person's prejudice.' For offences under this section, the problems identified in relation to the deception of a machine are overcome by express provision in the Act.

Gold and Schifreen were convicted, but appealed on the basis that no false instrument had been made. 'Instrument' is defined in s 8 of the Act and includes disks, tapes, etc, on which the material is stored by electronic means. The prosecution argument relied on the assertion that the dishonestly obtained password could constitute such an instrument, as it generated and was transmitted in the form of electrical impulses.

This contention was rejected for two reasons. First, it was felt that any instrument for the purposes of this Act had to be *ejusdem generis* with the other examples in the statutory definition, which were all physical objects, and, as the electrical impulses in question were only transient, this did not correspond well with the idea of the creation of an instrument. In addition to the difficulties with the definition of the instrument, the inapplicability of the charge was also held to be due to the nature of the offence of forgery. In this case, the password was not false – it was genuine – there was just no entitlement to use it. Both the Court of Appeal and the House of Lords were of the view that the use of this statute was inappropriate, as it was not intended to apply to this type of case. Lord Brandon of Oakbrook, giving judgment in the House of Lords, referred with approval to the speech of Lord Lane in the Court of Appeal, which is given below.

R v Gold and Schifreen
[1987] QB 1116, p 1124

Lord Lane CJ In our judgment the user segment in the instant case does not carry the necessary two types of message to bring it within the ambit of forgery at all. Moreover, neither the report nor the Act, so it seems to us, seeks to deal with information that is held for a moment whilst automatic checking takes place and is then expunged. That process is not one to which the words 'recorded or stored' can properly be applied, suggesting as they do a degree of continuance.

There is a further difficulty. The prosecution had to prove that the appellants intended that someone should accept as genuine the false instrument which they had made. The suggestion here is that it was a machine (under section 10(3)) which the appellants intended to induce to respond to the false instrument. But the machine (ie, the user segment) which was intended, so it was said, to be induced seems to be the very thing which was said to be the false instrument (ie, the user segment) which was inducing the belief. If that is a correct analysis, the prosecution case is reduced to an absurdity.

We have accordingly come to the conclusion that the language of the Act was not intended to apply to the situation which was shown to exist in this case. The submissions at the close of the prosecution case should have succeeded. It is a conclusion which we reach without regret. The Procrustean attempt to force these facts into the language of an Act not designed to fit them produced grave difficulties for both judge and jury which we would not wish to see repeated. The appellants' conduct amounted in essence, as already stated, to dishonestly gaining access to the relevant Prestel databank by a trick. That is not a criminal offence. If it is thought desirable to make it so, that is a matter for the legislature rather than the courts.

The wholehearted and unanimous endorsement of this passage by the House of Lords shows the disdain with which the attempt to squeeze the activity of computer hacking into the framework of an inappropriate statute was treated. The clear message was that, although it might be appropriate in some areas of the law to expand and develop the interpretation of existing legal provisions to take account of advances in technology, such provision had to be consonant with the alleged 'offence', in order not to stretch the law beyond its breaking point.[42]

In an attempt to bring a number of antisocial computer users to book, various persons were charged with offences under the Criminal Damage Act 1971. Was there any greater likelihood of success in these cases, or were they to be treated with the same contempt as the charges made under the Forgery Act?

The question for the court in *Cox v Riley*[43] was whether the deliberate erasure, by a disgruntled employee, of a computer program from a plastic card controlling a computerised saw, so as to render the saw inoperable, could be construed as criminal damage for the purposes of s 1(1) of the Criminal Damage Act 1971. It was agreed by all parties that the card was 'property' within the meaning of s 10(1), but had it been damaged? At first instance, damage was found in the fact that the card could no longer be used to operate and control the saw. On appeal, the opposing argument was again placed that, in reality, it was not the card that had been damaged but the program; the physical state of the card was unchanged. As the program was intangible, it was argued that it could not, of itself, be construed as 'property' within the meaning of s 10(1).

Stephen Brown LJ found, however, that the card was indeed damaged, in that it had been deprived of its usefulness and it would take both time and money to remedy this situation. In arriving at this conclusion, he relied on *dicta* of Cantley J in the case of *Henderson and Battley*,[44] which took the definition of 'damage' from the *Concise Oxford Dictionary* as 'injury impairing value or usefulness'. Both Stephen Brown LJ and Cantley J relied also on the much earlier precedent of *Fisher*,[45] concerning a discontented employee who put a steam engine out of action in such a way as not to damage the engine as such, but to ensure that considerable time and effort was needed to make it operative again. The use of this reasoning to reach the decision in *Cox v Riley* was later criticised by the Law Commission on the basis that it was decided under the provisions of the Malicious Damage Act 1861,[46] an Act which contained a different concept of damage. However, notwithstanding the applicability of this case to the situation in *Cox v Riley*, the inherent pragmatism in this approach and its application to

---

42 This should, however, be distinguished from the situation in *R v Governor of Brixton Prison ex p Levin* [1997] 1 Cr App R 355, where it was held that the word 'disk' was within the definition of 'instrument' in the Forgery and Counterfeiting Act 1981, s 8(1)(d) and embraced the information stored, as well as the medium on which it was stored. By entering false instructions on the disk, it was, in the court's opinion, falsified, and the applicant had thereby created a false instrument.
43 (1986) 83 Cr App R 54.
44 (1984) unreported, ICA.
45 (1865) LR 1 CCR 7.
46 See below, p 445.

rather more modern technology can be seen in the concluding remark that 'it seems to me quite untenable to argue that what this defendant did on this occasion did not amount to causing damage to property ...'.[47]

As will be appreciated, this does not really attack the crux of the opposing argument, which is directed at where the damage lies,[48] and is perhaps more informed by the fact that it was well established that the defendant had the requisite *mens rea* rather than confirmation that the necessary *actus reus* had been proved.

A rather different approach was to be taken to the application of the Criminal Damage Act 1971 in computer-related cases in *R v Whiteley*,[49] but, on any assessment, this was a radically different type of case. In brief,[50] Whiteley's hobby was hacking into computer networks and a particular target of his was JANET, the Joint Academic Network. Whilst engaged in such activities, he assumed the identity of Alan Dolby, the 'Mad Hacker', and deleted and changed data and 'locked out' authorised users by effecting changes of passwords, etc. He was eventually traced, following monitoring of the system at Queen Mary College, one of his prime targets, and charged with criminal damage.

Again, the argument was put that the damage was not to the tangible parts of the computer system but, rather, to the information contained on the disk. The manner in which such disks store information is in the arrangement of magnetic particles on the surface – if the information is changed (maliciously or otherwise), then this pattern will be altered. The court found that such a change could be sufficient to found a charge of criminal damage.

R v Whiteley
(1991) 93 Cr App R 25, p 27

... the disks are so constructed as to contain upon them thousands, if not millions, of magnetic particles. By issuing commands to the computer, impulses are produced which magnetise or demagnetise those particles in a particular way. By that means it is possible to write data or information on the disks and to program them to fulfil a variety of functions. By the same method it is possible to delete or alter data, information or instructions which have previously been written on to the disk. The argument advanced on behalf of the appellant, when reduced to its essence, seems to us to be this. That since the state of the magnetic particles on the disk is not perceptible by the unaided human senses, for instance of sight or touch, therefore the appellant's admitted activities only affected the 'intangible information' contained on the disk itself. Even if the absence of such a change is not fatal to the prosecution, goes on the submission, interference with the particles cannot amount to damage in law.

It seems to us that that contention contains a basic fallacy. What the Act requires to be proved is that tangible property has been damaged, not necessarily that the damage itself should be tangible. There can be no doubt that the magnetic particles upon the metal disks were a part of the disks and if the appellant was proved to have intentionally and without lawful excuse altered the particles in such a way as to cause an impairment of the

47 (1986) 83 Cr App R 54, p 58, *per* Stephen Brown LJ.
48 For discussion of these rules in a different context see above, p 142.
49 (1991) 93 Cr App R 25. See, also, Cowley, 1992.
50 For a more detailed account of events see Clough and Mungo, 1993, p 42 *et seq.*

value or usefulness of the disk to the owner, there would be damage within the meaning of section 1. The fact that the alteration could only be perceived by operating the computer did not make the alterations any the less within the ambit of the Act.

... Any alteration to the physical nature of the property concerned may amount to damage within the meaning of the section. Whether it does so or not will depend upon the effect that the alteration has had upon the legitimate operator (who for convenience may be referred to as the owner). If the hacker's actions do not go beyond, for example, mere tinkering with an otherwise 'empty' disk, no damage would be established. Where, on the other hand, the interference with the disk amounts to an impairment of the value or usefulness of the disk to the owner, then the necessary damage is established.

This reasoning might have provided a suitable avenue for the use of existing legal provisions to deal with cases of computer hacking – particularly of the more antisocial variety which involve rather more than mere browsing in the contents of files. However, by the time this decision had been reached, the Law Commission's recommendations for reform of the law in this area had resulted in the passing of the Computer Misuse Act 1990, which effectively removed such cases from the ambit of the Criminal Damage Act 1971.

The Law Commission reviewed the application of the existing criminal law and considered the desirability of criminalising activities such as hacking by the creation of specific offences. In so doing, they took into account the findings of the Scottish Law Commission, which had already reported on this topic.[51] It also had to come to terms with both the notion of computer crime and whether it was either necessary or desirable to create new criminal offences in this area, especially with regard to the activities of hackers. The Scottish Law Commission had recommended in its Report that the problem could be tackled by the creation of an unauthorised access offence, although this received a mixed reception in some quarters.

'Computer crime': Scotch mist
Colin Tapper
[1987] Crim LR 4, p 8
Possible responses

There seem to be three main possibilities. The first is for the legislature to do nothing, but instead to rely upon the judiciary to interpret the existing rules in such a way as to embrace computer-related crimes. The second is for the legislature to assist the task of the judiciary by modifying the definitions and conditions for liability of existing offences, but without enacting new ones. The third is to enact new offences specifically aimed at computer-related crime. This third alternative should perhaps be further subdivided between new offences which are intended to supplant existing offences in the computer-related area, and those which are intended to supplement them. Choice between these various alternatives must largely be determined by some perception of the particular uses or abuses of computers which fall outside the ambit of existing offences. Some general considerations are, however, apposite here.

The principal argument for the first alternative is that it is in many ways the most flexible. Development can proceed by minute steps, and those steps can often be retraced if a new perspective shows them to have started out in the wrong direction. It is also likely to be

---

51   Scottish Law Commission, 1987.

the method most congenial to the judiciary and so most likely to be accorded a sympathetic reception by them. It is much rarer to find determined opposition and destructive interpretation offered to a new common law development than to a new and unwelcome statute. It has the further advantage that the pace of development automatically reflects the incidence of the relevant situation. If no cases come to court for decision, the law stands still; but if many cases come, then some development, or at least crystallisation, is inevitable. This method is also least likely to foster anomalies, either between different applications of the same offence, or between different offences.

The disadvantages are in some ways the converse of the advantages. Just because the law proceeds in a flexible, and reversible, manner, it may lose some of its deterrent effect. It can be argued that in order to influence conduct, potential actors must have some clear idea of when the law is likely to intervene, and that this will be denied if each new situation gives rise to a new decision. Such an argument can be overstated however. Criminal law is concerned with morally reprehensible conduct, and the effect of uncertainty may be to restrain potential actors from doing anything remotely reprehensible in the area. Nevertheless, there remains a constraint upon the judges in this respect. They will be reluctant to depart very far from established rules. In general it is not the province of the judges to create new criminal offences, and this general policy is embodied in rules requiring all doubts to be resolved in favour of the accused, a maxim just as applicable to the establishment of rules as to the finding of facts. It may also be thought that the process of litigation is unlikely to lead to the development of the best-informed rules, rules of relevance confine lawyers to the proof of facts clearly and closely applicable to the particular facts before the court, and neither counsel nor judiciary may be thought sufficiently computerate to be trusted to understand the subject well enough to develop the best rules.

The third alternative lies at the opposite extreme. New legislation can be moulded to fit the precise delineation of the perceived need. It can come replete with exact definitions and explicit exceptions. The range of procedures, forms of proof and level of penalty are all capable of being adapted to the special problems of the situation. It may also be argued that it is just as, if not more, flexible than common law development, since legislation can always be amended, or, if necessary, repealed and replaced. However true this may be in theory, it is, given the pressure on parliamentary time, less than practically possible.

The principal disadvantages are those of creating anomalies and, by so doing, injustice. It is unlikely to be acceptable if criminality, or even sentence or procedure, depends upon whether a computer happens to have been involved ... Nor is it clear that legislators and draftsmen are so much more conversant with the technology of computing than counsel and judges, though they do have more opportunity to seek expert advice. Even so, the encapsulation of the burgeoning technology within the strait-jacket of the ordinary language and comprehensible structure ideally characterising Acts of Parliament, constitutes a formidable task. It is made more formidable still by the hinterland of presumptions, policies and principles customarily bestowed upon the construction of Acts of Parliament establishing new criminal offences, especially if recourse to anything beyond the words themselves is artificially restricted.

The middle course of tailoring definitions and conditions mitigates both advantages and disadvantages of the two extremes. It is likely to reduce anomalies when compared to the creation of wholly new offences, but it can often achieve this only at the expense of some distortion of the pattern of existing offences. The principal point of engagement in the legislative process is also perhaps the most hazardous in terms of drafting, namely in the casting of definitions.

It can be seen from this account that in the abstract there is no clear choice to be made between these different approaches. All must depend upon the array of conduct which is sought to be suppressed, and the aptitude of application of such crimes as already exist.

In order to explore the reasons for and against the use of the criminal law in this context, the Law Commission for England and Wales pointed out the differences between computers and other information storage and retrieval systems.

Reforming the Present Law – Hacking
Law Commission Working Paper No 110, Pt VI

6.3   The possible criminalisation of conduct which is not at present directly covered by the criminal law must involve a consideration of whether it is in the public interest that such conduct should be regarded as criminal. This in turn may involve consideration of whether it can be adequately controlled in some other way, in particular by the civil law ...

1 The arguments for an offence

6.8   One argument in favour of an offence ... acknowledges the importance of computers for society as a whole and suggests that those who use and rely on computers may be inhibited from making full use of them, if they fear that others might obtain unauthorised access to information held on them. For this reason, it is in the public interest that society must try to deter hacking generally, or at the very least in respect of computers holding certain kinds of information.

6.12   ... further argument in favour of an unauthorised access offence ... rests on the possible consequences of hacking to a computer system. Where the computer system is especially important, or the information stored on it especially valuable, these consequences will be more serious, but hacking could lead to an inadvertent damaging of any computer system. An offence of obtaining unauthorised access to a computer would signal society's disapproval of those who deliberately set out to breach security measures, and amount to a rejection of the claim that hacking is a harmless intellectual pastime. This rejection would have beneficial consequences beyond the number of successful prosecutions likely to be brought ...

6.13   Another positive side-effect of a hacking offence would be that its prohibition may serve to deter conduct which is made possible by the obtaining of unauthorised access to a computer, such as computer assisted fraud or theft, or the corruption of data or programs. An offence which may reduce the number of opportunities for subsequent (illegal) activities is worthy of further consideration.

2 The arguments against an offence

6.15   The main argument against the introduction, in any form, of a criminal offence of obtaining unauthorised access to a computer is that, although such conduct may constitute an invasion of privacy, it is not a matter in which the criminal law should interfere. No general right of privacy exists in English law even in the law of tort, and while obtaining unauthorised access to a computer may appear to be akin to the tort of trespass, such behaviour is generally not subject to criminal sanction without some further aggravating feature. Information is not property in English law ... and it is no offence, as such, to read someone else's correspondence or files ...

6.16   A further argument against the creation of a hacking offence is that the offence may be very difficult to enforce. We understand that it is possible for a hacker to obtain access to data on a computer and to ensure that the fact that he has obtained access remains undetected, or a least can be discovered only after a very time-consuming search ... Sometimes conduct may be so serious and so socially damaging that it clearly merits a criminal sanction whatever the problems of enforcement. In other cases where the harm caused by the relevant conduct is not so great, the case for providing a criminal sanction will be weakened by problems of enforcement. It is arguable that mere hacking falls into the latter category.

Further discussion and debate, together with further evidence received following the publication of the Working Paper, led to the conclusion that, taking all the circumstances into account, the creation of further criminal offences was in fact necessary.[52]

Computer Misuse[53]
Law Commission

1.37 ... the main argument in favour of a hacking offence does not turn on the protection of information, but rather springs from the need to protect the integrity and security of computer systems from attacks from unauthorised persons seeking to enter those systems, whatever may be their intention or motive. It is for that reason that we propose, as a deterrent counter to hacking, two offences: the first, a broad offence that seeks to deter the general practice of hacking by imposing penalties of a moderate nature on all types of unauthorised access; and the second a narrower but more serious offence, that imposes much heavier penalties on those persons who hack with intent to commit, or to facilitate the commission of, serious crime.

Thus, the Law Commission came to the conclusion that the existing criminal remedies were inadequate to deal with many instances of computer crime and misuse, although it conceded that a number of charges under the Theft Act might be appropriate in cases of computer fraud. However, despite the completion of the Law Commission Report, the Government seemed to have no plan to introduce legislation, and the Computer Misuse Act eventually saw the light of day as a consequence of a Private Members' Bill introduced by Michael Colvin. This Bill followed fairly closely the Law Commission's proposals – in particular, it took the two tier approach that is common in such legislation in other jurisdictions, namely, the creation of a basic hacking offence plus an ulterior intent offence to cover situations where there is some intent to commit a further crime.

Computer Misuse Act 1990
1 Unauthorised access to computer material

(1) A person is guilty of an offence if –
  (a) he causes a computer to perform any function with intent to secure access to any program or data held in any computer;
  (b) the access he intends to secure is unauthorised; and
  (c) he knows at the time when he causes the computer to perform the function that that is the case.

(2) The intent a person has to have to commit an offence under this section need not be directed at –
  (a) any particular program or data;
  (b) a program or data of any particular kind; or
  (c) a program or data held in any particular computer.

---

52 Whether this outcome is desirable has been questioned. See, eg, Wasik, 1991.
53 Cmnd 819, 1989.

2 Unauthorised access with intent to commit or facilitate commission of further offences

(1) A person is guilty of an offence under this section if he commits an offence under section 1 above ('the unauthorised access offence') with intent –

    (a) to commit an offence to which this section applies; or

    (b) to facilitate the commission of such an offence (whether by himself or by any other person) ...

(2) This section applies to offences –

    (a) for which the sentence is fixed by law; or

    (b) for which a person ... may be sentenced to imprisonment for a term of five years ...

(3) It is immaterial for the purposes of this section whether the further offence is to be committed on the same occasion as the unauthorised access offence or on any future occasion.

(4) A person may be guilty of an offence under this section even though the facts are such that the commission of the further offence is impossible.

These sections demonstrate the structure of the offences created. Sections 1 and 2 are hierarchical and, when charges are brought under s 2, it is still possible to convict under s 1, even where the necessary intent for a s 2 offence is not proved. Note, however, that certain activities do not fall within the ambit of the statute, in particular, reading of the contents of files non-interactively, for example, unauthorised reading after printing out in cases where the print operation had been performed by an authorised user, or mere reading of information on a computer screen. Depending on the nature of the material, such acts could fall within the scope of the Data Protection Act 1998.[54] A potentially more serious omission as the technology becomes ever more sophisticated is computer eavesdropping, and it may be that, in the future, action may be needed to remedy this lacuna.[55] In common with statutes in other jurisdictions, the Act does not define the word 'computer',[56] but a lengthy interpretation section demonstrates the wide reaching scope of some of the other crucial concepts in the Act:

17 Interpretation

(2) A person secures access to any program or data held in a computer if by causing a computer to perform any function he –

    (a) alters or erases the program or data;

    (b) copies or moves it to any storage medium other than that in which it is held or to a different location in the storage medium in which it is held;

    (c) uses it; or

    (d) has it output from the computer in which it is held (whether by having it displayed or in any other manner),

and references to access to a program or data (and to an intent to secure such access) shall be read accordingly.

---

54 See above, Chapter 7.

55 Law Commission, Working Paper No 119, *Computer Misuse* 1989; Wasik and Piperaki, 1987, p 112; Beale, 1986.

56 One exception is the legislation in Singapore. See, eg, Endeshaw, 1999; Mahalingham-Carr and Williams, 2000.

(3) For the purposes of subsection (2)(c) above a person uses a program if the function he causes the computer to perform –

   (a) causes the program to be executed; or

   (b) is itself a function of the program.

(4) For the purposes of subsection (2)(d) above –

   (a) a program is output if the instructions of which it consists are output; and

   (b) the form in which any such instructions or any other data is output (and in particular whether or not it represents a form in which, in the case of instructions, they are capable of being executed or, in the case of data, it is capable of being processed by a computer) is immaterial.

(5) Access of any kind by any person to any program or data held in the computer is unauthorised if –

   (a) he is not himself entitled to control access of the kind in question to the program or data; and

   (b) he does not have consent to access by him of the kind in question to the program or data from any person who is so entitled.

(6) References to any program or data held in a computer include references to any program or data held in a removable storage medium which is for the time being in the computer; and a computer is to be regarded as containing any program or data held in any such medium.

(7) A modification of the contents of any computer takes place if, by the operation of any function of the computer concerned or any other computer –

   (a) any program or data held in the computer concerned is altered or erased; or

   (b) any program or data is added to its contents; and any act which contributes towards causing such a modification shall be regarded as causing it.

(8) Such a modification is unauthorised if –

   (a) the person whose act causes it is not himself entitled to determine whether the modification should be made; and

   (b) he does not consent to the modification from any person who is so entitled.

Thus, as far as access is required, it appears that any sort of activity will suffice other than merely reading a screen and that the Act extends to access to, or modification of, the contents of floppy disks if this occurs while they are in any computer. The issue of authorisation is unlikely to be controversial in relation to a remote hacker, but where, as is frequently the case, the alleged unauthorised access occurs in employment, the Law Commission considered that:

> ... an employer should only have the support of the hacking offence if he has clearly defined the limits of authorisation applicable to each employee, and if he is able to prove that the employee had knowingly and recklessly exceeded that level of authority.[57]

It was made clear in *Ellis v DPP*[58] that a person's subjective belief that they should have access to a computer network was not sufficient to provide the requisite authorization. Ellis was an alumnus of a university and had thus previously been authorized to use the university's computer network. Several years after graduating he continued to use the system via terminals which had been left logged on by a previous

---

57 Law Commission, 1989 Cmnd 819, para 3.37.
58 [2001] EWHC Admin 362.

user. It was concluded that, although he thought that he should have such access, he did not honestly believe that he was so authorized. The question as to how far authorisation could extend was raised in *DPP v Bignell*,[59] where no criminal liability was found on the basis of lack of authorisation even though the consequent access was then exploited in an unauthorised manner. The reasoning in this decision, although not the outcome as such, was criticized by the House of Lords in *R v Bow Street Magistrates Court and Allison ex parte United States* as, in attempting to distinguish the control of access from the authority to access, it introduced 'a number of glosses which are not present in the Act'. This was summed up as follows:

R v Bow Street Magistrates Court and Allison ex parte United States
[2000] 2 AC 216, 225
House of Lords

Lord Hobhouse. The use of the phrase 'data of the kind in question' seems to derive from a simple misreading of section 17(5) and a confusion between kinds of access and kinds of data. Nor is section 1 of the Act concerned with authority to access kinds of data. It is concerned with authority to access the actual data involved. Because section 1(1) creates an offence which can be committed as a result of having an intent to secure unauthorised access without in fact actually succeeding in accessing any data, section 1(2) does not require that the relevant intent relate to any specific data. But that does not mean that access to the data in question does not have to be authorised.

Lord Hobhouse went on to point out that Kennedy LJ in the Court of Appeal judgment in *Allison* had fallen into the same trap, so that, by misreading s 17(5), he had failed to give effect to the plain words of s 1 when in fact the 'meaning of the statute is clear and unambiguous.' Despite the apparent clarity of the provisions the explanation was set out in some detail:

R v Bow Street Magistrates Court and Allison ex parte United States
[2000] 2 AC 216, 223
House of Lords

Section 17 is an interpretation section. Subsection (2) defines what is meant by access and securing access to any program or data. It lists four ways in which this may occur or be achieved. Its purpose is clearly to give a specific meaning to the phrase 'to secure access.' Subsection (5) is to be read with subsection (2). It deals with the relationship between the widened definition of securing access and the scope of the authority which the relevant person may hold. That is why the subsection refers to 'access of any kind' and 'access of the kind in question.' Authority to view data may not extend to authority to copy or alter that data. The refinement of the concept of access requires a refinement of the concept of authorisation. The authorisation must be authority to secure access of the kind in question. As part of this refinement, the subsection lays down two cumulative requirements of lack of authority. The first is the requirement that the relevant person be not the person entitled to control the relevant kind of access. The word 'control' in this context clearly means authorise and forbid. If the relevant person is so entitled, then it would be unrealistic to treat his access as being unauthorised. The second is that the relevant person does not have the consent to secure the relevant kind of access from a person entitled to control, that is authorise, that access.

Subsection (5) therefore has a plain meaning subsidiary to the other provisions of the Act. It simply identifies the two ways in which authority may be acquired – by being oneself

---

the person entitled to authorise and by being a person who has been authorised by a person entitled to authorise. It also makes clear that the authority must relate not simply to the data or program but also to the actual kind of access secured. Similarly, it is plain that it is not using the word 'control' in a physical sense of the ability to operate or manipulate the computer and that it is not derogating from the requirement that for access to be authorised it must be authorised to the relevant data or relevant program or part of a program. It does not introduce any concept that authority to access one piece of data should be treated as authority to access other pieces of data 'of the same kind' notwithstanding that the relevant person did not in fact have authority to access that piece of data. Section 1 refers to the intent to secure unauthorised access to any program or data. These plain words leave no room for any suggestion that the relevant person may say: 'Yes, I know that I was not authorised to access that data but I was authorised to access other data of the same kind'.

A further criticism was that Kennedy LJ had confined the operation of s 1 to 'hacking', rather than using the wider concept of using a computer to secure unauthorised access. This had been an issue in the very first case under the Computer Misuse Act 1990, that of *R v Cropp*.[60] Cropp had used his knowledge of his ex-employer's computer system to give himself a 70% discount on goods. On a charge under s 2(1), a submission of no case to answer was made, on the grounds that, in order to contravene s 1(1) (and, therefore, s 2(1)), it had to be established that the accused had used one computer with intent to secure unauthorised access into another computer. This represents the usual definition of 'hacking', which was popularly supposed to be the activity that was proscribed by this new legislation. This argument succeeded at trial but the Attorney General sought clarification from the Court of Appeal on the basis that the Act had been drafted so as to deal not only with the situation in which indirect access to a computer system is gained by using another computer, but also with the situation where a person misuses a computer to which he or she has direct (but unauthorised) access.

AG's Reference (No 1 of 1991)
[1992] WLR 432, p 437
Court of Appeal

Lord Taylor of Gosforth CJ The ordinary canons of construction require this court to look at the words of the section and to give them their plain and natural meaning. Doing that, we look again at the relevant words. They are, 'he causes a computer to perform any function with intent to secure access to any program or data held in any computer'.

Mr Lassman argued successfully before the judge, and sought to argue before this court, that that final phrase, 'held in any computer', should really be read as 'held in any other computer', or alternatively should be read as 'held in any computer except the computer which has performed the function'.

To read those words in that way, in our judgment, would be to give them a meaning quite different from their plain and natural meaning. It is a trite observation, when considering the construction of statutes, that one does not imply or introduce words which are not there when the plain and natural meaning is clear. In our judgment there are no grounds whatsoever for implying, or importing the word 'other' between 'any' and 'computer', or excepting the computer which is actually used by the offender from the phrase 'any computer' at the end of the subsection (1)(a).

---

60 (1991) unreported, but see case note at (1991) 7 CLSR 168.

If the court had not arrived at such an interpretation, the potential usefulness of the Computer Misuse Act 1990 could have been severely curtailed, resulting in what has been described as 'total emasculation'.[61] The dramatic effect that this might have had is particularly apparent with hindsight, as the majority of prosecutions that have been brought since then have far more in common with the situation in *Cropp* than with hacking.

In its Report, the Law Commission had also recommended an offence of unauthorised alteration or destruction of data, having come to the conclusion that the interpretation of the Criminal Damage Act 1971 as seen in *Cox v Riley*[62] (which they had appeared to endorse in the Working Paper[63] – 'Our provisional view is that this reasoning is correct and in accordance with the wide meaning which damage was intended to bear') was in need of clarification. It should be noted that this was written before the decision in *R v Whiteley*.[64]

Computer Misuse
Cm 819, 1989
Law Commission

2.27 Our provisional view was that the wide meaning attributed by the courts to the word 'damage', including as it did any injury impairing the value or usefulness of the property, had had the effect of extending the law of criminal damage to cover the tangible property … on which programs or data were stored. On this reasoning any unlawful interference with the data or program would amount to damage to the tangible storage medium, providing that its value was thereby diminished.

2.28 It does not seem to have been seriously questioned that the unauthorised destruction of data and the reprogramming of operational computers ought to be criminal … Alteration or erasure of data without authority has, in the absence of specific justifications provided by law, no social value; it involves deliberate interference with the property of others, and not merely trespassing on their premises or looking at their information; … it can cause substantial loss and, in the case of operational systems, physical danger. While it is clear therefore that these activities ought to be outlawed, it is more controversial whether the present law of criminal damage is an adequate response in the way that we provisionally suggested. Our conclusion on further consideration, which was supported by the weight of opinion on consultation, is that clarification of the law is required. The main reasons for that conclusion are as follows.

2.29 'Property' means, for the purposes of the Criminal Damage Act 1971, property of a tangible nature. In *Cox v Riley*, the deleted computer program had been stored on a plastic circuit card, which latter could be and was identified as the tangible property which had been damaged. … there may be more difficulty in other cases in pointing to a physical medium on which the altered or erased data has been held; … in some cases data is stored by means of electrical impulses that are only very notionally attached to any tangible property. For the commission of a criminal offence to depend on whether it can be proved that data was damaged or destroyed while it was held on identifiable tangible property not only is unduly technical, but also creates an undesirable degree of uncertainty in the operation of the law.

---

61 Dumbill, 1992.
62 (1986) 83 Cr App R 54; see, also, above, p 435.
63 Law Commission Working Paper No 110, 1988, para 3.38.
64 (1991) 93 Cr App R 25; see, also, above, p 436.

The report went on to criticise the reasoning employed in *Cox v Riley* and the eventual outcome was s 3 of the Act.

Computer Misuse Act 1990
Section 3 Unauthorised modification of computer material

(1) A person is guilty of an offence if –

    (a) he does any act which causes an unauthorised modification of the contents of any computer; and

    (b) at the time when he does the act he has the requisite intent and the requisite knowledge.

(2) For the purposes of subsection (1)(b) above the requisite intent is an intent to cause a modification of the contents of any computer and by so doing –

    (a) to impair the operation of any computer;

    (b) to prevent or hinder access to any program or data held in any computer; or

    (c) to impair the operation of any such program or the reliability of any such data.

(3) The intent need not be directed at –

    (a) any particular computer;

    (b) any particular program or data or a program or data of any particular kind; or

    (c) any particular modification or a modification of any particular kind.

(4) For the purposes of subsection (1)(b) above the requisite knowledge is knowledge that any modification he intends to cause is unauthorised.

(5) It is immaterial for the purposes of this section whether an unauthorised modification or any intended effect of it of a kind mentioned in subsection (2) above is, or is intended to be, permanent or merely temporary.

(6) For the purposes of the Criminal Damage Act 1971 a modification of the contents of a computer shall not be regarded as damaging any computer or computer storage medium unless its effect on that computer or computer storage medium impairs its physical condition.

The concepts contained in this section are further amplified in s 17(7) and (8).[65] Section 3 creates an offence of doing any act which causes unauthorised modification of the contents of any computer with the requisite intent and knowledge as defined by the section. Interestingly enough, the new Act does not actually amend the Criminal Damage Act 1971 as originally suggested by the Law Commission, but in s 3(6) contains a proviso as to the application of that Act to modification of computer material. It therefore appears that if another case like *Cox v Riley*[66] were to occur, it would have to be taken under this section, notwithstanding the successful prosecution argument in the later case of *Whiteley*.[67]

Section 3 of the Computer Misuse Act 1990 appears to be capable of catching a wide variety of types of activity. It would be expected to embrace the type of modification and erasure seen in *Cox v Riley* but should also be capable of covering the

65 See above, p 442.
66 (1986) 83 Cr App R 54; see, also, above, p 435.
67 (1991) 93 Cr App R 25; see, also, above, p 436.

intentional introduction of viruses, worms, Trojan horses[68] and other programs of a potentially destructive nature. Since the intent need not be directed at any particular computer, the liability of the person who originates the virus or worm should be unaffected if, in the event, a virus is introduced to a system by means of an infected disk innocently acquired by a third party. On the other hand, it would appear that anyone knowingly introducing an infected disk has a clear intent to modify the contents of a computer. These issues will be explored more fully below.

Computer Misuse Legislation in Practice

On first examination, it can appear that the bespoke Act has not had any more conspicuous success at deterring or apprehending computer misuse than the hotch potch of offences in use prior to its enactment. The number of prosecutions is small and yet the apparent incidence of computer misuse is large and increasing.[69] Significant problems of detection and enforcement, an issue not really addressed by the Law Commission reports, remain notwithstanding some element of inter-state cooperation and attempts at an international approach as evinced in Council of Europe Cybercrime Convention.[70] It is not only the detection and apprehension of offenders that has given rise to problems, but also the attitude of the courts. An early example is found in the case of *Bedworth*.[71] Bedworth was a teenager whose hacking activities started when he was given a computer for his fourteenth birthday in 1987. By the time he was arrested in 1991, together with fellow hackers who had all communicated under pseudonyms via an electronic bulletin board, he had hacked into an impressively long list of computer systems including the *Financial Times*, a cancer research institute in Brussels, the EC offices in Luxembourg and many others, resulting in significant financial losses being incurred by the institutions involved. At his trial, he made no attempt to deny what he had done. His defence was that he was obsessed; he was subject to compulsive behaviour, so that, although he knew that what he was doing was unlawful, his obsession denied him the freedom to stop – in other words, he was addicted to hacking. To the surprise of the prosecution, the jury acquitted him, a

---

68 These, and similar terms, are sometimes used interchangeably in non-technical parlance. A virus is a self-replicating program which may not be immediately apparent on examination of a system but copies itself into the computer memory and, from there, to any disks which are subsequently loaded and/or in the memory of other computers attached to the same network as data is exchanged. The type of program commonly referred to as a 'worm' is an example of a program that was developed for exploring the capabilities of computer systems and networks and may adversely affect systems on which it is unwanted by consuming resources. A 'Trojan horse' is a program which appears as a program performing an innocuous function but hides the fact that it also has another, usually more sinister, function. See further discussion below at p 449.

69 See eg, The Home Office Evidence submitted to the All Party Internet Group reviewing the operation of the Computer Misuse Act. The statistics on Computer Misuse Act prosecutions submitted as part of this evidence show, not only a relatively small number of cases in total but also a conviction rate of only just over 50% in 2002 compared with a rate of 74% for all offences in the same year. See, in particular, www.apig.org.uk/Home Office – total conviction rates.xls and www.apig.org.uk/Home Office Appendices.xls. In the light of this evidence the reference in the final APIG report to the 'substantial case law' on the Act (at para 26) is a little surprising.

70 See discussion below at p 480.

71 (1993) unreported. See, further, Charlesworth, 1993; 1993a; Christian, 1993; Fisch-Nigri, 1993.

verdict which was widely referred to at the time as if it drove the proverbial 'coach and horses' through the enforcement of the Computer Misuse Act 1990.

Accepting that it can never be known on what basis the jury came to their conclusion, there seem to be three main possibilities. The first of these was that they were intending to signal their disapproval of the Computer Misuse Act in much the same way as the surprise acquittal of Ponting[72] had discredited parts of the Official Secrets Act 1911. This seems unlikely; although there were certain aspects of the investigation of this case which had perhaps aroused the concern of the jury, the case had not been preceded by the history of criticism and bad publicity surrounding the statute in question which had set the scene prior to *Ponting*.

The second possibility is that the members of the jury were persuaded by the defence of addiction to computers, notwithstanding the judge's summing up. For addiction to be a sufficient defence to a criminal charge, the individual should be affected to such an extent that the affliction may be viewed as a 'disease of the mind', sufficient to prevent the formation of the requisite *mens rea*. this would then effectively equate with a defence of insanity. Whether or not there is clinical evidence to support any finding of addiction to computer hacking is not a subject which can be debated here, although supporting evidence had been produced during the trial. It is certainly the case that, at the trial, Bedworth gave repeated assertions, not only that he had committed the acts at issue, but also that he was aware that these acts were wrong and would not be repeated. If he were truly addicted, would he be able to make this latter promise? Charlesworth,[73] citing the case of *Lawrence*,[74] points out that courts are unlikely even to take addiction into account in mitigation. *Lawrence* was, of course, a case in which the offence (of burglary) was committed to feed the addiction rather than being directly related to that addiction. Whilst it can be problematic to draw analogies between such cases and those, such as *Bedworth*, in which the addiction is to the criminal behaviour itself, nonetheless there is confirmation for the absence of a general defence of addiction in *Kopsch*[75] – 'The defence of uncontrollable impulse is unknown in English law'.

Finally, it is entirely possible that what acquitted Bedworth was the 'sympathy vote'. There was evidence at the trial that the police had utilised tactics such as 'dawn raids' on his home in their apprehension of Bedworth and it may be that the jury thought that he was only a young, fresh faced boy and that, in the particular circumstances of the case, the police had overreacted.

Whilst we can never be sure of the precise reasoning on which this acquittal was based, it is clear that no such sympathy was extended to his co-defendants, Strickland and Woods, who, having pleaded guilty, were sentenced to six months' imprisonment – a recognition, perhaps, of the fact that the behaviour in question resulted in significant financial loss, can cause serious damage to the systems affected and should be viewed seriously. It is also significant that, notwithstanding the success of Bedworth's defence there has not been any further attempt to plead such a defence despite anecdotal references to addiction to computers.

---

72 *R v Ponting* [1985] Crim LR 318.
73 Charlesworth, 1995.
74 [1989] Crim LR 309.
75 (1925) 19 Cr App R 50.

Even taking into account the provisions provided in the Computer Misuse Act,[76] a further problem which could have surfaced in the case of Bedworth and many other hacking cases is that of jurisdictional problems; some of the computer systems into which they hacked were in other countries. The reverse situation is obviously equally likely: hackers in other countries can hack into computers and networks in the UK. How is this problem to be addressed? The evidence is that such situations have been dealt with by co-operation between police forces. European police forces have agreed with Interpol that hackers or originators of viruses can be prosecuted in their country of residence, even if the hack or the virus has wreaked havoc in another jurisdiction. As discussed below, the Cybercrime Convention contains more precise provisions on international cooperation and mutual assistance in the investigation of cybercrime but the extent to which this Treaty is likely to be ratified by all signatories is unclear at present.

Viruses and Similar Programs

Reports from a number of jurisdictions identify virus and similar attacks as the most prevalent form of computer misuse and abuse[77] and so it is unsurprising that this is an area in which there has been considerable investigatory and enforcement activity. Although the word 'virus' is often used as a generic term to encompass all programs which can be used in this way, there are some important differences between the major categories of such programs. A virus program can replicate itself and so spread from computer to computer although this does not usually occur spontaneously but the virus is passed on by e-mail attachments or file-sharing. The effects of the virus may vary from the comic message to serious damage. The 'ILOVEYOU' virus for instance sought out all MP3 and jpeg (image) files, deleted them and replaced them with a copy of itself. A worm is a similar program to a virus but needs no positive action to spread through a network. A worm can travel very quickly through a system and replicate in great volume so that, even if no other damage were done, the system would still become choked and its speed and efficiency of operation drastically reduced or even halted. Another common program is the 'Trojan Horse' which masquerades as a useful program but which hides other features and may cause a breach of the security features allowing subsequent entry of a virus or worm. In a distributed denial of service attack, the perpetrator sets up a system which will generate a high volume of traffic to the target site.[78]

Although the law originally had to respond to hacking and unauthorisd access, virus attacks and denial of service are now far more prevalent and familiar threats to computer systems and their effects are exacerbated by the increasing size and reach of current computer networks. To distinguish it from unauthorised access, this has been

---

76 The Computer Misuse Act 1990, s 4 makes it immaterial (subject to certain conditions detailed in subsequent sections and subsections) (a) whether any act or proof of which is required for conviction of the offence occurred in the home country concerned; or (b) whether the accused was in the home country concerned at the time of such an act or event. See, also, Kelleher, 1997.

77 See Audit Commission, 2001; CSI/FBI Computer Crime and Security Survey 2003, available via www.cybercrime.gov/CSI_FBI.htm

78 For further discussion see eg, Katyal, 2001, pp 1023–1027.

referred to by Katyal as 'unauthorised disruption'[79] – although disruption by its nature is likely to be unauthorised. To what extent is the law developed primarily as a response to 'hacking' able to deal with these more recent threats?

The first worm[80] to be released onto the embryonic internet was created in 1988 by a Cornell University student, Robert Morris, who was subsequently successfully prosecuted under the US Computer Fraud and Abuse Act 1986 (18 USC § 1030). This decision was upheld by the US Court of Appeals for the Second Circuit[81] which found that Morris had both exceeded the authorisation for those computers which he was allowed to access and, because the program was designed to spread to other machines, had also accessed computers which he had no authority to access. A short while later, not long before the Computer Misuse Act 1990 was passed in the UK, the strange case of Dr Lewis Popp hit the headlines. A large number of people associated with computer use received disks through the post, purporting to contain important information about the AIDS virus. If, in fact, the disks were used, although they did reveal information on that subject, they also contained a Trojan horse which was programmed to activate after the computer had been used about 100 times.[82] Although the contents of the hard disk would have been destroyed, at that time there would have been little action which could have been taken as a result of this particular activity, unless the courts would have been happy to use the reasoning in *Whiteley*.[83] This incident was referred to in the Parliamentary debates on the Bill and it is also evident that, at this stage, it was intended that the new legislation would cover such activities: '... circulation of an infected disk, such as this is not an offence. However, the Bill will make it one.'[84] Despite this, there was some discussion after the statute was enacted as to whether it was suitable for apprehending those who introduced viruses into computer systems for whatever reason even though it appears that in practically every case the effect of such programs will be to cause an unauthorized modification to a computer system.[85]

The fact that s 3 could, in principle, be used in this way was put beyond doubt in the case of *R v Pile*.[86] Pile, who referred to himself as the 'Black Baron', developed two particular viruses, Queeg and Pathogen, and also Smeg, a guide to writing viruses. He placed these on bulletin boards with the message, 'That's all there is to it. Have fun. The Black Baron'. Although there is an element of the comic in this, the viruses themselves were extremely sophisticated and capable of masquerading as other, innocent programs. He was even successful in incorporating a virus into an anti-virus scan program. This was the first time that a person had appeared in court as a result of intentionally introducing computer viruses to a system and the court had no problems

---

79   *Ibid*, p 1023.
80   For a history of viruses see eg, Klang, 2003, pp 163–7.
81   *US v Morris* 928 F 2d 504 (2nd Cir 1991).
82   See, eg, Akdeniz, 1996.
83   In fact, Dr Popp was eventually arrested in Ohio and charged with extorting money with menaces, as those affected were also directed to transfer sums of money to a bank account in Panama. In the event, there was evidence that Popp's mental condition had deteriorated to such an extent that he was pronounced unfit to plead.
84   Michael Colvin, *Hansard*, Vol 166 Col 1139, 1990.
85   See, eg, Wasik, 1996.
86   (1995) unreported. For further details see, eg, Jones, 1996; Akdeniz, 1996.

in finding a breach of s 3. In addition, by allowing a defence application to seek an expert opinion on the amount of damage caused by Pile's activities in advance of deciding on sentence, it was clear that the judge considered the likely losses to affected users as a very serious matter and subsequently imposed a custodial sentence of 18 months.

Since these early days, many virulent virus programs have been unleashed on the world's computer networks causing damage estimated at many billions of dollars. The originators of some of the more high profile attacks have been detected, although not necessarily apprehended. The creator of the Melissa virus, the major effect of which was to cause infected computers to send emails containing an infected attachment to the first 50 names in the user's computer address book, was prosecuted under 18 USC § 1030 and sentenced to 20 months imprisonment together with a fine of $5,000.[87] On the other hand, although Filipino ex-computer science student Onel de Guzman was identified as the creator of the ILOVEYOU virus, no appropriate charges could be brought against him in the Philippines. New law has since been enacted in the Philippines, but it does not have retrospective effect.[88] However the writer of the Anna Kournikova virus voluntarily confessed and was charged and convicted in the Netherlands. Two people have appeared in court in connection with the Blaster worm,[89] and in the UK, a man was jailed for two years for releasing viruses onto the internet.[90] In the unsuccessful appeal against sentence in the latter case, Penry-Davey remarked that 'criminal conduct of this kind has the capacity to cause disruption, consternation and even economic loss on an unimagined scale'[91] showing that courts are aware of the potential severity of such activities.[92]

Trojan horses can be installed on a computer without the user's knowledge and can then initiate a range of different actions which may or may not come to the notice of the user. The operation of this type of program was at issue in three separate cases in the UK, those of *Green* (2002), *Caffrey* (2003) and *Schofield* (2003).[93] The common feature in all of these cases was that the defendant alleged that the acts complained of resulted from the installation of a Trojan on their computers of which they were unaware. Both *Green* and *Schofield* were charged with possession of indecent images of children, but succeeded in bringing evidence that the presence of the images on their computers was due to them having been infected with Trojans which then downloaded the images whenever the internet was accessed. *Caffrey*, on the other hand, was a prosecution under Computer Misuse Act s 3 in which Caffrey was acquitted for a denial of service attack on the Port of Houston computer network. The result of the attack was to impair the operation of the network to such an extent that necessary navigation data was inaccessible. There was no dispute that Caffrey's

87   *US v Smith* DNJ 2 May 2002 see www.cybercrime.gov/ccases.html.
88   For further discussion see eg, Sprinkel 2002, Goodman and Brenner, 2002 which also contains details of the new law in the Appendix.
89   *US v An unnamed juvenile* WD Washington 26/9/2003 and *US v Parson* WD Washington 29/8/2003 see www.cybercrime.gov/ccases.html
90   *R v Vallor* [2004] 1 Cr App R (S) 54.
91   *Ibid*, para 7.
92   For a more detailed consideration of the application of the law to computer viruses together with some alternative points of view see eg, Klang, 2003.
93   All unreported but see discussion in Hill, 2003 and Brenner, *et al*, 2004.

computer was not the source of the attack, but the prosecution argued that it was initiated by Caffrey as a misdirected attack on a fellow chatroom user, whereas the defence argument was that the attack was the result of the activity of a Trojan which had infected Caffrey's machine. No trace of the Trojan was found, but evidence was accepted that the Trojan had self-deleted after launching the attack, despite the prosecution's view that such technology did not exist. These cases all demonstrate the evidential difficulties for both sides when it is possible that the acts, harm or damage complained of could have originated from a Trojan. Certainly a browse through a virus library shows that there are Trojan programs which exhibit some of the properties alleged in the above cases.[94] The mere facts of the case may not provide any indication of whether or not the act complained of occurred with or without the user's knowledge or consent.

One of the issues raised by the case of *Caffrey* was whether or not Computer Misuse Act s 3 covered denial of service attacks. In so far as the requirements of s 3 hinge on unauthorised modification, the natural conclusion is that those attacks which result in data or program modification will fall within the Act, but those which merely clog up the system with excessive traffic will not. The undesirability of the legality of such an action depending of the precise mode of execution was one of the issues discussed by the All Party Internet Group (APIG) in its public inquiry into the operation of the Computer Misuse Act 1990. There had been many calls for such a review to establish whether the Act's provisions were still appropriate and APIG focused particularly on the following:

whether the CMA is broad enough to cover the criminality encountered today;

whether the CMA's generic definitions of computers and data have stood the test of time;

whether there are 'loopholes' in the Act that need to be plugged;

what revisions may be needed to meet our international treaty obligations; and,

whether the level of penalties within the CMA is sufficient to deter today's criminals.[95]

Interestingly, the general impression from APIG's report is one of satisfaction with the way in which the CMA is perceived to have stood the test of time, and a finding that some of the expressed dissatisfaction with the statute was due to misapprehension about its provisions. For instance, a number of respondents asked for the statute to be extended to deal with hacking and disturbing viruses, despite the fact that there have been successful prosecutions under ss 1 and 3 with respect to both activities. 'We can only conclude that there must be widespread ignorance of the current law and what types of activity its provisions already address. This is an entirely undesirable state of affairs.'[96] Concluding that the absence of definitions had not been shown to be an impediment to application of the Act by the courts which understood the relevant terms to 'have the appropriate contemporary meaning',[97] the need was for the Home

---

94 Troj/Newsflood, for instance, is a Trojan horse that continually posts messages about child pornography to Usenet newsgroups, see www.sophos.com/virusinfo/analyses/.

95 *APIG Report,* 2004, para. 2 Also available at: www.apig.org.uk/CMAReportFinal Version1.pdf.

96 *Ibid,* para 23.

97 *Ibid,* para 17.

Office to 'prioritise the provision of website material about the CMA because it is directly relevant to Internet users and because it is clearly widely misunderstood'.[98] On more specific issues, the report noted that the revisions suggested by the Law Commission report on Fraud (see above) would address the concerns on computer fraud; that expediting the Law Commission work on misuse of trade secrets would allow the 'theft' of data to be criminalized; and that the problems with the interpretation of unauthorised access had been aired extensively by the House of Lords in *Allison* (see above) suggesting that no further clarification was required. However, a specific recommendation was made to enact an 'explicit 'denial-of service' offence of impairing access to data' which would cover all instances of deliberate denial of service, whether or not they would currently fall within s 3 and thus remedy the deficiency noted above.[99] The Report also suggests that there is a strong case for increasing the penalties available for the s 1 offence, to allow more realistic reflection of the damage which might be done, and to convey 'a clear message that society now takes hacking offences rather more seriously than in 1990'.[100] The report makes a number of other recommendations to assist with computer crime investigations,[101] but those referred to above are the only ones which might lead to the enactment of new substantive provisions. In the light of this report, together with the a report from the Internet Crime Forum[102] and the consideration of the legal issues in the Eurim-IPPR e-crime study[103], the Home Office is now considering appropriate amendments to the 1990 legislation.[104]

A similar pattern has been observed in the operation of computer crime statues in other jurisdictions. Brunnstein and Fischer-Huebner, for instance, have observed a similar lack of prosecutions in other jurisdictions,[105] and Conley and Bryan have identified similar enforcement problems in the US.[106] In addition to these specific concerns, a continuing topic of academic debate focuses on the more fundamental issues of whether the behaviour in question should be criminalised and whether or not this should be accomplished by means of specially designed statutes.

Wasik[107] suggested in 1996 that, in reviewing the operation of the law in this area, attention should be focused on two key issues:

> What is the proper role of the criminal law in this area? Should the continuing trend towards criminalisation of computer misuse be society's main response to that behaviour? What should be the priority between that approach and, say, the development of ethical codes and regulatory structures, which would impinge upon manufacturers and others to ensure compliance with higher levels of security in IT products? Might civil liability and/or regulatory arrangements offer a more subtle, and perhaps more effective approach, than further criminalisation? Do we need more law, or less?

---

98 *Ibid*, para. 25.
99 *Ibid*, para. 75.
100 *Ibid*, paras 98 and 99.
101 See summary of recommendations on pp 18–19.
102 *Reform of the Computer Misuse Act 1990*, 2003. Available at: www.internetcrimeforum.org.uk/cma-icf.pdf.
103 www.eurim.org/consult/e-crime/dec03/ECS_WP6_web_031209.htm.
104 See www.homeoffice.gov.uk/crime/internetcrime/compmisuse.html.
105 Brunnstein and Fischer-Huebner, 1995.
106 Conley and Bryan, 1999.
107 Wasik, 1996.

To the extent that criminalisation is appropriate in this area (and few would deny that it does offer an important element within a range of responses) we should be concerned to predict, to identify and to remedy the various shortcomings of the law. Will the criminal law as currently drafted cover, for example, the malicious dissemination of computer viruses? This requires us to look, not just at the substantive criminal law but also at the rules of admissibility of evidence in court and the provisions relating to enforcement, search and seizure of evidential material. We should also be concerned to identify new criminal trends associated with widespread computerisation, such as the organised theft of computer hardware and the spread of pornographic material through IT networks.

The Law Commission Reports evaluated some of the arguments for and against the introduction of criminal offences and their activity was paralleled in a number of other jurisdictions, which, on the whole, came to similar conclusions.[108] Nevertheless this did not curtail the debate over both the extent to which this was necessary and the shortcomings of the new laws.[109] Such discussions centre on whether criminalisation is an appropriate response, on the practical problems of detection and enforcement and the availability and imposition of appropriate sanctions.

To what extent should computer related crimes be the subject of specific legislative attention?
Douglas H Hancock
(2001) 12 Alb LJ Sci & Tech 97, 123

The need for specific computer crime was manifest in most jurisdictions, however, prosecutors have faced a number of difficulties in applying existing criminal laws. In part, this challenge related to the systemic bias in favor of the accused. An additional challenge was the criminal law's fixation on the tangible and its inability to adapt to technological change.

Laws that existed prior to the passage of specific computer crime legislation were wholly inadequate. ... computer crime legislation avoids [such] problematic arguments, like the arguments that damage was not done to property. ...

Furthermore, previous criminal laws frequently did not carry sanctions that were commensurate with the harm inflicted. Society's notion, that the hacker is an anti-hero is ebbing; ... specific legislation resolves ambiguities and allows for penalties that are appropriate ... specific computer laws avoid complex issues of intent ...

Ultimately, the most persuasive argument that can be brought favoring specific computer crime legislation is for the evolution of our information society. Businesses and societies have become immensely dependent upon the information infrastructure. Great value is now rightly ascribed to the intangible.

The enactment of the Computer Misuse 'Acts' in various jurisdictions ... represent necessary legislative interventions to address actual and manifest inadequacies in the criminal law. The extent to which this intervention was required cannot be assessed with mathematical precision. What can be said, however, is that it was clear that the existing criminal laws in many jurisdictions were entirely ill-suited to deal with the myriad of issues.

However not all commentators are so unequivocal in their analysis. Many continue to question the use of the criminal law for mere hacking without further damage and

108 For a survey of 'cybercrime specific legislation' in a number of other jurisdictions see Goodman and Brenner, 2002.
109 See, eg, Jackson, 1995. For a survey of the US situation see Conley and Bryan, 1999.

others have questioned some of the concepts which are habitually used in such legislation. Thus Kerr has considered the problems of interpreting commonly used words within computer misuse legislation such as access and authorization.

Cybercrime's scope: interpreting 'access' and 'authorization' in computer misuse statutes
Orin S Kerr
(2003) 78 NYUL Rev 1596, 1642

The history of computer crime law shows courts and legislatures trying to define a legal response to a problem that they only partially understand. In the first two decades, courts struggled to apply preexisting laws against theft and other property crimes to computer misuse. While they reached sensible outcomes in particular cases, no clear principles emerged. When computer misuse threatened or caused substantial harms, courts tended to find it criminal; when it did not, courts interpreted the law narrowly to avoid punishing the computer users. In response to these uncertainties, legislatures enacted computer crime statues that prohibited accessing computers without authorization, and in some cases, exceeding authorized access.

While proponents of the new laws believed that they would cure the old ills, the old ills have re-emerged, albeit in a slightly different form.

REGULATION OF CONTENT
ON COMPUTER NETWORKS

Thus far, the focus of discussion in this chapter has been on crimes related to computer use, either as the means of perpetration for example, fraud, or as newly identified criminal acts for example, hacking or other unauthorized access. The Computer Misuse Act 1990, and similar statutes in other jurisdictions are a particular example of the law's response to some of these activities and, despite the differences between the jurisdictions, shows, in many respects, a remarkable consistency of philosophy and approach. This is especially apparent in relation to the almost universal choice of criminal sanctions as appropriate to penalise such actions.

However, these are not the only activities facilitated by the burgeoning use of computers that have caused discussion and concern. The increase in both the size and the capability of computer networks and, in particular, the development of the internet and the world wide web, have raised a certain amount of disquiet as to the extent to which these media can be used for the propagation of undesirable material. In order to appreciate some of these problems, it is useful to have a rudimentary understanding of the way in which such systems function. The manner of operation of the Internet was set out in *ACLU v Reno I*.[110]

---

110 929 F Supp 824 (ED Pa 1996). See, also, Communication to the European Parliament, the Economic and Social Committee and the Committee of the Regions, *Illegal and Harmful Content on the Internet 2: How does the Internet Work?* COM (1996) 487.

ACLU v Reno I
929 F Supp 824
US DC Penn (1996)
Findings of Fact
The Nature of Cyberspace

The Creation of the Internet and the Development of Cyberspace

1. The Internet is not a physical or tangible entity, but rather a giant network which interconnects numerable smaller groups of linked computer networks. It is thus a network of networks. This is best understood if one considers what a linked group of computers – referred to here as a 'network' – is, and what it does ...

2. Some networks are 'closed' networks, not linked to other computers or networks. Many networks, however, are connected to other networks, which are in turn connected to other networks in a manner which permits each computer in any network to communicate with computers on any other network in the system. This global Web of linked networks and computers is referred to as the Internet.

4. ... The resulting whole is a decentralised, global medium of communications – or 'cyberspace' – that links people, institutions, corporations, and governments around the world. The Internet is an international system. This communications medium allows any of the literally tens of millions of people with access to the Internet to exchange information. These communications can occur almost instantaneously, and can be directed either to specific individuals, to a broader group of people interested in a particular subject, or to the world as a whole ...

9. Messages between computers on the Internet do not necessarily travel entirely along the same path. The Internet uses 'packet switching' communication protocols that allow individual messages to be subdivided into smaller 'packets' that are then sent independently to the destination, and are then automatically reassembled by the receiving computer. While all packets of a given message often travel along the same path to the destination, if computers along the route become overloaded, then packets can be re-routed to less loaded computers ...

11. No single entity – academic, corporate, governmental, or non-profit – administers the Internet. It exists and functions as a result of the fact that hundreds of thousands of separate operators of computers and computer networks independently decided to use common data transfer protocols to exchange communications and information with other computers (which in turn exchange communications and information with still other computers). There is no centralised storage location, control point, or communications channel for the Internet, and it would not be technically feasible for a single entity to control all of the information conveyed on the Internet.

The findings of fact in this case then went on to discuss the different routes by which people might gain access to the internet and the different methods by which they might communicate or retrieve information. These include email, newsgroups, real time interactions, use of distributed databases and remote information retrieval. The most advanced example of this last category is the world wide web, which was described as follows:

The World Wide Web

33. A third approach, and fast becoming the most well known on the Internet, is the 'World Wide Web'. The Web utilises a 'hypertext' formatting language called hypertext markup language (HTML), and programs that 'browse' the Web can display HTML documents containing text, images, sound, animation and moving video. Any HTML document can include links to other types of information or resources, so that while viewing an HTML document that, for example, describes resources available on the Internet, one can 'click' using a computer mouse on the description of the resource and

be immediately connected to the resource itself. Such 'hyperlinks' allow information to be accessed and organised in very flexible ways, and allow people to locate and efficiently view related information even if the information is stored on numerous computers all around the world.

34. *Purpose.* The World Wide Web (W3C) was created to serve as the platform for a global, on-line store of knowledge, containing information from a diversity of sources and accessible to Internet users around the world. Though information on the Web is contained in individual computers, the fact that each of these computers is connected to the Internet through W3C protocols allows all of the information to become part of a single body of knowledge. It is currently the most advanced information system developed on the Internet, and embraces within its data model most information in previous networked information systems ...

45. ... The Web links together disparate information on an ever-growing number of Internet-linked computers by setting common information storage formats (HTML) and a common language for the exchange of Web documents (HTTP). Although the information itself may be in many different formats, and stored on computers which are not otherwise compatible, the basic Web standards provide a basic set of standards which allow communication and exchange of information. Despite the fact that many types of computers are used on the Web, and the fact that many of these machines are otherwise incompatible, those who 'publish' information on the Web are able to communicate with those who seek to access information with little difficulty because of these basic technical standards.

46. ... Running on tens of thousands of individual computers on the Internet, the Web is what is known as a distributed system. The Web was designed so that organisations with computers containing information can become part of the Web simply by attaching their computers to the Internet and running appropriate World Wide Web software. No single organisation controls any membership in the Web, nor is there any single centralised point from which individual Web sites or services can be blocked from the Web. From a user's perspective, it may appear to be a single, integrated system, but in reality it has no centralised control point.

Computer networks thus facilitate communications between both individuals and groups, as well as providing the means to access and retrieve extensive information from a variety of sources across the globe. Not surprisingly, this does not only include educational and informative material, but also includes information that might be undesirable or antisocial. Such material might be defamatory,[111] obscene or pornographic, racist, malicious, threatening or abusive, or may constitute undesirable religious or political propaganda. The following list of areas which might give rise to concern in this respect and are likely to be covered by different national and international legal regimes was provided by the European Commission:[112]

- national security (instructions on bomb making, illegal drug production, terrorist activities);
- protection of minors (abusive forms of marketing, violence, pornography);
- protection of human dignity (incitement to racial hatred or racial discrimination);
- economic security (fraud, instructions on pirating credit cards);
- information security (malicious hacking);

111 See discussion above, Chapter 7.
112 Communication to the European Parliament, fn 110.

- protection of privacy (unauthorised communication of personal data, electronic harassment);

- protection of reputation (libel, unlawful comparative advertising);

- intellectual property (unauthorised distribution of copyrighted works, for example, software or music);

It was suggested that these were 'pressing issues of public, political, commercial and legal interest' which could not be ignored, even while recognising that 'the benefits of the Internet far outweigh its negative aspects'. Such comments have fuelled speculation about the extent to which the law might be able to intervene and regulate the actual content of information that is available on the internet and the world wide web.

It may be that the existing law is not tailored appropriately for application to computer networks but, whatever the law may be in a particular jurisdiction, it is clear that there is unlikely to be consensus between jurisdictions over acceptable standards. Certain governments may be sensitive about the expression of some political or religious views and it is evident that acceptable standards and definitions of obscene or pornographic material will vary from place to place. The practical effect of such divergence was noted by McGuire, in a consideration of the relevant regulatory regimes in Germany and the US. Both of these states provide a constitutional guarantee of freedom of expression but do not exhibit any agreement over what content should be regulated on the internet.[113] Delacourt concurred in this view, noting that 'Germany and the US are at least on the same page with regard to pornography but ... their treatment of divisive political propaganda differs dramatically'.[114] Given the ease of accessing information which originates in another jurisdiction, is it possible to control the propagation of such material or to enforce national laws on a medium which does not recognise national boundaries?

There are also a number of divergent views about the nature of the medium that colour the debate surrounding the basis on which the law might intervene. At one extreme is the view that this global network of computers is a fundamentally anarchic medium which is not, nor should it be, subject to any type of control or regulation. This has even found expression in such comments as 'no law applies to the internet'. Notwithstanding the sentiments of those who espouse this view of the internet, the fallacy behind such a statement should be obvious. Far from there being no law that applies, it is clear that there are a multitude of laws which apply in numerous jurisdictions.[115] However, the application and enforcement of those laws in this area may be so fraught with difficulties as to give the outward appearance that no law applies. Even for those who do not see the internet as completely anarchic, there is a problem in assessing the appropriate analogy to draw with other fora for the access and exchange of information. Is an encounter in cyberspace the equivalent to exchanging gossip at the village meeting place or to participating in a high level conference? Should the same standards be applied as are applied to publishing of hard copy, or to television and radio broadcasts? The fundamental difference between the internet or world wide web and these other forms of communication is that the global

---

113 McGuire, 1999, p 791.
114 Delacourt, 1997, p 214.
115 See above, Chapters 6 and 7, and below, Chapter 9.

network is capable of fulfilling all of these functions simultaneously; thus, in some circumstances, it may be appropriate to utilise similar rules as are used for traditional publication, but at other times such an attempt may be felt to be a violation of the right to free speech, or even the right to privacy.[116]

A centrally important question is, therefore, whether to regulate the internet at all, and if so, in what manner. There is an increasing amount of academic discussion concerning this issue from both a theoretical and practical point of view. Although it is beyond the scope of this book to explore the debate in depth, a brief review of the arguments will serve to place the ensuing discussion of the substantive law in context.

It has become common to speak of the 'online community' and it might be expected that any putative regulation would take this into account.[117] Indeed, the concept of community is a vital one in US jurisprudence for defining the legal meaning of 'obscenity'. The court in *US v Thomas*[118] rejected the notion of a community defined by the linkage of its members in cyberspace and retained the traditional connection between a community and its geographical location, although some commentators take the concept of such a community for granted, if not its identification – 'Due to the very nature of the internet, defining a community by which to judge potentially offensive material is impossible'.[119] Indeed, the very difficulty of connecting activity in cyberspace with a specific physical jurisdiction has led some commentators to suggest that the rules which pertain to cyberspace should evolve in relation to that medium, rather than out of an artificial connection to some geographical location.[120]

For those who think that regulation by law is either infeasible, over-restrictive or simply not appropriate, the alternative is non-regulation or some form of self-regulation.[121] A number of commentators have espoused a variety of self-regulatory regimes with regard to content regulation but, as yet, these have not received any universal acceptance.[122] One possibility is not to regulate at all. Delacourt, whilst acknowledging that this way forward might leave some important concerns unresolved, can nevertheless see some virtues in such an approach.

**The international impact of
Internet regulation
John T Delacourt
(1997) 38 Harv Int LJ 207, p 219**

The most obvious, and most controversial, alternative to this cumbersome web of national and local regimes is to leave the Internet completely unregulated ...

---

116 See, eg, Rowland, 1998.

117 See below, p 465.

118 *US v Thomas* 74 F 3d 701 (6th Cir 1995).

119 Gobla, 1997, p 129; See, also, discussion below of *ACLU v Reno I* and *ACLU v Reno II*.

120 See, eg, Johnson and Post, 1996; Oberding and Norderhaug, 1996. Burk, 1997. Lessig, 1999. Compare, also, Kohl, 1999.

121 See, also, above, p 309 on self-regulatory regimes in the context of privacy regulation.

122 For examples, see, eg, Delacourt, 1997; Gobla, 1997; Akdeniz, 1997. Burton, 1995; McGuire, 1999. See, also, the *Report on Self-Labelling and Filters* at www.ispo.cec.be/iap/INCOREexec. html and below, p 477 et seq on European initiatives.

While far from imaginary ... the dangers of objectionable on-line expression have been overstated. Although some would argue that any amount of obscenity or hate speech is cause for concern, the amount of such expression as a proportion of the enormous total volume of on-line expression does not warrant the amount of attention it has received. The argument that novel features of the new technology magnify the social impact of such expression is similarly one-sided, for there are an equal number of features which minimize such impact. The interactive nature of the Internet will often provide the user with the opportunity to respond instantaneously to the hate speech espoused in a usegroup or Web site, making such postings far less effective than the traditional leaflet. Additionally, the scope and relative complexity of navigating the Internet will often prevent users from finding what they are looking for, much less what they are trying to avoid. Someone who comes across obscenity was probably looking for obscenity and is no more likely to stumble across it than to stumble across song lyrics, techno-babble, or an infinite variety of other things. The relative chaos of the Internet demonstrates another point: the system is in its infancy. As it matures, several developments will take place to limit the amount of objectionable on-line expression ... the demographics of Internet users will diversify. In response to diversification, service providers will vary their offerings, with the elimination of objectionable material as a major selling point ...

An argument for regulation of the Internet to stem the flow of objectionable material also privileges the chaff at the expense of the wheat.

Despite this view, Delacourt nevertheless acknowledges the practical reality that, 'although the arguments for complete non-regulation are compelling, the fact remains that the political pressures which spurred the creation of the national regulatory regimes are not likely to disappear'. Indeed the political and cultural debate concerning internet censorship continues unabated and seems largely unaffected by whatever method of regulation is favoured in a particular jurisdiction. For, as observed by Arasaratnam, 'the debate is confused, emotive and polarised. The protagonists mark out their territory based on flawed assumptions and a passionate belief in the absolute truth of their principles. Conservative groups preach family values, industry focuses on e-commerce and civil libertarians obsess with free speech. It is a collision of values and interests, without room for compromise, pragmatism and discretion.'[123] Notwithstanding, however, some of the perceived problems inherent with application of legal rules to the internet, not all commentators favour a complete abandonment of legal regulation and many commentators combine elements of both pragmatism and idealism. Blume, for instance, points out that there are many areas where legal rules are not fully efficient ... although it must be recognised that the Internet is impossible to regulate completely this does not mean there should be no rules.'[124] On the other hand, influential commentators such as Lessig[125], have suggested that the solution does not lie in law, as such, or at least not solely in law, but in other devices which have a controlling or regulating effect on behaviour. Particular examples are social norms (for example, netiquette within the 'cybercommunity') or what Lessig refers to as 'architecture'[126] – the particular way in which the cyber environment is constructed – which channels users into a single specific mode of conduct, for example use of passwords, filters etc. A detailed assessment of these different regulatory techniques is

---

123 Arasaratnam, 2000, p 205.
124 Blume 2000, p 82.
125 Lessig has written frequently on this topic. See eg, Lessig, 1999.
126 *Ibid* p 509.

beyond the scope of this chapter, suffice it to say that very few areas of regulation would succeed by relying solely on one regulatory method but would respond instead to an appropriate 'regulatory mix'. So, for instance, a mix of legal rules and other regulatory mechanisms may be suitable to achieve the desired result.

Concentrating specifically on legal rules, as discussed below, there have been a variety of ways, all exhibiting varying degrees of success, in which legal regimes have been utilised for the regulation of the internet. These include application of pre-existing law, amendment of existing provisions and also the creation of new law.

Arguably, it is the use of the internet as a medium for the circulation of various types of pornography that has caused the greatest concern and controversy amongst both politicians and the public, and a study of the response to these concerns raises a number of the fundamental issues surrounding regulation of the internet as a whole. In the US, the challenge to the Communications Decency Act of 1996 as being unconstitutional on its face highlighted some of these tensions. This Act included provisions aimed at preventing young people from accessing indecent material over computer networks. It made it a criminal offence to engage in communication on computer networks that is either 'indecent' or 'patently offensive' if the contents of that communication can be viewed by a minor. Neglecting the not inconsiderable difficulty of ascertaining the age of those accessing the material, this was regarded by many as an unacceptable intrusion into the right to free speech, which is protected by the First Amendment to the US Constitution. Accordingly, the American Civil Liberties Union (ACLU) filed a legal challenge to the statute and the case was heard in June 1996.

Having discussed both the mode of operation of the internet and the world wide web and the way in which they were used,[127] the court went on to make some observations that related to the way in which analogies might be drawn between the internet and other methods of obtaining and exchanging information.

ACLU v Reno I
929 F Supp 824
US DC Penn (1996)

75. The internet is not exclusively, or even primarily, a means of commercial communication. Many commercial entities maintain Web sites to inform potential customers about their goods and services ... but many other Web sites exist solely for the dissemination of non-commercial information. The other forms of Internet communication – e-mail, bulletin boards, newsgroups, and chat rooms – frequently have non-commercial goals. ...

79. Because of the different forms of Internet communication, a user of the Internet may speak or listen interchangeably, blurring the distinction between 'speakers' and 'listeners' on the Internet. Chat rooms, email and newsgroups are interactive forms of communication, providing the user with the opportunity both to speak and to listen.

80. It follows that unlike traditional media, the barriers to entry as a speaker on the Internet do not differ significantly from the barriers to entry as a listener. Once one has entered cyberspace, one may engage in the dialogue that occurs there. In the argot of the medium, the receiver can and does become the content provider, and vice versa.

---

127 Extracted above, p 456.

81. The Internet is therefore a unique and wholly new medium of worldwide human communication ...

85. Once a provider posts content on the Internet, it is available to all other Internet users worldwide. Similarly, once a user posts a message to a newsgroup or bulletin board, that message becomes available to all subscribers to that newsgroup or bulletin board ...

86. Once a provider posts its content on the Internet, it cannot prevent that content from entering any community. Unlike the newspaper, broadcast station, or cable system, Internet technology necessarily gives a speaker a potential worldwide audience. Because the Internet is a network of networks ... any network connected to the Internet has the capacity to send and receive information to any other network ...

87 ... it takes several steps to enter cyberspace. At the most fundamental level, a user must have access to a computer with the ability to reach the Internet (typically by way of a modem). A user must then direct the computer to connect with the access provider, enter a password, and enter the appropriate commands to find particular data. On the World Wide Web, a user must normally use a search engine or enter an appropriate address. Similarly, accessing newsgroups, bulletin boards and chat rooms requires several steps.

88. Communications over the Internet do not 'invade' an individual's home or appear on one's computer screen unbidden. Users seldom encounter content 'by accident'. A document's title or a description of the document will usually appear before the document itself takes the step needed to view it, and in many cases the user will receive detailed information about a site's content before he or she need take the step to access the document. Almost all sexually explicit images are preceded by warnings as to the content ...

89 Evidence adduced at the hearing showed significant differences between Internet communications and communications received by radio or television. Although content on the Internet is just a few clicks of a mouse away from the user, the receipt of information on the Internet requires a series of affirmative steps more deliberate and directed than merely turning a dial.

The court then moved on to an analysis of the legal issues in the case. Notwithstanding the guarantee of free speech provided by the First Amendment, it is well established that this guarantee will be forfeited in the case of obscenity and pornography, and there is Federal law which proscribes such activities. The court observed that the existing law was capable of application to whatever medium was used for the dissemination of this type of material and, therefore, could equally be applied to propagation via the internet.[128] Commercial distributors of pornography were unlikely to be caught by the provisions of the Communications Decency Act 1996, as their usual practice was to require credit card validation, thus reducing the likelihood of the material being accessed by minors; in addition, the target of the Act was not

---

128 See, eg, *US v Thomas* 74 F 3d 701 (6th Cir 1995), affirmed by US Court of Appeals Sixth Circuit (29 January 1996). *Thomas* concerned obscene material made available on a bulletin board held on a computer in California. The case came to court in Memphis, Tennessee, where the bulletin board was accessed, on the basis that, in cases involving transportation of obscene material between States, the proper standard to apply is that of the community of the geographic area where the materials are sent. It had been suggested that the 'community standard' test for obscenity set out in *Miller v California* 413 US 15 (1973) should be modified in the light of the creation of 'cyber communities' but this was considered irrelevant on the facts of this particular case, as membership was required before the bulletin board was accessed, which, in practice, meant that some control could be exerted over the likely destination of the files in question. For the law relating to child pornography, in particular, see discussion below at pp 473 and 484.

obscene material but that which was 'indecent' or 'patently offensive'. Although 'obscene' had a recognised meaning,[129] this was not the case with regard to 'indecent' and neither was it defined in the statute. Given the criminal penalties attached to breach of the Act and the difficulties in ascertaining what material would be covered and the range of defendants, the court was unanimously of the opinion that the statute was unconstitutional for reasons of vagueness. In arriving at this conclusion, the judges found evidence that the internet had more in common with telephone conversation than with broadcasting, for instance, and that, based on this reasoning, the Government had little valid pretext for regulating the content.

ACLU v Reno I
929 F Supp 824, 872
US DC Penn (1996)

District Judge Dalzell ... The Internet is a new medium of mass communication. As such, the Supreme Court's First Amendment jurisprudence compels us to consider the special qualities of this new medium in determining whether the CDA is a constitutional exercise of governmental power. Relying on these special qualities, which we have described at length in our findings of fact above, I conclude that the CDA is unconstitutional and that the First Amendment denies Congress the power to regulate protected speech on the Internet ...

Four related characteristics of Internet communication have a transcendent importance to our shared holding that the CDA is unconstitutional on its face ... First, the Internet presents very low barriers to entry. Second, these barriers to entry are identical for both speakers and listeners. Third, as a result of these low barriers, astoundingly diverse content is available on the Internet. Fourth, the Internet provides significant access to all who wish to speak in the medium, and even creates a relative parity among speakers ...

The CDA will, without doubt, undermine the substantive, speech-enhancing benefits that have flowed from the Internet ... The diversity of the content will necessarily diminish as a result. The economic costs associated with compliance with the Act will drive from the Internet speakers whose content falls within the zone of possible prosecution. Many Web sites, newsgroups and chat rooms will shut down, since users cannot discern the age of other participants. In this respect, the Internet would ultimately come to mirror broadcasting and print, with messages tailored to a mainstream society from speakers who could be sure that their message was likely decent in every community in the country ...

The CDA's wholesale disruption on the Internet will necessarily affect adult participation in the medium. As some speakers leave or refuse to enter the medium, and others bowdlerise their speech or erect the barriers that the Act envisions, and still others remove bulletin boards, Web sites and newsgroups, adults will face a shrinking ability to participate in the medium. Since much of the communication on the Internet is participatory, that is, a form of dialogue, a decrease in the number of speakers, speech fora, and permissible topics will diminish the worldwide dialogue that is the strength and signal achievement of the medium ...

... It is no exaggeration to conclude that the Internet has achieved, and continues to achieve, the most participatory marketplace of mass speech that this country – and indeed the world – has yet seen. The plaintiffs in these actions correctly describe the 'democratising' effects of Internet communication: individual citizens of limited means

---

129 *Ibid.*

can speak to a worldwide audience on issues of concern to them. Federalists and Anti-Federalists may debate the structure of their government nightly, but these debates occur in newsgroups or chat rooms rather than in pamphlets. Modern day Luthers still post their theses, but to electronic bulletin boards rather than the door of the Wittenberg Schlosskirche. More mundane (but, from a constitutional perspective, equally important) dialogue occurs between aspiring artists, or French cooks, or dog lovers, or fly fishermen.

Indeed, the Government's asserted 'failure' of the Internet rests on the implicit premise that too much speech occurs in that medium, and that speech there is too available to the participants. This is exactly the benefit of Internet communication, however. The Government, therefore, implicitly asks this court to limit both the amount of speech on the Internet and the availability of that speech. This argument is profoundly repugnant to First Amendment principles ...

The Internet is a far more speech-enhancing medium than print, the village green, or the mails. Because it would necessarily affect the Internet itself, the CDA would necessarily reduce the speech available for adults on the medium. This is a constitutionally intolerable result.

Some of the dialogue on the Internet surely tests the limits of conventional discourse. Speech on the Internet can be unfiltered, unpolished and unconventional, even emotionally charged, sexually explicit and vulgar – in a word, 'indecent' in many communities. But we should expect such speech to occur in a medium in which citizens from all walks of life have a voice. We should also protect the autonomy that such a medium confers to ordinary people as well as media magnates ...

Cutting through the acronyms and argot that littered the hearing testimony, the Internet may fairly be regarded as a never-ending worldwide conversation. The Government may not, through the CDA, interrupt that conversation. As the most participatory form of mass speech yet developed, the Internet deserves the highest protection from governmental intrusion.

True it is that many find some of the speech on the Internet to be offensive, and amid the din of cyberspace many hear discordant voices that they regard as indecent. The absence of governmental regulation of Internet content has unquestionably produced a kind of chaos, but as one of the plaintiffs' experts put it with such resonance at the hearing: what achieved success was the very chaos that the Internet is. The strength of the Internet is that chaos.

Just as the strength of the Internet is chaos, so the strength of our liberty depends upon the chaos and cacophony of the unfettered speech the First Amendment protects.

This decision of the Pennsylvania Court was appealed by the US Government and the Supreme Court upheld the judgment in June 1997, noting that the 'community standards' criterion as applied to the internet means that any communication available to a nationwide audience will be judged by the standards of the community most likely to be offended by the message. Justice Stevens, giving the judgment of the court drew particular attention to factors already underlined in the lower court such as the democratising effect on speech and the growth and acceptance of this mode of communication as well as important issues of proportionality.

Reno v ACLU
136 L Ed 2d 436
US Supreme Court (1997)

This dynamic, multifaceted category of communication includes not only traditional print and news services, but also audio, video, and still images, as well as interactive, real time dialogue. Through the use of chat rooms, any person with a phone line can become a town crier with a voice that resonates farther than it could from any soapbox. Through the use of Web pages, mail exploders, and newsgroups, the same individual can become a pamphleteer ... Given the vague contours of the coverage of the statute, it unquestionably silences some speakers whose messages would be entitled to constitutional protection. That danger provides further reason for insisting that the statute not be overly broad. The CDA's burden on protected speech cannot be justified if it could be avoided by a more carefully drafted statute. ... In order to deny minors access to potentially harmful speech, the CDA effectively suppresses a large amount of speech that adults have a constitutional right to receive and to address to one another. That burden on adult speech is unacceptable if less restrictive alternatives would be at least as effective in achieving the legitimate purpose that the statute was enacted to serve ... The record demonstrates that the growth of the Internet has been and continues to be phenomenal. As a matter of constitutional tradition, in the absence of evidence to the contrary, we presume that governmental regulation of the content of speech is more likely to interfere with the free exchange of ideas than to encourage it. The interest in encouraging freedom of expression in a democratic society outweighs any theoretical but unproven benefit of censorship.

Still considering that the appropriate way forward was by means of legislation to address the perceived problems, in 1998, Congress produced another enactment, the Child On-line Protection Act (COPA), intending to rectify the specific concerns raised in the CDA litigation. The provisions of COPA made it a Federal crime to propagate material online that was 'harmful to minors' for 'commercial purposes' (47 USC s 231(1)). By virtue of 47 USC s 231(e)(2)(A), it would only be inferred that the communication was for commercial purposes if the person was 'engaged in the business of making such communication'. The meaning of this phrase was itself expanded upon in 47 USC s 231(e)(2)(B) in the following terms:

> A person will be deemed to be 'engaged in the business' if the person who makes a communication, or offers to make a communication, by means of the World Wide Web, that includes any material that is harmful to minors, devotes time, attention, or labor to such activities, as a regular course of such person's trade or business, with the objective of earning a profit as a result of such activities (although it is not necessary that the person make a profit or that the making or offering to make such communications be the person's sole or principal business or source of income). A person may be considered to be engaged in the business of making, by means of the World Wide Web, communications for commercial purposes that include material that is harmful to minors, only if the person knowingly causes the material that is harmful to minors to be posted on the World Wide Web or knowingly solicits such material to be posted on the World Wide Web.

The term 'contemporary community standards' was referred to in 47 USC s 231(e)(6), which defined 'harmful to minors' as:

> ... any communication, picture, image, graphic image file, article, recording, writing, or other matter of any kind that is obscene or that –
>
> (A) the average person, applying contemporary community standards, would find, taking the material as a whole and with respect to minors, is designed to appeal to, or is designed to pander to, the prurient interest;
>
> (B) depicts, describes, or represents, in a manner patently offensive with respect to minors, an actual or simulated sexual act or sexual contact, an actual or simulated normal or perverted sexual act, or a lewd exhibition of the genitals or post-pubescent female breast; and
>
> (C) taken as a whole, lacks serious literary, artistic, political, or scientific value for minors.

Defences were available where it could be shown that attempts had been made, in good faith, to restrict access to minors by requiring, for example, credit card verification or identity number, or age verification by digital certificate or other appropriate technological means.

This statute was again the subject of an immediate challenge by the ACLU and others, on the basis that it was:

(a) invalid on its face and as applied to them under the First Amendment for burdening speech that is constitutionally protected for adults;

(b) invalid on its face for violating the First Amendment rights of minors; and

(c) unconstitutionally vague under the First and Fifth Amendments.

The government had put forward the view that the provisions challenged were aimed at commercial pornographers and that the interpretation of the statute could be restricted in this way, an argument which was given short shrift by the court.

ACLU v Reno II
31 F Supp 2d 473
ED Pa (1999)

5. There is nothing in the text of the COPA, however, that limits its applicability to so called commercial pornographers only; indeed, the text of COPA imposes liability on a speaker who knowingly makes any communication for commercial purposes 'that includes any material that is harmful to minors', and defines a speaker that is engaged in the business as one who makes a communication 'that includes any material that is harmful to minors … as a regular course of such person's trade or business (although it is not necessary that the person make a profit or that the making or offering to make such communications be the person's sole or principal business or source of income)'. Because COPA applies to communications which include, but are not necessarily wholly comprised of material that is harmful to minors, it logically follows that it would apply to any Web site that contains only some harmful to minors material.

Like its predecessor, the CDA, the court was of the view that COPA infringed the right of adults to freedom of speech and expression, concluding, albeit somewhat reluctantly, that 'the protection of children from access to harmful to minors materials on the web, the compelling interest sought to be furthered by Congress in COPA, particularly resonates with the court' and that its decision to allow an injunction against enforcement would 'delay once again the careful protection of our children'. However, the court was 'acutely cognizant of its charge under the law of this country not to protect the majoritarian will at the expense of stifling the rights embodied in the Constitution' and so issued a preliminary injunction.

This injunction was upheld by the US Court of Appeals for the Third Circuit but, interestingly, for the purposes of the academic debate on community in cyberspace, Circuit Judge Garth focused on the impossibility of determining 'contemporary community standards'.

ACLU v Reno II
217 F 3d 162, 166
US Ct App 3rd Cir (2000)

Because material posted on the Web is accessible by all Internet users worldwide, and because current technology does not permit a Web publisher to restrict access to its site based on the geographic locale of each particular Internet user, COPA essentially requires that every Web publisher subject to the statute abide by the most restrictive and conservative state's community standards in order to avoid criminal liability. Thus, because the standard by which COPA gauges whether material is 'harmful to minors' is based on identifying 'contemporary community standards' the inability of Web publishers to restrict access to their Web sites based on the geographic locale of the site visitor, in and of itself, imposes an impermissible burden on constitutionally protected First Amendment speech ...

We base our particular determination of COPA's likely unconstitutionality, however, on COPA's reliance on 'contemporary community standards' in the context of the electronic medium of the Web to identify material that is harmful to minors. The overbreadth of COPA's definition of 'harmful to minors' applying a 'contemporary community standards' clause – although virtually ignored by the parties and the amicus in their respective briefs but raised by us at oral argument – so concerns us that we are persuaded that this aspect of COPA, without reference to its other provisions, must lead inexorably to a holding of a likelihood of unconstitutionality of the entire COPA statute. ...

Unlike a "brick and mortar outlet" with a specific geographic locale, and unlike the voluntary physical mailing of material from one geographic location to another, as in Miller, the uncontroverted facts indicate that the Web is *not geographically constrained.* ...

In fact, *Miller*, the very case from which the government derives its 'community standards' concept, has made clear that community standards are to be construed in a localized geographic context.

The court thus came to the conclusion that the concept of contemporary community standards, derived from *Miller*, was not applicable in this situation although it remained 'a useful and viable tool in contexts *other than* the Internet and the Web'. Since the statute depended heavily on this concept the decision was that COPA was also too broad. Nevertheless, the court referred to 'Congress' laudatory attempt to achieve its compelling objective of protecting minors from harmful material on the World Wide Web'. This decision was not, however, the last word on the case. The Supreme Court considered specifically the rejection of the *Miller* test and disagreed with the finding that it was not appropriate in the context of the internet.

Ashcroft v ACLU
535 US 564, 583
US Supreme Court (2002)

Justice Thomas: If a publisher chooses to send its material into a particular community, this Court's jurisprudence teaches that it is the publisher's responsibility to abide by that community's standards. The publisher's burden does not change simply because it decides to distribute its material to every community in the Nation ... Nor does it change because the publisher may wish to speak only to those in a 'community where *avant garde* culture is the norm ... but nonetheless utilizes a medium that transmits its speech from coast to coast. If a publisher wishes for its material to be judged only by the standards of particular communities, then it need only take the simple step of utilizing a medium that enables it to target the release of its material into those communities ...

The scope of our decision today is quite limited. We hold only that COPA's reliance on community standards to identify 'material that is harmful to minors' does not *by itself* render the statute substantially overbroad for purposes of the First Amendment. We do not express any view as to whether COPA suffers from substantial overbreadth for other reasons, whether the statute is unconstitutionally vague, or whether the District Court correctly concluded that the statute likely will not survive strict scrutiny analysis once adjudication of the case is completed below.

The decision was not reached without dissent, Justice Stevens emphasising some of the material differences between cyberspace and real space:

community standards originally served as a shield to protect speakers from the least tolerant members of society. By aggregating values at the community level, the test eliminated the outliers at both ends of the spectrum and provided some predictability as to what constitutes obscene speech. But community standards also serve as a shield to protect audience members, by allowing people to self-sort based on their preferences. Those who abhor and those who tolerate sexually explicit speech can seek out like-minded people and settle in communities that share their views on what is acceptable for themselves and their children. This sorting mechanism, however, does not exist in cyberspace; the audience cannot self-segregate. As a result, in the context of the Internet this shield also becomes a sword, because the community that wishes to live without certain material rids not only itself, but the entire Internet, of the offending speech.

As the decision had focused on merely one possible avenue for a finding of unconstitutionality, the case was remanded to the Third Circuit for further consideration. On this occasion, the court[130] considered both whether COPA could withstand strict scrutiny, that is, whether the statute served a compelling governmental interest, whether it was narrowly tailored to achieve that interest and was the least restrictive means of advancing that interest, and also whether it was overbroad. Although accepting that there was a compelling interest, the court found a number of the provisions not to be narrowly tailored eg, the definitions of 'material harmful to minors' and 'commercial purposes'. In addition, in considering less restrictive means of achieving the same objective, there was significant discussion of the use of technological devices such as filters in place of legislation and the conclusion was reached that 'the various blocking and filtering techniques ... may be substantially less restrictive than COPA ...'.[131] By this route the case arrived back at the Supreme Court having not yet been the subject of a full trial. The Supreme Court affirmed the decision of the Third Circuit Court of Appeals, upholding the basis for the injunction. Justice Kennedy began the judgment of the court by making the general comment that 'content-based prohibitions, enforced by severe criminal penalties, have the constant potential to be a repressive force in the lives and thoughts of a free people'. The decision then focused particularly on the 'least restrictive means' and the use of filtering software. The court seemed particularly keen that the use of filters should be considered in more detail on the basis that they could potentially be both less restrictive and more effective.

Ashcroft v ACLU
124 S Ct 2783, 2792
US Supreme Court (2004)

Filters are less restrictive than COPA. They impose selective restrictions on speech at the receiving end, not universal restrictions at the source. Under a filtering regime, adults without children may gain access to speech they have a right to see without having to identify them-selves or provide their credit card information. Even adults with children may obtain access to the same speech on the same terms simply by turning off the filter on their home computers. Above all, promoting the use of filters does not condemn as criminal any category of speech, and so the potential chilling effect is eliminated, or at least much diminished. All of these things are true, moreover, regardless of how broadly or narrowly the definitions in COPA are construed.

---

130 322 F 3d 240, (3rd Cir. 2003).
131 *Ibid*, p 265.

Filters also may well be more effective than COPA. First, a filter can prevent minors from seeing all pornography, not just pornography posted to the Web from America. ... COPA does not prevent minors from having access to those foreign harmful materials. That alone makes it possible that filtering software might be more effective in serving Congress' goals. Effectiveness is likely to diminish even further if COPA is upheld, because the providers of the materials that would be covered by the statute simply can move their operations overseas. It is not an answer to say that COPA reaches some amount of materials that are harmful to minors; the question is whether it would reach more of them than less restrictive alternatives. In addition, the District Court found that verification systems may be subject to evasion and circumvention, for example by minors who have their own credit cards. ... Finally, filters also may be more effective because they can be applied to all forms of Internet communication, including e-mail, not just communications available via the World Wide Web.

What are we to make of all the judicial activity on this topic? As pointed out by Justice Breyer, dissenting in *Ashcroft v ACLU*, 'after eight years of legislative effort, two statutes and three Supreme Court cases the Court sends this case back to the District Court for further proceedings. What proceedings? I have found no offer by either party to present more relevant evidence. What remains to be litigated?'.[132] What is clear is that there are strong lobbies on either side of the argument and that the strong judicial protection for free speech continues to be upheld by the Supreme Court. However, in the latest judgment, it was noted that the opinion 'does not hold that Congress is incapable of enacting any regulation of the Internet designed to prevent minors form gaining access to harmful materials.' Further, despite Justice Breyer's view, the court's opinion did not 'foreclose the District Court from concluding, upon a proper showing by the Government, ... that COPA is the least restrictive alternative available to accomplish Congress' goal.' In considering the role of the criminal law and the 'persistent efforts by Congress to restrict the access of minors to pornographic material on the Internet', Husak suggests that the answer may lie in a combination of techniques rather than success for one lobby and failure for the other.

The criminal law as last resort
Douglas Husack
[2004] OJLS 207

Is criminal liability for persons who post obscene depictions that are accessible to children a necessary means to achieve this objective? Those who challenge such proposals argue that filters are equally effective in shielding minors from pornography. But existing filtering technology is imperfect, and some obscene sites are bound to slip through the cracks. Why, then, not ask whether criminal prohibitions and filters do a better job than either device by itself? As far as I can tell, courts do not entertain this option; they strike a challenged proscription after concluding that filtering technology is at least as successful as a criminal statute in restricting the access of minors to pornography. Presumably, the alternative that represents the union of criminal and non-criminal strategies is not evaluated because the prohibitions burden a fundamental liberty of adult users and website operators. Fundamental liberates are so important that they may be burdened only when necessary; slight gains in attaining the legislative objective are insufficient to satisfy the demanding standard when non-criminal alternatives do nearly as well.

---

132 124 S Ct 2783, 2805.

Many other jurisdictions have also introduced legislation purporting to regulate the content and use of information on the internet. Below is just a sample of that activity, but there are a number of sources which can be accessed for an overview of legislative activity on this topic in many more states.[133] Reaction to this legislative activity has been mixed, although none has precipitated the volume of litigation that has been seen in the US. A number of States in Australia, for example, introduced legislation in the 1990s aimed both at restricting access to certain material on the internet and controlling content, but with little opportunity for public debate on the issue.[134] In the belief that 'responsible online content regulation will help to create an environment in which the Internet's positive opportunities and advantages are able to be nurtured, developed and accessed by a growing number of citizens, while allowing the proper concerns of current and future users to be addressed',[135] this was followed by action at Commonwealth level in the Broadcasting Services Amendment (Online Services) Act 1999 (the 'Online Services Act').[136] This statute came into force at the beginning of 2000 and applies the same level of censorship to the internet as is applied to films and videos by using the same classification system. Action under the statute is mainly initiated as a result of complaints. The Australian Broadcasting Agency, which is the enforcing authority, is empowered to make its own investigations, but is not required to actively police the network for unsuitable content. The Act applies to material hosted both within and without Australia, although there are different procedures which are initiated depending on the origin of the prohibited or restricted material. The Act has had a mixed reception; criticism has been based on a questioning of the underlying rationale;[137] of the difficulties of ensuring compliance;[138] and on wider concerns about restrictions on freedom of expression.[139] On the other hand, some have taken the pragmatic approach that, whatever the imperfections of the new regime, it should be welcomed because 'the internet's power and (potential) persuasiveness make it crucial to immediately begin trying to develop an effective and usable system for extending classification to it. ... the "Online Services Act" represents a useful first step in that direction.'[140]

In Singapore, the preferred method has been to introduce 'a licensing scheme that aims to safeguard public morals, political stability and religious harmony'.[141] This is now administered by the Singapore Media Development Authority.[142] It describes

---

133 For a general consideration of the situation in a number of jurisdictions see eg, 'Internet censorship: law and policy around the world' www.efa.org.au/Issues/Censor/cens3.html, 'The internet under surveillance: obstacles to the free flow of information online' www.rsf.org/rubrique.php3?id_rubrique=378, 'Free expression on the internet' www.hrw.org/advocacy/internet/index.htm

134 See, eg, Greenleaf, 1996.

135 Corker, et al, 2000.

136 See www.austlii.edu.au/au/legis/cth/num_act/bsasa1999n901999476/sch1.html.

137 See eg, Chen, 2000; Heitman, 2000, expresses the view that making an analogy with television and film was a tragic fallacy.

138 See eg, Chen, ibid, Arasaratnam, 2000 and also Argy, 2000.

139 See eg, Voon, 2001; Trager and Turner, 2000.

140 Handsley and Biggins, 2000.

141 www.mda.gov.sg.

142 'Internet regulation to start on Monday' (1996) Straits Times, 13 July.

itself as providing a 'three-pronged approach comprising of joint government and industry initiatives as well as public involvement to encourage the healthy development of the Internet' which emphasises a light regulatory touch, the promotion of industry self regulation and the increasing of public awareness.[143] All ISPs are subject to a class licence[144] and must, *inter alia*, block access to any site which is considered to be against the public interest, public order or national harmony, offends against public decency or violates a relevant code of practice. The Singapore Internet Code of Practice[145] defines prohibited material as follows:

Internet Code of Practice
Paragraph 4

Prohibited material

(1) Prohibited material is material that is objectionable on the grounds of public interest, public morality, public order, public security, national harmony, or is otherwise prohibited by applicable Singapore laws.

(2) In considering what is prohibited material, the following factors should be taken into account:

(a) whether the material depicts nudity or genitalia in a manner calculated to titillate;

(b) whether the material promotes sexual violence or sexual activity involving coercion or non-consent of any kind;

(c) whether the material depicts a person or persons clearly engaged in explicit sexual activity;

(d) whether the material depicts a person who is, or appears to be, under 16 years of age in sexual activity, in a sexually provocative manner or in any other offensive manner;

(e) whether the material advocates homosexuality or lesbianism, or depicts or promotes incest, paedophilia, bestiality and necrophilia;

(f) whether the material depicts detailed or relished acts of extreme violence or cruelty;

(g) whether the material glorifies, incites or endorses ethnic, racial or religious hatred, strife or intolerance.

(3) A further consideration is whether the material has intrinsic medical, scientific, artistic or educational value.

(4) A licensee who is in doubt as to whether any content would be considered prohibited may refer such content to the Authority for its decision.

In practice, although Internet Content Providers have to exercise their judgment and not place anything on the internet defined as prohibited materials under the code of practice, the main concern of the MDA seems to be with pornography, violence and incitement of racial or religious hatred.[146] However there have been reports that censorship also takes place of sites which are critical of the government.[147]

---

143 See www.mda.gov.sg/medium/internet/i_framework.html.
144 For conditions see www.mda.gov.sg/medium/internet/i_classlicence.html.
145 See www.mda.gov.sg/medium/internet/i_codenpractice.html.
146 See app.mda.gov.sg/scripts/MDA/faq/faq.asp?category=Internet.
147 See *The internet under surveillance* www.rsf.org/article.php3?id_article=7247.

In recent years China has issued many regulations attempting to censor the internet and restrict access only to sites which will assist in the economic development of the country. In the rest of the world this has been most apparent when sites outside China have been blocked,[148] but it appears that the Chinese authorities are far more effective at enforcing the law within China as then direct action can be taken against both content and service provider.[149]

Reference has already been made to the difference in approach between Germany and the US. At the end of 1995, a situation arose in Bavaria which was subsequently to receive worldwide attention. In November, a police search on a court order showed that customers of the ISP, CompuServe Germany, could access certain pornographic sites. As a result of this search, the police produced a list of unacceptable newsgroups containing representations of violent, child or animal pornography and, after communication with the parent company, CompuServe USA, access to these sites was blocked from 22 December 1995 until 13 February 1996. During this, albeit short, period, no customers of CompuServe worldwide could access the sites in question, showing the potential for the actions of a small jurisdiction to have a global effect. In February, access was restored but customers in Germany were offered free blocking software.

Despite the provision of this software, the offending sites could still be accessed by German customers and, eventually, the local manager of CompuServe Germany, Felix Somm, was charged with assisting in the dissemination of pornographic writings contrary to s 184 of the German Penal Code. Section 5 of the German Telecommunications Service Law, which came into force on 1 August 1997,[150] provides exemption from liability for 'access providers' and in other cases restricts liability to those situations where the ISP is aware of the content and does not take reasonable steps to deal with the situation.[151] At the trial in May 1998, neither of these provisions assisted Somm. CompuServe Germany was held not to be an access provider, as it did not connect customers to computer networks as such, but merely to its parent company. On the issue of the requisite knowledge, an interesting debate occurred due to the evidence of an expert witness, who pointed out that Somm could not have been expected to be aware of the actual content of the material, which was placed on the server in the US.[152] As a result of this testimony, even the State prosecutor argued against a finding of guilt. The court did not agree and Somm was given a two-year suspended sentence. This led to both prosecution and defence appealing and he was eventually acquitted at the appeal before the Landgericht München in November 1999. The defence for Somm commented that the case showed that, for effective regulation of the internet, 'there are no alternatives to international legal harmonisation and international co-operation'.[153]

148 For example, the search engine 'Google' was blocked by China for a period in 2002.
149 See http://en.wikipedia.org/wiki/Internet_censorship_in_China and the relevant parts of the reports cited in fn 133.
150 Available in English at www.iid.de/rahmen/inkdgebt.html.
151 Cf the Defamation Act 1996, discussed above, p 408.
152 See www.eim.de/sep-98-3.htm.
153 Available at www.apic.net/mailing-lists/apple/9911/msg00010.html; see, also, Palfrey, 1996, who suggests international co-operation to combat those who disseminate illegal and harmful material via the internet, along the same model as is currently in use for policing of money laundering activities.

In the UK, the debate has centred on the extent to which existing laws are adequate to deal with the distribution of pornography on the internet,[154] and also the extent to which they are capable of dealing with instances in which children are exposed to material intended only for an adult audience, as well as instances when the internet is used to propagate child pornography. Parliament recognised the widespread concern surrounding the perceived proliferation of 'indecent' material available via the internet and convened a Home Affairs Committee to investigate the matter.[155] The Committee defined pornography as 'obscene and indecent images and sounds which are stored, transmitted or viewed using computer technology'. They were given a wide brief to examine and assess the extent of the problems caused by the use of information technology to disseminate such material, and the likelihood of additional problems arising as a result of the development of the relevant technologies, and, in particular, to ascertain whether any changes in legislation were required to deal with existing and potential concerns relating to computer pornography. In the event, although the possibility of dedicated legislation at some future date was not ruled out, the Committee decided that it was possible to deal with the matter by amending the existing legislation to make it clear that it applied equally to the dissemination of material via computer networks. Their recommendations were given effect in the Criminal Justice and Public Order Act 1994, which amended certain sections of the Obscene Publications Act 1959 and the Protection of Children Act 1978.

Section 1(1) of the Obscene Publications Act 1959 makes it a criminal offence to publish any obscene article. 'Article' is defined as 'any description containing or embodying matter to be read or looked at or both, any sound record, any film etc'. Unlike the standard in the US, which allows for different standards in different communities, such matter will be obscene if, taken as a whole, it is such as to 'tend to deprave and corrupt persons likely to read, see or hear matter contained or embodied in it'. To avoid any possibility that 'article' could be construed as not including information on computer, this section was amended by the Criminal Justice and Public Order Act 1994 to include the transmission of electronically stored data which, on resolution into user-viewable form, is obscene. As the definition of 'publication' includes distribution, circulation, etc, this could have the effect of making a network provider liable for obscene material, as well as the originator of that information.

There may be more specific offences applicable to particular types of material, for example, offences under the Children and Young Persons (Harmful Publications) Act 1955, which applies to any book, magazine or other like work which is of a kind likely to fall into the hands of children and young persons. Such publications have to be pictorial in the main to attract the provisions of this Act and include stories portraying 'the commission of crimes, acts of violence or cruelty or incidents of a repulsive or horrible nature in such a way that the work as a whole would tend to corrupt a child or young person'. In the absence of specific amendments, the application of this statute will rest on whether an interpretation of 'other like work' includes material available on computer.

Provisions that criminalise paedophilia are also likely to be of relevance, especially as this is a type of behaviour of which there appears to be universal condemnation and whose adherents have made full use of the facilities for dissemination of material

---

154 See, eg, Manchester, 1995; Gibbons, 1995.
155 HC No 126, *Computer Pornography*, 1993–94.

offered by the internet. The Protection of Children Act 1978 creates offences relating to the display and distribution of indecent photographs of children. These provisions have also been amended by the Criminal Justice and Public Order Act 1994 to include both photographs and pseudo-photographs, the latter referring to computer generated or partially computer generated images of children.

Protection of Children Act 1978 s 1
as amended

It is an offence for a person –

(a) to take, or permit to be taken, or to make any indecent photograph or pseudo-photograph of a child; or

(b) to distribute or show such indecent photographs or pseudo-photographs; or

(c) to have in his possession such indecent photographs or pseudo-photographs with a view to their being distributed or shown by himself or others; or

(d) to publish or cause to be published any advertisement likely to be misunderstood as conveying that the advertiser distributes or show such indecent photographs or pseudo-photographs or intends to do so.

Section 160(1) of the Criminal Justice Act 1988 goes further and makes the mere fact of possession of such material an offence an offence. Data stored on a computer disk or other electronic means that is capable of conversion into a photograph or 'pseudo-photograph' is also included.[156] The interpretation of these sections has been discussed in *R v Fellows and Arnold*.[157] Here, the Court of Appeal dismissed an appeal against convictions for possessing indecent photographs of a child, having an obscene article for publication and distributing indecent photographs, the material in question being available over a computer network. The defendants had contended that such computer data did not constitute a photograph for the purposes of s 1 of the 1978 Act and that the data were not, in any event distributed or shown merely by reason of being made available for downloading. Evans LJ decided that:

> ... although the computer disk was not a photograph it was a copy of an indecent photograph. The disk contained data not visible to the eye, which could be converted by appropriate technical means into a print which exactly reproduced the original photograph from which it was derived. It was a form of copy which made the original photograph, or a copy of it, available for viewing by a person with access to the disk.[158]

In the case of *R v Bowden* the Court of Appeal (criminal division) considered whether downloading such images from the internet should be construed as 'making ' or 'possessing'. Although both are offences making a pseudo-photograph is considered a more heinous offence and is subject to a more severe sentence than mere possession.[159]. It could be argued that downloading images is more analogous to possession since, if the material were acquired by traditional means, there would be no suggestion of 'making' of an image.[160] However because of the nature of the technology and the objective of the statute, the court inclined to the view that

---

156 Protection of Children Act 1978 s 7(4)(b). For a review of cases relating to child pornography on the internet see, eg, Akdeniz, 1997.

157 [1997] 2 All ER 548 and see case note by Cobley, 1997; Palfrey, 1997.

158 [1997] 2 All ER 548.

159 Cf. Obscene Publications Act where there is no offence based on mere possession.

160 See also Gillespie, 2003.

a person who either downloads images onto a disk or who prints them off is making them. The Act is not only concerned with the original creation of images but also their proliferation. Photographs or pseudo-photographs found on the internet may have originated from outside the United Kingdom; to download or print within the jurisdiction is to create new material which hitherto may not have existed therein.[161]

Atkins v DPP,[162] an appeal by way of case stated, concerned not only downloading from the internet, but also the question of whether images stored in the computer's cache were either 'made' or 'possessed'. It was submitted in this case that *Bowden* was wrongly decided but, although the divisional court declined to follow this, it did decide that this could not be extended to the inadvertent storing or unintentional making of images in the cache, an issue which had not been raised in *Bowden*. Neither could the storage in the cache constitute possession in the absence of the knowledge of the defendant.[163] It will thus be a matter of fact, to be decided in every case, whether the defendant had the requisite knowledge. *Bowden* and *Atkins* were considered in the later cases of *Smith* and *Jayson*. This appeal considered two separate cases, both involving the alleged making of indecent pseudo-photographs of a child, one by opening an email attachment, and the other by downloading directly from the internet. In each case, temporary copies were also made in the computer cache. The judgment underlined how important the factual matrix is in such cases, since it was shown that the defendant, Smith, had good reason to believe that the attachment in question contained illicit images. But it seems that the every fact of opening such an attachment will not inevitably criminalise the unsuspecting and the unwary.

R v Smith, R v Jayson
[2003] 1 Cr App R 13
Court of Appeal (Criminal Division)

19. If this were a case ... of a person simply opening an unsolicited e-mail message and opening the attachments to it in ignorance of their actual or likely contents, we would have no difficulty in holding that the facts did not disclose an offence of making, contrary to s. 1(1)(a) of the 1978 Act, or indeed of being in possession contrary to s. 160(1) of the 1988 Act. For the reasons given by Simon Brown LJ in Atkins, these are not absolute offences. He held that the offence of making did not encompass the unintentional making of copies by images being automatically stored in the cache; and the offence of being in possession did not encompass having images stored in the cache, the existence of which was unknown to the appellant. By parity of reasoning, it seems to us that if the appellant had not known that the attachment contained or was likely to contain indecent photographs or pseudo-photographs of a child, he could not be guilty of the offence of making those photographs or pseudo-photographs when he opened the e-mail and its attachments. Nor could he have been guilty of making the photographs by the automatic storing of them in the cache if he was unaware of the existence of the cache.

The above cases suggest that downloading of images and copying onto disk or other storage medium will be regarded as the more serious offence of making a pseudo-photograph, notwithstanding analogies which could be made with activities using

---

161 [2000] 1 Cr App R 438; [2000] 2 All ER 418.
162 [2000] 2 Cr App R 248; [2000] 1 WLR 1427.
163 See also Criminal Justice Act 1988 s 160(2)(b) and compare also the situation in the Trojan horse cases discussed above at p 451.

traditional media. Since the above cases there has been general amendment and enhancement of the law relating to child pornography and, more generally, in relation to sexual offences involving children in the Sexual Offences Act 2003. This amends the definition of child in the Protection of Children Act (from 16 to 18 yrs), introduces new offences relating to child pornography[164] and provides new defences in respect of indecent images.[165] These are general offences and so will apply to the internet as to other methods of creation and dissemination. A further offence introduced by s 15 of the 2003 Act is directed at the conduct known as 'grooming', in which adults gain the confidence of children on prior occasions with the intention of committing a sexual offence at a later date.[166] This preparatory behaviour often takes place in internet chatrooms and so this new provision is expected to close the previous loophole in the law in this respect.[167]

Notwithstanding the applicability of the offences described above to material made available over the network, a problem may arise where the source of the material is outside the UK jurisdiction. Where the offence is one in which mere possession of the offending material is sufficient, there may be still a defendant who can be apprehended in the UK courts. This may not be the case where the offence is one of 'publication'. In such a case, the relevant issue may be whether the offending material can be construed as an 'article' for the purposes of s 46 of the Customs Consolidation Act 1876, which prohibits the importation into the UK of 'indecent or obscene prints, paintings, books, cards, lithographic or other engravings, or any other indecent or obscene articles'. HM Customs and Excise believe that this section would not apply where the offending material was made available in the UK via telephone lines, although it would be expected to apply to pornographic material which entered the country on disk.[168] Manchester, mindful of the wide construction of certain concepts that the courts have used in other cases involving pornography, suggests a possible avenue for judicial creativity in this area which is remarkably reminiscent of arguments voiced in other areas of law, discussed elsewhere in this work.[169]

Computer pornography
Colin Manchester
[1995] Crim LR 546, p 553

... it is not inconceivable for the terms 'articles' and 'goods', as defined [in s 46 of the Customs Consolidation Act 1876], to be used to describe intangible matter such as information held on computer disks. Both terms make reference to 'property' and the concept of intangible property is well recognised in law, for example, copyright in published works. If the reference to 'property' is widely interpreted, this could encompass intangible information held on computer disk and this could certainly be 'movable property', thereby falling within the definition of 'goods', since it can be moved (electronically) from a computer in one place to a computer in another place. Similarly, the term 'item' in the definition of 'article' might be employed to describe an 'item of

---

164 Ss 48–50.
165 Ss 45 and 46; See discussion in Gillespie, 2004.
166 For a review of this provision see Spencer, 2003.
167 See eg, Gillespie, 2001.
168 See eg, Manchester, 1995, p 552.
169 See, eg, the discussion above, p 435, of the decision in *Cox v Riley*, and the discussion of software as goods, above, p 138 et seq.

information', even though the information is not in tangible form. Further, if particular information is held on computer disk along with other information, the particular information might constitute a 'separate element, member or part of anything' viz part of the information held on the disk. If this article on 'Computer pornography' had been written abroad on a word processor, saved on computer disk and transmitted electronically to the *Criminal Law Review*, would it really be straining language too far to say that there had been an importation of an article into the country?

EUROPEAN AND INTERNATIONAL INITIATIVES

The so called information society is an important phenomenon for the European Union (EU), representing as it does a whole new market in services and products. The institutions of the EU have, therefore, not been slow to realise the importance of a suitable legal framework within which the new technology can operate. The major thrust of such initiatives is facilitatory – to enable enterprises within the EU to gain full advantage of new technologies and to ensure that any barriers to the provision of services or threats to competitiveness are removed or minimised.

This does not mean that any negative aspects of the market in information and services available via computer networks have been ignored, and there has been significant activity which demonstrates this fact. In 1996, a Green Paper on the *Protection of Minors and Human Dignity in Audiovisual and Information Services* was published,[170] which was followed by the Commission's communication, *Illegal and Harmful Content on the Internet*.[171] As there is no competence, as such, to legislate on criminal matters, it is for the Member States to respond as appropriate, although competence will be retained where the regulation of the activity in question might threaten the operation of the internal market:

> As regards the distribution of illegal content on the Internet, it is clearly the responsibility of Member States to ensure the application of existing laws. What is illegal off-line remains illegal on-line, and it is up to Member States to enforce these laws ... At another level, the presence of illegal and harmful content on the Internet has direct repercussions on the workings of the internal market. In particular, the adoption by Member States of regulations of new Internet services intended to protect the public interest may also create risks of distortions of competition (for example, through widely divergent responses to the question of potential liability of Internet service providers), hamper the free circulation of these services, and lead to a re-fragmentation of the internal market. If unsolved, such problems may justify Community intervention.

The communication goes on to advocate a combination of self-regulation supplemented by technical solutions to deal with 'illegal content' on the internet, but encounters problems when considering 'harmful content', due to the potential conflicts with the right to freedom of expression and also with the legal framework of the internal market, the competition rules and the principle of the free provision of services. This discussion also implicitly presumes that there is no overlap between what is actually illegal and what might be considered merely harmful either in individual Member States or between Member States, and that there will be some

---

170 COM (1996) 483 final.
171 Communication to the European Parliament, fn 110.

consensus about what is included in these terms. In respect of the free movement of goods, the European Court of Justice has already been able to extend a wide margin of appreciation to Member States to enable them to define acceptable standards for their own territory, even where this might restrict the free movement of goods.[172] The basic position is set out in the case of *R v Henn and Darby*.

Case 34/79 *R v Henn and Darby*
[1979] ECR 3795, p 3813
European Court of Justice

Under the terms of Article 36 of the Treaty the provisions relating to the free movement of goods within the Community are not to preclude prohibitions on imports which are justified *inter alia* 'on grounds of public morality'. In principle, it is for each Member State to determine in accordance with its own scale of values and in the form selected by it the requirements of public morality in its territory … Each Member State is entitled to impose prohibitions on imports justified on the grounds of public morality for the whole of its territory … whatever the structure of its constitution may be and however the powers of legislating in regard to the subject in question may be distributed.

This general statement is subject to the proviso that such measures should not constitute arbitrary discrimination, as explained in the later case of *Conegate v HM Customs and Excise*.

Case 121/85 *Conegate v HM Customs and Excise*
[1986] ECR 1007, p 1022
European Court of Justice

… although Community law leaves Member States free to make their own assessments of the indecent or obscene character of certain articles, it must be pointed out that the fact that goods cause offence cannot be regarded as sufficiently serious to justify restrictions on the free movement of goods where the Member State concerned does not adopt, with respect to the same goods manufactured or marketed within its territory, penal measures or other serious and effective measures intended to prevent the distribution of such goods in its territory. It follows that a Member State may not rely on grounds of public morality in order to prohibit the importation of goods from other Member States when its legislation contains no prohibition as to manufacture or marketing of the same goods on its territory.

This approach has effectively been reiterated by the Commission in relation to the provision of information services:

What is considered to be harmful depends on cultural differences. Each country may reach its own conclusion in defining the borderline between what is permissible and not permissible. It is therefore indispensable that international initiatives take into account different ethical standards in different countries in order to explore appropriate rules to protect people against offensive material whilst ensuring freedom of expression.

However, in the event of substantial differences in attitude between different Member States, it is more difficult to see how this might be accommodated in practice, in relation to information services, without compromising the free market in those services.

---

172 See the EC Treaty, Arts 28, 30.

These early initiatives have been developed further and, interestingly in the light of the approach taken in some other jurisdictions, more recent documents, in particular, have stressed the value and role of self-regulatory mechanisms, both within and without a more formal regulatory framework. This is particularly evident in Decision 276/1999 of the European Parliament and Council, which puts forward a four year plan to combat illegal and harmful content on global networks.

Adopting a Multiannual Community Action Plan on
Promoting Safer Use of the Internet by Combating
Illegal and Harmful Content on Global Networks
Decision No 276/1999/EC, 25 January 1999
[1999] OJ L 33/1

Article 2

The action plan has the objective of promoting safer use of the Internet and of encouraging, at European level, an environment favourable to the development of the Internet industry.

Article 3

In order to attain the objective referred to in Article 2, the following actions supporting and promoting measures to be taken in the Member States shall be undertaken under the guidance of the Commission ...

– promotion of industry self-regulation and content-monitoring schemes ...;

– encouraging industry to provide filtering tools and rating systems, which allow parents or teachers to select content appropriate for children in their care while allowing adults to decide what legal content they wish to access ...;

– increasing awareness of services provided by industry among users ... ;

– support actions such as assessment of legal implications;

– activities fostering international co-operation in the areas enumerated above;

– other actions furthering the objective set out in Article 2.

Further, in Annex 1 to the Decision, it is pointed out (in para 1.1) that 'co-operation from the industry and a fully functioning system of self-regulation are essential elements in limiting the flow of illegal content on the internet'. Later in 1999, the Council further concluded,[173] *inter alia*, that 'self-regulation systems, in accordance with national cultural and legal traditions and practices, may ... make a contribution to safeguarding public interests' and that 'self-regulation could usefully complement regulation in the context of the future development of new media services'.[174]

If this seems to be a rather different approach than might have been noted from other jurisdictions, it is perhaps important at this juncture to consider the problem in perspective. Although the issues surrounding the dissemination and propagation of illegal and/or harmful material via the internet are deserving of resolution, in comparison with the total of all information available on global networks, the proportion that would be likely to fall into these categories is very small. As with access to similar information available on more traditional media, the answer may be

173 Document 399 Y 1006 (02), *Council Conclusions of 27 September 1999 on the Role of Self-Regulation in the Light of the Development of New Media Services* OJ 1999 L 283/3.
174 See, also, above Chapter 7 on self-regulation in the context of privacy protection.

based more in a reassessment of society and community values, perhaps backed up by technological methods, than in the drafting of unenforceable legislation.

The current state of play thus seems to be somewhat confusing and there is an inherent tension emerging between the implementation of self-regulation and the desire of governments to impose external regulation on the internet.

The European Union has a particular interest in addressing issues which may prejudice the working of the free market in information services. A more intransigent problem at the international level is providing suitable procedures for policing global criminal activity and even allowing for a degree of harmonisation of criminal law. Criminal laws can be very particular to a state and, aside from a number of particularly heinous acts over which there is consensus, such as murder and other violent crime, for instance, criminal offences often reflect the particular cultures and mores of the society which caused them to be enacted. Thus far in this chapter, we have been considering certain jurisdictionally based laws which have been used, or attempted to be used, to apprehend the perpetrators of what can be termed computer crime or cybercrime. Unlike the scope of the jurisdictionally based laws which are pressed into service, the criminal acts which are committed in or via cyberspace cannot always be confined within convenient jurisdictional boundaries. The territoriality of many criminal provisions, together with the global reach and spread of the technology, provides an almost perfect environment for the perpetrator to be situated in one jurisdiction while the effect of their acts is felt in another or others. This can hamper enforcement efforts quite dramatically since 'while the Internet is borderless for criminals, law enforcement agencies must respect the sovereignty of other nations'.[175] To the extent that cybercrime and cybercriminals have scant regard for national borders then, arguably, the appropriate legal response should be one which also transcends these boundaries. Unless there are in place agreements with respect to cooperation, bilateral or multilateral enforcement and/or extradition, it will be practically difficult, if not impossible, to apprehend those responsible and many writers have testified, in principle at least, to the desirability of an international regime which could address, and hopefully begin to combat, cybercrime on a global scale.

The Council of Europe has been active in this area since the second half of the 1980s and issued recommendations in both 1989 and 1995.[176] This work continued and culminated in the Cybercrime Convention[177] which was opened for signature on 23 November 2001. Although it has been suggested that 'the inherent difficulties of formulating satisfactory global internet regulation result in model treaties taking years to approve,[178] in fact the cybercrime was drafted in a relatively short time in international agreement terms and was completed in 4 years and 27 drafts.[179] The explanatory report on the Convention refers to this earlier work, but expresses the view that 'only a binding international instrument can ensure the necessary efficiency

---

175 Keyser, 2003, p 326.
176 See above fn. 7 and also recommendation No. R (95) 13.
177 www.conventions.coe.int/Treaty/en/Treaties/Html/185.htm.
178 Sprinkel, 2002, p. 509.
179 See further Keyser 2003, p. 296.

in the fight against these new phenomena'.[180] The report also summarises the rationale for international action in this area:

Explanatory Report to the Convention on Cybercrime

4. The ease of accessibility and searchability of information contained in computer systems, combined with the practically unlimited possibilities for its exchange and dissemination, regardless of geographical distances, has lead to an explosive growth in the amount of information available and the knowledge that can be drawn there from.

5. These developments have given rise to an unprecedented economic and social changes, but they also have a dark side: the emergence of new types of crime as well as the commission of traditional crimes by means of new technologies. Moreover, the consequences of criminal behaviour can be more far-reaching than before because they are not restricted by geographical limitations or national boundaries. The recent spread of detrimental computer viruses all over the world has provided proof of this reality. Technical measures to protect computer systems need to be implemented concomitantly with legal measures to prevent and deter criminal behaviour.

6. The new technologies challenge existing legal concepts. Information and communications flow more easily around the world. Borders are no longer boundaries to this flow. Criminals are increasingly located in places other than where their acts produce their effects. However, domestic laws are generally confined to a specific territory. Thus solutions to the problems posed must be addressed by international law, necessitating the adoption of adequate international legal instruments. The present Convention aims to meet this challenge, with due respect to human rights in the new Information Society.

Participation in this Convention was not confined to the Member States of the Council of Europe itself and the US, Canada, Japan and South Africa were also parties to the negotiations. In one sense, the Convention can be viewed as ground-breaking and pioneering in that it is the first attempt at an international level to address the problems arising from computer crime. As the Convention has now been ratified by five signatories,[181] it came into force for Albania, Croatia, Estonia, Hungary and Lithuania on 1 July 2004. However, the Convention has not been without its critics and some of the arguments on both sides of the debate are reviewed below after a discussion of the contents of the Convention itself.

The Convention adopts a three-pronged approach and contains provisions relating to the harmonisation of substantive criminal law,[182] the necessary domestic procedural powers for investigation and prosecution,[183] and also provisions aimed at facilitating international co-operation and mutual assistance.[184] The list of substantive offences is not exhaustive or comprehensive and follows a fairly conventional classification scheme in being divided into sections relating to the integrity of computer systems such as access, interception etc,[185] 'computer-related' crimes such as computer-related

---

180 Explanatory   Report   to   the   Convention   on   Cybercrime   para   9 http://conventions.coe.int/Treaty/en/Reports/Html/185.htm.
181 Article 36(3) requires that five states of which three must be members of the Council of Europe must ratify before the Treaty can be brought into force.
182 Articles 2–13.
183 Articles 14–22.
184 Articles 23–35.
185 Articles 2–6.

forgery and computer-related fraud;[186] content-related offences although these relate exclusively to child-pornography;[187] and copyright crime subject to the provisions of the Berne Convention, TRIPS, the WIPO copyright treaty etc.[188]. In addition, there are provisions covering aiding and abetting,[189] corporate liability[190] and sanctions,[191] which should be 'effective, proportionate and dissuasive' and include the possibility of 'deprivation of liberty'.

To assist the implementation of the substantive provisions, the procedural provisions include, *inter alia*, provisions allowing 'expeditious preservation of specified computer data, including traffic data',[192] together with a number of articles providing powers to require production of such data, empowerment to search and seize relevant data, to collect data in real time and to intercept data.[193] Some of these provisions necessarily require the co-operation and participation of third parties and private organisations such as ISPs.

Significantly for the subsequent discussion, these provisions are expressed to be subject to the provisions of article 14, detailing the overall scope of the provisions, and article 15, which contains the following conditions and safeguards:

Convention on Cybercrime
Article 15

1. Each Party shall ensure that the establishment, implementation and application of the powers and procedures provided for in this Section are subject to conditions and safeguards provided for under its domestic law, which shall provide for the adequate protection of human rights and liberties, including rights arising pursuant to obligations it has undertaken under the 1950 Council of Europe Convention for the Protection of Human Rights and Fundamental Freedoms, the 1966 United Nations International Covenant on Civil and Political Rights, and other applicable international human rights instruments, and which shall incorporate the principle of proportionality.

2. Such conditions and safeguards shall, as appropriate in view of the nature of the power or procedure concerned, inter alia, include judicial or other independent supervision, grounds justifying application, and limitation on the scope and the duration of such power or procedure.

3. To the extent that it is consistent with the public interest, in particular the sound administration of justice, a Party shall consider the impact of the powers and procedures in this Section upon the rights, responsibilities and legitimate interests of third parties.

The preamble to the Convention also makes reference to the international human rights instruments referred to in article 15(1) and in addition reaffirms 'the right of everyone to hold opinions without interference, as well as the right to freedom of

---

186 Article 7 and 8.
187 Article 9.
188 Article 10.
189 Article 11.
190 Article 12.
191 Article 13.
192 Article 16.
193 Articles 17–20.

expression, including the freedom to seek, receive, and impart information and ideas of all kinds, regardless of frontiers, and the rights concerning the respect for privacy'. Despite the fact that earlier drafts were modified to take into account the concerns of a number of lobby groups,[194] and, notwithstanding both the ideals expressed in the preamble and the content of Article 15 above, much of the criticism of the Convention has centred on the extent to which it is, or is not compatible, with the general protection of human rights and civil liberties guaranteed by other international treaties or national constitutions.

To what extent has an appropriate balance of rights actually been preserved within the provisions of the Cybercrime Treaty? The major concerns have been voiced in the US in relation to a perceived clash with protected First Amendment rights in that jurisdiction. The apparent problems relate both to the substantive provisions on content, the associated procedural provisions and also to the requirement of co-operation and mutual assistance. Keyser[195] suggests that the criticisms of the Convention can be categorised as follows: it curtails freedom of expression; it overextends the powers of the enforcement agencies; it requires private persons and organisations to provide and retain much further information than previously; it infringes civil liberties. These issues have been brought to a head by the transmittal of the Convention to the US Senate in November 2003 for consent to ratify.[196]

The decision of the US government to participate in the drafting of the Cybercrime Convention was made in the belief that the US had 'much to gain from a strong well-crafted multilateral instrument that removes or minimises the many procedural and jurisdictional obstacles that can delay or endanger international investigations and prosecutions of computer-related crimes' and further that 'the central provisions of the Convention are consistent with the existing framework of US law'.[197] To what extent then are the above criticisms legitimate and well-founded? It is certainly the case that the First Amendment of the US Constitution offers substantial protection to free expression. Indeed, although the US originally participated in the subsequent protocol of the Cybercrime Convention concerning the criminalisation of acts of a racist and xenophobic nature committed through computer systems,[198] it did not become a party to the final version believing that it was inconsistent with First Amendment guarantees of free expression. However, restrictions on content under the Convention, itself, are limited to child pornography, presumably because it was not possible to obtain a consensus between negotiating states on other content-based offences.

194 See further Sprinkel, 2002, p. 510 and for general comments on how the convention has been received at various periods of gestation see, eg, Cybercrime Treaty Bibliography at www.wildernesscoast.org/bib/treaty-by-date.html.
195 Keyser, 2003, p 324.
196 At the time of writing evidence in support of ratification had been heard by the Senate Foreign Relations Committee in June 2004 but no actual decision had been made, see, eg, the testimony of Samuel Witten www.foreign.senate.gov/testimony/2004/WittenTestimony/040517.pdf.
197 www.usdoj.gove/criminal/cybercrime/COEFAQs.htm.
198 www.conventions.coe.int/Treaty/en/Treaties/Html/189.htm.

Convention on Cybercrime
Article 9 – Offences related to child pornography

1. Each Party shall adopt such legislative and other measures as may be necessary to establish as criminal offences under its domestic law, when committed intentionally and without right, the following conduct:

  (a) producing child pornography for the purpose of its distribution through a computer system;

  (b) offering or making available child pornography through a computer system;

  (c) distributing or transmitting child pornography through a computer system;

  (d) procuring child pornography through a computer system for oneself or another;

  (e) possessing child pornography in a computer system or on a computer-data storage medium.

2. For the purpose of paragraph 1 above "child pornography" shall include pornographic material that visually depicts:

  (a) a minor engaged in sexually explicit conduct;

  (b) a person appearing to be a minor engaged in sexually explicit conduct;

  (c) realistic images representing a minor engaged in sexually explicit conduct.

Child pornography is already illegal in the US by virtue of the provisions of 18 USC §§ 2252 and 2252A (Protection of Children from Sexual Predators Act), but as can be seen from the definitions in article 9(2) above, the Cybercrime Convention proscribes not only child pornography as such but also 'virtual child pornography', that is, material which has been created without the use of actual children. In other words it has been made either by computer manipulation of images of adult actors or altering innocent pictures of children. Earlier attempts in the US to outlaw such virtual child pornography in the Child Pornography Protection Act of 1996 were struck down as unconstitutional by the Supreme Court in *Ashcroft v Free Speech Coalition*, which found that the law as it stood was unacceptably broad. Virtual child pornography could be distinguished from actual child pornography and the law outlawed, *inter alia*, images which were produced without the involvement of actual children, and also images which might pass the community standards test for obscenity. It was in consequence an unacceptable restriction on free expression.

Ashcroft v Free Speech Coalition
535 U.S 234, 250-254
US Supreme Court (2002)

Virtual child pornography is not 'intrinsically related' to the sexual abuse of children … While the Government asserts that the images can lead to actual instances of child abuse … the causal link is contingent and indirect. The harm does not necessarily follow from the speech, but depends upon some quantified potential for subsequent criminal acts. … The mere tendency of speech to encourage unlawful acts is not a sufficient reason for banning it. … The Government has shown no more than a remote connection between speech that might encourage thoughts or impulses and resulting child abuse. Without a significantly stronger, more direct connection, the Government may not prohibit speech on the grounds that it may encourage pedophiles to engage in illegal conduct.

Following this decision Congress has been attempting to address the deficiencies which led to this result and the Prosecutorial Remedies and Tools against the Exploitation of Children Today (PROTECT) Act passed Congress in April 2003 and is expected to be signed into law. It will outlaw morphed child pornography provided that it can be proved beyond reasonable doubt that there was an intention to make others believe that the children depicted were genuine. It also contains an amendment introduced by the Child Obscenity and Pornography Protection Act of 2003 which proscribes any solicitation to buy or sell child pornography whatever its origin.

However, whether or not the US Congress is successful in outlawing virtual child pornography while still satisfying the stringent requirements of First Amendment jurisprudence, is not really directly relevant in whether or not to ratify the Cybercrime Convention. Although as shown, the Convention contains provisions dealing with virtual child pornography, Article 9(4) also provides that states can reserve the right not to apply in whole or in part these particular provisions. This suggests that it would be possible for the US to ratify without fear of diluting its strong constitutional protection for free speech.

Another frequent criticism is that the Convention does not satisfactorily provide a balance between the objectives of investigating cybercrime and the privacy of those who use the internet and world wide web. Such critics highlight the data preservation requirements in the Convention and their potential to infringe the privacy of innocent internet users and, in addition, Aldesco suggests that the data preservation requirements may also infringe freedom of expression by exerting a chilling effect on anonymous online speech.[199] Since 11 September 2001, many countries have passed laws which allow data preservation or data retention in an attempt not to lose data which might be relevant to the investigation of international terrorism. Interestingly, in response to such fears, the US has favoured data preservation over the mandatory retention of data which has received favour in many European states.[200] Both techniques have the propensity to infringe privacy but, arguably, expeditious preservation is more likely to meet the proportionality requirement in Art 15(1), to which all of the provisions on expedited preservation of stored computer data are expressly subject, than the data retention regimes being introduced in Europe, including the UK.[201] Taylor suggests that a 'vague reference to proportionality will not be adequate to ensure that civil liberties are protected'[202] and Jarvie remarks that 'the European Cybercrime Convention is regrettably silent on the appropriate safeguards'.[203] Arguably it is difficult in an international convention to be anything other than aspirational and rely on the will of the individual participants to translate and implement the provisions appropriately.

The final stumbling block for many US civil liberties organisations such as EPIC, ACLU etc. is the provisions requiring mutual assistance and international coperation. This objection is largely predicated on a distrust of other states to provide a basic level of human rights protection. Thus although Keyser[204] suggests that 'it seems very important for an international regime to be set up to combat these types of crimes in a

---

199 Aldesco, 2002, p 110.
200 See Rowland, 2004, and discussion in Chapter 7.
201 See Anti-terrorism, Crime and Security Act 2001 and the associated Code of Practice on Data Retention brought into effect in December 2003.
202 Taylor, 2002.
203 Jarvie, 2003.
204 Keyser 2003, p 296.

growing and integrated global society which is becoming ever more vulnerable to cyber attacks, nevertheless he still espouses the view that 'although it may not be such a big deal to have the United States government wield greater power, the same new powers will also be given to member countries that may not 'have a strong tradition of checks and balances on police power'.[205] The ACLU have been even stronger in their opposition to the mutual assistance provisions stating that 'ratification of the Council of Europe's Convention on Cybercrime will put the United States in the morally repugnant position of supporting the actions of politically corrupt and evil regimes'[206] and, in their submission to the Senate Foreign Relations Committee considering the ratification, 'the Senate should carefully consider what it means to agree to provide mutual legal assistance to countries whose substantive laws and procedures do not comport with American understandings of justice'.[207]

In contrast, unlike the situation in the US, there has been little controversy over that UK's plans for ratification of the Cybercrime Convention as indicated in the comment in the APIG report that the inquiry 'received very few comments on the implications on the CMA of ratifying the Convention on Cybercrime, suggesting that this is not widely seen as a contentious issue.'[208] The Report suggests that the government will ratify the Convention by 2005 and proposes that the Home Office, which considers that the 'Computer Misuse Act already covers the majority of the requirements of the Convention',[209] continues with the current approach.[210] In a written answer to a question about which Council of Europe Conventions had not yet been ratified by the UK, the Secretary of State said that new legislation would be required and that, because of problems of finding Parliamentary time, the earliest possible date was late 2004.[211] Nevertheless, there are certainly concerns which could arise if the Cybercrime Convention were transposed into the national law of any of the contracting parties without appropriate safeguards for individual rights and liberties but this is not necessarily something which is confined to this international convention. There are powerful lobby groups, notably in the US, on both sides of the debate and it will be interesting to see whether further ratifications occur in the future or whether the cybercrime convention joins the archives of international treaties which have been ratified by only a few signatories.

CONCLUDING REMARKS

The discussion in this chapter shows that there are a number of different responses to the phenomenon of so-called 'computer crime'. Aside from the not insignificant

---

205 *Ibid*, p 316.
206 16 June 2004 www.aclu.org/news/NewsPrint.cfm?ID=15954&c=39.
207 16 June 2004 www.aclu.org/news/NewsPrint.cfm?ID=15954&c=39.
208 APIG Report 2004, para. 82.
209 www.homeoffice.gov.uk/crime/internetcrime/compmisuse.html.
210 *Ibid*, para 77.
211 See www.parliament.the-stationery-office.co.uk/pa/cm200203/cmhansrd/vo030514/text/
      30514w13.htm and www.homeoffice.gov.uk/crime/internetcrime/compmisuse.html.

difficulties of detection and enforcement, for some crimes, notably those based on theft and fraud, it seems that, for the most part, existing law with some amendment may provide a suitable solution. Computer specific legislation addressed at activities such as hacking and the introduction of viruses has met with a mixed reception and, although there have been some successful cases, it seems likely that the majority of incidents of this type are not redressed. The inherently jurisdictionally based nature of criminal law meets its greatest challenges in relation to content based offences. There is little prospect of global consensus on a number of relevant concepts and definitions of offending behaviour and it is significant that, for this type of conduct, the Cybercrime Convention contains only provisions relating to child pornography. Further it is perhaps ironic that, in an area which stands to benefit most from international cooperation, it is these very provisions which are creating the greatest stumbling block to ratification.

CHAPTER 9

ASPECTS OF THE PROTECTION OF INTELLECTUAL PROPERTY RIGHTS ON THE INTERNET

INTRODUCTION

The questions arising out of the application of existing intellectual property rights to the development of computer software and databases were explored in Chapter 2. This chapter considers some of the challenges for the protection of intellectual property rights created by global networks. Just as computer networks created new ways of committing traditional crime, so they provide new ways of infringing intellectual property rights. A number of the issues raised are those which are generally common to the regulation of the internet and have been referred to in connection with the application of legal principles to other activities on the internet and the world wide web. Examples are the problems of jurisdiction, detection and enforcement and the liability of service providers.[1]

Other problems are specific to the realm of intellectual property. Cornish and Llewellyn have referred to the internet and copyright as 'the most inflamed issue in current intellectual property'[2] and this medium has certainly raised significant issues in this respect. This chapter considers some general issues arising out of the application of copyright principles to a new medium, together with associated changes in the law in both Europe and the US, and also considers the application of existing copyright principles using such examples as file sharing and hypertext links. This will be followed by a consideration of domain name disputes and the attempts to accommodate the rights in a new property, the domain name, within existing legal frameworks.

COPYRIGHT

Copying of material from the vast information source that is the internet is a trivial matter, but application of traditional copyright principles has not always proved to be straightforward.

Copyright and the internet
Hector L MacQueen
in *Law and the Interne a framework for electronic commerce*
Lilian Edwards and Charlotte Waelde (eds)
2000, Oxford: Hart, p 181

The issues are manifold. Is the ease of perfect reproduction and manipulation of material in the digital form used by our communication systems the death-knell of the whole basis of copyright? Are we going to have to reconsider such fundamentals of copyright law as what constitutes publication, reproduction and public performance, or the old distinctions between categories of work such as literary, artistic, sound recording and film? What rights should users enjoy? Are the rights accorded them in the analogue

---

1   See above, Chapters 6 to 8. See Dutson, 1997.
2   Cornish and Llewellyn, 2003, p. 795.

world so ill-defined that they will undermine the utility of copyright as a source of income for digital authors and their publishers? Will we see the emergence of a genuine market place in which producer and user bargain about the price for individual transfers of information and cultural goods, rather than requiring intermediaries such as publishers? Given the ready flow of material across national frontiers, does the international harmonisation of copyright laws need intensification, and should the classic rules of private international law on jurisdiction and choice of law be adapted to enable a party confronted with infringements in another country to sue effectively in his own country and have judgments recognised abroad?

This extract demonstrates the multiplicity of issues. Has copyright, which was developed in a very different era to the present, outlived its usefulness? Some would say yes.[3] On the other hand, Mackaay, in likening traditional copyrights and other legal rights to fences which separate those with entitlement from those without, answers the question thus:

> Does the Internet spell the end of property rights? The old fences may not work so well any more. Yet information, while apparently abundant once in existence, still needs to be created and the creator needs be encouraged.[4]

This suggests a belief that the concept of copyright is not dead, as such, but that the 'fencing techniques' may need modification or repair. Schønning[5] points out that the internet is unlikely to lead to a mass breakdown in the copyright system any more than has happened when it had to deal with other forms of piracy and illicit copying of easy-to-copy media, such as videos, audiotapes, computer software, etc, and simply concludes thus: ' ... surely copyright will survive even this legal and technological challenge.' More recently Wiese having reviewed the arguments on both sides has come to the conclusion that there are still reasons to rely on copyright law.

The justification of the information society in the digital age
Henning Wiese
[2002] EIPR 387, p. 390

... it seems to be a misconception ... to regard the law as a threat to the internet society. It is one of the law's major functions, if not its main function, to make life in society easier and worth living for each individual. It does so by providing axioms that can be applied to everyone, and that everyone can apply and rely on, thereby creating certainty and, to a certain extent, equality of treatment and opportunity. In doing so, the law, in an ideal world, takes into consideration the interests of all parties involved and weighs them against each other to find a proper balance, taking into account factors such as ethics, morality and practicality. This need for rules to allow something like 'peaceful coexistence' on the (P2P) net has been recognised by some, but only some, of those early internet evangelists labelled as digital revolutionaries themselves.

... Why abolish a whole piece of legislation that has been built over decades and seems to work reasonably well, rather than adjust it to changes in (virtual) reality? ...

There are several other arguments supporting the view that in a digital environment, there is still the need for intellectual property laws in general, and copyright laws in particular. Copy protection technology alone, while capable of addressing some of the

---

3   For representative arguments see, eg, Barlow, in Hugenholtz, (ed), 1996; Kergévant, 1996.
4   Mackaay in *ibid*, Hugenholtz, p 18.
5   Schønning, 1999. For a summary of the challenges facing copyright law see, also, Sterling, 2000 and Fitzpatrick, 2000, pp 214–218.

problems raised by the advent of the internet as a medium of fast, cheap and high-quality reproduction and distribution, cannot be the final answer to the problems that have arisen. One of such arguments is that the problems posed by the internet are not as alien to copyright law as some authors would like to make us think. Files still contain expressions (sounds, words, pictures; limited by our number of senses) of ideas. A file … is just another way of storing the expressed idea, just like storage on a video/audio tape, or a CD. The fundamentals of copyright remain the same, regardless of the format of storage. It is very likely that copyright will adapt to the internet just as it did to printed media, TV and music.

The question is not so much whether copyright law can adapt at all, but rather how it should adapt.

How should the copyright principles already enshrined in national laws be applied and how is the lack of global harmonisation to be dealt with when the medium, itself, is a global one? Is the necessary solution inevitably a global one? This is the view of Millé[6] who suggests that copyright law needs to find answers to the questions posed by the presence of new modes of intellectual creation, of distribution to the public and of use and enjoyment of the works; that there is a need to make the treatment given to intangible property uniform at world level; and that administration by an international organisation appears essential.

However, some other commentators, having considered the various arguments, have sounded a note of caution about the consequences of being in too much haste to introduce new or amended legislative rules. This is illustrated by the following extract, written in response to the EC initiatives on copyright in the information society (see below).

Copyright and the information society in Europe:
a matter of timing as well as content
Lionel Bently and Robert Burrell
(1997) 34 CMLR 1197, p 1208

… it would be sensible to delay any reform of copyright law until we have a good idea of exactly what impact the new forms of creation, distribution and consumption will have on authors, right holders, distributors and consumers. Some predict the 'death of copyright', that it is a concept that emerged in an era of print and is built upon print-informed notions of a fixed text. For such commentators copyright is a medium which is intrinsically incapable of accommodating impending/ongoing changes in the ways intellectual creation is conceived and the challenge for the future lies in devising new ways of providing incentives to creators of information. At the opposite extreme are those who argue that copyright has shown itself flexible enough to adapt to repeated technological changes since 1710 (both in expanding the scope of protected works and extending the rights given to new modes of distribution), and that it can, with a few minor modifications, adapt to the new digital environment.

However, even if we assume that copyright can be adapted to the new technologies, it is not clear as yet whether such adaptation requires a strengthening or weakening of the rights at present afforded to content holders. While … most of the calls for action have been from content holders concerned that their rights will be undermined by digitisation, other commentators have predicted that one of the effects of electronic distribution will be to strengthen the economic position of copyright owners. This is because digitisation

---

6   Millé, 1997.

may give rise to more effective ways of administering rights. One of the advantages of the developments in information processing may be that the transaction costs of obtaining licences will be reduced. While the cost of tracking down and obtaining many licenses is prohibitive when traditional methods are employed, the reduction in transaction costs presented by electronic licensing may open new valuable streams of revenue to content holders. At present it is difficult to predict which of these prognoses is more accurate and consequently, it would seem unwise to act until we have a better understanding of what the information society will look like ...

It is also unwise to act hastily when many people are working towards a technological solution to the problems that digital technologies are alleged to present. One such solution being developed involves the encryption of works that are currently protected by copyright. It is envisaged that users would then pay for access codes either for the works or group of works to which they wish to have access. A technological response, it is argued, would have the positive consequence of allowing for the evolution of mechanisms of supervision best suited to the new environment. Some commentators have even predicted that technological solutions could replace copyright altogether. Critics of those who hope to find a technological solution to the problem of unauthorised copying over electronic networks would undoubtedly argue that anti-copy systems can be overcome. If successful, however, a technological response could confine the need for legislative intervention to the laying down of certain standards, together with providing support through, for example, criminalising the use and sale of devices designed to circumvent copy-protection ...

Finally, and more abstractly, we do not know how the information society will affect many of the concepts we currently take for granted as underpinning our copyright laws or, as importantly, what new social constructs will gain conventional acceptance. Notions of authorship, of the work, of public and private may well be transformed in the 'electronic environment'.

Whilst at one level it might be sensible to delay legislating until the nature of the beast is better understood, technology is advancing all the time, and not always in the direction expected, such that there could always be a reason for legal inaction which could be confused with legal impotence. At a practical level, legislative change is frequently a long time in gestation and the Directive on copyright which prompted the above comments was not, in the event, adopted until 2001.[7] However there are some occasions where existing copyright principles have been applied to activities on the internet without any obvious need for amendment or distortion of existing concepts. A good example of this is found in *Kelly v Arriba Software*.[8] The case concerned a search engine which displayed thumbnail reproductions of images in response to an image search. The search engine was developed to provide a catalogue of and improved method of locating images on the internet. The original images at issue were artistic works. Although the search engine used exact replicas of the original image they were much smaller, lower resolution images which could not be enlarged to the size of the original without significant loss of clarity.[9] In applying the fair use factors the Ninth Circuit, agreeing with the District Court,[10] found that, even though the images were

---

7   Directive 2001/29/EC on the harmonisation of certain aspects of copyright and related rights in the information society.
8   336 F 3d 811 (9th Cir. 2003).
9   *Ibid* at 818.
10   77 F Supp 2d 1116 (CD Cal 1999).

reproduced exactly and entirely, it was for a completely different purpose. To that extent the use could be considered transformative – it was not merely a question of retransmission of the work in a different form. Although the creative works at issue were entitled to strong copyright protection, there was no evidence that the use of the thumbnails would damage the market for the original works and found that, overall, the use was fair. Interestingly, in relation to the transformative nature of the use the District Court had commented that where 'a new use and new technology are evolving, the broad transformative purpose of the use weighs more heavily than the inevitable flaws in its early stages of development.'[11]

The above example shows that the US doctrine of fair use, relying as it does on the application of general principles on a case by case basis, may produce an outcome which does not overly inhibit the new uses to which copyright material may be subject on the internet. It is, however, by no means certain that there would be the same outcome in other jurisdictions. In the absence of global harmonisation, there is little option for those seeking a remedy but to rely on the vagaries of national law and its interpretation. This can create complications and difficulties for the courts, as is evident in the comment from the US District Court for the Central District of California that it was 'mindful of the difficulty of applying well established doctrines to what can only be described as an amorphous *situs* of information, anonymous messenger of communication, and seemingly endless stream of commerce'.[12] As with other copyright infringements, there may be problems of mass piracy and easy commercial exploitation. At the other end of the scale, it is a trivial matter for the individual user to download copies of material from the internet and world wide web. For material which is already in digital form on the internet, copying may occur initially[13] when the material is uploaded by the provider. In this case, any potential illegality would fall to be judged in accordance with legislation in the jurisdiction of the provider's server. There will then be further copying when the material is downloaded by the user. In this case, whether or not the activity is lawful would be determined by the law in the geographical location of the user's computer. An awareness of the vagaries of national interpretation of copyright principles may thus be crucial. In between these two processes, transmission may be effected by means of a communication carrier, creating a further term in the equation. These and other issues have led to some significant legislative amendments to the existing law on copyright. In the US, the Digital Millennium Copyright Act (DMCA) was signed into law in 1998.[14] In the EU, relevant provisions are obtained in both Directive 2000/31/EC on certain legal aspects of information society services, in particular electronic commerce (the 'E-commerce Directive') and Directive 2001/29/EC on the harmonisation of certain aspects of copyright and related rights in the information society (the 'Copyright Directive').

---

11   *Ibid* at 1121.
12   *Playboy Enterprises v Netscape and Excite* 55 F Supp 2d 1070. See below, p 521.
13   See Schønning, 1999.
14   Full text available at: http://thomas.loc.gov/cgibin/query/z?c105:H.R.2281.ENR and see also www.copyright.gov/legislation/dmca.pdf.

LIABILITY OF INTERNET SERVICE PROVIDERS

Internet service providers (ISPs) have been a popular target for those wishing to gain some recompense for violation of their rights in situations when they cannot identify, cannot locate or there are other problems in bringing the actual offending party to justice. ISPs, in contrast, are in line because they fulfil all of these criteria being identifiable, locatable and frequently situated in the same jurisdiction. There are some very different approaches to the question of the extent of ISPs' liability for copyright infringement which to a great extent depends on whether they are acting merely as a communications carrier, providing the means of transmission between provider and user, or whether they have, or are capable of having, some input and control over at least some of the material to which they provide access. It has been fairly widely recognised that, when acting as a mere communications carrier, there is a very strong case for exemption 'from any type of copyright liability in respect of the provision of Internet infrastructure'[15] but that the situation may not be so clear cut for ISPs who retain some control. The US, having made provision in the Communications Decency Act in 1996 for limiting liability for substantive content,[16] addressed the issue of liability for copyright infringement in 1998 in the DMCA. This statute introduces a new § 512 into the US Copyright Act which limits ISP liability for copyright infringement in a number of situations. The first of these is for transient communications. Transient and incidental copies are vital to the operation of computers and computer networks and yet would nevertheless be an infringement of traditional copyright rules. During the gestation of the 1996 WIPO Copyright Treaty, a proposed new Art 7 would have made the definition of 'reproduction' include both direct and indirect reproduction, whether permanent or temporary, and in any manner or form. This did not make it into the final version of the Treaty but resulted in a spirited account of how such a definition would inhibit the functioning of information networks.

**The new WIPO Copyright Treaty:
a happy result in Geneva
Thomas C Vinje
[1997] EIPR 230**

The common denominator underlying objections to Article 7 were concerns that Article 7 would inappropriately tilt the balance in copyright law and hinder the growth of the information infrastructure ... most importantly, many ... feared that, unless properly circumscribed, Article 7 would threaten the legality of browsing and deprive infrastructure providers (such as Internet access and backbone providers) of legal security by threatening them with the risk that they would engage in copyright infringement by unknowingly making ephemeral copies ... of infringing works put on their systems by users. ... It is far preferable to the hasty adoption of an unbalanced provision that, rather than encouraging the creation and dissemination of works in the digital environment threatened to stifle the Information Infrastructure ...

The digital revolution by its very nature will inexorably lead to the making of vast numbers of ephemeral copies ... But should every one of those ephemeral copies

---

15 Macmillan and Blakeney, 1998.
16 See Chapters 7 and 8.

constitute an infringing reproduction? Are not many, perhaps most, ephemeral copies different in their fundamental nature from permanent reproductions, and should not the law reflect that difference? Will every, or even most, of those ephemeral copies have economic significance justifying their characterisation as an infringing act? What would be the social, technological and economic consequences of deeming the vast numbers of essential ephemeral copies to fall within the copyright holder's exclusive right of reproduction. Assuming the conclusion is reached that certain temporary copies should be excluded in the reproductive right, how should that result be achieved? Would it not be preferable to follow an approach whereby most temporary copies fall outside the reproductive right, and those that are covered be treated as the exception rather than the rule? ... If all these questions are debated broadly and soberly it should be possible to reach a wise and balanced legislative solution to this difficult and complex dilemma ...

To reflect the concern that transient copies could potentially lead to liability for ISPs, the following section was included in the DMCA.

Digital Millennium Copyright Act 1998
Title II Online Copyright Infringement Liability Limitation
Sec 512 Limitations on liability relating to material online

Transitory Digital Network Communications – A service provider shall not be liable for ... infringement of copyright by reason of the provider's transmitting, routing, or providing connections for, material through a system or network controlled or operated by the service provider or, by reason of the intermediate and transient storage of that material in the course of such transmitting, routing or providing connections, if –

(1) the transmission of the material was initiated by or at the direction of a person other than the service provider;

(2) the transmission, routing, provision of connections, or storage is carried out through an automatic technical process without selection of the material by the service provider;

(3) the service provider does not select the recipients of the material except as an automatic response to the request of another person;

(4) no copy of the material made by the service provider in the course of such intermediate or transient storage is maintained on the system or network in a manner ordinarily accessible to anyone other than anticipated recipients, and no such copy is maintained on the system in a manner ordinarily accessible to such anticipated recipients for a longer period than is necessary for the transmission, routing, or provision of connections; and

(5) the material is transmitted through the system or network without modification of its content.

Unlike the DMCA, the E-commerce Directive is capable of applying to a wider range of illegal activity than just copyright infringement. The parallel provision is to be found in Article 12.

Directive 2000/31/EC
Section 4: Liability of intermediary service providers
Article 12

'Mere conduit'

1.   Where an information society service is provided that consists of the transmission in a communication network of information provided by a recipient of the service, or the provision of access to a communication network, Member States shall ensure that

the service provider is not liable for the information transmitted, on condition that the provider:

(a) does not initiate the transmission;

(b) does not select the receiver of the transmission; and

(c) does not select or modify the information contained in the transmission.

2. The acts of transmission and of provision of access referred to in paragraph 1 include the automatic, intermediate and transient storage of the information transmitted in so far as this takes place for the sole purpose of carrying out the transmission in the communication network, and provided that the information is not stored for any period longer than is reasonably necessary for the transmission. …

That, in general, temporary reproduction will still fall within the scope of prohibited acts for the purposes of copyright law is underlined by its inclusion within the scope of the reproduction right defined in Art 2 of the Copyright Directive. This ostensibly follows the broad definition which proved so controversial in an early version of the WIPO copyright treaty referred to above. However this definition is ameliorated by an exception for transient reproduction occurring as part of a technical process, and is of wider application than that provided by Art 12 of the E-commerce Directive in that it removes relevant transient copies from the ambit of copyright law, rather than merely exempting from liability.

Directive 2001/29/EC
Article 5
Exceptions and limitations

1. Temporary acts of reproduction … which are transient or incidental [and] an integral and essential part of a technological process and whose sole purpose is to enable:

(a) a transmission in a network between third parties by an intermediary, or

(b) a lawful use

of a work or other subject-matter to be made, and which have no independent economic significance shall be exempted from the reproduction right …

A related issue, which can challenge traditional copyright principles, is the practice of 'caching'. 'Caching … is the automatic creation of temporary copies of digital data (in a 'cache') in order to make the data more readily available for subsequent use.'[17] This procedure enables ISPs to retain, for instance, the most frequently accessed web pages on their own servers in order to increase the speed of retrieval for users. The cache is space limited and, once full, the storage of new pages involves the deletion of older pages in the cache. Consequently the copies will not be held permanently but are likely to be held for longer periods than the transient copying already discussed.

Digital Millennium Copyright Act 1998
Title II Online Copyright Infringement Liability Limitation
Sec 512 Limitations on liability relating to material online

(b) **System Caching** –

(1) A service provider shall not be liable for … infringement of copyright by reason of the intermediate and temporary storage of material on a system or network controlled or operated by or for the service provider in a case in which –

---

17 Hugenholtz, 2000.

(A) the material is made available online by a person other than the service provider;

(B) the material is transmitted from the person described in subparagraph (A) through the system or network to a person other than the person described in subparagraph (A) at the direction of that other person; and

(C) the storage is carried out through an automatic technical process for the purposes of making the material available to users of the system or network who, after the material is transmitted as described in subparagraph (B) request access to the material from the person described in subparagraph (A). ...

This provision is subject to a number of conditions which effectively ensure that the material must be viewed by the end user as if it came straight from the originator, and that any information received from the user, for example, by submission of forms etc, is not retained by the ISP. Thus the material must not be modified; no material other than that made publicly available by the originator for viewing must be cached; if the originator imposes restrictions such as passwords then these must continue to be observed; and the ISP must not cache material which is itself in breach of copyright in situations where either the material has been or has been ordered to be removed for this reason from the original site. Further, it is possible for the originator to specify (via http protocols) that the material is not to be cached. Again a similar provision is to be found in the E-commerce Directive.

Directive 2000/31/EC
Section 4: Liability of intermediary service providers
Article 13

'Caching'

1. Where an information society service is provided that consists of the transmission in a communication network of information provided by a recipient of the service, Member States shall ensure that the service provider is not liable for the automatic, intermediate and temporary storage of that information, performed for the sole purpose of making more efficient the information's onward transmission to other recipients of the service upon their request, on condition that:

    (a) the provider does not modify the information;

    (b) the provider complies with conditions on access to the information;

    (c) the provider complies with rules regarding the updating of the information, specified in a manner widely recognised and used by industry;

    (d) the provider does not interfere with the lawful use of technology, widely recognised and used by industry, to obtain data on the use of the information; and

    (e) the provider acts expeditiously to remove or to disable access to the information it has stored upon obtaining actual knowledge of the fact that the information at the initial source of the transmission has been removed from the network, or access to it has been disabled, or that a court or an administrative authority has ordered such removal or disablement. ...

The provisions of the DMCA and the relevant European Directives go farther than exempting from liability for transient and temporary copies. They also extend to exempting from liability for the actual hosting of material which is in breach of copyright, providing that, where there is knowledge of infringing material that material is removed 'expeditiously'.[18]The DMCA clarifies this duty with a very detailed 'take down' procedure. It should be noted that these exemptions also differ in that that provided by the DMCA applies only to copyright infringement whereas the exemption provided for illegal content by the Communications Decency Act is of considerably wider scope.[19] In contrast, the relevant provision of the E-commerce Directive applies more generally to 'illegal activity'.

Digital Millennium Copyright Act 1998
Title II Online Copyright Infringement Liability Limitation
Sec 512 Limitations on liability relating to material online

Information residing on systems or networks at direction of users –

(1) In general – A service provider shall not be liable for … infringement of copyright by reason of the storage at the direction of a user of material that resides on a system or network controlled or operated by or for the service provider, if the service provider –

(A)(i) does not have actual knowledge that the material or an activity using the material on the system or network is infringing;

(ii) in the absence of such actual knowledge, is not aware of facts or circumstances from which infringing activity is apparent; or

(iii) upon obtaining such knowledge or awareness, acts expeditiously to remove, or disable access to, the material; …

Directive 2000/31/EC
Section 4: Liability of intermediary service providers
Article 13

'Hosting'

1. Where an information society service is provided that consists of the storage of information provided by a recipient of the service, Member States shall ensure that the service provider is not liable for the information stored at the request of a recipient of the service, on condition that:

(a) the provider does not have actual knowledge of illegal activity or information and, as regards claims for damages, is not aware of facts or circumstances from which the illegal activity or information is apparent; or

(b) the provider, upon obtaining such knowledge or awareness acts expeditiously to remove or disable access to the information.

The DMCA has a further provision dealing with information location tools which are not covered by the E-commerce Directive. This includes providing exemption from liability for, *inter alia*, 'linking users to an online location containing infringing material or infringing activity by using information location tools including a directory, index, reference, pointer or hypertext link'. The extent to which hypertext and other links could give rise to such liability is considered in more detail below.

---

18 Although in Europe the substantive provisions relating to ISPs are found in the E-commerce Directive. Art 8(3) of the Copyright Directive does require Member States to ensure that injunctions are available against intermediaries whose services are used by a third party to infringe copyright. In *SABAM v Tiscali*, this provision was relied on by the Court of First Instance of Brussels in November 2004 in a file-sharing case, even though the Directive had not yet been transposed into Belgian law. For details see e.g. Debusseré, 2005.

19 See, e.g. discussion of *Zeran* and other defamation cases in Chapter 7.

TECHNOLOGICAL CIRCUMVENTION

Digital technology allows the creation of endless copies of works that are indistinguishable from the original and also copies of copies with no subsequent deterioration in quality. Copying of materials by download from the internet or other means has never been easier. It is hardly surprising, therefore, that, as this technology has developed, so have technological devices been developed which prevent copying, thereby providing an additional method of protection an author's works. However technology has no way of divining the difference between copying which is an infringement of copyright and that which is not because, for instance, it falls within one of the exceptions to copyright such as fair use or fair dealing. Technological devices on their face thus have the potential to prevent copying in an indiscriminate way. This fact is probably the factor most capable of creating significant perturbations in the traditional balance which copyright law has tried to establish between the rights of the copyright holder and the public interest in providing and maintaining access to copyright works.

The advent of such technological protection mechanisms has been paralleled by legal provisions supporting their use. Fitzpatrick summarises the difficulties of dealing with such devices within the legislative framework of copyright whilst, simultaneously, attempting to preserve the appropriate balance between authors' and users' rights.

Copyright Imbalance:
US and Australian Responses to the WIPO Digital Copyright Treaty
Simon Fitzpatrick
[2000] EIPR 214, 219

... the spectre of greater control for the copyright holder, which these sorts of technological measures raise, must be examined closely by anyone interested in achieving and maintaining an appropriate copyright balance. ... In order to facilitate social progress, copyright has always ensured the existence of a healthy public domain. Therefore, if it is now appropriate to add to the armoury of protection granted to rightholders under copyright law technical protection systems, care should be taken not only to provide clarity and fairness to device manufacturers through legislation, but also not to upset the existing balance in the law by allowing rightholders to eliminate copyright exceptions and to eviscerate the public domain through technical means.

Notwithstanding such issues, following the 1996 WIPO Copyright Treaty, a number of jurisdictions have enacted legal provisions dealing with the technical circumvention of copy protection.

WIPO Copyright Treaty 1996
Article 11
Obligations concerning technological measures

Contracting parties shall provide adequate legal protection and effective legal remedies against the circumvention of effective technological measures that are used by authors in connection with the exercise of their rights under this Treaty or the Berne Convention and that restrict acts, in respect of their works which are not authorised by the authors concerned or permitted by law.

Importantly, this article implicitly allows circumvention of anti-copying measures for acts which would be permitted by law but, in the nature of the Treaty provision, gives no practical guidance as to how this should or could be accomplished. The circumvention of anti-copying devices raises specific issues in relation to the ability to decompile and the legality of decompilation or disassembly of a computer program,[20] but also has wider implications for the dissemination of copyright works and also those not protected by copyright on the internet and world wide web. In the US the provisions on anti-circumvention are contained in the DMCA. The provisions now in 17 USC §1201 envisage both technological devices intended to control access and those intended to control copying.

Digital Millennium Copyright Act 1998
Sec 1201
Circumvention of copyright protection systems

Violations regarding circumvention of technological measures

(1)(A) No person shall circumvent a technological measure that effectively controls access to a work protected under this title ...

(2) No person shall manufacture, import, offer to the public, provide, or otherwise traffic in any technology, product, service, device, component, or part thereof, that –

(A) is primarily designed or produced for the purpose of circumventing a technological measure that effectively controls access to a work protected under this tile;

(B) has only limited commercially significant purpose or use other than to circumvent a technological measure that effectively controls access to a work protected under this title; or

(C) is marketed by that person or another acting in concert with that person with that person's knowledge for use in circumventing a technological measure that effectively controls access to a work protected under this tile.

...

Additional violations

No person shall manufacture, import , offer to the public, provide, or otherwise traffic in any technology, product, service, device, component, or part thereof, that –

(A) is primarily designed or produced for the purpose of circumventing protection afforded by a technological measure that effectively protects a right of a copyright owner under this title in a work or a portion thereof;

(B) has only limited commercially significant purpose or use other than to circumvent protection afforded by a technological measure that effectively protects a right of a copyright owner under this title in a work or a portion thereof;

(C) is marketed by that person or another acting in concert with that person with that person's knowledge for use in circumventing protection afforded by a technological measure that effectively protects a right of a copyright owner under this title in a work or a portion thereof ...

These provisions then include a number of very specific and detailed exemptions and the whole effect has been criticised both for its complexity but also on a more general basis. Samuelson suggests that, notwithstanding the US commitment to the WIPO Treaty which it has been instrumental in drafting, it might not have been necessary to create such elaborate statutory provisions to give effect to the Treaty's intentions as the pre-existing law could be construed appropriately.

---

20   See discussion in Chapter 2.

Intellectual property and the digital economy:
Why the anti-circumvention regulations need to be revised
Pamela Samuelson
(1999) 14 Berkeley Tech LJ 519, 530

The WIPO treaty digital copyright norms were, however, mostly old news for US law. Its cases had already recognised the rights of authors to control digital reproductions of their works, as well as to control digital transmissions of their works to the public. Courts had invoked fair use in a number of digital copyright cases and had refused to hold online service providers liable for infringing activities of users about which the providers had no knowledge. ...

The US could have asserted that its law already complied with the WIPO treaty's anti-circumvention norm. This norm was, after all, very general in character and provided treaty signatories with considerable latitude in implementation. Moreover, anti-circumvention legislation was new enough to many national intellectual property systems, and certainly to international law, to mean that there was no standard by which to judge how to instantiate the norm. The US could have pointed to a number of statutes and judicial decisions that establish anti-circumvention norms. With US copyright industries thriving in the current legal environment, it would have been fair to conclude that copyright owners already were adequately protected by the law. Even many of those who favor use of technical systems to protect digital copyrighted works have expressed skepticism about the need for or appropriateness of anti-circumvention regulations, at least at this stage. Let content producers build their technical fences, advised one prominent information economist, but do not legislatively reinforce those fences until experience proves the existence of one or more abuses in need of a specific cure. However, the political reality and legislative dynamics of the WIPO Copyright Treaty implementation process were such that some sort of anti-circumvention provision appeared to be a necessary part of the bill.

She concluded that, although the way in which the US implemented the WIPO Copyright Treaty generally conformed to the spirit of the Treaty, which provided a 'predictable, minimalist, consistent and simple legal environment', this could not be said of the anti-circumvention provisions which were 'unpredictable, overbroad, inconsistent, and complex. The many flaws in this legislation are likely to be harmful to innovation and competition in the digital economy sector, and harmful to the public's broader interests in being able to make fair and other non-infringing uses of copyrighted works.'[21] This latter point has also been discussed by Foged, who is concerned that such provisions have the potential to effect a drastic change on the traditional balance between copyright owners' rights and public user privileges in favour of the copyright owner.

US v EU anti circumvention legislation:
preserving the public's privileges in the digital age
Terese Foged
[2002] EIPR 525, 526

Technological measures prevent access not only for potential infringers, but may additionally prevent access for those who have a legitimate right to access, for example because of fair use. Furthermore, technological measures effectively prevent access, not only to copyright material, but also to other information and ideas that may not be subject to copyright but may be protected by the same technological measures. Access controls

---

21   *Ibid*, p. 563.

may have consequences for the user of a work; those parts of the work in the public domain become inaccessible, except at the behest of the copyright owner. Technological measures may cause material to be protected that would not have been protected by copyright laws. Authors are enabled to create rights in their works that are not subject to the limitations historically imposed by copyright law. It is at the expense of the public interest in the creation and dissemination of creative works. The risk of reducing the public's privileges is something to be aware of when allotting extra legal protection to copyright owners in the digital age.

Foged goes on to discuss a number of instances when public user privileges may be diminished, including when anti-circumvention measures operate to prevent rights given by fair use provisions and the fact that access may, incidentally, be prevented to works which are not subject to copyright protection such as ideas, facts and scènes à faire. A number of writers have also suggested that these provisions are unconstitutional and are an unacceptable restriction on freedom of speech. In making out such a case, Mitchell points out that the goal of the copyright clause in the US Constitution is defined as promoting the 'progress of science and the useful arts'. The widespread dissemination of information via the Internet is capable of fulfilling this objective by generally promoting learning.[22]

In the European Union, parallel legal provisions have been introduced in Directive 2001/29/EC, the 'Copyright Directive', implemented in the UK by the Copyright and Related Rights Regulations 2003. Although asserting that 'no new concepts for the protection of intellectual property are needed' but that 'the current law on copyright and related rights should be adapted and supplemented to respond adequately to economic realities such as new forms of exploitation' (Recital 5), the preamble contains many references to the appropriate balance of rights which needs to be achieved. The need for incentives and appropriate regard for creative and intellectual endeavour is emphasised in Recitals 9–11; Recital 14 notes the simultaneous need to 'seek to promote learning and culture ... while permitting exceptions or limitations in the public interest ... ' and Recital 31 states explicitly that 'a fair balance of rights and interests between the different categories of rightholders, as well as between the different categories of rightholders and users of protected subject-matter must be safeguarded.'

Directive 2001/29/EC
Preamble

(47) Technological development will allow rightholders to make use of technological measures designed to prevent or restrict acts not authorised by the rightholders of any copyright ... The danger, however exists that illegal activities might be carried out in order to enable or facilitate the circumvention of the technical protection provided by these measures. ... there is a need to provide for harmonised legal protection against circumvention of effective technological measures and against provision of devices and products or services to this effect.

(48) Such legal protection should be provided in respect of technological measures that effectively restrict acts not authorised by the rightholders of any copyright ... Such legal protection should respect proportionality and should not prohibit those devices or activities which have a commercially significant purpose or use other than to circumvent the technical protection ...

---

22 Mitchell, 2004. For further discussion of the alleged unconstitutionality of the DMCA, see e.g. Schley, 2004.

(51) The legal protection of technological measures applies without prejudice to public policy ... Member States should promote voluntary measures taken by right holders ... to accommodate achieving the objectives of certain exceptions and limitations provided for in national law in accordance with this Directive. In the absence of such voluntary arrangements ... Member States should take appropriate measures to ensure that rightholders provide beneficiaries of such exceptions or limitations with appropriate means of benefiting from them, by modifying an implemented technological measure, or by other means.

These provisos are then given legal effect in Article 6 of the Directive. The extent to which this provision is successful at balancing these competing interests is open to question. The wording does not lend itself to easy comprehension as highlighted by the following comment: 'the InfoSoc Directive's eventual provision on the subject, Art 6, became during the legislative process so twisted by conflicting demands as to resemble Laocoon wrestling with the serpents. Legislation should never be so hideously contorted but here it writhes'.[23]

Directive 2001/29/EC
Article 6
Obligations as to technical measures

1. Member States shall provide adequate legal protection against the circumvention of any effective technological measures, which the person concerned carries out in the knowledge or with reasonable grounds to know, that he or she is pursuing that objective.

2. Member States shall provide adequate legal protection against the manufacture, import, distribution, sale, rental, advertisement for sale or rental, or possession for commercial purposes of devices, products or components or the provision of services which:

    (a) are promoted, advertised or marketed for the purposes of circumvention of, or

    (b) have only a limited commercially significant purpose or use other than to circumvent, or

    (c) are primarily designed , produced, adapted or performed for the purposes of enabling or facilitating the circumvention of,

any effective technological measures.

...

4. ... in the absence of voluntary measures taken by rightholders ... Member States shall take appropriate measures to ensure that rightholders make available to the beneficiary of an exception or limitation provided by national law in accordance with Article 5(2)(a), (2)(c), (2)(d), (2)(e), (3)(a), (3)(b) or (3)(c) the means of benefiting from that exception or limitation ...

The provisions of Article 6(1) and (2) although not distinguishing between access control and copy control devices are, nevertheless, very similar in essence to those of the DMCA. However, the effect of Art 6(4) in no way encompasses all possible exceptions and limitations to the exclusive rights granted to copyright holders; for example the right to use material for the purposes of criticism or review. This suggests

---

23 Cornish and Llewelyn, 2003, p. 810.

that, for fair dealing rights not included in Art 6(4), the Directive does not assist in maintaining a fair balance between authors' and users' rights.[24]

These are still comparatively early days to assess the full impact and implications of these provisions. The case law in the US is beginning to amass and most of the courts have enforced the DMCA provisions in the way that might be expected, despite (sometimes vigorous) pleadings to the contrary.[25] In this respect the result of legislative intervention may well be to create a diminution in fair use rights which can be contrasted with the application of more general fair use principles to other copyright issues as discussed in the next section.

COPYRIGHT AND FILE SHARING

The Digital Millennium Copyright Act 2000 and similar enactments do not prevent standard copyright principles being applied to activities on the internet. Given the quality of the copies which can be obtained by digitisation, it is not surprising that ever more inventive ways have been found to both copy and deal in copyright material. This is nowhere so apparent as in the growth in both sophistication and usage of peer-to-peer (P2P) file sharing software. Historically, copyright infringement was rarely pursued against individual infringers, not only because of difficulties of detection, but also because the amount of copying was relatively insignificant.[26] The advent of the perfect copy, which could be easily and simultaneously made available to multitudes of users, has moved the focus of litigation onto both the individual infringer and the means by which the infringement can occur; those who facilitate individual copying and file sharing. This has resulted in copyright owners, notably the music recording industry, taking action in a number of jurisdictions against not only those who make available various types of P2P file sharing software, but also individual infringers. The litigation thus spawned represents far more than merely a dispute over the application of copyright to new activities made possible by internet technology, but has been presented as a battle between those, usually individuals, who espouse the freedom to access information that the internet provides and corporate interests. As Cornish and Llewelyn remark: 'the *Napster* judgment in the US (see discussion below) has become a bleeding image much paraded in the campaigns to preserve the Internet as an unfettered instrument of free exchange.'[27] The following extract gives the background and some of the factors surrounding the advent of this phenomenon together with an explanation of the *modus operandi* of the software.

Peer-to peer file sharing and copyright infringement:
Danger ahead for individuals sharing files on the internet
Richard Swope
(2004) 44 Santa Clara L Rev 861

One Internet activity that has become popular over the last few years is file sharing, specifically peer-to-peer (P2P) file sharing. P2P file sharing's popularity is such that the

---

24 See also the more detailed discussion of this point in Foged 2002, pp 536–8 and Hart, 2002, pp 62–63.
25 See eg, *Universal City Studios Inc v Reimerdes* 111 F Supp 2d 294 (2000) (discussed further below at p 512), *US v Elcom Ltd* 203 F Supp 2d 1111 (2002) and *321 Studios v MGM Studios Inc* 307 F Supp 2d 1085 (2004).
26 See eg, Ginsburg, 1995; Wu, 2003 pp 711–716; Lemley and Reese 2004, pp 1373–1379.
27 Cornish and Llewelyn, 2003, p 804.

overall Internet bandwidth used by users sharing files dwarfs the bandwidth used by regular Internet users. File sharing is, as its name implies, the practice of sharing files between users connected to the Internet. The vast majority of files shared on these file-sharing networks are unlicensed copyright works. Currently, the file-sharing networks allow the sharing of not only music files, but any type of file, including video, images and software. ...

... In its simplest form, P2P is a technology that allows a computer connected to a network to both initiate communication and respond directly to queries from other computers connected to the same network without having to go through an intermediate server. A common application for a P2P network is file sharing. In a P2P network, a computer connected to the network can query the other computers on the network for a particular file and once the file is located, request a copy of the file directly from that computer. In addition, the computer can respond to queries from other computers, and if the file requested exists on the queried computer, that computer can send a copy of the file directly to the querying computer. In contrast, a non-P2P network generally uses a client-server communications architecture, in which a computer connected to the network sends queries to a server and can only communicate with other computers connected to the network via a server.

In standard client-server network architecture, access to particular types of data – such as copyrighted materials – can be limited to protect the rights of copyright holders. For example, copyrighted material on the server could be segregated from "free" material, and only persons with valid authorisation would be allowed to download the copyrighted material. In addition, since there is no way for individual client computers to communicate with one another directly, any unauthorised transfer of copyrighted material can be monitored or filtered at the server. In a P2P network, however, the ability to control access to copyrighted material is limited. The software itself can be designed to filter transfers, but this configuration requires each computer attached to the P2P network to perform checks on material being shared against a database of enumerated 'banned' files. If the file-sharing activity is high, the computers have to check many files, thereby slowing the system dramatically. Furthermore, this type of system is only effective if the enumerated lists of files are accurate and up-to-date.

The Internet itself is a type of global client-server network; software enables computers to communicate in a P2P fashion via the Internet. Any two users connected to the Internet who are running the same P2P software can communicate directly with each other as if they were on a separate P2P network. P2P communication over the Internet first became popular with the rise of companies offering free P2P networking over the web. The most notable of these companies was Napster; Napster offered its users free software to share their files easily with other Napster users via Napster's own P2P network.

Napster was, arguably, the most notable because it was the first to be pursued by the record companies who were concerned at the effect that this technology might have on record sales. Napster operated by means of a centralised server, which meant that the requests for the files passed through a central server although the actual file transfers were conducted between individual users.[28] As use of the Napster system grew in the late 1990s, a lawsuit was brought against those operating Napster by a number of record companies and music publishers making various claims, including contributory and vicarious liability for copyright infringement. Napster, for its part, responded that its users could avail themselves of the fair use defence on the basis of sampling the

---

28   See further Swope, 2004 and the explanation given in *MGM v Grokster* 380 F3d 1154, 1159 (9th Cir. 2004).

music before buying and also space-shifting, that is, using the Napster system to make a copy of an audio CD of which they were already the legitimate owner. The US Court of Appeals for the Ninth Circuit[29] considered the four fair use factors. In terms of the purpose and character of the use, the court found that a commercial use 'weighs against a finding of fair use but is not conclusive'. Although 'direct economic benefit was not required to demonstrate a commercial use' in relation to Napster 'commercial use is demonstrated by a showing that repeated and exploitative unauthorised copies of copyrighted works were made to save the expense of purchasing authorised copies.' In addition, merely retransmitting in a different format was not a 'transformative' use.[30] Given the creative nature of the works copied, the second fair use factor 'nature of the use' militated against a finding of fair use. The third factor requires a consideration of the portion used. Although copying a whole work can amount to fair use in certain situations, in general it militates against fair use. The final factor is the effect of the alleged fair use on the market. To assess this, the court assessed a number of reports on the use of Napster and its effect on the sale of recorded music and concluded that 'having digital downloads for free on the Napster system necessarily harms the copyright holders' attempts to charge for the same downloads'. The cumulative effect of these findings was that file sharing was not protected by the fair use provisions. Applying this reasoning to sampling, the court upheld the previous findings that 'sampling remains a commercial use even if some users eventually purchase the music ... even authorised temporary downloading of individual songs for sampling purposes is commercial in nature'. This was not affected by the fact that record companies, themselves, sometimes provided samples for users to try before purchase as 'free downloads provided by record companies consist of thirty to sixty second samples or are ... programmed to ... exist only for a short time on the downloader's computer'. In comparison, Napster users downloaded a full, free and permanent copy of the recording. Overall, Napster was found to have 'an adverse impact on the audio CD and digital download markets.' The space-shifting argument was made in analogy with the seminal case of *Sony v Universal City Studios*,[31] in relation to video recordings made for time-shifting purposes. In *Sony*, it was held that time shifting was fair use, but the same argument was held not to be applicable to Napster, because, in *Sony*, there was no question of also simultaneously making the copyright materials available to other members of the public. 'It is obvious that once a user lists a copy of music he already owns on the Napster system in order to access the music from another location, the song becomes available to millions of other individuals, not just the original CD owner.'

Having ascertained that there was no fair use and that Napster users were directly infringing copyright, the court went on to consider whether Napster could be liable for contributory infringement, which required an assessment of whether they knew or had reason to know of the direct infringement. In *Sony*, there was no evidence of actual knowledge of specific cases of infringement. Neither did the Supreme Court assign constructive knowledge to Sony for infringing uses of their video recorders on the

---

29 *A&M Records v Napster* 239 F 3d 1004 (9th Cir. 2001).
30 Following the judgment of the Supreme Court in *Campbell v Acuff-Rose* 510 US 569, L Ed 2d 500 (1994).
31 464 US 417, 78 Led 2d 574 (1984).

grounds that the equipment could be used for both infringing and 'substantial non-infringing' uses. The lower court had based liability on the fact that Napster had 'failed to demonstrate that its system is capable of commercially significant noninfringing uses', but the Court of Appeals departed from this reasoning and, instead, found that Napster had '*actual* knowledge that *specific* infringing material is available using its system, that it could block access to the system by suppliers of the infringing material, and that it failed to remove the material'. Neither was it willing to countenance Napster's attempt to avail itself of the DMCA 'safe harbor' for ISPs.

The outcome was that Napster was closed down although it has since been resurrected as a subscription service. The reason for Napster's demise was primarily due to its centralised architecture and its consequent ability to both control and to block access. As Wu has commented: 'Napster taught peer network designers that both lack of control and general functionality had to be comprehensive and credible to avoid contributory liability.'[32] However, the decentralised system, Aimster (since renamed Madster), did not escape liability when it came to be considered by the Seventh Circuit. The extract below shows how this system differs from Napster.

In re: Aimster Copyright Litigation
334 F 3d 643
US Court of Appeals for the Seventh Circuit (2003)

Aimster's server searches the computers of those users of its software who are online and so are available to be searched for files they are willing to share, and if it finds the file that has been requested it instructs the computer in which it is housed to transmit the file to the recipient via the Internet for him to download into his computer. Once he has done this he can if he wants make the file available for sharing with other users of the Aimster system by listing it as explained above. In principle, therefore, the purchase of a single CD could be levered into the distribution within days or even hours of millions of identical, near-perfect ... copies of the music recorded on the CD ... But because the copies of the songs reside on the computers of the users and not on Aimster's own server, Aimster is not a direct infringer of the copyrights on those songs.

The court was critical, however, of the Ninth circuit's interpretation of *Sony* since it was clear that, in that case, there was evidence that the technology was being used for both infringing and non-infringing uses, but the court did not wish to deny non-infringing users the benefit of the technology. It therefore disagreed with the suggestion that 'actual knowledge of specific infringing uses is a sufficient condition for deeming a facilitator a contributory infringer.' Instead, it took the view that 'when a supplier is offering a product or service that has non-infringing uses as well as infringing uses, some estimate of the respective magnitudes of these uses is necessary for a finding of contributory infringement.' Although the Aimster system could, in principle, be used for 'innocuous purposes such as the expeditious exchange of confidential business data' in fact the only examples given in the explanatory tutorial about Aimster involved the sharing of copyrighted material. Neither was the argument that encryption prevented the operators from knowing what was being copied persuasive – 'wilful blindness is knowledge in copyright law'. Aimster had 'failed to produce any evidence that its service has ever been used for a non-infringing use, alone evidence concerning the frequency of such uses ... its ostrich-like refusal to

---

32 Wu, 2003, p. 730.

discover the extent to which its system was being used to infringe copyright is merely another piece of evidence that it was a contributory infringer.' Even if it could be shown that there were substantial non-infringing uses, the operator would still have to show that it would have been disproportionately costly to prevent or substantially reduce the number of infringing uses.

At this point it appeared that whether the system was centralised or decentralised, in the absence of genuine evidence that a file sharing system both could, and did, have non-infringing uses, the courts were likely to find liability for contributory infringement. Concern was expressed that this application of the law could have an unfortunate effect on the development of the technology.

Reducing digital copyright infringement without restricting innovation
Mark A Lemley and R Anthony Reese
(2004) 56 Stan L Rev 1345, 1362

Like the Ninth Circuit's Napster opinion, Aimster's interpretation of Sony poses significant challenges for innovation. Someone who develops a new dual-use technology must be concerned about whether non-infringing use of that technology will not only be 'substantial' but perhaps whether it will be the primary use, as well as whether she will be able to prove that substantial or primary use in court. Perhaps more significantly, even if the innovator is confident as to how the technology will be used, she will have to consider ... whether she can design the technology to reduce or eliminate the possibility of infringing uses of the technology, what the costs of doing so are, and whether a court will decide that those costs are 'disproportionate' and therefore need not be expended.

This was, however, before the Ninth Circuit gave its opinion in *MGM v Grokster*. Grokster was an example of a peer-to-peer (P2P) sharing network based on 'the 'supernode' model in which a number of select computers on the network are designated as indexing servers. The user initiating a file search connects with the most easily accessible supernode, which conducts the search of its index and supplies the user with the results. Any computer on the network could function as a supernode if it met the technical requirements, such as processing speed.'[33] This was described by the lower court as being 'novel in important respects', but was nevertheless operating in 'a manner conceptually analogous to the Napster system' as explained below.

MGM v Grokster
259 F Supp 2d 1029, 1032
United States District Court, CD California, (2003)

In both cases, the software can be transferred to the user's computer, or 'downloaded' from servers operated by defendants. Once installed, a user may elect to 'share' certain files located on the user's computer, including, for instance, music files, video files, software applications, e-books and text files. When launched on the user's computer, the software automatically connects to a peer-to-peer network ... and makes any shared files available for transfer to any other user currently connected to the same peer-to-peer network. ... a user can select to search only among audio files, and then enter a keyword, title or artist search. ... The user may then click on a specific listing to initiate a direct transfer from the source computer to the requesting user's computer. When the transfer is complete, the requesting user and source user have identical copies of the file, and the

---

33 *MGM v Grokster* 380 F 3d 1154, 1159 (9th Cir. 2004).

requesting user may also start sharing the file with others. Multiple transfers to other users ('uploads'), or from users ('downloads'), may occur simultaneously to and from a single users' computer.

Although 'conceptually analogous' to Napster, the major distinguishing feature is that requests for files are not routed through a central server and neither, therefore, is there any possibility of controlling or preventing access to infringing material. Referring to both its previous judgment in *Napster* and that of the Supreme Court in *Sony*, the Ninth Circuit concluded that there was no liability for contributory infringement.

MGM v Grokster
380 F 3d 1154, 1160
US Court of Appeals for the Ninth Circuit, (2004)

Napster I held that if a defendant could show that its product was capable of substantial or commercially significant noninfringing uses, then constructive knowledge of the infringement could not be imputed. Rather, if substantial non-infringing use was shown, the copyright owner would be required to show that the defendant had reasonable knowledge of specific infringing files.

Thus, in order to analyze the required element of knowledge if infringement, we must first determine what level of knowledge to require. If the product at issue is not capable of substantial or commercially significant non-infringing uses, then the copyright owner need only show that the defendant had constructive knowledge of the infringement. On the other hand, if the product at issue *is* capable of substantial or commercially significant non-infringing uses, then the copyright owner must demonstrate that the defendant had reasonable knowledge of specific infringing files and failed to act on that knowledge to prevent infringement. ...

In this case, the Software Distributors have not only shown that their products are capable of substantial non-infringing uses, but that the uses have commercial viability. Thus applying *Napster I, Napster II and Sony-Betamax* to the record, the district court correctly concluded that the Software Distributors had established that their products were capable of substantial or commercially significant non-infringing uses. Therefore the district correctly reasoned, the Software Distributors could not be held liable for constructive knowledge of infringement, and the Copyright Owners were required to show that the Software Distributors had reasonable knowledge of specific infringement to satisfy the threshold knowledge requirement. ...

In the context of this case, the software design is of great import. ... the software at issue in *[Napster]* employed a centralised set of servers that maintained an index of available files. In contrast under ... Grokster's quasi-decentralised supernode ... no central index is maintained. As the district court observed: even if the Software Distributors 'closed their doors and deactivated all computers within their control, users of their products could continue sharing files with little or no interruption.' ...

... defendants also communicate with users incidentally, but not to facilitate infringement. All of these activities are too incidental to any direct copyright infringement to constitute material contribution. No infringing files or lists of infringing files are hosted by defendants, and the defendants do not regulate or provide access.

While Grokster ... may seek to be the 'next Napster', the peer-to peer file-sharing technology at issue is not simply a tool engineered to get around the holdings of *Napster I* and *Napster II*. The technology has numerous other uses, significantly reducing the distribution costs of public domain and permissively shared art and speech, as well as reducing the centralised control of that distribution. ...

... unlike Napster, Grokster ... [does] not operate and design an 'integrated service' which they monitor and control. ... The nature of the relationship between Grokster ...

and their users is significantly different from the nature of the relationship between a swap meet operator and its participants or prior versions of Napster and its users, since Grokster ... [is a] more truly centralised, peer-to-peer file-sharing network. ...

... we live in a quicksilver technological environment with courts ill-suited to fix the flow of internet innovation. The introduction of new technology is always disruptive to old markets and particularly to those copyright owners whose works are sold through well-established distribution mechanisms. Yet, history has shown that time and market forces often provide equilibrium in balancing interests, whether the new technology be a player piano, a copier, a tape recorder, a video recorder, a personal computer, a karaoke machine, or an MP3 player. Thus, it is prudent for courts to exercise caution before restructuring liability theories for the purposes of addressing specific market abuses, despite their apparent present magnitude.

The Ninth Circuit was 'mindful' that the outcome in the Seventh Circuit's deliberations on Aimster had been different, but noted that this decision had been arrived at as a result of a disagreement of the use of the *Sony* precedent in *Napster* and that they were compelled to follow the precedent set by their own Circuit. In commenting on the decision of the lower court, Wu suggested that, given its dependence on the interpretation of *Sony*, it might not survive appeal since Sony effectively corrected a market failure whereas 'file sharing looks more like a replacement for legitimate music sales; such reasoning may compel a court to find some way to assess liability on P2P developers ... '[34]. Nevertheless, as seen above the decision was upheld on appeal and, indeed, the final paragraph quoted seems to warn against and automatic reaction based on the perceived effect on the market for recorded music. Wu further suggested that final settlement of the filesharing argument may have to be a task for Congress and that this might be the outcome of a decision against the copyright owners.[35] However, this was not the end of the matter; a further appeal to the Supreme Court was granted and the case was heard in March 2005. In June 2005, a unanimous ruling overturned the previous decision holding that 'one who distributes a device with the object of promoting its use to infringe copyright as shown by clear expression or other affirmative steps taken to foster infringement, is liable for the resulting acts of infringement by third parties.'[36]

The supernode architecture, of which Grokster is an example, had been developed by a Dutch company, KaZaa, which itself distributed file sharing software via its website. This could be used for the exchange of text image and sound files. In a dispute with the licensing organisation BUMA-STEMRA, the Amsterdam Appeal Court found that, although individual users might infringe copyright when file sharing, the distributor of the software (KaZaa) was not liable as, unlike Napster, it did not use a central server and could not control what files were shared once the software had been installed on a user's computer. There was also evidence that the software was being used for legal purposes which included the exchange of both copyright material with the permission of the copyright owner and also non-copyright material. This reasoning was upheld by the Dutch Supreme Court in December 2003 and it is

---

34   Wu, 2003, p 739.

35   *Ibid*, p 740.

36   The decision of the 9th Circuit was overturned and the case was remanded for a rehearing in the light of the Supreme Court reasoning. The Supreme Court judgment was given too late for any substantive discussion to be included in this edition but the full text is available at http://a257.g.akamaitech.net/7/257/2422/27jun20051200/www.supremecourtus.gov/opinions/04pdf/04-480.pdf.

expected that the issues will now be aired in a full hearing.[37] The KaZaa file sharing system is also the subject of litigation in Australia, the outcome of which may be more indicative of the way in which English law concepts might be applied to these activities. At the time of writing the decision is still awaited.[38]

Because of the uncertainty of winning cases against the distributors of the software the recording and music industry has instead begun to initiate suits against the actual users of the software.[39] The Court of First Instance of Brussels, relying on Article 8(3) of the Copyright Directive, has ruled against the ISP, Tiscali, for file sharing of infringing music files via its service.[40] In practical terms, more and more sites are offering music downloads for a small fee per track. This may take the sting out of some of the litigation.

From entertainment to education
Charlotte Waelde and Hector MacQueen
[2004] IPQ 259, 274

Another important development in 2003 strongly supported and promoted by the music recording industry was the launch of a number of licensed music download websites. The IFPI report stated in January 2004 that the total number of subscribers to such sites had reached half a million, although consumer awareness was still low. Companies from outside the music industry were also establishing music download sites. ...

The issue which dogs the licensing of file-swapping websites is the restricted amount of material which the recorded music industry appears to be willing to allow into circulation by contrast with the 'world of almost limitless access to content' created originally by the likes of Napster. There have accordingly been arguments for the reintroduction of a system of compulsory licensing akin to the 'mechanical reproduction right' known in UK law between the 1911 and 1988 Copyright Acts, under which once the copyright holder had granted permission to make a recording of a musical work, third parties were also free to make such recordings subject to payment of a statutorily fixed licence fee. Such proposals are rejected by the recorded music industry on pretty much the grounds which explained their repeal in the 1988 Act, namely that they involve too great a constraint upon market freedom and competition; but if copyright is used to prevent the coming to market of products for which there is reasonable public demand, then there may indeed be grounds in competition law for intervention of some kind. Compulsory licensing would sit rather easily with automated contracting; it might also be thought of as compulsory blanket licensing of the repertoire of recording companies, akin to that which collecting societies already grant voluntarily to broadcasters.

ISSUES RAISED BY LINKING ON
THE WORLD WIDE WEB

A further feature of the relevant technology which has created challenges for traditional legal principles is the web link.[41] The phenomenon of hypertext linking,

---

37 See Bettink and Wentholt, 2004.

38 For preliminary hearings see *Universal Music Australia Pty Ltd v Sharman License Holdings Ltd* [2004] FCA 183; *Brilliant Digital Entertainment Pty Ltd v Universal Music Australia Pty Ltd* [2004] FCA 448; *Brilliant Digital Entertainment Pty Ltd v Universal Music Australia Pty Ltd* [2004] FCAFC 270. All available from www.austlii.edu.au. See also commentary in Oliver, 2005.

39 See eg, discussion in Swope, 2004, p. 873 and Waelde and MacQueen, 2004.

40 *SABAM v Tiscali*, above fn 18.

41 For a general overview see, eg, Stangret, 1997.

which allows the user to move from site to site, is now so familiar as to have lost all remaining vestiges of novelty, but is indisputably crucial to the existence and operation of the world wide web. Linking provides the way in which information is retrieved via search engines and is the way in which users move from site to site. A site which is not linked is less likely to be found by other users and its worth will be diminished to the user if he or she cannot travel from that site to another. Conversely, many people will bookmark sites which contain a collection of links to sites relevant to their interests.[42] The number of times different users arrive at a site (the number of 'hits') is a useful way of gauging the site's appeal and popularity as well as the efficiency of its links and, for commercial sites, the number of hits may be an important way of raising revenue.

Controlling world wide web links: property rights, access rights and unfair competition
Chris Reed
(1998) 6 Indiana J Global LS[43]

In order to analyse how the law might be applied to web links, it is necessary to understand the way in which a link works. Each link is part of a web page whose display is created on the viewer's computer by his browser software. The web page is built up using the instructions contained in the HTML file produced by the creator of the page, which is transmitted to the viewer's browser when he enters that page's URL. The HTML file contains text to be displayed as part of the page, the URLs for any images or other binary files (for example, sound files) that are to be incorporated automatically into the page, and instructions for laying out the page on the viewer's screen.

The HTML file may also contain code for a link. That code highlights some element of the page, normally either a piece of text or an image, which is selectable by the viewer with his mouse. The HTML file associates a URL with the page element. When the viewer selects that page element, the browser software sends a request to the associated URL for a file and, upon receipt, performs the appropriate action for that type of file. The simplest kind of link is to another web page; its selection by the viewer results in his browser receiving the new HTML file and, by following the instructions in its code, building a fresh page for display.

It is important to note that the creator of the web page containing the link does not transmit the linked-to page to the viewer. He merely provides the address from which the linked-to page can be obtained. It is the viewer, through the browser software, who requests the page, receives a copy of its code, and displays the resulting work; while it is the proprietor of the linked-to page who transmits the HTML code to the viewer via a web server.

Given the fact that the world wide web cannot function without links does the fact of launching a website create an implied licence to link to it? Or is there something akin to a right to link? Various real world analogies have been suggested for hypertext links. In *Universal City Studios v Reimerdes*,[44] it was said that: 'links bear a relationship to the information superhighway comparable to the relationship that roadway signs bear to roads but they are more functional. Like roadway signs, they point out the

---

42 For an example of such a site in the present context see the Link Controversy page at www.jura.uni-tuebingen.de/~s-bes1/lcp.html.
43 Available at www.law.indiana.edu/glsj/vol6/no1/reed.html.
44 111 F Supp 2d 294 (SDNY 2000).

direction.' An alternative analogy is that of the footnote or reference, Burk explains that: 'the hypertext link is in essence an automated version of a scholarly footnote or bibliographic reference: it tells the reader where to find the referenced material'[45] and Deveci has made the categorical comment that 'a link is no different from a citation in hard copy'.[46] However although a link may conceptually perform both of these functions, it accomplishes more than merely showing the user where to go. As the court in *Reimerdes* went on to say: 'unlike roadway signs, they take one almost instantaneously to the desired destination with the mere click of an electronic mouse'. The same is clearly true for the citation/reference analogy as graphically explained by Burk: 'the user's browser ... can then retrieve the material from its location, a process that is not only hidden from the user, but far more convenient than physically venturing into library stacks to retrieve hardcopy referenced in a plain footnote'. To what extent does this additional functionality affect liability? Writers would not expect to find themselves liable for copyright infringement on the basis of an infringement in a work cited in a footnote, why should a different situation pertain in relation to links?

The case of *Reimerdes* arose because the defendant had made available the decryption code for DVD recordings on his website. After removing this information he continued to maintain links to other sites where the relevant code could be found. As discussed above, the DMCA, prohibits, *inter alia*, the trafficking in anti-circumvention technology. The question for the district court was whether maintaining such links could be equated with trafficking, especially as in this case, where the linked-to sites contained no other material and indeed, where activating the link initiated an automatic download. The court found that in this case there can be 'no serious question. Defendants are engaged in the functional equivalent of transferring the DeCSS code to the user themselves.' Nor was it persuaded that there was any significant difference where users were offered a choice as to whether or not to download the offending code; 'the only distinction is that the entity extending to the user the option of downloading the program is the transferee site rather than defendants, a distinction without difference.' It was admitted that it might be more difficult if linked-to sites contained additional content such that any prohibition on linking could perhaps be construed as breaching First Amendment rights.

Universal City Studios v Reimerdes
111 F Supp 2d 294, 340
US District Court
SD New York (2000)

Links are ... used in ways that do a great deal to promote the free exchange of ideas and information that is a central value of our nation. Anything that would impose strict liability on a web site operator for the entire contents of any web site to which the operator linked therefore would raise grave constitutional concerns, as web site operators would be inhibited from linking for fear of exposure to liability. And it is equally clear that exposing those who use links to liability under the DMCA might chill their use, as some web site operators confronted with claims that they have posted circumvention technology falling within the statute may be more inclined to remove the allegedly offending link rather than test the issue in court. Moreover, web sites often contain a great

---

45   Burk, 1998.
46   Deveci, 2004.

variety of things, and a ban on linking to a site that contains DeCSS amidst other content threatens to restrict communication of this information to an excessive degree.

The possible chilling effect of a rule permitting liability for or injunctions against Internet hyperlinks is a genuine concern. But it is not unique to the issue of linking. The constitutional law of defamation provides a highly relevant analogy. The threat of defamation suits creates the same risk of self-censorship, the same chilling effect, for the traditional press as a prohibition of linking to sites containing circumvention technology poses for web site operators. Just as the potential chilling effect of defamation suits has not utterly immunised the press from all actions for defamation, however, the potential chilling effect of DMCA liability cannot utterly immunise website operators from all actions for disseminating circumvention technology. And the solution to the problem is the same: the adoption of a standard of culpability sufficiently high to immunise the activity, whether it is publishing a newspaper or linking, except in cases in which the conduct in question has little or no redeeming constitutional value.

...

... there may be no injunction against, nor liability for, linking to a site containing circumvention technology, the offering of which is unlawful under the DMCA, absent clear and convincing evidence that those responsible for the link (a) know at the relevant time that the offending material is on the linked-to site, (b) know that it is circumvention technology that may not lawfully be offered, and (c) create or maintain the link for the purpose of disseminating that technology. Such a standard will limit the fear of liability on the part of web site operators ... and it will not subject web site operators to liability for linking to a site containing proscribed technology where the link exists for purposes other than dissemination of that technology.

Thus, in this test, the knowledge element was crucial and it could, in principle, be extended to other cases of direct linking, involving other unlawful activities, where the person making the link was both aware of the existence of unlawful content and also, perhaps, was making the link for that purpose. When the matter was subsequently considered by the Second Circuit, however, there was agreement on the actual facts of the case, that is, that there was a violation of the anti-trafficking provisions of the DMCA given the nature of the links at issue, but the court felt that it had neither need to consider the use of such a test in a more general case, nor was it the appropriate forum as 'it is not for us to resolve the issues of public policy implicated ... Those issues are for Congress'.[47]

Notwithstanding the discussion on linking in *Reimerdes*, it is a case where the functionality of the link was crucial to the outcome and the extent to which it can be applied to the more general case of a direct link is doubtful. Whether the knowledge test can be used if the linkor knows that the link may result in a breach of copyright ultimately depends on an adjudication of the function of links and whether there exist legitimate restrictions on making links or whether there is something akin to a 'right to link'. On the latter, there is evidence that the courts may not wish to inhibit unduly the use and utility of the new technology. Indeed, in arriving at its decision, the court in *Kelly v Arriba*, discussed above, as well as suggesting a lenient approach when the technology is evolving, also referred to the 'established importance of search engines' indicating its awareness of the need to facilitate this type of linking. In addition, any knowledge test also has to be circumscribed if the linkor is not to run the risk of either

---

47   *Universal City Studios v Corley* 273 F 3d 429, 458.

being found liable for additional linked sites, or liable at a future date because the content of the linked-to site has changed. These issues were considered by the Higher Regional Court in Munich in a judgment which seemed to suggest that the fact of the establishment of a link itself creates a responsibility for the linked content, although it did not need to decide this in relation to the actual case before it.[48]

The crucial question for this chapter is whether, and in what circumstances, links to material on other sites can violate the intellectual property rights of the creator of the material or the proprietor of the site? One of the first cases to raise this issue was that of *Shetland Times v Wills*,[49] which, despite being only an interlocutory hearing, has received substantial debate and comment.[50]

The *Shetland Times* is an old established newspaper, serving the Shetland Islands. Wills, an ex-employee of the *Shetland Times*, started an electronic newspaper, the *Shetland News*. When its site was accessed, the reader would see a selection of headlines, on which he or she could click to read the full story. Some of these headlines were reproduced verbatim from the *Shetland Times* website and, when these particular hypertext links were followed, the reader would be taken directly to the story on the *Shetland Times* site, bypassing the *Shetland Times* home page, in other words it used what would now be referred to as a 'deep link'. Although there was no suggestion that the actual stories had been copied from one site to the other (a process made rather superfluous by the technology), the *Shetland Times* alleged infringement of its copyright.[51]

Shetland Times v Wills
1997 SLT 669, p 670
Outer House

Lord Hamilton The grounds of action are twofold. The pursuers maintain that the headlines made available by them on their web site are cable programmes within the meaning of s 7 of the Copyright, Designs and Patent Act 1988 ... that the facility made available by the defenders on their web site is a cable programme within the meaning of s 7, and that the inclusion of those items on that service constitute an infringement of copyright under s 20 of the Act. The pursuers also maintain that the headlines are literary works owned by them and that the defenders' activities constituted infringement by copying under s 17 of the Act, that copying being in the form of storing the works by electronic means ...

No detailed technical information was put before me in relation to the electronic mechanism involved. It was simply submitted [by the defenders] that there was not 'sending' in an ordinary sense and that a contrast could be made with cable television

---

48 Oberlandesgericht München MMR 2002 p. 65.
49 1997 SLT 669; [1997] FSR 604.
50 See, eg, Campbell, 1997; Connolly and Cameron, 1998; MacQueen, 1998. For comparison with other linking cases see, eg, Sableman, 1999.
51 This can be compared with the US case of *Ticketmaster Corp v Microsoft Corp* (1997) (www.jmls.edu/cyber/cases/ticket1.html), in which a website containing a city guide to Seattle linked directly to Ticketmaster pages providing details of events and tickets, bypassing the home page. Ticketmaster alleged that this link constituted trademark dilution and unfair competition but the case was settled by means of an agreement whereby any links would only be made directly to the home page. In *Playboy Enterprises v Universal Tel-a-Talk Inc* US Dist Lexis 8231 (1998) (www.bna.com/e-law/cases/playtele.html), the court found that the use of the word 'playboy' in a hypertext link from the defendant's to PEI's site did not constitute trademark infringement.

where there was sending by transmission from the provider to the customer. On the internet a caller electronically accessed information which was provided entirely passively.

In my view the pursuers' contention that the service provided by them involves the sending of information is prima facie well founded. Although in a sense the information, it seems, passively awaits access being had to it by callers, that does not, at least *prima facie* preclude the notion that the information, on such access being taken, is conveyed to and received by the caller. If that is so, the process may arguably be said to involve the sending of that information ...

... On the information that was available or on the basis of the arguments presented, the pursuers have, in my opinion, a *prima facie* case that the incorporation by the defenders in their web site of the headlines provided at the pursuers' web site constitutes an infringement of s 20 of the Act by inclusion in a cable programme service of protected cable programmes ...

... While literary merit is not a necessary element of a literary work, there may be a question of whether headlines, which are essentially brief indications of the subject matter of the items to which they relate, are protected by copyright. However, in light of the concession that a headline could be a literary work and since the headlines at issue (or at least some of them) involve eight or so words designedly put together for the purpose of imparting information, it appears to me arguable that there was an infringement, at least in some instances, of s 17.

So-called deep links have continued to be the subject of litigation. In an early dispute between Ticketmaster and Microsoft, Microsoft had created deep links that bypassed the Ticketmaster home page.[52] The case settled apparently by agreeing a licence which required any links to be to the home page, illustrating the fact that often the main issue for commercial sites may be that bypassing the home page results in a loss of revenue. In addition, the deep link may access material for which a password or some form of registration would normally be required, but this technology can also be used to prevent links other than to the home page altogether. In the later case of *Ticketmaster Corp v Tickets.com*,[53] both parties provided information and sold tickets for a variety of entertainment and sporting events. For events for which it did not sell tickets itself, Tickets.com listed alternative vendors and often deep linked to other similar sites such as that of Ticketmaster. On the copyright issue, the court applied the decision of the Supreme Court in *Feist*,[54] and reasoned that there was no copyright protection for facts or raw data. This limited the information that could be protected and further, the four elements of the fair use doctrine favoured Tickets.com. Tickets.com made temporary copies of the material from Ticketmaster's pages and the final webpage did not contain any infringing material. Ticketmaster thus gained very little assistance from the law of copyright in trying to prevent the deep links to its site.

A number of cases from Europe have not suggested that copyright law is a major tool in the regulation of hyperlinks. In *Algemeen Dagblad BV & ors v Eureka Internetdiensten*,[55] Eureka operated a website, www.kranten.com, containing a page of

---

52 No. 97-3055 DDP (CD Cal 1997).
53 2003 WL 21406289. See discussion in Zynda, 2004.
54 113 L Ed 2d 358 (1991) and see discussion in Chapter 2.
55 The 'kranten.com' case Case 139609/KGZA 00-846 District Court of Rotterdam 22 August 2000 www.ivir.nl/rechtspraak/kranten.com-EN.html. See also discussion in Chapter 2 at p 90.

national newspapers which listed news reports and articles matching that provided on the papers' own website. These were deep links taking the user straight to the story and bypassing the home page. In addition, Eureka also provided a daily email service with the latest news stories in the form of a list of these deep links. The court was unconcerned about the effect of deep linking, noting that the homepages of the newspapers were not made inaccessible by the deep link, that kranten.com did not take over the function of these home pages, nor did it prejudice the exploitation of the home pages. Its view was that, for the purposes of copyright law, adding a deep link could not be regarded as a reproduction of the works contained on the linked-to page. Although the complete taking of the list of stories might be afforded copyright protection, it would be subject to an exception for freedom of quotation for press surveys.

In *Belgacom Skynet v IFPI Belgium and NV Universal (formerly Polygram)*,[56] the defendants were ISPs who hosted a number of sites providing hyperlinks to sites providing distribution of musical recordings via the MP3 file format. It was unnecessary to decide whether the presence of links per se incurred liability because, as in *Reimerdes*, the fact of knowledge of linking to an infringing site was not in doubt. However the court laid down guidelines based on a notice and take down procedure as to when removal or prevention of access to offending links was appropriate which were not dissimilar to those now contained within the Copyright Directive. More recently, on similar facts to those in *Kranten.com*, the Bundesgerichthof (Federal Court of Germany) has not found copyright infringement for deep links. In *Handelsblatt Publishers Group v Paperboy*,[57] Paperboy provided access to a large number of news sites including those of newspapers, radio stations, political parties etc, by means of deep links, together with a daily e-mail service allowing users to create a personalise news service. Reproduction of the small parts necessary to make the links did not constitute copyright infringement as they were not sufficiently original, in themselves, to be copyrightable. Specifically on the functionality of links, the court said that the links provided by Paperboy merely made access easier, that is, they were not a prerequisite to access that could be obtained directly if the user knew the URL. Further, the court suggested that, given that there was no liability for the link if a URL was published as a footnote in a hardcopy publication, the situation should be no different if the URL was effectively made available via a deep link. Although copyright is under consideration here, the majority of deep linking cases base their actions on a number of claims. In Europe, these have usually been infringement of database rights[58] and unfair competition but with no more success. In the US, where there is, at present, no separate protection for databases, the more tortuous avenue of trespass has been attempted.[59]

---

56   Court roll no 1999/AR 13372, Appeal Court of Brussels 8th Division, 13 February 2001.

57   BGH, Paperboy 17 July 2003, I ZR 259/00. See Müller, 2003.

58   For instance in *DDF v Newsbooster*, [2003] ECDR 5, again on similar facts to the *Kranten.com* case, an injunction to prevent *Newsbooster* creating deep links to newspaper articles was upheld but on the basis of a violation of the database right rather than copyright infringement. See further discussion in Chapter 2 and in this context see also Dahm, 2004.

59   See, eg, *Register.com v Verio* 00 Civ 5747 (BSJ) (SDNY 2000) *Ticketmaster v Tickets.com* and *e-bay v Bidder's Edge* , all of which involved, *inter alia*, the collection of data from other websites by means of an automated software robot or 'spider'. See also discussion in Rowland and Campbell, 2002 and Dockins, 2005.

Slightly different issues arise when the links and references to other sites are made via the techniques of inline linking, in which images can appear as part of the viewed web page even though they originate elsewhere, or framing, where the viewed web page will appear divided into multiple, independently scrollable windows, some of which may come from other sites although appearing within the frame of the first site. These avoid the issues of bypassing the home page seen in deep linking cases but instead give rise to other problems.

Link law: the emerging law of internet hyperlinks
Mark Sableman
(1999) 4 Comm L & P 557

Framing technology and inline linking technologies raise particular copyright concerns. Each of these technologies permit a web publisher, to some extent, to display images or other content from another site, as if that content were maintained on the publisher's own site ... Inlined links ... allow one to essentially import a graphic from another website, and incorporate it in one's own website. The viewer will not know that the graphic comes from another site; rather to the viewer, the inlined graphic appears to be a seamless part of the web page he is viewing. It is a little bit like painting a picture of a gallery at the Louvre, simply by importing onto your canvas the Louvre's own digital reproductions of those drawings. at the very least, it *seems* sneaky ... As browsing technology develops, and as users get faster web access, other web page display and browsing technologies (particularly involving audio, music and other multimedia outputs) are likely to raise copyright infringement claims. Whatever the resolution of these issues, use of framing and inline linking technologies to create composite web pages is likely to raise more difficult copyright infringement issues than simple direct hyperlinks like those involved in the *Shetland News* case.

Sableman (above) refers to the case of *Washington Post Company v Total News Inc*, in which a number of publishers objected to the way in which Total News used framing technology to set a news story from another site within the overall Total News frame, in particular by blocking banner advertisements and other distinguishing features. The objection here was not to the link *per se*, but to the way in which the link was accomplished and presented. In common with many linking cases, the issue was settled by agreement between the parties, originating the notion of the 'linking licence' whereby Total News agreed to link to other sites only in certain specified ways.

Aside from the potential loss of advertising, etc, the question in the *Total News* case was essentially whether framing led to the creation of derivative works. This same issue also arose in *Futuredontics Inc v Applied Anagramics Inc*.[60] Applied Anagramics linked to the Futuredontics website in such a way that Futuredontics material appeared within frames on the Anagramics site. Futuredontics claimed that this was a copyright infringement and sought an injunction to restrain the link. The district court found insufficient reasons for granting an injunction, as Futuredontics had not demonstrated conclusively that the 'balance of hardships tips sharply in its favor' and no real evidence of significant injury had been presented. The US Court of Appeals for the Ninth Circuit affirmed this denial of injunctive relief, agreeing with the lower court on the application of the 'balance of hardships' test. Because of these factors, the question of whether the material on the Anagramics site constituted a derivative work

---

60   45 USPQ 2d (BNA) 2005 (1998), affirmed by 152 F 3d 925 (9th Cir 1998) See Tucker, 1999.

was not considered in any detail, but the district court suggested that the 'cases cited by the parties do not conclusively determine whether the defendant's frame page constitutes a derivative work'; and so, this assertion remains to be explored more fully by the courts at a later date.

There have been many cases filed in the US and elsewhere on matters associated with linking and framing,[61] and the majority appear to have reached a settlement based on an agreement related to the manner of framing. However, framing is arguably a special case because of the ease of confusion as to the origin of the material. Nonetheless, a number of other cases have also settled by agreeing a licence to link, despite the fact that there does not appear to be a strong case that links are likely to be unlawful, other than in the comparatively rare cases in which the connection is made with knowledge and indeed with intent to connect the user to infringing material of some sort. The extent to which an implied licence is a necessary device is thus open to debate.

Content and Access Agreements:
An analysis of some of the legal issues arising from linking and framing
Diane Rowland and Andrew Campbell
(2002) Int J LCT 171, 183

It is a moot question whether in the general case it is necessary to invoke the device of the implied licence to link. When someone posts information on the world wide web or the Internet a general acceptance seems to have arisen that this creates an implied licence to access or link to it but analysis seems to indicate that this is not actually the case. Merely posting such information on a freely accessible web site is more akin to placing a poster in a public place which can then be viewed by all who come across it, a situation in which invoking an implied licence to view would not be contemplated. Is there a difference if the person is going beyond viewing to actual linking? We need some conceptual acceptance of the purpose and effects of links – is their purpose beyond that of the 'signpost' referred to in *Reimerdes* and elsewhere? If not then surely no tacit permission is needed and the need to imply a licence is redundant assuming the link concerned is not of a deceptive nature and it is clear to the user that they are activating a link from one site to another.

The extent to which copyright, in particular, provides an appropriate legal mechanism for dealing with such disputes is debatable. However, intellectual property rights may also be infringed via embedded links or metatags. This is more an issue for the law relating to trademarks than copyright, but it is convenient to discuss it here along with the other aspects of linking. Metatags are the key words which are used by search engines. They can be written into the code for a website but will remain invisible to the user unless he or she examines the underlying code for that particular web page. This does not create a problem as long as the site uses ordinary, descriptive words or its own trademark, but some commercial sites also incorporate trademarks of their competitors. This means that, when a user employs a search engine to find a competitor's website, the results of the search will list both sites, even though there is apparently no overt mention of the search term on the face of the retrieved page. Further, when a search engine finds a correlation between a search term and a metatag,

---

61 See also the decision of the Landgericht Cologne, 2 May 2001, in which a poetry website was framed by the defendant. This had the result of circumventing banner advertisements and was deemed to cause damage to the website owner. See www.netlaw.de/urteile/lgk_19.htm.

it is likely to place that site high in the order of relevance, a fact which will also be of importance to a commercial site.

Cases on metatags have been proliferating in the US[62] and a representative idea of the issues which have been raised and the attitude and approach of the courts can be gained from a consideration of the *Playboy* litigation. Playboy Enterprises Inc (PEI) own the registered trademarks 'Playboy' and 'Playmate' and, in a number of actions in the US courts have alleged trademark infringement by others who have used these trademarks either as metatags or other labels to attract users to their sites. In *Playboy Enterprises Inc v AsiaFocus International Inc*,[63] the court found that the defendants had engaged in 'deceptive tactics' which warranted severe sanctions.

Playboy Enterprises Inc v AsiaFocus International Inc
No Civ A 97-734-A 1998 WL 724000 (ED Va)
10 April 1998

The Defendants specifically chose to copy famous trademarks for a well known source of 'adult' entertainment for use in their own 'adult' service. In doing so, they reaped the benefit of the public's established association of the trademarks PLAYMATE and PLAYBOY with adult entertainment. No other purpose appears for choosing PLAYMATE and PLAYBOY but to create that false association in the mind of the consuming public. The defendants' wilfulness is further established by their purposeful tactic of embedding the trademarks PLAYMATE and PLAYBOY in the hidden computer source code. This strategy epitomises the 'blurring' of PEI's trademarks. When a search engine led a consumer to the asian-playmates website in response to a search of PEI's trademarks, the consumer would probably believe that the defendants' website was affiliated with PEI.

Using a trademark as a metatag may both divert a user to another site and also lead to confusion over the ownership and relationship between the site and the legitimate trademark owner. This point was returned to in a later decision.

Playboy Enterprises Inc v Calvin Designer Label
985 F Supp 1220
US District Court (ND Cal 1997)

28 Metatags create confusion as to source despite an infringer's success in its unlawful venture. Infringement can be based upon confusion which creates initial customer interest, even though no actual sale is finally completed as a result of the confusion. That is, the web user is lured to a web site she is not looking for as a result of confusion and deception intentionally caused by the defendant who knows the limitation of the searching device used by the potential visitor.

The case law showed that the absence of evidence of actual confusion[64] did not automatically create an inference that there was no likelihood of confusion, and this was of particular relevance in internet cases, since:

[The] nature of the internet makes proof of actual confusion difficult to obtain because browsing on the internet is a private matter that may not involve any actual sales. The

---

62 For an early discussion see Chong, 1998.
63 No Civ A 97-734-A 1998 WL 724000 (ED Va).
64 A point which had already been made in *Playboy Enterprises Inc v Frena* 839 F Supp 1552 (MD Fla 1993) in which the issue concerned the use of 'playboy' and 'playmate' as file descriptors for photographs, breaching PEI's copyright, available on the defendant's bulletin board.

internet is different from a retail shopping environment, where evidence of actual confusion is easier to obtain through mall intercept surveys [para 39].

Note, however, the following extract from a UK case, involving domain names rather than metatags[65] but perhaps even more relevant in this context, and compare it with the notion of 'initial interest confusion', discussed in the extract from *Playboy Enterprises v Netscape and Excite*, below.

Avnet Inc v Isoact Ltd
[1998] FSR 16
High Court

Jacobs J ... it is a general problem of the internet that it works on words and not words in relation to goods and services. So whenever anyone searches for that word, even if the searcher is looking for the word in one context, he will, or may find web pages or data in a wholly different context ... Of course, users of the internet also know that is a feature of the internet and their search may produce an altogether wrong web page or the like. This may be an important matter for the courts to take into account in considering trademark and like problems.

Returning to *Playboy v Calvin*, the court held that the intent of the defendant in selecting the allegedly infringing marks was a key factor in determining the likelihood of confusion and, in this case, the defendants had actually admitted that they used 'Playboy' as a metatag. The court also derived further evidence of the defendant's intent from the fact that, as well as using the trademark in metatags, it had also been used as a background which contained multiple uses of the trademark in black text on a black background so that, although it was not visible to the user it was easily detectable by search engine. The court therefore issued a permanent injunction preventing the defendant from using PEI's trademarks in this way.

PEI was unsuccessful in a later case, in which they tried to obtain an injunction against some of the organisations which provide search engines and attempt to maximise the revenue gained from advertising by 'keying' banner advertisements to the search terms employed by the user.

Playboy Enterprises Inc v Netscape Communications Corp[66]
Playboy Enterprises Inc v Excite Inc
55 F Supp 2d 1070
US District Court (CD Cal 1999)

Defendants operate search engines on the internet. When a person searches for a particular topic in either search engine, the search engine compiles a list of sites matching or related to the user's search terms, and then posts the list of sites, known as 'search results'.

Defendants sell advertising space on the search result pages. Known as 'banner ads', the advertisements are commonly found at the top of the screen. The ads themselves are often animated and whimsical, and designed to entice the internet user to 'click here'. If the user does click on the ad, she is transported to the web site of the advertiser.

---

65   See, also, Hurdle, 1998.
66   Affirmed by 202F3d 278 (9th Cir 1999) See also *Playboy Enterprises v Netscape* 354 F 3d 1020 (9th Cir 2004) where a similar result was reached in relation to keying – allowing advertisers to target individuals with certain interests by linking adverts to pre-determined search terms.

As with other media, advertisers seek to maximise the efficacy of their ads by targeting consumers matching a certain demographic profile. Savvy web site operators accommodate the advertisers by 'keying' ads to search terms entered by users.

That is, instead of posting ads in a random rotation, defendants program their servers to link a pre-selected set of banner ads to certain 'key' search terms. Defendants market this context-sensitive advertising ability as a value-added service and charge a premium.

Defendants key various adult entertainment ads to a group of over 450 terms related to adult entertainment, including the terms 'playboy' and 'playmate.' Plaintiff contends that inclusion of those terms violates plaintiff's trademarks rights in those words.

PEI was asserting both trademark infringement and dilution and, in order to be awarded an injunction, it needed to show both likelihood of confusion and likelihood of resultant harm:

Assuming *arguendo* that defendants' use of 'playboy' and 'playmate' is use of plaintiff's marks, plaintiff must still show that confusion is likely to result from that use. Plaintiff has not so shown.

Rather, plaintiff relies on the recent case from the Court of Appeals for the Ninth Circuit, *Brookfield Communications Inc v West Coast Entertainment Corp*,[67] for the proposition that defendants cause 'initial interest confusion' by the use of the words 'playboy' and 'playmate.' Initial interest confusion, as coined by the Ninth Circuit, is a brand of confusion particularly applicable to the internet. Generally speaking, initial interest confusion may result when a user conducts a search using a trademark term and the results of the search include web sites not sponsored by the holder of the trademark search term, but rather of competitors. The Ninth Circuit reasoned that the user may be diverted to an unsponsored site, and only realise that she has been diverted upon arriving at the competitor's site. Once there, however, even though the user knows she is not in the site initially sought, she may stay. In that way, the competitor has captured the trademark holder's potential visitors or customers.

Brookfield is distinguishable from this case, and where applicable, supportive of defendants' position. ...

As English words, 'playboy' and 'playmate' cannot be said to suggest sponsorship or endorsement of either the websites that appear as search results (as in *Brookfield*) or the banner ads that adorn the search results page. Although the trademark terms and the English language words are undisputedly identical, which, presumably, leads plaintiff to believe that the use of the English words is akin to use of the trademarks, the holder of a trademark may not remove a word from the English language merely by acquiring trademark rights in it.[68] ... the analogy is quite unlike that of a devious placement of a

---

67   174 F 3d 1036 (9th Cir 1999), noting the point that words routinely used in English such as 'movie buff' could legitimately be used in metatags, but not if they were confusingly similar to a trademark – in this case, MovieBuff.

68   There are, however, some conflicting decisions as to whether the term 'playboy' could be construed as a word which has meaning independent of its association with PEI. In *Playboy Enterprises v Chuckleberry Publishing* 939 F Supp 1032 (SDNY 1996), the defendant had originally published a magazine in Italy entitled *Playmen*. This case was concerned with whether rulings made about the publication of the US version were violated by an internet site subsequently established by the defendant. However, the court noted that the 'Italian courts ruled that, "lexically", PLAYBOY was a weak mark and not entitled to protection in that country'. In contrast, in *Playboy Enterprises v Giannattasio* (1999), it was argued that those assessing the site in question would not automatically assume any connection with PEI, as the term 'playboy' had become a generic term. However, this was rejected by the court in Naples, which granted an injunction against the offending site. Summary available at www.arbiter.wipo.int/domains/guidelines/precedents.html.

road sign bearing false information. This case presents a scenario more akin to a driver pulling off the freeway in response to a sign that reads 'Fast Food Burgers' to find a well known fast food burger restaurant, next to which stands a billboard that reads: 'Better Burgers: 1 Block Further.' The driver, previously enticed by the prospect of a burger from the well known restaurant, now decides she wants to explore other burger options. Assuming that the same entity owns the land on which both the burger restaurant and the competitor's billboard stand, should that entity be liable to the burger restaurant for diverting the driver? That is the rule PEI contends the court should adopt.

So, the court found that, not only was there no likelihood of confusion, there was not even 'use' of the trademarks by the defendant. It was similarly dismissive of the arguments on dilution and tarnishment. The point was made that, even if the defendants could be said to 'use' the trademark, PEI would still have to show that that use caused harm, which it had not done, and, if such contentions were allowed, there was a danger of giving PEI near-monopoly control of placing their marks and associated goods and services on the internet. This would clearly be an undesirable outcome.

There are a number of other situations where it is entirely possible to use the trademark of another as a metatag. In *Playboy Enterprises Inc v Welles*,[69] PEI again tried to prevent the defendant from using its trademarks as metatags on her website. However, Terri Welles had, in the past, been a model for Playboy and had also been awarded the title 'Playmate of the Year' by the *Playboy* magazine. She therefore had a legitimate purpose in making use of these trademarks on her site and there was no likelihood of confusion with the PEI site, especially as her site contained a disclaimer which made it clear that there was no link with or official endorsement by PEI. In addition, the Ninth Circuit was concerned about the effect that not being able to use trademarks in a descriptive way might have on the use of search engines.

Playboy Enterprises v Welles
279 F 3d 796, 803
US Court of Appeals for the Ninth Circuit (2003)

Welles has no practical way of describing herself without using trademarked terms. In the context of metatags, we conclude that she has no practical way of identifying the content of her website without referring to PEI's trademarks.

A large portion of Welles' website discusses her association with Playboy over the years. Thus, the trademarked terms accurately describe the contents of Welles' website, in addition to describing Welles. Forcing Welles and others to use absurd turns of phrase in their metatags, such as those necessary to identify Welles, would be particularly damaging in the internet search context. Searchers would have a much more difficult time locating relevant websites if they could do so only by correctly guessing the long phrases necessary to substitute for trademarks. ... Similarly, someone searching for critiques of Playboy on the internet would have a difficult time if internet sites could not list the object of their critique in their metatags.

There is simply no descriptive substitute for the trademarks used in Welles' metatags. Precluding their use would have the unwanted effect of hindering the free flow of information on the internet, something which is certainly not a goal of trademark law. ...

---

69   279 F 3d 796 (9th Cir 2003).

The metatags use only so much of the marks as reasonably necessary and nothing is done in conjunction with them to suggest sponsorship or endorsement by the trademark holder. We note that our decision might differ if the metatags listed the trademarked term so repeatedly that Welles' site would regularly appear above PEI's in searches for one of the trademarked terms.

This illustrates that not only can the use of metatags relating to others trademarks or names be done for valid reasons, which can include activities such as comparative advertising, or even sites which are critical of the original site,[70] but also that not to allow the use of trademarks as metatags in certain situations could inhibit the functioning of search engines to the detriment of users. One rationale for this is that the metatag is an important device to assist the users in searching the web and, when conducting a web search, they may be just as interested in finding information about, or criticism of, the name searched for as information prepared by the owner of that name. In the commercial setting, this situation is replicated in more traditional markets and is considered as one of the outcomes of normal competition; so, no different standard would be expected to pertain in cyberspace in the absence of evidence of deception or unfair competition. This point of view was reinforced by Jacob LJ in *Reed Executive Plc v. Reed Business Information Ltd* saying that 'causing a site to appear in a search result, without more, does not suggest any connection with anyone else.'[71] However there have been some cases which, on their particular facts, have been held to violate the rights of the trade mark holder or be an example of unfair competition. Thus in *Road Tech Computer Systems Ltd v Mandata* it was noted that the use of a trade mark or name of another in a metatag can enable the offender to take a ride on the back of a successful website. Even though the marks had been removed upon notification, the court still awarded damages as 'the claimant had spent a great deal of money on the creation of the website ... this is not a use to which the claimant would ... in any circumstance, have contemplated or consented to.'[72]

DOMAIN NAMES

A domain name can be likened to an address on the global computer network, which both identifies and gives other information about a specific internet site. The term 'top level domain' (TLD) refers to either the generic descriptors '.com'; '.net'; '.org', etc, or an indication of the country in which the domain name has been registered, for example, '.uk'; '.de'; '.to', etc. Second level domain names then give further information which may be the name of the site in the case of the generic TLD, for example, 'cavendishpublishing.com', or further information about the type of site in the case of country TLDs, for example, '.co.uk'; '.ac.uk', etc.[73] In these latter cases, a

---

70 See, e.g. *Esso Societe Anonyme Francaise v Association Greenpeace France* [2003] ETMR 35 (Tribunal de Grande Instance, Paris); *Harris v Kassel* 253 F Supp 2d 1120 (ND Cal. 2003).
71 [2004] RPC 40, para 148.
72 [2000] ETMR 970, 974. See also *Trieste e Venezia Assicurazioni Genertel v Crowe Italia* [2001] ETMR 66 (Tribunal of Rome) and *Tdc Forlag v Medieforlaget Danmark*. [2003] ETMR 13 (Maritime and Commercial Court, Copenhagen).
73 The courts have provided agreed explanations of the operation of domain names in, eg, *Pitman Training Ltd v Nominet UK* [1997] FSR 797 and *Panavision International LP v Toeppen* 141 F 3d 1316 (9th Cir 1998). See also descriptions in, e.g. Black, Ch. 6 in Edwards and Waelde (eds) 2000; Froomkin, Ch. 11 in Marsden, (ed) 2000, pp 213 *et seq*; Maniatis, 2002, pp 398 *et seq*.

further domain name will then identify the actual site, for example, 'aber.ac.uk'. Each domain name can identify only one site and so is unique to that site, so that two companies who might trade under the same name quite successfully in the 'real world' cannot have exactly the same domain name in cyberspace.

There are many organisations, for instance, which use the initials FSA. Only one of these can have the domain name fsa.com although there are, of course, other possible registrations and fsa.gov.uk, fsa.co.uk, fsa.org and fsa.org.uk are all owned by different concerns.[74] Conversely, it is common for the same company to register in more than one TLD; for example, butterworths.com and butterworths.co.uk are both owned by the same legal publisher. Osborne notes the following:

> ... in practice, few companies will be prepared to register their names in all registries around the world ... and indeed may not be eligible under local rules. However, because the Internet is truly international, it may be possible for well known domain names to be registered by third parties in unusual countries where the well known company does not have a registration, and then use it worldwide; for example, 'wellknowntradename.is' could be registered in Iceland but used everywhere. This could be particularly troublesome if the same goods and services were sold by the newcomer or if the trademark was so distinctive (for example, Kodak) that a perceived connection with the trade owner is likely, whatever the newcomer's business.[75]

As more and more commercial enterprises trade or advertise their presence on the web, domain names have become more and more valuable and the potential for dispute is high. Whereas a large number of trademarks containing the same name can comfortably co-exist because they are associated with different products, belong to business in different jurisdictions etc, the distinctive nature of the domain name providing global exclusivity is much sought after.[76] The fact that many consumers searching for a particular site are likely, in the first place, to try and guess its domain name has further enhanced this value. For instance, as seen in *British Telecom & ors v One in a Million*, discussed below, the retail store Marks & Spencer could be identified in a domain name not only by marks-and-spencer.com but also by marksandspencer.com. This has led to disputes between those who wish to claim the entitlement to the use of a particular domain name, and also to the emergence of 'cybersquatting', in which domain names incorporating famous names are registered by those with no interest in using the domain name other than to transfer it to the 'rightful owner' for an appropriately large sum.[77] If businesses do not wish to be at the mercy of cybersquatters, they need to ensure registration of all names which could conceivably be used to identify their website. Both well known commercial

---

74 See the Findlay Steele Associates website www.fsa.co.uk and further discussion below at p 530. Findlay Steel Associates succeeded in retaining this registration in an acrimonious dispute with the Financial Services Authority (www.fsa.gov.uk). Compare the situation in *WWF-World Wide Fund for Nature v. World Wrestling Federation Entertainment Inc* [2002] FSR 33.

75 Osborne, 1997.

76 See, eg, Griffin, 1998, commenting on the fact that there are apparently 100,000 trademarks in the world which use the word 'Prince', but only one of these can have the domain name 'prince.com'.

77 For further discussion of the way in which such disputes arise see, eg, Waelde, Edwards and Waelde (eds), 1997, p 48; Osborne, 1997.

enterprises, such as Harrods, and famous personalities, including Julia Roberts, the actress, and Ronaldinho Gaúcho, the footballer, have been victims of such activity.[78]

As disputes over the registration and use of domain names began to proliferate, litigants and potential litigants looked to the law for a suitable remedy. Many disputes in the commercial sector arose from the use of trademarks and trade names, and so answers were sought in the law relating to trademarks,[79] unfair competition and passing off.

The cases which have come before the courts can basically be divided into two types: those in which both parties have some legitimate interest in the name; and the more common 'cybersquatting' cases. The latter category includes both those cases where the defendant merely shelved the acquired domain names in order to block use by the 'rightful owner' and extract a high price for the transfer, and also those where the defendants used the name to maximise visits to their own sites, or to cause damage to the victim as a result of the confusion created.[80]

TRADEMARKS AND DOMAIN NAMES

It is understandable that companies who own trade marks in different jurisdictions will want to register the same name as a domain name. However it has to be borne in mind that, when a word is used as a domain name, it is not performing the same function as when it is used as a trademark. At the most basic level a domain name is an address used to facilitate access to an internet site whereas a trademark is a jurisdictionally based intellectual property right which enables consumers to distinguish between different products and services. They should not, therefore, be regarded as serving the same purpose. Nevertheless, given that many companies are inevitably closely associated with either the trade marks of the business or its products, it is not surprising that there is some blurring of function. As summed up by Froomkin 'a system that relies on geographic distance and sectoral differentiation maps badly to a borderless world in which every participant on the global network needs a unique address.'[81] Generally, trademark law can still be applied where a word used as a domain name is also used as a trade mark. If, then, a trademark registered in one jurisdiction is incorporated into a website in another jurisdiction, can this constitute 'use' in the course of trade so that the website owner becomes liable for trademark infringement?

In *Euromarket Designs Inc v Peters* the claimant had stores in the US called 'Crate and Barrel', had a UK registered trademark from 1988 for household goods and also held a Community mark. Peters had a store in Dublin with the same name. In theory, a website could be taken as an indication of trading in a world wide market whereas, in fact, for most undertakings, the actual market is very little different geographically

78 See below, p 539.
79 See, also, Stoodley, 1997.
80 The issue of confusion has also been discussed in actions for trademark infringement in relation to the unauthorised use of trademarks as metatags (see above). For a consideration of the difference in the relevant factors suggesting confusion in metatag and domain name cases see, eg, *Brookfield Communications Inc v West Coast Entertainment Corp* 174 F 3d 1036 (9th Cir 1999).
81 Froomkin, Ch. 11 in Marsden, (ed) 2000.

than it was before the internet. The dispute centred on whether the name 'Crate and Barrel' was *used* in the UK, although in substance neither of the parties traded in the UK. Jacob J, although advising that settlement was the most appropriate course of action in the particular case, nevertheless suggested that 'some of the points involved are of great importance even though they are trivial in the context of the real dispute between the parties.' One of these important points was whether, given that the internet is accessible all over the world, the use of a trademark on a website constituted use in other jurisdictions.

Euromarket Designs v Peters
[2001] FSR 20
High Court

22 Now a person who visited that website would see 'ie'. ... So what would the visitor understand? Fairly obviously that this is advertising a shop and its wares. If he knew 'ie' meant Ireland, he would know the shop was in Ireland: otherwise he would not. There is no reason why anyone in this country should regard the site as directed at him. So far as one can tell, no one has.

23 Now almost any search on the net almost always throws up a host of irrelevant 'hits'. You expect a lot of irrelevant sites, moreover you expect a lot of those sites to be foreign. Of course you can go direct to a desired site. To do that, however, you must type in the exact address. ...

24 Whether one gets there by a search or by direct use of the address, is it rational to say that the defendants are using the words "Crate & Barrel" in the United Kingdom in the course of trade in goods? If it is, it must follow that the defendants' are using the words in every other country of the world. [counsel for the claimant] says that the Internet is accessible to the whole world. So it follows that any user will regard any website as being 'for him' absent a reason to doubt the same. ... I think it is not as simple as that. ... [counsel for the defence] here used another analogy. He said using the internet was more like the user focusing a super-telescope into the site concerned; he asked me to imagine such a telescope set up on the Welsh hills overlooking the Irish Sea. I think [this] analogy is apt in this case. Via the web you can look into the defendant's shop in Dublin. Indeed the very language and the Internet conveys the idea of the user going to the site – 'visit' is the word. Other cases would be different – a well-known example, for instance, is Amazon.com. Based in the US it has actively gone out to seek world-wide trade, not just by use of the name on the Internet but by advertising its business here, and offering and operating a real service of supply of books to this country. These defendants have done none of that.

The dispute in *Flowers Inc v Phonenames* was essentially concerned with the question of whether the name '800 FLOWERS', which on an alphanumeric phone connected to a service providing flowers, was sufficiently distinctive, as opposed to merely descriptive.[82] However, there was also discussion of whether there had been use in the UK and, in particular, whether inclusion of the name on a website hosted in the US would constitute use in the UK if accessed from this jurisdiction.

Flowers Inc v Phonenames Ltd
[2002] FSR 12
Court of Appeal

Buxton LJ ... The implications of Internet use for issues of jurisdiction are clearly wide-ranging, and will need to be worked out with care both in domestic and in private

---

82 See also discussion on distinctiveness in *efax.com v Oglesby The Times*, 16 March 2000.

international law. … Without presuming to enter into detailed discussion … I do venture to suggest that the essence of the problem is to fit the factual circumstances of Internet use into the substantive rules of law applying to the many and very different legal issues that the Internet affects. It is therefore unlikely, and it is nowhere suggested, that there will be one uniform rule, specific to the Internet, that can be applied in all cases of Internet use. That consideration is of importance in our present case, because it was a significant part of the applicant's submissions that, for instance, "publication" of statements in a particular jurisdiction by downloading from the Internet according to the rules of the law of defamation or of misrepresentation was of at least strong analogical relevance to whether a trade mark downloaded from the Internet had been "used" in the jurisdiction to which it was downloaded; and, even more directly, that when A placed a mark on the Internet that was downloaded by B, the same criteria should apply in determining whether A thereby used the mark as determine whether A thereby infringed the same mark in the jurisdiction where B was located.

I would wish to approach these arguments, and particularly the last of them, with caution. There is something inherently unrealistic in saying that A 'uses' his mark in the United Kingdom when all that he does is to place the mark on the Internet, from a location outside the United Kingdom, and simply wait in the hope that someone from the United Kingdom will download it and thereby create use on the part of A. By contrast, I can see that it might be more easily arguable that if A places on the Internet a mark that is confusingly similar to a mark protected in another jurisdiction, he may do so at his peril that someone from that other jurisdiction may download it; though that approach conjured up in argument before us the potentially disturbing prospect that a shop in Arizona or Brazil that happens to bear the same name as a trademarked store in England or Australia will have to act with caution in answering telephone calls from those latter jurisdictions.

However that may be, the very idea of 'use' within a certain area would seem to require some active step in that area on the part of the user that goes beyond providing facilities that enable others to bring the mark into the area. Of course, if persons in the United Kingdom seek the mark on the Internet in response to direct encouragement or advertisement by the owner of the mark, the position may be different; but in such a case the advertisement or encouragement in itself is likely to suffice to establish the necessary use.

DOMAIN NAME DISPUTES

Entitlement to use the name on both sides

Pitman Training Ltd v Nominet UK Ltd,[83] concerned a dispute between Pitman Training and Pitman Publishing over the use of the name 'Pitman'. Pitman Publishing had been using the name 'Pitman' in association with publishing since 1849. The business had originally been a training business, which was sold in 1985 to Pitman Training Ltd. Pitman Publishing became one of the divisions of Pearson Professional Ltd, a wholly owned subsidiary of Pearson plc. By virtue of an agreement made at the time that the businesses were divided, both Pitman Training and Pitman Publishing were allowed to use the name 'Pitman' in connection with their respective businesses, as long as

---

83 [1997] FSR 797.

Pitman Training used it only in connection with training and correspondence courses and agreed not to publish books or engage in any other trade under that name.

The facts that led to the dispute were as follows. Pitman Publishing applied to Nominet, which administers registrations for the '.uk' domain, for use of the domain name 'pitman.co.uk', which was allocated to them on the usual 'first come, first served' basis in February 1996. It was intended that a website would be designed and constructed but would not be ready for launch until December 1996. The domain name was not used in the interim except for advertising in connection with promotions.

In March 1996, Pitman Training was told that 'pitman.co.uk' was still unallocated; its ISP therefore procured the name and began to use the email address 'enquiries@pitman.co.uk'. As noted by the court, the question of how this could have occurred was not resolved:

> No one – neither of the two experts who have given evidence in this case nor anyone else – has come up with any clear explanation beyond mere speculation as to how this could have happened. It should not have been possible but it did happen.[84]

Pitman Publishing became aware of the situation in December 1996 and requested immediate restoration of the domain name from Nominet, which acceded. Pitman Training commenced proceedings. Scott VC was not impressed by the argument that the actions of Pitman Publishing could constitute passing off:

> This strikes me as a strange proposition given that Pitman Publishing has traded under the style Pitman for nearly 150 years ... The evidence does not even begin to support the contention that the public associates the domain name pitman.co.uk with PTC ... That there may be some confusion by some members of the public is undoubtedly so. But that confusion results from the use by both companies ... of the style 'Pitman' for their respective trading purposes.[85]

So, although the court appeared to accept that inappropriate use of a domain name might sometimes constitute passing off, that was not the case in these particular circumstances; any confusion which might have arisen had its origin in another source, namely, the agreement voluntarily entered into by both parties concerned.

Another case where, as in *Pitman*, the dispute had arisen because both parties felt that they had a legitimate entitlement to the use of the domain name in question was *Prince plc v Prince Sportswear Group Inc*.[86] When the US firm, Prince Sports Group Inc, tried to register the domain name 'prince.com', it found that it had already been registered by Prince plc, a UK computer services firm which had also registered the domain name 'prince.co.uk'. Prince Sports Group was the owner of the trademark 'Prince' and, although the registration of the '.com' domain is done on a first come, first served basis, if another party is able to show that it has a Federal registered trademark, then the first party will lose its registration. The dispute led to proceedings being filed in both the US and the UK. In the UK, Prince plc sought a ruling that the allegations of Prince Sports Groups that its registration of the domain name had resulted in trademark dilution were unfounded and constituted groundless threats in

---

84   *Ibid*, p 804.
85   *Ibid*, p 807.
86   [1998] FSR 21 and see, eg, Orange, 1999.

relation to s 21 of the Trademarks Act 1994. The High Court found for Prince plc and issued an injunction preventing Prince Sports from continuing with the threats, but there was no discussion of whether the UK trademarks held by Prince Sports were being infringed. The parties subsequently agreed a settlement in which Prince plc retained the domain name, and so the legal arguments were not developed any further.

In most cases where there is entitlement on both sides to use the name, the significant factor will be first use. It was for this reason that the dispute between Findlay Steele Associates and the Financial Services Authority was decided in favour of Findlay Steele. Findlay Steele had registered the domain name fsa.co.uk in 1997.[87] A website was not launched until 2002, but the domain was used for e-mail communications. The Financial Services Authority, which has the domain name fsa.gov.uk, was created six months after Findlay Steele's registration of its domain name. It subsequently sought to obtain fsa.co.uk on the grounds that the similarity between the domain names might lead to confusion for the consumer who was trying to contact the Financial Services Authority. In the absence of evidence of bad faith, the first use principle will be the usual determinant. This principle has been adhered to in cases where the choice of domain name registered was more dubious. An example of this is found in the case of *French Connection v Sutton*.[88] In 1997, French Connection began the advertising campaign which established the use of 'fcuk' as representing the company. Around the same time, Sutton registered the domain name fcuk.com. He alleged that he intended to use in connection with his IT consultancy business, First Consultants UK. His evidence was that he thought he would get more hits as a result of the use of this acronym. Subsequently, French Connection, who had registered the trademark but had overlooked registration of the domain name, sought to have the domain name transferred. Although the judge found the facts of the case from both parties 'unpalatable in the extreme' there was no evidence of bad faith. Sutton had not offered to sell fcuk.com to French Connection for vast sums of money and neither had he acquired any other domain names which might have been indicative of cybersquatting (see below). A similar outcome occurred in *MBNA America Bank v Freeman*,[89] in which MBNA Bank which had the domain name mbna.com failed to obtain either an injunction against Freeman to prevent him using the domain name, mbna.co.uk, or an order to transfer this domain name which had been legitimately registered in anticipation of supporting his business 'Marketing Banners for Net Advertising'.

Cybersquatting

In cybersquatting cases, the typical behaviour is to register numerous domain names corresponding with well known names and marks and then attempt to sell them to the rightful owner. On occasions the names are merely shelved rather than used. Cases in a number of jurisdictions have shown that this behaviour will not be viewed

---

87   The dispute was adjudicated by Nominet under the Uniform Dispute Resolution Policy.
88   Chancery Division December 1999, unreported.
89   Chancery Division July 2000, unreported.

sympathetically by the courts. The first cybersquatting case in the UK was that of *Harrods plc v UK Network Services Ltd*.[90] The domain name 'harrods.com' was registered but not used by unrelated third parties, with the intention of selling the name to Harrods at an inflated price. Harrods sued for trademark infringement, passing off and conspiracy. In agreeing to issue an injunction, the legal arguments were not aired extensively but Lightman J accepted the principle that the law relating to trademarks and passing off can be applied to domain names. He referred, by analogy, to the case of *Glaxo plc v Glaxowellcome Ltd*,[91] in which a company called 'Glaxowellcome' was registered in anticipation of the merger of Glaxo and Wellcome and a sum of £100,000 was demanded for transfer of the name. Even though the company had not traded, the court in that case was not prepared to tolerate a price being demanded for a name in which another party had goodwill. In both cases, the court appeared to be heavily influenced by the perceived dishonest intentions of the defendants. In the *Harrods* case itself, the defendant had accumulated a range of domain names corresponding to famous names and a number of commentators have noted that the court had little sympathy with the defendants. Policy issues may loom large in these cases, since 'most would agree that some remedy should exist against a domain name pirate seeking to extract payment from the 'rightful owner' in return for a domain name which the pirate possesses'.[92]

The issues were aired more extensively in the *One in a Million* cases. One in a Million had registered domain names associated with a number of famous enterprises, including Marks & Spencer, Ladbrokes, Sainsbury, Virgin Enterprises and British Telecommunications, for the apparent purpose of extracting a high price for transferring them. Actions were brought on behalf of the all the companies concerned, on the basis of passing off. If the only action of such cybersquatters is to shelve the domain names and not to make use of them for trading purposes, it appears that it could be difficult to establish the classic ingredients of passing off, namely, misrepresentation in the course of trade, damage to goodwill and consumer confusion. In the High Court, Sumption J appeared at first to be taking this line of argument:

> The mere creation of an 'instrument of deception' without either using it for deception or putting it into the hands of someone else to do so is not passing off ... it follows that the mere registration of a deceptive company name or a deceptive internet domain name is not passing off.[93]

However, he then went on to grant an injunction on the basis that 'there is only one possible reason why anyone who was not part of the Marks & Spencer plc group should wish to use such a domain address, and that is to pass himself off as part of that group or his products as theirs'.[94] Note that the alleged action has changed from that of registering to that of use, even though there was no evidence as such that there had been any trading, or even any other activity on websites associated with these domain names. Nonetheless, the potential for passing off rather than the genuine

---

90   (1996) unreported (Ch D) but discussed in, eg, Morton, 1997; Osborne, 1997.
91   [1996] FSR 388.
92   Meyer-Rochow, 1998.
93   *Marks & Spencer plc v One in a Million Ltd* [1998] FSR 265, 271.
94   *Ibid*.

threat seemed to be sufficient to allow the injunction to be granted. Again, as in the *Harrods* case, there was clearly little sympathy for this practice:

> The history of the defendants' activities shows a deliberate practice followed over a substantial period of time of registering domain names which are chosen to resemble the names and marks of other people and are primarily intended to deceive. [95]

In the Court of Appeal, Aldous LJ reviewed the history of both trademark legislation and the action for passing off, leading to the five familiar characteristics itemised by Lord Diplock in *Erven Warnink BV v J Townend and Sons (Hull) Ltd*.[96]

British Telecommunications plc and Another
v One In A Million Ltd and Others
[1998] 4 All ER 476, CA, p 497

Aldous LJ It is accepted that the name 'Marks & Spencer' denotes Marks & Spencer plc and nobody else. Thus anybody seeing or hearing the name realises that what is being referred to is the business of Marks & Spencer plc. It follows that registration by the appellants of a domain name including the name 'Marks & Spencer' makes a false representation that they are associated or connected with Marks & Spencer plc. This can be demonstrated by considering the reaction of a person who taps into his computer the domain name marksandspencer.co.uk and presses a button to execute a 'whois' search. He will be told that the registrant is One In A Million Ltd. A substantial number of persons will conclude that One In A Million Ltd must be connected or associated with Marks & Spencer plc. That amounts to a false representation which constitutes passing off.

Mr Wilson submitted that mere registration did not amount to passing off. Further, Marks & Spencer plc had not established any damage or likelihood of damage. I cannot accept those submissions. The placing on a register of a distinctive name such as marksandspencer makes a representation to persons who consult the register that the registrant is connected or associated with the name registered and thus the owner of the goodwill in the name. Such persons would not know of One In A Million Ltd and would believe that they were connected or associated with the owner of the goodwill in the domain name they had registered. Further, registration of the domain name including the words 'Marks & Spencer' is an erosion of the exclusive goodwill in the name which damages or is likely to damage Marks & Spencer plc.

Mr Wilson also submitted that it was not right to conclude that there was any threat by the appellants to use or dispose of any domain name including the words Marks & Spencer. He submitted that the appellants, Mr Conway and Mr Nicholson, were two rather silly young men who hoped to make money from the likes of the respondents by selling domain names to them for as much as they could get. They may be silly, but their letters and activities make it clear that they intended to do more than just retain the names. Their purpose was to threaten use and disposal sometimes explicitly and on other occasions implicitly. The judge was right to grant *quia timet* relief to prevent the threat becoming reality.

I also believe that domain names comprising the name 'Marks & Spencer' are instruments of fraud. Any realistic use of them as domain names would result in passing

---

95   *Ibid* p 273.
96   [1979] 2 All ER 927, p 932.

off and there was ample evidence to justify the injunctive relief granted by the judge to prevent them being used for a fraudulent purpose and to prevent them being transferred to others.

Ignoring the question of whether there is any likelihood that a consumer looking for the Marks & Spencer website would actually type the 'whois' command, a person might well guess the domain name as 'marksandspencer.com'. Nevertheless, despite the belief of the Court of Appeal that misrepresentation and confusion could be found, this decision seems rather out of line with other passing off cases. It has, however, been suggested that the *One in a Million* decisions may lead to a refinement of the tort of passing off on the basis that 'the essence of passing off is to provide a remedy against a party which is perceived as unjustly reaping where it has not sown'.[97]

Whether or not this occurs remains to be seen, but there is no doubt that, where the domain pirate has done more than merely shelve the domain name, identifying the constituents of passing off is less controversial, as can be seen from two cases decided by the courts in New Zealand. In *Oggi Advertising Ltd v McKenzie*,[98] Oggi sought to restrain the use of the domain name 'oggi.co.nz' by the defendant, registered allegedly on behalf of a Mr Elliott Oggi from Canada, whom the plaintiffs believed to be bogus. The court found that the defendant's association with the name 'Oggi' and also with a home page referring to a similar business was sufficient to constitute a misrepresentation. It was made to prospective customers in the course of trade, was calculated to injure goodwill, caused actual damage and the elements of passing off were thus made out.

Oggi was referred to in the later case of *NZ Post v Leng*.[99] The domain name 'nzpost.com' was registered by Leng, an New Zealand citizen, with InterNic, which administers the '.com' domain name. In this case, a website was created which corresponded to the domain name which hosted a range of material, some of which was similar to that provided by the New Zealand Postal Service, NZ Post, on its website at 'nzpost.co.nz'. NZ Post alleged passing off and breaches of the New Zealand Fair Trading Act 1986. The evidence was accepted that, if looking for the website of NZ Post, a New Zealand resident might guess 'nzpost.co.nz', but that others were very likely to try 'nzpost.com'. Having considered the elements of passing off and the conduct necessary for deceptive conduct under the statute, the High Court in Auckland had little difficulty in concluding that the continued existence of 'nzpost.com' would lead to confusion. The court concluded that the requirements for passing off were made out, or that, at a minimum, there was an arguable case, and so felt that it was obliged to issue an injunction.

As Leng's website was hosted on a server in California, the court also considered issues of jurisdiction and enforceability.[100] It noted that, in the US case of *Panavision International v Toeppen and Network Solutions Inc*,[101] the Court of Appeals for the Ninth circuit had rejected Toeppen's assertions that the damage had occurred in cyberspace.

---

97 Meyer-Rochow, 1998.
98 [1999] 1 NZLR 631.
99 [1999] 3 NZLR 219. See, also, Elliott and Gravatt, 1999.
100 See, also, Garnett, 2000.
101 141 F 3d 1316 (9th Cir 1998).

The *One in a Million* cases were also considered and the court concluded that not only did it have jurisdiction to issue an injunction, but it was obliged to do so. Leng had registered a domain name containing NZ Post's mark and showed no inclination to change it. A very real chance of confusion existed and there was no suggestion that Leng had a legitimate personal interest in the 'NZ Post' name. The domain name was an instrument of deception and was appropriating NZ Post's goodwill, at least in New Zealand. The issues of enforcement outside of the jurisdiction did not arise, as Leng resided in New Zealand and there was therefore no need to discuss what might have happened if that had not been the case.

In the courts in the US, domain name piracy has been discussed in terms of infringement of trademarks. Again, in *Panavision International LP v Toeppen*, referred to in *NZ Post v Leng*, Toeppen had done more than merely register the disputed domain name; he had a website with the address 'panavision.com', on which there were photos of the town of Pana in Illinois. Panavision said that this was an infringement of their trademark and required him to transfer the domain name. He refused to do so unless paid $13,000. When Panavision would not co-operate, Toeppen registered another domain name using their other trademark, panaflex.com – the website for this address just said 'hello'. As with many other cybersquatters and domain name pirates, Toeppen had a history of registering names corresponding to well known enterprises, some of which he had tried to sell to the 'rightful owner'.[102]

The Federal Trademark Dilution Act (15 USC) provides in § 1125(c) that:

> The owner of a famous mark shall be entitled … to an injunction against another person's commercial use in commerce of a mark or trade name, if such use begins after the mark has become famous and causes dilution of the distinctive quality of the mark …

The corresponding California statute is couched in similar terms. It prohibits dilution of 'the distinctive quality' of a mark, regardless of competition or the likelihood of confusion. The protection extends only to strong and well recognised marks.

Toeppen's argument was that the domain name was merely an address and he referred the court to a number of cases which were authority for the fact that neither the registration of a domain name nor the acceptance for registration constituted a 'commercial use' within the meaning of the Trademark Dilution Act. The court, however, was of the view that Toeppen's use was not 'as benign as he suggests'.

Panavision International LP v Toeppen
and Network Solutions Inc
141 F 3d 1316
US Court of Appeals (9th Cir 1998)

24   In order to prove a violation of the Federal Trademark Dilution Act, a plaintiff must show that (1) the mark is famous; (2) the defendant is making a commercial use of the mark in commerce; (3) the defendant's use began after the mark became famous; and (4) the defendant's use of the mark dilutes the quality of the mark by diminishing the capacity of the mark to identify and distinguish goods and services …

… Toeppen traded on the value of Panavision's marks. So long as he held the internet registrations, he curtailed Panavision's exploitation of the value of its trademarks on

---

102 A number of other cases were also brought against him in other States.

the internet ... and that it did not matter that his use had not been attached to a product ...

Trademark dilution on the internet was a matter of Congressional concern. Senator Patrick Leahy (D-Vt) stated:

> ... it is my hope that this anti-dilution statute can help stem the use of deceptive internet addresses taken by those who are choosing marks that are associated with the products and reputations of others.

We reject Toeppen's premise that a domain name is nothing more than an address. A significant purpose of a domain name is to identify the entity that owns the web site. 'A customer who is unsure about a company's domain name will often guess that the domain name is also the company's name.' (*Cardservice International v McGee* 950 F Supp 737, 741 (ED Va 1997)). '[A] domain name mirroring a corporate name may be a valuable corporate asset, as it facilitates communication with a customer base.' (*MTV Networks Inc v Curry* 867 F Supp 202, 203–204 n 2 (SDNY 1994)). ...

31 Using a company's name or trademark as a domain name is also the easiest way to locate that company's web site. Use of a 'search engine' can turn up hundreds of web sites, and there is nothing equivalent to a phone book or directory assistance for the internet. See *Cardservice*, 950 F Supp at 741.

32 Moreover, potential customers of Panavision will be discouraged if they cannot find its web page by typing in 'Panavision.com', but instead are forced to wade through hundreds of web sites. This dilutes the value of Panavision's trademark ...

33 Toeppen's use of 'Panavision.com' also puts Panavision's name and reputation at his mercy.

While the justice of the result may not be in doubt,[103] as with the UK passing off cases, it would appear that the court had no sympathy for the defendant and so was willing to put a broad construction on the meaning of 'commercial use'.

Electronic commerce and trademarks in the US: domain names,
trademarks and the 'use in commerce requirement' on the Internet
Giorgio Nicolò Vergani
[1999] EIPR 450

... the courts have stretched the 'use in commerce' requirement to the 'vanishing point'. One reason for this interpretation may be (and probably is) the tendency towards a conception of trademarks as property granting the trademark owner broader protection than under traditional trademark doctrine. One possible justification of such a construction is that the courts addressed the Internet explosion in a very short period of time while facing usurpers, religious and political extremists and various exploiters with the only instrument arguably available, the trademark law.

The efforts of UK courts to deal with cybersquatting have been described as both 'short-sighted' and 'ad hoc'[104], in contrast, in 1999, the US Congress the Anticybersquatting-Consumer Protection Act (ACPA) which introduces new provisions[105] into the Lanham Act on trade marks.

103 For further discussion of this case and other US domain name cases see, eg, *op cit*, Tucker, 1999.
104 Magee, 2003.
105 15 USC § 1125(d) and see www.gigalaw.com/library/anticybersquattingact-1999-11-29-p1.html

Anticybersquatting Consumer Protection Act
Sec 3002 Cyberpiracy Prevention

(a) IN GENERAL – Section 43 of the Trademark Act of 1946 (15 U.S.C. 1125) is amended by inserting at the end the following:

(d)(l)(A) A person shall be liable in a civil action by the owner of a mark, including a personal name which is protected as a mark under this section, if, without regard to the goods or services of the parties, that person –

(i) has a bad faith intent to profit from that mark, including a personal name which is protected as a mark under this section; and

(ii) registers, traffics in, or uses a domain name that –

(I) in the case of a mark that is distinctive at the time of registration of the domain name, is identical or confusingly similar to that mark;

(II) in the case of a famous mark that is famous at the time of registration of the domain name, is identical or confusingly similar to or dilutive of that mark; or

(III) is a-trademark, word, or name protected by reason of section 706 of title 18, United States Code, or section 220506 of title 36, United States Code.

(B)(i) In determining whether a person has a bad faith intent described under subparagraph (A), a court may consider factors such as, but not limited to –

(I) the trademark or other intellectual property rights of the person, if any, in the domain name;

(II) the extent to which the domain name consists of the legal name of the person or a name that is otherwise commonly used to identify that person;

(III) the person's prior use, if any, of the domain name in connection with the bona fide offering of any goods or services;

(IV) the person's bona fide noncommercial or fair use of the mark in a site accessible under the domain name;

(V) the person's intent to divert consumers from the mark owner's online location to a site accessible under the domain name that could harm the goodwill represented by the mark, either for commercial gain or with the intent to tarnish or disparage the mark, by creating a likelihood of confusion as to the source, sponsorship, affiliation, or endorsement of the site;

(VI) the person's offer to transfer, sell, or otherwise assign the domain name to the mark owner or any third party for financial gain without having used, or having an intent to use, the domain name in the bona fide offering of any goods or services, or the person's prior conduct indicating a pattern of such conduct;

(VII) the person's provision of material and misleading false contact information when applying for the registration of the domain name, the person's intentional failure to maintain accurate contact information, or the person's prior conduct indicating a pattern of such conduct;

(VIII) the person's registration or acquisition of multiple domain names which the person knows are identical or confusingly similar to marks of others that are distinctive at the time of registration of such domain names, or dilutive of famous marks of others that are famous at the time of registration of such domain names, without regard to the goods or services of the parties; and

(IX) the extent to which the mark incorporated in the person's domain name registration is or is not distinctive and famous within the meaning of subsection (c)(1) of section 43.

(ii) Bad faith intent described under subparagraph (A) shall not be found in any case in which the court determines that the person believed and had reasonable grounds to believe that the use of the domain name was a fair use or otherwise lawful.

There have been a number of cases under the ACPA[106] which have considered the nature of the evidence required to show bad faith in the light of the guidance given in the ACPA. In *Virtual Works Inc v Volkswagen of America Inc*, the Fourth Circuit found both circumstantial and direct evidence of establishing bad faith. Virtual Works Inc had registered vw.net even though both vwi.org and vwi.net were available, it had never done business as VW and the name was clearly similar to the famous Volkswagen brand. Nonetheless the court proceeded with caution:

> we do not suggest that these four facts would alone resolve the question of Virtual Works' intent on summary judgment. The fact that a domain resembles a famous trademark, for example, hardly in and of itself establishes bad faith. Moreover, domain names that are abbreviations of a company's formal name are quite common. To view the use of such names as tantamount to bad faith would chill Internet entrepreneurship with the prospect of endless litigation.[107]

However there was also evidence that Virtual Works foresaw the ability to profit from the natural association with Volkswagen which these initials would bring and there was also evidence that there was an intention to sell the domain name for 'a lot of money'. Unsurprisingly Virtual Works could not take advantage of the provision in §1125 d(1)(B)(ii). Although there might be some legitimate explanation, 'all but the most blatant cybersquatters will be able to put forth at least some lawful motives for their behavior' and the court declined 'to construe the safe harbor so broadly as to undermine the rest of the statute'.[108]

Shields v Zuccarini,[109] concerned a dispute over five domain names registered by Zuccarini which were not, as in the previous case, identical to the contested name. Instead the domain names in question, joescartoon.com, joecarton.com, joescartons.com, joescartoons.com and cartoonjoe.com, closely resembled Shield's domain name 'joecartoon.com'. The evidence was that Zuccarini had knowingly registered thousands of Internet domain names that were identical to, or confusingly similar to, the distinctive marks of others. In so doing he earned between $800,000 and $1,000,000 per year from their use. Zuccarini's argument was that the ACPA did not apply to his activities as its purpose was the prevention of cybersquatting, which he defined as 'registering someone's famous name and trying to sell the domain name to them or registering it to prevent the famous person from using it themselves'. The court gave this argument short shrift pointing out that it ignored 'the plain language of the statute and its stated purpose as discussed in the legislative history'. It clearly covered domain names that were 'confusingly similar' and the intentional registration of domain names that were misspelt or had other slight modifications was a reasonable interpretation of that.

---

106 For a review see eg, Mota, 2003.
107 238 F3d 264, 269 (4th Cir. 2001).
108 *Ibid* p. 270.
109 254 F3d 476 (3rd Cir 2001).

Zuccarini was also to feature in later litigation. Of his many domain names which were misspellings of other names (a practice which had been christened 'typosquatting') many of these directed the unwary user, who was looking for the genuine site, to pornographic sites. Given that many of the sites with which there was confusion were ones which were attractive to children, for instance www.bobthebiulder.com and www.teltubbies.com, this was the cause of considerable concern. A later statute the 'Truth in Domain Names Act'[110] was intended to address this problem by making it a criminal offence to use a 'misleading domain name with the intent to attract a minor into viewing a visual depiction of sexually explicit conduct on the Internet'. Zuccarini was arrested and, in December 2003, pleaded guilty to 49 counts of using domain names to direct minors to sexually explicit or nude content on web sites.[111]

Uniform Dispute Resolution Policy (UDRP)

The various organisations that register domain names are accredited to ICANN (Internet Corporation for Assigned Names and Numbers), which was created in October 1998 and now coordinates the assignment of internet domain names.[112] As a result, all registrars of the generic top level domains must follow the Uniform Domain Name Dispute Resolution Policy (UDRP). The UDRP provides that, before any action can be taken to suspend the use of a domain name, all disputes involving trade marks should be resolved by agreement, court action or arbitration. Disputes involving abusive registration for example cybersquatting (with the object of selling the name to the rightful owner at an inflated price), or 'typosquatting' (involving the registration of a domain name the same or similar to a famous name with the purpose of diverting the user searching for the 'official site' to another site) may be addressed by an alternative dispute resolution service provider such as the WIPO Arbitration and Mediation Centre. To date, approximately 10,000 disputes have been adjudicated by such providers.[113] To obtain the transfer of a domain name, the claimant must show that the respondent has acted in bad faith which can include, *inter alia*, registering the domain name for the purpose of selling to the rightful owner; preventing the holder of the corresponding trade mark registering the domain name; disrupting the business of the claimant; or intending to use it for commercial gain by means of confusion with the claimant's mark.[114]

The advantage of the UDRP is that it is much quicker than other methods and is less expensive, neither are jurisdictional issues of importance. It has frequently been used by famous individuals wishing to take action against those trying to capitalise on their reputations. In March 2000, Mark Hogarth, a Cambridge academic, registered a number of domain names corresponding to the names of famous writers, including

---

110 18 USC §2252B.
111 See www.usdoj.gov/criminal/cybercrime/zuccariniSent.htm, news.findlaw.com/cnn/docs/ cyberlaw/uszuccarini82903cmp.pdf and discussion in Clark, 2004.
112 For a more wide-ranging analysis of the role of ICANN than is possible here see e.g. Caral, 2004.
113 See www.icann.org/udrp/proceedings-stat.html.
114. See also Gey, 2001.

'jeanettewinterson.com', 'jeanettewinterson.org' and 'jeanettewinterson.net'. He alleged that he intended to create unofficial sites devoted to providing extracts of the writings of the author, other details, etc, but he also wrote to a number of them, asking if they wished to purchase the domain name associated with their name. Winterson filed a complaint against Hogarth on the basis that she had a common law right to her name. The WIPO Arbitration Panel considered the situation in the UK and referred to a number of cases, including those involving One in a Million, discussed above:

> 6.9 ... the issue is not whether the Respondent has committed passing off by registering the three domain names at issue, it is merely whether under English common law unauthorised use of a mark can be restrained other than by a action for infringement of a trademark. The mere fact that the right to sue for infringement of an unregistered trademark is not available under English law does not affect a person's right of action against another for passing off ... applying English law the Complainant clearly would have a cause of action to prevent unauthorised use of the mark JEANETTE WINTERSON in passing off.[115]

In addition to the rights of the complainant in her name, the panel found that the domain name had been both used and registered in bad faith and that the respondent had no legitimate rights of interests in the name, and accordingly ordered that all three domain names be transferred.

A similar result occurred in a hearing involving the actress Julia Roberts.[116] As this related to the situation in the US, it was argued on the basis of the existence of a common law trademark. In this case, the respondent alleged that the fact of registration and use of the domain name 'juliaroberts.com' was of itself sufficient to give him rights and a legitimate interest in the name. The panel referred to the *Winterson* case and decided that 'registration of her name as a registered trademark or service mark was not necessary and that the name 'Julia Roberts' has sufficient secondary association with the complainant that common law trademark rights do exist under US trademark law'. Further, the respondent had 'failed to show: (a) use of the domain name in connection with the offering of any goods or services; (b) common knowledge that he is known by the domain name; (c) legitimate, non-commercial or fair use of the domain name; or (d) any other basis upon which he can assert rights or a legitimate interest' and the court further found that both use and registration had been in bad faith. Thus, as might be expected, a similar result was obtained to that in the *Winterson* case, but by considering relevant law and precedent in the jurisdiction of origin. In contrast the singer, Sting, was not able to have the domain name sting.com transferred to him. Sting is a common word and the evidence was that the person to whom it was registered had used it as a nickname on the internet for about eight years, he had acquired the name five years before the action was commenced, and there had been no attempt to sell it. In these circumstances the panel was unable to find the requisite use in bad faith.[117]

---

115 *Jeanette Winterson v Mark Hogarth* (2000), available at arbiter.wipo.int/domains/ decisions/html/2000/d2000-0235.html. See, also, Osborne, 2000.

116 *Julia Fiona Roberts v Russell Boyd* (2000), available at arbiter.wipo.int/domains/ decisions/html/2000/d2000-0210.html.

117 arbiter.wipo.int/domains/decisions/html/2000/d2000-0596.

Unlike the above cases, *Pierce Brosnan v Network Operations Center*[118]concerned the use of the domain name piercebrosnan.com to divert traffic to a commercial website which contained some biographical details of actors, although nothing about Pierce Brosnan. It did however have a large number of banner advertisements etc. which created revenue for the holder. *Ronaldo de Assis Moreira v Goldmark Cd Webb*,[119] involved a serial typosquatter who had repeatedly registered domain names corresponding to the names and trade marks of others and used them to divert business to his commercial sites. This case involved the footballer, Ronaldinho Gaúcho, described by the panel as such a well-known footballer that 'rather than an unfortunate coincidence, it is clear that the Respondent was aware of the Complainant's reputation and aimed at misleading consumers and unfairly benefiting from it'. Both of these cases were found to be clear examples of use in bad faith.

There is no internal appeal system under the UDRP, but use of the procedure does not preclude an adjudication by the courts. In *Sallen v Corinthians Licentiamentos LTDA*, Sallen had unsuccessfully defended his registration of the domain name corinthians.com in proceedings under the UDRP.[120] He subsequently sought to obtain a ruling that his registration of the domain name was not a breach of the Anticybersquatting Consumer Protection Act (ACPA) court. The district court found that federal courts had no jurisdiction in such cases but this decision was reversed by the First Circuit. The relationship between the application of the UDRP and the ACPA is summed up in the following extract.

Sallen v Corinthians Licentiamentos LTDA
273 F 3d 14, 28
US Court of Appeals, First Circuit (2001)

A finding by a federal court that Sallen was within his rights would necessarily undermine the panel's conclusion that he used the domain name in bad faith. More generally, a court's decision that a party is not a cybersquatter under the ACPA, and that a party has a right to use a domain name, necessarily negates a WIPO decision that a party is a cybersquatter under the UDRP. The conclusion that a federal court's interpretation of the ACPA supplants a WIPO panel's interpretation of the UDRP is further reinforced by the fact that WIPO does not create new law – it applies existing law. In fact, the application of the "lowest common denominator of internationally agreed and accepted principles concerning the abuse of trademarks," rather than the creation of new law, is part of the UDRP's fundamental structure.

In the subsequent case of *Excelentisimo Ayuntamiento de Barcelona v Barcelona.com Inc*, the City of Barcelona sought to have the domain name, barcelona.com, transferred from a registrant who was using it for a website which promoted links between US, Europe and South America, where there are several places also called Barcelona. At a hearing under the UDRP, the Panel, on rather tenuous grounds, made an order for transfer.[121] In the subsequent court case, the district court upheld the order, but this was reversed by the Fourth Circuit on the basis that the district court had applied Spanish rather than US law. Further clarification of the relationship of the UDRP with national law was also provided.[122]

---

118 arbiter.wipo.int/domains/decision/html/2003/d2003-0519.html.
119 arbiter.wipo.int/domains/decision/html/2004/d2004-0827.
120 see arbiter.wipo.int/domains/decision/html/2000/d2000-0461
121 arbiter.wipo.int/domains/decision/html/2000/d2000-0505
122 See also discussion in Efroni, 2003; Moreira 2003.

Excelentisimo Ayuntamiento de Barcelona v Barcelona.com Inc
330 F3d 617, 625
US Court of Appeals, Fourth Circuit (2003)

... domain names are issued pursuant to contractual arrangements under which the registrant agrees to a dispute resolution process, the UDRP, which is designed to resolve a large number of disputes involving domain names, but this process is not intended to interfere with or modify any "independent resolution" by a court of competent jurisdiction. Moreover, the UDRP makes no effort at unifying the law of trademarks among the nations served by the Internet. Rather, it forms part of a contractual policy developed by ICANN for use by registrars in administering the issuance and transfer of domain names. Indeed, it explicitly anticipates that judicial proceedings will continue under various nations' laws applicable to the parties.

The ACPA recognizes the UDRP only insofar as it constitutes a part of a policy followed by registrars in administering domain names, and the UDRP is relevant to actions brought under the ACPA in two contexts. First, the ACPA limits the liability of a registrar in respect to registering, transferring, disabling, or cancelling a domain name if it is done in the "implementation of a reasonable policy" (including the UDRP) that prohibits registration of a domain name "identical to, confusingly similar to, or dilutive of another's mark." ... Second, the ACPA authorizes a suit by a domain name registrant whose domain name has been suspended, disabled or transferred under that reasonable policy (including the UDRP) to seek a declaration that the registrant's registration and use of the domain name involves no violation of the Lanham Act as well as an injunction returning the domain name.

Thus, while a decision by an ICANN-recognized panel might be a condition of, indeed the reason for, bringing an action under 15 U.S.C. § 1114(2)(D)(v), its recognition *vel non* is not jurisdictional. Jurisdiction to hear trademark matters is conferred on federal courts by 28 U.S.C. §§ 1331 and 1338, and a claim brought under the ACPA, which amended the Lanham Act, is a trademark matter over which federal courts have subject matter jurisdiction. ...

Moreover, any decision made by a panel under the UDRP is no more than an agreed-upon administration that is not given any deference under the ACPA. To the contrary, because a UDRP decision is susceptible of being grounded on principles foreign or hostile to American law, the ACPA authorizes reversing a panel decision if such a result is called for by application of the Lanham Act.

Opinion is divided on how successful ICANN and the UDRP have been to date. It has certainly proved popular with those seeking to resolve disputes over domain names and many more cases are decided by this mechanism than ever come before national courts. There have been criticisms of the procedural aspects of the policy[123] and more fundamentally, the reasoning and outcomes have also been the subject of criticism. The Barcelona.com case, for instance, is often cited as an example of a 'bad' decision. Magee points out, however, that it is not necessarily representative and that there has been an improvement in quality in the decisions under the UDRP with accumulated experience.[124] Armon, on the other hand, although remarking that the UDRP could be used to resolve domain names disputes efficiently and fairly in the manner intended at its inception, suggests that 'bias, mistakes, and poorly reasoned decisions characterise the interpretation of the UDRP'.

---

123 See, eg, Armon, 2003.
124 Magee, 2004.

Orion Armon
As good as it gets? An appraisal of the Uniform Domain Name Dispute Resolution Policy
(2003) 20(12) Computer and Internet Law 1, 3

The UDRP is a bold experiment, arguably too bold. It expands trademark rights in cyberspace. It tests the outer limits of the feasibility of Internet self-governance. It establishes uniform global rules for domain name dispute resolution. It promises to reduce the cost of resolving domain name disputes and to make the dispute resolution process quicker than litigation. In short, the UDRP's goal is to do everything national court systems do to resolve domain name disputes but to do it on a global scale, for less money, in less time, all to prove that an alternative dispute resolution system designed by Internet users for Internet users is superior to relying on legislatures in various countries to impose solutions for Internet problems from the outside. To say the least, the standard for success set by the UDRP's creators is a high one, and like many other Internet experiments that were rolled out with fanfare and early acclaim, the UDRP has been only a partial success.

SUMMARY

This chapter has considered the current legal response to some of the problems of intellectual property law associated with digitisation and the developing information society. The legal reaction to these technological changes is seen, generally, to be one of pragmatism. While the appropriateness of a copyright regime has been debated, the practical response to some of the fundamental copyright issues has been to develop legislative proposals, with the further possibility of supplementing the legal framework with technical requirements. Nevertheless, the situation with regard to ISP liability remains far from clear.

Attitudes to linking vary, from the proponents of the view that the *raison d'être* of the world wide web is indicative of the creation of a 'right to link', to those who take a rather more circumspect view of the way in which their work might be disseminated to a wider audience. This has resulted in a flurry of litigation, which has usually resulted in an agreement on the manner of linking, leading to the emergence of the so called 'licence to link'.

Finally, with respect to domain names, the use of mediation and alternative dispute resolution has removed the imminent threat of the courts being bombarded with disputes over domain name registration and use. However, as is revealed by a browse through the list of hearings on the ICANN website,[125] this has not stemmed the tide of disputes but has merely transferred them to other fora.

As the information society progresses, the law will have to continue to be flexible and adaptable in the face of continuous technological evolution. The prospect of a complete review of the framework and rationale of intellectual property law in the face of such changes seems remote at present, if, indeed, it is even desirable.

---

125 See www.icann.org/udrp/proceedings-list.htm.

BIBLIOGRAPHY

Computer programs as goods under the UCC' (1979) 77 Mich L Rev 1149).

Chalton SNL et al (eds) *Encyclopedia of Data Protection 1988–2005,* London: Sweet & Maxwell.

Report of the Committee on Data Protection, Cmnd 7341, 1978, London: HMSO.

Privacy and Related Matters, (the Calcutt Report) Cmnd 1102, 1990, London: HMSO.

Report of the Commitee on Privacy, (The Younger Report) Cmnd 5012, 1972, London: HMSO.

Computers: Safeguards for Privacy, Cmnd 6354, 1975, London: HMSO.

Akdeniz, Y, 'Section 3 of the Computer Misuse Act 1990: an antidote for computer viruses!' [1996] 3 Web JCLI, available at webjcli.ncl.ac.uk/1996/issue3/akdeniz3.html.

Akdeniz, Y, Taylor, N, and Walker, C, 'BigBrother.gov.uk: State surveillance in the age of information and rights' [2001] Crim L Rev 73.

Albert, MR, 'E-Buyer beware: Why online auction fraud should be regulated' (2002) 39 Am Bus LJ 575.

Aldesco, AI 'The demise of anonymity; A constitutional challenge to the Convention on Cybercrime' (2002) 23 Loy. LA Ent L Rev 81.

Aldhouse, FGB, 'UK data protection – where are we in 1991?' (1991) 5 LCT Yearbook 180.

Alongi, EA, 'Has the US canned Spam?' (2004) 46 Ariz L Rev 263.

Arasaratnam, N, 'Brave New (Online) World' (2000) 23 UNSWLJ 205.

Arden J, 'Electronic commerce' (1999) 149 NLJ 1685.

Argy, P, 'Internet content regulation: an Australian Computer Society perspective' (2000) 23 UNSWLJ 265.

Armon, O, 'As good as it gets? An appraisal of the Uniform Domain Name Dispute Resolution Policy ' (2003) 20(12) Computer & Internet Law 1.

Arnold-Moore, T, 'Legal pitfalls in cyberspace: defamation on computer networks' (1994) 5 JLIS 165.

Asarch, CG, 'Is turnabout fair play? Copyright law and the fair use of computer software loaded into RAM' (1996) 95 Mich L Rev 654.

Atiyah, PS, Sale of Goods, Adams, JN and MacQueen, H (eds), 10th edn, 2000, Harlow: Longman.

Attridge, DJM 'Challenging claims! Patenting computer programs in Europe and the USA' [2001] IPQ 22.

Auburn, F, 'Usenet news and the law' (1995) 1 Web JCLI, available at webjcli.ncl.ac.uk/articles1/auburn1.html.

Audit Commission *Your Business @ risk,* 2001, London: HMSO.

Audit Commission, *Computer Fraud Survey,* 1985, London: HMSO.

Bainbridge, D, 'Computer programs and copyright: more exceptions to infringement' (1993) 56 MLR 591.

Bainbridge, D, *Introduction to Computer Law,* 2000, London: Longman.

Baldwin, R and Cave, M, *Understanding Regulation: Theory, Strategy and Practice*, 1999, Oxford: OUP.

Baldwin, R and McCrudden, C, *Regulation and Public Law*, 1987, London: Weidenfeld & Nicholson.

Barlow, JP, 'Selling wine without bottles: the economy of mind on the global net', in Bernt Hugenholtz, P (ed), *The Future of Copyright in a Digital Environment*, 1996, The Hague: Kluwer.

Beale, I, 'Computer eavesdropping: fact or fantasy' (1986) 1 CLSR 16.

Bennett, C, 'Convergence revisited', in Agre, PE and Rotenberg, M (eds) *Technology and Privacy: the New Landscape*, 1998, Cambridge, Mass: MIT.

Bettink, WW, and Wentholt, F, 'Kazaa victory leaves permissibility of file-sharing software undecided' (2004) Houthoff Buruma Newsletter, March.

Black, W, 'The Domain Name System' in Edwards, L and Waelde, C (eds) 2000 *Law and the Internet: A framework for Electronic Commerce,* Oxford: Hart.

Blanke, JM, (2004) 'Assessment Technologies of WI, LLC v WIREdata Inc: Seventh Circuit decision reinforces the non-copyrightability of facts in a database'. 20 Santa Clara Computer & High Tech LJ 755.

Blume, P, 'Transborder data flow: is there a solution in sight?' (2000) 8 IJLIT 65.

Booton, D, and Mole, P, 'The Action freezes? The draft directive on the patentability of computer related inventions.' [2002] IPQ 289.

Bott, F, Coleman, A, Eaton J, and Rowland, D, *Professional Issues in Software Engineering*, 3rd edn, 2000, London: Taylor & Francis.

Braithwaite, N, 'The internet and bulletin board defamations' (1995) 145 NLJ 1216.

Braithwaite, N, and Carolina, R, 'Multimedia defamation' (1994) 12 Int Media Law 19.

Brenner, SW, Carrier, B, and Henninger, J, 'The Trojan Horse defense in cybercrime cases' (2004) 21 Santa Clara Computer & High Tech LJ 1.

Brunnstein, K, and Fischer-Huebner, S, 'How far can the criminal law help to control IT misuse?' (1995) 9 LC & T Yearbook 111.

Burk, DL, 'Jurisdiction in a world without borders' (1997) 1 Va JLT, available at www.student.virginia.edu/~vjolt/vol1/BURK.htm.

Burk, DL, 'Proprietary Rights in Hypertext Linkages' (1998) 2 JILT available at www2.warwick.ac.uk/fac/soc/law/elj/jilt/1998_2/burk/.

Burton, PF, 'Regulation and control of the Internet: is it feasible? Is it necessary?' (1995) 21 J Inf Sci 413.

Calleja, R, 'The E-Bill and the E-Directive' [2000] CL Feb/Mar 27.

Campbell, KJ, 'Copyright on the Internet: the view from Shetland' [1997] EIPR 255.

Caral, JMA, 'Lessons from ICANN: Is self-regulation of the internet fundamentally flawed?' (2004) 12 Int'l JL & Info Tech 1.

Carter-Ruck, P, and Starte, H, *Carter-Ruck on Libel and Slander*, 5th edn, 1997, London: Butterworths.

Cerina, P, 'The originality requirement in the protection of databases in Europe and the United States' (1993) 24 IIC 579.

Cesare, K, 'Prosecuting computer virus authors: The need for an adequate and immediate international solution' (2001) 14 Transnat'l Law 135.

Chalton, S, 'Interpretation in the UK of EC Directive 96/9 on the Legal Protection of Databases' (2000) 5 Comm L 79.

Chandrani, R, 'RIP e-commerce' (2000) 11 C & L 30.

Chapman, M, 'Can a computer be deceived? Dishonesty offences and electronic transfer of funds' (2000) 64 J Crim L 89.

Charlesworth, A, 'Addiction and hacking' (1993) 143 NLJ 540.

Charlesworth, A, 'Between flesh and sand: rethinking the Computer Misuse Act 1990' (1995) 9 LC & T Yearbook 31.

Charlesworth, A, 'Clash of the data titans? US and EU data privacy regulation' (2000) 6 EPL 253.

Charlesworth, A, 'Legislating against computer misuse: the trials and tribulations of the UK Computer Misuse Act 1990' (1993a) J L & IS 80.

Chen, P, 'Pornography, protection, prevarication: the politics of internet censorship' (2000) 23 UNSWLJ 221.

Chissick, M, and Kelman, A, Electronic Commerce: Law and Practice, 2nd edn, 2000, London: Sweet & Maxwell.

Chisum, DS, 'The patentability of computer algorithms' (1986) 47 Pitt UL Rev 959.

Chitty on Contracts H Beale ed 29th ed Sweet & Maxwell, London (2004).

Chong, S, 'Internet meta-tags and trade mark issues' [1998] EIPR 275.

Christian, C, 'Down and out in cyberspace' (1993) 90 Law Soc Gazette 2.

Clark, CG, 'The Truth in Domain Names Act of 2003 and a preventative measure to combat typosquatting' (2004) 89 Cornell L Rev 1476.

Clarkson, CMV, and Hill, J, Jaffey on the Conflict of Laws, 1997, London: Butterworths, p 236.

Clough, B, and Mungo, P, Approaching Zero: Data Crime and the Computer Underworld, 1993, London: Faber & Faber.

Cmnd 5012, 1972, London: HMSO.

Cmnd 5012, 1972, London: HMSO.

Cmnd 7341, 1978, London: HMSO.

Cohen, J, 'The patenting of computer software' [1999] EIPR 607.

Cobley, C, 'Child Pornography on the Internet' (1997) 2 Comm L 30.

Colombe, M, and Meyer, C, 'Seeking interoperability: An industry response' [1990] EIPR 79.

Colombe, M, and Meyer, C, 'Interoperability still threatened by EC Software Directive: A Status Report' [1990] EIPR 325.

Communication to the European Parliament, the Economic and Social Committee and the Committee of the Regions, Illegal and Harmful Content on the Internet 2: How does the Internet Work? COM (1996) 487.

Conley, JM, and Bryan, RM, 'Computer Crime Legislation in the US' (1999) 8 ICTL 35.

Connolly, JP, and Cameron, S, 'Fair dealing in webbed links of Shetland Yarn' [1998] JILT, available at www2.warwick.ac.uk/fac/soc/law/elj/jilt/1998_2/connolly/.

Consultation Paper of the Lord Chancellor's Department, Review of Press Regulation, Cmnd 2135, 1993, London: HMSO.

Cooke, J, 'Architects and engineers: practising in the public interest' (1991) 14 NSW ULJ 73.

Coote, B, 'Correspondence with description in the law of sale of goods' (1976) ALJ 154.

'Copyright protection for computer software' (1964) 64 Colum L Rev 1274.

Corker, J, Nugent, S, and Porter, J, 'Regulating Internet Content: A co-regulatory approach' (2000) 23 UNSWLJ 198.

Cornish, WR, 'Interoperable systems and copyright' [1989] EIPR 391.

Cornish, WR, 'Computer program copyright and the Berne Convention' [1990] EIPR 129.

Cornish, WR, 'Computer program copyright and the Berne Convention', in Lehmann, M and Tapper, CF (eds), *Handbook of European Software Law*, Pt I, 1993, Oxford: Clarendon.

Cornish, WR, and Llewellyn, D, *Intellectual Property* 5th edn, 2003, London: Sweet & Maxwell.

Cornish, WR, *Intellectual Property*, 4th edn, 1999, London: Sweet & Maxwell.

Council of Europe Convention for the Protection on Individuals with regard to the Automatic Processing of Personal Data, available at www.conventions.coe.int/treaty/EN/cadreprincipal.htm.

CSI/FBI Computer Crime and Security Survey 2003, available via www.cybercrime.gov/CSI_FBI.html.

Czarnota, B, and Hart, RJ, *Legal Protection of Computer Programs in Europe: A Guide to the EC Directive*, 1991, London: Butterworths.

Dahm, AL, 'Database protection v Deep linking' (2004) 82 Tex L Rev 1053.

Daniels, DWT, 'Learned Hand never played Nintendo: a better way to think about non-literal, non-visual software copyright cases' (1994) 61 Chicago UL Rev 613.

Data Protection: The Government's Proposals, Cm 3725, 1997, London: HMSO.

Davidson, DM, 'Common law, uncommon software' (1986) 47 Pitt UL Rev 1037.

Davies, D, 'Anatomy of a disaster' (1990) 6 CL & Security Rep 27.

Davies, L, 'A model for internet regulation', 1998, available at www.scl.org.

Davies, L, 'Contract formation on the internet: shattering a few myths', in Edwards, L, and Waelde, C, (eds), *Law & the Internet*, 1997, Oxford: Hart.

Davies, S, 'Computer program claims' [1998] EIPR 429.

Debusseré, F, 'Court finds peer-to-peer music file-sharing illegal' Stibbe ICT Law Newsletter No. 18, January 2005 available at www.stibbe.be/upload/b6e39f0101b6616168014a5a.pdf.

Delacourt, JT, 'The international impact of Internet regulation' (1997) 38 Harv Int LJ 207.

Derclaye, E, 'Databases *sui generis* right: Should we adopt the spin off theory?' [2004] EIPR 402.

Deveci, HA, 'Hyperlinks oscillating at the crossroads' (2004) 10 CTLR 82.

Deveci, HA, 'Databases: Is sui generis a stronger bet than copyright?' (2004) 12 Int'l JL & Info Tech 178.

Dockins, M, 'Internet links: the good, the bad, the tortuous and a two-part test' (2005) 36 U Tol L Rev 367.

Dommering, EJ, and Hugenholtz, PB, (eds), *Protecting Works of Fact: Copyright, Freedom of Expression and Information Law*, 1991, The Hague: Kluwer.

Dooley, S, 'Defamation on the internet' (1995) 1 CTLR 191.

Dorsett, R, *Risks Digest: Forum on Risks to the Public in Computers and Related Systems* (1990) 9(72) ACM Committee on Computers and Public Policy.

Douma, E, 'The Uniform Computer Information Transactions Act and the issue of preemption of contractual provisions prohibiting reverse engineering, dissassembly or decompilation' (2001) 11 Alb LJ Sci & Tech 249.

Downing, S, and Harrington, J, 'The postal rule in electronic commerce: a reconsideration' (2000) 5(2) Comm L 43.

Drexl, J, 'What is protected in a computer program? Copyright protection in the US and Europe' (1994) 15 IIC Studies in Industrial Property & Copyright Law, Munich: VCH.

DTI, *Guide to the Consumer Protection Act 1987*, 1987, London.

Dumbill, EA, 'Computer Misuse Act 1990 – recent developments' (1992) 8 CLSR 105.

Dutson, S, 'The Internet, the conflict of laws, international litigation and intellectual property: the implications of the international scope of the Internet on intellectual property infringements' [1997] JBL 495.

Edwards, J, 'Has the dreaded data doomsday arrived?: Past, present, and future effects of the European Union's database directive on database and information availability in the European Union' (2004) 39 Ga L Rev 215.

Edwards, L, 'Canning the Spam: Is there a case for legal control of junk electronic mail' in Edwards, L, and Waelde, C, (eds.) *Law and the Internet: A framework for electronic commerce*, 2000, Oxford: Hart.

Efroni, Z, 'Barcelona.com analysis: Towards a better model for adjudication of international domain name disputes' (2003) 14 Fordham Intell Prop Media & Ent LJ 29.

Eighth Report of the Data Protection Registrar, 1992, London: HMSO,

Electronic Commerce: Formal Requirements in Commercial Transactions Advice from the Law Commission, 2001, December, para 3.28

Eleventh Report of the Data Protection Registrar, 1995, London: HMSO.

Elliott, C, and Gravatt, B, 'Domain name disputes in a cross-border context' [1999] EIPR 417.

Endeshaw, A, 'Computer misuse law in Singapore' (1999) 8 ICTL 5.

Englund, SR, 'Idea, process or protected expression? Determining the scope of copyright protection of the structure of computer programs' (1990) 88 Mich L Rev 866.

European Parliament Session News, available at www.europarl.eu.int/dg3/sdp/pointses/en/ps000703_ens.htm#19.

Ewing, M, 'The perfect storm: the Safe Harbor and the Directive on data protection' (2002) 24 Hous J Int'l L 315.

Feldman, D, 'Secrecy, dignity or autonomy? Views of privacy as a civil liberty' (1994) 10 CL & P 41.

Fellas, J, 'The patentability of software-related inventions in the US' [1999] EIPR 330.

Fisch Nigri, D, 'Computer crime: why should we still care' (1993) 9 CLSR 274.

Fitzpatrick, S, 'Copyright imbalance: US and Australian responses to the WIPO Digital Copyright Treaty' [2000] EIPR 214.

Foged, T, 'US v EU anti circumvention legislation: Preserving the public's privileges in the digital age' [2002] EIPR 525.

Fong, K, 'Non-literal copying infringes copyright in software: *Data Access Corporation v Powerflex Services Pty Ltd*' [1997] EIPR 256.

Foss, M and Bygrave, LA 'International consumer purchases through the Internet: Jurisdictional issues pursuant to European Law' (2000) 8 Int Jo Law.

Fourteenth Report of the Data Protection Registrar, 1998, London: HMSO.

Fraud Law Reform: Consultation on Proposals for Legislation Home Office, 2004, May.

Freed, RN, 'Information Technology – the birth, life and death of computer law: Part 3', (1992) 8 CL & Security Rep 19.

Freed, RN, 'Legal interests' relation to software programs' (1986) 3 CL & P 141.

Freed, RN, 'The protection of computer software in the USA' (1982) C & L 6.

Freed, RN, The birth, life and death of computer law' (1990–91) 7 CL & Security Rep 107.

Froomkin, AM 'Semi-private international rule-making' in Marsden, C (ed) *Regulating the Global Society*, 2000, London: Routledge.

FTC Report, *Privacy Online: A Report to Congress*, available at www.ftc.gov/ reports/privacy3/toc.htm.

Fuller 'Consideration and form' (1941) 41 Col LR 799.

Gall, G, 'European Patent Office Guidelines 1985 on the Protection of Inventions Relating to Computer Programs' (1985) 2 CL & P 2.

Garnett, R, 'Are foreign interest infringers beyond the reach of the law?' (2000) 23 NSW ULJ 105.

Garrigues, CC, 'Databases: a subject matter for copyright or for a neighboring rights regime?' [1997] EIPR 3.

Gavison, R, 'Privacy and the limits of law' (1980) 89 Yale LJ 421.

Geake, E, 'Did ambulance chiefs specify safety software?' (1992) 136 *New Scientist* 5.

Gellman, R, 'Does privacy law work?', in Agre, PE, and Rotenberg, M, *Technology and Privacy: the New Landscape*, 1998, Cambridge, Mass: MIT.

Gey, P 'Bad faith under ICANN's Uniform Domain Name Dispute Resolution Policy' [2001] EIPR 507.

Gibbons, T, 'Computer-generated pornography' (1995) 9 LC & T Yearbook 83.

Gibbons, T, 'Defamation reconsidered' (1996) 16 OJLS 587.

Gibson, J 'Re-reifying data' (2004) 80 Notre Dame L. Rev. 163.

Gillespie, A, 'Children, chatrooms and the law' [2001] Crim LR 435.

Gillespie, A, 'Sentences for offences involving child pornography' [2003] Crim LR 81.

Gillespie, A, 'The Sexual offences Act 2003: (3) Tinkering with 'child pornography' [2004] Crim LR 361.

Ginsburg, J, 'Creation and commercial value: copyright protection of works of information' (1990) 90 Col L Rev 1865.

Ginsburg, JC, 'Putting cars on the information superhighway: authors, exploiters and copyright in cyberspace (1995) 95 Colum L Rev 1466.

Ginsburg, JC, 'Four reasons and a paradox: the manifest superiority of copyright over *sui generis* protection of computer software' (1994) 94 Colum L Rev 2559.

Glatt, C, 'Comparative issues in contract formation' (1998) 6 Int JLIT 34.

Gobla, KA, 'The infeasibility of Federal internet regulation' (1997) 102 Dickinson L Rev 93.

Gobla, KA, Akdeniz, Y, 'The regulation of pornography and child pornography on the Internet' [1997] 1 JILT, available at elj.warwick.ac.uk/jilt/internet/97_1akdz.

Goldstein, P, 'The EC Software Directive: a view from the USA' in Lehmann, M and Tapper, CF (eds), Handbook of European Software Law, Pt I, 1993, Oxford: Clarendon.

Goodman, MD, and Brenner, SW, 'The emerging consensus on criminal conduct in cyberspace' (2002) UCLA J L & Tech 3.

Gordon, SE, 'The very idea? Why copyright is an inappropriate way to protect computer programs' [1998] EIPR 10.

Greenbaum, DS, 'The database debate: In support of an inequitable solution' (2003) 13 Alb LJ Sci & Tech 431.

Greenleaf, G, 'Law in cyberspace' (1996) 70 Aust LJ 33.

Griffin, TM, 'Internet domain names and trademarks: strategies for protecting brand names in cyberspace' (1998) 32 Suffolk UL Rev 47.

Guest, AG, (ed), Benjamin's Sale of Goods, 4th edn, 1992, London: Sweet & Maxwell.

Haaf, J, 'The EC Directive on the Legal Protection of Computer Programs: decompilation and security for confidential programming techniques' (1992) 30 Col J Transnat L 401.

Handa, S, and Buchan, J, 'Copyright as it applies to the protection of computer programs in Canada' (1995) 26 IIC 48.

Handsley, E, and Biggins, B, 'The sheriff rides into town: A day of rejoicing for innocent westerners' (2000) 23 UNSWLJ 257.

Harrington, D, 'The engineers have it! Patenting computer programs in the USA' (1996) 1 Comm L 232.

Hart, M, 'The copyright in the information society directive: An overview' [2002] EIPR 58.

Harvey, BW, and Franklin, F, Auctions Law and Practice, 2nd ed. 1995, Oxford: OUP.

Haslam, E, 'Contracting by electronic means' (1996) 146 NLJ 549.

Hatton, L, 'Software failures, follies and fallacies' (1997) IEE Rev, p 49.

Hayes, DL, 'What's left of look and feel: a current analysis' (1993) 10 CL 1.

Heitman, K 'Vapours and Mirrors' (2000) 23 UNSWLJ 246.

Hidalgo, PG, 'Copyright protection of computer software in the European Community: current protection and the effect of the adopted Directive' (1993) 27 Int Lawyer 113.

Hill, S 'Driving a trojan horse and cart through the Computer Misuse Act' (2003) 14(5) C&L 31.

Hirschbaeck, J, 'Is software a product?' (1989) 5 CL & P 154.

Hodges, C, Product Liability; European Laws and Practice, 1993, London: Sweet & Maxwell.

Huet, J, and Ginsburg, JC, 'Computer programs in Europe: A comparative analysis of the 1991 EC Software Directive' (1992) 30 Col J Transnat L 327.

Hugenholtz, PB, 'Caching and Copyright: The right of temporary copying' [2000] EIPR 482.

Hugenholtz, PB, 'Program Schedules, Event data and Telephone subscriber listings under the Database Directive' Eleventh Annual Conference on International IP Law and Policy, 2003, Fordham University School of Law, New York.

Hunter, 'Reverse engineering computer software – Australia parts company with the world' (1993) 9 CL & P 122.

Hunter, D, 'Mind your language: copyright in computer languages in Australia' [1998] EIPR 98.

Hurdle, H, 'Domain names – the scope of a trademark proprietor's monopoly' [1998] EIPR 74.

Inman, JA, and Inman, RR, 'Responsibility as an issue in internet communication: reading flames as defamation' (1996) 1 J Tech L & P 5.

Jackson, M, 'Computer crime laws: are they really needed? The Australian experience' (1995) 9 LC & T Yearbook 47.
Jackson, R, and Powell, J, *Jackson and Powell on Professional Negligence*, 4th edn, 1997, London: Sweet & Maxwell.
Jarvie, N, 'Control of cybercrime – is an end to our privacy in the internet a price worth paying? Part 2 (2003) 9 CTLR 110.
Jawahitha, S, 'Negligent liability and e-consumers in Malaysia' (2004) 10 CTLR 200.
Jay, R, and Hamilton, A, *Data Protection: Law and Practice*, 2nd edn, 2003, London: Sweet & Maxwell.
Johnson, DR, and Post, D, 'Law and borders – the rise of law in cyberspace' (1996) 48 Stan L Rev 1367.
Jones, S, 'Computer terrorist or mad boffin?' (1996) 146 NLJ 46.

Karjala, DS, 'Copyright protection of computer software in the US and Japan, Part I' [1991] EIPR 195.
Karjala, DS, 'Distinguishing Patent and Copyright Subject Matter' (2003) 35 Conn L Rev 439.
Karjala, DS, 'Recent US and international developments in software protection, Part 2' [1994] EIPR 58.
Katyal, NK 'Criminal law in cyberspace' (2001) 149 U Pa L Rev 1003.
Kelleher, D, 'International computer crime' (1997) 147 NLJ 445.
Kergévant, C, 'Are copyright and *droit d'auteur* viable in the light of information technology?' (1996) 10 Int Rev LCT 55.
Keyser, M, 'The Council of Europe Convention on cybercrime' (2003) 12 J. Transnat'l L. & Pol'y 287.
Kirby, M, 'Privacy in cyberspace' (1998) 21 NSW ULJ 323.
Klang, M, 'A Critical Look at the Regulation of Computer Viruses' (2003) 11 IJLIT 162.
Koffman, L, and Macdonald, E, *The Law of Contract*, 5th edn, 2004, Butterworths.
Kohl, U, 'Legal reasoning and legal change in the age of the Internet – why the ground rules are still valid' (1999) 7 Int JLIT 123.
Koo, D, 'Patent and Copyright Protection of Computer Programs' [2002] IPQ.
Krocker, ER, 'The Computer Directive and the balance of rights' [1997] EIPR 247.
Kwiatkowski, FJ, 'Hacking and the criminal law revisited' (1987) 4 CL & P 15.

Laakkonen, A, and Whaite, R, 'The EPO leads the way, but where to?' [2001] EIPR 244.
Lai, S, 'Database protection in the United Kingdom – the new deal and its effect on software protection' [1998] EIPR 32.
Lai, S, *The Copyright Protection of Computer Software in the United Kingdom*, 2000, Oxford: Hart.
Lake, WT, et al 'Seeking compatibility or avoiding development costs? A reply on software copyright in the EC' [1989] EIPR 431.
Lannetti, DW, 'Toward a revised definition of 'product' under the Restatement (Third) of Torts: Products Liability' (2000) 35 Tort & Ins LJ 845.

Lavenue, LM, 'Database rights and technical data rights: the expansion of intellectual property for the protection of databases' (1997) 38 Santa Clara L Rev 1.

Law Com Rep No 154. *The Parol Evidence Rule.*

Law Commission *Report on Liability for Defective Products,* Law Com 82, 1977, London: HMSO (Scottish Law Commission Report No 45).

Law Commission, *Reforming the Present Law–Hacking,* Working Paper No 110, 1988, London: HMSO

Law Commission, *Report on Computer Misuse,* Working Paper No 119, 1989, London: HMSO.

Law Commission, *Report on Formalities for Contracts for Sale of Land,* No 164, 1987, London: HMSO.

Law Commission, *Report on Offences of Dishonesty: Money Transfer,* Law Com 243, 1996, London: HMSO.

Law Commission, Consultation Paper No 155 'Legislating the criminal code: fraud and deception' 1999.

Law Commission, *Report on Fraud,* No 276, 2002.

Law Commission, *Unfair Terms in Contracts,* Consultation Paper No 166, London: HMSO (Scottish Law Commission Discussion Paper No 119).

Lemley, MA and Reese, RA 'Reducing digital copyright infringement without restricting innovation' (2004) 56 Stan L Rev 1345.

Lemley, MA, 'Intellectual property and shrink wrap licenses' (1995) 68 S Cal L Rev 1239.

Lenno, MJ, 'US patent rights in financial services software' (1994) 10 CL & P 17.

Lessig, L, 'The law of the horse: What cyberlaw might teach' (1999) 113 Harv. L. Rev. 501.

Leveson, NG, Safeware: *System Safety and Computers,* 1995, Reading, Mass: Addison-Wesley.

Likhovski, M, 'Fighting the patent wars' [2001] EIPR 267.

Lipton, J, 'Databases as intellectual property: New legal approaches' [2003] EIPR 139.

Lloyd, I, 'Legal barriers to electronic contracts: formal requirements and digital signatures', in Edwards and Waelde, *Law & the Internet* 1997, Oxford: Hart.

Lloyd, I, 'Liability for defective software' (1991) 32 Reliability Engineering and System Safety 193.

Lloyd, I, 'Patenting software – Humpty Dumpty rules' [1995] SLT 163.

Lloyd, I, and Simpson, M, *Law on the Electronic Frontier: Hume Papers on Public Policy,* 1994, Edinburgh: Edinburgh UP.

Lloyd, I, *Information Technology Law,* 4th ed, 2004, Oxford: Oxford University Press.

Lloyd, I, *Legal Aspects of the Information Society,* 2000, London: Butterworths.

Lowrie, AD, 'Developments in US case law' (1997) 28 IIC 868.

Loy, JA, 'Database and Collections of Information Misappropriation Act of 2003: Unconstitutionally Expanding Copyright Law?' 7 NYUJ Legis & Pub Pol'y 449.

Ludbrook, T, 'Defamation and the Internet: where are we now and where are we going? Parts I and II (2004) 15 Ent LR 173 and 203.

Lunney, GS, '*Lotus v Borland*: copyright and computer programs' [1996] Tul L Rev 239.

Macdonald, E, '"In the course of a business" – a fresh examination' (1999a) 3 Web JCLI.

Macdonald, E, 'Exclusion clauses: the ambit of s 13(1) of the Unfair Contract Terms Act 1977' (1992) 12 LS 277.

Macdonald, E, 'Incorporation of contract terms by a consistent course of dealing' (1988) 8 LS 48.

Macdonald, E, 'Mapping the Unfair Contract Terms Act 1977 and the Directive on Unfair Terms in Consumer Contracts' [1994] JBL 441.

Macdonald, E, 'The Emperor's old clauses' [1999b] CLJ 413.

Macdonald, E, 'Unifying unfair terms legislation' (2004) 67 MLR 69.

Macdonald, E, 'Bugs and Breaches' (2005) 13 International Journal of Law and Information Technology 118.

Macdonald, E and Poyton, D 'E-commerce: Recognizing the Context' in *Issues in Interaction of Commercial Law*, I. Davies ed, 2005, Ashgate: Aldershot.

Mackaay, E, 'The economics of emergent property rights on the Internet', in Bernt Hugenholtz, P (ed), *The Future of Copyright in a Digital Environment*, 1996, The Hague: Kluwer.

Macmillan, F, and Blakeney, M, 'The Internet and communication carriers' liability' [1998] EIPR 52.

MacQueen, HL, 'Copyright in cyberspace: *Shetland Times v Wills*' [1998] JBL 297.

Magee, J, 'Domain names disputes: an assessment of the UDRP as against traditional litigation' (2003) U Ill JL Tech & Pol'y 203.

Mahalingham Carr, I, and Williams, KS, 'A step too far in controlling computers? The Singapore Computer Misuse (Amendment) Act 1998' (2000) 8 Int JLIT 48.

Maltz, T, 'Customary law and power in Internet communities' (1996) 2 J Computer-mediated Comm, available at www.ascusc.org/jcmc/vol2/issue1/custom.html.

Manchester, C, 'Computer pornography' [1995] Crim LR 546.

Maniatis, S, 'Trade Mark Law and Domain Names: back to basics' [2002] EIPR 397.

Marchini, R, '*Navitaire v easyJet*: What now for look and feel?' (2005) 15(6) Computers and Law 31.

Marston, G, 'The parol evidence rule: the Law Commission speaks' [1986] CLJ 192.

Mashima, R, 'Examination of the interrelationship among the software industry structure, Keiretsu and Japanese intellectual property protection for software' (1999) 33 Int LJ 119.

McGuire, JF, 'When speech is heard around the world: internet content regulation in the United States and Germany' (1999) 74 NYUL Rev 750.

McKendrick, E, 'Product liability and the development risks defence' [1990] Law for Business 252.

Menell, PS, 'An analysis of the scope of copyright protection for application programs' (1989) 41 Stan L Rev 1045.

Meyer-Rochow, R, 'The application of passing off as a remedy against domain name piracy' [1998] EIPR 405.

Millard, C, 'Shrink wrap licensing' (1988) 4 CL & Security Rep 8.

Millé, A, 'Copyright in the cyberspace era' [1997] EIPR 570.

Miller, AR, 'Copyright protection for computer programs, databases and computer-generated works: is anything new since CONTU?' (1993) 106 Harv L Rev 977.

Miller, AR, *The Assault on Privacy: Computers, Databanks and Dossiers*, 1971, Ann Arbor, Mich: Michigan UP.

Mitchell, TA, 'Copyright, congress and constitutionality: How the Digital Millennium Copyright Act goes too far' (2004) 79 Notre Dame L Rev 2115.

Moreira, J, 'Making an informed choice between arbitration or litigation: the Uniform Domain-name Dispute Resolution Policy vs the Anti-Cybersquatting Act' (2003) 44 IDEA 147

Morgan, R, and Burden, R, *Morgan and Burden on Computer Contracts*, 6th edn, 2001, London, Sweet & Maxwell.

Morton, J, 'opinion.com' [1997] EIPR 496.

Mossoff, A, 'Spam – Oy, what a nuisance' (2004) 19 Berkeley Tech LJ 625.

Mota, SA, 'The Anticybersquatting Consumer Protection Act: An analysis of the decisions from the Courts of Appeals' (2003) 21 J Marshall J Computer & Info L 355.

Moutsatsos, SS, and Cummings, JCR, '*Apple v Microsoft*: has the pendulum swung too far?' (1993) 9 CL & P 162.

Moxon, J, (1991) *Flight International*, May, p 20.

Murdoch, J, *Law of Estate Agency and Auctions*, 4th edn, 2003, London: Estates Gazette.

Nehf, JP, 'Borderless trade and the consumer interest: protecting the consumer in the age of e-commerce' (1999) 38 Col J Transnat Law 457.

Newdick, C, 'Risk, uncertainty and "knowledge" in the development risks defence' (1991) 20 Anglo-Am L Rev 309.

Newdick, C, 'The development risk defence of the Consumer Protection Act 1987' [1988] CLJ 455.

Newell, A, 'The models are broken, the models are broken' (1986) 47 Pitt UL Rev 1023.

Newman, J, 'The patentability of computer-related inventions in Europe' [1997] EIPR 701.

Newton, J, 'Software patents in the UK' (1996) 1 Comm L 202.

Nicholl, CC, 'Can computers make contracts?' [1998] JBL 35.

Oberding, JM, and Norderhaug, T, 'A separate jurisdiction for cyberspace?' (1996) 2 J Computer-mediated Comm.

Ogilvie, JWL, 'Defining computer program parts under Learned Hand's abstractions tests in software copyright infringement cases' (1992) 91 Mich L Rev 526.

Ogus, AI, *Regulation: Legal Form and Economic Theory*, 1994, Oxford: Clarendon.

Oliver, J, 'Kazaa on trial in Australia' (2005) 15(6) Computers and Law 36.

Orange, A, Developments in the domain name system: for better or for worse', [1999] 3 JILT, available at www2.warwick.ac.uk/fac/soc/law/elj/jilt/1999_3/orange/.

Osborne, D, 'Domain names, registration and dispute resolution and recent UK cases' [1997] EIPR 644.

Osborne, D, 'Don't take my name in vain! ICANN dispute resolution policy and names of individuals' (2000) 5 Comm L 127.

Page, AC, 'Self-regulation: the constitutional dimension' (1986) 49 MLR 141.

Palfrey, T, 'Pornography and the possible criminal liability of internet service providers under the Obscene Publication(s) and Protection of Children Act' (1997) 6 ICTL 187.

Pangiotidou, E, 'The patentability of computer programs according to the Commission's new proposals for a directive and to the EPO Boards of Appeal decisions' (2003) 9 CTLR 126.

Perri 6, *The Future of Privacy Volume 1: Private Life and Public Policy*, 1998, London: Demos.

Poullet, Y *et al*, *Preparation of a Methodology for Evaluating the Adequacy of the Level of Protection of Individuals with regard to the Processing of Personal Data*, 1998, Luxembourg: OOPEC.

Poullet, Y, 'Data protection between property and liberties', in Kaspersen, HWK and Oskamp, A (eds), *Amongst Friends in Computers and Law*, 1990, The Hague: Kluwer.

Press, T, 'Patent protection for computer-related inventions', in Reed, C (ed), *Computer Law*, 3rd edn, 1996, London: Blackstone.

Prestin, D, 'Where to draw the line between reverse engineering and infringement: *Sony Computer Entertainment Inc v Connectix Corp.*' (2002) 3 Minn Intell Prop Rec 137.

Price, SA, 'Understanding contemporary cryptography and its wider impact upon the general law' (1999) 13 Int Rev LC & T 95.

Privacy Online: Fair Information Practices in the Electronic Marketplace, 2000, May available at www.ftc.org/reports/privacy2000/privacy2000text.pdf.

Pun, KH, 'Five years since the Software Regulations – China's recent developments in software copyright' (1997) 28 IIC 347.

Raab, C *et al*, *Application of a Methodology Designed to Assess the Adequacy of the Level of Protection of Individuals with regard to Processing Personal Data*, 1998, Luxembourg: OPEC.

Raab, C, 'The governance of data protection', in Kooiman, J (ed), *Modern Governance*, 1993, London: Sage.

Ramberg, C, *Internet marketplaces: The Law of Auctions and Exchanges Online*, 2002, Oxford: OUP.

Raskind, LJ, 'The uncertain case for special legislation protecting computer software' (1986) 47 Pitt UL Rev 1131.

Reed, C, 'Reverse engineering computer programs without infringing copyright' [1991] EIPR 47.

Reed, C, and Slatter, G, 'E-Commerce' in Reed, C, and Angel, J, (eds), *Computer Law* OUP 2003.

Reed, C, and Welterveden, A, 'Liability', Ch. 3 in Reed, C and Angel, J (eds), *Computer Law*, 5th edn, 2003, Oxford: OUP.

Reed, C, *Digital Information Law – Electronic Documents and Requirements of Form*, 1996, Centre for Commercial Law Studies, Queen Mary and Westfield College, University of London.

Report on Self-Labelling and Filters at www.ispo.cec.be/iap/INCOREexec.html.

Report on the Convention on Law Applicable to Contractual Obligations, (Guiliano-Lagarde Report) OJ 1980 C 282/1.

Rinck, GM, 'The maturing US law on copyright protection for computer programs: *Computer Associates v Altai* and other recent case developments' [1992] EIPR 351.

Rodau, A, 'Computer software: Does Article 2 of the Uniform Commercial Code apply?' (1986) Emory LJ 853.

Rowe, H, *Data Protection Act 1998: A Practical Guide*, 2000, Croydon: Tolley.

Rowland, D, 'Cyberspace: a contemporary utopia?' [1998] JILT, Pt 3, available at www.law.warwick.ac.uk/jilt/98-3/rowland.html.

Rowland, D, 'Data retention and the war against terrorism – a considered and proportionate response?' [2004] JILT 3. Available at www2.warwick.ac.uk/fac/soc/law/elj/jilt/2004_3/rowland/

Rowland, D, 'Free expression and defamation' in Klang, M and Murray, A (eds) *Human Rights in the Digital Age*, 2005, London: Glasshouse Press.

Rowland, D, 'Liability for defective software' [1991] Cam L Rev 78.

Rowland, D, 'Negligence, professional competence and computer systems' [1999] 2 JILT.

Rowland, D, 'Privacy, freedom of expression and CyberSLAPPs: Fostering anonymity on the Internet?' (2003) 17 Int Rev LCT 303.

Rowland, D, 'The EC Database Directive: an original solution to an unoriginal problem?' [1997] Web JCLI,

Rowland, D, and Campbell, A, 'Content and Access Agreements: An analysis of some of the legal issues arising out of linking and framing' (2002) 16 Int Rev LCT 171.

Rowland, D, and Rowland, JJ, 'Competence and legal liability in the development of software for safety related applications (1993) 2 Computers and Artificial Intelligence 229.

Rusch, LJ, 'Products liability trapped by history: Our choice of rules rules our choices.' (2003) 76 Temp L Rev 739.

Rustad, ML, and Koenig, TH, 'Cybertorts and legal lag: an empirical analysis' (2003) 13 S Cal Interdisc LJ 77.

Sableman, M, 'Link law: the emerging law of Internet hypertext links' (1999) 15 CL & P 557, available at www.ldrc.com/cyber2.html.

Safety-Related Systems: A Professional Brief for the Engineer, 1992, London: IEE.

Safety-Related Systems: Guidance for Engineers, 1995, London: Hazards Forum.

Samek, RA, 'Contracts for work and materials' (1962) 36 ALJ 66.

Samuelson, *et al*, 'A manifesto concerning the legal protection of computer programs' (1994) 94 Colum L Rev 2308.

Saxby, S (ed), *Encyclopedia of Information Technology Law*, 1990, London: Sweet & Maxwell.

Schley, GM, 'The Digital Millennium Copyright Act and the First Amendment: How far should courts go to protect intellectual property rights?' (2004), 3 J High Tech L 115.

Schønning, P, 'Internet and the applicable copyright law: a Scandinavian perspective' [1999] EIPR 45.

Schriver, RR, 'You cheated, you lied: The Safe Harbor agreement and its enforcement by the Federal Trade Commission' (2002) 70 Fordham L Rev 2777.

Schwarz, PM, 'Property, Privacy and Personal Data' (2004) 117 Harv L Rev 2055.

Scottish Law Commission, *Report on Computer Crime*, Cmnd 174, 1987, London: HMSO, para 2.4.

Seaman, A, 'E-commerce, jurisdiction and choice of law' [1999–2000] CL Dec/Jan 29.

Self-Regulation and Privacy Online, available at www.ftc.gov/os/1999/9907/privacy99.pdf.SG/EC (1998) 14 final, available at www.oecd.org/dsti/sti/it/consumer/prod/cpguidelines_final.pdf.

Selis, P, Ramasastry, A, and Sato, A, 'Bidder Beware: Towards a fraud-free marketplace – best practices for the online auction industry', www.atg.wa.gov/consumer/auctions/home.htm28.

Sherwood-Edwards, M, 'Seven degrees of separation: the Software Directive and UK implementation' (1993) 9 CL & P 169.

Shillito, R, 'Making bones of sticks and stones law' (1994) 91(38) Law *Soc Gazette*, 19 October.

Sieber, U, 'Legal Aspects of computer-related crime in the information society' *Report for the European Commission of the Outcome of the COMCRIME Study* 1998, available at www.europa.eu.int/ISPO/legal/en/comcrime/sieber.html.

Smith, GP, 'Shrinkwrap licensing in the Scottish courts' (1990) 4 Int JLIT 131.

Smith, GP, 'Tear open licenses – are they enforceable in England?' (1986) 3 CL & P 128.

Smith, JC, *Law Of Theft*, 8th edn, 1997, London: Butterworths.

Smith-Ekstrand, V, 'Drawing swords after Feist: Efforts to legislate the database pirate' (2002) 7 Comm L & Pol'y 317.

Software in Safety-Related Systems, 1989, London: IEE.

Son, S, 'Can black dot (shrinkwrap) licenses override federal reverse engineering rights?: The relationship between copyright, contract and antitrust laws' (2004) 6 Tul J Tech & Intell Prop 63.

Sookman, BB, 'The liability of information providers in negligence' (1989) 5 CL & P 141.

South West Thames RHA, *Report of the Inquiry into the London Ambulance Service*, February 1993.

Spencer, JR, 'The Sexual Offences Act 2003: (2) Child and family offences' [2003] Crim LR 347.

Sprinkel, SC, 'Global internet regulation: the residual effects of the 'iloveyou' computer virus and the draft convention on cyber-crime' (2002) 25 Suffolk Transnat'l L Rev 491.

St Oren, J, 'Jurisdiction over Consumer Contracts in e-Europe' (2003) 52 ICLQ 665.

Stallworthy, M, 'Data protection: regulation in a deregulatory State' [1990] Statute L Rev 130.

Stangret, LA, 'The legalities of linking on the world wide web' (1997) 2 Comm L 202.

Stanton, KM, and Dugdale, AM, 'Design responsibility in civil engineering work' (1981) 131 NLJ 583.

Stanton, KM, *The Modern Law of Tort*, 1994, London: Sweet & Maxwell.

Stapleton, J, 'Products liability reform – real or illusory?' (1986) 6 OJLS 392.

Stapleton, J, 'Software, information and the concept of product' (1989) 9 Tel Aviv U Stud L 147.

Stapleton, J, *Product Liability*, 1994, London: Butterworths.

Sterling, JAL, 'Philosophical and legal challenges in the context of copyright and digital technology' (2000) 31 IIC 508.

Stern, RH, 'An ill-conceived analysis of reverse engineering of software as copyright infringement: *Sega Enterprises v Accolade*' [1992] EIPR 107.

Stern, RH, 'Reverse engineering of software as copyright infringement – an update: *Sega Enterprises v Accolade*' [1993] EIPR 34.

Stern, RH, 'The bundle of rights suited to the new technology' (1986) 47 Pitt UL Rev 1229.

Sterne, RG, Sokohl, RE, and Axenfield, RR, 'The shifting sands of section 101 and section 112 requirements for computer program-related inventions' [1994] Int Lawyer 29.

Stoodley, J, 'Internet domain names and trademarks' [1997] EIPR 509.

Storey, N, *Safety-Critical Computer Systems*, 1996, Harlow: Addison-Wesley.

Sullivan, JD, and De Leeuw, MB, 'Spam after CAN-SPAM: How inconsistent thinking has made a hash out of unsolicited commercial e-mail policy' (2004) 20 Santa Clara Computer & High Tech LJ 887.

Surfer Beware III: Privacy Policies without Privacy Protection, December 1999, available at www.epic.org/reports/surfer-beware3.html.

Susman, AM, 'International Electronic Trading: Some Legal Issues' [2000] CL Feb/Mar 29.

Swire, PP, and Litan, RE, *None of Your Business: World Data Flows, Electronic Commerce and the European Privacy Directive*, 1998, Washington DC: Brookings Institution.

Swope, R, 'Peer-to-peer file sharing and copyright infringement: Danger ahead for individuals sharing files on the internet' (2004) 44 Santa Clara L Rev 861.

Tapper, CF, 'Computer crime: Scotch mist?' [1987] Crim LR 4.

Tapper, CF, 'United Kingdom' in Lehmann, M and Tapper, CF (eds), Handbook of European Software Law, Pt II, 1993, Oxford: Clarendon.

Taylor, G, 'The Council of Europe Cybercrime Convention: A Civil Liberties Perspective' 2002 www.crime-research.org/library/CoE_Cybercrime.html.

Tenth Report of the Data Protection Registrar, 1994, London: HMSO.

Terry, NP, 'State of the art evidence: from logical construct to judicial retrenchment' (1991) 20 Anglo-Am L Rev 285.

Teter, TS, 'Merger and the machines: an analysis of the pro-compatibility trend in computer software copyright cases' (1993) 45 Stan L Rev 1061.

Thakur, N, 'Database protection in the European Union and the United States: the European Database Directive as an optimum global model' [2001] IPQ 100.

Tiberi, L, and Zamboni, M, 'Liability of Internet Service Providers (2003) 9 CTLR 49.

Trager, R, and Turner, S, 'The Internet down under: Can free speech be protected in a democracy without a Bill of Rights? (2000) 23 U Ark Little Rock L Rev 123.

Tucker, RL, 'Information superhighway robbers: The tortious misuse of links, frames, metatags and domain names' (1999) 4 Va JLT 8.

Van Overstraten, T, and Szafran, E, 'Data protection on the internet: technical considerations and European legal framework' (2001) 5 CTLR 56.

Vass, S, 'Lessons from Robertson's victory' *Sunday Herald*, 12 September 2004 www.sundayherald.com/44642

Velasco, J, 'The copyrightability of non-literal elements of computer programs' (1994) 94 Col L Rev 242.

Vinje, T, 'The legislative history of the EC Software Directive', in Lehmann, M and Tapper, CF (eds) Handbook of European Software Law Pt 1, 1993, Oxford: Clarendon.

Von Helfeld, A, 'Protection of inventions comprising computer programs by the European and German Patent Offices – a confrontation' (1986) 3 CL & P 182.

Voon, T, 'Online pornography in Australia: Lessons from the First Amendment (2001) 24 UNSWLJ 141.

Wacks, R, *Privacy and Press Freedom*, 1995, London: Blackstone.

Waelde, C, and MacQueen, H, 'From entertainment to education' [2004] IPQ 259.

Waelde, C, 'Trademarks and domain names: what's in a name?', in Edwards, L and Waelde, C (eds), *Law and the Internet: Regulating Cyberspace*, 1997, Oxford: Hart.

Warren, S, and Brandeis, L, 'The right to privacy' (1890) 4 Harv L Rev 193.

Wasik, M, (1996) 9 LC & T Yearbook p ix.

Wasik, M and Piperaki, A, 'Computer crime: the Scottish Law Commission proposals' (1987) 3 LC & T Yearbook 109.

Wasik, M, 'Misuse of information technology: what should the role of the criminal law be?' (1991) 5 LC & T Yearbook 158.

Wasik, M, *Crime and the Computer*, 1990, Oxford: Clarendon.

Waters, P, and Leonard, PG, 'The lessons of recent EC and US developments for protection of computer software under Australian law' [1991] EIPR 125.

Watkins, T, and Rau, A, 'Intellectual property in artificial neural networks – in particular under the EPC' (1996) 27 IIC 447.

Westin, AF, *Privacy and Freedom*, 1967, London: Bodley Head.

Wiebe, A, 'European copyright protection of software from a German perspective' (1993) 9 CL & P 79.

Wilkins, JS, 'Protecting computer programs as compilations under *Computer Associates v Altai*' (1994) 104 Yale LJ 435.

Williams, AWS, 'European Commission: Proposed directive for patents for software-related inventions' [2004] EIPR 368.

Wu, T, 'When code isn't law' (2003) 89 Va L Rev 679.

Zadra-Symes, LJ, '*Computer Associates v Altai*: the retreat from *Whelan v Jaslow*' [1992] EIPR 327.

Zimmerman, D, 'Global limits on 'look and feel': defining the scope of software copyright protection by international agreement' (1996) 34 Col J Transnat L 503.

Zynda, T, 'Ticketmaster corp v Tickets.com inc: Preserving minimum requirements of contract on the internet.' (2004) 19 Berkeley Tech LJ 495.

INDEX

Information Technology Law

568

Information Technology Law

Information location tools

498

Innocent dissemination defence

defamation, and

408–09

Insurance

reasonableness test, and

198

Intellectual property rights

databases, in. see Databases

domain names, and. see Domain names

hypertext linking, and

511–24

appropriate legal mechanism

519

creation of derivative works

518–19

deceptive tactics

520

deep link

515–16

framing

518

functionality

514

implied licence as necessary device

519

implied licence to link

512

inline linking

518

ISPs hosting sites providing

517

keying banner advertisements

521

knowledge element

514

legal use of trademarks as metatags

523

likelihood of confusion

522

linking to infringing sites

513

metatags

519

restrictions on making

514

use of copyright law

516–17

use of hidden trademark images

521

use of trademark as metatag

520

uses

512

violating intellectual property rights, whether

515

internet, on

489–542

copyright. see Copyright

practical test of Petersen J

5

software

5–100

abuse of innovations

8

advent of microcomputers

5

copyright, use of,

6

see also Copyright

false icon of sui generis protection

9–10

Model Provisions approach

6

programmes as texts

8

purpose of Model Provisions

6

reasons for using copyright

8

vulnerability of

6

World Intellectual Property Organisation (WIPO), and

5

software as goods, and

145–46

Interface commands

copyright protection of

57–58

Internet

acquisition of software from shrink wrap licences, and

113

censorship

460

commerce. see E-commerce

data protection on. see Data protection

intellectual property rights on. see Intellectual property rights

Internet service provider (ISP)

defamation

liability for publication

402–03

liability of

copyright, and. see Copyright

Invention

meaning

73

Invitation to treat

meaning

273

Japan

copyright protection of computer software in

7

Journalism

data protection, and

376

Jurisdiction

e-commerce. see E-commerce

Legislation

impact on entire agreement clauses

136

software copyright, for

20–21

Legitimate expectations

concept of

350

Libel

392–93

Licence

106–07

see also Software licence

EC Directive

110–13

back-up copies

111

basic use of software

110–11

error correction

112–13

shrink wrap licence,

113–19

see also Shrink wrap licence

source code

107–09

definitions

107

escrow agreement

107

significance of

107

supply of

109

use for error correction

107–08

terms

106–07

Linking

intellectual property rights, and. see Intellectual property rights

Literal copying

computer programmes, of

15

Literature

data protection, and

376

Merchantability

definition

164